Drafting Commercial Agreements

AUSTRALIA
LBC Information Services—Sydney

CANADA and USA
Carswell—Toronto

NEW ZEALAND
Brooker's—Auckland

SINGAPORE and MALAYSIA
Thomson Information (S.E. Asia)—Singapore

Drafting Commercial Agreements

Second Edition

Richard Christou
Solicitor (M.A. Cantab.)

LONDON
SWEET & MAXWELL
1998

Published in 1998 by Sweet & Maxwell Limited of
100 Avenue Road, Swiss Cottage,
London NW3 3PF
(http://www.smlawpub.co.uk)

First edition 1993
Reprinted 1996 (twice)
Second edition 1998

No natural forests were destroyed to make this product;
only farmed timber was used and replanted.

A CIP catalogue record for this book is available from the British Library.

ISBN 0 421 654 104

Printed and bound in Great Britain by MPG Books Ltd, Bodmin, Cornwall

Contents

Preface

In the five years since *Drafting Commercial Agreements* was first published, commercial law in the United Kingdom has continued to develop rapidly. Legislation and case law emanating from the European Union, particularly in the area of agency and distribution, competition, merger control and consumer protection, have had a significant impact. So far as local law within the UK itself is concerned, there have been new and interesting developments in the judicial interpretation of commercial contracts and liability for negligent misstatements. In addition, the Office of Fair Trading has been given increased powers under the Unfair Terms in Consumer Contract Regulations 1994, and is starting to exercise these vigorously, with a marked impact on the way consumer contracts are now being drafted.

Last but not least, the change in government has led to a detailed review and wholesale changes in the areas of employment law and competition law, which are still in process at the time this book is being published. For instance, the Competition Bill 1997, which completely changes the competition law regime in the UK is on course to receive Royal assent in October 1998.

Although the precedents have by and large stood the test of time, I have taken the opportunity of a second edition to revise and update both commentary and precedents in the light of all of these developments. The law is generally current as at April 1998, but my publishers have, in view of the state of flux mentioned above, been kind enough to allow me to incorporate a series of footnotes, referred to in the text, and gathered together in an Appendix at the end of the book, which brings in significant developments up to July 1998.

Richard Christou
London, July 1998

This book is dedicated to my family, with many thanks for their support and encouragement, but most of all to Sapphire who kept me company while I was working and waited patiently until I had finished.

Table of Cases

Table of European Cases

Table of Statutes

Table of Statutory Instruments

Table of European Community Legislation

Notices

Part I

Supply of Goods and Services

Chapter 1

Basic principles

1.1 Introduction

The first Part of this book deals with standard sets of conditions covering various relationships that can arise in the context of the supply of goods and services in the course of a business, ranging from short form standard conditions for the supply of goods and the provision of services, to a full contract for the supply of a turnkey system.

The negotiation of the contractual terms of such relationships is all too often regarded as a contest in which the supplier attempts to exclude the maximum possible liability to the customer, and the customer to impose the maximum possible liability on the supplier; the only rules are those imposed by the Unfair Contract Terms Act, and the contest is finally decided by the relative bargaining power of the two parties. From a commercial point of view, this is not the most fruitful way to approach a continuing business relationship, since it normally leaves one of the parties unsatisfied with the deal that was struck. It is far better to look upon the purpose of such negotiations as to define the risks which each party is willing to accept, and what benefits or rewards he requires from the other party in order to accept those risks. For instance, at the most basic level, the higher the profit margin the supplier receives for performing a contract, the greater the liability he can reasonably be asked to accept for failure to perform as promised.

Following from these considerations, Chapters 2 and 3 both contain precedents for use in non-consumer transactions, prepared from the point of view of the supplier and the customer respectively, to show examples of the different approaches that each party has in a situation where he has the preponderance of bargaining power, and wishes to use it. Chapter 4 sets out, by way of contrast, an approach to the allocation of risk and reward between the parties, based on a compromise which attempts to satisfy the reasonable aspirations of both parties. Such compromises are particularly important where the parties are embarking on the long-term and complicated relationship required for the supply of a turnkey system. Chapter 5, finally, deals with some aspects of contracting with consumers.

Nevertheless, whether the parties want compromise or a contest, their legal advisers cannot satisfy them without a thorough knowledge of the Unfair Contract Terms Act 1977 ('UCTA'), and of the underlying principles contained in the Sale of Goods Act 1979 (as amended by the Sale of Goods (Amendment) Act 1994 and the Sale of Goods (Amendment) Act 1995) (collectively 'SGA'), the Supply of Goods And Services Act 1982 ('SGSA') and the Sale and Supply of Goods Act 1994 ('SSGA 1994') which introduced important amendments to the SGA and the SGSA. The last three Acts will be referred to as necessary in this and the following chapters, and, needless to say, no legal adviser should be without copies of these Acts, as well as a standard reference work on the subject, when drafting conditions or contracts for the supply of goods and services. However, the UCTA is so intimately connected with the process of negotiation and drafting in the areas covered by the next four chapters that, as a preliminary to detailed analysis of the precedents, it was felt essential to lay out the principles contained in the UCTA and discuss their application in the light of the case law that has evolved in the 20 years or so since the UCTA came into effect.

The UCTA is concerned to regulate the use of clauses which exclude liability for failure to perform, for certain other types of tortious acts, and for failure to comply with certain warranties implied into contracts for the supply of goods and services under the SGA and SGSA (for instance as to good title under the SGA). The UCTA covers not only clauses which exclude such liability in whole, but also those which exclude or restrict it partially (eg a limitation as to the monetary amount to be paid by way of compensation for such a liability when incurred). For the purposes of this chapter such clauses are generally called 'exemption clauses' and references to 'exclusion' of liability include partial exclusion or restriction as well as total exclusion.

1.2   Basic rationale of the UCTA

In dealing with exemption clauses the UCTA has three possible reactions: the imposition of a total ban on all exemption clauses of that category; the imposition of a ban on all such clauses unless in the circumstances the clause satisfies the criterion of 'reasonableness'; and no imposition of a ban at all.

The relevant factors in deciding how the UCTA deals with an exemption clause are: the type of contract, the identity of the parties, the subject matter of the contract, and the presence or absence of a foreign element. These factors can be broken down into a number of sets for the purposes of different sections of the UCTA, and probably form the most useful framework under which to analyse its effect. They can be summarised as follows:

(*a*) Types of contract:
- (i) all contracts;
- (ii) all contracts where the party ('businessman') seeking to rely on the exemption clause entered into the contract in the course of a business (except those businesses excluded under Sched 1 to the UCTA—basically those which have some other form of statutory regulation such as insurance contracts, contracts for the carriage of goods by sea, or contracts whose subject matter is specialised, and which therefore have a particular body of law governing them, such as real property or intellectual property). ('Business contracts');
- (iii) all contracts for sale or hire purchase of goods;
- (iv) all business contracts for sale or hire purchase of goods;
- (v) all contracts for the hire or barter of goods, and for the supply of labour and materials;
- (vi) all business contracts for the hire or barter of goods, and for the supply of labour and materials.

(*b*) Identity of parties:

Party relying on clause	*Party protected by UCTA*
(i) any party	any party
(ii) businessman	any party
(iii) businessman	non-consumer (standard terms)
(iv) businessman	non-consumer (negotiated terms)
(v) businessman	consumer

(*c*) Subject matter of the contract:
- (i) all goods in general;
- (ii) goods ordinarily supplied for private use or consumption ('consumer goods').

(*d*) Foreign element:
- (i) contracts containing governing law clauses;
- (ii) international contracts for the supply of goods;
- (iii) contracts regulated by certain international conventions.

In addition to the regulation of exemption clauses, the UCTA also makes some alterations to the general law of contract in relation to the contracts affected by it, and regulates the exclusion of tortious liability, in business situations, for death, personal injury or other damage caused by negligence. Although this regulation of tortious liability is not of itself a contractual issue, there are some situations where it has great importance for business contracts, for instance in the area of pre-contract negotiations.

One word of warning needs to be given about the extent of the exclusion of contracts whose subject matter is covered by Sched 1 to the UCTA. Just because the contract relates to some extent to subject matter excluded by Sched 1, it does not mean that all of its terms will necessarily escape scrutiny under the UCTA. For instance, the creation and subsequent licensing of the use of software to a customer under a bespoke development contract relates in part to the creation and transfer of an intellectual property right which is one of the areas of subject matter excluded under Sched 1. In this case the provisions relating to the license may well escape scrutiny (eg exclusion of liability for infringement of third party intellectual property rights), but if the software is supplied on a tangible medium (eg floppy disks or tape) as opposed to merely being downloaded into the customer's computer, there may also be a supply of goods, the terms of which are subject to s 6 of the UCTA, and, in any event, the supply of the development service itself will be subject to ss 2 and 7 of the UCTA. (See *The Salvage Association v CAP Financial Services Ltd* [1995] FSR 654 and *St Albans and District Council v International Computers Ltd* [1997] FSR 251, CA.)

1.3   The test of reasonableness under the UCTA

The definition of 'reasonableness' applied by the UCTA is the key to understanding its approach to exemption clauses in general. Section 11(1) applies the test of reasonableness to an exemption clause by asking whether it is a 'fair and reasonable [exemption clause] to be included having regard to the circumstances which were, or ought reasonably to have been, known to or in the contemplation of the parties when the contract was made'. It is for the party who claims that a clause satisfies the test of reasonableness to show that it does (s 11(5)).

Section 11 reverses the previous legislation on the subject in the Misrepresentation Act 1967, and the Supply of Goods (Implied Terms) Act 1973, as well as the English Law Commission's initial recommendation on the subject. There the test to be applied was what was fair and reasonable 'in all the circumstances of the case'.

The test now embodied in the UCTA is thus a hypothetical test, which requires the court to put itself in the position of the parties as they were (and with the state of knowledge which they had) at the time when the contract was made. This prevents the court looking at the actual circumstances surrounding the breach in question. This hypothetical test was preferred on the grounds that it gave rise to less uncertainty, and avoided the possibility of the court acting on the basis of hindsight. The Scottish Law Commission, for instance, criticised the previous test as being 'a judicial dispensing power exercised possibly in the light of unforeseeable events subsequent in date to the contract'. In other words 'hard cases make bad law'.

The definition of what is 'fair and reasonable' has, however, given rise to some problems. First, it seems that in practice the word 'fair' adds little if anything to the definition, and that the courts have tended to focus in practice on what is 'reasonable'. Secondly, there are some express guidelines in the UCTA, but these are far from complete, are only indicative, and impose no restriction on the other matters which the court can take into account.

Section 11(4) requires regard to be had to the financial resources of a party claiming the protection of an exemption clause which limits liability by reference to a specified sum of money, and also to the extent to which he could cover his liability by insurance.

Schedule 2 contains some express guidelines for all contracts relating to the supply of goods, which inevitably have influenced thinking about reasonableness in relation to all types of contracts. They are:

(1) The relative bargaining strength of the parties.
(2) Whether the customer received an inducement to accept the exemption clause.
(3) Whether the customer knew or ought reasonably to have known of the term.
(4) Whether the customer could have found another party who would have contracted without the exemption clause.
(5) Where the term excludes liability if some condition is not complied with, whether it was reasonable at time of contract to expect that such condition could be complied with.
(6) Whether the goods were made or adapted to special order for the customer.

Additional guidelines were also mentioned in the Law Commission Report which led to the enactment of the UCTA (Report No 69, pp 71–73), which can be summarised as follows:

(1) Which party can most reasonably insure.
(2) '*Force majeure*' clauses are *prima facie* likely to be reasonable.
(3) When looking at clauses which require compliance with time limits (eg a time limit for notifying a warranty claim after a defect is discovered in goods supplied under the contract) the question to ask is whether the time limit has been imposed from a genuine need to protect the other party's position, or whether it is there to make it difficult, or practically impossible, for the other party to exercise its rights under the clause.
(4) Which party has the most experience in the transaction.
(5) To what extent has one party relied on the other's advice.

It was expected that case law would give rise to sufficient precedents to flesh out the relatively few guidelines available under the UCTA, but in fact cases have been few and not very helpful. The *dictum* in the *Mogul SS* case ((1889) 23 QBD 598, CA) equating reasonableness with 'the good sense of the tribunal' still seems to come closest to the mark.

The current cases have not resulted in rigid definitions of reasonableness. The court at first instance can always distinguish except in very similar cases, and appeal is not easy unless a judgment is so unreasonable as to be perverse (*Geo Mitchell (Chesterhall) Ltd v Finney Lock Seeds Ltd* [1983] 2 AC 803 and *St Albans and District Council v International Computers Ltd* [1997] FSR 251, CA at 264.)

The cases demonstrate that a clause can only be judged under s 11 in the context of the specific factual and legal matrix applying to the contract in which it is incorporated. For instance, in *First National Commercial Bank plc v Loxleys (A Firm)* [1996] NPC 158, the Court of Appeal said 'the true question was not ... the fairness and reasonableness [under s 11(3) of the UCTA] of the disclaimer itself, but whether it was fair and reasonable to allow [the defendant] to rely on it in all the circumstances'. On this basis, it is not possible to provide a set of rules which will produce clauses that will satisfy the test of reasonableness in all circumstances.

A striking example of this can be found in *Fillite Runcorn Ltd v APV Pasilac Ltd and APC Corporation Ltd* (1993) discussed in (1994) 11 *Building Law Monthly*, issue 1. Here, the same exclusion clause was incorporated in two different contracts between the same seller and the same buyer. The first contract was for a piece of machinery ('the original machinery') available from a number of suppliers. The buyers had the chance to shop around and chose to enter into the contract with the seller, even though it contained the exclusion clause. In the case of the first contract this circumstance rendered the exclusion clause reasonable, since there was equality of bargaining power between the parties. The machinery to be supplied under the second contract (the ancillary machinery') had to interwork with the original machinery. Once the seller was chosen for the first contract, no one other than the seller could supply machinery which could be guaranteed to interwork with the original machinery, unless the seller was willing to provide the buyer with detailed specifications of the original machinery, to enable a third party to manufacture and supply the ancillary machinery. This put the seller into what was effectively a monopoly position. The buyer had to accept the terms of the seller's contract for the ancillary machinery, including the exclusion clause, whether he liked it or not. This lack of equality of bargaining power rendered the same exclusion clause unreasonable in the context of the second contract.

However, various decisions can be examined to deduce guidelines as to the sort of factors to be taken into account when determining whether a clause is reasonable. First, it does seem that consumers are more likely to succeed in an assertion that a clause is unreasonable than a commercial undertaking. (Cf *Photo Production Ltd v Securicor Transport Ltd* [1980] AC 827, *R&B Customs Brokers Ltd v UDT Finance Ltd* [1988] 1 All ER 847 and *Omega Trust Co Ltd v Wright Son & Pepper* [1996] NPC 189.) Secondly, in general courts are more favourably disposed to clauses which limit liability rather than those which completely exclude it (Cf *Rasbora Ltd v JCL Marine Ltd* [1977] 1 Lloyd's Rep 645 and *RW Green Ltd v Cade Bros Farm* [1978] 1 Lloyd's Rep 602.)

One of the most useful cases is *Geo Mitchell* where the limitation of liability was by reference to the purchase price. It was clear from the type of contract entered into (purchase of seed to grow a commercial crop to be sold for profit) that the likely loss, caused if the defendants supplied defective seed, would exceed the purchase price by such an amount (namely the value of the ultimate crop) that the limitation really amounted to a total exclusion of liability. The defendants could have found product liability insurance easily (see also on this point *Flamar Interocean Ltd v Denmac* [1990] 1 Lloyd's Rep 434) and the term was universal in the trade (but had never been negotiated by any trade association) so that the plaintiff had no opportunity of obtaining product on other terms. Additionally, the defendants had of their own accord not relied on the clause in other customer disputes, which showed that they themselves tended to regard its limitation as unreasonable. Under these circumstances the House of Lords found the clause unreasonable.

Cases have also been helpful on some points of detail. Too tight time limits are likely to be unreasonable (see *Green*, above) as is small print, and unnecessarily convoluted drafting (see *Stag Line Ltd v Tyne Ship Repair Group Ltd* [1984] 2 Lloyd's Rep 211).

Finally, in *Harris v Wyre Forest District Council* [1989] 2 All ER 514, a case concerned with a disclaimer of liability in a surveyor's report, a variety of factors were taken into account in deciding reasonableness. The main point of the case was that it involved domestic property where the client would suffer (as a private purchaser) a relatively great loss if the report were negligent, while the risk that would have been undertaken by the surveyor, if he had accepted liability for negligence, would have been relatively low, since it was a routine survey of domestic property, and for him, as a businessman, the value of the property in question was not relatively a great amount of money. In any event, as a businessman, he could have taken out professional indemnity insurance against the risk without difficulty. The court commented that the situation could have been different if the property concerned was of a very high value, or of an unusual nature (eg industrial property) so as to impose too great a risk upon the surveyor if he accepted liability. Again, presumably, the fact that the plaintiff was a consumer also affected the result. This approach has been followed in by the Court of Appeal in *Omega Trust Co Ltd v Wright Son & Pepper* [1996] NPC 189.

1.4   General effects of the UCTA

The UCTA has, in the area of commercial transactions, had most impact where standard form contracts are in use, and very little in arms-length, one-off negotiated contracts where the parties are presumed to have access to proper legal advice, and to be able to take care of themselves. However, it is certainly still possible to see many sets of standard terms which contain clauses which could well be either banned or subject to the reasonableness test under the Act. In part this is due not to ignorance of the Act, but rather to the not unreasonable proposition that, since the Act prescribes no penalty for inserting such clauses, in cases of doubt it is better to have the clause present '*in terrorem*', even if, in the ultimate event of legal proceedings, it is held invalid.

The most obvious sign of the Act's influence is the presence of statements along the lines of 'this guarantee does not affect your statutory rights' which are now added in close proximity to all consumer guarantees. The practice in fact originally arose out of the combined effect of the Sale of Goods (Implied Terms) Act 1973 and the Consumer Transactions (Restrictions on Statements) Order 1976 (SI No 1813) made under the Fair Trading Act 1973. However, it was the great increase in statutory rights granted to consumers under the UCTA which caused the practice to become so widespread. These provisions have been one of the major forces responsible for the complete change in standard terms and conditions for dealing with consumers that came in after the passing of the UCTA. Because of them, unlike the case of business contracts discussed above, the practice of the insertion of possibly invalid or unreasonable exclusion clauses *'in terrorem'* is not possible in consumer contracts, since failure to notify a consumer of his statutory rights, or misleading him as to what they are, is a criminal offence.

Thus, as was intended, the Act has had most impact on consumer transactions, and its effect, together with the Consumer Protection Act 1987, has been to make it hardly worthwhile to exclude liability in consumer transactions. The more fruitful course is not to promise to undertake liability in the first place (to the extent that the law permits this) rather than to make promises and exclude liability for their subsequent breach. For the rest, the only refuge is in insurance. The particular approach to consumer contracts for the supply of goods and services will be discussed in detail in Chapter 5.

1.5   A detailed analysis of the UCTA

Having dealt with the general principles of the UCTA it is now possible to analyse its effect in detail on various contractual relationships using as a framework the definitions and different combinations of the factors set out above in the section devoted to the basic rationale of the UCTA.

1.5.1   Party protected by UCTA: any party; category of contract: all contracts

Section 8 of the UCTA provides that there can be no exclusion of liability for misrepresentation prior to entry into a contract under the Misrepresentation Act 1967, s 3 or the Misrepresentation (Northern Ireland) Act 1967, s 3 unless the exemption clause passes the test of reasonableness. This section is of the very widest application. It is not limited, as are ss 2–7 of the UCTA, either by s 1 to business-to-business and consumer transactions, or by the exception of the operation of those sections from the classes of contracts set out in Sched 1 to the UCTA. The ambit of s 8 is thus defined purely by the 1967 Acts, and they apply to all contracts of any nature, whether business-to-business, or entered into with a consumer, or non-business transactions between private individuals. Subject, then, to the extent, if any, to which the conflict of laws provisions of ss 26 and 27 of the UCTA apply, the 1967 Acts, as amended, would appear to regulate all of the contracts dealt with in this book, if they are governed by the law of England and Wales or of Northern Ireland.

Section 8 has most application in the area of whole agreement (or entire agreement) clauses which limit the bounds of the relationship of the parties to the particular contract in question. Such clauses exclude all prior representations and negotiations, and, usually, ancillary documentation, such as sales literature, as well. Under the test, the question is how reasonable such clauses are at the time the contract is made. They should not be put in automatically, but only after consideration as to the circumstances surrounding the formation of the contract.

The situation where such clauses are most likely to be reasonable is one where prior negotiations have been complex, with many oral discussions and lots of paper work passing between the parties, so that it is equally to the advantage of both parties to create certainty by describing all of their rights and liabilities in one defined set of documents and excluding all extraneous issues. A further factor which would tend to make such clauses reasonable would be adequate protection by warranties in the final express contract documents. Finally, probably the most decisive factor of all is whether both parties were properly advised legally, of equal bargaining power and equally skilled technically and commercially, so that they should have been capable of adequately assessing the risks and rewards they were undertaking in the transactions and of producing a contract document which properly reflected this. (See *W Photoprint Ltd v Forward Trust Group Ltd* (1993) 12 TrL 146, QBD.)

However, it has also been held that where a pre-contract representation was the vital factor which induced a party to enter into the contract, exclusion of liability for such a representation by a general whole agreement clause in a set of standard conditions was unreasonable, and that the only type of exclusion which would have been reasonable was one which referred specifically to the representation in question. (See *St Marylebone Property Co Ltd v Payne* [1994] 45 EG 156, Mayors and City of London Court, *Lease Management Services Ltd v Purnell Secretarial Services Ltd* [1994] CCLR 127, (1994) 13 TrL 337, and *Miljus (t/a A&Z Engineering) v Yamazaki Machinery UK Ltd* (1996) unreported, QBD (OR), transcript reference 1994 Orb. No 774.)

There are two other unreported decisions on the question of the more general type of whole agreement clause. The first held that a whole agreement clause which only stated that the agreement 'sets forth the entire agreement and understanding of the parties' is not sufficient to exclude a claim for rescission or damages based upon a pre-contractual misrepresentation, although there was no reason why appropriate wording could not have been added which would have had this effect (*Alman and Benson v Associated Newspapers Ltd* (1980) unreported, 20 June, Browne-Wilkinson J). The second held that a whole agreement clause could not preclude the plaintiff from seeking rescission or claiming damages on a tortious basis, in addition to his right to claim damages for breach of contract, unless the clause contains express provision to this effect (*Witter Ltd v TBP Industries Ltd* (1994) unreported, Ch 1990-W-5354, 15 July, Jacob J).

In the second case, the learned judge went on further to consider the effect of the clause more generally. In his opinion (contrary to the remarks of Browne-Wilkinson J) merely stating that a party has not relied on pre-contract negotiations was not sufficient to exclude liability; the clause would have to go further and expressly exclude any remedy, other than breach of contract, in respect of any untrue statement in reliance upon which the other party had entered into the contract. He also remarked that, in any event, in his view, the clause failed to satisfy the reasonableness test under s 8 of the UCTA because it was so wide that it excluded fraudulent misrepresentation which was clearly unreasonable.

There has been considerable discussion as to the effect of these two unreported cases, and, in particular, as to the validity of the *obiter dicta* in Jacob J's judgment in *Witter*. However, in the last year or so whole agreement clauses which take these two cases into account, including the remark about fraudulent misrepresentation, have become increasingly common in the legal profession in the UK.

1.5.2   Party protected by UCTA: any party; category of contract: all business contracts

Section 2(1) of the UCTA imposes a complete ban on any exemption clause giving protection against liability for death or personal injury caused by negligence. Section 2(2) prevents the use of an exemption clause to escape liability for other loss or damage (in general this is taken to refer to property damage and economic loss) caused by negligence, unless the clause can satisfy the test of reasonableness.

There is some question as to the true extent of s 2. First of all it is necessary to decide the type of party whose attempts to exclude liability are regulated by the section. Here s 1, which defines the application of various parts of the UCTA, must be looked at. Sections 2–5 of the UCTA apply only to 'business liability', which is defined by s 1(3) as 'liability for breach of obligations or duties arising (*a*) from things done or to be done by a person in the course of a business (whether his own or another's); and (*b*) from the occupation of premises used for business purposes of the occupier'. This sort of liability can obviously only be incurred by someone acting in the course of a business (a 'businessman').

Where the contract is between a businessman and a party who is not a businessman, usually a consumer, it seems from s 1(3)(*a*) that the businessman will incur 'business liability' (and hence is caught by s 2(1)), while the other party cannot incur 'business liability', since by definition he is not acting in the course of a business, and therefore will not be caught by the section. Obviously where no party to the contract is acting as a businessman (eg sale of a second-hand car between two natural persons by way of private treaty) the contract cannot be a business contract (as defined above), neither party can incur 'business liability', and both parties can exclude liability without reference to the section.

However, where both parties are acting as businessmen, both parties could in theory incur 'business liability', and thus become subject to s 2(1). Take installation of machinery at a factory. The installer is caught under s 1(3)(*a*). The factory owner may possibly be caught under the same provision, and he can certainly be caught in respect of occupier's liability for business premises under s 1(3)(*b*).

The second problem is to decide whether a particular exemption clause relating to liability for death or personal injury is to be dealt with under s 2(1) or 2(2). Where the exemption clause seeks to exclude such liability suffered by a party to the contract (the 'innocent party') who is a natural person (most usually, but not always, a consumer), because of the negligence of the other party (the 'party in default') (whether or not a natural person), then s 2(1) clearly applies, and the exemption clause will be regarded as void for the benefit of the innocent party should he suffer such personal injury or death.

However, the other category of liability for personal injury or death which the party in default can seek to pass on to the innocent party is that relating to claims made against the party in default by third parties, who have suffered death or personal injury by reason of the negligence of the party in default. Exemption clauses shifting liability (from the party in default to the innocent party) for third party claims of this nature relate in fact (as between the parties to the contract, and whether or not they are natural persons) to economic loss, so that s 2(2) will apply rather than s 2(1). Here the basic question is who (as between the parties to the contract) will indemnify the third party. Such clauses have no effect on the primary liability to the third party for the death or personal injury he has suffered. This liability is owed to the third party in tort by the party in default, and the terms of the contract between the party in default and the innocent party can have no effect on it.

Some case law was required in this area to supplement the bare provisions of the UCTA. First, the simple clause which seeks to exclude liability for death or personal injury caused by the party in default to the innocent party can only have application where the innocent party is a natural person. Such a clause is clearly banned under s 2(1). The only other type of clause which operates to shift liability is a counter-indemnity whereby the innocent party ('indemnifier') indemnifies the party in default ('indemnitee') for any claim made in respect of death or personal injury caused by the indemnitee's own negligence. Here two cases are possible. If the indemnifier is a natural person, the death or personal injury in question could either be suffered by the indemnifier himself, or by a third party who has suffered it by reason of the indemnitee's negligence and is claiming against the indemnitee in tort. If the indemnifier is not a natural person, only the situation relating to third party claims can arise.

Section 4 of the UCTA subjects any such counter-indemnity granted by a consumer to the test of reasonableness, so that in cases other than death or personal injury the situation is identical to that subsisting under s 2(2) but this left the operation of s 2(1) unclear in relation to a counter-indemnity granted by a consumer in respect of death or personal injury suffered by himself. It was not settled whether the indemnity be void under s 2(1) or only subject to a reasonableness test under s 4. The general situation with regard to such counter-indemnities granted by businessmen was also unclear. Were they somehow caught by s 2, or, because s 4 had no application, did they fall outside the Act?

Phillips Products Ltd v Hyland [1978] 2 All ER 620 solved the problem in respect of all such counter-indemnities, where the loss or damage was suffered personally by the indemnifier, whether or not a consumer. They were to be treated as exclusion clauses. Their effect was to cause the indemnifier to suffer the loss or damage caused by the indemnitee's negligence towards the indemnifier. This was tantamount to an exclusion of the liability otherwise owed by the indemnitee to the indemnifier in respect of the indemnitee's negligence. Therefore, counter-indemnities relating to death or personal injury suffered by the indemnifier were void under s 2(1), without the need to consider s 4, and all counter-indemnities relating to other loss or damage suffered directly by the indemnifier were subject to the reasonableness test under s 2(2), and/or s 4 if the indemnifier was a consumer.

However, where the indemnifier grants an indemnity to the indemnitee (under a contract between them) in respect of third party claims made against the indemnitee by reason of the indemnitee's own negligence, different considerations arise. First, if the indemnifier is a consumer, then s 4 (which regulates all indemnities granted by consumers, whoever the indemnitee) subjects the clause to the test of reasonableness. In the case of an indemnifier who is not a consumer, the question to be asked is whether, in the absence of the indemnity, the indemnitee would have been obliged at common law to compensate the indemnifier for the economic loss suffered as a result of having to pay out on the third party claim. If no such obligation existed then the indemnity is not transferring liability, and falls outside the Act (See *Thompson v T Lohan (Plant Hire) Ltd (J W Hurdiss Ltd third party)* [1987] 2 All ER 631.)

The situation is otherwise where there is an underlying liability owed by the indemnitee to the indemnifier, so that in the absence of the indemnity the indemnitee would be legally obliged to compensate the indemnifier for the economic loss suffered as a result of the third party claim. A good example is a manufacturer who sells to a reseller and requires the reseller to grant him an indemnity in respect of third party claims for product liability made against the manufacturer arising in relation to the products of the manufacturer that are sold on by the reseller. In the absence of such an indemnity, the manufacturer would be legally obliged to compensate the reseller for product liability claims made by the reseller's customers as a result of products which were defective due to the manufacturer's negligent workmanship. Section 2(1) can have no application in these circumstances, since any liability owed to a third party victim who suffers the death or personal injury remains unaffected by the indemnity (*Thompson*). Nevertheless, such an indemnity, whether relating to third party claims based on death, personal injury or damage, still acts to shift liability for economic loss, thus acts as an exclusion clause, and should therefore be controlled under s 2(2) (*Phillips*).

Leaving aside the position of the consumer who is party to a business contract, who clearly needs some special protection, the question of exemption clauses under s 2 is not merely one of regulating an unfair desire on the part of a party to exclude liability for his own negligence. It is much more concerned with the question, as between two businessmen, and their insurers, as to which side shall accept liability and insure for a particular risk.

As an example, property insurance is cheaper than liability insurance, so that it makes more sense, for instance, for a site-owner to insure against the fire risk of a fire caused by an installer, under fire insurance, than it does for the installer to insure against liability for causing the same risk, under a public liability or contractor's all risks policy. In any case, since the site-owner and his insurer will never be sure they can prove the liability of the installer, the existence of the installer's liability cover will not reduce the fire premium, so that the only alternative to the site-owner bearing the risk will be double insurance, which benefits neither side. (Also, just because of the difficulty of proving who caused the damage, fire insurers generally find it easier to give the necessary consent to waiver of their subrogation rights, without which the arrangements could not work.)

Where only death or personal injury are concerned, the need for counter-indemnities in the context of insurance is not as great. Each side will probably already be covered under appropriate employers', occupiers' and public liability policies, and, since the liability to be covered in each side's case is the same type, the shift from one side to the other will not result in an overall increase of premiums. Indeed, in most cases there is no effect at all on the premium as these sort of policies give cover of a type that will not result in a reduced premium just because a few people more or less are covered at any one time in a particular situation.

Insurance considerations will not be very relevant in deciding whether to exclude liability (for loss or damage other than death or personal injury) to a consumer to the extent that it is regarded as reasonable under s 4 and permitted under s 2(2). Even if the consumer can cover the risk by insurance, the position is much more complicated for him, and his insurers are going to be less likely to waive their rights of subrogation, without which his assumption of liability and his taking on of the insurance for the risk will not work.

Finally, s 2(3) should be noted. It provides for a partial abolition of the rule '*volenti non fit injuria*', without which ss 2(1) and 2(2) could not properly operate. The rule states that willing, knowledgeable assumption of a risk, freely undertaken, bars the right to compensation if damage is suffered as a result. The rule is used basically in tort, but it can also apply in contract (*Chapman v Ellesmere* [1932] 2 KB 431).

The point of s 2(3) is to spell out clearly the restrictions on the operation of the doctrine. At common law awareness plus action which implied consent was often enough (*Smith v Baker* [1891] AC 325). Section 2(3) seems to go further by saying that just because a party has entered into a contract with a term imposing risk on him, this 'is not of itself to be taken as indicating his voluntary acceptance' of that risk. This, of course, would be particularly applicable in standard term contracts, or where there was a marked inequality in bargaining power. There is some argument that the UCTA is doing no more than spell out a rule about what is really voluntary acceptance, which is already in the common law (*ICI v Shatwell* [1965] AC 656).

The provision as drafted is not entirely clear, and the use of the words 'is not of itself to be taken' might be construed to imply that some other type of truly voluntary acceptance could override s 2(1) or 2(2) by the operation of the rule. The Law Commission's original suggested draft sections (paras 132–135 of Report No 69) were clearer in that they specifically stated the purpose of preventing the enforcement of clauses, invalid under the preceding subsections, by calling in the rule.

1.5.3   Party protected by UCTA: consumers; category of contract: all business contracts

Sections 3(1) and 3(2) of the UCTA prevent the use of an exemption clause to exclude liability for breach, deviation or failure to perform a contract, in whole or part, unless it satisfies the test of reasonableness.

Section 3(2)(*a*) restricts the exclusion of liability for breach when the party relying on the clause is actually in breach. Therefore this section cannot catch clauses which define the obligations to be performed under the contract in a restrictive way. For instance, in an unreported case, *Fillite Runcorn Ltd v APV Pasilac Ltd and APC Corporation Ltd* (1993) discussed in (1994) 11 *Building Law Monthly*, issue 1, Judge Bowsher QC said 'terms which are drafted as defining the contractual obligations themselves, whether or not drafted as "exemptions" or "exceptions", are not caught by [section 3]'.

Section 3(2)(*b*)(ii) restricts clauses permitting a party to render no performance in respect of contractual obligations. The same points apply as to s 3(2)(*a*).

As an example, contrast a contract to paint the whole of a house, but containing a clause exempting the contractor from liability if he fails to paint certain parts (caught under s 3(2)(*a*)), and a contract to paint a whole house with the exception of certain parts (not caught). Clauses which impose only an obligation to exercise reasonable endeavours to attain a specific result (eg the contractor is only to make reasonable endeavours to paint the whole of the house) achieve the same effect.

Clauses imposing an obligation to exercise 'best endeavours' to achieve a particular result are to be treated in the same way as a 'reasonable endeavours' clause. However, the use of the term 'best endeavours' is generally believed to impose a more stringent obligation to achieve performance, but still does not impose an absolute liability to perform. In *Davis Ltd v Tooth & Co Ltd* [1937] 4 All ER 118, a form of words was used which was held to be equivalent to this term: 'to devote the principal part of their energies ... to pushing the sale' was held to mean 'to do the best it could to sell as much as could be sold'. This term thus does not impose an obligation to do everything possible, regardless of whether or not it is practicable. Looking at *Davis Ltd v Tooth & Co Ltd*, there also seems to be a suggestion that what is practicable is judged subjectively by reference to the particular entity undertaking the obligation.

The same approach was taken in *Midland Land Reclamation Ltd v Warren Energy Ltd* (1997) unreported, 20 January, QBD (OR), Judge Bowsher QC. The facts of the case are complicated, but among the issues was a discussion of best endeavours obligations. The plaintiffs had undertaken a contractual obligation to use their best endeavours to 'maintain, develop and operate at its own cost' a gas extraction plant, and the defendants had undertaken to use their best endeavours 'to maximise the use of the gas' delivered by the plant.

The learned judge stated that a best endeavours provision is sufficiently certain to be enforceable and relied on *Walford v Miles* [1992] 2 AC 128 at 138C for this proposition (see the extract from Lord Ackner's judgment mentioned below).

He held that 'best endeavours' imposes a duty to do what can reasonably be done in the circumstances, and the standard of that reasonableness is that of a reasonable and prudent board of directors acting properly in the interests of their company (see *Terrell v Mabie Todd & Co* 69 RPC 234). He also quoted *Sheffield District Railway v Great Central Railway* 27 TLR 451: 'Best endeavours means what it says—it does not mean second best endeavours.' He rejected the argument that a 'best endeavours obligation is the next best thing to an absolute obligation or guarantee'. In his view:

> 'To be satisfied of a breach of a best endeavours clause ... I would wish to hear evidence that in the light of the knowledge available at the time of the alleged default the party alleged to be in default was culpable. In assessing culpability I also take into account the unfriendly nature of the environment ... The question is, does the room for improvement which has been demonstrated by the [expert] evidence show that the plaintiffs have been in breach of contract by failing to use the best endeavours required by the contract? The answer to that question is No. There is much evidence that the parties on both sides could now in their present state of knowledge make improvement.'

However, the learned judge found that there was no evidence that either the plaintiffs or the defendants had failed to use best endeavours in the past given their level of technical knowledge at the time complained of.

This discussion of the use of the phrases 'reasonable endeavours' and 'best endeavours' must be distinguished from the use of such phrases in cases like *Phillips Petroleum Company UK Ltd v ENRON Europe Ltd* (1996) *New Law Digest*, 10 October, CA.

In *Phillips* the parties undertook to use reasonable endeavours to agree a delivery date for supplies of natural gas, as soon as possible, and, in default of agreement specified a longstop date on which deliveries would commence in any event. The buyer refused to agree a date because the market price of gas had fallen since the contract was entered into, and it was financially advantageous for him to delay the agreement of the delivery date as long as possible. The Court of Appeal, relying on *Walford v Miles*, in overturning the judgment at first instance, held that the buyer was entitled to refuse to agree a date for purely selfish commercial and financial reasons.

The distinction between cases like *Phillips* and *Midland Land Reclamation* can be found by going back to *Walford v Miles*, which was relied upon in both of these cases, but only to reach what at first sight appears to be diametrically opposed conclusions. The key to understanding how this can occur is that the distinguishing feature between the two cases is that *Phillips* was concerned with an agreement to negotiate while *Midland Land Reclamation* was concerned with an undertaking to perform a defined a contractual obligation. The fact that both obligations can be couched in terms of 'best endeavours', 'reasonable endeavours' or even 'good faith' is actually irrelevant. What made the court decide that the obligation in *Phillips* was unenforceable was the fact that the obligation was an agreement to negotiate. The fact that the obligation was couched in terms of using reasonable endeavours to come to an agreement was not the issue.

This distinction comes out clearly in Lord Ackner's judgment in *Walford v Miles* when he criticises the Court of Appeal for confusing in their decision the two concepts of an exercise of best endeavours and an obligation to negotiate. He said:

> 'While accepting that an agreement to agree is not an enforceable contract, the Court of Appeal appears to have proceeded on the basis that an agreement to negotiate in good faith is synonymous with an agreement to use best endeavours and as the latter is enforceable so is the former. This appears to me, with respect, to be an unsustainable proposition. The reason why an agreement to negotiate, like an agreement to agree, is unenforceable, is simply because it lacks the necessary certainty. The same does not apply to an agreement to use best endeavours … How can a court be expected to decide whether subjectively a proper reason existed for the determination of the negotiations? The answer suggested

depends upon whether the negotiations have been determined in "good faith". However, the concept of a duty to carry on negotiations in good faith is inherently repugnant to the adversarial position of the parties when involved in negotiations. Each party to the negotiations is entitled to pursue his or her own interest, so long as he avoids making misrepresentations. To advance that interest he must be entitled to threaten to withdraw ... from further negotiations or to withdraw in fact ... how is a vendor ever to know that he is entitled to withdraw? ... [If there is an obligation to negotiate in good faith] how is the court to police such an "agreement". A duty to negotiate in good faith is as unworkable in practice as it is inherently inconsistent with the position of a negotiating party. It is here the uncertainty lies.'

The judgment in *Phillips* clearly has this passage in mind when it is stated: 'A court cannot decide by reference to any objective consideration or criteria whether subjectively a proper reason exists for the termination of the negotiations. A provision requiring a party to use its best endeavours to agree will in general be equally unenforceable.'

In contrast, where there is an obligation to perform a particular action set out in a contract, the arguments relating to agreements to negotiate become irrelevant. The party required to perform the obligation has undertaken to perform it when entering into the contract. The obligation is thus set out as part of a legally enforceable contract, and the only issue is the standard of performance expected of the party concerned in order to discharge that obligation. Is it an absolute obligation to perform in all circumstances? Is it an obligation to perform unless excused by *force majeure*? Is it an obligation only to use best or reasonable endeavours to perform?[1]

When the specified standard of performance is something less than absolute, the only question is whether the standard specified is sufficiently certain to be capable, if necessary, of application by the court in the event of a dispute. This was clearly the case, where the phrase 'best endeavours' is concerned, in *Tooth* and in Lord Ackner's opinion stated in his judgment in *Walford v Miles*, which was relied upon by Judge Bowsher in *Midland Land Reclamation*. So far as the phrase 'reasonable endeavours' is concerned, it should be no more difficult for the court to judge whether reasonable endeavours has been exercised than it is for them to judge any other of the many instances of reasonableness which they are required to deal with (for instance the question of the exercise of reasonable care in the tort of negligence). The only problem to be observed here is the definition of 'best endeavours' put forward in *Midland Land Reclamation* relies heavily upon the use of a reasonableness test. If this is correct where does it leave the definition of 'reasonable endeavours'? Does *Midland Land Reclamation* mean that in substance there is no difference between the standard required for reasonable endeavours or best endeavours?

The phrase 'all reasonable endeavours' was considered in *Lambert v HTV*

Cymru (Wales) Ltd (1998) *The Times*, 17 March, which neatly confirms the distinction between the line of cases from *Walford v Miles* up to *Phillips*, relating to agreements to negotiate, and confirms the approach of Judge Bowsher in *Midland Land Reclamation*, in relation to a unilateral obligation to exercise best or reasonable endeavours to achieve an objective specified in the contract. In this case, the defendant undertook a contractual obligation, under a copyright assignment by the plaintiff in favour of the defendant, to use 'all reasonable endeavours' to obtain for the plaintiff first rights of negotiation for certain book publishing rights from any person to whom the defendant subsequently assigned all or part of the rights which were the subject of the first assignment. The defendant sold certain rights to third parties and did not obtain from them first negotiating rights for the plaintiff. The plaintiff sued for breach of the 'all reasonable endeavours obligation', but the court at first instance struck out part of his claim on the ground that English law would not enforce a right to negotiate. The Court of Appeal allowed the plaintiff's appeal against this decision. The Court of Appeal distinguished this case from *Walford v Miles*, as the plaintiff was not seeking enforcement of a right to negotiate. The defendant was obliged to endeavour to secure negotiation rights for the plaintiff. The obligation to exercise all reasonable endeavours to secure those rights was enforceable, even if, once the plaintiff had them, he could not force the third parties concerned to come to an agreement with him. What he had lost was the chance to negotiate. The Court of Appeal then stated clearly that an obligation to 'use all reasonable endeavours' was not unenforceable for lack of certainty. It was clear what was required of the defendant and he had failed to exercise any efforts at all to achieve the rights in question.

Lambert does not, however, give much guidance on the different standards required for reasonable as opposed to best endeavours, and, therefore, given the uncertainty in this area raised by *Midland Land Reclamation*, there must be some uncertainty as to how a court would interpret either the phrase 'reasonable endeavours' or the phrase 'best endeavours'. The safest course for a draftsman who wishes to ensure the enforceability of such obligations is to include a definition of the phrase in his agreement, specifying particular actions that should be performed or sets of criteria that should be applied, against which the court can judge if the obligation has been discharged.

However, the really important provision in s 3 of the UCTA is s 3(2)(*b*)(i), restricting exclusion of liability to perform what is reasonably expected of the party concerned under the contract. The Law Commission said (Report No 69, p 175) 'In [this] case the terms of the contract will not be decisive—regard will be had to all the circumstances'. The strict construction of the contract is thus not the conclusive factor. In this instance watering down the contractual obligation to use reasonable or even best endeavours, whatever degree of enforceability or lack of enforceability such a phrase may have, may not be sufficient to escape scrutiny under this provision.

As an example, take two parties agreeing to the painting of a house, where, in law, the contract finally made amounts only to an obligation to exercise reasonable endeavours to paint the house. The question to be answered is what was the consumer reasonably expecting, not what are his strict legal rights. For instance, if the clause imposing the obligation only to exercise reasonable endeavours were hidden away in a set of standard terms on the back of a quotation offering in unequivocal terms to paint the house, and the job was otherwise obviously a straightforward one, it is hard to see how reliance on the clause would be reasonable. However, where the job was a very difficult one involving areas where it might be impossible to gain access even with scaffolding, and the reservation had been specifically drawn to the consumer's attention, then it would seem reasonable to rely on the clause.

The state of knowledge that the supplier has of the buyer's requirements is also an important factor here. In *Zockoll Group Ltd v Mercury Communications Ltd* (1997) unreported, ChD (discussed in the periodical (1998) 9 PLC, issue 1, 47), Mercury in its standard terms of business reserved the right to withdraw or change any telephone number given to a customer subject to reasonable notice in writing. The customer protested the withdrawal of certain telephone numbers which it had applied for since, when dialled, they spelled out certain words, such as 'Flight', which it used in its marketing activities. Mercury had no knowledge of this, and regarded the telephone numbers as of no particular significance. The customer contended that the clause was invalid under s 3(2)(*b*)(i), as this enabled Mercury to change numbers of significance to the customer, and this was something that rendered the performance substantially different from what the customer could reasonably expect. The court refused to accept this contention. The customer had not told Mercury of this particular requirement. All that could he could reasonably expect of Mercury under the terms of the contract would be to provide telephone numbers of the quantity required. This Mercury had done.

Before discussing in more detail the types of exclusion clauses that are likely to pass the reasonableness test under s 3, one preliminary point must be made. Before the court even has to consider the reasonableness of an exclusion clause, the party relying on the clause has to convince the court that the clause is drafted in such a way that it covers the breach in question.

Liability for any type of breach arising from any cause, including total failure to perform caused by wilful default, can (leaving aside the impact of s 3 of the UCTA) be excluded, provided the clause is drafted widely enough. Section 9 of the UCTA provides for the partial abolition of the doctrine of fundamental breach in relation to contract terms which have to satisfy the element of reasonableness under the UCTA, such as exclusion clauses governed by s 3. In such cases the doctrine no longer exists. Even if the contract is terminated, the offending party can still rely on the clause if reasonable to do so, but even if the contract is affirmed, he cannot rely on the term unless it is reasonable to do so. This has reversed the rule in *Harbutts Plasticine Ltd v Wayne Tank and Pump Co Ltd* [1970] 1 QB 447, but it has not affected the rule in the *Suisse*

Atlantique case [1967] 1 AC 61 that exemption clauses cannot be construed to apply to fundamental breach unless clearly stated to do so. This principle was followed in the *Securicor* case mentioned above, where an exclusion clause was found to be drafted so widely as to exclude liability for a wilful default which was also a fundamental breach of the contract. Similarly, in a recent decision, *Armitage v Nurse* [1997] 3 WLR 1046, the Court of Appeal held that a trustee exemption clause could validly exclude liability for gross negligence as it was sufficiently widely drafted to cover this contingency, and that there was no point of public policy that would otherwise cause such a clause to be unenforceable.[2]

Once the party seeking the protection of the exclusion clause has established that it applies to the type of breach in question, and the cause from which the breach arose, he then has to satisfy the court of its reasonableness under s 3. Here, there are three factors to take into account: the seriousness of the type of breach in question, the cause of that breach, and the extent of the exclusion of liability. Clearly, total exclusion of liability for failure to perform a contract at all because of wilful default will not be reasonable under s 3. Equally, total exclusion of liability for failure to perform a contract at all because of circumstances beyond the control of the party in default (ie reasons of *force majeure* or an act of the other party) will conversely be reasonable in nearly all circumstances. Total exclusion of liability for failure to perform a contract at all is unlikely to be reasonable where it occurs because of acts or omissions within the control of the party in default, which are caused by negligence, incompetence or inadvertence but not wilful default ('inadvertent default').

Looking at some recent decisions which have considered this issue, it does appear that exclusion clauses of this nature are likely to be regarded by the court as *prima facie* unreasonable, so that the party relying on them will have a particularly difficult task in proving that they should be considered reasonable in all the circumstances of the particular case. (See *Sovereign Finance Ltd v Silver Crest Furniture Ltd* [1997] CCLR 76 and *Miljus (t/a A&Z Engineering) v Yamazaki Machinery UK Ltd* (1996) unreported, QBD (OR), transcript reference 1994 Orb. No 774). However, it is possible to succeed in this task, particularly in the context of a business transaction. In *Monarch Airlines Ltd v London Luton Airport Ltd* [1997] CLC 698, QBD (Admiralty Court), where an aircraft was damaged by loose paving blocks at the airport, the defendant sought to escape liability by relying on its standard terms which excluded liability for damage to aircraft caused by any act, omission, neglect or default. The court held that the clause was drafted widely enough to cover negligent acts by the defendant and that the clause satisfied the test of reasonableness because it had been generally accepted in the market, its meaning was clear, and both parties could make insurance arrangements on the basis of the clause.

Where the breach is of a less serious type, a clause which totally excludes liability for it is still likely to be reasonable where the breach is caused by *force majeure* and unreasonable if the breach is caused by wilful default. Where the breach is caused by inadvertent default the more serious the type of breach covered by the clause, the less likely it is to be reasonable.

Some exclusion clauses do not totally exclude liability for a breach but only restrict it. Such clauses are of three main types: liquidated damages clauses, clauses excluding liability for pure economic loss and clauses capping liability for the breach by reference to a monetary figure.

True liquidated damages clauses should by definition be reasonable under s 3 of the UCTA, since they are a genuine pre-estimate of the damage suffered as a result of the type of breach in question. If they are not, then they are regarded as penalty clauses which are unenforceable at common law, so that the question of the applicability of s 3 of the UCTA never arises. In this case, the question of the cause and the seriousness of the type of breach should have little relevance.

Clauses which limit liability for a particular type of breach, by excluding any liability for pure economic loss, such as loss of profit or business (often loosely called consequential loss clauses) should in most cases pass the test of reasonableness, whatever the cause of the breach, where the transaction is a non-consumer transaction. This is because economic loss can be of unforeseen proportions, can far exceed, in many cases the total contract value, and thus be a risk which it is for all practical purposes beyond the financial strength of most businessmen to assume, particularly if they were to accept such risks routinely in all their business dealings. It is also difficult to obtain insurance cover in substantial amounts to cover this type of liability. (For a discussion of these issues in the context of a business transaction see *Fillite Runcorn Ltd v APV Pasilac Ltd and APC Corporation Ltd* (1993) discussed in (1994) 11 *Building Law Monthly*, issue 1, and *The Salvage Association v CAP Financial Services Ltd* [1995] FSR 654.)

However, it could be that, in some transactions, where economic loss is suffered because of a breach caused by wilful default (or perhaps even inadvertent default), such clauses would not be regarded as reasonable where a consumer suffered economic loss. The amount of loss suffered by the consumer could be very large in relation to his financial resources, while not serious for the businessman who caused the breach, and in any event the businessman could (in cases of breach caused by inadvertent default, at any rate) possibly obtain insurance cover for such liability, since it is likely to be of a very low level (see *Harris v Wyre Forest District Council* [1989] 2 All ER 514).

The remaining type of clause is that which limits liability by reference to an overall monetary figure. The reasonableness of such clauses depends mainly upon the questions raised by s 11(4) of the UCTA—is the amount a reasonable one having regard to the financial resources of the party seeking its protection, and the extent to which he could insure against the relevant liabilities? Here the question of the seriousness of the type of breach, and its cause, seems less relevant. If the amount passes the test of s 11(4), then that amount is all that the party in breach can reasonably be expected to pay, however much loss the other party suffers, and even for total failure to perform caused by wilful default. Nevertheless, the insertion of a trivial amount to restrict liability for a serious breach (for wilful or inadvertent default) is unlikely to be regarded as reasonable.

A final point on this type of clause: if what is regarded as an initially reasonable figure is inserted in standard conditions and remains unchanged for a number of years it may well have become unreasonable through the impact of inflation, either in an absolute sense, or because average contract values have increased. Alternatively, applying one standard figure to a variety of contract values may in itself be unreasonable. What is appropriate for a contract worth £1,000 will be unreasonable for one worth £1,000,000 (see the *George Mitchell* case).

The safest course is to limit liability to a monetary figure which seems generally reasonable in the light of the business concerned or the value of the contract, whichever is the higher. An alternative approach which can also be recommended is to set the limit at x per cent of the contract price, where x is always greater than 100 per cent. This approach allows potentially for the return of all money paid under the contract plus some compensation for other loss (eg loss of profit or bargain) suffered as well. Limiting liability to a figure or the contract value whichever is the lower is unlikely to be reasonable. (See *St Albans and District Council v International Computers Ltd* [1997] FSR 251, CA.) In any event the relevant figure should be reviewed regularly to take account of inflation.

So far we have looked at exclusion clauses which exclude or restrict liability for a particular type of breach arising from a particular cause. Such clauses are common in contracts, but equally common are general exclusion clauses which exclude or restrict liability for all breaches, however caused ('general exclusion clauses'). General exclusion clauses will obviously be effective, if they are drafted properly, subject only to s 3 of the UCTA. However, because of their wide scope, when judging such clauses under s 3 of the UCTA, one has to treat them on the basis that they exclude or restrict liability for total failure to perform by reason of wilful default. A general exclusion clause which excludes liability altogether is thus very unlikely to be reasonable under s 3. A general exclusion clause which restricts liability to a monetary figure, or by reference to a liquidated damages formula, could well be reasonable, depending upon the actual figure or formula, which should be judged on the criteria relating to such limitations of liability discussed above. The same would be true of a general exclusion clause which excluded liability for economic loss, where, again, one would have to consider the issues as to reasonableness discussed above.

As stated above, the only principle that can be deduced is that a clause can only be judged under s 11 of the UCTA in the context of the specific factual and legal matrix applying to the contract in which it is incorporated. Therefore, it is not possible to provide a set of rules that will enable the draftsman to produce exclusion clauses which will always pass the test of reasonableness under s 11. However, by analysing the examples of general and specific exclusion clauses discussed in this section, it is possible to consider a strategy for drafting exclusion clauses which has a greater probability of being reasonable in a wider range of factual and legal matrices.

This strategy is based upon understanding the effect of setting the three parameters common to all exclusion clauses at different levels. These parameters are:

(1) the *type* of breach for which liability is excluded;
(2) the *cause* of the breach for which liability is excluded; and
(3) the *extent* of the exclusion of liability.

At one end of the range is the clause which applies to all *types* of breaches, however *caused* and *extends* to all liability for such breaches. Here all three parameters can be said to be set 'high'. It is almost impossible to envisage circumstances under which such a clause would pass the test of reasonableness under the UCTA. At the other extreme is a clause which applies only to one *type* of breach, *caused* by circumstances beyond the reasonable control of the party concerned where the *extent* of the exclusion of liability for the breach is limited to a genuine pre-estimate of the direct damage suffered by the other party. An example would be a liquidated damages clause expressed to be in full and final satisfaction of delay in delivery caused by *force majeure*. Here all the parameters are set 'low'. Such a clause is likely to be reasonable in most factual and legal matrices which can be envisaged.

Clauses with parameters set at differing levels will fall somewhere between these two clauses as to the range of situations in which such clauses are likely to be reasonable. For instance a clause applying to all *types* of breach *caused* by *force majeure* which *extends* to exclude all liability for such breaches has the *type* and *extent* parameters set 'high', but the *cause* parameter set 'low'. Similarly, a clause applying to all *types* of breaches *caused* for any reason but only *extending* to exclude liability for loss of profit, has the *type* and *cause* parameters set 'high' and *extent* parameter set 'low'. It would be likely to be reasonable in many matrices, but the chance of it so being would be increased if the *cause* parameter were set 'lower' by making it clear that the exclusion clause did not apply in circumstances where the cause of the breach was wilful default.

The three parameters can also be used to assess clauses which limit contract liability by a monetary cap. Where the clause covers all *types* of breaches ('high') from all *causes* ('high'), then it is unlikely to be reasonable unless the *extent* of the exclusion is set 'low'. This is achieved by capping the liability at a monetary sum which is at the least as high as the contract value, and preferably higher. The higher the cap, the 'lower' the parameter is set, and the greater the likelihood of the clause being reasonable in a greater variety of matrices.

Three working principles can be derived from this discussion. First, it is impossible to draft an exclusion clause which will always pass the reasonableness test in any factual and legal matrix. Secondly, the further each of the parameters of an exclusion clause is set towards the 'low' end of the scale, the more likely is a court to find the clause reasonable. Thirdly, general exclusion clauses which cap all liability should not normally have the parameter of *extent* set at less than the contract price.

Given that these principles are imprecise, how should the draftsman proceed? The first point is never to forget the common law rule that exclusion clauses are construed *contra proferentem*. One will never have to ask whether an exclusion clause is reasonable if the court finds that its provisions failed to cover the relevant breach in the first place. The second point is to place reliance on the principles of severance and draft a battery of clauses with their various parameters set at different points on the low-high scale. For instance there could be a liquidated damages clause covering late delivery, clauses excluding specific warranties that would otherwise be implied under the SGA, a clause excluding liability for loss of profit, however caused, a clause excluding liability for failure to perform because of *force majeure* and finally a clause capping all liability at 125 per cent of the contract price. Each of these clauses has to be tested separately for reasonableness. Some may fail the test, but others may survive to provide whole or at least partial cover in respect of the breach that has occurred.

1.5.4   Party protected by UCTA: non-consumers contracting on other party's standard terms and conditions; category of contract: all business contracts

The provisions of s 3 of the UCTA apply equally in these circumstances, and the protected party is placed in the same position as a consumer, even if he is acting as a businessman. The justification for protection in these circumstances is that a businessman who is willing to deal on the other party's standard terms and conditions is probably unable to negotiate a special deal due to an inequality of bargaining power.

The problem is to decide when one party is dealing on the other party's standard terms and conditions. There is no definition in the UCTA of the phrase used in s 3(1) 'written standard terms of business'. The Law Commission was against one, on the grounds that a rigid definition could be more easily evaded, and that, in individual cases, the courts and legal advisers would recognise standard terms and conditions when they saw them.

Standard contracts issued by trade or professional associations for the use of their members will be caught (RIBA contracts for example) as will individual standard conditions of the type often printed on the back of quotation forms or invoices. The terms of a performance bond have also been held to fall within the definition, since it was a form regularly used by the issuer of the bond when providing such a facility to its customers (*Oval (717) Ltd v Aegon*

Insurance Co (UK) Ltd (1997) 54 Con LR 74).

The hallmarks seem to be conditions which are not drafted with any particular parties or transaction in mind, that are used for a series of contracts, and in respect of which the person who puts them forward does not expect much, if any, negotiation to take place. Nevertheless, all these matters are only indicative, and cannot be said to be conclusive. (See *Chester Grosvenor Hotel v Alfred MacAlpine Management* (1993) 56 BLR 115.)

1.5.5 Party protected by UCTA: non-consumers not contracting on other party's standard terms and conditions; category of contract: all business contracts

This heading comprises the vast majority of commercial contracts, where the parties have presumably an equality of bargaining power and have freely entered into properly negotiated contracts. In these circumstances, s 3 has no application, and the parties (subject to the caveats surrounding the exclusion of liability for death, personal injury and other loss caused by negligence, as regulated under s 2) are free to make whatever bargain as to liability for breach, non-performance or failure to perform as they choose.

Here the problem is to decide when a party is not dealing on the other's standard terms. The resolution of this issue depends upon both the definition of 'dealing' and the definition of 'standard terms'. These are questions of strict definition. Thus when determining what contracts fall within or outside the ambit of s 3, issues of reasonableness, equality of bargaining power and the possibility of negotiation are in fact not very relevant, except in so far as they could move a judge to finding that terms were standard or not in borderline cases.

So far as the definition of 'dealing' is concerned, in *St Albans and District Council v International Computers Ltd* [1997] FSR 251, CA at 262–263, Nourse LJ stated that: 'as a matter of plain English "deals" means "makes a deal" irrespective of any negotiations that have preceded it. Thus in order that one of the contracting parties may deal on the other's written standard terms ... it is only necessary for him to enter into the contract on those terms.' This solves the problem where, despite previous negotiations, the standard terms are finally incorporated without alteration. However, the court gave no guidance as to the effect of partial renegotiation. For instance would renegotiation of only one or more clauses remove just that clause or clauses (if relevant) from the ambit of s 3, or would it render the whole set of terms no longer standard. The safest argument (in the absence of further authority) is that only the renegotiated clauses would be so removed. Thus, on this basis, it would be imprudent to regard an exclusion clause in a set of standard terms as outside the ambit of s 3 just because some clauses, other than the exclusion clause itself, had been renegotiated.

The discussion in the previous paragraph is concerned with whether the terms in question fall within the ambit of s 3 or not. Nevertheless, even if the negotiation in question has not resulted in any alteration to the exclusion clause, so that s 3 applies, the substance of the negotiations may well affect the finding of whether or not the clause is reasonable under s 11. For instance, the other party may have been offered and accepted a substantial price reduction in return for agreeing to accept the standard terms in question.

St Albans provided no particular help with the definition of 'written standard terms of business'. However, apart from the *indicia* of a set of standard terms and conditions discussed in the previous section, it is possible to identify certain commercial transactions which are so structured that it cannot be said that the parties are dealing on written standard terms at all.

First, an oral contract can never be caught, since s 3(1) specifies dealing on 'written standard terms of business'. Oral contracts are possibilities in situations where well-established trade customs can be proved, and contain principles of exemption from liability upon which the party in default can rely.

Secondly, a unique situation, with a unique typed or manuscript contract would be outside the provision. Even using the same terms on more than one occasion with the same customer would seem not to amount of itself to trading on standard terms.

However, the matter is less clear cut where a party uses typed precedents drawn up by its lawyers as a basis for starting negotiations. For instance, a businessman could habitually send customers a typed standard contract and then negotiate on that, or, having had his lawyers draw up a special contract on one occasion, he could start to use this on subsequent occasions as if it were a precedent. Whether such a use results in the businessman trading on written standard terms and conditions, is probably a matter of degree. Critical factors here would be the number of times such documents were sent out, and the amount of negotiation that took place in the relevant case. A great many contract negotiations that started from a written set of terms and conditions sent with an offer to negotiate, which in fact produced mainly contracts upon the original terms offered, with little evidence of variations introduced by negotiation, would seem likely to be caught. Trifling variations of printed conditions, or an expressed as opposed to an actual willingness to negotiate, will not avoid the section. (See *Fillite Runcorn Ltd v APV Pasilac Ltd and APC Corporation Ltd* (1993) discussed in (1994) 11 *Building Law Monthly*, issue 1, and *The Salvage Association v CAP Financial Services Ltd* [1995] FSR 654 at 671–672 which was approved in *St Albans*.)

The conclusions seem to be that printing in general is fatal, draft standard conditions sent for negotiation are very often caught, but there is not a problem with the unique situation, even if the starting point is a set of standard terms and conditions. From this it follows that far more transactions could well be caught under the section than at first appears.

Thirdly, the parties may have started with the contract or conditions of the party who is now seeking the protection of the UCTA against an exemption clause. They may have then negotiated from these to produce a final contract in which the other party introduced the exemption clause in question through negotiation. Here it seems hard to say that the party seeking to rely on the exemption clause is contracting on his own written standard terms.

Fourthly, if the standard terms upon which the contract was made were put forward by the party seeking protection, then he has no protection under s 3 against an exclusion clause which he himself has put in his conditions, if the other party chooses to rely on it. This is of course because the party seeking protection is not dealing on the other party's standard terms and conditions and the section can therefore have no application.

Lastly, the question as to whose standard terms govern the contract, or even if there is a contract at all, is a difficult one to solve under English law where the parties exchange standard form contracts and then do not negotiate on them. This so-called 'battle of the forms' is discussed further in Chapter 2.

1.5.6 Party protected by UCTA: any party; category of contract: all contracts for sale or hire purchase of goods; subject matter of contract: all goods

Having dealt with the question of exclusion clauses in general, the UCTA then deals with the question of the extent to which liability for breach of certain warranties implied into contracts for the supply of goods and services under the SGA, the SGSA and the Supply of Goods (Implied Terms) Act 1973 can be excluded by express provision in the relevant contract.

It will be recalled that by and large this body of legislation provides that such warranties are to be implied into the relevant contracts unless the contract itself expresses a contrary intention. Sections 6 and 7 of the UCTA override these provisions, and, in effect, provide for mandatory inclusion of such warranties in the contracts covered by these sections, since the easiest way to exclude liability for breach of such warranties is to exclude them altogether from the terms of the contract. However, the effect of ss 6 and 7 goes further because their wording is also wide enough to regulate contracts which permit the inclusion of such warranties, but then seek to nullify that inclusion by excluding liability for breach of the warranties so included.

Section 6(1) of the UCTA states that (under any contract for the sale or hire purchase of goods, not merely business contracts—see s 6(4)) liability for breach of the obligations arising from the warranties as to title and quiet possession implied under SGA 1979, s 12 (in relation to sale of goods) and s 8 of the Supply of Goods (Implied Terms) Act 1973 (in relation to goods disposed of on hire purchase) cannot be excluded or restricted by reference to any contract term.

In some cases (for instance distress sales by receivers, in situations of insolvency) both parties may know there is a doubt as to title but want to take the chance anyway. The correct approach here is to cut down the obligation to perform undertaken under the contract, rather than attempt to impose an exemption clause covering the liability for a breach committed. This has already been discussed when considering s 3 of the UCTA. Thus one could contract to pass a restricted title, or whatever title one has in the goods. This is envisaged by SGA 1979, s 12(3), although even here SGA 1979, s 12(4) and (5) imply a warranty that the seller has disclosed known encumbrances, and warranties promising no disturbance of quiet possession by the seller or the person on whose behalf he is selling, or by third parties claiming through them (except by reason of an encumbrance disclosed to the buyer). These warranties are also covered by the UCTA 1979, s 6(1).

Section 6(1) of the UCTA gives rise to particular problems in the area of infringement of third party intellectual property rights and in relation to clauses which attempt to exclude by blanket wording all warranties implied by the SGA, or which provide for exclusion of liability generally (such as those excluding liability for economic loss or capping total liability under the contract by reference to a monetary amount). These issues are discussed in Chapter 2 in relation to the clauses in the precedents in that chapter which are affected by this issue.

1.5.7   Party protected by UCTA: consumers; category of contract: business contracts for sale or hire purchase of goods; subject matter of contract: consumer goods

Section 6(2) of the UCTA prevents exclusion of liability for breach of the warranties relating to conformance to description, conformance to sample, satisfactory quality and fitness for purpose which are implied by ss 13, 14 and 15 of SGA, for sale of goods contracts, and ss 9, 10 and 11 of the Sale of Goods (Implied Terms) Act 1973, for hire purchase contracts, as amended by SSGA 1994. UCTA, s 30, which prevents exclusion of obligations relating to safety under consumer safety legislation should also be noted in this context.

Although the UCTA does not say so, the section must here only be dealing with sales or hire purchase of goods made to the consumer in the course of a business, because s 6(2) only protects persons dealing as consumers, and a person can only deal as a consumer if the person with whom he is dealing deals in his turn in the course of a business. (See s 12(1)(*b*).)

Under this provision, the same points about stating limited obligations (subject to UCTA, s 3(2)(*b*)(i)), as opposed to restricting liability for breach, will apply. The most usual examples of this are the sales of second-hand or shop-soiled goods where the vendor clearly states their condition and sells them 'as seen'. This is not really a case of excluding the warranties which would otherwise be implied by the relevant legislation, but rather one of making sure that the warranty given is properly tailored to the subject matter of the contract. For instance, the standard of satisfactory quality of second-hand or shop-soiled goods is clearly less than of brand new goods, and a vendor who spells out that he is selling second-hand or shop-soiled goods is still warranting conformance with description, but it is a different description from the one he would have applied to brand new goods.

The most difficult point about this section is that its application is necessarily limited to goods 'of a type ordinarily supplied for private use or consumption' by the operation of s 12(1)(*c*). The Law Commission thought that this would exclude products 'designed and normally bought for commercial use', but that there might be borderline cases.

However, this definition does in practice cause some problems. For instance, some items, such as raw materials like wood, sand and cement, or products such as glass and bricks, clearly can be purchased both for private use and consumption (eg DIY sales) and by businessmen (eg builders). The same problem can arise with finished products such as tools, or personal computers. The problem is not helped by the fact that the UCTA refers to the type of goods, not the type of outlet they are bought from, or the quantity in which they are bought. Because of this it is not possible to make a distinction based on the difference between wholesale and retail sales. In any event some outlets (eg cash and carry or the large DIY chains) are used both by consumers and tradesmen. The only possible wholesale/retail distinction relating to the type of goods that might have some application would seem to be in the area of packaging for retail as opposed to wholesale sale.

The only really satisfactory way to solve the whole problem is to assume that there are certain types of goods which can at the same time be 'ordinarily' for private use and for commercial use. A standard personal computer which can be used both for business and home purposes (for instance with a standard word processing package) would be a good example.

1.5.8 Party protected by UCTA: persons not dealing as consumers; category of contract: all contracts for the sale or hire purchase of goods; subject matter of contract: all goods

Section 6(3) of the UCTA prevents exclusion or restriction of liability for breach of the warranties relating to conformance to description, conformance to sample, satisfactory quality, and fitness for purpose which are implied by ss 13, 14 and 15 of SGA, for sale of goods, and ss 9, 10 and 11 of the Sale of Goods (Implied Terms) Act 1973, for hire purchase contracts, unless such exclusion or restriction passes the test of reasonableness.

The scope of this section is wide, since there are three reasons why a person may be dealing otherwise than as a consumer: first, because he is a businessman (see s 12(1)(*a*)); secondly, because the other party is not a businessman (see s 12(1)(*b*)); and, thirdly, because the goods are not of a type ordinarily supplied for private use or consumption (see s 12(1)(*c*)). The first category covers business contracts, the second private contracts, and the third could cover either.

From these categories it is possible to construct a matrix for different combinations of types of parties and classes of goods. For the purposes of this analysis, goods 'ordinarily' supplied for private use or consumption are referred to as 'consumer goods', and all other goods are referred to as 'commercial goods'.

Protected Party	*Party Relying On Clause*	*Class of Goods*
Non-consumer	Business	Commercial
Business	Non-consumer	Consumer/Commercial
Non-consumer	Non-consumer	Consumer/Commercial
Business	Business	Consumer/Commercial

Prima facie, it would appear that a court would be likely to find exclusions more reasonable as one proceeds down the matrix, and exclusions relating to consumer goods more reasonable than those relating to commercial goods.

The first category covers a businessman disposing of commercial goods to a private person. This would be a consumer sale except for the fact that the goods are not consumer goods within the meaning of s 12(1)(c). Here the exclusion of liability is obviously least likely to be reasonable. However, since the private person has chosen to deal in commercial goods (and presumably has some expertise in relation to the subject matter of the contract) such exclusion is more likely to be reasonable than if consumer goods were the subject matter of the contract, and hence the transaction were a consumer transaction governed by s 6(2).

The analysis in relation to the first category shows the correct way of solving the problems, under s 6(2), of the borderline cases as to what are consumer goods. Where the only disqualifying element under s 6(2) is the type of goods, then the overwhelming likelihood will be that, when considering the transaction under s 6(3), the court will find the exclusion unreasonable.

The second category relates to a transaction whereby a private person disposes of goods to a businessman. The businessman should be better able to take care of himself in the transaction, and therefore should require little protection. As for the class of goods, it should make little difference here, since the businessman should be better able than the private party to assess them. However, in most cases, the private person, even if not acting in the course of a business, is still really entering into a commercial transaction and it seems more likely that there will be more cases than in the first category where it will be reasonable that he accept some liability.

The third category relates to private transactions, where an equality of bargaining power is usually to be presumed. In any event, in many cases, courts will (in the absence of fraud) be less likely to wish to intervene in non-commercial dealings between private individuals. As for the class of goods, where commercial goods are concerned the party acquiring them presumably has some expertise in relation to them which gives him the capability to assess their quality or to understand if he needs to call in an expert assessor, so that less protection should be required in this case.

In the final category, both parties to the transaction are acting in the course of business, and are presumably able to take care of themselves. It seems, *prima facie*, most reasonable that they deal with the question of liability in this area as they think fit, irrespective of the goods concerned. For instance a manufacturer and a wholesaler could enter into a contract for the supply of domestic refrigerators (consumer goods) for onward sale by the wholesaler to retailers, while a factory owner could enter into a contract with a manufacturer for the supply of a machine for use in his factory (commercial goods). In neither case does the category of goods seem likely to affect the reasonableness of any exclusions of liability to be agreed as between the two parties to the relevant contract.

1.5.9 Party protected by UCTA: all parties; category of contract: contracts for the barter of goods, and for the supply of labour and materials; subject matter of contract: all goods

The SGSA, s 2 implies warranties as to title and quiet possession into all contracts 'for the transfer of goods' which are equivalent to those implied into contracts for the sale of goods under s 12 of the SGA. The SGSA defines such contracts as those 'under which one person transfers or agrees to transfer to another person the property in goods' except in pursuance of a contract of sale, a hire purchase contract, and 'a contract under which property in goods is transferred in exchange for trading stamps on their redemption' (see s 1). (Under the SGA and the UCTA 'trading' stamp redemption contracts are treated as sale of goods contracts.) The contracts covered by SGSA, s 2 are thus in practice contracts of exchange or barter, and contracts for the supply of labour and goods or materials (eg building contracts). It should be noted that the SGSA, s 2 is not limited to business contracts.

Section 17 of the SGSA inserts a new subsection 3A in s 7 of the UCTA, which is equivalent in its operation to s 6(1) of the UCTA, and thus prevents exclusion of liability for breach of the warranties implied by s 2 of the SGSA. Section 2 of the SGSA applies to all contracts, and the wording of the new s 7(3A) imposes an absolute prohibition on exclusion of liability for breach of the warranties implied by s 2 of the SGSA. Thus, despite the limitation of s 7 of the UCTA (prior to its amendment by the addition of s 7(3A)) to business contracts (see s 1(3)), the better argument would seem to be that the new s 7(3A), like the old s 6(1), applies to all contracts, not just business contracts. On this basis, all contracts under which property in goods passes from one party to the other receive the same treatment in relation to prevention of exclusion of liability for breach of warranty of good title and quiet possession.

Section 7(3A) of the UCTA gives rise to the same issues as s 6(1) of the SGA, in relation to infringement of third party intellectual property rights, clauses excluding all implied warranties, and clauses limiting liability under the contract as a whole. Again these issues are discussed in Chapter 2.

1.5.10 Party protected by UCTA: all parties; category of contract: business contracts for the hire, rental, lease or bailment of goods; subject matter of contract: all goods

Prior to the passing of the SGSA, s 7(4) of the UCTA prevented exclusion of liability for breach of warranties of title and quiet possession 'arising by implication of law' (see s 7(1)), in business contracts (other than for the sale and hire purchase of goods) under which possession or ownership of goods was transferred, unless such exclusion passed the test of reasonableness. However, as discussed above, in relation to contracts under which ownership of goods is transferred, so far as such contracts are not governed by s 6 of the UCTA, they are now governed by the new s 7(3A). Section 7(4) has thus been rendered partially otiose. This is recognised by s 17(3) of the SGSA which amends s 7(4) of the UCTA so that it applies only in cases where s 7(3A) has no application.

Given the provisions of s 6 of the UCTA and the way in which SGSA, s 17 has dealt with the warranties of title and quiet possession to be implied into other contracts under which property in goods is transferred, there do not in practice seem to be left any other types of contract under which property in goods can be transferred. Thus s 7(4) is now restricted in practice to business contracts where possession of goods passes, but not title, namely contracts of hire, rental, lease or bailment.

The SGA has no provisions implying warranties as to title or quiet possession into such contracts, but s 7 of the SGSA implies certain warranties as to the right to transfer possession into a 'contract for the hire of goods' (which under s 6 of the SGSA is defined as a contract of bailment by way of hire for a consideration of any nature). The bailor warrants that he has the right to transfer possession for the period of the bailment, and that the bailee will enjoy quiet possession for the period of the bailment except so far as possession is disturbed by the owner or other person entitled to the benefit of any charge or encumbrance disclosed or known to the bailee before the contract was made. The definition of 'contract for the hire of goods' in s 6 of the SGSA is not all-encompassing, and there may well be some contracts of bailment which fall outside it. In these cases the general case law must be looked at to decide what warranties are to be implied in this area.

Thus s 7(4) now acts, in respect of these warranties under business bailment contracts alone, to prevent exclusion of liability for their breach unless reasonable. It should be noted that, although ss 6 and 7 of the SGSA apply to all contracts, not just business ones, there is no provision in s 17 which overrides the restriction of s 7(4) to business contracts only.

1.5.11 Party protected by UCTA: consumers; category of contract: business contracts for the barter of goods, for the supply of labour and materials, and for the hire, lease rental or bailment of goods; subject matter of contract: all goods

Section 7(2) prevents the exclusion of liability as against a consumer for breach of warranties arising by implication of law from the form of the contract as to the goods' correspondence to description or sample, or their quality or fitness for any particular purpose. Prior to the passing of the SGSA what warranties could be implied was the subject only of case law. The SGSA implies warranties as to conformance with description (ss 3 and 8) and with sample (ss 5 and 10), and (in the case of business contracts only) as to quality and fitness for purpose (ss 4 and 9).

Since s 7(2) applies only to business contracts, the fact that ss 3, 5, 8 and 10 of the SGSA apply to all contracts is of no relevance in this context. There may still be some other warranties implied at common law in contracts of these types, both those covered by, and those outside the scope of, the SGSA. However, in the area of quality and fitness for purpose, the SGSA prescribes that any such warranties relating to those matters shall no longer have effect in such contracts to the extent that they fall within the scope of the SGSA.

Finally, it should be noted that the whole of s 7 of the UCTA, and, indeed, the relevant sections of the SGSA discussed above, only apply to contracts under which possession or ownership of the goods passes to the other party. Where one party to a contract contracts to use certain goods for the purposes of the contract, considerations of title and quiet possession may be irrelevant, but conformity to description, sample, quality and fitness for purpose may well not be. For instance, quality and fitness for purpose could well be vitally important in a contract whereby, eg a dry cleaner agrees to use particular solvents upon a customer's clothes, or the owner of an art gallery agrees to use special chemicals to restore and clean a painting. The Law Commission thought that the use of such goods, which operate by chemical action without their substance attaching to the article cleaned, with no transfer of ownership or possession, should also be caught by s 7. Section 7 clearly does not cover such contracts, although the SGSA (treating them as contracts for the supply of services) would imply an obligation to use reasonable care and skill under s 13.

It may be arguable that some part of the substance used does attach to the article cleaned, even if the rest is rinsed off, so that ownership in that part passes by adhesion to the article. If this is so, s 7 may apply in some cases. However, given the implied term of reasonable care and skill under SGSA, s 13, both ss 2 and 3 of the UCTA may well apply in any event to avoid an exclusion of liability if the wrong substance is used, or it does not produce the result contracted for.

1.5.12 Party protected by UCTA: non-consumers; category of contract: business contracts for the barter of goods, for the supply of labour and materials, and for the hire, lease rental or bailment of goods; subject matter of contract: all goods

Section 7(3) regulates the same warranties as those covered by s 7(2). All of the same considerations apply, except that here since the protected parties are non-consumers, the section permits the exclusion of liability to the extent that the exemption clause satisfies the requirement of reasonableness. It should be noted that, although s 7(3A) applies to all contracts, not just business contracts, as discussed above, this is not the case with s 7(3). Section 7 contains no provision equivalent to s 6(4) which would apply s 7(3) to all contracts, and, since s 7(3) was not introduced by the SGSA, the arguments relating to s 7(3A) as outlined above can have no application.

1.6 Treatment of contracts with a foreign element

Having analysed the main provisions of the UCTA in relation to specific types of contracts it remains to consider the extent to which contracts with a foreign element are caught by its provisions.

Section 27(1) of the UCTA excludes from its operations contracts which are governed by the law of any part of the UK only because the parties inserted an express governing law clause to that effect. This provision thus excludes contracts which, apart from such a governing law clause, would, under the general provisions of conflict of laws prevailing under private international law as applied in the UK, be governed by a foreign proper law. For an example of the application of this provision see *Surzur Overseas Ltd v Ocean Reliance Shipping Co Ltd* (1997) unreported, QBD (Commercial Court), transcript reference 1997 F-No 83.

On the other hand, a contract which, under such conflict of laws provisions, would be governed by the laws of any part of the UK, except for the fact that the parties inserted a governing law clause specifying a foreign proper law, may still be caught by the UCTA. Section 27(2)(*a*) permits the court or the arbitrator a discretion to ignore the governing law clause if it appears that it has been included only for the purpose of evading the provisions of the UCTA.

Section 27(2)(*b*) goes further than this by negating absolutely any governing law clause imposing a foreign proper law where the contract was concluded in the UK by a consumer then habitually resident in the UK. In a sense, this provision simply imposes the result that would have arisen under general conflict of law principles if the governing law clause had never existed. By implication all other contracts with a foreign element are exempt.

There is an alternative line of attack to that contained in s 27, available in business transactions, which can be mounted against governing law clauses imposing a foreign law, where the clause is contained in written standard terms. Such a clause can be regarded as a kind of indirect exemption clause, since its effect would be to exclude the operation of the UCTA entirely. Such a clause can then be regarded as equivalent to an exemption clause under s 13 of the UCTA, and would therefore fall to be considered in terms of its reasonableness under s 3 of the UCTA just like any other exemption clause. (See *Surzur Overseas Ltd v Ocean Reliance Shipping Co Ltd*, above.)

A contract genuinely governed by a foreign proper law is obviously exempt (whether or not it contains a foreign proper law clause), whether so specifically stated in the UCTA or not. Also exempt would be a contract which could or should have been governed by one of the systems of law in the UK, where s 27(2)(*b*) does not apply, and the parties have chosen a foreign proper law for a genuine reason other than evasion of the UCTA (eg because the other party was a foreigner who insisted on using the law of his own jurisdiction as the governing law of the contract).

The conclusion seems to be that where one wishes the UCTA not to apply, one should, where possible, by observing the relevant conflict of law rules, create a contract genuinely governed by a foreign proper law, so that there is no need for an express choice of law clause which can be attacked or negated under s 27(2).

International contracts for the supply of goods, even if *prima facie* caught under s 27, will be exempt under s 26 of the UCTA, if they fulfil its rather strict requirements. Although there is no exemption for a contract which consists exclusively of the international supply of services, a mixed contract (eg supply and installation, or supply and supervision of installation, of plant abroad) will come under s 26. Therefore in such cases, where it is desired that the UCTA not apply, one method is to draft one contract for both goods and services, and not two separate contracts for each element.

International distributorship agreements will also fall under s 26 since they are pure agreements for the sale of goods, and thus fall within the SGA (see SGA, s 1(3)). An arrangement where an agent works on a commission with a consignment stock, is obviously not an agreement for the sale of goods, but is a contract under or in pursuance of which *possession* of goods passes (UCTA, s 26(3)(*a*)). and would also be caught. Contracts with commission agents, indenting agents and canvassers will not be caught under s 26, as no goods pass between them and their principal. They merely collect orders and pass them back to their principal who fulfils the orders direct. Their contract is not one *under* which possession or ownership of goods passes. Nor, it is submitted, can it properly be regarded as one in *pursuance* of which possession or ownership passes either.

Finally, ss 28 and 29 exclude from the UCTA contracts governed by international conventions (eg Athens Convention regulating sea carriage of passengers) and contracts governed by any other statutory scheme of regulation in the UK which permits specific exclusions of liability.

1.7   General considerations relating to the law of contract

The UCTA also deals with some general considerations relating to the law of contract.

First, evasion of the UCTA by means of secondary contracts, which contract out of rights under the UCTA, is controlled by UCTA, s 10.

Secondly, s 13(1) of the UCTA prevents a further possibility of evasion by creating an extended definition of exemption clauses. Another type of evasion would be to create a situation where there was no contract at all, so that only certain liabilities under tort, in accordance with UCTA, s 2, would remain. The Law Commission admitted that it would be difficult to cope with this, and the UCTA does not do so. However, the Law Commission expressed the hope that if the practice became widespread, the Office of Fair Trading would prevent it under the powers granted by the Fair Trading Act 1973. In practice the problem does not seem to have arisen so far, and s 13(1) is still restricted to secondary contracts.

Another problem under s 13(1) is the status of the liquidated damages clause. This is, by definition, neither a penalty clause, nor a limitation of liability up to a certain amount, because it is supposed to be a genuine pre-estimate of the damage. In theory, then, and in genuine cases, such clauses should be completely untouched by the UCTA, and by s 13 in particular, since they are only helping the parties to quantify their loss. In practice, in many industries, particularly the construction industry, such clauses have become standard, and both the courts and the parties have tended to accept them without argument as to their status or the effect of s 13. In flagrant cases, the best argument open to a party wishing to escape liability is still that such a clause is a penalty and hence unenforceable under general principles of law.

The effect of s 13(1) in relation to set-off was discussed in *Stewart Gill v Horatio Myer Co* [1992] 2 All ER 257, CA. Depending upon the relative bargaining powers of the parties many commercial contracts either contain set-off clauses permitting set-off of cross claims between the parties, or clauses forbidding such set-off. Although rights of set-off subsist at law, the inclusion of set off clauses is common, and equally common are clauses excluding those rights. Until *Stewart Gill v Horatio Myer Co*, however, no one doubted clauses preventing set-off were enforceable, without any consideration of the UCTA applying.

In this case the clause provided that 'the customer shall not be entitled to withhold payment of any amount due to the company under the contract by reason of any payment credit set-off or counterclaim'. The plaintiff tried to obtain collection of a debt under the contract by way of summary judgment, and, when the defendant attempted to raise a counterclaim for breach which would entitle him to defend the case, relied on this clause.

At first instance the court held that such a clause was an exclusion clause within the meaning of s 13 of the UCTA, since it clearly excluded one of the methods by which the defendant could otherwise, at law, have enforced his counterclaim, namely by set-off. Thus the clause could be considered under s 3 of the Act, since it was contained in the plaintiff's standard conditions upon which the contract was entered into. The court held that such a clause was *prima facie* unreasonable under s 3, and that, as he had not discharged the burden of proof upon him to show that the clause was reasonable under the circumstances, the plaintiff could not rely on it in order to obtain summary judgment. The Court of Appeal upheld this decision.

A good example of the way the UCTA cases depend upon the particular factual matrix surrounding the contract is provided by another recent case on set-off, *Overland Shoes Ltd v Schenkers Ltd; Overland Shoes Ltd v Schenker International Deutschland GmbH* (1998) *The Times*, 26 February. Here the same type of clause preventing set-off was included in standard conditions, in just the same way as in *Stewart Gill v Horatio Myer Co*. The court at first instance agreed that the clause was an exclusion clause caught by s 3 of the UCTA. However, profiting by the error in *Stewart Gill v Horatio Myer Co*, the defendants had led evidence to show that the clause was reasonable, and, on this evidence, the court was satisfied that the clause passed the reasonableness test, since the parties were of equal bargaining power. The Court of Appeal refused to disturb the finding at first instance, and commented that, in this case, as a clause in common use in the relevant trade, it reflected a general view of what was reasonable in that trade.

Arbitration clauses are specifically excluded from the ambit of s 13(1) by s 13(2). In theory (subject to the general powers of the court to control arbitration in the areas of misconduct) even a very unfair arbitration clause (eg offending party chooses arbitrator, and victim must agree) is not controlled. However, despite the initial expressions of fear that this practice could cause problems, it does not in fact seem to have become widespread. In any event, the Consumer Arbitration Agreements Act 1988 now provides that in most domestic consumer contracts any arbitration clause cannot be enforced against a consumer without the leave of the court unless the consumer has consented in writing to submit the contract dispute to arbitration after it has arisen. Presumably, it was felt that businessmen could take care of themselves in this area, and the fact that such clauses are not in common use in business contracts seems to bear this out. In addition ss 89–91 of the Arbitration Act 1996 provide that for the purposes of the Unfair Terms in Consumer Contracts Regulations 1994 (SI No 3159) (discussed in more detail in section 1.10 below) an arbitration agreement in a consumer contract is unfair for purposes of the Regulations so far as it relates to a claim for a pecuniary amount which does not exceed that amount specified by order for the purpose of the section. The aim of this provision is to prevent consumers being forced to go to arbitration where only a modest amount is sought and they would probably be better off applying under the procedure for small claims in the county court.

Finally, s 5 regulates the attempts to evade the UCTA by use of the manufacturer's so-called 'guarantee'. Before the passing of the UCTA such guarantees in theory were supposed to offer the purchaser of defective goods a remedy additional to that of suing the person from whom he bought the goods. The manufacturer would offer various remedies for defective goods returned direct to him, for instance, repair, replacement or money back at his option. However, in order to take advantage of such guarantees, the customer would have to sign and return a portion of the guarantee form or certificate to signify that, in consideration of the granting of the guarantee, he would accept that his legal remedies against the manufacturer were limited to the express ones contained in the guarantee. In practice the express remedies were actually in many cases fairly limited, so that the effect of such guarantees was rather to avoid the manufacturer's liability than to provide an additional remedy.

Section 5 prevents this practice completely, by providing that avoidance of liability for defective goods caused by negligence of the person involved in their manufacture or distribution cannot be excluded by a term or notice in a 'guarantee' of goods ordinarily supplied for private use or consumption as against a person who has found the goods to be defective while he was using them, or while they were in his possession, otherwise than exclusively for the purposes of a business. Section 5 refers to such use or possession as 'consumer use'.

The section does not apply to contractual guarantees, as between a seller and a purchaser, as these are obviously caught under the appropriate sections of the UCTA relating to contracts, in so far as they should be caught at all (see s 5(3)).

The section imposes a double test. First, the goods have to be 'consumer goods' within the meaning of s 12(1)(c), with all of the problems that this definition entails. Even if they pass that test they still have to pass the second hurdle of being 'in consumer use' when the defect arises. The definition of 'consumer use' is very wide, and looks at the actual facts of the case, even if the other party did not know them, or could not be expected to know them. Obviously a person who first acquired consumer goods as a businessman, and then chose to put them into consumer use for his own private uses could take advantage of this section.

1.8   EC law considerations

In concluding this chapter it is necessary to mention five pieces of EC law which are of vital significance in relation to consumer contracts: the General Product Safety Directive (92/59/EC), the Unfair Contract Terms Directive (93/13/EC), the Directive to Protect the Consumer in Respect of Contracts Negotiated away from Business Premises (85/577/EC), the Directive on the Protection of Consumers In Respect of Distance Contracts (97/7/EC) and the Proposal for a Directive on the sale of consumer goods and associated guarantees which has been circulating since late in 1997.

1.9   General Product Safety Directive (92/59/EC)

The General Product Safety Directive (92/59/EC) is designed to ensure that products placed on the market in member states are safe for consumers to use. Producers and distributors are required to tell consumers relevant information concerning their products, to monitor the safety record of their products while in use, and to take the necessary steps to protect consumers from defective products, including, if necessary by withdrawal.

Member states are obliged to police the Directive and the safety of products put on the market. This will entail monitoring and sampling activity, and carries with it the power to ban the sale of dangerous products and to organise their withdrawal and destruction. The Directive prescribes that there should be criminal penalties for its breach, but leaves it to the implementing legislation in each member state to decide what these should be. The Directive, which member states had to implement by 29 June 1994, imposes a detailed and strict regulatory system on all producers and distributors of consumer products within the EC.

1.10   The Unfair Contract Terms Directive

The effect of this Directive on drafting consumer contracts is very far reaching, and no consideration of the general principles of law relating to the drafting of commercial contracts in the UK would be complete without an examination of its provisions.

The lengthy preamble makes it clear that this Directive is a harmonisation measure requiring member states to equalise the level of protection granted to consumers when they enter into contracts with traders, businessmen or professionals. The preamble stresses that it is the responsibility of member states to ensure that contracts concluded with consumers do not contain unfair terms. The intention is that consumers (who generally are unfamiliar with the law in other member states) should be able to buy goods and services as consumers throughout the EC while feeling confident that whatever laws govern those contracts, the relevant member state will have ensured that such contracts do not contain unfair terms. The Directive requires the adoption of uniform rules of law by all member states in the matter of unfair terms, which should apply to all contracts between sellers or suppliers, of goods and services, and consumers, whether such contracts are oral or written. The Directive does make it clear, however, that other types of contracts such as those relating to employment, family law, company law and partnership, should be excluded from the Directive. Insurance and financial services contracts are partially but not wholly excluded.

It should be noted that the Directive applies to trades, businesses and professions of both a public and a private nature, so that state owned enterprises are included within its ambit.

The basis of the Directive is to fix, in a general way, the criteria for assessing the unfair character of contract terms taking into account, in particular, whether the relevant term was individually negotiated, the relevant strength of the bargaining position of the parties, whether the consumer had an inducement to agree to the term, and whether the goods or services were sold or supplied to the special order of the consumer.

The Directive, however, does not attempt to assess the bargain which the consumer has made under the contract and therefore excludes assessment of the unfair character of terms which relate to 'the main subject matter of the contract' and 'the quality/price ratio of the goods or services supplied'.

The Directive also provides that contracts must be drafted in 'plain intelligible language, the consumer should be given a proper opportunity to examine all the terms', and any ambiguities in drafting should be interpreted in favour of the consumer.

Article 1 states the purpose of the Directive as approximating the law regulations and administrative provisions of the member states relating to unfair terms in contracts concluded between the seller or supplier and the consumer.

Article 2 defines 'consumer' as 'any natural person who, in contracts covered by this Directive, is acting for purposes which are outside his trade, business or profession'. It similarly defines 'seller or supplier' as 'any natural or legal person who, in contracts covered by this Directive, is acting for purposes relating to his trade, business or profession, whether publicly owned or privately owned'.

Article 3 provides that a contract term which has not been individually negotiated shall be regarded as unfair if, contrary to the requirements of good faith, it causes significant imbalance in the parties' rights and obligations arising under the contract, to the detriment of the consumer.

A term is *always* to be regarded as not individually negotiated where it has been drafted in advance and the consumer has therefore not been able to influence the substance of the term, particularly in the context of a pre-formulated standard contract.

The article also states that the burden of proof that a standard term has been individually negotiated falls on the seller or supplier, but given the provisions set out in the previous paragraph, it is hard to see how this burden can ever be discharged, unless there has been an individual negotiation at which both parties actually discussed and wrote out the clause in question for the first time.

Article 4 gives some guidelines for the 'unfairness test' as follows: 'If necessary the unfairness of a contractual term shall be assessed taking into account the nature of the goods or services for which the contract was concluded and by referring, *at the time of conclusion of the contract*, to all the circumstances attending the conclusion of the contract and to all the other terms of the contract or of another contract on which it is dependent'. The guidelines exclude the possibility of assessment of the bargain under the contract as described above.

Article 5 imposes the plain language requirement and the obligation to interpret ambiguities in the way most favourable to the consumer.

Article 6 provides that unfair terms shall *not bind the consumer* but that the contract shall continue to bind the parties upon the remaining terms if it is capable of continuing in existence without the unfair terms. The article also requires member states to enact measures to prevent working around the Directive by imposing artificially, as the proper law of the contract, the law of a non-member state, where the contract has a close connection with the territory of the member states of the community.

Article 7 appears to give the right to consumer groups or organisations to take action against organisations of suppliers or sellers who draw up and use standard terms and conditions which contain unfair terms. The article gives the possibility of legal action against individual sellers or suppliers, or groups of them from the same economic sector, or against their trade associations. This remedy is particularly interesting since it applies to public sector suppliers (such as utilities) as well as private business.

Article 8 provides that member states may adopt more stringent provisions than those set out in the Directive if they so wish.

Article 10 requires the member states to adopt the laws, regulations and administrative provisions necessary to comply with this Directive no later than 31 December 1994.

Finally, in the Annex there are set out a number of terms which, according to the previous draft of art 3(3), was to be an indicative list of terms which may be regarded as unfair. The most significant amendment still to be discussed on the Directive prior to its adoption related to the status of this list. The July 1992 text regarded it as giving non-mandatory guidelines. Consumer groups wished to give the Annex the status of a blacklist. The final text adopts a compromise position which changes its status to 'an indicative and non-exhaustive list of the terms which may be regarded as unfair'. This wording, and the relevant wording in the preamble, means that the burden of proof is shifted onto the trader, businessman or professional relying on a clause falling within the Annex to prove that it is not unfair.

Thus while generally speaking all terms listed can be presumed to be unfair, this presumption may be contested by a seller who uses this type of term in specific situations.

At the very least drafting of consumer contracts which avoid the types of clauses set out in the Annex will go most of the way towards ensuring that such contracts are fair within the terms of the Directive. Further discussion of the drafting of a consumer contract in the light of the Directive is covered in Chapter 5.

So far as UK law is concerned, the Directive has been implemented through the passing of the Unfair Terms in Consumer Contracts Regulations 1994 (SI No 3159) which came into force on 1 July 1995 (six months after the date mandated in the Directive) and by and large follow closely the wording of the

Directive. The only really controversial issue relates to the implementation of art 7(1) (powers to prevent the general use of unfair terms) and art 7(2) (representative actions by consumer associations). The DTI originally did not intend to implement these two provisions on the grounds that, so far as the first was concerned, anyone who was personally aggrieved could bring a civil action, and the judgments in such actions would build up a group of precedents which would deter future use of offending provisions, and that, so far as the second was concerned, since UK law does not provide for representative or class actions, no action to implement this section was possible or necessary in the UK.

As a result of further lobbying the DTI were finally persuaded that the statutory instrument should implement art 7(1) by giving the Director General of the Office of Fair Trading statutory powers to consider complaints that 'any contract term drawn up for general use is unfair, unless the complaint appears to the Director to be frivolous or vexatious'. He then has power, in appropriate cases, to bring proceedings before the courts for an injunction to prevent the use of the term by 'any person appearing to him to be using or recommending the use of such a term in contracts concluded with consumers'. Such injunctions 'may relate not only to use of a particular term drawn up for general use but to any similar term, or a term having like effect, used or recommended for use by any party to the proceedings'.

However, the DTI had no such change of opinion, despite considerable lobbying by consumer associations, in relation to representative actions under art 7(2). It considered that it had gone far enough in giving powers to the Director General of Fair Trading and that it should not alter the general law in the UK by granting a right, even in these special circumstances, for consumer groups to bring representative actions.

With the change of government in 1997 came a change in policy. The DTI has issued in January 1998 a consultation paper on widening the scope for action under art 7(2) while still preserving the powers of the Office of Fair Trading. The proposal is to add a provision to permit the court to admit other bodies whose function is to protect the interests of consumers so as to allow such bodies to bring a representative action under the Regulations. There would be a list of criteria set out in a new schedule to the Regulations which the court may use in deciding whether to recognise a body. The system to be applied will have to be compatible with the proposed EC Directive on Injunctions for the Protection of Consumers' Interests which is expected to be adopted towards the end of 1998, and enables member states to designate as 'qualified entities' one or more independent public consumer bodies (as well as private consumer bodies) which will be able to seek injunctions in the courts of other member states to stop traders contravening consumer rights under the nine current EC consumer policy directives, including the Unfair Contract Terms Directive.

The Regulations have now been in force for nearly three years and in this time the Office of Fair Trading has proved to be far more vigorous in the area of enforcement that was first thought by many of the consumer associations who lobbied for a direct role under art 7(2). It publishes periodical reports on its activities including cases in which it has found various clauses objectionable under the Regulations and required the users to modify or drop them. This is discussed in more detail in Chapter 5. As a general indicator of the Office of Fair Trading's activity level, it should be noted that in the period from July 1995 to May 1997 it examined 1,660 cases, and has made some significant changes to consumer contract terms particularly in the area of double glazing, mobile phones and satellite broadcasting.

The main problem with implementation in the UK was that the UCTA already regulates various types of contractual relationships, namely freely negotiated commercial contracts, commercial contracts on standard terms and conditions and consumer contracts whether or not freely negotiated. However, in implementing the Directive through the 1994 Regulations, the decision was taken by the DTI not to amend the UCTA in any way, so that the protection offered by the UCTA would remain. They considered that the test of fairness in the Directive had similarities to the test of reasonableness to which a majority of the terms within the scope of the UCTA were subject. In their view, the extent of this similarity would reduce any problems arising from the overlap between the two measures. A comparison of the details of the two tests set out in Appendix 1 shows that there is considerable similarity and overlap. The biggest difference is the express inclusion in the test for unfair terms of the requirement to assess whether the supplier dealt in good faith and fairly and equitably with the consumer. There is currently no case which has compared the two tests, and consumers, in any relevant legal proceedings, would be well advised to proceed both under the UCTA and the Regulations. However, it must be observed that in principle it is hard to see how the UCTA test, which requires the term to be 'fair and reasonable' will differ very much from a test which considers whether the term is 'unfair'.

The DTI considered that although the title of the Directive applies to all contracts involving consumers, the recitals and indeed parts of the text, imply that it can only apply to contracts for the supply of goods and services, and this is made clear in the 1994 Regulations. In some circumstances the UCTA can have a wider application (for example ss 2 and 8). The DTI also pointed out that the definition of a consumer in the Directive was narrower than that in the UCTA, which talks of 'dealing as a consumer'. The courts have thus interpreted the UCTA as giving protection in certain circumstances to companies dealing as consumers, while the Directive only applies to natural persons. (See *R&B Customs Brokers Ltd v UDT Finance Ltd* [1988] 1 All ER 847 and *Chester Grosvenor Hotel v Alfred MacAlpine Management* (1993) 56 BLR 115.)

Thus, although the regime under the Regulations and the regime under the UCTA will overlap in most cases concerning consumers, there are circumstances where only one regime will provide a remedy and the other will not apply. A summary comparison of the application of the two regimes is provided in Appendix 2 to this chapter.

1.11   Contracts Negotiated Away From Business Premises Directive

The Directive applies (art 1) to contracts for the supply of goods and services by a trader to a consumer which are concluded during an excursion organised by the trader away from his business premises, or during a visit to the consumer's home, or to that of another consumer, or to the consumer's place of work, where the visit does not take place at the express request of the consumer. The Directive also applies where, during a visit covered by the Directive, the contract is not concluded but the consumer makes an offer which is later turned into a contract by the trader's acceptance.

The Directive does not apply (art 2(a)) to contracts for the construction, sale and rental of immovable property or to contracts concerning other rights relating to immovable property, other than contracts for the supply of goods and for their incorporation into immovable property or contracts for repairing immovable property. The Directive does not apply (art 2(b)) to contracts for the supply of foodstuffs or beverages or other goods intended for current consumption in the household and supplied by regular roundsmen. The Directive does not apply (art 2(c)) to sales made out of a catalogue, provided that the consumer has had a proper opportunity of reading the catalogue in the absence of the trader's representative, there is intended to be continuity of contact between the trader's representative and the consumer, either for that or any subsequent transaction, and both the catalogue and the contract clearly inform the consumer of his right to return the goods within a period of not less than seven days of receipt, or otherwise cancel the contract within that period, without any obligation other than to take reasonable care of the goods.

The Directive also does not apply to insurance contracts (art 2(d)) nor to contracts for securities (art 2(e)). Article 3(1) provides that, by way of derogation from art 2, member states may provide that the Directive should not apply to contracts unless they exceed 60 ECU nor (art 3(2)) to contracts for the supply of goods or services having a direct connection with goods or services in respect of which the consumer requested the visit of the trader.

Article 5(1) provides the consumer with a right to cancel contracts controlled by the Directive. This right cannot be waived (art 6). Article 4 requires traders to give consumers written notice of this right of cancellation. Article 5 then provides that the consumer can exercise his right of cancellation by sending notice to the trader within a period of not less than seven days from the receipt by him of the relevant notice under art 4. It is sufficient if the notice is despatched within this period even if it is not received before the end of the period. Article 5(2) states that the giving of notice releases the consumer from any obligations under the cancelled contract, although art 7 provides that the legal effect of the consumer's cancellation of the contract (particularly in regard to payment for goods or services provided and the return of goods received) shall be governed by the national law of the member states.

Article 8 permits the member states to enact in local law provisions in relation to the matters dealt with in the Directive which are more favourable to consumers than those detailed in the Directive. Article 9 requires the Directive to be implemented by member states within 24 months of its publication. The Directive was implemented in the UK by the Consumer Protection (Cancellation of Contracts Concluded Away From Business Premises) Regulations 1987 (SI No 2117).

By and large the Regulations merely implement the terms of the Directive, with some clarification. They are particularly important in dealing with the interaction between the rights under this Directive and the rights of cooling off and cancellation already given to consumers in the UK under the Consumer Credit Act 1974. Where the transaction is one which is governed by the Act, the Act applies rather than the Regulations (reg 4(2) and see reg 9). The Regulations also specify (reg 3(2)(*f*)) the amount under art 3(1) of the Directive, currently £35. The Regulations also deal in more detail than the Directive with the precise form and procedure for the notification to the consumer of the right of cancellation and as to the way in which the consumer can exercise that right (see arts 4 and 11 and the Schedule to the Regulations). The Regulations also specify the relevant provisions to take effect under national law (see art 7 of the Directive) in relation to recovery of money paid by the consumer (reg 5), repayment of credit received by the consumer (reg 6), return of goods received by the consumer (reg 7) and return to the consumer of goods given to the trader in part exchange (reg 8). Finally, art 10 deals with the fact that, either directly or indirectly, the consumer cannot contract out of his rights under the Regulations.

Clearly the Directive and the Regulations have limited impact, since the exclusions provided under the Directive have a wide scope, particularly the fact that they only apply to transactions over the specified amount, and the limited exclusion for catalogue sales. Many door-to-door transactions which would otherwise be caught are likely to be excluded by one or both of these exceptions. The exclusions relating to financial services and real-property transactions will also exclude many transactions (eg unsolicited invitations by estate agents to view and buy houses or to attend events intended to persuade consumers to lease time-share holiday apartments).

The most difficult issue is the question of when the consumer rather than the trader was responsible for initiating the visit. At one end of the spectrum, the trader will have called uninvited, or will have invited the consumer to visit him at some place away from his business premises. At the other end, the consumer will have initiated the transaction by expressly requiring the trader to attend at his premises or workplace. The grey area results when the invitation by the consumer takes place after he has already had some contact with the trader. The Directive is not very helpful here, but the Regulations are more specific. Regulation 2(3) defines an 'unsolicited visit' (ie one covered by the Regulations) as 'a visit by a trader, whether or not he is the trader who supplies the goods or services, which does not take place at the express request of the consumer and includes a visit which takes place after a trader telephones the consumer (otherwise than at his express request) indicating expressly or by implication that he is willing to visit the consumer'.

Regulation 2(3) thus seems to provide guidelines for most scenarios. The trader who calls uninvited or invites the consumer to an event away from his business premises is clearly covered. The consumer who invited the trader entirely of his own accord is not protected. What happens where the trader and the consumer discuss a visit by the trader and the consumer finally invites him or agrees to a visit? The trader who persuades the consumer to agree to a visit by means of an unsolicited telephone call ('cold calling') is expressly caught. A trader who took silence for consent and did not receive an express invitation would also be caught since reg 2(3) only talks about an 'express' request. However, reg 2(3) does not appear to catch the situation where the consumer communicates with the trader otherwise than by telephone (for instance by letter, or face-to-face on the trader's business premises or elsewhere, provided it is not the home or workplace of the consumer or the home of another consumer—because otherwise the visit will already have taken place) and at last expressly requests the trader to make a visit. In this situation, it can perhaps be said that the consumer has, when at last issuing the express invitation, either in a sense brought it on himself (by visiting trade premises for a discussion in the first place) or had enough time to say no to a visit without pressure (eg if the invitation finally comes after an exchange of correspondence).

1.12   Distance Contracts Directive

The Directive covers any contract concerning goods or services concluded between a supplier and a consumer under an organised distance sales or service-provision scheme run by the supplier and concluded exclusively by one or more means of distance communication up to and including the moment at which the contract is concluded. The definitions of consumer and supplier are similar to those in the Unfair Contract Terms Directive. Consumers are defined as natural persons acting outside the course of their trade, business or profession. Suppliers are defined as any natural or legal person acting in his commercial or professional capacity. The definition of distance communication is very wide, and clearly covers all forms of electronic comm..erce, including sales over the internet: 'any means which, without the simultaneous physical presence of the supplier and the consumer may be used for the conclusion of a contract between the parties'. There is an indicative but non-exhaustive list of such means in Annex 1 to the Directive, including sales through mail shots, press advertisements containing order forms, catalogues, telephone, videophone, videotext, radio, electronic mail, fax and television (teleshopping).

The Directive does not apply to contracts relating to financial services, contracts concluded by means of automatic vending machines or automated commercial premises, contracts concluded with telecommunications operators through the use of public payphones, contracts for the construction and sale of immovable property (except for rental), nor to contracts concluded at an auction.

The Directive requires suppliers to give to the consumer essential information about the contract before it is made (art 4), written confirmation of such information in a durable form after the contract has been concluded (art 5) and, subject to some detailed exceptions, a period of at least seven working days in which to withdraw from the contract without penalty and without giving any reason (art 6). The only charge that may be made to the consumer because of the exercise of his right of withdrawal is the direct cost of returning the goods. This cooling-off period begins from the day when the consumer has received the written confirmation of the contract terms, or, if no such information has been delivered, three months from delivery of the relevant goods or, in the case of the supply of services, three months from the date on which the contract was concluded. Exceptions to the cooling-off right are as follows: contracts for the supply of services, where the consumer has agreed to the performance of the services beginning before the cooling-off period has expired; contracts for the supply of goods or services subject to fluctuations in the financial market outside the supplier's control; contracts for goods made to the consumer's specifications, or clearly personalised, or which, by their nature, are liable to deteriorate, to expire rapidly or cannot be returned; contracts for the supply of audio or video recordings or computer software once unsealed by the consumer; contracts for the supply of newspapers, periodicals and magazines; and contracts for gaming and lottery services.

The Directive requires the supplier to perform the contract within a maximum of 30 days from the day following that on which the consumer forwarded his order to the supplier (art 7(1)). In the event the goods or services are unavailable, the supplier must inform the consumer of the situation and refund any money paid as soon as possible and in any case within 30 days (art 7(2)). Member states may provide that the supplier can supply substitute goods or services of equivalent price and quality provided this right is included in the relevant contract and the consumer has been informed of it in a clear and comprehensible manner. In this case, if the consumer exercises his right of withdrawal in relation to substitute goods, the cost of their return must be borne by the supplier (art 7(3)).

It should be noted that arts 4, 5, 6 and 7(1) do not apply to contracts for the supply of foodstuffs, beverages or other goods intended for everyday consumption supplied to the home of the consumer, to his residence or to his workplace by regular roundsmen. Nor do they apply to contracts for the provision of accommodation, transport, catering or leisure services, where the supplier undertakes, when the contract is concluded, to provide these services on a specific date or within a specific period. Exceptionally in the case of outdoor leisure events the supplier can also reserve the right not to apply art 7(2) in specific circumstances.

Article 8 of the Directive provides for the consumer's right to request cancellation of a payment where fraudulent use has been made of his payment card and to be recredited with the sums paid or have them returned. Article 9 prohibits the supply of unsolicited goods or services to consumers (inertia selling). Article 10 restricts the use of automated calling machines, or of fax machines as a means of distance communication for the purposes of the Directive, without the prior consent of the consumer. Article 11 provides for judicial or administrative redress on behalf of consumers against suppliers who contravene the Directive, including through the actions of consumer or professional associations and public bodies or their representatives. One such body in the UK would clearly be the Office of Fair Trading, which already acts to police the Unfair Contract Terms Directive. Article 12 provides that the consumer cannot waive the rights conferred upon him by the Directive. Article 13 provides that the Directive shall be overridden by any more specific Community rules governing any particular aspects of the supply of particular goods or services. Article 14 provides that member states may provide for more stringent provisions than those contained in the Directive, provided that they are compatible with the Treaty of Rome. One area suggested is the prohibition of the sale of certain medicinal products by means of distance contracts.

Member states are required to implement the Directive within three years of its publication in the *Official Journal* (art 15) and to provide adequate information to consumers about the existence of their rights under the implementing legislation (art 16). The Directive was published on 4 June 1997, so the end date for implementation is 4 June 2000, but the Department of Trade and Industry has already indicated that it intends to implement the Directive much more quickly than that, and is in the process of circulating a consultation paper prior to drafting the necessary statutory instrument.

Three initial comments may be made about this Directive. First, the whole purpose of electronic commerce is to conclude transactions at a distance speedily and easily. This does not sit so easily with the provisions of art 6 which requires written confirmation of the contract terms. However, there seems no reason why the pre-contract information required under art 5 could not be sent to the consumer by electronic means, and the right of withdrawal under art 7 in respect of the supply of goods (ie seven days after delivery) raises no real issues. In fact consumers now partially enjoy this right under the SSGA 1994. Under s 2(2) and (3) of the SSGA 1994, a consumer, who has not had a prior opportunity to examine the relevant goods, has the right (which cannot be waived) to reject them if they are not in conformance with the contract. (See

Chapter 2.) Secondly, the Directive in fact only supplies partial protection to consumers, since a consumer may order goods or services through 'distance communication' (for instance over the internet) from suppliers situated outside the European Union. In these circumstances the supplier cannot be compelled to comply with his obligations under the Directive, nor, arguably, to recognise the consumer's rights of withdrawal. Perhaps a court within the European Union could refuse to enforce a contract against the consumer if the supplier had refused to comply with the terms of the Directive, even though the supplier was based outside the European Union. However, this is a debatable point which depends on quite complicated issues in the area of private international law, and is only one aspect of the desirability and feasibility of international controls over the internet. At present, and until an enabling statutory instrument is brought into force in the UK, it is premature to conjecture how a court in the UK would deal with such issues.

1.13   Proposal for a directive on consumer guarantees

The Proposal for an EC Directive on the sale of consumer goods and associated guarantees would create a mandatory two-year guarantee for consumer goods (excluding buildings) for all consumer contracts in the EU. The guarantee would have to provide that the goods should be 'in conformity with the contract' throughout this period. The definition of conformity is broadly in line with the warranties as to conformity to description and sample and as to satisfactory quality and fitness for special purpose now contained in ss 13, 14 and 15 of the SGA. Where goods fail so to conform, the consumer would be entitled to require the seller to repair the goods free of charge or provide a price reduction throughout the guarantee period. In addition, for the first year of the period only, the consumer would be entitled to opt for a refund or replacement of the goods (where possible) instead. Any failure of the goods to conform with the contract which manifests itself within six months of delivery is assumed to be the fault of the seller, unless he can prove otherwise. Member states can include a provision restricting the consumer's rights in the case of a minor nonconformity (compare s 15A of the SGA which applies this same provision but only in the case of business contracts).

The current draft of the proposal clearly requires some further discussion. In particular, the two-year guarantee and the rights given to the consumer under it seem more suited to durable goods, rather than consumable or perishable goods, or goods which are obviously of a nature (for instance with a particular sell-by date or shelf life) which means that they are not intended to last for two years.

The current timetable for the implementation of the Directive envisages European Council and European Parliament approval in August 1998, with final publication of the Directive in the *Official Journal* in January 1999. The member states would then be required to implement the Directive by January 2001. Once this Directive is implemented express guarantees will clearly have to comply with its provisions as finally published.

1.14   Construction of commercial contracts

Finally, certain developments in recent cases make it desirable to conclude this chapter with a short discussion on the approach which the courts in the UK are now adopting to the construction of commercial contracts. These are points which need to be borne in mind by the draftsman in dealing with any of the contracts covered within this book.

The classic approach of the common law is to construe a contract according the plain and ordinary meaning of the words contained in it, without reference to extraneous circumstance such as the prior negotiations or intentions of the parties, except in the specific instance where a claim of rectification is being made to correct a manifest error in the contract.

This approach has been somewhat altered as a result of a number of recent decisions. In *Charter Reinsurance Co Ltd v Fagan* [1996] 2 WLR 726, the House of Lords held that a provision providing that a reinsurer had to pay out to the insurer for the 'sum ... *actually* paid in settlement' did not mean that the reinsurer was only liable to pay when the insurer had *actually* paid. All it meant was that the amount the reinsurer had to pay was to be calculated by what the insurer paid. In this decision, the court chose to interpret a term in the contract in a way which it felt better implemented the intention of the parties even though it perhaps went beyond the plain and ordinary meaning of the word 'actually'.

In *Mannai Investment Co Ltd v Eagle Star Life Assurance Co Ltd* [1997] 2 WLR 945, HL, a tenant served a notice to terminate which contained the wrong date of termination. The correct break date was 13 January 1995 and the notice specified 12 January 1995. The House of Lords held that the notice was valid as any reasonable landlord would have understood what was meant by it and when the break clause was to be exercised. Lord Steyn said: 'If a notice unambiguously conveys a decision to determine, a court may nowadays ignore immaterial errors which would not have misled a reasonable recipient.' Lord Clyde said: 'The standard of reference is that of the reasonable man exercising his common sense in the context and the circumstances of the particular case ... The test is an objective one ... the actual understanding of the parties is beside the point.'

In *Investors Compensation Scheme Ltd v West Bromwich Building Society* (1997) *The Times*, 24 June, HL, the court went further in this approach. The case concerned the interpretation and effectiveness of a clause whereby certain investors assigned to the Investors Compensation Scheme any rights they might have against third parties in respect of negligent advice, including the

West Bromwich Building Society. Lord Hoffmann described the principles of interpretation of documents under the common law as follows:

> 'Interpretation is the ascertainment of the meaning which the document would convey to a reasonable person having all the background knowledge which would reasonably have been available to the parties in the situation in which they were at the time of the contract ... subject to the requirement that it should have been reasonably available to the parties ... [the background] includes absolutely anything which would have affected the way in which the language of the document would have been understood by a reasonable man ... The law excludes from the admissible background the previous negotiations of the parties and their declarations of subjective intent. They are admissible only in an action for rectification ... the meaning which a document would convey to a reasonable man is not the same thing as the meaning of its words ... the meaning of the document is what the parties using these words against the relevant background would reasonably have been understood to mean ... The rule that words should be given their "natural and ordinary meaning" reflects the common sense proposition that we do not easily accept that people have made linguistic mistakes, particularly in formal documents. On the other hand, if one would nevertheless conclude that something must have gone wrong with the language, the law does not require judges to attribute to the parties an intention which they plainly could not have had.'

The principles in these cases were followed and approved in *Atari Corporation (UK) Ltd v Electronics Boutique (UK) Ltd* (1997) unreported, 10 July, in the Court of Appeal. The case concerned the interpretation of a fax purporting to exercise a right to reject goods supplied on sale or return. The court stated that the principles in *Mannai* could apply to contracts for the sale of goods and that 'reading the fax in a common sense commercial way' the plaintiff must have understood that the defendant was rejecting the goods.

In *Dukeminster (Ebbgate House One) Ltd v Somerfield Properties Co Ltd* (1997) *The Times*, 13 August, the Court of Appeal construed a rent review clause, which operated on the basis of a valuation of notional premises. The court said that valuation of notional premises operated in the real world and not in one of fantasy. Thus in the absence of clear words, notional premises cannot be taken to be such as would produce a valuation, whether it be too low or too high, which cannot reasonably have been intended to apply to the actual premises. The court relied on background evidence as to the lack of actual comparables for leased property and decided that the wording was intended to achieve a market rent, even though there were no comparables, and was not intended to allow the landlord to achieve a rent above the market value. It therefore construed the clause so as to give effect to this intention, and wording was, in effect, inserted in the clause by the court to make this point clear.

However, there are signs in two recent cases that the Court of Appeal is reluctant to embrace Lord Hoffmann's approach in its entirety. These are *Scottish Power plc v Britoil (Exploration) Ltd* (1997) *The Times*, 2 December and *Total Gas Marketing Ltd v Arco British Ltd* (1997) *The Times*, 22 December. In *Scottish Power* Lord Staughton referred to the matrix of fact or the background against which the contract should be interpreted, but stated this should only comprise what the parties had in mind and what was going on around them when they entered into the contract. In *Total Gas*, the court proceeded on the basis of 'the factual background known to the parties at the time at which [the contract] was entered into'. Lord Gibson stated that he reached his decision 'on the true construction of the letter of the contract'. He did not adopt Lord Hoffmann's approach of good commercial sense which he said 'was often like a chameleon, taking its hue from the environment'.

Finally, it is important to stress that arguments as to the plain and ordinary meaning of a document, for instance a notice, will have no effect on the validity of the document if it is required to comply with some statutory regime as to its form and content and fails to do so. In that event, the document is invalid even if the recipient understands perfectly what is intended by it. (See *Sabella Ltd v Montgomery* (1997) *The Times*, 15 December, CA, which concerned a notice served pursuant to s 25 of the Landlord and Tenant Act 1954, which failed to comply with the relevant statutory instrument prescribing the form and content of such notices, and was therefore invalid.)[3]

Looking at this line of cases in the round, two important points can be deduced. The first is that, although the courts still have a reluctance to interpret documents on a more flexible basis than their 'plain and ordinary meaning', they are increasingly unwilling to carry this to the extreme of attributing 'to the parties an intention which they plainly could not have had'. It is clear that careful, clear and unambiguous drafting, which properly represents the intention of the parties, is of more importance than ever. Where 'something must have gone wrong with the language' and the court allows itself a more flexible approach to interpretation, instead of refusing to deal with the issue at all, the result may not please either party, and least of all the party on whose behalf the term in question was drafted. Secondly, the courts are feeling increasingly uncomfortable in allowing a party to escape from what are clearly his contractual obligations purely by relying on a technicality, particularly a procedural one. This is of most importance in the area of service of notices, and the drafting of notice clauses with as much clarity and as little procedural complication as possible is highly desirable both for those who serve notices and those who receive them.

Comparison of the two tests

UCTA reasonableness test under s 11

The term shall be:
- *fair* and reasonable
- *having regard to the circumstances*
- which were,
- or ought reasonably to have been,
- known to, or in the contemplation of, the parties
- *when the contract was made.*

Non-exhaustive criteria to be applied for the purposes of the test:
- *strength of the bargaining positions of the parties*;
- could the customer go elsewhere?
- *did the customer receive an inducement to agree to the term?*
- could the customer have entered into a similar contract with a third party without the term?
- whether the customer knew or ought reasonably to have known of the existence and extent of the term;
- where the terms excludes liability if a condition is not complied with, whether it was reasonable at the time the contract was entered into to expect that compliance with that condition would be practical;
- *whether the goods were manufactured processed or adapted to the special order of the customer*;
- resources which the party relying on the exclusion clause could expect to be available to meet the liability should it arise; and
- how far could a person seeking to exclude liability have covered that liability by insurance?

Fairness test under the Directive/Regulation

Definition of 'unfair term':
- contrary to the requirement of good faith;
- causes a significant imbalance in the parties' rights and obligations under the contract;
- to the detriment of the consumer;
- taking into account nature of goods or services;
- referring, *as at the time of conclusion of the contract*;
- to *all the circumstances attending the conclusion of the contract*; and
- to all other terms of the contract or of another contract on which it is dependent.

Non-exhaustive criteria to be applied for the purposes of the test:
- *strength of the bargaining position of the parties*;
- *whether the consumer had an inducement to agree to the term*;
- *whether the goods or services were supplied to the special order of the consumer*;
- the extent to which the seller or supplier has dealt *fairly* and equitably with the consumer.

NOTE: areas which are broadly similar in both tests have been highlighted by the use of *italics*.

Overlap between Directive/Regulation and UCTA

1 Definitions of contracting parties

A As defined in the Directive/Regulation:

'Consumer' (art 2) (reg 2):
  (1) natural person
  (2) acting for purposes outside his trade business or profession.

'Seller or Supplier' (art 2) (reg 2):
  (1) natural or legal person
  (2) acting for purposes relating to his trade business or profession.

B As defined in the UCTA:

'Contracting Party/Person dealing as a consumer' (s 12):
  (1) neither makes the contract in the course of a business nor holds himself out as doing so; and
  (2) the other party does make the contract in the course of a business; and
  (3) in the case of a contract governed by [ss 5, 6 or 7 of the Act] the goods passing under or in pursuance of the contract are of a type ordinarily supplied for private use or consumption; but
  (4) on a sale by auction or by competitive tender the buyer is not in any circumstances to be regarded as dealing as a consumer.

'Goods in Consumer Use' (s 5):
  (1) goods of a type ordinarily supplied for private use or consumption;
  (2) where loss or damage arises from the goods proving defective; and
  (3) while the goods are being used by or in the possession of a person otherwise than exclusively for the purposes of a business.

'Business Liability' (s 1):
Liability for breach of obligations or duties arising:
(1) from things done or to be done by a person in the course of a business (whether his own or another's); or
(2) from the occupation of premises used for business purposes of the oc-cupier.

'Business' (s 14):
Business includes a profession and the activities of any government department or local or public authority.

2 Contracts caught under the two regimes

A Contracts caught under the Directive/Regulation

There are a number of general exclusions:
- employment contracts;
- contracts relating to succession rights;
- contracts relating to rights under family law;
- contracts relating to the incorporation and organisation of companies or partnerships; and
- contracts containing terms incorporated to comply with mandatory or statutory or regulatory provisions of the UK or the provisions or principles of international conventions to which the member states or the Community are a party.

Apart from this all contracts between *'Consumers'* and *'Sellers or Suppliers'* of goods or services are covered. (The Regulation assumes that the Directive does not apply to any general types of contracts other than commercial contracts concluded with consumers for the sale or other supply of goods or services. This appears to be the case from the preamble, but is not completely clear from the articles of the Directive itself.) Regulation A achieves this result as follows:
- *'Seller'* means a person who sells *goods* and who, in making a contract to which these Regulations apply, is acting for the purposes relating to his business.
- *'Supplier'* means a person who supplies *goods or services* and who, in making a contract to which these Regulations apply, is acting for the purposes relating to his business. (It is assumed that the 'or' here can be read to include 'and' to cover mixed contracts for work and materials.)
- *'Consumer'* means a natural person who, in making a contract to which these Regulations apply, is acting for purposes which are outside his business.
- *'Business'* includes a trade or profession and the activities of any government department or local or public authority.

Note: It appears from the Directive's language (and the DTI concurs in this) that oral contracts are covered as well as written ones.

B Contracts caught under the UCTA

Schedule 1 to the UCTA: general exclusions

Sections 2–4 do not extend to:
- contracts of insurance;
- contracts for creation transfer or termination of interests in land;
- contracts for creation transfer or termination of an interest in intellectual property rights; and
- contracts relating to the formation or dissolution of companies and partnerships, and the rights of their members.

Also by operation of Sched 1, s 2 does not extend to a contract of employment except in favour of the employee, nor to the waiver of future claims for pneumoconiosis by persons in the coal industry who have received a settlement in compensation for their disease.

Each section of the UCTA has application in particular circumstances, governed by the way in which the various definitions discussed above are applied. A summary of this application is as follows:

Section 2: Liability for death personal injury or other loss or damage caused by negligence
- Only *business liability* is covered, but subject to this any natural or legal person can claim the protection of the section.

Secrion 3: Exclusion clauses

Section 4: Unreasonable indemnity clauses
- Only *business liability* is covered, and any natural or legal person *dealing as a consumer* can claim protection of the section.

Section 5: Control of manufacturers' guarantees
- Only *business liability* is covered, and any natural or legal person can claim protection of the section if he can show that he holds the *relevant goods in consumer use*.

Sections 6: Implied warranties in sale and hire purchase of goods
- Section 6(1) applies to prevent any exclusion of warranties as to title

and quiet possession in all contracts for the sale or hire purchase of goods, not just those giving rise to *business liability* (s 6(4)).

- Section 6(2) which only applies to contracts giving rise to *business liability* prevents exclusion of the other warranties implied by the Sale of Goods (Implied Terms) Act 1973, as against any natural or legal person *dealing as a consumer*.
- Section 6(3) protects any natural or legal person not dealing as a consumer from exclusion of the other warranties implied by those Acts in all contracts for the sale of goods, not just those giving rise to *business liability*, unless such exclusion passes the reasonableness test (s 6(4)).

Section 7: Implied warranties in other contracts for the supply of goods

- Section 7(2) which only applies to contracts giving rise to *business liability* prevents exclusion of the warranties (other than those relating to title and quiet possession) implied by the SGSA 1994 in other contracts for the supply of goods as against any natural or legal person *dealing as a consumer*.
- Section 7(3) protects any natural or legal person not dealing as a consumer from exclusion of the other warranties implied by those Acts in other contracts for the supply of goods which give rise to *business liability*, unless such exclusion passes the reasonableness test. (Note: there is no provision equivalent to s 6(4) which would apply s 7(3) to all contracts.)
- Section 7(3A) applies to prevent any exclusion of warranties as to title and quiet possession in all contracts for the supply of goods other than by way of sale or hire purchase, not just those giving rise to *business liability*.
- Section 7(4) applies in the case of a bailment of goods, giving rise to *business liability* and not covered by s 7(3A), to prevent exclusion of warranties as to the right to give possession (and perhaps quiet possession) unless such exclusion passes the reasonableness test.

Section 8: Exclusion of liability for misrepresentation

- Applies to all contracts.

Note: Sections 2–8 do not provide (so far as consumers are concerned) that there is any exclusion of oral contracts from the scope of the UCTA.

Chapter 2

Standard conditions for the supply of goods to business customers

2.1 Introduction

This chapter will concentrate on the drafting of standard conditions for the supply of goods in business as opposed to consumer transactions.

Precedent 1 is a set of standard conditions for the sale of goods written from the viewpoint of the seller. Thus it is referred to, as is customarily the case, as a set of standard conditions of sale. Precedent 2 covers the same type of transaction, but it is drafted more widely to cover not only the supply of goods, but also the supply of work and materials and the supply of services. It is written from the point of view of the purchaser, and therefore, as again is customary, is referred to as a set of standard conditions of purchase. It will be treated rather as a set of conditions relating to the sale of goods or the supply of work and materials for the purposes of the comparative analysis carried out in this chapter. Precedent 3 is a framework agreement governing the continuous supply of goods under a number of orders placed over a period of time. Finally, Precedent 4 deals with particular points relevant to the sale of second-hand goods in a business context.

The chapter commences with a comparative analysis of Precedents 1 and 2, and then finishes with a commentary on Precedents 3 and 4.

Conditions of sale and conditions of purchase are two different sides of the same coin. The obligations to be dealt with are the same, but the approach is very different as between the buyer and the seller. Thus, the most useful way of analysing the first two precedents is to compare the provisions in each of them which relate to the same contractual issues and consider the two different approaches. This exercise is valuable not only to enable the draftsman to produce a set of conditions which is most to the advantage of his client (whether his client be buyer or seller), but also to enable him to understand the motivation of the other side when he is in negotiation with their advisers.

The use of standard conditions gives rise to two special problems under the common law. The first relates to whether a set of standard conditions should govern the contract in the first place, and the second (in the case where the parties exchange their respective sets of standard conditions) to the question of which set shall govern the contract between the parties (the so-called 'battle of the forms'). These issues will be considered first before turning to an analysis of the remainder of the clauses in Precedents 1 and 2.

2.2   Incorporation of standard conditions in the contract

The problem of incorporation of standard terms and conditions has been dealt with in a series of cases generally known as the 'ticket cases', which arose from the practice of printing terms and conditions on a variety of documents from railway or steamship tickets, to deck chair or swimming pool tickets, which were intended to govern the contract between the proprietor and the person using his services (see for instance *Parker v South Eastern Railway* (1877) 2 CPD 416, *Hood v Anchor Line (Henderson Brothers) Ltd* [1918] AC 837, *Chapelton v Barry UDC* [1940] 1 KB 532 and *Thornton v Shoe Lane Parking Ltd* [1971] 2 QB 163).

The special issues in the ticket cases revolve around whether the party whom it is sought to bind under the conditions on the ticket had actual or constructive knowledge of their existence. The question of constructive knowledge is dealt with in part by asking whether or not, in the circumstances of the particular case, the ticket was the sort of document on which one would reasonably expect to find legally binding terms and conditions, and in part by asking whether or not the party issuing the ticket made reasonable attempts to bring the existence of the conditions to the notice of the other party.

The first relevant principle to be derived from the ticket cases in the case of contracts placed on standard terms and conditions is that, if the party whom it is sought to bind knows that there is a set of standard terms which the other party intends should apply to the contract, and he enters into the contract on this basis, he will be bound by them. This will be so whether he takes the trouble to read them or not, and whether they are actually set out in a document in his possession, or (subject to the question of the need to offer an opportunity to inspect, which is discussed below) merely incorporated into the contract by a reference in such a document.

The question of constructive knowledge is more difficult. On the principles relating to constructive knowledge in the ticket cases, the documents upon which standard terms and conditions are usually printed (quotations, order forms and acknowledgments) are clearly the sort of document where one would expect to find terms and conditions, and which a reasonable man would read carefully. Thus, *prima facie*, the party who receives such a document should be bound by relevant standard terms and conditions, even if he never reads the document, and is unaware that they exist.

However, the hostility of the courts towards 'unreasonable or onerous clauses' has led them to ignore this principle, where such a clause is printed on the reverse of a document, or incorporated by reference. Here they rely on the principles in the ticket cases which require a reasonable attempt to give notice to a party of the existence of terms and conditions by which it is intended to bind him. If such notice is required and not given, and the party has no actual knowledge of the terms and conditions, he cannot be fixed with constructive knowledge of its existence (see for instance *Spurling (J) Ltd v Bradshaw* [1956] 1 WLR 461 and *Interfoto Picture Library Ltd v Stiletto Visual Programmes Ltd* [1988] 2 WLR 615).

It is hard to see why reasonable notice should be an additional requirement where the document concerned is one which a reasonable man would regard as a legal document, to be read carefully for its terms and conditions. However, it is the job of the draftsman to produce certainty for his client rather than to rely on general legal principles. For this reason, all documents which have standard terms and conditions on the reverse should have a clear statement on the front to the effect that the contract is to be subject to the terms and conditions on the reverse. Examples of relevant statements are given at the beginning of Precedents 1 and 2. Where conditions are incorporated by reference it is also prudent and, according to some authorities, necessary, to offer to the party whom it is sought to bind by them a reasonable opportunity for inspection (see *Parker v South Eastern Railway*, above). This issue is discussed further, below, in the section relating to the effect of subcontracts.

Finally, as a preliminary issue, it is important to establish that actual or constructive knowledge of the relevant conditions occurred before the contract concerned came into existence. This is elementary contract law, because, obviously, once the contract has been formed it is too late to try to change it by adding additional terms (see *Olley v Marlborough Court Ltd* [1949] 1 KB 532). Many of the ticket cases failed because the ticket was not issued until after the contract was formed.

2.3   The battle of the forms

The problems associated with the battle of the forms arise because the common law principles governing the formation of contracts are based on the concept of a bargain arrived at through a process of negotiation, while the whole purpose of standard conditions is to minimise or exclude the process of negotiation.

In the process, according to the common law, one party indicates his interest in the transaction (invitation to treat), the other party then proposes the terms upon which he is willing to complete the transaction (offer), and the first party then indicates his agreement to those terms (acceptance) whereupon the contract comes into existence. However, in order to create the contract, the acceptance must be a total and unconditional acceptance of the offer. If the offer is not acceptable, then it is up to the other party to make a different proposal (counter-offer). The two parties will then exchange counter-offers, until one party accepts the counter-offer of the other, whereupon the contract then comes into existence.

The common law is not well adapted to the use of standard terms because their use is inconsistent with a freely negotiated bargain. Thus the process of contract formation arising out of the exchange of documents containing or referring to standard terms creates considerable problems when one tries to fit it into the framework of offer and acceptance. There are two leading cases on the battle of the forms, *BRS v Arthur V Crutchley Ltd* [1968] 1 All ER 811 and *Butler Machine Tool Co Ltd v Ex-Cell-O Corporation (England) Ltd* [1979] 1 WLR 401.

The first step is for the seller to send out a quotation, on the back of which will be printed his standard conditions of sale. The quotation will state that any contract entered into as a result of the quotation will be on these standard conditions of sale, to the entire exclusion of those of the buyer (see the preliminary statement of Precedent 1). In most cases the quotation will also state that the sending back by the buyer of an acceptance of the quotation will not automatically result in a contract; a contract will only come into existence upon acceptance of the order by the seller. Precedent 1 is a typical set of standard conditions of sale which would be found upon the back of a seller's quotation, and cl 1 adopts this approach. Where the quotation is not capable of immediate acceptance by the buyer it is thus an invitation to treat, and, at this stage, the seller has kept all of his options open. Absent this provision, the quotation will be an offer.

Whether the quotation be an invitation to treat or an offer is actually immaterial, because the buyer will, in response, send back his purchase order with his standard conditions of purchase on the back. Even though the purchase order accepts on its face all of the terms of the seller's quotation, and even if the quotation had the status of an offer, the purchase order will not qualify as an acceptance. This is because in the purchase conditions there will be a provision stating that any contract entered into pursuant to the purchase order will be on the standard conditions of purchase on the back of the order (see the preliminary statement and cl 1.1 of Precedent 2). This contradicts the requirement on the quotation that the contract be on the standard conditions of the seller. Thus the purchase order is either an offer or a counter-offer, but in neither event does the contract come into existence at this stage.

The seller will on receipt of the order normally send back an order acknowledgment. If the order acknowledgment contains no reference to the standard conditions on the back of the quotation, the acknowledgment will become the unconditional acceptance needed to create the contract. In this case, contrary to the wishes of the seller, the buyer's conditions will govern the contract, because the seller has, in effect, accepted the counter-offer of the buyer, contained in the purchase order, to do business on the buyer's conditions.

In fact the acknowledgment in most cases either has the seller's conditions printed on the back, or refers to the execution of the contract in accordance with the quotation in such a way that the seller's conditions on the back of the quotation are incorporated by reference. In this case the acknowledgment is another counter-offer, and at this stage no contract has been created.

In some cases, on receipt of the seller's acknowledgment the buyer will send back another acknowledgment. If the seller's acknowledgment amounted to an unconditional acceptance then this further acknowledgment has no effect on the contract which has already been concluded. However, if the seller's acknowledgment was a counter-offer, the buyer's acknowledgment will, again, either be an unconditional acceptance (ie no further reference to the buyer's standard conditions) or a further counter-offer.

If it is supposed that the last acknowledgment to pass between the parties is a counter-offer then at this stage no contract has been created. However, in nine cases out of ten the parties do not appreciate this fact. They will have exchanged their pieces of paper with their attention on the specific terms on the front, and the administrative process of placing and logging an order, but, in many cases, they will not have the legal training to make the proper analysis of the situation. If asked, at this stage, each side would be likely to reply that its standard conditions governed the transaction.

The above analysis is based upon a combination of the principles in *BRS* and *Butler*, but the two cases do have some differences.

In *BRS* the final exchanges took place just as the goods were being delivered. Prior to delivery there had been an exchange of counter-offers which the court held did not result in a contract. At the time of delivery the plaintiff's employee tendered a delivery note for signature which made it clear that the contract was to be on the plaintiff's conditions. However, the defendant's employee stamped the note with a statement that delivery would be accepted subject to the defendant's conditions and then signed it. Following that, the plaintiff's employee made delivery of the goods. The court held that the tendering of the delivery note was another counter-offer, and that the defendant's employee made a further counter-offer when he over-stamped the delivery note and signed it. When the plaintiff's employee then chose to accept the delivery note and deliver the goods his conduct constituted an unconditional acceptance of the last counter-offer and the defendant's terms were held to apply.

In *Butler* there was a similar exchange of counter-offers, but here the last communication between the parties, sent by the seller, was a copy of the buyer's order, signed by way of acknowledgment, together with a covering letter stating that the order was acknowledged, and was being 'entered into in accordance with the offer'. The court held that the covering letter had not made it clear that the seller was intending to contract on his own terms and conditions, and that he had merely mentioned the offer by way of reference for its main terms (eg quoted price and delivery). Thus the seller's return of the signed copy order, containing the buyer's terms and conditions, was an unconditional acceptance, and the contract came into existence on the buyer's terms and conditions.

Butler thus agrees with *BRS* to the extent that both cases see the battle of the forms as an exchange of counter-offers, which can only result in a contract when one side makes an unconditional acceptance, either intentionally, or in error. The lesson from *Butler* is that not every document sent between the parties is in fact a counter-offer. Only those documents which clearly state that the contract is to be entered into upon the terms and conditions of the sender, and either have those terms and conditions printed on them, or clearly incorporate them by reference, will rank as counter-offers. In *Butler* the seller lost the battle of the forms because he was careless and failed to make his last document a counter-offer instead of an acceptance.

The decision in *Butler* turned on the fact that the battle of the forms was ended because the last document exchanged was construed as an unconditional acceptance, but what if the last document exchanged is a counter-offer, as discussed in the analysis set out above? In this case, as can be seen from *BRS*, all is not lost. Acceptance can be signified not only by a written document, but also by conduct. If the last counter-offer came from the buyer, then the seller will signify acceptance (depending on the type of goods and the nature of the transaction concerned) when he either appropriates goods to the contract, puts their manufacture in hand, or delivers them to the buyer. Where the last counter-offer came from the seller, the buyer will accept that offer, and create the contract, when he takes delivery of the goods from the seller, or (if earlier) when he pays for them.

On this analysis the contract will always be governed by the standard conditions attached to the last genuine counter-offer to pass between the parties, although (as seen from *Butler*) this may not actually be the last document to pass between the parties. Where there is no document constituting an unconditional acceptance, *BRS* tells us that the contract will actually come into existence when this last counter-offer is accepted by performance.

Since in most cases, the last counter-offer is an acknowledgment of order from the seller, it is his conditions of sale that will most often prevail. If the purchaser is to try to ensure that his is the last counter-offer, so that it will be accepted by the conduct of the seller, the device of sending back another acknowledgment does not work well in practice. In many cases, it does not fit into the administrative systems of the parties, nor is it a usual way of doing business. Not only is this burdensome and difficult to administer, but it becomes very noticeable to the seller. The seller is then likely specifically to reject the buyer's acknowledgment, and a detailed negotiation as to whose conditions are to govern the contract will probably ensue. This defeats the purpose of doing business on standard conditions (speed and efficiency in dealing with a large number of transactions), and the purchasing departments of both the buyer and the seller will probably be unable to cope with the work load imposed if there are many such special negotiations.

Clause 1.2 of Precedent 2 (copying the buyer's approach in *Butler*) approaches the problem in a different way, by seeking to pre-empt the seller's administrative processes. The buyer provides the seller with, and encourages him to return, a standard acknowledgment which acts as an unconditional acceptance of the purchase order, thus bringing the contract into existence on the standard terms on the back of the purchase order. Following *BRS* the buyer also makes explicit the common law rules on acceptance by conduct, in case the seller simply fails to send back any acknowledgment at all.

Clause 1.2 is not foolproof. If the seller ignores it, and returns his own acknowledgment form, then the seller will simply have made another counter-offer, either precipitating a special negotiation, or, if the buyer is not alert, leaving the way open for an unconditional acceptance on the part of the buyer when the seller delivers the goods to him. In one situation where such a provision was used in practice, on a large scale, over a number of years, it was found to operate successfully in more than 50 per cent of the cases. The only practical problem encountered (apart from cases where the proffered acknowledgment form was ignored, and the seller returned his own acknowledgment form or called for a special negotiation) was that some sellers' administrative systems required the issue of their own acknowledgment form before an order could be logged. They therefore issued their own form and sent back both the buyer's form and their own form. Under these circumstances, unless the seller's own acknowledgment was poorly drafted (as was the case in *Butler*), without a special negotiation it was almost impossible to decide in individual cases which set of conditions prevailed.

There is no sure way under English law of winning the battle of the forms. Some civil code jurisdictions get around the problem by looking for a consensus which blends the two sets of conditions, and uses the power of the court to resolve contradicting conditions. Another view of some civil law courts is that neither set of conditions can apply to the contract (since the parties manifestly wanted the contract to exist, acted as if it did, but could not agree as to which of their sets of standard conditions should apply to it). In these circumstances, the general provisions of the code will apply to the contract instead. There are *obiter dicta* in *Butler* which explore these possibilities, but they are possibilities alien to the common law, and unlikely to be applicable. Certainly they are not part of the *ratio decidendi* of *Butler*, so that here *BRS*, which applies the common law principles in its *ratio* is to be preferred. Since the civil law options are not open to the English courts, it is likely that by the application of the doctrines of offer and acceptance, they will, in the end, find in each case one winner and one loser for each particular battle of the forms, even though that winner may not be the one who fires the last shot.

The battle of the forms has been discussed more recently in three cases in the Court of Appeal, all of which in varying aspects confirm the above analysis. They are *G Percy Trentham v Archital Luxfer* [1993] 1 Lloyd's Rep 25, CA, *Nissan UK Ltd v Nissan Motor Manufacturing (UK) Ltd* (1994) unreported, CA, discussed in (1995) 12 *Building Law Monthly* issue 5, and *Hitchins (Hatfield) Ltd v H Butterfield Ltd* (1995) unreported, CA, discussed in (1995) 12 *Building Law Monthly* issue 7.

The only sure way to avoid the problem is to negotiate, either in advance, or on a case by case basis, to determine whose conditions will apply. This is however, not always practical, and, in the absence of a change in the law through statute, the battle of the forms will continue to be a feature of the formation of contracts placed on standard terms and conditions.

2.4   The effect of subcontracts

In addition to the problems raised by the battle of the forms, there is the need to consider the relationship between prime contract conditions and subcontract conditions. In many cases the contract under consideration between the buyer and the seller will be a subcontract (for instance to provide components) which will be used by the buyer to fulfil part of his obligations under a prime contract where he is in his turn acting as the seller. The buyer's greatest exposure will come not so much from the fact that he has accepted the seller's standard conditions as governing the contract between them, but from situations where there is a mismatch between the obligations undertaken by the seller in favour of the buyer under the subcontract and the obligations undertaken by the buyer to his customer under the prime contract.

A simple example would be a delivery date, under a subcontract for the supply of components, which was too late to enable the buyer to fulfil his delivery obligations under a prime contract for the supply of a machine in which the components were to be incorporated. A proper matching of these liabilities is known as a back to back arrangement and the best way of dealing with this issue is to negotiate a full back to back subcontract rather than rely on standard conditions.

Of course, a seller is not interested in the buyer's liabilities under any potential or actual prime contracts. In fact, at common law, it is better for the seller if he is not fixed with actual knowledge of such contracts, since he is then more likely to escape liability for loss suffered by the buyer if the seller's default prevents the buyer from fulfilling his obligations under those contracts.

The buyer naturally has the opposite concern and, in the absence of a formal back to back contract, when one is dealing with standard conditions of purchase the best that can be accomplished is to incorporate a provision like cl 1.3 of Precedent 2, which notifies the seller of the possibility of prime contracts and attempts to impose their terms upon the seller, coupled with an opportunity for the seller to examine them and a warning that they will apply, even if not examined. This clause relies upon the ticket cases discussed above (see particularly *Parker v South Eastern Railway*). If such clauses are to stand it is vital that attention be drawn to them on the face of the order, and wording for this purpose is also provided at the commencement of Precedent 2.

2.5 Delivery, the passing of property and risk, and payment

The discharge of the basic obligations under the contract, relating to delivery, passing of risk and property, and payment, are partly a matter for negotiation between the parties (although the SGA provides guidelines) but must also be looked at in relation to s 3 of the UCTA, with its restrictions on clauses excluding liability for breach.

On the question of delivery, cl 2.1 of Precedent 2 imposes the strict obligations of compliance with a specified delivery date upon the seller, which a buyer will normally try to require. The provision making time of the essence will enable the buyer to cancel the contract for breach, without notice, if the seller does not deliver exactly in accordance with the contract. In the absence of an express (or possibly an implied) provision to this effect, the SGA provides that time of delivery is not of the essence (see SGA 1979, s 10(2)). So far as the seller is concerned he would prefer not to accept liability to deliver by a particular date in the first instance. However, s 3 of the UCTA would control a clause which would exempt the seller from liability for failure to comply with a specified delivery date. Clause 4.2 of Precedent 1 deals with the matter by not taking on the obligation to deliver to a specific date in the first place.

For both the seller and the buyer the question of who pays the costs of delivery is really only a matter related to the negotiation of the price. This is reflected in the terms of cl 2.1 of Precedent 2 and cl 4.1 of Precedent 1. Similarly the question of the need to store the goods in third party premises, if the buyer cannot accept delivery when they are ready for delivery, really comes down to who pays for the storage charges. The matter is addressed from the point of view of the buyer in cl 2.2 of Precedent 2 and of the seller in cl 6 of Precedent 1, but apart from the time when the buyer becomes responsible to pay the storage charges, the principles are much the same.

Under the SGA 1979, s 17 property in the goods under a contract of sale generally passes when the parties intend it to pass (although s 18 of the SGA lays down rules which apply if the intention of the parties cannot be ascertained). Unless otherwise agreed risk passes when property passes (whether or not delivery has occurred) under s 20(1) of the SGA. The tension between the buyer and the seller in this area occurs around retention of title clauses. A detailed discussion of such clauses is beyond the scope of this chapter, but it should be said that the case law shows that use of such clauses to provide security in the event of failure to pay the purchase price is surrounded with many pitfalls. The more complicated and far-reaching that the clause is, the more likely it is to be ineffective. A simple clause reserving title in the goods to the seller until the buyer has paid their purchase price in full is probably the type of clause most likely to be effective. In large measure its effectiveness depends upon the types of goods concerned. Goods whose identity can be easily determined (eg capital goods) as the subject matter of the contract to which the retention of title clause relates are most suitable for this type of clause. Commodity goods (eg bricks or cement) give rise to severe problems of identification.

In Precedent 1, cl 5.5 gives an example of a simple retention of title clause, coupled with the express grant of a power to sue for the price, once the due date for payment has come, even though property has not passed. Section 49(1) of the SGA in general makes the passing of property a precondition for suing for the price, but s 49(2) permits an express provision of this type, provided that the price is stated in the contract to be due on a 'date certain'. By contrast cl 4.1 of Precedent 2 provides (as the buyer would prefer) for property to pass on delivery, and does not couple either the passing of property or delivery with the obligation to make payment. In this connection s 28 of the SGA should be noted; unless otherwise agreed delivery of the goods and payment of the price are concurrent conditions, and must therefore occur at the same time. Such a provision is not normally practical, and certainly not favourable to buyers. Hence the need to exclude it (both in Precedent 1 and Precedent 2) by express provisions. The specification of payment terms, currencies and dates has to be dealt with in much the same way, whether looked at from the point of view of the buyer or the seller, as can be seen by a comparison of Precedent 1, cl 5.4, and Precedent 2, cl 5.1.

From the point of view of both the buyer and the seller, it makes more sense for risk to pass on delivery than upon the passing of property, and this is provided for in cl 4.3 of Precedent 1 and clause 4.1 of Precedent 2. The SGA 1979, s 20(2) provides that where delivery has been delayed through the fault of one of the parties, the goods are at the risk of that party until delivery. This is reflected in cl 2.2 of Precedent 2, where risk remains with the seller until delivery to the buyer notwithstanding delivery to storage. On the other hand cl 6 of Precedent 1 deems delivery to store to be delivery for the purposes of the contract, so that risk passes despite s 20(2) of the SGA. It is a mistake to look at the provisions relating to the passing of risk as in some sense enabling one party to score over the other. What is at stake here is which party is to carry the insurance to cover the risk, and this is, presumably, once again reflected in the price.

One final area of risk is that relating to goods damaged in transit. Precedent 2 does not deal with this expressly, since the thrust of cl 2.1 is that delivery will normally be to the buyer's premises. Since risk does not pass till delivery, in most cases, then any damage in transit will automatically be for the account of the seller. Clause 7 of Precedent 1 expressly specifies that this is to be the case. For both the buyer and the seller this tends to make sense, since it is more efficient for the seller to insure against the risk under an insurance policy covering the risk of damage to goods in transit than for the buyer to cover the goods under an all risks policy relating to his moveable property.

2.6   Warranty of good title and quiet possession

As discussed in Chapter 1, ss 6(1) and 7(3A) of the UCTA prevent the exclusion of liability in relation to the warranties of title and quiet possession implied by s 12 of the SGA and s 2 of the SGSA. The combination of cll 6.3 and 7.3 with cl 1.4 of Precedent 2 in fact imposes both express and implied warranties and an indemnity in this area, but they are hardly necessary, given the operation of the UCTA. Apart from the special area of infringement of third party intellectual property rights, which is discussed in detail below, most sellers do not even attempt to exclude such liability, and this approach is followed in cl 5.1 of Precedent 1.

As discussed in Chapter 1, certain classes of sellers, mainly receivers and liquidators, do take advantage of the provisions of s 12(3) of the SGA or s 2(3) of the SGSA to pass only such title as they may have in the goods, subject to disclosure of known encumbrances, and a warranty of quiet possession so far as they are concerned. However, although in theory any seller could take advantage of these sections generally, it would not be commercially practicable in most cases for ordinary sellers to do so.

Precedent 1 does, however, exclude liability for infringement of third party intellectual property rights, and the relevant provisions are analysed in the section relating to this subject. Clauses 5.1 (including both phrases in square brackets), 5.2 and 5.3 are necessary if one intends to exclude that liability otherwise the bracketed phrases in cl 5.1 and the whole of cl 5.2 and 5.3 should be deleted and cl 5.4. and 5.5 should be renumbered accordingly.

2.7   Conformance to specification, quality, fitness for purpose

The most important aspect of the discharge of the obligations under the contract is the supply of the goods that are the subject matter of the contract, in compliance with the specifications contained in the contract. To the extent that the contract leaves these matters undefined, the warranties implied by the SGA as to quality, suitability, and compliance with description or sample will apply.

Some changes have been made in the warranty of merchantable quality implied by s 14(2) of the SGA which has been amended, with effect from 3 January 1995, so as to replace the implied warranty of merchantable quality by one of satisfactory quality. By s 1 of the SSGA 1994, s 14(2) of the SGA now reads: 'Where the seller sells goods in the course of a business, there is an implied term that the goods supplied under the contract are of satisfactory quality.' The new s 14(2A) defines 'satisfactory quality' as 'the standard that a reasonable person would regard as satisfactory, taking account of any description of the goods, the price (if relevant) and all other relevant circumstances', and s 14(2B) goes on to provide that 'fitness for all the purposes for which goods of the kind in question are commonly supplied, appearance and finish, freedom from minor defects, safety and durability' are all 'in appropriate cases aspects of the quality of goods'.

Section 14(2C) provides that the implied term does not extend to 'any matter making the quality of goods unsatisfactory' if it is 'specifically drawn to the buyer's attention before the contract is made', if it is one which 'where the buyer examines the goods before the contract is made ... that examination ought to reveal [it]' or, where the contract is one of sale by sample, 'which would have been apparent on a reasonable examination of the sample'.

Purely as a consequential amendment, s 1(2) of the SSGA 1994 amends s 15 of the SGA (sales by sample) so that references in that section to defects which render the goods 'unmerchantable' are replaced by references to making the quality of the goods 'unsatisfactory'. The new standard of satisfactory quality does not differ to a great extent from that of the old one of merchantable quality, but it has taken account of some of the case law built up around the concept of merchantable quality to provide a standard which is better defined, and should give contracting parties greater certainty.

Equivalent changes have been made by the SSGA 1994 to the Trading Stamps Act 1964, the Uniform Laws on International Sales Act 1967, the Supply of Goods (Implied Terms) Act 1973 (which governs hire purchase sales) and the Supply of Goods and Services Act 1982. The treatment accorded to all of the relevant sections under the Unfair Contract Terms Act 1977 remains unchanged, so that the new standard of satisfactory quality is dealt with in exactly the same way (so far as relates to its possibilities of exclusion) as was the old standard of merchantable quality.

It should be noted that the concept of merchantable quality was originally created by the common law, and later brought into statute by the Sale of Goods Act 1893. Thus the SSGA 1994 has not abolished the common law concept. In some cases, for instance where the statutes do not apply, there is no reason why the common law rules as to implied warranties relating to merchantable quality or fitness for purpose cannot still be invoked. (See, for instance, *St Albans and District Council v International Computers Ltd* [1997] FSR 251, CA, and *Amstrad plc v Seagate Technology Inc [1998] Masons CLR 1*.) This is why, when drafting clauses to exclude implied warranties, it is important to exclude not only warranties implied by statute, but also those implied by common law as well. The seller is anxious to insure that, above all else there is certainty as to the extent of his obligations in this area. Clause 2 of Precedent 1 proceeds on this basis. This provides for a sale by description, but the description is one which has been carefully drafted by the seller for general use when selling that particular product. Any further specifications must be specifically set out in the relevant order. Equally important is the last sentence of the clause which excludes prior representations and extraneous material, such as sales catalogues. Given that the aim is one of certainty, and that here the contract is not with a consumer, the likelihood is that s 8 of the UCTA will have no effect on this clause. Clause 2 cannot operate effectively without an exclusion of the other warranties otherwise implied by the SGA in the area of quality and fitness for purpose. Clause 9.3 operates to provide this. Again given that these conditions deal with a business sale, these exclusions are likely to pass the test of reasonableness imposed in such cases by s 6 of the UCTA.

While the buyer is also anxious to ensure certainty, his desire is to surround the contract and impose upon the seller as many express warranties as possible to ensure that the goods supplied under the contract are satisfactory to him in every way. Clauses 3.1 and 3.5 of Precedent 2 achieve this aim. In fact they spell out many of the warranties which would (in the absence of exclusion) be implied under the SGA anyway. Finally, since the buyer is also anxious not to exclude any of his rights implied at common law or under the SGA in addition to the express rights which he has included in the contract, he makes it absolutely clear that all such implied rights will also apply to the contract. This is accomplished by cl 1.4 of Precedent 2.

There is a rule of construction which is sometimes quoted ('*inclusio unius, exclusio alterius*'). This states that where specific clauses are included in a contract, which deal with matters which would otherwise be implied into the contract by law or statute, the very fact of the inclusion of a specific clause dealing with those matters, by implication, excludes the provisions which would otherwise be implied by law or statute in respect of them. Nevertheless, as will be seen from both Precedent 1 and Precedent 2, neither the buyer nor the seller has chosen to rely on this maxim. The seller expressly excludes implied provisions and the buyer expressly includes them. In general this rule should only be used as a last resort in legal proceedings over a contract where the parties have failed to make an express provision as to the status of implied terms.

One particular point should also be made here about the implied warranty of fitness for purpose. Many businessmen suppose that there is a general obligation on the seller (in the absence of exclusion clauses to the contrary) to ensure that the goods are fit for the purpose for which the buyer intends to use them. Thus whenever goods turn out to be unsatisfactory, they immediately attack the seller with the complaint that they are unfit for purpose.

This concept is in fact incorrect, although the issue is now somewhat complicated by the amendments to s 14(2) of the SGA made by SSGA 1994. Following these amendments there are now in fact two kinds of fitness for purpose warranties that may be implied under s 14. The first is implied indirectly through the new warranty of satisfactory quality implied under s 14(2). Section 14(2B) when defining the concept of 'quality' provides that one of the aspects of quality of goods is, in 'appropriate cases', the 'fitness [of the goods] for all the purposes for which goods of the kind in question are commonly supplied'. This test is clearly an objective test and has no necessary relation to the purpose for which the buyer intends to use the goods.

Section 14(3) of the SGA in fact does provide an implied warranty of the fitness of goods for the purpose for which the buyer intends to use them, but this is quite a restricted remedy. First, the buyer has to make known to the seller, expressly or by implication, the purpose for which he intends to use the goods. Secondly, even where this is the case, no warranty is implied if the circumstances show that the buyer does not rely, or it is unreasonable for him to rely, on the skill or judgment of the seller in deciding whether or not the goods are in fact suitable for that purpose. This warranty is obviously much easier for a consumer to invoke than a businessman. Not only is the purpose for which the consumer buys consumer goods more likely to be known to the seller (particularly by implication) but it is far more likely that the consumer will rely on the seller's judgment and skill.

In a business sale, the buyer will be less likely to be able to take advantage of the implied warranty, particularly because he may well be as expert as the seller in dealing with the goods which are the subject matter of the contract, and so will not (or it will not be reasonable for him to) rely on the seller's judgment and skill. A good example is the purchase of components or sub-assemblies for incorporation in apparatus manufactured and sold by the buyer to third parties. In such cases, where the component is unsuitable for its purpose, it is quite unlikely that the seller will even know what its intended use was, and, even if he did, it would frequently be clearly unreasonable for the buyer to place any reliance on the judgment and skill of the seller in relation to use in apparatus in respect of which the buyer himself was an expert, since he was its manufacturer.

It is true that, in some cases, the buyer may be able to invoke the general fitness for purpose warranty under s 14(2) as amended, but the buyer is far better advised to include an express statement of the purpose for which the goods are intended, and an express warranty as to their suitability for it. In this way, the question of suitability is really only another aspect of the description or specification with which the goods are to conform, and it is up to the seller to accept or reject this term as he sees fit.

Buyers often attempt to include express warranties stating that goods will be suitable for the purpose for which they are intended to be used by the buyer, or suitable for the purpose for which they are ordinarily or generally used. The latter warranty is in any event now implied under s 14(2) as amended. The seller should of course resist such warranties because of their vagueness, and insist that, if he is to give such a warranty, the purpose should be clearly specified in the contract, with sufficient detail to enable him to be sure that the goods that he supplies are in fact suitable for that purpose.

The conclusion must be that both the general and the specific implied warranties of fitness for purpose are too vague to be of much help to the buyer or the seller, except perhaps as a last resort in litigation if their contract does not cover the point specifically, either by express inclusion or express exclusion. The best course for both parties is to decide as part of their negotiations the extent to which the seller will warrant the fitness of the goods for the purpose which the buyer intends to use them and then to embody this warranty expressly in the contract. Sections 14(2) and (3) will clearly be of most application in the area of consumer transactions.

2.8   Acceptance and rejection

Bound up with the question of compliance with specification is the question of acceptance, since, until the goods have been accepted by the buyer, the seller cannot be sure that he has discharged his basic liability to perform the contract, even if he has delivered the goods to the buyer. The importance of acceptance is that once it has taken place, the buyer can no longer reject the goods, claim that the seller has failed to perform the contract, and refuse to pay the price. Instead he must rely upon a claim for damages, but is otherwise obliged to keep the goods and pay for them (see SGA 1979, s 11(4)).

The seller thus wants to make acceptance as quick, simple and decisive as possible. Section 27 of the SGA imposes upon the seller a duty to deliver the goods and upon the buyer to accept the goods in both cases in accordance with the terms of the contract. Clause 3 of Precedent 1 relies upon this provision, to specify that acceptance shall take place upon delivery. Given the wording of cl 6 relating to delivery to store, acceptance would also take place upon delivery to store.

The buyer, on the other hand, wishes to put off acceptance as long as possible, so that he can be sure the goods are totally satisfactory to him before he gives up the opportunity of rejecting them. He is somewhat aided in this objective by the changes which the SSGA 1994 has made to the SGA, ss 11, 33, 34 and 35 in relation to the law on acceptance and rejection.

Section 2 of the SSGA 1994 Act amends s 35 of the SGA, so that acceptance now takes place either when the buyer intimates to the seller that he has accepted the goods, or when (after delivery of the goods to him) 'the buyer does any act in relation to them which is inconsistent with the ownership of the seller'. So much is old law. However, the new amendments to s 35 now provide that the buyer who has taken delivery of the goods without previously having examined them, is not deemed to have taken delivery until he has had a reasonable opportunity to examine them to ascertain if they are in conformity with the contract or (if under a sale by sample) in conformity with the sample.

It is true that the buyer is still deemed to have accepted the goods if he has not (within a reasonable time after delivery) told the seller that he rejects them, but the question of whether a reasonable time has elapsed depends, *inter alia*, upon whether the buyer has had a reasonable opportunity of examining the goods. Finally, an important provision, s 35, now provides that the buyer is not deemed to have accepted the goods merely because he asks or agrees for the seller to repair or arrange for their repair, nor because he has delivered them to a third party under a sub-sale or other disposition.

A new s 35A has also been inserted which provides for a right of partial rejection, either of the goods delivered under the contract as a whole or in respect of one instalment where delivery is under a contract for delivery by instalments.

Section 35 is of mandatory application in the case of a sale to a person dealing as a consumer (the same definition as in the Unfair Contract Terms Act 1977 applies) but can be excluded by contract in the case of any other sale. Section 35A, however, only applies, in the case of all contracts of sale, 'unless a contrary attention appears in, or is to be implied from, the contract'.

Section 4 of the SSGA 1994 has made some changes to the classification of the warranties to be implied into a sale of goods contract under ss 13, 14 and 15 of the SGA, which affect the right of rejection in sales where the buyer does not deal as a consumer. A new s 15A(1) is inserted into the SGA which provides that, where the breach of the warranty is so slight that it would be unreasonable for the buyer to reject the goods, the breach is to be treated not as a breach of condition (giving a right of rejection) but as a breach of warranty (imposing an obligation to accept the goods, subject only to a claim for damages for any diminution in value caused by the breach).

Similarly, s 15A(2) modifies s 30 of the SGA, by providing that, where a buyer does not deal as a consumer, he cannot reject the whole of a delivery by reason of a shortfall or an excess, where the shortfall or excess 'is so slight that it would be unreasonable for him to do so'.

In both cases the burden of proof is on the seller to show that the breach, shortfall or excess is so slight as to fall within the provisions of the section. However, while s 15A(1) only applies if it is not displaced by a contrary intention which appears in, or is to be implied from, the contract, s 15A(2) does not contain this wording and therefore appears to be mandatory.

Section 7 and Sched 2 of the SSGA 1994 also make amendments, analogous to those contained in the new s 15A, to the Supply of Goods (Implied Terms) Act 1973 and to the SGSA, with the exception that there is no provision effecting an amendment analogous to s 15A(2).

Finally, it should be noted that, since the question of the extent to which the above provisions are to be mandatory has been covered in the provisions themselves, the SSGA 1994 has had no need to, and has not, made any consequential amendments in this respect to the UCTA.

Considering the impact of the mandatory and non-mandatory provisions of SSGA 1994, cl 3 of Precedent 1 remains silent on the various issues. The provisions of s 35 (as amended) are not mandatory, and the content of cl 3.1 will therefore displace them. The seller will be content to fetter the right of the buyer to reject for trivial breaches of warranty or for trivial variations between the quantity contracted for and the quantity delivered (now contained in s 15A of the SGA) and so will allow the standard conditions to remain silent on the matter.

So far as the buyer is concerned, despite the amendments to s 35 of the SGA, which clearly favour the buyer, most buyers are best advised to set out specific rights to inspect and test the goods, coupled with a formal procedure for acceptance or rejection, taking account of the mandatory nature of s 15A(2) and an exclusion of the operation of ss 11 and 35 of the SGA. This is dealt with in Precedent 2 in cll 3.2 and 3.3. Given the modifications to s 30 of the SGA mentioned, the buyer will want to exclude the restriction on his right to reject for any breach of warranty, however trivial, contained in s 15A(1) of the SGA, but will have to accept that he does not have the right to reject for trivial variations in quantity, given the provisions of s 15A(2). The clause therefore deals with s 15A(1) but is silent on s 15A(2)

It should be noted that cl 3.2 gives a right to reject for latent defects that could not have been discovered upon examination and which appear after a reasonable period of use. This right goes far beyond the rights of rejection otherwise granted by the SGA. Also, cl 3.3 deals with the right not only to reject the goods in question, but grants a right to cancel the balance of the order as well. This right does not arise under the SGA where the contract provides for delivery in more than one consignment, since there has been no breach in respect of goods not yet delivered, however reasonable it is for the buyer to fear that there will be in the future. The new s 35A actually deals only with the opposite issue, so that a buyer who accepts one instalment does not thereby lose his right to reject the rest. In most cases, the buyer thus prefers to include such a right expressly, which he can then invoke at his discretion in situations where the defects in the initial delivery of goods are so severe that he loses confidence in the ability of the seller to perform properly under the contract .

Finally, cl 3.4 deals with a common practice of sellers in relation to delivery notes. They often require the buyer to sign a delivery note which contains a statement to the effect that signature signifies that the goods have been delivered in compliance with the contract, and in good condition, and that therefore the buyer accepts them. Such notes are usually signed by the buyer's warehouse staff, who are not necessarily part of the buyer's purchasing department and may have no idea of what the requirement under the contract is in relation to the goods. Nevertheless, once signed by an authorised employee of the buyer, the statement on such delivery notes is often hard to rebut, subject to the discussion on the application of s 35 of the SGA (as amended by the SSGA 1994) set out in the next paragraph. Clause 3.4 thus negates the effect of such delivery notes, except in relation to matters (eg the number of boxes delivered) which the warehouse staff can properly check, and can be reasonably expected to sign for.

Incidentally, a clause in a purchase order which attempted to negate the effect of a delivery note purporting to apply the seller's terms and conditions to the transaction would have no effect on the 'battle of the forms'. Either the contract will already have been concluded, on whatever terms, in which case the delivery note's terms are irrelevant anyway, or else, if the contract has not yet been concluded, the delivery note, being a later 'shot' in the 'battle', would prevail over the conditions on the purchase order (see the *BRS* case, above) and the contract would come into existence when the buyer took delivery and signed the note. Note that s 35 (as amended) can only be displaced by contractual provisions: thus if the condition on the delivery note is not part of the contract, s 35 (as amended) will prevail, and the note will have no effect.

2.9   Warranties and guarantee

The terms warranty and guarantee have various meanings in different legal contexts. For instance in the context of the law relating to sale of goods, a warranty is usually understood to be a representation relating to the subject matter of the contract, which is of secondary importance, and whose breach therefore entitles the injured party to damages but not to terminate the contract. However, in the commercial world, in the context of conditions of sale and purchase, the terms are used interchangeably to refer to express remedies granted in the contract by the seller to the buyer in respect of defective goods or workmanship.

Superficially, the approach is the same whether the remedy is contained in conditions of sale or conditions of purchase, and in many cases the wording of the remedies may be very similar indeed. Clauses 9.1 and 9.2 of Precedent 1 set out a standard type of guarantee. This guarantee covers the period of time in which defects will be remedied, the procedure that the buyer must go through in order to take advantage of the guarantee, and the remedies which the seller offers in respect of the defects. Clause 3.2 and the first part of cl 3.3 of Precedent 2 cover the same principles, but, as would obviously be preferred by the buyer, in cl 3.3 the procedures are more flexible and the buyer's rights are somewhat greater. In particular, there is no limitation of the remedy by reference to some period of time during which defects will be remedied.

Care should be taken with the phrase in square brackets in cl 9.1.2 of Precedent 1. If it is not included, cl 3.2 becomes what is known as a 'revolving warranty', with the effect that each time the goods are replaced or repaired, the new or repaired goods enjoy another warranty for the whole of the period in cl 9.1.1. This will go on indefinitely, unless and until one of the repaired or replaced goods manages to last for the whole of the period. Some manufacturers (particularly of mass-produced goods) do not take this point, and are happy to replace goods (it is cheaper than repairing them) until the buyer is satisfied.

Both buyers and sellers prefer the inclusion of express remedies. From the buyer's point of view, the warranties implied by the SGA, the SGSA or the common law, leave something to be desired. First, there are the problems of the remedies available to the buyer after he has accepted the goods, discussed above. Once the right to reject the goods has lapsed, the buyer's only remedy is to sue for damages for breach of contract. This is an unsatisfactory position when what he really wants is to have the defective goods repaired or replaced. From the seller's point of view, rather than expose himself to the vagaries of litigation, and the need to negotiate with each buyer as to exactly what remedies are appropriate in each case, it is preferable to set out a specific and detailed procedure which deals with the remedying of defects. Also, apart from legal considerations, in most situations, a seller who does not provide such a remedy is likely to be at a significant commercial disadvantage compared to his competitors, since the giving of such guarantees and warranties has really become standard commercial practice.

Warranties and guarantees also address the question of product lifetimes which is one issue, of equal concern to the buyer and the seller. The new implied warranty of satisfactory quality does provide some assistance on the question of product lifetimes. As discussed above, s 2B(e) of the SGA now makes durability one of the aspects of the quality of goods which is 'in appropriate cases' to be taken into account in determining if the goods are of 'satisfactory quality'. Presumably, the wording 'in appropriate cases' is there to deal with goods (such as fresh food or other perishables) where durability is not something the parties can reasonably be concerned with, unlike the case of, for instance, consumer durables like washing machines or motor vehicles, or capital goods like computers or plant and machinery.

In any event, clearly the standard of durability to be met must vary with 'the description of the goods, the price (if relevant), and all other relevant circumstances (see s 14(2A) of the SGA). For instance, a low-priced felt tip pen with no facility for a refill can be expected to write for a reasonable but short period of time after purchase, while an expensive fountain pen can be expected to continue to be serviceable for a much longer period. Similarly, second-hand goods, sold as seen, should not have to meet the same standard of durability as the equivalent goods when purchased new.

Nevertheless, in the absence of any specific legislative provisions laying down specific lifetimes for specific products, the definition of the period must be vague and the relevant standard of durability will obviously be a question of fact to be determined (perhaps with the assistance of trade custom or usage) variously according to the different types, prices and qualities of products.

It is far better for the buyer and the seller to avoid all these arguments by providing for an express period of time in which defects will be remedied. This period is thus, in effect, the lifetime of the product, during which it can be expected to function normally without the need for repair (other than, of course, in appropriate cases, replacement of consumables—such as ribbons on a printer, and routine or preventive maintenance—such as the need to service a car in accordance with the maker's guidelines).

Warranties and guarantees are thus generally to the benefit of both the buyer and the seller but there is one area where their interests do not coincide. A seller will prefer that the buyer's only remedy in respect of defective goods should be the express one granted under the contract. He will thus insert an additional clause specifying that the express remedy is the sole remedy, and that all other remedies express or implied by law or statute are excluded. In Precedent 1 this exclusion clause is set out in cl 9.3. On the other hand, the buyer will wish to have the comfort of the guarantee, and, in addition, whatever rights law and statute grant him in the particular circumstances of the case. This is achieved in Precedent 2 by the inclusion of cl 1.4 which expressly protects these additional rights notwithstanding the specific remedies granted by cll 3.2 and 3.3.

Where the seller is successful in adding his additional clause, the guarantee obviously acts as an exclusion of liability. In this case, s 3 of the UCTA will regulate a guarantee as excluding liability for breach or failure to perform a contractual obligation. However, it is clear that, as discussed above, an express warranty is in the interests of both parties, so that, provided the guarantee grants what can be regarded as a reasonable remedy under the particular circumstances of the contract, no problems under s 3 of the UCTA should arise.

The reasonableness of the guarantee has two aspects. First, is the procedure that the buyer has to go through to claim the remedy a proper one from an administrative point of view, or is it designed to make it difficult or impossible in practice for the buyer to invoke the clause? Secondly, is the period for which the seller promises to remedy defects a reasonable one given the nature of the goods and any other relevant factors under the contract? For instance, a year may be a reasonable period for a washing machine, but five years, or even ten, may be expected for building works.

The guarantee in cll 9.1 and 9.2 of Precedent 1 is designed (subject of course to the question of agreeing a specific period for the remedying of defects appropriate to the particular circumstances of the case) to pass the test of reasonableness imposed by s 3 of the UCTA. The only contentious area is the requirement in cl 9.1.1.2 that the defects must be found 'to the Seller's satisfaction to have arisen solely' from the seller's default. This restriction is often imposed to avoid prolonged arguments between seller and buyer. However, with one eye on s 3 of the UCTA, it would probably be prudent either to delete the words 'to the Seller's satisfaction' and perhaps also 'solely', so that the test to be met becomes an objective one, or, at the very least, to provide that the test be 'to the Seller's reasonable satisfaction'. Such an addition could well be implied into the contract by the court anyway, in instances where the seller refused to recognise responsibility for a defect even though he was clearly responsible, so that the refusal amounted to clear unreasonableness or even bad faith.

In most cases, where the guarantee is a reasonable one both parties are better off excluding other remedies express or implied by law or statute. The seller appreciates the clear specification of his liability for defects under the contract and the buyer should be willing to trade his somewhat uncertain remedies at law for the ease and certainty of remedy provided by the guarantee. The only area where this may work to the buyer's detriment is in the area of the product lifetime. For instance, if a car manifests a defect outside the express period for the correction of defects, where the guarantee excludes other legal remedies, this is (subject to s 3 of the UCTA) the end of the matter. However, in the absence of such an exclusion, it might be possible to show that the failure was due to a latent defect present in the car at the time of delivery (particularly possible in the area of negligent design) and this could then be the basis for a claim that there was a breach of the warranty of satisfactory quality at the time of delivery.

2.10 Cancellation and termination

So far as cancellation and termination are concerned, in most conventional types of contracts, the seller would wish to perform, or be given the opportunity to perform the contract. It is not in his interest to terminate the contract prematurely, nor would he wish to give the buyer the opportunity to do so. The seller might wish to cancel the contract if it proves too difficult or costly to perform, but this is not a feature of the straightforward contracts that would be covered by the use of Precedent 1. The issue arises in relation to more complicated or long-term contracts such as the system contract dealt with in Chapter 4, and the matter is discussed there. The seller may also wish to cancel in the event of the buyer's insolvency or impending insolvency, but in this case the remedies granted by the SGA coupled with cl 5 are sufficient to deal with the issue in most cases. In any event most sellers prefer, as a commercial issue, not to discuss such questions with their buyers, and instead to protect themselves by the use of appropriate credit vetting procedures, or else, where possible, by requiring payment upon delivery or even in advance of delivery.

The buyer, as always, has a different view. Circumstances may change, and he may no longer want the goods and services that he has ordered, or the seller may appear to be doing a poor job, and the buyer may have lost confidence in him. Precedent 2 tackles two aspects of this issue. Clause 10.1 permits cancellation (by either party) after a reasonable extension of time where one party or the other cannot complete the contract through circumstances outside that party's control. This is not a contentious clause and benefits both buyer and seller equally. It is in neither's interest for the contract to be kept in suspense indefinitely in circumstances where it clearly cannot be performed. (However, it must be said that even here, the seller would probably not want the contract to be terminated too quickly or easily by the buyer, as the seller has more to lose by being denied the chance to perform and get full payment for the supply of his goods.) Clause 10.2 of Precedent 2 provides an express right for the buyer to cancel in the event of breach by the seller. It is arguable that this clause does no more that restate the remedies available at common law to the buyer in the event of the seller's breach of contract. However, the common law right to terminate depends upon showing a sufficiently serious breach of contract to justify termination in the eyes of the court. It is far better for the buyer to have an express right which applies to any breach of contract. Further, the clause gives additional flexibility by permitting the cancellation of the order in whole or part. The common law right to terminate does not extend this far.

The remedy of purchase from a third party, with the consequent obligation on the seller to pay the increase in the purchase price, is broadly similar to that available at common law, but, again, the express clause imports a certain amount of flexibility in the area of the price paid for third party goods (for instance a premium might have to be paid for quick delivery to meet the buyer's original timescales) and as to how closely their specification need resemble the original goods.

The final point, not covered by either precedent, relates to cancellation at will for convenience. The system contract in Chapter 4 deals with this question at some length, but it is not unusual in standard terms and conditions to find a simple clause which permits the buyer to cancel the order in return for payment of a cancellation fee. The cancellation fee is usually expressed as a percentage of the contract price, and varies on a sliding scale. For some goods it may be appropriate to permit cancellation at no charge provided sufficiently long notice is given. However, such notice is usually longer than the lead time that the seller requires to fulfil an order. This is because until the commencement of the lead time period, the seller has probably not started work on the order, and so has incurred no expense. Equally, at some point before delivery, the seller will require the scale to rise to 100 per cent, because he will by then have completed the products ready for delivery, and cancellation will no longer relieve him from incurring the costs associated with performing the contract. Of course at this stage, rather than pay the cancellation charge, the buyer might as well take delivery.

2.11   General exclusions of liability

The supplier of goods or services can become liable for breach of contract in a variety of ways. The main types of breach are obviously failure to supply goods or services of the nature or quality promised under the contract, late delivery and failure to pass a good title to items sold under the contract. A less common type is some act or omission of the seller under the contract which lays the buyer open to legal action from third parties (for instance because goods which have been negligently manufactured injure a third party while they are being used by the buyer).

The exclusion of liability for all of these issues can be dealt with either on a piecemeal basis by writing a particular exclusion or limitation into the contract conditions dealing with each issue, or, alternatively or in addition, by the use of blanket exclusion clauses covering the whole contract. In practice most sets of conditions use a mixture of the two solutions. In Precedent 1, this is the approach that has been followed. As already discussed above, limitation of liability in respect of specification, delivery and defects in the goods have been dealt with specifically in cll 2, 4 and 9 respectively.

The specific exclusions of liability referred to above should in theory be sufficient for nearly all purposes, since it is unrealistic of the seller to suppose (and indeed contrary to s 3 of the UCTA) that he can exclude all liability for his failure to perform in all circumstances. No set of contract conditions can or should protect the seller totally against his own incompetence. However, as discussed in Chapter 1, a clause excluding liability for failure to perform due to circumstances beyond his control (usually called a *'force majeure'* clause) is considered reasonable both commercially, and for the purposes of s 3 of the UCTA. Clause 8 of Precedent 1 is a typical short form *force majeure* clause. In addition, more as an added insurance than anything else, many sellers also include a general exclusion clause which limits total liability under the contract by reference to a monetary figure. These general exclusion clauses are discussed in Chapter 1, and a typical example is included in Precedent 1 as cl 13. As noted in Chapter 1 extreme care must be taken in setting the monetary figure in order to pass the reasonableness test imposed by s 3 of the UCTA.

The final type of general exclusion clause which is also frequently included is one which restricts or excludes liability for various kinds of economic loss. Such clauses are often called 'consequential loss' clauses, but the term is not entirely accurate, since economic loss under a contract can be both direct and consequential under the common law (see *Victoria Laundry (Windsor) Ltd v Newman Industries Ltd* [1949] 2 KB 528, *Trans Trust SPRL v Danubian Trading Co* [1952] 2 QB 297, *Croudace v Cawoods Concrete* [1978] 2 Lloyd's Rep 55, CA, Allied Maples Group Ltd v Simmons and Simmons [1995] 1 WLR 1603, *Amstrad plc v Seagate Technology Inc* [1998] and *British Sugar plc v NEI Power Projects Ltd* (1997) unreported, CA, 8 October). Thus the common conception that has prevailed in commercial circles for many years, that consequential loss is the same thing as loss of business, profits, revenues or contracts is incorrect.

Looking at *Victoria Laundry* and *British Sugar* it would appear that the term 'consequential loss' equates to damage which was in the reasonable contemplation of the parties at the time the contract was entered into, but which did not flow naturally from the breach (the second limb of the rule in *Hadley v Baxendale*). In both cases, the plaintiff claimed damages because the defendant's breach in relation to the supply of machinery to be used by the plaintiff for the purposes of his business had caused loss of profits and increased production costs. In both cases this loss was held by the court to flow directly and naturally from the breach (ie the first limb of the rule in *Hadley v Baxendale*), and therefore to be recoverable despite an exclusion for consequential loss. However, in *Victoria Laundry*, the loss of a particularly profitable contract, outside the ordinary course of business, which was not known to the defendant, was held to be consequential loss, so that the exclusion clause prevented the recovery of damages for its loss,

Given these cases, it may be argued that the correct course is to draft exclusion clauses which deal solely with concepts such as economic loss, loss of profit or loss of revenue, and to avoid using such terms as direct, indirect or consequential loss. However, the use of these terms has become so ingrained in our contracts that the best course is to specify the types of economic loss to be excluded (eg loss of profit, revenue or contracts) and then to also exclude indirect and consequential loss, as well. Using only the terms 'consequential loss' or 'indirect loss' should exclude economic loss falling under the second limb of the rule in *Hadley v Baxendale*, but it will certainly not exclude economic loss falling under the first limb of that rule.

Clause 12 of Precedent 1 deals with the point in the correct way to avoid this problem. The point of such clauses is to put the buyer in the position where his remedies for failure to perform or defective performance under the contract are limited in fact to compelling either proper performance under the contract (by way of rework, repair or replacement) or the return of his money. Additionally, in the case of a complete failure to perform to contract at all, the buyer will usually have the right to go elsewhere to a third party for the same goods and to charge the seller for any increase in the price paid to the third party over that payable to the seller. Such clauses are often fiercely resisted by the buyer, but in most cases without reason. The seller can only obtain a limited profit margin on the goods or services that he supplies, while the economic loss suffered by the buyer for his failure to perform may be unknown to the seller, not easily forecast, and far greater than the profit margin the seller enjoys on the transaction. A seller who accepted an unlimited liability for economic loss on many of his transactions would soon go out of business. In appropriate circumstances, and where the profit margin admits of the taking of such a risk, sellers do sometimes accept liability for economic loss, but then it is usually with some upper limit, or through the operation of a liquidated damages clause. Liquidated damages clauses are discussed in Chapter 4.

From the point of view of the buyer, general exclusion clauses are obviously less popular, and, in general he sees little need for them to protect his own position. Precedent 2 reflects this position, as discussed above. However, even buyers tend to adopt some form of *force majeure* clause (often a mutual one benefiting both parties) and this has been included in cl 10.1 of Precedent 2.

The general exclusion clauses discussed in this section which impose blanket exclusions of liability give rise to particular problems under the UCTA. Where the UCTA controls exclusion clauses its approach is either to state that liability for the matter in question 'cannot be excluded or restricted by reference to any contract term' (imposition of a total ban) or to state that such liability cannot be so excluded or restricted unless the relevant contract term 'satisfies the test of reasonableness'.

As discussed in Chapter 1, the total ban, in the case of non-consumer transactions applies only to liability for death or personal injury (UCTA 1977, s 2(1)) and liability for breach of the implied warranties of good title and quiet possession implied by the SGA and the SGSA (UCTA 1977, ss 6(1) and 7(3A)). Exclusion of other types of liability (for damage other than personal injury or death, for breach generally, for breach of implied warranties other than title or quiet possession, and for pre-contract misrepresentation: ss 2(2), 3, 6(3), 7(3) and 8 of the UCTA) is governed by the requirement of reasonableness.

Where an exclusion clause controlled by the UCTA is specific to a particular liability the effect of the UCTA is either to render the clause unenforceable (if the UCTA imposes a total ban), or (if the UCTA imposes the requirement of reasonableness) to render the clause unenforceable if it fails to satisfy that requirement. For all practical purposes a specific exclusion clause which is rendered unenforceable under these circumstances can be regarded as void. However, the UCTA does not state that such clauses are void, merely that the relevant liability cannot be excluded or restricted by reference to them. Thus, in the case of a general exclusion clause, is it possible that a clause could be enforceable in respect of some classes of liability controlled by the UCTA, but not in respect of others?

The question is easily answered where the two types of liability to be excluded are covered by sections of the UCTA which only render the clause unenforceable if it fails to satisfy the requirement of reasonableness (for instance s 2, property damage, and s 6(3), implied warranty of quality). Section 11(1) of the UCTA states that the test for reasonableness is that the term must have been 'a reasonable and fair one ... having regard to the circumstances which were, or ought reasonably to have been, known to or in the contemplation of the parties *when the contract was made*'. This means that the court cannot take account of the various breaches actually committed, for which the defendant is seeking protection under the clause, to decide if the clause is reasonable or not, either generally, or separately in relation to each breach. The test is one test, applied on the factors known to the parties at the time of the breach. Thus, if the clause is reasonable it will stand for all the classes of liability under the UCTA for which exclusion is permitted if the requirement of reasonableness is satisfied. If the clause fails the test it will be unenforceable in respect of all of those classes.

The position is more complicated where one of the classes of liability concerned is one for which the UCTA forbids exclusion or restriction. For instance, take a clause which imposes a total cap on liability under a contract. Let us suppose that an action is brought for breach of contract by a party to a contract who is a natural person who has suffered both personal injury and property damage as a result of the breach. Section 2(1) of the UCTA forbids exclusion or restriction of the liability for personal injury, but s 2(2) permits the exclusion or restriction of liability for other loss or damage if the clause satisfies the requirement of reasonableness. Under these circumstances could the court refuse to enforce the exclusion clause in respect of the personal injury, but, subject to the requirement of reasonableness, enforce it in relation to the property damage? Alternatively would the court regard the clause as so tainted by its attempt to exclude the liability for personal injury that it would also become unenforceable in respect of the liability for property damage as well?

Theoretically, on the wording of the UCTA, this former course would seem correct. The UCTA does not render the clause void, under s 2(1). It merely overrides it and makes it unenforceable for the purposes of excluding liability for death or personal injury. However, one has to ask whether the court would not be tempted to hold that the clause was not only unenforceable under s 2(1) but also failed the reasonableness test under s 2(2). One of the circumstances which was known, or ought to have been known, to the parties at the time they were entering into the contract was that in certain circumstances the clause would clearly be unenforceable (namely, in the area of liability for death or personal injury). Is a clause which is known to be unenforceable in certain circumstances an unreasonable one? See *Witter Ltd v TBP Industries Ltd* (1994) unreported, ChD, 15 July (Ch 1990-W-5354).

The first way to avoid such danger is not to plead any general exclusion clause as a defence to an action for a class of liability for which the UCTA renders exclusion clauses unenforceable. However, this is not free from danger if one then seeks to rely on the clause for another class of liability, in the same action, for which exclusion is permitted, subject to the requirement of reasonableness. The plaintiff may himself raise the arguments in the previous paragraph about the unreasonable nature of the clause and seek to render it unenforceable for all classes of liability under the action.

A recent judgment in the Court of Appeal has shown the dangers to the defendant in trying to avoid raising the issue of the applicability of the UCTA when pleading an exclusion clause. In *Sheffield v Pickfords Ltd* (1997) *The Times*, 17 March, the court held that the plaintiff can raise this issue during the course of the action even if neither he nor the defendant had raised the matter in the pleadings. Once the defendant has raised as a defence terms which are subject to the UCTA, there is an implication that the terms were those upon which he was entitled to rely having regard to the provisions of the UCTA. Further, the court strongly recommended that, where an exclusion clause is pleaded, and is appropriate, the defendant should state expressly that he regards the terms upon which he is relying as subject to the UCTA and should state that he considers them reasonable within the meaning of s 11(3). It is then open to the plaintiff in a reply to clarify his position. The matter can then be properly argued at trial if the plaintiff contends that the terms are unreasonable and the defendant can prepare the necessary evidence to attempt to rebut this contention.

The only totally safe way to proceed is to exclude from the operation of the general exclusion clauses all those classes of liability for which the UCTA imposes a total ban on exclusion clauses. Then, provided the exclusion clause as a whole passes the general requirement of reasonableness as discussed above, the clause will be effective to exclude liability for all the other classes of liability for which the UCTA permits exclusion subject to the requirement of reasonableness. This is the basis adopted in Precedent 1 by the inclusion of cl 14. With regard to cl 14.2, there is in fact no need to include such a clause unless one is actually contracting with a natural person, hence the limitation on the operation of the clause in the phrases in square brackets. However, since the liabilities covered by cl 14.2 are easy to insure against, many sellers offer this clause without any of the limitations in the phrases in square brackets, as a marketing advantage over their competitors.

Finally, the overall reasonableness of this type of clause, which excludes or limits liability for all breaches under a contract, however caused, is discussed in Chapter 1, under the heading relating to s 3 of the UCTA, to which regard should be had. Clauses 12 and 13 of Precedent 1 rely on the principles in that discussion to pass the test of reasonableness and are drafted in such a way that they apply to all types of breach, however caused (including by reason of wilful default).

2.12 Indemnities for third party claims

The one area of liability which really concerns the buyer is the possibility of claims made against him by third parties which arise because of some act or omission of the seller. These can arise from a great variety of causes. A particularly specialised area is that relating to infringement of third party intellectual property rights, and this is discussed in detail in the next section. Here the discussion is confined to more general types of tortious liability, such as that arising from negligent acts or omissions.

For instance, a manufacturer may sell defective goods which the buyer then sells on to a third party who suffers loss or injury because of the defect. The third party will probably sue the buyer under the contract of sale between them, and the manufacturer in tort for negligence. Another example is the contractor who negligently injures an employee of his customer while on that customer's premises. The employee is likely to sue the contractor in tort for negligence, and the customer as his employer for failing to provide safe working conditions. The issues surrounding these indemnities under the UCTA have been discussed in Chapter 1. However, in general, where he can prevail, the buyer will wish to have an indemnity from his seller against all such third party claims and their consequences.

Clause 7 of Precedent 2 provides an extensive example of such an indemnity. Were a seller to accept such an indemnity he would probably want to add further clauses requiring the buyer to give prompt notification of such claims, to permit him to take over conduct of the claim, not to admit liability, and to render him any necessary assistance in contesting the claim. Although there are more elaborate clauses, copying the wording at the beginning of cl 10.2 of Precedent 1 would suffice in most cases.

It should be noted that cl 7.3 goes beyond granting an indemnity for third party claims, since it also grants an indemnity for loss suffered by the buyer as a result of breaches of the contract by the seller. The purpose of such an indemnity is to aid the buyer in recovering all relevant damages in the event of litigation against the seller. In the absence of such a clause the buyer would have to prove for the damage suffered under the normal common law rules. The inclusion of this clause enables him to recover all loss, however remote (provided he can prove causation) suffered as a result of the seller's wrongful acts, since the seller has, by the clause, undertaken an express obligation to compensate him for such loss. This clause is the exact opposite of the seller's clause excluding economic loss included in cl 12 of Precedent 1.

2.13   Intellectual property rights

As stated above, ss 6(1) and 7(3A) of the UCTA provide that liability for breach of the obligations as to title and quiet possession implied by the SGA and the SGSA cannot be excluded or restricted by reference to any contract term. This gives rise to special problems in the area of the supply of goods which infringe third party intellectual property rights, where the UCTA applies. It has been held that such supply amounts to a breach of these warranties (see *Niblett v Confectioners' Materials* [1921] 3 KB 387 and *Microbeads v Vinhurst* [1976] RPC 19). This being the case, it is not possible simply to exclude or, indeed, restrict, liability for the supply of goods which infringe third party intellectual property rights.

Rather as in the case of the warranty given for defective goods, both buyer and seller find it advantageous to set out the procedure and remedies to be followed in the event of any claim of infringement being made by a third party. The seller normally wishes to have the conduct of the claim at his expense, and its ultimate litigation or settlement, since it concerns his business generally, and it is usually impractical for the buyer to deal with the issue anyway, since all of the relevant knowledge is in the possession of the seller.

Thus most such clauses provide for the seller to have the conduct of the action at his expense, on the basis that he will bear the costs of conduct and pay any resulting settlement or judgment against him and the buyer. In addition such clauses also normally give the seller the options of trying to alter the goods so that they are no longer infringing, buying the third party claimant out by obtaining a licence from him, or, in the last resort, taking back the goods in return for a refund of their purchase price; all of these at the seller's expense.

Many such clauses then go on to provide, rather as in the case of the warranty in relation to defective goods, that the express remedies in the clause are the only remedies granted to the buyer in respect of infringement of third party intellectual property rights, and that all other remedies implied by law are excluded. Where the UCTA applies, this final clause is obviously unenforceable by reason of s 6(1) or 7(3A) of the UCTA. It is also at least arguable that these sections of the UCTA prevent the seller from imposing an obligation on the buyer to permit the seller to exercise the options of alteration of the goods or taking them back for a refund, because such actions by the seller would be in breach of his warranty of quiet possession.

Where the UCTA applies, despite such an exclusion clause, the buyer will be able to enjoy the express remedies under the clause, and any other remedies available to him at law as well. For instance, in addition to the express remedies, he would be able, in appropriate cases, to claim damages for lost profits or contracts or other interruption caused to his business if he were unable finally to use or resell the goods concerned. As discussed under the section relating to general exclusion clauses, not only would the specific exclusion in the infringement clause be unable to bar such claims, but general exclusion clauses (eg those relating to economic loss) would be ineffective as well.

From the buyer's point of view this is a totally acceptable situation, and it will be seen from cll 6.1, 6.2 and 6.3 of Precedent 2 that the buyer here provides for express warranties against infringement, coupled with an indemnity against the consequences of such infringement. The general indemnity in cl 7.3 of Precedent 2 would also assist the buyer in appropriate cases, and would have the effect of permitting recovery of compensation for all damage flowing from the infringement, subject only to proving causation, as discussed in the previous section. In addition, any other rights the buyer may have at law are reserved to him by the operation of cl 1.4.

The one exception, provided for the benefit of the seller in these clauses, is where the infringement is caused because of a design, specification or other instructions supplied by the buyer for the seller to work to. This exception is not only totally fair and reasonable, but it is hard to see how the seller could be in breach of a warranty of title or quiet possession since the problem is caused by the buyer not the seller. Such exceptions should be untouched by s 6(1) or 7(3A) of the UCTA.

If the seller wishes to restrict or exclude liability for infringement of third party intellectual property rights there are, however, some options open to him.

First of all, he can include a patent indemnity, without any exclusion clause tacked on to it, along the lines set out above, providing express but limited remedies, and, in particular, not putting forward an express right to compensation for economic loss. If the seller honours the express remedies, the buyer will have to prove any loss that he has suffered in addition to that covered by the clause, subject to the ordinary common law rules relating to remoteness. This will not be easy, and, where the seller has solved the problem of infringement by obtaining a licence, or redesigning the goods so as to put an end to the infringement, there may not be any other damage suffered in any event.

Also, it should not be forgotten that in order for the buyer to be able to claim any additional damage at all, he must first prove that there has indeed been a breach of the warranties of title or quiet possession. If the allegation of infringement proves unfounded, there will have been no breach. Not only is it hard to see how the buyer can then bring an action for breach of contract, as opposed to invoking the express remedies of the clause, but, even if he were able to, there is no reason why general exclusion clauses capping liability or excluding liability for economic loss should not be effective, since they would then only have to pass the reasonableness test. Section 6(1) or 7(3A) of the UCTA could have no application in this situation.

A seller who wishes to exclude liability for third party infringement can do so to some extent by relying on SGA 1979, s 12(3) and (4) or SGSA 1982, s 2(3) and (4) (contracting to pass only such title as the seller may have, subject to disclosure of known encumbrances and a warranty of no interference in quiet possession by the seller). He can include a clause stating that, while he is not aware of any intellectual property right which may be infringed by the possession or intended use of the goods being sold, he takes no responsibility for the existence of relevant third party intellectual property rights, and the buyer must assume the risk of infringement of the same.

Additionally, of course, where a seller is aware of any infringement (and, to be prudent, any allegation or potential for an allegation of infringement) he should give specific notice of this to the buyer, either in the clause, or separately. Failure to do this will, in the event of a third party claim based on such an undisclosed infringement, expose him to damages at large for breach of the warranties relating to disclosure of known encumbrances under s 12(4) of the SGA or s 2(4) of the SGSA, as the case may be.

Such a clause is not attractive to the seller, because he loses control of the conduct of the claim of infringement, and it is often a difficult clause to persuade the buyer to accept unless there is a problem which is so well-known in a particular industry that many sellers tend to include a reservation relating to it. The best way to proceed is to include the clause as described above, but then to add a further clause, covering the issues normally included in an intellectual property rights indemnity, and stating that these express remedies are offered (on, as it were, an *ex gratia* basis) even though the seller takes no responsibility for the infringement.

There is no case law on such a combination of clauses. However, given that the disclaimer of responsibility is valid under the UCTA, it is hard to see why such a solution, which puts the buyer in a better position than he would have been in if no express remedies were available, should fall foul of the UCTA.

Precedent 1 adopts this approach of a combination of an exclusion of liability for infringement pursuant to s 12(3) of the SGA and s 2(3) of the SGSA (set out in cll 5.1, 5.2 and 5.3) and an express but limited remedy for such infringement (set out in cl 10). If one wished to adopt the approach of a limited express remedy with no exclusion of liability, one would retain cl 10 (except for cl 10.6) and delete the phrases in square brackets in cl 5.1 and the whole of cll 1, 5.2 and 5.3. In this case cl 14.1 should refer to s 12(1) of the SGA and s 2(1) of SGSA, and not ss 12(3) and 2(3) respectively. It would then operate to preserve the express warranty in cl 5.1 (as amended) and the implied warranties in s 12(1) and s 2(1).

Finally, with regard to cl 10, it should be noted that no obligation to permit alteration of the goods to make them non-infringing is imposed on the buyer, and that the obligation to return infringing goods, subject to a refund of the price, is only imposed on the buyer where it arises not at the option of the seller but because of a judgment or settlement relating to the claim of infringement (which is presumably not entirely within the seller's control). This is to avoid the problem about breach of the seller's warranty of quiet possession discussed above.

2.14 Boilerplate, choice of law and confidentiality

It will always be the case that sets of standard terms and conditions contain a number of miscellaneous conditions, falling either within the popular designation of 'boilerplate', or else specifically tailored to the type of transaction that the standard set of terms is designed to cover. So far as boilerplate conditions are concerned, the draftsman can add these to the extent that they seem appropriate and necessary, although he should be sparing given that the aim of the exercise is to produce a relatively short set of commercially acceptable terms and conditions. These could cover items such as interpretation, waiver of rights, severability, forum for settling disputes, an arbitration clause and so on.

In general most of these clauses are not highly desirable in short form standard conditions. The most useful is probably a choice of law clause (see cl 15 of Precedent 1, and cl 1.4 of Precedent 2). It should not be forgotten that there are different systems of law even within the UK, so that even for domestic sales such a clause avoids a potential source of confusion.

Another area of boilerplate that is probably useful to include as a general rule is that relating to confidentiality, although, where the parties are specifically exchanging and dealing with large volumes of confidential information a separate full confidentiality agreement is much more appropriate. Short confidentiality clauses in standard conditions are really only precautionary measures to be relied upon in an emergency. Clause 11 of Precedent 1 is a very short form of confidentiality clause, which is mutually binding, while cl 11.1 of Precedent 2 is inserted by the buyer only to bind the seller. Additionally this clause forbids the seller to use the order or his connection with the buyer as a reference sale or generally for advertising or publicity purposes. In practice most buyers are prepared to have their names used for publicity purposes provided that this is done in a controlled manner and with their prior consent.

2.15   Assignment and subcontracting

One area of boilerplate which concerns the buyer rather more than the seller is the question of the right to assign or subcontract all or part of the order. The basic principle of law is that assignment of a contract is not possible where the identity of the assignor is an important factor for the other party to the contract either as a reason for his entering into the contract in the first place, or because it is for some reason significant for the proper discharge of the contract.

Buyers prefer not to leave such issues to the general law. They would contend that in nearly all cases the identity of their supplier was an important factor, and therefore would prefer to permit no assignments without their prior consultation and consent. Clause 24 of Precedent 1 achieves this aim. Even sellers may prefer their buyer not to have the option to assign the contract, given that one of the important factors for sellers when deciding to enter into a contract may well be the creditworthiness of the buyer. Although it is true that the general law would in most cases not permit assignment by a buyer to a less creditworthy assignee (since creditworthiness would be an important factor relating to the identity of the contracting party) many sellers would prefer to insert a non-assignment clause and avoid the argument. In standard conditions of sale, therefore, many sellers would choose the option of a clause forbidding both parties to assign (in whole or part) as the most commercially acceptable way of proceeding.

Clauses forbidding assignment of the contract do not, however, prevent a seller from factoring or otherwise assigning the debts due to him from his buyer as a result of his performance of the contract. Most buyers in any event have little interest in preventing such an assignment, and most sellers, at least in today's economic climate, desire to retain the flexibility to sell off or secure their debts to assist their cash flow. Thus clauses which use wording forbidding the seller to assign the 'benefit or burden' of the contract are undesirable. As long as the seller cannot assign the contract itself, he should be free to deal with the benefit thereof (ie the resulting revenue stream and book debts) as he sees fit.

Subcontracting is a more complex issue. In the absence of a clause forbidding this, a seller can subcontract his performance of the contract without reference to, or sometimes even the knowledge of, the buyer. The theory is that such subcontracting should not concern the buyer, because the seller still remains liable to him for the discharge of the main contract in accordance with its terms. Most sellers will not wish to contract out of the right to subcontract, since this gives them a very necessary flexibility in times of high demand, or if their own facilities cannot produce the required goods for some reason. A buyer, on the other hand, may well be concerned about such subcontracting, since one of the factors on which he decided to place the contract with the seller may well have been his perception of the seller's own quality standards and competence to carry out the contract. A subcontractor may not be able to satisfy the buyer in this regard. Clause 9.2 of Precedent 2 contains a standard clause preventing subcontracting. Note, however, that even this clause does contain some exceptions to allow either for nominated subcontractors or subcontracting customary in the trade, since, in practice, the seller probably will not perform every part of the contract himself.

2.16   Tooling, the supply of hazardous goods

It is not possible to discuss all of the possible specially-tailored clauses that may be needed in standard terms and conditions, but these can cover such issues as special acceptance tests, compliance with particular quality standards, or special methods of manufacture or delivery. In Precedent 2 there are two such special clauses which are, however, felt to be of some general application.

The first relates to the provision by the buyer of jigs, tools and gauges. Where the buyer places an order with a seller for what is essentially subcontract manufacture, it is very common either for the seller to require the buyer to provide such items for use in the manufacture, or to have such items made himself. In the latter case this is often at the buyer's expense (either by way of a lump sum payment, or an amortisation by way of an increase in the unit price of the goods to be manufactured using such items). A good example would be a contract for the seller to manufacture injection-moulded plastic components for the buyer, which requires one party or the other to provide the mould to be used in such production.

The buyer's concerns here are that these items be properly used and cared for by the seller, that they be used only for the purposes of the subcontract (ie that the seller does not use them to make goods for third parties which can then be sold by them in competition with the buyer), and that they be returned to him at the end of the subcontract. Although in this case the seller will find it hard to argue with the buyer's concerns, where the seller himself provides the items (even if he charges the buyer directly or indirectly for their provision) he may well wish to keep ownership himself, either to tie the buyer to him for future orders, or to enable him to use the items for sales to third parties, even if this is to the buyer's detriment, and against his consent. Such use may be an infringement of any design rights that the buyer has in the designs embodied in these tools, but he will in general prefer to avoid the attempt to invoke these rights, and instead to rely on a provision like cll 8.1 and 8.2 of Precedent 2.

A final clause, which is of general application is that relating to the supply of hazardous goods in accordance with the proper safety regulations, particularly in the area of the proper hazard markings and warnings. This is set out in cl 12.1 of Precedent 2.

2.17   Framework supply agreements

Where the parties have a continuing relationship based on a large volume of business under regular orders the most efficient way to proceed is to enter into a framework agreement which regulates the mechanism for placing orders and decides in advance the terms and conditions which will govern each order. Such agreements are useful because they make order placing easier, and usually also contain a mechanism enabling the seller to have visibility of his buyer's future requirements and to make some preparation to meet them. Additionally, since such agreements are usually only entered into by the seller with his most important customers, the special negotiation of a set of terms and conditions of supply is worth the effort of both sides, and, incidentally, is the best way of avoiding the battle of the forms. Precedent 3 is a typical framework or 'umbrella' supply agreement.

Clauses 1, 2 and 3 of Precedent 3 deal respectively with the identity of the parties, the period of validity of the agreement, and the general purpose of the agreement, all of which are self-explanatory. It should be noted that cl 3 details the subject matter of the agreement (ie the products to be supplied and their particular specifications) by incorporating the contents of Scheds 1 and 2 to the agreement. This is a useful mechanism which allows the agreement to be easily updated by replacing schedules as old products are dropped and new ones added.

Clause 4 is the heart of the agreement, dealing as it does with the mechanism for the forecasting of requirements and the placing of orders. The forecast mechanism proposed here is one which is much to the advantage of the buyer, since it carries no obligation upon the buyer to purchase all or any of the forecast quantities. To the extent the seller uses it to manufacture stock for the buyer ahead of any orders he does so at his own risk. Also the mechanism for updating the forecast is not a very accurate one.

One commonly used alternative is a rolling forecast. As an example, every three months the buyer gives a 12 months forward forecast. Thus the forecast's window of 12 months rolls forward three months every time the forecast is updated, and the balance of the previous periods' forecasts still within the new window are automatically updated as well. In some versions of this type of forecasting, the buyer is obliged to purchase the requirements detailed in the first three months of the rolling forecast, so that, in effect, as he rolls his forecast on, he places an order for the first three months' requirements and forecasts those of the next nine months.

Where forecasts are not legally binding on the buyer, another commonly used alternative is for the buyer to agree to compensate the seller (up to some agreed limits) for excess inventory of the products covered by the agreement which are still in the seller's hands on termination of the agreement, but which he cannot reasonably dispose of elsewhere. Clause 7.4 of Precedent 3 is a simple example of such a clause. It is weighted in the seller's favour, as it has no upper limit, or other pre-conditions to the obligation to purchase.

The remainder of cl 4 deals with order placing. Although a variety of provisions is possible, the position taken in Precedent 3 is that the seller is obliged to accept all orders placed for delivery subject to agreed lead times. This type of provision is suitable for commodity goods which are produced by a continuous production process. The seller has no difficulty in producing them for the buyer in any quantity provided he has sufficient notice to schedule production, and purchase needed materials and components.

For some types of goods, particularly those made to order this may not be appropriate. In such cases, the seller will provide that no order is to become binding unless he has specifically accepted it. Another variation is to impose on the seller the obligation to accept all orders placed in accordance with the buyer's forecast, even though that forecast is not binding on the buyer. However, in such a case, since the seller may well have to take on commitments, either to purchase materials and components or to manufacture without order cover, so that he can be ready to supply the forecast requirements if ordered, the buyer must take some responsibility if he does not purchase up to his forecast. This may take the form of an agreement to purchase a minimum percentage of the forecast, or to compensate the seller for excess work in progress or inventories. Sellers in a strong bargaining position will attempt to impose such a clause even where they are not obliged to supply the forecast requirements. In this connection, Precedent 3 imposes a minimum purchase obligation (see cl 4.6) and, as already stated, a buy-back on termination provision (see cl 7.4).

Lastly, cl 4.5 provides for the terms and conditions of supply which will govern all orders placed under the agreement. These are set out in Sched 3. Any standard set of conditions (such as Precedent 1 or Precedent 2) can be attached.

Clause 5 covers pricing, and incorporates a price variation formula to cover increases in future years. In the absence of a firm formula, the parties will either tie themselves to a fixed price for the duration of the agreement (which is clearly usually undesirable) or else have to provide an agreement with a shorter duration, but with an option of renewal if new prices can be agreed. A clause which merely imposes on the parties an obligation to renegotiate prices from time to time, once an initial period has elapsed, will simply turn the agreement, on the lapse of the initial period, into an agreement to agree, which is then void for uncertainty. Where such clauses are included at the wish of the parties it is always as well to go on to spell out the consequences of the failure to agree. The usual formula is that for a period of time ending on the expiry of the initial period the parties will attempt to renegotiate the prices to apply for a further fixed period. If they agree, the agreement is renewed for that period, if they fail to agree by the expiry of the initial fixed period, then the agreement terminates automatically.

Clause 6 is a clause which sellers often try to impose. Exclusive purchase obligations are in general permissible under various competition law regimes, but buyers, for obvious reasons, tend to avoid them. The usual *quid pro quo* for this clause is found in cl 7.2. If the seller cannot supply, for any reason, even if it is outside his control, then the buyer must be entitled to terminate the agreement and look elsewhere. As an alternative, the seller sometimes agrees that the agreement can be suspended during the period of his inability to supply, so that the buyer can go elsewhere during that period, but is obliged to return to the seller (subject to any transition period needed to take delivery of and consume orders placed with third parties) when he is next in a position to supply. This type of clause usually only grants the right of suspension, as opposed to termination, where the seller cannot deliver because of *force majeure*.

Apart from the points already discussed, the remainder of cl 7 is a standard termination clause. It should be noted, however, that termination does not affect the status of orders wholly or partially outstanding at the date of termination. This is a provision which is usually inserted, since, once an order has been placed, it becomes a separate contract, with a life of its own, and stands or falls on the terms and conditions which govern it.

Clause 8 provides the necessary precautionary provision to prevent the buyer claiming that he has the right to intellectual property arising out of any development work which the seller has had to effect in order to put himself in a position to supply the goods under the contract. The law generally would provide (unless the contract specifically stated to the contrary) that such intellectual property would vest in the seller, but it is as well to clarify the point ahead of time.

Precedent 3 is intentionally a minimalist document, which contains little boilerplate, and little by way of exclusion clauses. Obviously, once the principle of the document has been understood it is possible to create more elaborate framework agreements depending upon the client's requirements. However, in most cases, the best approach is to keep the framework agreement rather along the lines of Precedent 3 for length and simplicity, and to attach a more elaborate set of standard terms and conditions to govern each order.

Although the details of the law on electronic commerce, particularly over the internet, are outside the scope of this book, it should be noted that a framework agreement is one way to simplify many of the problems relating to electronic commerce where the transactions contemplated are between two business parties and intended to continue for a reasonable period of time. The framework agreement can be used to solve problems like which governing law applies in international transactions, whose terms and conditions apply to orders, and when do orders placed electronically turn into binding contracts. This last point is a particularly difficult issue.

In the UK, absent specific provisions to the contrary, where the medium of acceptance entails a delay in delivery, such as post or telegram, acceptance takes place when and where the message is posted or handed to the telegraph office for transmission (the so-called 'postal rule'). However, where the means of communication is instantaneous (eg telex, fax, telephone or video conference) the general rule is that acceptance takes place when and where the message is received. (See *Entores v Miles Far Eastern Corporation* [1955] 2 QB 327.) Recent cases have cast some doubt on this rule. In *Tradax Co v Reinante SA* [1973] 1 WLR 386, there was some consideration of whether a telex sent outside business hours was received when sent, or when the office next opened for business. The remarks, however, were only *obiter*. The same point fell to be decided in *Mondial Shipping and Chartering BV v Astarte Shipping Ltd* [1995] CLC 1011. Brandon J proceeded on the principle that the notice was received when its content 'reached the mind of the other party'. However, he added the proviso that, if the telex had been sent during business hours, then the party sending it had the right to assume that the receiving party had seen and understood it, and the receiving party could not then 'contend that it did not come to his attention'. The telex was sent late at night (just before the deadline for serving notice expired), and was read the next day when the office opened for business. However, if this rule were generally applied to telexes, it would seem as if either the postal rule needs some revision or telexes fall to be treated worse than less efficient means of communication. For instance, if the notice in *Mondial* had been sent at the same time as the telex, but by telegram, the postal rule would suggest that notice had been served when the telegram was handed in for transmission at the telegraph office, rather than the next day when the recipient opened for business. Electronic commerce can not only suffer from the same problems as telex (ie e-mails sent and received without delay but outside business hours) but e-mails are also not always instantaneous means of communication. Messages are sometime stored and forwarded later, or may take some time to work their way through the internet, although many systems do provide proof of date and time of delivery and even of whether or not the recipient has read the message. Given the legal uncertainties surrounding these issues the framework agreement is obviously a good place to deal with them. Precedent 3 provides an optional clause covering such issues.

2.18   Sale of second-hand goods

The problems relating to the sale of second-hand goods are basically no different from those of any other type of goods, except in the area of quality. Second-hand goods clearly have different standards of quality than new goods. Precedent 4 shows how this point should be dealt with. Usually, second-hand goods should be sold on an 'as is' or 'as seen' basis. Precedent 4 is a document which would be used where second-hand goods were sold, for instance, at auction or over the counter, rather than in the context of a sale governed by a set of standard terms and conditions. Where second-hand goods were sold regularly under standard terms, the correct approach would be to include a provision equivalent to Precedent 4 in the set, either as an alternative to or instead of the standard clauses applying to the quality standards for new goods.

The main area of exposure with second-hand goods is their use at work. Section 6 of the Health and Safety at Work Act 1974 imposes liabilities on those who supply equipment for use at work to ensure that it is 'so far as reasonably practicable … safe and without risks to health when properly used'. It should be noted that s 6 does not impose a civil liability, but only a criminal one (see s 47(1)(*a*) of the 1974 Act). When second-hand goods are sold on the 'as is' basis of Precedent 4, the question arises as to the extent to which the seller can disclaim responsibility for their condition if they are to be used at work either by the buyer, or by someone to whom the buyer sells them.

Section 6(8) of the 1974 Act can relieve the seller of responsibility in these circumstances provided that he obtains a written undertaking from the buyer that the buyer will himself take the necessary steps in relation to the safety of the goods. Where the seller obtains such an undertaking it will relieve him from his liability 'to such extent as is reasonable having regard to the terms of the undertaking'. Precedent 4 contains such an undertaking and explains the steps that should be taken to obtain the benefit of s 6(8).

Precedent 1

Standard conditions for business sale of goods

Statements on front of quotation

THE CONDITIONS OVERLEAF SHALL APPLY TO THIS QUOTATION
AND TO ANY CONTRACT BETWEEN US FOR THE SUPPLY OF ITEMS
DETAILED IN THIS QUOTATION (SEE CONDITION 1). [PLEASE READ
ALL OF THEM CAREFULLY.]

Statement on front of acknowledgment

YOUR ORDER [REFERRED TO ABOVE] [NO [   ] DATED
[   ]] IS ACCEPTED ON THE BASIS THAT THE CONDITIONS
[OVERLEAF] [ON THE REVERSE OF OUR QUOTATION NO
[   ] DATED [   ]] SHALL APPLY TO THE CON-
TRACT BETWEEN US FOR THE SUPPLY OF THE ITEMS DETAILED IN
YOUR ORDER (SEE CONDITION 1). [PLEASE READ ALL OF THEM
CAREFULLY.]

1   Formation of contract

1.1 Any order sent to the Seller by the Purchaser shall be accepted entirely at
the discretion of the Seller, and, if so accepted, will only be accepted upon
these conditions (hereafter referred to as the 'Conditions') and by means of
the Seller's standard order acknowledgment form.

1.2 Each order which is so accepted shall constitute an individual legally binding contract between the Seller and the Purchaser and such contract is

hereafter referred to in these Conditions as an 'Order'.

1.3 These Conditions shall override any contrary different or additional terms or conditions (if any) contained on or referred to in an order form or other documents or correspondence from the Purchaser, and no addition alteration or substitution of these terms will bind the Seller or form part of any Order unless they are expressly accepted in writing by a person authorised to sign on the Seller's behalf.

2   Specification

All goods supplied by the Seller shall be in accordance with (i) the current edition of the relevant Product Description Leaflet as published from time to time by the Seller (copies of which are available from the Seller upon request) and (ii) those further specifications or descriptions (if any) expressly listed or set out on the face of the Order. No other specification, descriptive material, written or oral representation, correspondence or statement, promotional or sales literature shall form part of or be incorporated by reference into the Order.

3   Acceptance

The Purchaser shall be deemed to have accepted all goods upon their delivery by the Seller to the address specified in the Order.

4   Delivery and risk

4.1 Unless otherwise stated in the Order, the price quoted includes delivery to the address specified in the Order, provided that the Seller reserves the right to make an additional charge to cover any increase in transport costs occurring before the date of delivery.

4.2 Any time or date for delivery given by the Seller is given in good faith, but is an estimate only.

4.3 Risk in the goods shall pass to the Purchaser upon delivery.

5   Title and payment

5.1 The Seller warrants that [(except in relation to intellectual property rights of third parties as referred to in Condition 5.3)] the Seller has good title to the goods [and that (pursuant to s 12(3) of the Sale of Goods Act 1979, or s 2(3) of the Supply of Goods and Services Act 1982, whichever Act applies to the Order) it will transfer such title as it may have in the goods to the Purchaser pursuant to Condition 5.5].

[**5.2** The Seller warrants that it is not aware of any actual or alleged infringements of any intellectual property rights of third parties which relate to the goods other than those (if any) which the Seller has disclosed to the Purchaser prior to acceptance of the Order.]

[**5.3** The Seller shall have no liability to the Purchaser (other than as provided in Condition 10) in the event that the goods to be supplied under the Order infringe any intellectual property rights of a third party (including without limitation by reason of their possession, sale or use, whether alone or in association or combination with any other goods); the Seller gives no warranty that the goods to be supplied under the order will not infringe as aforesaid, and all conditions, warranties, stipulations or other statements whatsoever relating to such infringement or alleged infringement (if any), whether express or implied, by statute, at common law or otherwise howsoever, are hereby excluded.]

5.4 Unless otherwise stated in the Order, payment of the price of the goods comprised in each consignment delivered pursuant to an Order shall become due at the end of the month following the month in which that consignment is delivered.

5.5 Title to the goods comprised in each consignment shall not pass to the Purchaser until the Purchaser has paid their price to the Seller, but, even though title has not passed, the Seller shall be entitled to sue for their price once its payment has become due.

6   Storage

If the Seller shall be unable, through circumstances beyond its control (including without limitation lack of shipping instructions from the Purchaser), to deliver the goods within 14 days after notification to the Purchaser or its agent that the goods are ready for delivery, the Seller shall be entitled to arrange storage on behalf of the Purchaser, whereupon delivery shall be deemed to have taken place, all risk in the goods shall pass to the Purchaser, and delivery to the Purchaser of the relevant warehouse receipt shall be deemed to be delivery of the goods for the purposes of Condition 4. All charges incurred by the Seller for storage or insurance shall be paid by the Purchaser within 30 days of submission of an invoice.

7   Damage in transit

The seller will replace free of charge any goods proved to the Seller's satisfaction to have been damaged in transit provided that within 24 hours after delivery both the Seller and the carriers have received from the Purchaser notification in writing of the occurrence of the damage and also, if and so far as practicable, of its nature and extent.

8   Force majeure

8.1 The Seller shall not be under any liability for any failure to perform any of its obligations under the Order due to *Force Majeure*. Following notification by the Seller to the Purchaser of such cause, the Seller shall be allowed a reasonable extension of time for the performance of its obligations.

8.2 For the purposes of this Condition, '*Force Majeure*' means fire, explosion, flood, lightning, Act of God, act of terrorism, war, rebellion, riot, sabotage, or official strike or similar official labour dispute, or events or circumstances outside the reasonable control of the party affected thereby.

9   Guarantee

9.1 For goods which are manufactured by the Seller or which bear one of the Seller's trade marks, the Seller grants the following guarantee:
9.1.1 The Seller shall free of charge either repair or, at its option, replace defective goods where the defects appear under proper use within [12 months] from the date of delivery, *provided that*:
9.1.1.1 notice in writing of the defects complained of shall be given to the Seller upon their appearance; and
9.1.1.2 such defects shall be found [to the Seller's [reasonable] satisfaction] to have arisen [solely] from the Seller's faulty design, workmanship or materials; and
9.1.1.3 the defective goods shall be returned to the Seller's factory at the Purchaser's expense if so requested by the Seller.
9.1.2 Any repaired or replaced goods shall be redelivered by the Seller free of charge to the original point of delivery but otherwise in accordance with and subject to these Conditions of Sale [save that the period of [twelve months] referred to in Condition 9.1.1 shall be replaced by the unexpired portion of that period only].
9.1.3 Alternatively to Condition 9.1.1, the Seller shall be entitled at its absolute discretion to refund the price of the defective goods in the event that such price shall already have been paid by the Purchaser to the Seller, or, if such

price has not been so paid, to relieve the Purchaser of all obligation to pay the same by the issue of a credit note in favour of the Purchaser in the amount of such price.

9.2 In respect of all goods manufactured and supplied to the Seller by third parties the Seller will pass on to the Purchaser (in so far as possible) the benefit of any warranty given to the Seller by such third parties and will (on request) supply to the Purchaser details of the terms and conditions of such warranty and copies of any relevant product information sheets, technical data sheets or product leaflets issued by such third parties and the Purchaser shall be solely responsible to the entire exclusion of the Seller for complying with all of these.

9.3 The Seller's liability under this Condition shall be to the exclusion of all other liability to the Purchaser whether contractual, tortious or otherwise for defects in the goods or for any loss or damage to or caused by the goods, and (subject to Condition 14) all other conditions, warranties, stipulations or other statements whatsoever concerning the goods, whether express or implied, by statute, at common law or otherwise howsoever, are hereby excluded; in particular (but without limitation of the foregoing) the Seller grants no warranties regarding the fitness for purpose, performance, use, nature or quality of the goods, whether express or implied, by statute, at common law or otherwise howsoever.

10   Intellectual property rights

10.1 In the event that any claim is made against the Purchaser for infringement of Intellectual Property Rights arising directly from the use [or sale] by the Purchaser of the goods, the Seller at its own expense shall conduct any ensuing litigation and all negotiations for a settlement of the claim. The Seller will bear the costs of any payment (either by way of a lump sum or a continuing royalty payment) made in settlement, or as a result of an award in a judgment against the Seller in the event of litigation.

10.2 The benefit of Condition 10.1 is granted to the Purchaser by the Seller only in the event that the Purchaser shall give the Seller the earliest possible notice in writing of any such claim being made or action threatened or brought against it, shall make no admission of liability or take any other action in connection therewith, shall permit the Seller to have the conduct of the claim pursuant to Condition 10.1, and shall (at the Seller's expense) give all reasonable information, co-operation and assistance to the Seller (including without limitation lending its name to proceedings) in relation to the conduct of the claim. In addition, if it is made a condition of any settlement made by the

Seller, or judgment awarded against the Purchaser, pursuant to Condition 10.1, the Purchaser shall return or destroy, as applicable, all infringing goods still under its control subject to a refund by the Seller of any payment for such goods already made [less a reasonable allowance for depreciation of the goods by reason of their use (if any) by the Purchaser prior to their return or destruction as aforesaid].

10.3 The provisions of Condition 10.1 shall not apply to any infringement caused by the Seller having followed a design or instruction furnished or given by the Purchaser nor to any use of the goods in a manner or for a purpose which shall have been specifically prohibited in writing by the Seller, nor to any infringement which is due to the use of such goods in association or combination with any other product.

10.4 Any design or instruction furnished or given by the Purchaser shall not be such as will cause the Seller to infringe any intellectual property rights.

10.5 For the purposes of this Condition, the capitalised term 'Intellectual Property Rights' means Patents, Registered Designs, Unregistered Designs, Registered Trademarks and Copyright only, having effect in the United Kingdom.

[**10.6** The foregoing states the Seller's entire liability to the Purchaser and the Purchaser's sole and exclusive remedies against the Supplier in connection with claims based on or resulting from the infringement of intellectual property rights, of any kind whatsoever, of third parties.]

11   Confidentiality

Both the Seller and the Purchaser shall each keep confidential and shall not without the prior consent in writing of the other disclose to any third party any technical or commercial information which it has acquired from the other as a result of discussions, negotiations and other communications between them relating to the goods and the Order.

12   Economic loss

Subject to Condition 14, and notwithstanding anything contained in these Conditions (other than Condition 14) or the Order, in no circumstances shall the Seller be liable, in contract, tort (including negligence or breach of statutory duty) or otherwise howsoever, and whatever the cause thereof (i) for any loss of profit, business, contracts, revenues, or anticipated savings, or (ii) for any special indirect or consequential damage of any nature whatsoever.

13   Limitation of liability

Subject to Condition 14, and notwithstanding anything contained in these Conditions (other than Condition 14) or the Order, the Seller's liability to the Purchaser in respect of the Order, in contract, tort (including negligence or breach of statutory duty) or howsoever otherwise arising, shall be limited to [[125]% of the price of the goods specified in the Order] [the price of the goods specified in the Order or £[   ] whichever is the greater].

14   Unfair Contract Terms Act 1977

14.1 If and to the extent that s 6 and/or s 7(3A) of the Unfair Contract Terms Act 1977 applies to the Order, no provision of these terms and conditions shall operate or be construed to operate so as to exclude or restrict the liability of the Seller for breach of the express warranties contained in Condition 5, or for breach of the applicable warranties as to title and quiet possession implied into the terms and conditions of the Order by s 12(3) of the Sale of Goods Act 1979, or s 2(3) of the Supply of Goods and Services Act 1982, whichever Act applies to the Order.

14.2 [Where the Purchaser is a natural person] [and if and to the extent that s 2(1) of the Unfair Contract Terms Act 1977 applies to the Order,] nothing in these terms and conditions shall operate or be construed to operate so as to exclude or restrict the liability of the Seller for death or personal injury caused [to the Purchaser] by reason of the negligence of the Seller or of its servants, employees or agents.

15   Applicable law

The Order shall be considered a contract made in England and shall be governed in all respects by the law of England and the parties agree to submit to the non-exclusive jurisdiction of the English courts.

Purchase conditions

Statements on front of orders

1 THE CONDITIONS OVERLEAF SHALL APPLY TO THIS ORDER (SEE CONDITION 1.1). [PLEASE READ ALL OF THEM CAREFULLY.]

2 [IN ADDITION TO THE CONDITIONS OVERLEAF, THIS ORDER IS SUBJECT TO THE APPLICABLE TERMS OF A CONTRACT, BETWEEN US AND [   ], FOR WHICH THESE ITEMS WILL BE USED. PLEASE READ CONDITION 1.3 OVERLEAF.]

1   Formation of contract

1.1 No addition alteration or substitution of these terms will bind us or form part of any contract unless they are expressly accepted in writing by a person authorised to sign on our behalf.

1.2 Acknowledgment of this order must be made by signing the duplicate order, enclosed with it, and the duplicate must be received within fourteen days of the date of this order. Should you despatch goods to us or perform work for us in accordance with this order without such an acknowledgment, this shall of itself be deemed an acknowledgment falling within this paragraph.

1.3 If the goods and/or the work the subject of this order are to be used in carrying out or otherwise in connection with another contract specified overleaf this order shall be subject to the contract conditions of such specified contract in so far as the same are applicable and do not conflict with these purchase conditions. Details of any such contract conditions will be supplied by us on request, but you will be deemed to have accepted the same as part of the terms of this order, whether such request has been made by you or not.

1.4 Nothing in these conditions shall prejudice any condition or warranty expressed or implied, or any legal remedy to which we may be entitled, in relation to the goods and/or the work the subject of this order, by virtue of any statute or custom or any general law or local law or regulation.

1.5 The construction validity and performance of these conditions and this order shall be governed by the law of England.

2   Delivery

2.1 In regard to performance of this order by you time is of the essence. The goods shall be delivered and/or the work performed on the date and at the place stated overleaf, and in accordance with the instructions specified overleaf, during normal business hours unless previously arranged otherwise. Delivery of goods shall be to the place specified overleaf and terms of carriage shall be as specified overleaf.

2.2 If for any reason, we are unable to accept delivery of the goods on or after the agreed delivery date, you will store the goods, safeguard them and take all reasonable steps to prevent their deterioration until delivery. In cases where Condition 10.1 does not apply, we shall be obliged to pay you in accordance with the terms specified overleaf upon delivery of the goods to storage, and (where such storage exceeds 30 days) we shall reimburse you for your reasonable expenses (including insurance) of such storage.

3   Specifications, quality tests, rejection

3.1 The goods and/or the work must conform in all respects with the drawings, specifications and other requirements or descriptions stated. All goods must be of sound materials, workmanship and (where you are responsible for this) design, and shall be equal in all respects to relevant samples, or patterns provided by or accepted by us. All work must be performed in a sound manner, and be free from all defects including (to the extent if any that you are responsible for design) defects in design.

3.2 All of the goods and/or the work must pass the acceptance tests of our inspector. We shall be entitled to reject all goods and/or work which do not conform completely in every respect with the terms of this order and in particular (but without prejudice to the generality of the foregoing) Conditions

3.1 and 3.5. Furthermore, if by the nature of the goods and/or the work, any defects therein or any failure thereof to conform as aforesaid does not or would not become apparent (despite the carrying out of any examination and/or such tests) until after use we may reject the same even after a reasonable period of use. It is agreed that in the case of goods we may exercise the aforesaid rights of rejection notwithstanding any provision contained in ss 11, 15A(1) or 35 of the Sale of Goods Act 1979, but subject to s 30(2A) of that Act.

3.3 Any goods and/or work rejected under Condition 3.2 must at our request be replaced or re-performed as the case may be, by you at your expense; alternatively we may elect (at our option) to cancel this order as provided in Condition 10.2 both in respect of the goods and/or the work in question and of the whole of the undelivered balance (if any) of the goods and/or the remainder of the work (if any) covered by this order. All rejected goods will be returned to you at your expense.

3.4 Our signature, given on any delivery note, or other documentation, presented for signature in connection with delivery of the goods, is evidence only of the number of packages received. In particular, it is no evidence that the correct quantity or number of goods has been delivered or that the goods delivered are in good condition or of the correct quality.

3.5 You will ensure that in all respects (except by way of design or specification where we have supplied the same) the goods and/or the work comply with all relevant requirements of any statute, statutory rule or order, or other instrument having the force of law, which may be in force when the goods are delivered and/or the work performed as the case may be. In particular, without prejudice to the generality of the foregoing, all goods capable of use as, or in any way likely to be used in the preparing or packing of, food, toiletries, perfume, cosmetics, pharmaceutical products or any other goods for human consumption or for use upon the human body shall contain nothing rendering them unsuitable for their purpose and shall comply with all relevant requirements relating to their sale and composition and to the use of preservative or colouring matter therein.

4   Property and risk

Property and risk in the goods shall pass to us, when they are delivered in accordance with Condition 2.1. Such passing of property and risk shall be without prejudice to any right of rejection arising under these Conditions, in particular (but without prejudice to the generality of the foregoing) under Conditions 3.1–3.5 inclusive.

5 Prices and payment

Prices, payment terms and currency shall be those specified overleaf.

6 Intellectual property rights etc

6.1 You warrant that neither the sale nor the use of the goods nor the performance of the work will infringe any British or foreign patent, trademark, registered design, or other intellectual property rights whether or not similar to any of the foregoing.

6.2 You shall indemnify us from all actions, costs, claims, demands, expenses and liabilities whatsoever resulting from any actual or alleged infringement as aforesaid in Condition 6.1, and at your own expense will defend or (at our option) assist in the defence of any proceedings which may be brought in that connection, provided that you shall be under no liability under Condition 6.1 or this Condition in respect of any infringement as aforesaid occasioned by use of a design or specification supplied to you by us.

6.3 No goods covered by orders shall be manufactured sold or disposed by you in violation of any right whatsoever of third parties, and in particular, but without prejudice to the generality of the foregoing, of any patent right, trademark or similar right, or of any charge, mortgage or lien, provided that you shall be under no liability under this Condition in respect of a violation as aforesaid occasioned by use of a design or specification supplied to you by us.

7 Indemnities, third party liabilities

7.1 You shall indemnify us against all loss, actions, costs, claims, demands, expenses and liabilities whatsoever (if any) which we may incur either at common law or by statute in respect of personal injury to or the death of any person or in respect of any loss or destruction of or damage to property (other than as a result of any default or neglect of ourselves or of any person for whom we are responsible) which shall have occurred in connection with any work executed by you against this Order or shall be alleged to be attributable to some defect in the goods.

7.2 Should you use any personnel to execute work on our premises they shall be required to abide by the safety rules and other relevant regulations laid down by us from time to time. This order is given on the condition that (without prejudice to the generality of Condition 7.1) you will indemnify us against all loss, actions, costs, claims, demands, expenses and liabilities whatsoever (if any) which we may incur either at common law or by statute (other than as a result of any default or neglect of ourselves or of any person for whom we are responsible) in respect of personal injury to, or the death of, any such employees, agents, subcontractors or other representative while on our premises whether or not such persons are (at the time when such personal injury or deaths are caused) acting in the course of their employment.

7.3 You will indemnify us against any and all loss, costs, expenses and liabilities caused to us whether directly, or as a result of the action, claim or demand of any third party, by reason of any breach by you of these conditions or of any terms or obligations on your part implied by the Sale of Goods Act 1979, by the Supply of Goods and Services Act 1982 or by any other statute or statutory provision relevant to the order or to goods or work covered thereby. This indemnity shall not be prejudiced or waived by any exercise of our rights under Condition 3.3.

7.4 Whenever any sum of money is recoverable from or payable by you to us as a result of the operation of any of these conditions or any breach by you of the same, such sum may be deducted by us from any sum then due or which at any time thereafter may become due to you under any other order or transaction placed or entered into by us with you.

8   Jigs, tools, gauges, etc

8.1 If any jigs, tools, dies, patterns, moulds, gauges, components, materials or any other items of whatsoever nature are supplied to you by us for use in connection with this order, the same shall be at your risk from the time they leave our premises until they are returned thereto, but shall remain our property. We shall have the right of reasonable access to your premises to inspect such items while they are there. You shall not use any of the foregoing except in connection with our orders, and you shall maintain the same in good condition and return them to us at any time on demand or otherwise automatically on completion of this order. Gauges are issued as reference standards only. All jigs, tools, dies, patterns, moulds and gauges manufactured or supplied by you for us in connection with this order shall become our property and shall be retained by you until disposal instructions are given by us to you which instructions shall be complied with forthwith.

8.2 You shall indemnify us against any loss or damage to the items mentioned in Condition 8.1, arising while such items are in your possession or before redelivery to us. You will insure the aforesaid items against all risks and (if necessary) note our interests on your policy.

9   Assignment and subcontracting

9.1 You may not assign or transfer this order or part thereof to any other person without our written consent.

9.2 You may not, without our written consent, subcontract this order or part thereof, other than for materials, minor details, or for any part of the goods in respect of which the makers are specified overleaf, or to the extent to which subcontracting is a trade custom in relation to the subject matter of the order.

10   Cancellation

10.1 If either you or we are delayed or prevented from performing our obligations under this order, by circumstances beyond the reasonable control of either of us (including without limitation any form of government intervention, strikes and lock-outs relevant to this order, breakdown of plant or delays by subcontractors concerned) such performance shall be suspended, and if it cannot be completed within a reasonable time after the due date as specified in this order, this order may be cancelled by either party. We will pay to you such sum as may be fair and reasonable in all the circumstances of the case in respect of work performed by you under this order prior to cancellation, and in respect of which we have received the benefit. This Condition can only have effect if it is called into operation by the party wishing to rely on it giving written notice to the other to that effect.

10.2 Subject to Condition 10.1, we reserve the right to cancel the whole or any part of this order or any consignment on account thereof, if the same is not completed in all respects in accordance with the instructions and specifications stated in the order and with the foregoing conditions, in particular (but without prejudice to the generality of the foregoing) with Conditions 2.1, 3.1 and 3.5, compliance with which by you is of the essence. In the event of our cancelling this order as to all or any of the goods and/or the work covered thereby we shall be entitled to purchase from a third party a like quantity of goods of similar description and quality, or a reasonable alternative thereto, bearing in mind our need to take delivery of the goods by the date specified overleaf, or to contract with a third party to perform work of a similar description and quality, and in that event you shall be liable to reimburse to us on demand all expenditure incurred by us in connection with our said cancellation, including any increase in the price over that stated overleaf.

11   Confidentiality

11.1 You will keep secret and will not disclose to any third party (except subcontractors accepting a like obligation of secrecy, and then only to the extent necessary for the performance of the subcontract) all information given by us in connection with this order, or which becomes known to you through your performance of work under this order. You will not mention our name in connection with this order or disclose the existence of this order in any publicity material or other similar communication to third parties without our prior consent in writing.

12   Hazardous goods

12.1 You will mark all hazardous goods with international danger symbols where they exist, and display the name of the material in English. Transport and other documents must include declaration of the hazard and name of the material in English. Goods must be accompanied by emergency information in English in the form of written instructions, labels or markings. You shall observe the requirements of UK legislation and any relevant international agreements relating to the packing labelling and carriage of hazardous goods. All information held by or reasonably available to you regarding any potential hazards known or believed to exist in the transport handling or use of the goods supplied shall be promptly communicated to us prior to delivery.

Framework supply agreement

---

1   Parties

[   ] LIMITED of [   ]
('the Company') and
[   ] LIMITED of [   ]
('the Supplier').

2   Date and term

This Agreement commences on [   ] and will continue for a fixed period of three years and thereafter will continue from year to year unless terminated by at least sixty days' written notice by either party to the other, such notice to expire on any anniversary date of the commencement of this Agreement falling after the expiry of the fixed period aforesaid.

3   Purpose of agreement

The Supplier will supply to the Company during the currency of this Agreement the products set out in Schedule 1 hereto in the form and to the specifications (including packaging) set out in Schedule 2 hereto (hereinafter called the 'Products') in accordance with the provisions hereinafter contained.

4   Sales forecasts and placing of orders

4.1 The Company will provide the Supplier on the date of commencement hereof and thereafter on each anniversary of the said date with a forecast for the following twelve months of the Company's requirements for the Products.

4.2 The Company will give three months' notice to the Supplier of any alterations to the above forecast should it wish to revise the same during any twelve month period.

4.3 The above forecasts shall be given by the Company to the Supplier on the basis that they are for information only, and the Company shall be under no obligation (legal or otherwise) to order all or any of or no more than the quantities shown in the said forecasts.

4.4 The Company will place purchase orders with the Supplier for quantities of the Products as and when required, and the Supplier shall accept the same, provided that all such orders will be placed so as to allow to the Supplier at least 90 days for delivery.

4.5 All such orders will be placed by the Company on the terms and conditions set out in Schedule 3 hereto, which shall govern and form part of every contract for the supply of the Products by the Supplier to the Company and prevail over any express or implied terms or conditions of the Company. Any variation, waiver or cancellation of the said terms and conditions must be in writing and signed by a duly authorised representative of the Supplier.

4.6 The Company undertakes, notwithstanding the foregoing provisions of this Clause, to purchase in each year of the currency of this Agreement not less than the minimum amount of the Products (by value) set out for that year in Schedule 4 hereto.

5   Pricing

5.1 The Supplier will supply the Products hereunder initially at the ex works prices set out in Schedule 5 hereto.

5.2 The above prices shall be subject to increase in accordance with the price variation formula set out in Schedule 6 hereto.

6   Third parties

While this Agreement is in force the Company undertakes not to purchase the Products from any person other than the Supplier or to manufacture the Products itself whether directly or indirectly.

7   Termination

7.1 This Agreement may be terminated by either party immediately upon the happening of either of the following events:
  (i) if either party shall pass a resolution for winding up or the court shall make an order that either party shall be wound up (in either case other than for the purpose of reconstruction) or if a receiver or manager on behalf of a creditor be appointed, or if circumstances shall arise which would entitle a court or a creditor to appoint a receiver or manager or which would entitle a court to make a winding up order; or
  (ii) on either party assigning or attempting to assign this Agreement other than to a subsidiary or associated company.

7.2 If the Supplier shall become substantially unable, whether for reasons within or beyond its control, to fulfil its obligations to supply the Products to the Company in accordance with any purchase orders outstanding at any time and (after the Company has notified the Supplier in writing of such default) the Supplier shall not have remedied the same within a period of 90 days from the receipt of such notice, then the Company shall be entitled to terminate this Agreement forthwith, and obtain supplies of the Products from third parties.

7.3 Termination under this Clause shall be without prejudice to the fulfilment of purchase orders wholly or partially outstanding at the date of such termination, and likewise shall not prejudice or affect any right of action or remedy which shall have accrued or shall accrue thereafter under this Agreement to either party.

7.4 In addition to its obligations under cl 7.3, upon termination of this Agreement for whatever cause (including effluxion of time) the Company shall purchase from the Supplier all stocks of finished Products held by the Supplier which are not covered by purchase orders together with all stocks of unused packaging materials for the Products which are either held by the Supplier or which the Supplier is already obliged to purchase from third parties. The said finished Products shall be purchased at the prices laid down in cl 5 and the said packaging materials at direct cost to the Supplier plus five percent.

8   Intellectual property rights

Any and all patents, registered designs, unregistered designs, copyright, or other intellectual property rights whether or not similar to any of the foregoing in or resulting from any work carried out by the Supplier under or in pursuance of this Agreement shall belong exclusively, throughout the world, to the Supplier.

9   Notice

Any notice direction or communication (including the placing or acceptance of an order) given hereunder by one party to the other:

9.1 if sent by post to the last known place of business of the other party shall be deemed to have been served on the date when in the ordinary course of post it would have been delivered to the other party; and

9.2 if sent by electronic mail shall be deemed to have been served at the time and date when the electronic mail message is delivered to the electronic mail box of the intended recipient, as evidenced by an advice of delivery message automatically returned to the sender by the relevant system and network used for the transmission of such message.

SCHEDULE 1
The Products

SCHEDULE 2
The Specification

SCHEDULE 3
Terms and Conditions of Sale

SCHEDULE 4
Minimum Purchase Commitments

First Year
Second Year
Third Year
Fourth Year
and thereafter in each year [   ] per centum
more than in the previous year

SCHEDULE 5
The Prices

SCHEDULE 6
Price Variation Formula

IN WITNESS WHEREOF the duly authorised representatives of the parties have set their hands on
[   ] For and on behalf of the Company
[   ] For and on behalf of the Supplier

Standard conditions for the business sale of second-hand goods

HEALTH AND SAFETY AND WORK, ETC ACT 1974

UNDERTAKING IN ACCORDANCE WITH SECTION 6(8)

The items sold to the Buyer under this contract of sale are second-hand, having already been used by the Seller in the Seller's business. Accordingly, the Buyer agrees to take the goods in their current state, after having satisfied himself by inspection, as to their quality and fitness for the purpose for which the Buyer requires them.

Accordingly, the Seller gives no warranties in relation to the quality of the goods or their suitability for any purpose, and all such warranties, whether express or implied by statute, common law or otherwise howsoever, are hereby excluded. The Seller shall be under no liability, whether at contract or in tort or otherwise, in respect of the quality of the goods or their fitness for any purpose, save that, if the Buyer is a natural person, in accordance with the provisions of s 2(1) of the Unfair Contract Terms Act 1977, the Seller accepts and does not seek to limit or exclude liability for any death or personal injury caused to the Buyer by reason of the Seller's negligence.

Where the Buyer intends to use the goods at work, the Seller supplies the goods on the basis that the Buyer will ensure, so far as reasonably practicable, that the goods will be safe and without risks to health when properly used, and that prior to delivery the Buyer will sign and return the written undertaking attached hereto as Annex A obliging the Buyer to take the steps specified in that undertaking to ensure this.

Where the Buyer purchases the goods with the intention of selling them to a third party for the use by that third party of the goods at work, the Buyer undertakes to supply the goods to the third party on the basis that the third party will ensure, so far as reasonably practicable, that the goods will be safe and without risks to health when properly used, and the Buyer further undertakes to procure the signature by the third party (prior to delivery of the goods to the third party) of the written undertaking attached hereto as Annex A obliging the third party to take the steps specified in that undertaking to ensure this. The Buyer shall upon obtaining such signature send a copy of the signed undertaking to the Seller.

ANNEX A

Undertaking under Section 6(8) of Health and Safety at Work, etc Act 1974, I/ we [   ] of [   ] having agreed to purchase [   ] ('the Article') for use at work, hereby undertake in accordance with the above Section that I/we will implement the Specified Steps as set out below in order to ensure, so far as reasonably practicable, that the Article will be safe and without risks to health when properly so used.

Specified Steps

[*Note*: the Seller must fill in here the specified steps which are relevant to the particular machinery in order to take advantage of the Section of the Act. This would include things like providing adequate guarding, wiring up properly in accordance with electrical regulations, installing fume extractor equipment, etc. If the properly specified steps are not inserted, then the undertaking has *no* effect.]

Chapter 3

Standard conditions for the supply of services

3.1   Introduction

The SGSA defines contracts for the supply of services simply as contracts under which the supplier agrees to carry out a service (s 12(1)). For the purposes of this chapter such contracts will be referred to as service supply contracts, and the person supplying the service under such contracts will be referred to as the supplier.

Part II of the SGSA implies three terms into service supply contracts. First, where the supplier is acting in the course of a business, there is an implied term that he will carry out the service with reasonable care and skill (s 13); secondly, again where the supplier is acting in the course of a business, that in the absence of specific provisions as to the time for performance of the service, it will be performed within a reasonable time (s 14); thirdly, that in the absence of specific provisions as to consideration for the performance of the service, the party contracting with the supplier will pay a reasonable charge (s 15). Section 15 applies to all service supply contracts, not just those where the supplier is acting in the course of a business.

However, s 16(1) of the SGSA provides that (subject to relevant terms of the UCTA) these implied terms may be negatived or varied by express agreement, by virtue of the course of dealing between the parties, or by 'such usage as binds both parties to the contract' (which can be broadly interpreted as trade custom). Section 16(2) provides a clarification of the term 'negatived' by stating that an express provision in a contract does not negative one of the implied terms unless it is inconsistent with it.

It should be noted that Part II of the SGSA applies to oral as well as written service supply contracts, so that both the specific provisions as to performance and price mentioned in ss 14 and 15, and the express agreement and express term referred to in s 16 may be oral, although prudence would require that a documentary record (if not a full written contract) be created for evidentiary purposes. Since ss 14 and 15 only apply when there is no relevant express provision in the contract, s 16 has less scope for application here. So far as the implied term of reasonable care is concerned, most service supply contracts are unlikely to exclude this, but may well limit the extent of the supplier's liability for its breach. Clearly s 16 permits complete exclusion of this term, since an express clause exluding the implied term would be inconsistent with the 'negative' it within the definition of s 16(2). Section 16 also permits limitations on liability for breach of the term, if included. Section 16(2) prevents an express clause from negativing the implied term unless inconsistent, but lays down no such requirement for a clause which varies the term. A general limitation of liability (eg by reference to an overall sum of money, or by way of exclusion of liability for loss of profit) is not inconsistent with an obligation to use reasonable care in performing the relevant service. To the extent that such limitation can be said to affect this term at all, the most that can be said is that it varies it.

It can thus be seen that in practice the SGSA need not be considered as particularly relevant to the drafting of service supply contracts (provided due note is taken of s 16(2)), and that the provisions of Part II of the SGSA are in fact only truly of relevance for those service supply contracts where the parties have chosen not to specify the terms of their contract in sufficient detail to deal with the matters otherwise covered by the SGSA.

This leaves the provisions of the UCTA, where that Act applies to the contract. Section 2 (avoidance of liability for negligence) and s 3 (avoidance of liability for breach of contract) will be of the most relevance. However, the UCTA has to be considered as a whole when dealing with service supply contracts, since the provisions of the UCTA governing liability arising from the supply of goods cannot always be ignored.

A service supply contract may also entail the supply of goods. For instance a contract for the supply and installation of a central heating or air conditioning system in a building would be both a service supply contract (the supply of installation services) and a contract for the supply of goods (the actual plant and equipment installed). Section 12(3) of the SGSA expressly provides that contracts for the supply of services, 'under which goods are transferred or to be transferred, or bailed or to be bailed by way of hire', have a dual nature. They are both contracts for the supply of goods and contracts for the supply of services. Such contracts cannot be contracts for the sale of goods, and hence are not governed by the SGA (see SGSA 1982, s 1(2)). They are, however, governed by Part I of the SGSA (see SGSA 1982, s 1(1)), as well as Part II. Thus service supply contracts which also entail the supply of goods will have to take account of s 7 of the UCTA and its limitations on the exclusion of liability for breach of the warranties implied by Part I of the SGSA in relation to the goods supplied under the contract.

Under some service supply contracts no goods are supplied at all. For instance a contract for the supply of technical advice or assistance may be discharged purely by the physical activities of the supplier, or by his giving oral advice, or, at the most, by the provision of a written report. For all practical purposes the provisions of Part I of the SGSA and s 7 of the UCTA can be ignored, even in respect of any documents which pass under the contract from the supplier to his customer. At the other extreme a contract for the supply and installation of plant and equipment is probably as much, if not more, concerned with the conditions surrounding the supply of the goods under the contract, as with those relating to the supply of the installation service, which may well be a minor component of the contract only. When drafting such contracts, the focus should be on the UCTA and Part I of the SGSA. Part II of the SGSA will have little relevance, given that express provisions in the contract will deal with the supply of the service in detail, thus negativing or varying the implied terms of Part II pursuant to s 16 of the SGSA.

In this context it should be remembered that the SSGA 1994 has made amendments to Part I of the SGSA relating to the substitution of the warranty of satisfactory quality for that of merchantable quality, identical to the amendments made to the SGA. The substance of these amendments was discussed in Chapter 2.

The precedents in this chapter concentrate upon service supply contracts in a business relationship. Precedent 1 is a contract for the supply of maintenance service. It is also a contract for the supply of goods, since spare parts are supplied and installed as part of the maintenance service. It thus has a dual nature, and in terms of importance of the two components it probably falls about midway on the scale between a contract for the provision of services alone and one for the supply and installation of plant and equipment. Precedents 2 and 3 cover different contracts for the supply of technical or professional services, with no obligations relating to the supply of goods at all. Finally, Precedent 4 is a contract for the design and development of a semi-conductor device, where the supply of services is most important (the design and development aspect), but which also entails significant obligations in relation to the supply of goods. Prototypes of the device are to be supplied so that they can be used as reference samples for the production quantities of the device, which will be supplied under a subsequent contract of sale whose terms are set out in the precedent.

3.2   Precedent 1

Precedent 1 is a standard agreement for the provision of maintenance service, which is one of the commonest instances of a service supply contract to be found. Its format is that of a formal agreement which on its face specifies the parties and the machinery to be maintained, and signifies the obligation of the supplier to provide maintenance service, and of the customer to accept it, in accordance with the attached terms and conditions. Both parties formally sign this front page to the contract, thus avoiding the battle of the forms and bringing the contract into force upon the date of its signature.

Clause 1 contains a number of definitions, most of which are self-explanatory, but two require discussion. From the point of view of both parties the most important issue is how to define the standard of the maintenance service provided by the supplier. The definition of 'Good Working Order' is crucial to this. The definitions in square brackets show a number of possibilities. Tying the definition to a specification (the first two definitions) provides the greatest certainty for both sides. The last two definitions are vaguer and probably only appropriate where the function or purpose of the system is obvious. Another alternative is to have no definition at all, and use the words 'good working order' in their ordinary dictionary sense. This could be possible, for instance, with standard appliances, such as dishwashers or refrigerators, or automobiles, where it is simple to determine what good working order means. In any event, the draftsmen for both parties should take particular care to create a definition of 'Good Working Order' which is appropriate to the equipment to be maintained, and satisfactory both to the supplier and the customer.

The definition of 'User Routine Maintenance' also requires care, for the same reasons as that of 'Good Working Order'. The latter defines the maintenance obligations of the supplier, the former those of the customer. The alternatives in square brackets are suggestions only, and again a mutually satisfactory definition should be drawn up to fit the circumstances of the particular case.

Maintenance contracts are of two types. First, there are those provided by the supplier of equipment, and entered into either upon delivery or installation of the equipment, or upon expiry of the relevant warranty period (during which, in effect, maintenance will have been provided free of charge). Secondly, there are those, often known as third party maintenance contracts, which are provided by undertakings whose business consists solely of the provision of maintenance services in respect of equipment manufactured and supplied by others.

Clause 2 should not be necessary in the case of maintenance contracts provided by the equipment supplier, since he is responsible for the good working order of the equipment he supplies in any event, but it is vital for third party maintainers. Before the latter can undertake to keep equipment in good working order, they must be sure that it is in good working order to start with, and capable of being so maintained. The maintenance fee that they charge will be calculated on the basis that the equipment is in good working order at the start of the contract. Clause 2 enables the third party maintainer to inspect the equipment and decide whether initial remedial work is required to bring the equipment up to standard, and to charge an inspection fee for this. The customer then has the choice of paying the third party maintainer to carry out any necessary work, or refusing to do so. In the latter event the contract is cancelled automatically, and the supplier retains the inspection fee as some compensation for his trouble. If the equipment is in fact found to be in good working order, or if and when the remedial work is carried out, the supplier issues his confirmatory certificate under cl 2.2 or 2.4. and the initial fixed period of the maintenance agreement commences pursuant to cl 3.2.

Where the supplier is also the supplier of the equipment to be maintained, it is likely that cl 2 would be deleted, and cl 3 adjusted so that the fixed term commenced either on signature, or on some predetermined date (eg upon expiry of the relevant warranty period). However, the terms of cl 3 as shown in the precedent are important for third party maintainers from a commercial point of view. It would be possible for a third party maintainer to inspect, and, if necessary and agreed, carry out remedial work on equipment outside the terms of a maintenance agreement, and then enter into the agreement once these issues have been dealt with. However, in practice, the conclusion of a contract dealing with the provision of maintenance subject to satisfactory initial condition gives him greater certainty of continuing with the contract, while safeguarding him from wasting his time with equipment that in fact cannot be properly maintained because of its condition, and ensuring that, even if the contract is cancelled, he receives a fee for his initial inspection. Moreover, it is a fact of human nature that, once all the details of the contract have been negotiated and it has been signed, where initial remedial work is necessary, the customer is far more likely, through inertia and dislike of having to renegotiate an agreement with someone else, to agree to have the remedial work put in hand, unless the project is truly impractical or the supplier's demands are extortionate.

The provisions for the term of the agreement in cl 3.2 are quite usual, in that most maintenance agreements run from year to year, or perhaps quarter to quarter. The termination provision somewhat favours the supplier in that the agreement will continue for a renewal period unless terminated by 60 days' notice expiring at the end of the relevant period. Again, inertia on the part of the customer makes it more likely that he will let the contract run for a new period, unless he is seriously displeased with the supplier. However, this provision should be read in conjunction with cl 5.2 which provides for the supplier to revise the charges for maintenance upwards by 90 days' notice expiring at the end of the relevant period. In effect this gives the customer 30 days to decide if he agrees or not with the increase, and, if the supplier agrees, to renegotiate the increase. If no renegotiation takes place, and the customer is unhappy with the proposed increase, he still has time to give 60 days' notice to terminate the agreement.

The heart of the agreement is cl 4, in which the supplier sets out his obligations to provide maintenance service. Clause 4.1. is more or less severe depending upon the stringency of the definition of 'Good Working Order', but the obligations are always serious in that, in return for a fixed fee, the supplier must supply whatever services and spare parts are necessary to keep the equipment in good working order. Clause 4.2 sets out for the convenience of the parties the basic services which the supplier will provide and the terms upon which he will supply them. Note that, as a matter of drafting convenience, the defined term 'Maintenance Service' includes the initial remedial work carried out under cl 2, so that the exclusions of liability under cl 8 can be applied easily to this work as well as to the ongoing maintenance service. Clause 4.3 sets out a list of standard exclusions, for which the supplier will not provide service, or at least not without extra charges. Clauses 4.4 and 4.5 provide standard approaches to the times at and within which maintenance service is to be provided. It is not unusual to provide stricter standards for on-call remedial maintenance (cl 4.5), for instance by specifying the number of hours within which the engineer will appear on site after the call has been logged by the supplier. Obviously more stringent standards are usually accepted only in return for a higher fee, since they necessitate the supplier having a larger number of staff, and probably paying overtime to them as well.

As stated above, this contract is not only for the supply of services, but also for the supply of goods, since spare parts are supplied and installed by the supplier as part of the service. Clauses 4.6 and 4.7 deal with certain issues relating to spare parts, in a standard manner for such contracts, and in particular give an express warranty of good title as required by s 7 of the UCTA. The supply of spare parts is included within the definition of maintenance service, so that, once again, the limitations on liability in cl 8 apply also to the supply of spare parts.

Clause 5 contains the relevant payment and invoicing provisions under the contract. It should be noted that most maintenance contracts provide for payment in advance, rather than arrears, although it is true that a year's payment in advance, while not unusual, is not always negotiable. If the period of payment is quarterly in advance it is probably not advisable for the supplier to have the periodic renewal of the agreement under cl 3 also adjusted to a quarterly basis. This is probably too short-term an arrangement for either party. It is usually better to retain the 12 month renewal period, and accept that the supplier has to stay with a fixed quarterly payment for the whole of the current renewal period.

Some suppliers require payment by direct debit or standing order. Where this is accepted (and the supplier does not require a price increase) automatic renewal of the term under cl 3.2 becomes very likely, since no action at all is required on the part of the customer at the time of renewal.

Clause 4.3 lists services which the supplier was not responsible for providing as part of the maintenance service. Clause 6 is the other side of the coin, in that it imposes certain positive obligations on the customer, particularly the carrying out of 'User Routine Maintenance'. The supplier may not want to terminate the agreement if the customer fails to carry out these obligations, but failure will certainly make maintenance more costly for the supplier, and may even entail additional remedial work. He will want to be in the position of being able to threaten to cancel the contract for breach, so that he can, if possible, negotiate additional fees for remedying the situation, or, at least, cut his losses by terminating the arrangement.

Clause 7 is a standard *force majeure* exclusion clause, and cl 8 limits or excludes the liability of the supplier for other breaches of contract. This is on the basis that the profit margin derived from the maintenance charges under the contract, and, presumably, the insurance cover the supplier can obtain and reasonably pay for, do not make it reasonable for him to undertake unlimited or excessive risks. This is particularly important in maintenance contracts for factory or office machinery, where failure of the machine could cause business interruption to the customer (eg downtime on computer or production machinery) or could cause physical damage to property (eg exploding boiler or failure in a crane while hoisting plant and machinery) out of all proportion to the value of the maintenance charges received by the supplier. Clause 8.2 lists various heads of liability under which compensation will be paid up to certain limits which are, in practice, likely to be set in individual cases by reference to the supplier's insurance policy. The same issues with regard to liability for death or personal injury under s 2(1) of the UCTA arise in maintenance agreements as were discussed in general in relation to that section in Chapter 1. Clause 8.2.5 should not be included at all where the customer is a legal entity.

Clause 8.4 is a general exclusion of all liability except for the specific provisions in cll 4, 8 and 9. This is considered, in general, reasonable under ss 2, 3 and 7 of the UCTA. On the one hand, cl 8.2 (subject to the financial limitations of cl 8.3) provides reasonable remedies for damage caused to the customer by defective provision of the maintenance service or the negligent acts or omissions of the supplier. On the other hand, because cl 4.1 provides that the supplier must do everything necessary to keep the equipment in good working order in return for a fixed fee, it is unnecessary and inappropriate for the supplier to warrant, for instance, that maintenance services will be performed in a workmanlike fashion, or that spare parts will be fit for their purpose. The customer's remedy is that the supplier will have to come back to site (on a remedial call if necessary) to remedy any defects in his service.

The only other issue on cl 8 relates to the effect of the provisions of s 7 of the UCTA which prevent the exclusion or restriction of liability for breach of warranty of good title in relation to spare parts supplied under the contract, which would be implied by s 2 of the SGSA. In fact, an express warranty to this effect is included in cl 4.7, so the only issue is the extent to which cl 8 overall restricts liability for its breach. On a careful reading nothing in cl 8 has this effect, except, possibly the proviso to condition 8.4 excluding loss of profit and consequential loss. It is hard to see how breach of warranty of good title to spare parts could lead to such loss. It is unlikely that the true owner could go on the customer's premises in the short term to remove them, and presumably the supplier would remedy the situation before any actual interruption occurred.

Thus, in reliance on the arguments relating to general exclusion clauses in Chapter 1, the proviso could reasonably be left unqualified. However, a cautious draftsman could in appropriate circumstances include cl 14.1 from Precedent 1 in Chapter 2 (suitably adapted) to avoid any doubt on the issue.

The final question of liability relates to what happens in the event of material breach by either party. The combination of cl 8.4 and 9 means that the remedy for such breach is in effect limited to direct damages. Under cl 9.2 the customer gets the balance of his money back, and under cl 9.3 the supplier keeps the whole of his maintenance fee up to the end of the current maintenance period as compensation for his lost bargain. (The figure of 365 in the formula in cl 9.2 is based on the fact that, in this Precedent, the period of the agreement is 12 months.)

Clauses 10, 11 and 12 provide the final necessary 'boilerplate' provisions for the operation of the agreement, and may be adapted as necessary to fit the circumstances of particular contracts. In regard to cl 11, some suppliers may need to have more elaborate provisions relating to requests for service calls, as opposed to formal notice under the contract for matters such as renewal or price changes. It is not uncommon for all requests for service to be addressed by customers over the telephone to a specified telephone help desk, and, where this is the case, the particular arrangements should be specified in the notice clause, and, for clarity and convenience, on the front sheet of the contract.

3.3   Precedent 2

This precedent is a short form set of standard conditions for the supply of consultancy and testing services. It is appropriate where the relationship between the supplier and the customer is not a very close one, and where the supplier is in the business of providing a large number of customers with similar services on a regular basis. Examples of such services would be the routine testing of equipment to see that it complied with various British Standards, the provision of technical advice in relation to the running of a machine in a factory, or the suitability of particular tools, equipment, materials or components for specified purposes. The Precedent can of course be adapted and is suitable for the provision of most types of advice on this basis.

The real issue for the supplier in such arrangements is the extent to which he lays himself open to civil liability, and, perhaps, in some cases, criminal liability (for example under the Health and Safety at Work Act 1974) for errors in the advice given. Given the impact of the UCTA it is obviously an open question as to the extent to which the supplier can protect himself completely against civil liability by means of disclaimers where advice is given negligently. Obviously, disclaimers are, of themselves, unlikely to affect criminal liability.

Thus, before even considering the contract, any supplier should take certain necessary practical steps to counter any claims that negligent advice has been given. First, the supplier must obtain professional indemnity insurance to cover him in the event of a claim made in respect of negligent advice. Then he should ensure, so far as practicable, that advice is given by competent persons, formalise the procedure for giving critical or complex advice and record properly the advice given and the context within which, and the caveats subject to which, it was given. These precautions should help refute charges of negligence, and virtually remove the risk of criminal liability. They would also be regarded as good housekeeping provisions by the supplier's insurers, and, as such, even if not actually part of the supplier's duty under the contract of insurance, would certainly make such insurance easier to obtain or reduce the premium required.

So far as qualified personnel are concerned, certain professional or technical areas are so complicated, or have such significant consequences in the event of error, that they should only be dealt with by persons that can be regarded as true experts who can either reply out of their own knowledge, or are able to obtain, and understand properly, specialised information from third parties, and then produce a full and proper reply to the query. The supplier should ensure that he or his staff who supply such advice have these qualifications, and that other members of staff, if any, understand their personal limitations, and do not attempt to deal with such matters. This approach is best embodied in a policy statement document, or standing instruction, which should be distributed very widely throughout the supplier's business, so that every employee should either be given a copy, or at least have a chance to see one on a notice board. It should be specifically brought to the attention of persons who are likely to be asked for such advice in the course of their work. Provision should also be made on a continuing basis to notify new starters. Unqualified staff should not answer requests for such advice, but should refer them to the relevant experts, who would enter into a formal relationship with the customer concerned, along the lines of Precedent 2.

Obviously, not all advice requires such elaborate precautions. Advice which is of sufficiently straightforward a nature that the possibility of error is not great, and the consequences of such error would not be significant in financial or other terms, may well be given by almost any employee of the supplier without any formal contract. In any case, it is obviously impractical for all advice to be centralised, and most professional indemnity insurance policies would recognise and accept this fact, covering all liability for advice given by all employees.

Even with all that has been said above, Precedent 2 should not be used as it is for types of advice where the consequences of error are very great (for instance the structural design of a building or a bridge, or advice relating to the design of a new aeroplane). It is emphasised that the advice should be of a relatively routine and straightforward nature where the risk of exposure is not excessive and the consequences of error are not great.

The terms and conditions of Precedent 2 would appear on the reverse of a proposal, or offer, from the supplier setting out the specification of the service to be offered and the price, timescales and deliverables involved. As shown on the heading to Precedent 2, there would be suitable wording on the face of the proposal drawing attention to the conditions on the reverse. In fact, it is un- likely that all of the contents of the proposal could be contained on the face of the proposal, which is more likely to incorporate specification documents, or previous preliminary reports, by reference, to define the scope of the work.

Clause 2.1 deals with the battle of the forms by requiring the customer to sign a duplicate of the proposal and return it by way of unqualified acceptance, in order to create the contract. Contracts for the supply of advice are much less likely than contracts for the supply of goods to involve the battle of the forms. The supplier will not usually embark upon the contract inadvertently, since in most cases he needs the active co-operation of the customer to give him pre- liminary information or other items before he can start work. The most likely result of counter-offers by the customer which contain conflicting conditions is that there will be a special negotiation. The balance of cl 2 recognises this situation and provides for it.

Clause 3 covers the procedure for the provision of technical assistance. It takes the approach of not accepting liability to deliver by a particular date. The supplier only accepts an obligation to make reasonable endeavours to deliver by the estimated date, and there are provisions for notification of delays and a revised delivery schedule. The customer has an option to cancel upon notifica- tion, subject to paying the supplier's reasonable cancellation charges, but if he does not exercise the option, the customer is deemed to have accepted the new delivery schedule. Clause 4 also provides certain extensions of time as of right for the supplier in the event of *force majeure*, but with the ultimate right for the customer to cancel, after a period of inactivity.

Do cll 3 and 4 negate s 14 of the SGSA? Certainly they vary it, but it is questionable if they negative it within the meaning of s 16(2) of the SGSA. There seems little doubt that, if the supplier were, in the absence of *force ma- jeure*, to take an unreasonably long time to fulfil the contract, and failed to make any notification, or offer a revised delivery schedule under cl 3.2, the customer would be able to cancel the contract for breach of the term implied by s 14 of the SGSA, as well as, possibly, for breach of cl 3.2 itself. This analysis shows that short of an express exclusion of s 14, or the specification of a precise delivery schedule in the contract, it is not so easy to displace the implied term under s 14 as it may first appear.

Clause 5 contains standard payment terms for such service supply contracts, namely monthly in arrears for work done during that month. Clause 6 is a sweeping exclusion of liability for errors in the advice. Apart from the remedy of requiring the supplier to re-perform the service and correct the errors free of charge, cl 6.2 excludes all other liability for such errors.

Is such an exclusion likely to be reasonable under ss 2 and 3 of the UCTA?

This is a difficult question to answer in the abstract, but the answer appears to depend upon the nature of the advice given, and the likely extent of the loss or damage that would be caused if the advice turned out to contain errors. This is why the precedent as it stands is not really suitable for situations where errors in the advice given could cause serious loss or damage. In such cases, the best way to proceed is probably to add additional clauses providing for an exclusion of liability for economic loss and an overall limitation of liability under the contract by reference to a monetary limit that is tied into the amount of insurance cover that the supplier can obtain. Clauses 7 and 8 take this approach. Either or both of cll 7 and 8 could be included in the contract, in addition to cl 6, depending upon the circumstances of the case. Another alternative would be to draft more elaborate provisions along the lines set out in cl 8 of Precedent 1, or to consider adopting Precedent 1 in Chapter 4.

Finally, the supplier should also be aware of the need to structure the advice that he gives in such a way as to minimise the possibility of claims. The key to this is not so much to disclaim responsibility for negligent advice, but to circumscribe and define precisely the request for advice coming from the customer, as well as the purpose for and the circumstances and assumptions under which the advice is given. The customer should be asked to agree the accuracy and correctness of these matters, which should, ideally, form part of the specifications referred to on the face of the relevant proposal, or in a specification incorporated in the proposal by reference. The customer will thus finally signify his agreement to these issues when he returns the signed copy of the proposal to the supplier and the contract comes into existence.

If the advice is based upon incorrect information supplied by the customer, or the customer uses it for some purpose other than one he specified, and as a result the advice either contains errors or is inapplicable for the purpose for which the customer uses it, the supplier has some basis for claiming that any resulting loss is really the responsibility of the customer. Of course if the technical advice given by the supplier really does contain an error which is caused rather by the supplier's negligence than because he relied on incorrect information recorded in the proposal, a claim for negligence would still lie, except in so far as the limitations of liability in the relevant contract passed the test of reasonableness under ss 2 or 3 of the UCTA.

One point of some concern to a supplier of advice is the extent to which he can be liable to third parties if he gives his customer negligent advice, and the customer then either uses this in a way which causes loss or damage to a third party, or passes it on to a third party who uses it himself and suffers loss or damage as a result.

The third party can obviously only claim against the supplier in tort, since he is not in a contractual relationship with the supplier. His right to do so depends upon a number of factors, but the nature of the loss or damage which he is suffers is of paramount importance. The principles can best be explained by way of some examples.

Imagine that the supplier is a structural engineer giving professional advice to a building contractor on the way a building is to be constructed. His advice is negligent, and after the contractor has constructed the building in reliance upon it, the building collapses. Mr A, who is visiting an office in the building, is injured. Mr B's car, which was parked outside, is crushed. C Ltd, which employed the contractor to construct the building for it, finds that it cannot carry on its business without its offices, is faced with a large repair bill to put the building back into a useable state, becomes insolvent and is wound up. D Ltd, a venture capitalist who was principally financing C Ltd, has to write off its investment in C Ltd and suffers a large financial loss in doing so. The loss and damage suffered by all four victims has been caused ultimately by the supplier's negligence. Can they recover their loss or damage from the supplier by an action in tort?

The law of negligence as it has developed during the late 1980s and early 1990s finds no difficulty in giving a remedy to Mr A and Mr B, under the original principles in *Donoghue v Stevenson* [1932] AC 562, which can be summarised as a duty to take reasonable care not to cause physical harm to the person or property of people who (in the words of Lord Atkin) could be regarded as the 'neighbours' of the tortfeasor. Mr A and Mr B are clearly 'neighbours' of the supplier for the purpose of *Donoghue v Stevenson* since the supplier could clearly foresee that if his advice were defective, and the building collapsed, people inside it would be injured, and that people who had property close to it would suffer damage to that property. They will be able to recover compensation for the direct damage they have suffered (eg compensation for pain and suffering, or physical impairment for Mr A, and the value of his car for Mr B) together with any economic loss flowing from such damage such as loss of earnings for Mr A or the cost of a hire car to use while Mr B's car is being repaired (see for instance the Australian case *Voli v Inglewood Shire Council* (1963) 110 CLR 74 and *Spartan Steel & Alloys Ltd v Martin & Co (Contractors) Ltd* [1973] QB 27).

The position of C Ltd is not so simple. It is clearly a 'neighbour' of the supplier as the owner of the building, but is the element of physical harm, also required by *Donoghue v Stevenson*, present here? The building has been damaged, and, as a result, C Ltd has suffered the economic loss relating to the cost of the repair. Up until recently, C Ltd would have been entitled to recover the cost of the repair of the building on the basis that the physical harm necessary to bring it within the principles of *Donoghue v Stevenson* was the collapse of the building. Thus it would be able to recover the economic loss flowing from that physical damage, namely the cost of repair. On this basis its position would be no different from that of Mr A and Mr B (see *Dutton v Bognor Regis UDC* [1972] 2 QB 373 and *Anns v Merton LBC* [1978] AC 728).

Unfortunately for C Ltd this type of extension of the principle in *Donoghue v Stevenson* (to provide compensation for the diminution in value of a defective product not actually supplied by the tortfeasor) led to what the courts regarded as too wide an exposure for potential tortfeasors, by an attempt to impose a liability that should only really be assumed under a contract, and the two above decisions were overruled by a combination of two House of Lords cases, *D&F Estates Ltd v Church Commissioners* [1989] AC 177 and *Murphy v Brentwood DC* [1991] 1 AC 398. The essence of these decisions is that where the loss suffered is really the cost of repairing property which is inherently defective, the loss suffered should be regarded as pure economic loss not flowing from physical damage. Given other recent developments in case law, such economic loss is rarely recoverable by way of an action in negligence (but see the discussion of the so-called 'complex structure exception' in *Murphy* and in *Jacobs v Moreton* (1994) 72 BLR 92 at 103). Thus C Ltd, like D Ltd, has suffered pure economic loss, and the possibility of recovery for this is limited for both of them.

Hedley, Byrne & Co Ltd v Heller & Partners Ltd [1964] AC 465 held that, where the victim suffered only pure economic loss, provided there was a close relationship between the parties, the victim could be regarded as a 'neighbour' of the tortfeasor, and then the duty of care under *Donoghue v Stevenson* would extend to a duty to take reasonable care not to cause pure economic loss to that victim. This duty was widened by applying a much looser definition of the neighbour test (based only on foreseeability of the likelihood of harm to the victim), and dropping the requirement of a specially close relationship, in *Junior Books Ltd v Veitchi Co Ltd* [1983] 1 AC 520. However, again, the potential exposure of the tortfeasor to a wide and potentially unlimited liability to an indeterminate class of victims caused the courts to restrict these decisions. In *Caparo Industries plc v Dickman* [1990] 2 AC 605 Lord Oliver explained that the duty of care had to be linked with the type of damage suffered. The duty of care in *Donoghue v Stevenson* was a duty to take care to avoid physical harm, and not just a duty to take care in the abstract. The wide definition of neighbour (ie anyone whom it was reasonably foreseeable would be harmed as a result of the negligent act) was appropriate for a duty of this nature, but not for a duty to take care to avoid pure economic loss unconnected with physical damage. In *Murphy v Brentwood DC* Lord Harwich spoke of the need for 'a special relationship of proximity ... sufficiently akin to contract to introduce the element of reliance, so that the duty embraced purely economic loss'. Thus the recent cases on pure economic loss have returned to the restricted test of proximity in *Hedley Byrne*.

The proximity requirement can be described best by following Lord Bridge in *Caparo*. The defendant giving advice or information must be fully aware of the nature of the transaction which the plaintiff had in contemplation, know that the information or advice would be communicated to him directly or indirectly, and know it was very likely that the plaintiff would rely on that advice or information in deciding whether or not to enter into the transaction in question. At most, if the defendant did not know of a particular plaintiff to whom his advice would be communicated for a specific purpose, he must be aware that it would be communicated to an identifiable class of people, and in respect of an identifiable class of transaction.

The approach taken in *Caparo* (ie the proximity test) appears to have been more recently displaced at least in some circumstances by a return to the concept of 'assumption of responsibility'. In *Henderson v Merrett Syndicates Ltd* [1995] 2 AC 145, HL, where underwriting agents and sub-agents of 'names' at Lloyd's of London were found to have been negligent in the management of their principals' affairs, and liable for the economic loss so caused, Lord Goff saw *Hedley Byrne* as resting:

> 'on a relationship between the parties, which may be general or specific to the particular transaction ... All of their Lordships [in the *Hedley Byrne* judgments] spoke in terms of one party having assumed or undertaken a responsibility towards the other ... In subsequent cases concerned with liability under the *Hedley Byrne* principle in respect of negligent misstatements, the question has frequently arisen whether the plaintiff falls within the category of persons to whom the maker of the statement owes a duty of care ... there has been some tendency ... to criticise the concept of "assumption of responsibility" as being "unlikely to be a helpful or realistic test in most cases" (see ... *Caparo Industries plc v Dickman* [1990] 1 All ER 568 at 582–583 *per* Lord Roskill). However, at least in cases such as the present, in which the same problem does not arise, there seems to be no reason why recourse should not be had to the concept, which appears after all to have been adopted, in one form or another, by all of their Lordships in [*Hedley Byrne*] ... the principle in *Hedley Byrne* ... has been expressly applied to a number of different categories of persons who perform services of a professional or quasi-professional nature ... the relationship between name and managing agent appears to provide a classic example of the type of relationship to which the principle in *Hedley Byrne* applies.'

Caparo received further discussion in *White v Jones* [1995] 2 AC 207, HL, where a solicitor was held liable for negligent omission in failing to prepare a revision to a client's will in a timely fashion. The client died leaving his will unchanged and the solicitor was held liable for the loss of legacies suffered by the persons who would have received them as beneficiaries under the new will. The decision in the House of Lords was a narrow one in favour of the plaintiff beneficiaries (by three to two). Lord Goff, Lord Browne-Wilkinson and Lord Nolan all saw *Hedley Byrne* as being concerned at least in part with the concept of the assumption of responsibility. Indeed Lord Browne-Wilkinson helpfully showed the relationship between the proximity test and the assumption of responsibility when he said: 'the special relationship [ie the sufficient degree of proximity] is created by the defendant voluntarily assuming to act in the matter by involving himself in the plaintiff's affairs.' He then quoted with approval Lord Bridge's statement in *Caparo* recognising that the law would develop novel categories of negligence 'incrementally and by close analogy with existing categories'. He then proceeded to find that this was a case where 'such development should take place since there is a close analogy with existing categories of special relationship giving rise to a duty of care to prevent economic loss'. He also stated that as a matter of public policy it would be 'unacceptable, if, because of some technical rules of law, the wishes and expectations of testators and beneficiaries generally could be defeated by the negligent actions of solicitors without there being any redress'.

Lord Goff was also much influenced by the injustice of not providing a remedy on this case, and was ready 'to fashion a remedy to fill a lacuna in the law'. He was again influenced by the fact that 'the beneficiaries are a small number of identified people'.

Lord Nolan again saw a close relationship between the question of the degree of proximity and the assumption of responsibility. The solicitor was acting in the role of family solicitor. Although the contract was with the head of the family, '[it] would be astonishing if [the solicitor] owed a duty of care to him alone, to the exclusion of the other members of the family [the beneficiaries]. In the particular circumstances of the case the degree of proximity to the plaintiffs could hardly have been closer. Carol White the first plaintiff had spoken to [the solicitor] about the revised wishes of [the testator] and the letter setting out those wishes was written [for the testator] by the husband of the second plaintiff. It would be absurd to suggest they placed no reliance upon the [solicitor] to carry out the instructions ... I simply point to the facts as being relevant to the pragmatic case by case approach which the law now adopts to negligence claims.'[4]

A further example of this pragmatic approach is *Marc Rich & Co AG v Bishop Rock Marine Co Ltd* [1995] 2 AC 207, HL. In this case a surveyor working for a marine classification society negligently advised that a ship could be made seaworthy by temporary repairs. They were insufficient, and the ship sunk with the loss of cargo. The cargo owners sued the society for its employee's negligent advice. Their Lordships found that both the elements of foreseeability and proximity were present. However, a majority of their Lordships (with Lord Lloyd of Berwick dissenting) found against the cargo owners for reasons of public policy. They considered it to be unjust, unfair and unreasonable to impose a duty of care on a defendant which was a non-profit-making organisation created and operated for the sole purpose of promoting the safety of lives and ships at sea. Lord Steyn (with whose judgment rest of the House, with the exception of Lord Lloyd, agreed) was, however, also influenced because the facts of the case showed no assumption of responsibility towards the cargo owners.

A further case in the Court of Appeal decided at the end of 1995 after the previous cases (*McCullagh v Lane Fox and Partners Ltd* (1995) *The Times*, 22 December) followed the line of these cases. Here a surveyor acting for a seller was saved from liability to the purchaser for a negligent misstatement made to the seller, but relied upon by the purchaser, because of a disclaimer of liability on the document containing the statement. The court stated that the disclaimer negatived one of the essential elements for establishing the requisite duty of care, namely an assumption of liability. The court concluded that it was clear from the more recent authorities that *Hedley Byrne* was still the governing authority in cases such as the present and that the elements of reasonable foreseeability and reliance were fundamental as was the element of assumption of liability. In more recent cases there has continued to be a primary emphasis on the question of assumption of responsibility.

In *ADT Ltd v BDO Binder Hamlyn* [1996] BCC 808, a partner in BDO attended a meeting with his clients who were selling a company to the plaintiff. The partner confirmed to the plaintiff that the target company's audited accounts showed a true and fair view of the company. This subsequently proved not to be so, and the plaintiff sued BDO for the negligent misstatement. The court found for the plaintiff on the basis that the partner in BDO had directed his statements to the plaintiff and assumed responsibility for them to the plaintiff.

By contrast, in *Peach Publishing v Slater & Co* (1997) unreported, 7 February, CA, the facts were similar, except that the partner made a statement relating to unaudited management accounts very reluctantly and only for the purpose of advising his own client, the seller, that the seller could make a warranty as to their accuracy. Even though the statement was made to the buyer (it was a joint pre-completion meeting) the court held that under the circumstances, and given the reason that the statement was made, it was for the benefit only of the seller, and the partner had assumed no responsibility to the buyer in respect of it.

In *Secured Residential Funding plc v Nationwide Building Society* (1997) *New Law Digest Property Communication*, 21 October, the plaintiff's agent instructed the defendant to prepare a valuation of property. The valuer did so and gave it to the agent who subsequently gave it to plaintiff who relied upon it to his detriment and sued the defendant for negligent advice. The defendant had no knowledge of the plaintiff, nor that the plaintiff would be shown and would rely upon the report. It thought it was acting for the agent who had commissioned and paid for the report. Under these circumstances it had assumed no responsibility towards the plaintiff and was under no liability to the plaintiff.

In *Haddow v Secretary of State for the Environment* (1998) unreported, QBD, 29 January, the Department had given some advice over the telephone to the plaintiff about the conduct of a planning application. In the outcome, the plaintiff followed the advice and the application failed. She claimed that the advice was negligent. The court held that there was no relationship between the Secretary of State and the plaintiff, whereby he assumed responsibility for advising her about the conduct of the planning application. It was entirely reasonable for him to assume that in such a major planning application as in this case, the plaintiff would not act solely on advice given casually over the telephone, but would have appointed proper advisers. In any event the advice given was not negligent or careless. Accordingly the application failed.

In summary there now seem to be three possible tests to decide if the relationship between the plaintiff and defendant is one where it is appropriate to compensate the plaintiff for pure economic loss arising as a result of a negligent act or omission: proximity, assumption of responsibility and public policy. However, on closer inspection it can be seen that these tests are at least to some extent interdependent and overlapping. The concept of proximity described by Lord Bridge in *Caparo* ('sufficiently akin to contract to introduce the element of reliance') clearly imports an assumption of responsibility and public policy considerations are clearly more likely to find liability where there has been such assumption of responsibility.[5]

Let us now use the method of proceeding by analogy under the pragmatic incremental approach favoured in *Caparo*, and the flexible approach that use of these three overlapping tests can allow us, to consider the position of C Ltd and D Ltd. C Ltd (since he cannot rely on the damage to his building to bring him within *Donoghue v Stevenson*) and D Ltd (as an investor who has suffered no physical damage at all) would only be able to recover their economic loss if they can show that they have a special relationship with the supplier, which either falls within the one of the existing categories of relationship where liability has already been found to exist or which can be said, proceeding incrementally and by analogy, to be close to one of such categories. Let us assume that they never saw the supplier's advice and in no way relied upon it. In this case no special relationship between either C Ltd or D Ltd and the supplier can arise. There is no degree of proximity between them and there was certainly no assumption of responsibility towards them on the part of the supplier. What if C Ltd had been concerned about the structural integrity of the proposed building, and D Ltd had wanted to be sure that C Ltd was entering into a well-thought-out building project before investing, and both had asked the customer to pass on a copy of the supplier's advice on the subject, and had then gone ahead with the project and the investment in reliance on the advice? Even here, the supplier could not be liable to C Ltd and D Ltd unless the supplier knew his advice would be communicated to C Ltd for the purpose of reassuring C Ltd about the structural integrity of the proposed building and to D Ltd for the purpose of its assessment of the investment in C Ltd.

If the supplier provides the advice in the knowledge that the purpose of its preparation is for C Ltd and D Ltd to receive it and to act in reliance upon it, the element of knowledge will create the special relationship which is required. This can be looked at either in terms of proximity between the parties or as an assumption of liability on the part of the supplier. The only questions left are then whether this type of relationship is one which is sufficiently close to existing relationships where liability has been found to exist in previous cases. There seems little difficulty in finding that the relationship, between a structural engineer and persons who rely upon his advice in relation to the sound-ness of a building in which they are financially concerned, is a relationship which falls within or very close to the categories of professional adviser who have already been found to have liability for negligent discharge of their pro-fessional responsibilities. Nor would there appear to be any public policy con-siderations which would militate against a finding of responsibility in the con-text of this relationship. It can therefore be seen that the best defence for the supplier against third party claims for pure economic loss is to build on the procedures discussed above for restricting the purpose for which the advice is to be used by the customer. For instance, a prohibition upon the customer showing such advice or transmitting it orally to third parties, would presum-ably be helpful in the extreme in putting the supplier outside of any relation-ship at all with any third party. He will certainly have assumed no responsibil-ity to any third parties who may see the advice, if he has forbidden the cus-tomer to disclose it to them.

One final distinction needs to be made. This is between someone who gives information and someone who gives advice in a more general sense. This dis-tinction was set out in *South Australia Asset Management Corporation v York Montague Ltd* [1996] 3 All ER 365, HL. In this case, Lord Hoffmann distin-guished between the provision of information where the duty was to take rea-sonable care that it was correct, and the giving of advice where the duty is to take reasonable care to consider all the potential consequences of the course of action advised. In the former case the negligent provider of information is liable only for the loss caused by the information being wrong, but not neces-sarily for all the loss suffered by the person who relied upon the information in order to decide to embark upon a particular course of action. In contradistinc-tion, where someone embarks upon a particular course of action because they are advised to do so, and this advice is negligent, the provider of the advice is liable for all the loss suffered (subject to the rules on foreseeability) as a result of the course of action taken. This is not to impose a higher standard of care upon persons who give advice as opposed to those who provide information, as it really turns upon questions of causation. However, clearly one way to limit the potential for recovery of damages is to make sure, wherever possible, that what is given is information rather than information plus advice. Suppose a valuer simply gave an opinion as to the value of property, but did not advise upon the investment in that property, and the property subsequently fell in value so that the plaintiff suffered loss on his investment as a result. Since the valuer had not advised the plaintiff to make the investment, provided the valu-ation was correct at the time in question, there could be no question of the valuer having any liability for the subsequent falls in value. Furthermore, even if the valuation were not correct, the valuer would only be liable for the differ-ence between his valuation and the actual value at the time the investment was made. He would still not be liable for subsequent falls in value.

Clause 6.3 proceeds on this basis, and also, for good measure, includes an indemnity from the customer to the supplier in the event of any third party claims against the supplier for loss caused by negligent advice given by the supplier, whether or not such advice was passed on to that third party by the customer, contrary to the prohibition. This applies whether or not such claims relate to death, injury, property damage, or pure economic loss. Where it is intended that the supplier's advice be passed on then the prohibition would obviously be deleted, or at least modified so that an exception was granted to permit passing on only to the designated recipient or class of recipients, for the specified purpose. However, even in this case, an indemnity from the customer should be sought against third party claims (again in respect of death, injury, property damage, or pure economic loss) in case the advice turns out to be defective. If this can be negotiated, and the customer is sufficiently substantial, it is a good solution.

Finally, and in addition, the supplier should of course make sure he is covered under his professional indemnity insurance policy in such cases.

3.4   Precedent 3

Precedent 3 is for a service supply contract where there is a closer connection between the customer and the supplier. It is more appropriate for a supplier who works as an independent contractor supplying general professional services for one, or at most a few customers, on a long term regular basis, and who takes up a considerable amount of his personal time in so doing. The example in Precedent 3 is of a physician who supplies medical services to a company at one of its factories, but it could equally well apply to any of the other professions, such as lawyers, accountants, or architects, or to the provision of technical, engineering or marketing expertise.

Clause 1 of the precedent specifies the services and the fees to be paid for them by reference to detailed schedules to be attached to the agreement. Clause 2(*a*) builds upon the general implied term of s 14 of the SGSA as to the degree of skill and care with which the supplier will perform his duties. This clause imposes, arguably, a higher standard of skill and care than s 14, and thus, pursuant to s 16(2) of the SGSA will displace the term implied by s 14 from the contract. Clause 2(*b*) imposes a strict indemnity upon the physician for breach of cl 2(*a*) and his other obligations under the agreement.

The question of limitation of liability is a difficult one where the supplier of the service is, as is most likely to be the case in such contracts as this, a natural person. It is unrealistic of the customer to impose unlimited liability, but, at the same time, not fair that the supplier should escape with no responsibility at all. The proviso to cl 2(*b*), together with cl 2(*c*) takes a middle way by imposing upon the supplier the liability to take out professional indemnity insurance, and to produce proof of current cover on demand, while, at the same time, capping the supplier's liability at the assumed limit of cover under the insurance.

However, cl 2(*c*) makes it clear that the supplier is liable up to the relevant limit, even if he has in fact neglected to take out the policy. This provides the proper incentive for the supplier to take out and maintain the cover. Of course, in practice, the customer might find he were suing a man of straw, if he attempted to enforce liability in the absence of insurance cover, but failure to take out or maintain insurance cover would enable the customer to terminate for breach, if he so wished, pursuant to cl 8(*b*). Some customers feel so strongly about the question of insurance cover that they are prepared to pay themselves for the cost of the supplier's professional indemnity insurance, and, in relevant cases, such a provision can be included in cl 2(*c*).

Clauses 3 and 4 contain administrative provisions to enable the supplier to provide his services in a manner which is properly supervised by his customer.

Clauses 5 and 6 relate to confidentiality and the ownership of intellectual property rights arising from work carried out by the supplier pursuant to the provision of services to the customer. The supplier has a much closer association with the customer than a supplier whose relationship is governed by Precedent 2, and it is likely that he will have a far more intimate contact with the customer, and a far greater knowledge of his affairs. Thus, it is appropriate for the supplier under this precedent to undertake greater obligations of confidentiality, and to agree that ownership of any intellectual property rights arising as a result of performance by him of work under the contract (including copyright in any reports prepared for the customer) should vest in the customer.

Clause 7 provides for reimbursement of expenses, and cl 8 for the term and termination of the agreement. Clause 9 is a useful clause for permitting what is in effect a kind of subcontracting by the supplier to enable him to fulfil his duties under the contract even when incapacitated or on leave. Clauses 11 and 12 are useful formal provisions, which may be added to with further boilerplate or interpretative provisions as appropriate.

Clause 10, however, requires further discussion. It has been stated above, and the clause so provides, that the supplier, even though a natural person, is in fact working as an independent contractor, and is not therefore an employee of the customer. The consequences of the supplier being regarded as an employee of the customer are twofold. First, with the course of time he may secure rights not to be unfairly dismissed, and to be paid redundancy payments in the event that the contract is terminated. Secondly, the customer will become liable to deduct income tax from the supplier's fees at source, and account for them to the Inland Revenue under the PAYE scheme. He will also become liable for the payment of employer's and employee's social security contributions in respect of the supplier.

In these circumstances, although the Inland Revenue can, if it chooses, pursue the supplier direct for payment of income tax, it may also require the customer to pay the tax, even though no deduction from the supplier's fees has been made. In these circumstances the customer may not be able to recover the tax from the supplier by way of a civil action (see *Bernard & Shaw Ltd v Shaw*

(1951) 30 ATC 187, *R v CIR, ex parte Chisholm* (1981) 54 TC 722 and *R v CIR, ex parte Sims* [1987] STC 211).

Interestingly one indication of an independent contractor is that he is entitled to subcontract to a third party the supply of his services to the customer under the service supply contract. An employee is obliged to discharge his duties personally and cannot send a substitute (see *Ready-Mixed Concrete (South East) Ltd v Minister of Pensions and National Insurance* [1968] 1 All ER 433). Thus, in the case of this precedent, the inclusion of cl 9 would certainly help the court to hold that the supplier is an independent contractor, even if it is not entirely conclusive.

Whether a supplier of services is an independent contractor or an employee is in each case a question of fact, and is to be decided by the court upon the circumstances of each case, without regarding as conclusive any provision of the contract which declares that the supplier is not an employee. Thus cl 10 has no real use except to focus the minds of the parties on the issue, and, perhaps, to provide to a court some evidence of their intention. The basic criterion applied by the court is one of the degree of control exercised by the employer over the person in question, but other factors have to be taken into account. There is no one overall simple test that can be applied. (See the *Ready-Mixed Concrete* case above and *Lee v Chung and Shun Shing Construction and Engineering Co Ltd* [1990] IRLR 236, a Privy Council decision which neatly summarises and discusses the tests to be applied.) However, one rule of thumb is to compare the supplier with employees of the customer. If the only distinguishing feature between them is not what they do or how they are managed, but the nature of the contract with the customer, then the supplier will almost certainly be an employee.

3.5 Precedent 4

This precedent (for the development and supply of prototypes of a custom integrated circuit chip) is a more specialised contract than the three preceding precedents, but the general principles on which it is based are applicable to a large variety of service supply contracts relating to design and development services which are preliminaries to the supply of the resultant product in production quantities.

After designation of the parties in cll 1 and 2, cl 3 of the contract proceeds to specify the supplier's obligations for design and development of the chip to the customer's specification which sets out the functions which he intends the chip to perform (a 'functional specification'). The obligations of the supplier are tied to the functional specification and to a programme which sets out the key events in the development programme and timescales by which one party or the other must perform them. The last item in the list of key events is the making of the mask from which the chip can be manufactured.

Clause 4 thus leads on to deal with the supply of the prototype or sample chips to be made with the mask. The purpose of the prototypes is to enable the supplier to test them to demonstrate to the customer that the supplier's design produces chips which perform in accordance with the functional specification. Clause 4.2 also deals with the obligations of the supplier to design the correct equipment and methods to enable such tests to take place. However, the customer also has the right to conduct whatever further tests he deems necessary to assure himself that the chips not only perform in accordance with the functional specification which he has provided, but also that they are in all other respects satisfactory for his purposes (cll 4.4 and 4.5). Clause 5 provides for the provision to the customer by the supplier of all necessary information relating to the design and development process, and the manufacture of the prototypes, other than the manufacturing techniques and processes which are proprietary information of the supplier.

Clause 6 then provides an option for the customer to purchase the chip under a new contract in production quantities. The purpose of the procedure in cl 4 is to make the contract of sale as simple a one as possible. The contract will in fact become a sale by reference to a sample (the prototypes—see cl 6.5), since the customer has satisfied himself as to the compliance of the chip with its technical specification and its suitability for its intended purpose. Thus all of the implied warranties under the SGA, except, of course, those in s 12 relating to title, can quite reasonably be excluded. Clause 6 thus lays down all of the necessary conditions for the future contract or contracts, except for quantity and pricing, either by the express provisions in the clause, or by the application to the contract of the terms of the SGA, and the common law. Given the exclusion of all implied warranties other than that of title, this position is quite fair and reasonable for both the supplier and the customer. It favours neither, but provides a useful shorthand way of setting up the contract of sale with negotiation limited to the two important issues of price and quantity only. Thus, if the UCTA applies to the contract, its provisions should not cause any problems. It should be noted that cl 6.7 provides for a revolving warranty for defective chips, so that each replaced chip will receive the benefit of a full warranty period.

Clause 7 deals with payment to the supplier for the design and development work. As usual in such agreements, cl 7.1 ties payment to successful completion of key milestones in the programme, cl 7.2 provides that defective work must be re-performed free of charge, and cl 7.3 states that where performance of a milestone is delayed no payment will be made until completion is satisfactorily achieved.

The essence of design and development contracts which lead to production contracts is that the supplier makes his profit out of the production contract and is therefore willing to enter into a design and development contract at a very keen price, and, sometimes, even at or below cost. In any event, his business is usually the supply of items in production quantities, and he is not therefore interested in taking design and development contracts for their own sake. His greatest fear is that the customer will obtain the design generated by him, and have the item manufactured by a third person, thus depriving him of his intended profit. The customer's greatest fear is that the supplier will put him in a position where the only source of supply for the items is the supplier, and that the supplier will then be able to charge virtually any price he likes for the subsequent supply contract.

The aim of most agreements of this type is to keep a balance of terror between the two parties so that they are forced into striking a fair bargain. In this agreement, this is achieved as follows. Clause 6.9 prevents the supplier selling chips to any one other than the customer during the option period. Conversely, cl 10 makes it clear that the supplier owns the design in the chip, so that the customer cannot manufacture it himself or through a third person without the supplier's consent. It is true that the first sentence of cl 10 means that the customer owns the functional specification of the chip, so that he could go elsewhere, and ask another supplier to design him from scratch a new chip which complied with that functional specification, but this is hardly likely to be in the customer's interest unless he is seriously displeased with the current supplier. Thus, during the option period, the supplier can only sell chips to the customer, and the customer can in practice only buy chips from the supplier. This is the best situation for ensuring that the two parties will come to a reasonable bargain over the supply contract, because both of their interests are best served by doing so.

The situation described above does need some relaxation. If the supplier goes out of business, the customer should be free to have the chip manufactured elsewhere, and should be granted the necessary copyright licences, and access to the necessary tools and information to do this. Further, certain end users may require that equipment they purchase from the customer should only incorporate key chips which can be obtained from two sources. This requirement ensures both security of supply, and also provides for competitive pricing of key components. Clause 8 provides for both of these matters in what is essentially the customary way.

Clause 9 deals with a small but important point. Most customers who purchase essential or important components from a vendor go through an exercise of vendor qualification to ensure that the way the vendor carries on his business and manufactures the relevant product is satisfactory from the point of quality and conformance to specifications. Once this exercise has taken place, and particularly since here the customer will have qualified the prototypes, and is then purchasing production quantities of the chip in conformance with the prototype samples, the supplier must not be permitted to change his methods and processes in an uncontrolled manner, which may be detrimental to the quality of the items he produces, or may render them different from the original samples which the customer qualified as the basis for his supply contract. Clause 12 also adds weight in this area since it forbids any assignment or subcontract of any part of the supplier's duties under the contract without the consent of the customer. The customer does not want a vendor, whom he has qualified, to allow part or all of the contract to be performed by an unqualified, unknown and unapproved third party, even if the supplier is ready to vouch for him.

One very important area of liability is that relating to infringement of intellectual property rights. Each side could cause the other to infringe third party rights. The customer's instructions to the supplier in the functional specification could cause the supplier to infringe when he produces a design in conformance with that specification. Clause 11.1 deals with this issue. It is a mutual clause, so it would also cover the customer in the (presumably unlikely) event that information given by the supplier to the customer under cl 5 caused the customer to infringe. However, the real exposure to the customer is that the design of the chip produced by the supplier will infringe third party rights, so that he will not be able to make use of the production quantities of the chip once he has obtained them. As discussed in Chapters 1 and 2, the causing of such infringement would be a breach of the warranty of good title implied into this contract by s 12 of the SGA, in respect of which liability under the UCTA cannot easily be limited. However, in addition to the cause of action under this implied warranty, cl 11.2 provides an express indemnity, still unlimited. Even were s 6 of the UCTA to have no application to the contract it is still usual for the supplier to bear this responsibility. He is responsible for the design, and he is taking the profit margin on the sale of the chip. It is only fair that he should deliver a useable item to the customer. If the supplier is able to negotiate some limitations on his liability then the approach discussed in Chapter 2 in relation to this issue should be adopted and provisions equivalent to cll 5 and 10 of Precedent 1 should be used, and cl 15.3 amended to refer to s 12(3) and s 2(3) of the SGA and the SGSA respectively.

The problem of termination in design and development contracts is a difficult one. The most usual instance of breach is failure to perform milestones in accordance with the contractual dates. In some cases this will be due to genuine *force majeure*, in others, but rarely, to wilful default, but in most cases no real cause can be assigned. Despite what appears to be due diligence on the part of the supplier the task has turned out to be harder or technically more complex than he, and, indeed, often the customer, envisaged. Matters have just dragged on, despite hard work on the part of the supplier, so that various milestones cannot now be met.

Termination in the case of *force majeure* is normally on the basis that the supplier is entitled to payment for work performed up to the date of termination. This is provided for in cl 14. Termination for wilful default normally entitles the customer to have the work performed elsewhere, with any increased costs for the account of the supplier. This is provided for in cl 13.2.

Failure to perform which lies in between these two extremes is dealt with in two ways. Certain events which can generally be described as unforeseen technical difficulties are set out in square brackets in cl 14.1 under the definition of *force majeure*. If these are included within that definition, then the supplier will be excused from performance if they occur, and cancellation will occur in the same way and on the same basis as for any other event of *force majeure*. This still leaves a middle ground between unforeseen technical difficulties and wilful default, which can be described, perhaps, as lack of technical or managerial competence.

Many customers would punish lack of managerial or technical competence in the same way as wilful default, but there is one issue here which needs clarification. The biggest risk for a supplier under a design, development and production contract is damages for loss of profits or business. In the event that the contract is terminated early so that production never takes place, can the supplier be held liable for all of the profits which the customer lost because he never obtained the items in production quantity, and therefore was unable to use them in his contracts with end-users? Certainly the supplier is in theory liable for such losses, subject to the ordinary common law rules of remoteness. Even more obviously, is he liable for such losses if he fails to perform on the production contract after the development is finished?

For the purposes of compensation of increased cost to the customer of having the work performed elsewhere ('direct damages') it appears fair that a line should be drawn between termination for *force majeure*, including for unforeseen technical problems (no direct damages payable) and termination for all other causes, ie technical or managerial incompetence and wilful default (direct damages payable). This is the approach taken in cll 13 and 14.

However, the same is not true of loss of profits or business ('economic loss'). Here the line could well be drawn differently in a development contract. It is at least arguable that the supplier should bear all the consequences of wilful default, including economic loss, but that he should be excused liability for economic loss in the case where, despite good faith and reasonable endeavours, technical and managerial competence was just not up to the task. True, the supplier is to blame, and should compensate the customer for the direct consequences of his incompetence, but the customer did after all choose the supplier in the first place, and did or should have made some reasonable assessment of his competence. The customer should also have considered some fall-back plans in the event the supplier did not perform whether in the event of *force majeure* or for any other reason. Under these circumstances, it is hard to see why, as between the parties, the supplier should bear the liability for the customer's economic loss.

For these reasons, cl 15 proceeds on the basis that the supplier has no liability for economic loss for failure to perform under the contract for any reason at all, while the words in square brackets, if included, would provide that he had no such liability except in the event of his own wilful default.

The remarks relating to cll 13, 14 and 15 should be considered as well in the light of the discussion on general exclusion clauses in relation to the UCTA contained in Chapter 1. It is considered that cll 13, 14 and 15 would pass the test of reasonableness as applied by s 3 of the UCTA, however the liability for breaches arising from wilful default were dealt with.

The remaining clauses in the contract relate to the standard areas of notice, whole agreement clauses and other boilerplate. Clause 16 which applies English law to the contract is particularly important if it is an international contract, given the application of the SGA and of the common law to the supply contract entered into pursuant to cl 6.

Precedent 1

Maintenance services agreement

AGREEMENT NO [   ] dated [   ] day of
[   ] 19 [   ] BY AND BETWEEN [   ] LIMITED
of [   ] (the 'Company')
AND [   ] of [   ] (the 'Customer')

The Customer hereby requests the Company to provide (in consideration of
the payment by the Customer to the Company of the Initial Inspection Fee, the
Annual Charge, and the other charges referred to overleaf) a maintenance service
in respect of the machinery (including each and every part thereof) listed below and the Company hereby agrees to render such service upon and subject
to the terms and conditions overleaf.

Description   Serial Number   Location

Initial Inspection Fee: £ [   ]

Annual Charge: £ [   ]

Signed on behalf of the Customer   Signed on behalf of the Company
[   ]   [   ]
AUTHORISED SIGNATORY   AUTHORISED SIGNATORY
FULL NAME [   ]   FULL NAME [   ]
POSITION [   ]   POSITION [   ]

Terms and conditions of maintenance

1   Definitions

'Effective Date' means the date on which a certificate is issued pursuant to Condition 2.2 or 2.4;

'Good Working Order' means [functioning in accordance with the applicable specification of the manufacturer of the System] [functioning in accordance with the specification annexed hereto as Appendix A] [functioning in a manner which enables the System to fulfil the purpose for which it was designed] [performing the functions for which the System is ordinarily used, in a reasonably efficient manner];

'Maintenance Service' is defined in Conditions 4.1, 4.2 and 4.3;

'Normal Working Hours' means 8:00 am to 5:00 pm, Monday to Friday inclusive, National and Bank Holidays excepted;

'Premises' means the location listed overleaf or (as the case may be) any other premises in which for the time being the System is installed with the consent of the Company;

'Spare Parts' means all parts and subassemblies of the System supplied and installed in the System by the Company pursuant to the provision of Maintenance Service;

'System' means the machinery and any associated items (including wiring) listed overleaf and includes (where appropriate) all replacements thereof and additions thereto;

'User Routine Maintenance' means maintenance which [the operating instructions for the System advise the user thereof to carry out as a matter of routine on a regular basis] [would customarily be carried out by the user of the System as part of the routine operation of the System].

2   Initial inspection

2.1 Upon signature of this Agreement and payment by the Custo...er to the Company of the Initial Inspection Fee, the Company shall thereupon forthwith carry out an inspection of the System to determine whether it is in Good Working Order.

2.2 If the System is found to be in Good Working Order, the Company shall forthwith issue a certificate to the Customer confirming this.

2.3 If the System is not found to be in Good Working Order, the Company shall set out in a written quotation (the 'Quotation') to the Customer the work (including the supply and installation of any necessary Spare Parts) which is required to be carried out, at the Customer's expense, to put the System into Good Working Order.

2.4 If the Customer accepts the Quotation, the Company shall carry out the said work in accordance with the Quotation and upon and subject to the terms of this Agreement, and, upon its completion, and receipt of payment therefor from the Customer, issue a certificate to the Customer confirming that the System is in Good Working Order.

2.5 If the Customer rejects the Quotation, then this Agreement shall thereupon terminate automatically without notice, and without liability to either the Customer or the Company, except that the Company shall be entitled to retain the Initial Inspection Fee.

3   Term

3.1 This Agreement shall come into force when it has been signed on behalf of the Customer and the Company.

3.2 This Agreement shall continue in force for a period of twelve months from the Effective Date ('the Fixed Period'). At the end of the Fixed Period, or of any subsequent period of twelve months during which this Agreement is in force pursuant to a renewal under this Condition (a 'Renewal Period'), this Agreement shall be automatically renewed for a further period of twelve months, unless terminated by either party giving to the other not less than sixty (60) days prior written notice to expire at the end of the Fixed Period or of the relevant Renewal Period, as the case may be.

3.3 This Agreement shall be subject to earlier termination as provided in Conditions 2.5 and 9.

4   Maintenance services

4.1 The Company agrees (subject to Condition 2) to provide on and from the effective date all maintenance services necessary to keep the System in Good Working Order (hereinafter referred to as 'Maintenance Service').

4.2 Maintenance Service includes but is not limited to:
4.2.1 all work (if any) carried out by the Company on the System pursuant to Condition 2.3 and 2.4;
4.2.2 scheduled preventive maintenance (including, without limitation, adjustments, modifications, and supply and installation of Spare Parts) of such a nature and at such times and frequency as shall be deemed necessary by the Company to keep the System in Good Working Order; and
4.2.3 unscheduled on-call remedial maintenance (including, without limitation, adjustments, modifications, and supply and installation of Spare Parts) due to malfunction of the System.

4.3 For the avoidance of doubt, Maintenance Service does not include:
4.3.1 user Routine Maintenance;
4.3.2 work other than to the System;
4.3.3 repair of damage to, or replacement of parts of, the System, caused by accident or misuse, or by the neglect, act or default of the Customer or any other user of the System (including, without limitation, because of failure to undertake User Routine Maintenance) or by any factor external to the System (including, without limitation, defective consumable items, or the failure of, or defects in, equipment which is not part of the System);
4.3.4 painting or refinishing the System or furnishing supplies for such purposes, or making specification changes or performing services connected with relocation of the System or any part thereof, or providing, adding or removing accessories, attachments, consumable items or other devices; and
4.3.5 such services as it may be impractical for the Company to render because of alterations to the System other than alterations carried out by the Company.

4.4 Maintenance Service under Condition 4.2.2. (scheduled preventive maintenance) will be provided by the Company during Normal Working Hours and subject to reasonable prior notice by the Company to the Customer.

4.5 Maintenance Service under Condition 4.2.3 (on-call remedial maintenance) will be provided by the Company as soon as reasonably practicable from the time the request from the Customer for such Maintenance Service is received by the Company, *provided that* the Company shall be under no obligation to provide such Maintenance Service outside Normal Working Hours and *provided further that*, in the event the Company agrees with the Customer so to provide it, the Customer shall pay to the Company, in addition to the relevant Annual Charge, the Company's then current standard extra charges for the provision of Maintenance Service outside Normal Working Hours.

4.6 Spare Parts supplied and installed in the System as part of the provision of Maintenance Service shall be so supplied and installed by the Company without any charge in addition to the Annual Charge, except for those Spare Parts supplied and installed as part of work carried out pursuant to Condition 2.3 and 2.4 in which case the charge for the same shall be as specified in the relevant Quotation.

4.7 All Spare Parts shall be either new, or reconditioned or reassembled Spare Parts which are equivalent to new Spare Parts in performance. The Company warrants that it has good title to such Spare Parts and that property in such Spare Parts shall vest in the Customer upon their installation in the System; and property in all parts and subassemblies of the System replaced by such Spare Parts shall vest in the Company upon their removal from the System.

4.8 If any replacement or repair included within Maintenance Service is normally effected by removal of the System or any part thereof from the Premises, and the Customer refuses to permit this, then the Company will be entitled to recover any additional costs incurred thereby and the Company shall incur no liability for any resultant delay or failure in providing the relevant Maintenance Service.

5   Maintenance and other charges

5.1 The Customer shall pay to the Company annual charges ('the Annual Charge') at the rate stated overleaf for the Maintenance Service in respect of the Fixed Term and in respect of each Renewal Term for which this Agreement remains in force.

5.2 The Company reserves the right to vary the Annual Charge by giving the Customer not less than ninety (90) days prior written notice to expire on the expiry of the Fixed Period or of any Renewal Period.

5.3 The Company shall issue to the Customer an invoice in respect of all sums payable by the Customer to the Company hereunder, in each case on or in advance of the date upon which the relevant sum becomes due, and each such invoice shall be payable [thirty] days after the relevant due date with the exception of that relating to the Initial Inspection Fee which shall be payable on the date on which it is due. The Initial Inspection Fee shall be due upon the signature of this Agreement. The Annual Charge shall be due on the commencement of the Fixed Period and of each Renewal Period. All other sums payable by the Customer to the Company under this Agreement shall be due on receipt by the Customer of the Company's invoice for the same.

5.4 If any amount due to the Company hereunder remains unpaid after the date on which it is payable pursuant to Condition 5.3, the Company shall be entitled [to charge interest on such sum at a rate of [3%] per annum above [base rate] from that date until the date of actual payment, and] to withhold any or all of the services to be provided by the Company hereunder until such time as payment of the said sum [and of the interest thereon] is received by the Company.

5.5 All charges to the Customer made by the Company under this Agreement (including, without limitation, the Initial Inspection Fee and the Annual Charge), exclude Value Added Tax. The Customer shall in addition to such charges pay to the Company (subject to the issue of the relevant Value Added Tax Invoice) the amount of Value Added Tax for which the Company will be accountable to HM Customs and Excise in respect of all such charges.

6   Customer's obligations and undertakings

The Customer shall throughout the period of this Agreement take good care of the System and operate the same in a proper manner, carry out all User Routine Maintenance; order and pay for such consumable items as he shall require to operate and use the System; permit the Company and any person authorised by the Company to have access to the System at all reasonable times; and not make or endeavour to make any alterations or additions to the System or any part thereof nor permit any other person to do so without the prior written consent of the Company.

7   Force Majeure

Neither party to this Agreement shall be under any liability to the other in respect of any failure to carry out or delay in carrying out any of its obligations hereunder attributable to any cause of whatever nature outside its reasonable control.

8   Limitation of liability

8.1 These conditions shall not be deemed to constitute or imply any warranty by the Company that the System will at all times operate satisfactorily without malfunction, and the Company gives no such warranty.

8.2 It is understood that the amounts payable to the Company under this Agreement are based upon the value of the Maintenance Service and the scope of the Company's liability as set forth in these Conditions. Accordingly the Company shall indemnify the Customer as follows:

8.2.1 against any loss of or damage to the System;

8.2.2 against any loss of or damage to the property of the Customer (other than the System);

8.2.3 against all claims made by third parties (including employees of the Customer) against the Customer in respect of death or personal injury;

8.2.4 against all claims made by third parties (including employees of the Customer) against the Customer in respect of loss of or damage to property;

[8.2.5 where the Customer is a natural person and Section 2(1) of the Unfair Contract Terms Act 1977 applies to this Agreement, against death or personal injury to the Customer;] and

8.2.6 to the extent that any of the foregoing are caused directly by (*a*) failure of the Company to provide Maintenance Service pursuant to and in accordance with Condition 4 or (*b*) by the negligent acts or omissions of the Company, its employees, subcontractors or agents.

8.3 The indemnities given by the Company under Condition 8.2 [(with the exception of the indemnity under Condition 8.2.5 where the liability of the Company shall be unlimited)] shall be limited to the following maximum amounts:

8.3.1 in respect of the indemnity under Condition 8.2.1 [a maximum amount of [twice] the relevant Annual Charge in respect of any one incident];

8.3.2 in respect of the indemnity under Condition 8.2.2 [a maximum amount of £[   ] in respect of any one incident or series of related incidents and a maximum amount of £[   ] in respect of all and any incidents (whether or not related) arising during the Fixed Period or the relevant Renewal Period as the case may be];

8.3.3 in respect of the indemnity under Condition 8.2.3 [a maximum amount of £[   ] in respect of any one incident or series of related incidents and a maximum amount of £[   ] in respect of all and any incidents (whether or not related) arising during the Fixed Period or the relevant Renewal Period as the case may be];

8.3.4 in respect of the indemnity under Condition 8.2.4 [a maximum amount of £[   ] in respect of any one incident or series of related incidents and a maximum amount of £[   ] in respect of all and any incidents (whether or not related) arising during the Fixed Period or the relevant Renewal Period as the case may be].

8.4 The Company's entire liability to the Customer in relation to the System,

Spare Parts, the Maintenance Service and any negligent act or omission of the Company (and of its employees, subcontractors or agents) and in respect of any death, injury, loss or damage caused by or resulting from any of the foregoing is set out in Conditions 4, 8 and 9, which apply to the total exclusion of any other conditions, warranties, stipulations or statements whatsoever, whether express or implied by statute, common law or otherwise howsoever, including, without limitation, any such conditions, warranties, stipulations or statements regarding the fitness for purpose, performance, nature or quality of Spare Parts. Without prejudice to the generality of the foregoing the Company accepts no liability for any loss of business, profits or contracts nor for any special indirect or consequential loss or damage.

9   Termination

9.1 In the event that either party (the 'party in default') commits a material breach of any of its obligations under this Agreement (and, where such breach is capable of remedy, has not remedied the same within fifteen days of receipt of a notice from the other party (the 'innocent party') requiring that the same be remedied) then the innocent party may by notice to the party in default terminate this Agreement, such termination to take effect immediately upon the receipt by the party in default of such notice.

9.2 Where the innocent party is the Customer, it shall be entitled to a refund from the Company of a proportion of the Annual Charge paid by the Customer in respect of the Fixed Period or the Renewal Period during which the relevant breach took place (the 'Relevant Period') calculated as follows:

$$\frac{\text{Relevant Annual Charge} \times \text{Days of Relevant Period Remaining After Termination}}{365}$$

9.3 Where the innocent party is the Company, it shall be entitled to retain the whole of the Annual Charge paid by the Customer in respect of the Relevant Period.

10   Entire agreement and applicable law

10.1 This Agreement constitutes the entire agreement between the Company and the Customer in respect of the System (including without limitation in respect of the provision of Maintenance Service) and supersedes all other agreements, statements, representations or warranties made by or between the parties or either of them concerning the same. The terms and conditions of this Agreement shall supersede any terms and conditions appearing on or referred to in any purchase order, acknowledgment or other document issued by the Customer in respect of the subject matter of this Agreement.

10.2 No waiver, alteration, variation or addition to the Agreement shall be effective unless made in writing on or after the date of signature of this Agreement by both parties and accepted by an authorised signatory of both parties.

10.3 The interpretation construction effect and enforceability of this Agreement shall be governed by English Law, and the parties agree to submit to the exclusive jurisdiction of the English courts.

11 Notices

All notices, documents or other communications (a 'Notice') to be given hereunder shall be in writing and shall be transmitted by first class registered or recorded delivery mail, or by telex, facsimile or other electronic means in a form generating a record copy to the party being served at the relevant address for that party shown overleaf. Any Notice sent by mail shall be deemed to have been duly served three working days after the date of posting. Any Notice sent by telex, facsimile or other electronic means shall be deemed to have been duly served at the time of transmission [(if transmitted during normal business hours) at the location of the recipient and (if not so transmitted) then at the start of normal business hours on the next business day commencing at such location after the time at which the transmission was made].

12 Miscellaneous

12.1 The headings in this Agreement shall not affect its interpretation.

12.2 Throughout this Agreement, whenever required by context, the use of the singular number shall be construed to include the plural, and the use of the plural the singular, and the use of any gender shall include all genders.

[**12.3** the Appendix to this Agreement constitutes an integral part hereof.]

12.4 Reference in this Agreement to a Condition is to a Condition of this Agreement.

12.5 If any term or provision in this Agreement shall be held to be illegal or unenforceable, in whole or in part, under any enactment or rule of law, such term or provision or part shall to that extent be deemed not to form part of this

Agreement but the validity and enforceability of the remainder of this Agreement shall not be affected.

12.6 The waiver or forbearance or failure of a party in insisting in any one or more instances upon the performance of any provisions of this Agreement shall not be construed as a waiver or relinquishment of that party's rights to future performance of such provision and the other party's obligations in respect of such future performance shall continue in full force and effect.

Precedent 2

Terms and conditions for supply of consultancy and testing services

Statement on front of proposal:

THE CONDITIONS OVERLEAF SHALL APPLY TO THIS PROPOSAL AND TO ANY CONTRACT BETWEEN US FOR THE SUPPLY OF THE SERVICES DETAILED IN THIS PROPOSAL (SEE CONDITION 2). [PLEASE READ ALL OF THEM CAREFULLY.]

1 Definitions

In these terms and conditions the following expressions shall (where the context so admits) have the following meanings:

'Supplier' shall mean [   ] Limited.

'User' shall mean the company, firm or person to whom Supplier supplies Technical Assistance under a Contract.

'Proposal' shall mean the proposal set out overleaf for the provision of Technical Assistance.

'Specification' shall mean the description, specifications and other details of the Technical Assistance set out, or incorporated by reference in, the Proposal.

'Technical Assistance' shall mean the technical assistance as detailed in the Specification.

'Contract' shall mean the Contract between Supplier and User entered into subject to these Conditions for the provision of Technical Assistance, comprising the Proposal (including the Specification) and User's acceptance thereof in accordance with Condition 2.1.

2   Contract for technical assistance

2.1 The Proposal shall be valid only if accepted by User by signing and returning to Supplier within 21 days the duplicate copy of the Proposal. If not so accepted, the estimated cost and estimated delivery schedule stated therein may be subject to change by Supplier, or Supplier may refuse to proceed with the Contract at all. The Proposal shall state the date(s) by which any information or other items to be supplied by User to enable Supplier to execute the Contract will be required from User in order for Supplier to meet the estimated delivery schedule stated in the Proposal.

2.2 The Contract shall be subject to these terms and conditions.

2.3 Supplier shall be under no obligation to take any action to progress the Contract unless and until Supplier shall have received from User all the information and other items referred to in 2.1 above.

3   Availability of technical assistance

3.1 Supplier shall be responsible for providing Technical Assistance to User in accordance with the requirements of the Contract. Although Supplier will use all reasonable endeavours to make the Technical Assistance available in accordance with the estimated delivery schedule set out in the Proposal, such delivery schedule is only an estimate and accordingly Supplier accepts no responsibility or liability, financial or otherwise, in the event that the said estimated delivery schedule is not complied with. In particular, for the avoidance of doubt, and without limitation of the generality of the foregoing, Supplier shall not be liable to reimburse User in respect of any delay payments or other penalties for which User may become liable to any customer of User as a result of delay or failure by Supplier, whether or not Supplier is aware of User's potential liability to pay the same.

3.2 Supplier shall use reasonable endeavours to notify User of any delay in the estimated delivery schedule for the provision of Technical Assistance, and to propose a revised estimated delivery schedule to User. Any onward notification of such delay to customers of User shall be the sole responsibility of User. Where the reasons for the said delay are other than those covered in Condition 4 (*Force Majeure*), User shall have the right (within twenty one days of the date of receipt of the notification) to advise Supplier in writing that it intends to terminate the Contract forthwith (which latter course User shall be entitled to take without liability to Supplier other than reimbursement to Supplier of all costs and expenses and of any cancellation charges of Supplier's subcontractors or suppliers) incurred by Supplier up to the date of termination. Subject as aforesaid the Contract shall be deemed to include the aforesaid revised estimated delivery schedule. Any revision proposed by User to the estimated delivery schedule shall be subject to mutual agreement.

3.3 User shall be responsible for making arrangements for the collection of any physical items required to be made available to User under any Contract from such premises as Supplier shall notify to User, and for the shipment of such items to User's premises.

3.4 If detailed in the Proposal, Supplier shall render progress reports to User at agreed intervals and progress meetings will be arranged to an agreed schedule.

4 Force Majeure

4.1 Supplier shall not have any liability in respect of any delay in carrying out or failure to carry out any of its obligations under the Contract caused by fire, strikes or other industrial action or dispute, acts of Government, default of suppliers or subcontractors, or any circumstances outside the reasonable control of Supplier.

4.2 Supplier shall have the right to extend the estimated delivery schedule by a period of time sufficient to take due account of the event occurring as set out in Condition 4.1. If, however, such extension continues for a period of [six months] User may, on the expiry of that period terminate the Contract forthwith without liability to Supplier other than reimbursement on the same terms as provided in Condition 3.2.

5 Prices and payment

5.1 Prices for the provision of Technical Assistance will be those set out in the Proposal.

5.2 Supplier shall be entitled to invoice User under the Contract at the end of each month for work by Supplier on the Contract during that month. Payment of all Supplier invoices shall be made in Pounds Sterling at the end of the month following the month in which the invoices are issued. At the request of User Supplier shall issue with all invoices submitted to User under this Condition, a statement of the work carried out by Supplier to which the invoice refers. Where chargeable, Value Added Tax and any other applicable taxes or duties shall be added to the invoices at the current rate or rates in force at the relevant times.

6   Defects

6.1 In respect of any error or defect in Technical Assistance provided by Supplier under the Contract which is notified to Supplier in writing by User within [six months] of the provision thereof, Supplier agrees that it will make resources available to investigate the defect and endeavour to rectify the defect. On receipt of notification of any suspected defect, Supplier shall free of charge as soon as possible carry out an investigation into the cause thereof, and thereafter rectify the same (if possible).

6.2 Except as set out in 6.1, Supplier accepts no liability in respect of any error or defect in any Technical Assistance, or the consequences thereof, and gives no warranty in respect thereof.

6.3 The Technical Assistance is provided by Supplier on the basis that it is for the sole use of User, for the purpose set out in the Specification. User shall not use the Technical Assistance or any information contained therein other than for the said purpose and shall not communicate the Technical Assistance or any information contained therein to any third party whether or not in connection with the said purpose., nor. Without prejudice to the generality of 6.2:
6.3.1 should User use the Technical Assistance or any information contained therein contrary to the foregoing other than for the said purpose Supplier accepts no liability in respect of any error or defect in any Technical Assistance, or the consequences thereof, and gives no warranty in respect thereof; and
6.3.2 should User communicate the Technical Assistance or any information contained therein to a third party, contrary to the foregoing, or use any such Technical Assistance or information in the performance of work for a third party, whether or not in accordance with the said purpose, User will be solely liable to such third party for any error or defect in such Technical Assistance or information, and or the consequences thereof, and will indemnify Supplier against all loss, actions, claims, costs, demands, expenses and liabilities whatsoever (if any) which Supplier may incur either at common law or by statute in respect of any loss, damage, personal injury or death suffered by a third party by reason of any error or defect in such Technical Assistance or information, or by reason of the consequences of any such error or defect.

7   Economic loss

In no circumstances shall Supplier be liable, in contract, tort (including negligence or breach of statutory duty) or otherwise howsoever, and whatever the cause thereof:
    (i) for any increased costs or expenses,
    (ii) for any loss of profit, business, contracts, revenues, or anticipated sav-

ings, or

(iii) for any special indirect or consequential damage of any nature whatsoever

arising directly or indirectly out of the provision by Supplier of Technical Assistance, or of any error or defect therein, or of the performance, non-performance or delayed performance by Supplier of the Contract.

8   Limitation of liability

Notwithstanding anything contained in the Contract, Supplier's liability to User
in respect of the Contract, in contract, tort (including negligence or breach of
statutory duty) or howsoever otherwise arising, shall be limited to £[   ].

Agreement for supply of professional services

THIS AGREEMENT is made the [   ] day of [   ]
between [   ] whose registered office is situated at [   ]
(hereinafter called the 'Company') of the one part and [   ] of
[   ] (hereinafter called the 'Physician') of the other part

WHEREAS:

The Company is desirous of obtaining the services of the Physician for the purpose of providing certain medical services upon the terms and conditions hereinafter contained.

NOW IT IS HEREBY AGREED as follows:

1(*a*) The Physician undertakes to provide the services detailed in Part I of the Schedule hereto (hereinafter called the 'Services'), in consideration of the payment detailed in Part II of the said Schedule.

(*b*) Should the Company request and the Physician agree to provide services additional to those specified in Part I of this Schedule, the fees for the same shall be mutually agreed between the parties, but otherwise for all purposes of this Agreement the said additional services shall be deemed to be included within the definition of Services.

2(*a*) The Services shall be carried out by the Physician with all due despatch, care, accuracy and attention, and in compliance with the highest standards of relevant established current professional medical practice.

(*b*) The Physician shall indemnify the Company from all claims, actions or demands made by third parties against the Company, and all liabilities of the Company to third parties (collectively 'Third Party Liabilities') and from all damage, losses, costs, expenses and payments whatsoever suffered or incurred by the Company either directly or in relation to Third Party Liabilities in respect of (i) personal injury to or the death of any person and any loss or destruction of or damage to property (not attributable to any default or neglect of the Company or of any person for whom the Company is responsible) which shall have occurred in connection with the provision of the Services under this Agreement, (ii) any defect in the Services, and (iii) any breach by the Physician of any of the terms of this Agreement, including, without limitation, cl 2(*a*) hereof PROVIDED THAT the liability of the Physician to the Company under this Agreement, including without limitation this cl 2(*b*), shall be limited to [a maximum amount of £[   ] in respect of any one incident or series of related incidents and a maximum amount of £[   ] in respect of all and any incidents (whether or not related) arising during the term of this Agreement].

(*c*)   The Physician shall take out and maintain during the currency of this agreement an insurance policy, with an insurance company [of repute] [satisfactory to the Company], upon terms which are [satisfactory to the Company and] sufficient to cover his liabilities under this Agreement, including, without limitation, his liabilities under cl 2(*b*). The Physician shall upon request produce to the Company a copy of the said insurance policy, and a receipt for the payment of the current premium. For the avoidance of doubt the Physician shall be liable under all of the provisions of this Agreement, including, without limitation, cl 2(*b*), whether or not he complies with the provisions of this cl 2(*c*).

3 The Physician shall furnish with all reasonable promptness to the Company Chief Medical Officer written reports on the discharge of his obligations under this Agreement as and when these may he requested, and shall as and when required by him discuss with the said Chief Medical Officer the progress in and methods of providing the Services, together with all medical problems and other medical matters relating thereto.

4 The Physician shall discuss with and report to concerning, and obtain from, the Location Site Administrator specified in Part I of the Schedule hereto all necessary and requisite facilities and arrangements for the operation of this Agreement and the discharge of the Physician's obligations hereunder.

5 All communications and all information whether written, visual or oral and all other material supplied to or obtained by the Physician in the course of or as a result of the discharge of his obligations under this Agreement and all information relating to any invention, improvement, report, recommendation or advice given to the Company by the Physician in pursuance of his obligations hereunder shall be treated by the Physician as confidential and shall not be disclosed by him to any third party or published without prior written consent of the Company.

6 All intellectual and industrial property rights throughout the world in patentable and non-patentable inventions, discoveries and improvements, processes and know-how, copyright works and the like discovered or created by the Physician in the course of or as a result of the discharge of his obligations hereunder and/or (as the case may be) based whether directly or indirectly on any item of information required to be kept confidential under cl 5 hereof shall vest in and be the absolute property of the Company. Upon the request of the Company the Physician shall (at the expense of the Company) execute all documents and do all acts and things required to vest or perfect the vesting of such property rights legally and exclusively in the Company or any nominee or assignee of the Company.

7 The Company will reimburse the Physician for all reasonable expenses (including without limitation travel expenses) incurred in the discharge of his obligations hereunder, provided that all such expenses will be subject to prior written approval by the Company. Expenses are to be accounted for and reimbursement will be made against vouchers approved by the Company and in accordance with relevant standard Company procedure as from time to time established and notified to the Physician.

8(*a*) This Agreement shall commence on [   ] and subject to cl 8(*b*) hereof shall terminate automatically without notice on [   ].

    (*b*) Irrespective of anything contained in cl 8(*a*) hereof each party shall be entitled to terminate this Agreement forthwith if the other party commits a material breach of any of its terms.

    (*c*) Termination of this Agreement shall be without prejudice to any obligation by one party hereof to the other which shall have accrued prior thereto.

9 The Physician undertakes that, in the event of his being unable personally to perform the Services in accordance with his obligations hereunder, he will provide by way of a substitute to perform the Services in his place a fully-qualified general medical practitioner acceptable to the Company ('Locum'), PROVIDED THAT the provision of the Locum shall be under a subcontract between the Physician and the Locum and that the rights and obligations of the Physician hereunder in relation to the Company (save as to the performance of the Services by the Physician personally) shall not be affected, nor shall the Company be obliged to pay any fees to the Locum for the provision by him of the Services.

10 For the avoidance of doubt both parties hereto confirm that the Physician enters into this Agreement as an independent contractor and that he is not nor shall for any purpose be regarded as an employee of the Company.

11 Any notice or letter sent hereunder by prepaid post to the last known address of the addressee shall be deemed to have been received three days after the day on which it was so posted.

12 The obligations imposed upon the Physician under cll 5 and 6 shall survive the expiry or termination of this Agreement.

SCHEDULE
Part I

The Physician shall provide the following medical services at the following locations and in accordance with the following time-table:-
Medical Services
Timetable
Location
Location Site Administrator

Part II

The Physician shall be paid for the provision of the Services hereunder a [quarterly] fee of £[   ] payable in arrears on the last day of each quarter, the first such payment to be made on the last day of [   ]

IN WITNESS WHEREOF the duly authorised representative of the Company and the Physician have set their hands the day and year first above written.

[   ] duly authorised representative of the Company
[   ] the Physician

Precedent 4

Agreement for design, development, testing and supply of a custom integrated circuit chip

1   Parties

1.1 [   ] Limited of [   ] ('Buyer')
1.2 [   ] Limited of [   ] ('Seller')

2   Date

This agreement shall commence on [   ] ('Commencement Date').

3   Design and development

3.1 Seller shall design and develop one custom integrated circuit chip ('the Chip') to comply with the functional specification supplied by Buyer and attached hereto as Appendix 1.

3.2 The programme for such design and development shall be as follows:

Milestone	Weeks elapsed after Commencement Date
(*a*) Seller to deliver Breadboard layout in conformity with Appendix 1 to Buyer together with detailed specificationevolved from Breadboard.	(*a*)
(*b*) Buyer to approve Breadboard and detailed specification.	(*b*)

(*c*) Seller to complete Chip layout.   (*c*)

(*d*) Seller to complete Digitising, Edits and Pattern
Generation.   (*d*)

(*e*) Seller to complete mask making.   (*e*)

4   Supply of prototypes of the Chip

4.1 Seller shall deliver to Buyer at [   ], upon the expiry of the
[   ] week after the Commencement Date the following prototypes
of the Chip:

4.2 During the fabrication of the prototypes Seller will design the hardware
and software required to test the prototypes and prepare a test schedule based
thereon to demonstrate compliance by the prototypes with the specifications
referred to in cl 3 and Seller shall submit copies of all of the aforesaid to Buyer
upon the expiry of the [   ] week after the Commencement Date.
Such test schedule shall be based upon the concept of 100% testing of production with a specified failure rate expressed in parts per million. Buyer shall
provide Seller with all reasonable assistance in drawing up the said test schedule.

4.3 Buyer shall approve the aforesaid design and test schedules upon the expiry of the [   ] week after the Commencement Date and Seller
shall test all of the prototypes in accordance with cl 4.2 and provide a signed
test report in duplicate demonstrating that all of the prototypes comply in full
with the functional specification set out in Appendix 1 hereto and the detailed
specification referred to in cl 3.2(*b*).

4.4 Buyer shall inspect the prototypes and verify the test report. Buyer shall
also carry out all further tests deemed necessary by it to verify that the circuit
contained in the Chip operates satisfactorily to Buyer in the equipment in which
it is designed to be incorporated.

4.5 Buyer shall complete the activities in cl 4.4 and formally notify Seller of
acceptance or rejection of prototypes by not later than the expiry of
[   ] weeks after receipt of the prototypes.

5   Information

Seller shall supply to Buyer all the information relating to the design, development, manufacture and use of the Chip set out in Appendix 2 hereto. Seller
shall supply the same in accordance with the time schedule also set out in the

said Appendix. For the avoidance of doubt nothing in this Agreement, including in the said Appendix, shall oblige Seller to disclose to Buyer information relating to the know-how, processes, methods or techniques used by Seller in the manufacture of the Chip.

6   Option for purchase of the chip in larger quantities

6.1 Upon completion of the activities referred to in cl 4.5 Seller and Buyer shall negotiate upon the supply of production quantities of the Chip to Buyer. If agreement is reached upon quantity and pricing (including without limitation minimum quantity per order), then orders shall be placed by Buyer on Seller in accordance with the remainder of this cl 6. If no such agreement is reached then the procedure in cl 13.1 shall apply.

6.2 Orders may be placed within a period of three years from prototype approval in accordance with cl 4.5.

6.3 Delivery for orders under this clause shall be ex works (packaging included) Seller's factory, and their terms and conditions shall unless otherwise agreed be governed by the law of England and in particular the Sale of Goods Act 1979, save in so far as the terms and conditions of this cl 6 are inconsistent therewith. In the case of any such inconsistency the terms of this cl 6 shall prevail.

6.4 Delivery time for the first such order placed hereunder shall be [   ] weeks from the date on which it is placed; and for all such orders placed thereafter [   ] weeks from the date on which they are placed.

6.5 All quantities of the Chip supplied under this clause shall conform strictly to the prototypes referred to in cl 4 and shall be manufactured in accordance with quality levels and manufacturing controls consistent with Seller's specifications under cl 3.2(*b*) and Buyer may reject all quantities of the Chip which do not comply with this subclause.

6.6 Buyer shall have the right to inspect and approve Seller's manufacturing lines and to audit Seller's quality assurance procedures.

6.7 Seller warrants that all quantities of the Chip supplied under this clause shall comply with the requirements of cl 6.5 and further warrants them to be free from all defects in material and workmanship for a period of [eighteen months] from date of delivery. All Chips which do not comply with the warranties contained in this subclause will be replaced free of all charges by Seller to the original point of delivery, but otherwise in accordance with and subject to this cl 6, as if they had been delivered pursuant to an order. Save as provided in this cl 6.7, all other conditions, warranties, stipulations or other statements whatsoever concerning the quantities of the Chip supplied under this clause (save as to title and quiet possession) whether express or implied, by statute, at common law or otherwise howsoever, are hereby excluded; in particular (but without limitation of the foregoing) Seller grants no warranties regarding the fitness for purpose, performance, use, nature or quality of the said quantities of the Chips, whether express or implied, by statute at common law or otherwise howsoever.

6.8 Seller hereby agrees that the option contained in this Clause may be exercised not only by Buyer but also by any company controlled by, controlling or in common control with Buyer.

6.9 Seller hereby agrees that for a period of three years from prototype approval in accordance with cl 4.5 it will not sell the Chip in any quantities other than to Buyer or (pursuant to cl 6.8) to any company controlled by, controlling or in common control with Buyer.

6.10 Clauses 11, 14 and 15 of this Agreement shall apply to each order for quantities of the Chips placed under this cl 6.

7 Payment terms

7.1 For the design development and supply of prototypes of the Chip, Buyer shall make the following payments to Seller:
7.1.1 £ [   ] upon the Commencement Date;
7.1.2 £ [   ] upon delivery of prototypes by Seller in accordance with cl 4.1;
7.1.3 £ [   ] upon completion of acceptance of prototypes of the Chip by Buyer in accordance with cll 4.4 and 4.5.

7.2 Where completion of the relevant activity within the original time for completion in accordance with cl 3 or 4 as the case may be has not been achieved by reason of any failure or delay on the part of Seller or the presence of any defect which in any such case results in delay or causes Buyer to reject instead of granting approval as required at any stage under this Agreement then Seller shall perform all necessary work at Seller's expense (unless Buyer terminates this Agreement pursuant to cl 13.2) to rectify such failure, delay or defect and enable the completion of the relevant activity by Seller or the grant of the relevant approval by Buyer to take place as the case may be.

7.3 Where completion of the relevant activity referred in cl 7.1 has been delayed as stated in cl 7.2 no payment shall be made under cl 7.1 until the relevant completion is achieved in accordance with cl 7.2.

7.4 Seller shall notify Buyer of completion of all milestones and scheduled activities, in accordance with cll 3 and 4, upon their completion, and shall also immediately notify Buyer of any actual or foreseeable difficulties which may affect completion of any activity in accordance with the relevant clauses.

8   Second sourcing

8.1 Seller shall retain the production photo masks, test tapes, interface boards for testing and all other manufacturing data reasonably required for another party to produce production quantities of the Chip. In the event that Seller shall elect no longer to produce the Chip for Buyer (including any company controlled by, controlling or in common control with Buyer) Seller will provide Buyer or its designee the foregoing documentation, material and information immediately upon demand, and provide Buyer or its designee with a non-exclusive royalty free licence to produce the Chip, and to use and copy the said documentation, material and information for this purpose.

8.2 Should any end user of equipment incorporating the Chip refuse to approve the equipment and/or the use of the Chip therein unless Buyer (or any company controlled by, controlling or in common control with Buyer as the case may be) guarantees that there will be a second source available for production of the Chip other than Seller then upon demand by Buyer (or any company controlled by, controlling or in common control with Buyer as the case may be), Seller will provide Buyer or its designee the foregoing documentation, material and information, and provide Buyer or its designee with a non-exclusive royalty free licence to produce the Chip, and to use and copy the said documentation, material and information for this purpose.

9   Changes

Seller shall not make any changes to its manufacturing process, materials, testing procedures and agreed tooling specifications which may affect the performance or reliability of the Chip without Buyer's written approval. Buyer's approval shall not be unreasonably withheld provided that Seller has at its own expense demonstrated that such change will have no detrimental effect on the performance and reliability of the Chip.

10   Copyright

The copyright of all drawings and documents supplied to Seller hereunder by or on behalf of Buyer are deemed to be the property of Buyer. All documents, drawings, programmes, artworks and photomasks generated by Seller for the purpose of fulfilling the obligations of this Agreement (and all intellectual property rights therein, of whatever nature and wherever in the world subsisting) shall be owned by and vest in Seller but subject to the rights of Buyer contained in cl 8 hereof. Further Buyer shall have a non-exclusive royalty free licence to use and copy all copyright material contained in the information to be transferred to Buyer by Seller under cl 3.2 hereof for all purposes throughout the world without limit of time.

11   Third party intellectual property rights

11.1 Each party undertakes and agrees to compensate the other for any expense, damage or loss suffered as a result of any claims or proceedings against the other, regarding patents, copyright or any other intellectual property rights owned by a third party, resulting from the use of any documentation or information supplied by that party hereunder to the other.

11.2 Seller undertakes and agrees to compensate Buyer for any expense, damage or loss suffered as a result of any claim or proceedings against Buyer regarding patents, copyright or any other intellectual property rights owned by a third party, resulting from the use or sale of the prototypes or any production quantities of the Chip purchased under cl 6 hereof, or by the exercise in any manner whatsoever of the rights enjoyed by Buyer under this Agreement.

12   Assignment

Seller shall not give, assign or sublet any part of the design or development of the Chip to a third party without prior consent of Buyer.

13   Termination

13.1 If no agreement is reached as to purchase of production quantities under cl 6.1, this Agreement shall terminate and Buyer will pay to Seller reasonable costs incurred by Buyer in carrying out his obligations hereunder up to the date of termination. Termination costs shall not exceed [   ], and payments made under cl 7.1 shall be deducted therefrom.

13.2 Termination of this Agreement by Buyer in the event of Seller's failure to perform its obligations under cll 3.2 and 4 other than by reason of an event covered by cl 14 (*force majeure*) shall excuse Buyer from any further payments not already made under cl 7.1 hereof at the date of such termination and further shall entitle Buyer to recover from Seller all reasonable increased expenses (if any) incurred by reason of the completion of the work contemplated hereunder by a third party.

13.3 Termination of this Agreement under this clause shall not be deemed to constitute termination of those provisions including but not limited to cll 8, 10 and 11, which envisage continued performance notwithstanding termination of the remainder of the Agreement.

14   Force majeure

14.1 Neither party shall be liable to the other party for loss, injury, delay, expenses, damages or other casualty suffered by the other party in the event of any delay or failure of the first party in performing its obligations under this Agreement or an order placed pursuant to cl 6 as a result of general strikes, riots, storms, fires, acts of God or Government, [technical problems which render it impracticable for the party concerned to perform in accordance with this Agreement or that order] or any reason beyond the reasonable control of the first party, provided that the first party shall have given the other party prompt notice in writing of the occurrence of any such event or cause and of its discontinuance.

14.2 In the event that such cause has prevented or is likely to prevent the party from performing its obligations for a period of more than 90 days then the other party may terminate this Agreement (and in such cases the procedure in cl 13.1 shall then apply), or may cancel the relevant order, as the case may be.

15   Limitations of liability

15.1 Subject to cl 15.3 and notwithstanding anything contained in this Agreement (other than cl 15.3), in no circumstances [except where Seller has wilfully refused to perform any of its obligations under this Agreement or under any order placed pursuant to cl 6] shall Seller be liable, in contract, tort (including negligence or breach of statutory duty) or otherwise howsoever, and whatever the cause thereof, (i) for any loss of profit, business, contracts, revenues, or anticipated savings, or (ii) for any special indirect or consequential damage of any nature whatsoever.

15.2 Subject to cl 15.3 and notwithstanding anything contained in this Agreement (other than cl 15.3), [except where Seller has wilfully refused to perform any of its obligations under this Agreement or under any order placed pursuant to cl 6] Seller's liability to the Purchaser, in contract, tort (including negligence or breach of statutory duty) or howsoever otherwise arising, shall in respect of this Agreement be limited to the total amounts payable under this Agreement pursuant to cl 7 or £[   ] whichever is the greater, and in respect of any order placed pursuant to cl 6 be limited to the value of the order or £[   ] whichever is the greater.

15.3 If and to the extent that s 6 and/or 7(3A) of the Unfair Contract Terms Act 1977 applies to this Agreement, or to an order placed pursuant to cl 6, no provision of this Agreement or that order (as the case may be) shall operate or be construed to operate so as to exclude or restrict the liability of Seller for breach of cl 11, or for breach of the applicable warranties as to title and quiet possession implied into this Agreement or that order (as the case may be) by s 12(1) of the Sale of Goods Act 1979, or s 2(1) of the Supply of Goods and Services Act 1982, whichever Act is applicable.

16 Notices

Any notice to be given hereunder shall be sent by first class mail, telex or telegram to the addresses set out in cl 1 or such other addresses as the parties may specify.

17 Non-waiver of rights

The failure of Buyer or Seller to insist, in any one or more instances, upon the performance of any provisions of this Agreement shall not be construed as a waiver or relinquishment of either party's right to future performance of such provision, and the other party's obligation in respect of such future performance shall continue in full force and effect.

18 Applicable law

The Agreement shall in all respects be governed by and construed in accordance with the laws of England.

19   Entire agreement

This Agreement sets forth and shall constitute the entire agreement between both parties with respect to the subject matter thereof, and (except in the case of fraud) shall supersede any and all promises and representations made by one party to the other concerning the work to be performed under this Agreement, and the terms applicable thereto. This Agreement may not be released, discharged, supplemented, interpreted, amended or modified in any manner, except by an instrument in writing, signed by a duly authorised officer or representative of each of the parties hereto, except as is specifically provided otherwise in this Agreement.

Signed for and on behalf of Seller by   Signed for and on behalf of Buyer by

Name [   ]   Name [   ]

Chapter 4

Standard conditions for the supply of a system

4.1   Introduction

This chapter puts together the matters discussed in the three preceding chapters, to produce a contract (set out as Precedent 2) for the supply of a complex turnkey system, including some civil works. Most of the issues discussed already arise again, and various versions of clauses already used in previous precedents will be seen, in a differing and, in some cases, more extended form. Thus this precedent can be used not only in its own right but also as a source for standard clauses to amplify the precedents in the preceding chapters, if longer standard form contracts are required. Therefore, the emphasis in this chapter will not be on issues which have already been covered (even though they will arise in relation to system contracts as well) but on the special problems thrown up by system contracts.

However, one of the most important issues relating to system contracts is the way in which the specification is drawn up for the system which is to be supplied. This is dealt with as a preliminary matter by the definition study contract set out as Precedent 1.

4.2   Precedent 1

When dealing with the supply of a system, the most common area of dispute between the parties relates to the specification of the system. There are two sorts of system specifications.

First, the functional specification spells out what the system does (eg a central heating and air conditioning system, which has the capacity to provide a uniform temperature of 25 degrees centigrade throughout a given building, when the exterior temperature is no higher than 40 degrees centigrade, and no lower than minus ten degrees centigrade). The functional specification is likely in most cases to be much more complex, and go into much more detail about the required parameters for the system's performance than the simple example given here.

Secondly, the system design specification, using the functional specification as a basis, describes in detail the plant and equipment which is needed to achieve a system which will perform in accordance with the functional specification (eg a boiler and a refrigeration plant, blowers, ducting and ventilation grills for the circulation of hot and cold air, and a thermostatic control system driven by a variety of micro-processors and computers, all of specified size and capacity to achieve the operating parameters of the functional specification, and of a size and layout which fits properly into the designated building).

If the customer later complains that the system is not performing satisfactorily, then, if one leaves aside the question of defective workmanship and materials, there are two reasons possible. Either the functional specification was not in accordance with the customer's requirements, but he did not understand this, or the system design specification was drawn up incorrectly and specified plant and equipment which did not deliver what was required in the functional specification.

A second area of dispute which can arise during the course of the performance of the system contract, also relates to a mismatch between the functional specification and the system design specification. The contractor may discover that the system design specification does not deliver the functional specification required, or, worse still, that it is technically impossible to design a system which does deliver the functional specification. If it is possible to deliver the functional specification with a different system design, who is responsible for any increased cost and delay occasioned by the change? If it is not possible to deliver the functional specification by any system at all, in the current state of the relevant technology, should the contract be terminated, and on what terms, and which party is responsible for abortive costs and expenses?

Such disputes, quite apart from customer dissatisfaction, can cost the contractor large sums of money, particularly if he has contracted to deliver a functional specification and has costed the contract price with reference to an incorrect system design specification. For instance, in the example above, if the boiler is of too small a capacity to heat the building to 25 degrees centigrade, the contractor would under these circumstances have to bear the cost of removing the existing boiler, and supplying and installing a larger and more expensive one of sufficient capacity.

The only way to avoid such disputes is to ensure (before the contract is entered into) that the functional specification is what the customer wants, that the functional specification is technically capable of realisation by a system design specification, and that the actual system design specification is capable of delivering the functional specification. It is not until all of these matters are sorted out that the contractor is really in a position to quote properly for the supply of the relevant system, and to take on the contractual liability to supply it at a fixed price.

The best method of dealing with these issues is to split the process into two stages. At the first stage, the customer and the contractor work together to evolve the functional specification and the system design specification under what is often called a definition study contract. At the second stage, based on these specifications, the parties enter into the system supply contract.

A standard definition study contract is set out in Precedent 1. The heart of the contract is cl 2. Under cl 2.1 the parties first produce the functional specification based upon a basic business requirement provided by the customer. This basic requirement must be the responsibility of the customer because he knows his own business requirements better than anyone else, and should take responsibility for defining them. Clause 2.1 provides for an interactive process by which the contractor draws up and submits, and, if necessary, resubmits, the functional specification to the customer until the customer approves it. The customer pays for any modifications and re-submissions, since presumably they are caused because he is changing his initial requirements, unless the need for changes arises because the contractor has misinterpreted the business requirements specification. Once approved, the functional specification is the responsibility of the customer (cl 2.1.3).

The creation of the system design specification under cl 2.2 follows the same process, using the functional specification as the basis. There are similar opportunities for approval by the customer, and provision for changes if required. Once approved, and subject to the negotiation and placing of the system contract (set out in Precedent 2) the contractor is obliged to supply the system in accordance with the system design specification. Clause 4 provides that under the system contract, the contractor will (notwithstanding the customer's approval of the system design specification) be responsible for ensuring that the system design specification specifies a system which will perform in accordance with the functional specification. Thus the customer is responsible for correctly specifying what he wants to achieve (functional specification) and the contractor is responsible for correctly specifying the means of achieving this (system design specification). This is an obvious and equitable distribution of responsibility. The only exception to this rule is if the customer chooses to meddle in the system design specification, and impose his view of the correct design against the advice of the contractor. To the extent that this occurs, the contractor should not be liable for the relevant elements of the system design specification (cl 3).

Clause 5 has standard provisions specifying milestones for performance of the contractual obligations, and excuses for delay caused by *force majeure*. However, in addition, cl 5.5 provides for the contractor to terminate the contract, on the same basis as if the contract were terminated for *force majeure*, if the contractor discovers that it is technically impossible to produce a system design specification which delivers the relevant functional specification. This clause is vitally important for the contractor, since it enables him, at an early stage, to avoid getting involved in projects which cannot be realised in practice.

Clause 7 provides that both the functional specification and the system design specification belong to the contractor. This prevents the customer taking them and using them to enter into a contract for the supply of the system with another party. The contractor will not wish, as a rule, to go through the work and expense of the definition study, often for very little profit, if he cannot realise the profits involved in the actual supply of the system.

Clause 8, in any event, imposes stringent limitations of liability, to ensure that no liability in respect of any specification arises under the definition study contract, but only under the system contract, in the event that it is placed with the contractor (see cl 8.2). As a safeguard, given the potential magnitude of the risk inherent in specifying systems, cll 8.3 and 8.4 contain standard provisions excluding economic loss, and capping liability by reference to a sum of money or the contract price, whichever is the greater, as additional safeguards. Even if the relevant definition study contract is placed on standard terms (as opposed to being fully negotiated) so that s 3 of the UCTA applies, there seems little prospect that, given the purpose of the definition study, and the clarity with which the exclusions of liability, and the reasons for them, are spelled out, that cl 8 will fail to pass the test of reasonableness. This is particularly so given that (under cl 2.2.3) the contractor offers to take on proper additional liabilities if he is awarded the system contract.

In some cases, the customer will agree with the contractor that, following the definition study and the creation of the specifications, the system contract will be put out to competitive tender to a number of contractors (including the contractor) based upon the specifications. Public authorities, for instance, are now required in many cases to put such contracts out to competitive tender under the EC public procurement directives. These directives may also constrain the customer in the instructions he gives to the contractor who draws up the specifications. For instance, he will not be able to permit the contractor to specify proprietary equipment which only that contractor can supply. To do so would be to prevent, in effect, other contractors from tendering, because they could not comply with the specification as drawn.

Where this procedure is agreed, it may be appropriate to vest ownership of the specifications in the customer, or at least for the contractor to permit their use in the manner contemplated. In either event cl 7 would be modified accordingly. However, if this occurs cl 8 is doubly important, because if the contractor does not win the tender, then the winning contractor and the customer should apportion the risk of inaccuracy in the specifications between them as they see fit. The contractor who drew them up should not take this risk, given that he will enjoy none of the profits of the system contract, and be unable to take advantage of the exclusion clauses (if any) built into it.

In these circumstances, the contractors should also seek an indemnity from the customer against third party claims in respect of inaccuracies in the functional specification and the system design specification, particularly from the successful tenderer who wins the system contract, and from his subcontractors. Clause 6.3 of Precedent 2 in Chapter 3, should be used, suitably adapted, and reference should be made to the discussion on that clause in that chapter.

4.3   Precedent 2

Having created and approved the functional specification and the system design specification for the system, the parties are in a position to negotiate the price and the timescales for its supply under the terms of the system contract set out as Precedent 2. Precedent 2 is a complicated and extensive document, and is probably best analysed clause by clause.

Clause 1 lists the principal definitions used in the contract. It builds upon the definitions used in Precedent 1. The operation of the contract is tied to three defined specifications, for the function of the system, for the design of the system, and for the civil works needed to make the site ready for the installation of the system. The other definitions support and interwork with these three main definitions, and are all to some extent interrelated. No changes should be made to any one of the definitions without considering the impact of the change on other definitions.

Clause 2 lists the basic obligations of both parties. The contractor supplies the system in accordance with the contract, and the customer pays the agreed price.

Clause 3 deals with the passing of ownership and risk. It should be noted that the provisions in this clause would not be acceptable to many customers, particularly given the schedule of payments set out in cl 6. Many customers require property to vest in equipment as it is delivered to site, or even, where advance payments are made, as it is constructed in the contractor's factory.

Clause 4 provides detailed provisions dealing with the apportionment of liability for loss, damage, death and personal injury caused during the course of the contractor's performance of the contract (including while on the customer's premises in the warranty period). The provisions of s 2(1) of the UCTA have no application, except in the unlikely event that the customer is a natural person. Where this is the case appropriate provisions providing unlimited liability for death or personal injury caused to the customer by the contractor's negligence should be added.

The price and payment terms in cll 5 and 6 are of the utmost importance to the contractor. Particularly crucial is to obtain a payment schedule which at least keeps pace with, if it is not in advance of, the cash spent by the contractor in the performance of the contract. It is not sufficient for the contractor to negotiate a favourable contract price, if the payment terms are so unfavourable that poor cashflow causes the contractor to lose all his profit in interest payments to his bank.

Clause 7 should be read in conjunction with cl 6. Many long term contracts require price adjustment clauses if the fixed price is not to be rendered unprofitable in the course of performance. Clause 7 deals not only with inflation or the fluctuation in material prices, but also with increased costs due to changes in legislation, or factors within the control of the customer. In the UK, inflation is currently less of a problem than in the past, but system contracts can often stretch over a number of years, in which case even modest inflation rates can eat into profits. In any event the other causes of cost increase are still an issue. In other countries, where inflation is much higher, such clauses are absolutely vital.

The provisions of cl 7 use examples of various indices and percentages, but, in practice, these, and indeed the actual terms of the clause, will have to be adjusted to deal with the particular issues on escalation affecting each contract.

Clauses 8–11 deal with the delivery schedule, and the consequences of delay, including a liquidated damages clause. Such clauses are of course of benefit to both parties, since the customer has a ready remedy, and the contractor has a cap to his liability for delay under the contract.

Clause 12 deals with that most difficult question of acceptance. Proper and simple methods of acceptance are vital to the contractor, because he is not discharged of his basic performance obligations under the contract until he has achieved acceptance. It follows that acceptance should come about as a result of compliance with objective, easily demonstrable criteria, and not as a result of persuading the customer that he should be satisfied with the contractor's performance. Clause 12 proceeds on the basis that the civil works and the system are all accepted at the same time by means of a series of acceptance tests that have been specified as a schedule to the contract. The key to the clause is cl 12.2. The purpose of the tests is to demonstrate compliance with the relevant specifications, and nothing else. If compliance is demonstrated, the customer must issue the acceptance certificate. This is obviously fair, given that after the work carried out under the relevant definition study contract, compliance with the relevant specifications should be all that the customer requires. The model of this clause should always be used where there has been a prior definition study contract. Where this provision is used, and the acceptance tests are agreed in advance, the contractor knows what he has to satisfy, and there is little room for dispute.

However, acceptance tests which are designed to deal with vaguer issues, such as that the system is operating both in accordance with the specification and 'to the satisfaction of the customer', should be avoided. This is especially so when acceptance tests to meet such criteria are not agreed before the contract is signed, and attached as a schedule to it, but left to be negotiated between the parties during the course of the contract. Here the contractor is at the mercy of the customer, and acceptance becomes a matter of satisfying the subjective demands of the customer rather than demonstrating compliance with objective criteria. Such provisions are, in particular, completely inappropriate where there has been a prior definition study contract, because, as stated previously, the customer has had all the opportunity he needed at that stage to see that his various requirements and concerns were built into the functional specification. Once this has been dealt with, nothing remains for the contractor except to demonstrate that the system supplied delivers a performance in accordance with that functional specification. If it does, the customer should have no alternative but to accept it, since he is getting what he contracted for.

Clause 13 is an elaborate warranty, but its basis is again simply that of the obligations in relation to the various specifications to which performance of the contract is tied. Clause 13.1 provides the warranty that the contractor undertook to give in the definition study contract (cl 8.2 of Precedent 1). Here the contractor now has to warrant that the system design specification specifies a system which will perform in accordance with the functional specification, and that the system he actually supplies complies with the system design specification. Additionally, the civil works, and individual components of the system are warranted to comply with the relevant specifications, and there are some more general warranties, in relation to these aspects of the contract, relating to materials and workmanship and reasonable care and skill in carrying out work under the contract. These latter may be adjusted to cater for the particular contract, but it is hardly likely that the contractor will be able to contract out of them.

The remainder of cl 13 is standard and self-explanatory, if somewhat detailed, but the definition of 'Defect' needs mention. The defined term 'Defect' relates only to those defects which the contractor is liable to remedy under the contract. The term 'defect' (uncapitalised) bears its general meaning. This is why the term 'defect' (uncapitalised) is used in cl 13.3 in the provisions relating to exclusion of liability.

The matters relating to spare parts, support and consumables covered by cll 14 and 15 are not part of the contractor's warranty obligations, but instead are chargeable items provided as a post-acceptance service. Such provision will require additional contract terms to be drawn up. This precedent provides either for the use of the contractor's standard terms and conditions of sale, or for the use of specimen contracts which would be attached as schedules to the contract. The maintenance contract, for instance, would be along the lines of Precedent 1 of Chapter 3 and the support service could be entered into under a contract based on Precedent 2 of Chapter 3.

Termination under system contracts usually takes place for three reasons: breach, insolvency or convenience. Clause 16 deals with all three issues. Its provisions are necessarily complicated because it has to deal with the unravelling of a complex contract which, it is likely, will have been part performed at the date of termination. Either party has the right to terminate for breach, but only the customer can terminate for convenience. This latter issue should not bother the contractor, since the question of impossibility of performance for technical reasons will already have been considered and dismissed upon the successful performance of the relevant definition study contract.

Under cl 16.4, where the customer terminates for breach or insolvency, he is entitled to recover his direct losses as a result of such termination, to have the contract performed by someone else, and to recover the additional costs of this course of action (if any) from the contractor. The provisions of cl 16.4 are designed to put the customer in the position of being able to have the work performed elsewhere, and to take advantage (if he wishes) of the contractor's part performance, subject to a fair and reasonable payment.

On the other hand, cl 16.5 enables the contractor who terminates for breach or insolvency of the customer, or who suffers a termination for convenience at the hands of his customer, to recover his lost bargain by charging cancellation charges which include an element of profit. Here cl 16.7.1.3 should be noted, which provides for compensation for loss of profits and overheads on the un-completed portion of the contract. Most contractors would regard this as fair, since full payment (even with profit element) of work completed to date (see cl 16.7.1.1) does not take account of the lost opportunity cost of the contractor; he could have entered into another contract which he would have performed in full, but instead he concentrated his resources on the customer. Customers find it hard to resist this provision in cases of breach, but often try to do so when contemplating termination for convenience. Clause 16.7 also provides that the contractor, may, but is not obliged, to permit the customer to make use of work performed to date, subject to payment.

Special note should be taken of cll 16.6 and 16.7.5. Whatever the circumstances of termination, the contractor should not permit copyright in software used on, or in the operation of, the system to fall into the ownership of the customer. These clauses provide that all such software remains subject to the relevant licence provisions set out in cl 17, and that the customer must pay a licence fee for their use. Clause 16.7.5 goes somewhat further than cl 16.6, in requiring a licence fee for all products not just software. Such extension may have little practical applicability, but is justified (where it does apply) because under cl 16.7 the relevant breach or termination is the responsibility of the customer.

Clause 17 deals with all of the issues in the contract relating to know-how and intellectual property rights. Clauses 17.1–17.5 inclusive deal with the question of the contractor's liability for claims that the system infringes third party intellectual property rights. The same considerations as to breach of the warranties of good title and quiet possession arise under this system contract as under the conditions of sale in Chapter 2, and the relevant discussions in Chapter 1, and in Chapter 2 in relation to cll 5 and 10 of Precedent 1, apply. In this precedent the option of warranting only such title as the contractor may have in relation to infringement of third party intellectual property rights has been followed. Given the complexity of systems, and the possible unknown and unquantifiable exposures, this seems the safest course.

Clauses 17.6 and 17.8, continuing the principles of cl 7 of Precedent 1, provide that ownership of the intellectual property rights in all items supplied under the contract, including the specifications and the system itself, remain with the contractor. This intellectual property is the contractor's most important resource for carrying on his business, and for fulfilling future contracts with other customers. Although many customers will seek to own at the least intellectual property generated or arising during the performance of work (eg special bespoke development work) under the contract, this should be resisted if at all possible. However, the customer does need certain rights to the contractor's intellectual property (particularly in relation to software) or he will not be able to use the system in the way that the contract intended. The contractor thus grants him suitable licences, in return for licence fees, and subject to suitable controls. Clause 17.7 deals with this, and references the pre-agreed licence terms which are attached as schedules to the contract. Finally, cl 17.9 provides short-form confidentiality obligations binding both parties.

Clauses 18–21 inclusive are concerned with procedural matters and the general implementation of the work under the contract.

Clause 18 provides for the two parties to appoint project managers, who will administer and monitor the progress of the contract. In order for the parties to co-operate smoothly in the discharge of the contract, information, defined in the contract as Contract Implementation Information, needs to pass between them, for instance in relation to the state and condition of the site. Errors in such information can cause delays to the contract and extra expense. Clause 19 provides that the party receiving such information is entitled to rely on it (although he should point out errors if he notices them) and that he should be compensated for any costs incurred because of errors in it; additionally, where relevant, he should be granted an extension of time to take account of the time lost through acting on incorrect information. However, neither party should be responsible for damages at large for such errors. This is particularly important for the contractor, since he must take care that such information does not somehow become embodied in the specifications for which he is responsible under the contract. Clause 19.3 and the definition of 'Contract Implementation Information' taken together obviate this danger.

Clauses 20 and 21 deal with both the carrying out of the civil works on the site where the system is to be installed, and the delivery, installation and commissioning of the system itself on the site. The definition of the 'Works' comprises all of these matters. It should be noted that this precedent is not as a whole suited to a situation where complex civil works are required, such as the building of a whole factory. The provisions in this precedent are adequate to cover the supply of a system accompanied by minor civil works, such as the installation of an environmentally controlled area in which a computer system is to be installed, or the engineering works associated with installing a central heating and air conditioning system. Where more complex civil works are required, the standard JCT or RIBA contract forms should be used as appropriate. Since the customer is in control of the site, cl 20 deals with the conditions for the contractor's access to the site, and how he will conduct the work on the site, while cl 21 permits the customer to suspend and resume performance of the Works, subject to appropriate notice and compensation.

Clause 22 sets out a procedure for contract variations. It is based on the principle that each variation may entail changes to the price, timescales and specifications of the contract, and that therefore no variation should be implemented until its effect on the contract has been assessed, and all these matters agreed. Clause 22.6 is particularly important. If the customer insists on a variation which would give rise to a defect (as defined—ie a defect (uncapitalised term) for which the contractor would be responsible under the contract) the contractor is under no obligation to implement such a variation, and if he does so may disclaim responsibility for the consequences of its implementation, and exclude his relevant liabilities under cl 13.1 (warranty). Following on from this concept, cl 23 makes it clear that the customer is totally liable for the functional specification (as was contemplated by cl 2.1.3 of Precedent 1).

Clauses 24–32 inclusive deal with those matters of general importance under the contract which are often referred to as boilerplate, and are largely self-explanatory. The matters that they cover are dealt with in other ways in many of the other precedents in Chapters 2 and 3, but the clauses used here are more detailed, given the importance and complexity of a system contract.

A few detailed points arise. It will be noticed that cll 25 and 30 are general exclusion clauses. Clause 25 deals with economic loss, while cl 30 is an entire agreement clause, drafted to deal with the issues raised by *Witter Ltd v TBP Industries Ltd* (1994) unreported, 15 July, ChD (Ch 1990-W-5354) as discussed in Chapter 1, which also excludes implied warranties and representations and all legal remedies for breach other than those expressly provided under the contract. It will have been noted that where clauses in the contract deal with a particular issue they also included a provision limiting the liability of the contractor to the express remedies in the clause (see for example cl 17.5 in relation to infringement of third party intellectual property rights). However, given the various issues which arise under the system contract and its complexity, the addition of general exclusion clauses as well is considered prudent.

The drafting of these general exclusion clauses takes account of the issues relating to blanket exclusion of liability under the UCTA discussed in Chapters 1 and 2, by the inclusion of cl 30.4.

Clause 25.2 is necessary because the remedies upon termination contained in cl 16 do have an element of compensation for economic loss, and, without the special provisions of cl 25.2, the general exclusion of economic loss under cl 25.1 would conflict with these provisions.

Clause 26 deals in detail with events of *force majeure*; not only those which delay or make it impossible to perform the contract, but also those which make it more difficult or expensive to perform, but do not preclude performance altogether. Because of the complex nature of a systems contract, it is not possible simply to permit suspension of the contract. The two parties must try to work around the problem, and treat extensions to timescale, and increased costs, as contract variations to be dealt with under cl 22.

Clause 28 deals with waiver and variation in a standard manner. Clause 28.2 prohibits all variations or amendments to the contract except in writing in the prescribed form. It is true that these clauses are of doubtful legal validity in that it is possible for the parties to agree to vary the contract by some different procedure (including an oral agreement). If the purported variation can be properly evidenced and is legally enforceable then it will have effect as varying not only the relevant parts of the contract, but also the variation procedure in cl 28.2 itself. The real point about cl 28.2 is that it lays down a procedure which the parties should follow as a matter of good contract management, and it makes it necessary for the party relying on any variation falling outside the clause to produce very strong evidence to rebut the presumption that the 'variation' was in fact regarded by the other party as an informal concession and not legally binding.

Clause 31 is a notice clause which deals with the points about service of notice which were discussed in Chapter 2 in relation particularly to service by electronic means and the judgment in *Mondial Shipping and Chartering BV v Astarte Shipping Ltd* [1995] CLC 1011.

Finally, it should be noted that cl 32 submits all disputes to the court for resolution after a period in which the parties try to solve the dispute themselves. Many system contracts favour the insertion of arbitration clauses, but in practice, in many cases, arbitration is more time consuming and expensive than litigation in court, and with a less certain outcome. Also, one of the best methods of concentrating the minds of the parties to solve their problem is for them to realise that, at least in the absence of actual agreement at the time to put the matter in question to an arbitrator, the only way forward is to go to court.

Precedent 1

Standard definition study contract relating to the design and specification of a system

Parties

[   ] Limited, whose registered office is at [   ] ('THE CONTRACTOR').

[   ] Limited, whose registered office is at [   ] ('THE CUSTOMER').

1   Definitions and interpretation

1.1 In this Contract the following terms shall have the following meanings:

'Contract Price' means the contract price (which excludes Value Added Tax) set out in Appendix B;

'Functional Specification' means the specification to be produced pursuant to and in accordance with the Contract, which sets out the functions which the Customer requires to be performed by means of a system to be obtained from the Contractor;

'Intellectual Property Rights' means patents, registered and unregistered designs, copyright and all other intellectual property protection (other than trade marks) wherever in the world enforceable;

'Know-how' means all inventions, discoveries, improvements and processes (whether patentable or non-patentable), copyright works (including without limitation computer programs), designs (whether or not registered or registrable) and all other technical information of whatever nature;

'Product Description' means that edition of a standard document published by THE CONTRACTOR, in force at the date of signature of the Contract, giving

the description and specifications of a standard Product which THE CON-
TRACTOR sells generally on the open market;
'Product Specification' means each of those specifications incorporated by
reference in, or attached as part of, the System Design Specification, which
give the description and specifications of a Product which is to be specially
developed, modified or adapted by THE CONTRACTOR for incorporation in
the System;
'Products' means all of the items of hardware and software comprising the
System, and 'Product' shall be construed accordingly;
'Programme' means the programme of dates, time scales and milestones set
out in Appendix B in accordance with which the parties are to discharge their
various obligations under the Contract;
'Specifications' means the Functional Specification, the System Design Specification, Product Descriptions and Product Specifications;
'System' means the system specified in the System Design Specification;
'System Design Specification' means the specification to be produced pursuant to and in accordance with the Contract, which specifies the description,
design, and specifications of a system which performs the functions set out in
the Functional Specification. The System Design Specification is not a Product Description, or Product Specification, but it will incorporate the same by
reference (as relevant) in respect of the Products.

1.2 The headings and titles in the Contract are for descriptive purposes only,
and shall not control or alter the meaning of the Contract as set forth in the text
thereof, and do not in any way limit or amplify the terms of the Contract.

1.3 Throughout the Contract, whenever required by context (including, without limitation, in relation to one of the aforesaid defined terms) the use of the
singular number shall be construed to include the plural, and the use of any
gender shall include all genders.

1.4 The Appendices to the Contract constitute an integral part thereof.

1.5 All references to Conditions or Appendices, are references to Conditions
or Appendices of the Contract.

2   Creation and approval of specifications

2.1 Functional Specification.
2.1.1 THE CONTRACTOR shall prepare the Functional Specification in consultation with THE CUSTOMER, based upon a business requirement specification produced by or on behalf of THE CUSTOMER, and submit the same to
THE CUSTOMER for approval.
2.1.2 After receipt of the Functional Specification, THE CUSTOMER shall

either approve it, or notify THE CONTRACTOR of the reasons why it does not approve it.

2.1.3 If THE CUSTOMER notifies THE CONTRACTOR that it does not approve the Functional Specification, THE CONTRACTOR shall modify and re-submit the Functional Specification for approval, at THE CUSTOMER's cost unless THE CONTRACTOR has incorrectly reflected the relevant business requirement specification in the Functional Specification; upon such resubmission the provisions of cl 2.1.2 above shall thereupon apply to such resubmission.

2.1.4 In any event, THE CUSTOMER shall be responsible for the Functional Specification, including, without limitation, for its accuracy and its compliance with THE CUSTOMER's requirements in respect of the use to which the System will be put by THE CUSTOMER and its fitness for such use.

2.2 System Design Specification.

2.2.1 After approval of the Functional Specification THE CONTRACTOR shall prepare and submit the relevant System Design Specification to THE CUSTOMER for approval.

2.2.2 After receipt of the System Design Specification, THE CUSTOMER shall either approve it, or notify THE CONTRACTOR of the reasons why it does not approve it.

2.2.3 If THE CUSTOMER notifies THE CONTRACTOR that it does approve the System Design Specification, then, subject to the agreement between and entry into by the parties of a formal legally binding contract for the supply of the System in accordance with such System Design Specification, THE CONTRACTOR shall proceed with the supply of the System in accordance with such System Design Specification.

2.2.4 If THE CUSTOMER notifies THE CONTRACTOR that it does not approve the System Design Specification, THE CONTRACTOR shall modify and re-submit the System Design Specification for approval, at THE CUSTOMER's cost unless THE CONTRACTOR has incorrectly reflected the Functional Specification in the System Design Specification; upon such resubmission the provisions of cl 2.2.2 shall thereupon apply to such resubmission.

3   Disclaimer of the customer's design

Where THE CONTRACTOR is required to include any design provided by THE CUSTOMER in the System Design Specification, THE CONTRACTOR shall be deemed to have accepted responsibility for such design as though it were part of the System Design Specification produced by THE CONTRACTOR unless within 30 days of receipt of the design, it notifies THE CUSTOMER that it does not accept such responsibility and specifies the reasons for non-acceptance.

4   The contractor's design responsibility

Subject to cl 3, THE CONTRACTOR will, under any contract for the supply of the System entered into between the parties pursuant to cl 2.2.3 assume responsibility (subject to and in accordance with the terms of the said contract) for ensuring that the System Design Specification correctly specifies a System which will perform in accordance with the relevant Functional Specification on which it is based.

5   The programme

5.1 The parties shall carry out their obligations under the Contract in accordance with the Programme, provided that a party (the 'performing party') shall not be obliged to take any action to perform any obligation under the Contract unless and until it shall have received from the other all the information and other items detailed in the Programme as required to be supplied by the other to enable the performing party to perform the relevant obligation.

5.2 Notwithstanding cl 5.1, each party shall use reasonable endeavours to notify the other of any delay in the performance of any of its obligations under the Contract which has arisen or is anticipated to arise.

5.3 THE CONTRACTOR shall render progress reports to THE CUSTOMER and progress meetings will take place in accordance with the Programme.

5.4 A party (the 'party in delay') shall not have any liability in respect of any delay in carrying out or failure to carry out any of its obligations under the Contract caused by fire, strikes or other industrial action or dispute, acts of Government, default of suppliers or subcontractors, or any circumstances outside the reasonable control of the party in delay. The party in delay shall have the right to extend the relevant dates, time scales or milestones set out in the Programme by a period of time sufficient to take due account of the event occurring as set out in this cl 5.4. If, however, such extension continues for a period of six months the other party may, on the expiry of that period terminate the Contract forthwith upon the terms set out in cl 5.6.

5.5 Where THE CONTRACTOR is unable to produce the System Design Specification because it is not reasonably practicable for legal, commercial or technical reasons to design a system which will perform in accordance with the Functional Specification, THE CONTRACTOR shall notify THE CUSTOMER to this effect, and the parties shall either agree an appropriate amendment to the Functional Specification, the Programme and the Contract Price within thirty days (or such longer period as the parties may agree) of receipt of the relevant notice by THE CUSTOMER, or THE CONTRACTOR shall have (upon the expiry of the relevant period) the right to terminate the Contract forthwith upon the terms set out in cl 5.6.

5.6 Upon termination pursuant to cl 5.4 or 5.5, THE CONTRACTOR shall, if THE CUSTOMER has already paid to THE CONTRACTOR all or part of the Contract Price pursuant to cl 6 (the 'prepayment') be entitled to deduct from the prepayment, all costs and expenses (including cancellation charges of sub-contractors or suppliers) incurred by THE CONTRACTOR up to the date of such termination ('termination costs'). If the termination costs are less than the prepayment, THE CONTRACTOR shall (within thirty days of such termination) refund the balance of the prepayment to THE CUSTOMER, and if the termination costs are greater than the prepayment THE CUSTOMER shall (within thirty days of such termination) make a further payment to THE CONTRACTOR of either (i) the balance of the termination costs or (ii) the amount by which the Contract Price exceeds the prepayment, whichever is the lesser. For the avoidance of doubt, if the amount under (ii) is zero and no repayment has been made, THE CUSTOMER shall (within thirty days of such termination) pay to THE CONTRIBUTOR the termination costs, THE CUSTOMER shall make no further payment to THE CONTRACTOR. Except as expressly set out in this cl 5.6, neither party shall have any liability to the other, in respect of termination pursuant to cl 5.4 or 5.5 as the case may be, whether in contract, tort (including negligence or breach of statutory duty) or otherwise howsoever arising.

6   Prices and payment

THE CUSTOMER shall pay THE CONTRACTOR the Contract Price in the amount, by the instalments and upon the dates set out in Appendix B. THE CUSTOMER shall in addition to the Contract Price pay all value added tax thereon, subject to the receipt from THE CONTRACTOR of the relevant value added tax invoices.

7   Intellectual property rights and know-how

7.1 All Intellectual Property Rights and Know-how in or relating to the Specifications, whether subsisting prior to the entry into the Contract or generated or arising in the course of the Contract shall (with the sole exception of any Intellectual Property Rights or Know-how belonging to THE CUSTOMER prior to the entry into the Contract which have been incorporated into the Functional Specification or the System Design Specification) remain or vest in THE CONTRACTOR.

7.2 THE CUSTOMER shall keep the Specifications confidential, not disclose them to a third party without the consent of THE CONTRACTOR, and use and copy them only for the purposes of evaluating whether or not to enter into, and, if so decided, of entering into and executing, a contract with THE CON-TRACTOR for the supply of the System pursuant to cl 2.2.3. In the event that no such contract as aforesaid is entered into within six months of the completion of the Contract in accordance with the Programme, THE CUSTOMER shall upon the request of the Contractor return the Specifications and all copies thereof to THE CONTRACTOR.

8   Limitation of liability

8.1 The Contract has been entered into, and the Contract Price agreed between the parties, upon the basis that except for its obligations set out in cll 2.1.3 and 2.2.4 THE CONTRACTOR accepts no liability in respect of any error or defect in any Specification, or of the consequences thereof, and gives no warranty in respect thereof.

8.2 THE CONTRACTOR is willing to undertake further liability in respect of the matters set out in cl 8.1 but only pursuant to and in accordance with the terms of a contract for the supply of the System entered into pursuant to cl 2.2.3.

8.3 Notwithstanding anything contained in the Contract, each party (the 'performing party') shall have no responsibility or liability whatsoever for any loss of profit, business, revenues, contracts or anticipated savings, or for any special, consequential or indirect loss incurred or suffered by the other, arising directly or indirectly out of the Contract, or the performance, defective performance, non-performance or delayed performance by the performing party of any of its obligations under the Contract (including, without limitation, in the case of THE CONTRACTOR, the creation and provision of the Specifications and any error or defect therein).

8.4 Notwithstanding anything contained in the Contract, THE CONTRACTOR's liability in contract, tort (including negligence or breach of statutory duty) or otherwise howsoever arising by reason of or in connection with this Contract shall be limited to the Contract Price or the sum of £[   ] whichever is the greater.

Signed by the authorised representatives of THE CONTRACTOR and THE CUSTOMER on [   ]

Signature [ ]	Signature [ ]
Name [ ]	Name [ ]
Title [ ]	Title [ ]
For and on behalf of THE	For and on behalf of THE
CONTRACTOR	CUSTOMER

Precedent 2

Contract for the supply, installation and commissioning of a system

---

This Agreement (hereinafter the 'Contract') is entered into the [   ] day of [   ] 19[   ], between [   ] Limited whose registered office is at [   ] (the 'Supplier') and [   ] Limited whose registered office is situate at [   ] (the 'Customer'),

WHEREBY THE PARTIES AGREE AS FOLLOWS:

1   Definitions and interpretation

1.1 In the Contract the following terms shall be defined as follows:

'Acceptance' means the successful completion of the Acceptance Tests;

'Acceptance Certificate' means the document in the form set out in Appendix A;

'Acceptance Date' means the date upon which Acceptance occurs;

'Acceptance Tests' means the acceptance tests detailed in Appendix B;

'Civil Works' means the civil works to be carried out on and to the Site in order to prepare them so that the delivery, installation, commissioning and Acceptance of the System can take place in accordance with the Contract;

'Civil Works Specification' means the specification, attached as Appendix C, detailing the Civil Works and the site where the Works (including but not limited to the Civil Works) are to be carried out;

'Civil Works Items' means all materials, plant and equipment to be incorporated in or installed upon the Site pursuant to the execution of the Civil Works in accordance with the Civil Works Specification;

'Consumable Supplies' means any discs, magnetic media, paper, printing ribbons, inks, fluids, disposable batteries and/or any other items (whether or not of a similar nature) which are consumed during the use of the System and replaced on a periodic basis;

'Contract Implementation Information' means information (in whatever form) supplied by one party to the other party, pursuant to the Contract, for the purpose of enabling that party to perform its obligations under the Contract. For the avoidance of doubt Specifications are not Contract Implementation Information;

'Contract Price' bears the meaning set out in Condition 5;

'Defect' means any defect in the Works, the Civil Works, Civil Works Items, the Products or the System for which the Supplier is responsible by reason of its breach of one or more of the express warranties granted by it pursuant to Condition 13 of the Contract;

'Defects Correction Period' means the period of [twelve months] from the Acceptance Date;

'Equipment' means all or any of the hardware forming part of the System;

'*Force Majeure*' bears the definition set out in Condition 26.1;

'Functional Specification' means the specification, attached as Appendix D, which sets out the functions which the Customer requires to be performed by means of a system to be obtained from the Supplier;

'Intellectual Property Rights' means patents, registered and unregistered designs, copyright and all other intellectual property protection (other than trade marks) wherever in the world enforceable;

'Know-how' means all inventions, discoveries, improvements and processes (whether patentable or non-patentable), copyright works (including without limitation computer programs), designs (whether or not registered or registrable) and all other technical information of whatever nature;

'Legislation' means all statutes, statutory instruments, bye-laws, regulations and directives which are relevant to the Civil Works, Civil Works Items, the Works, Products or the System;

'Product Description' means that edition of a standard document published by the Supplier, in force at the date of signature of the Contract, giving the description and specifications of a standard Product which the Supplier sells generally on the open market;

'Product Specification' means each of those specifications attached as part of Appendix E which give the description and specifications of a Product which has been specially developed, modified or adapted by the Supplier for incorporation in the System;

'Products' means Equipment and Programs;

'Programme' bears the definition set out in Condition 8;

'Programs' means all or any of the software forming part of the System;

'Project Manager' means a project manager appointed pursuant to Condition 18;

'Site' means the site detailed in the Civil Works Specification and situated at [   ] together with so much of the area surrounding the said site as shall be reasonably necessary for the Supplier actually to use in connection with the Works including without limitation for the purpose of access;

'Specifications' means the Functional Specification, the Civil Works Specification, the System Design Specification, Product Descriptions and Product Specifications;

'System' means the system specified in the System Design Specification;
'System Design Specification' means the specification, attached as Appendix F, which specifies the description, design, and specifications of a system which performs the functions set out in the Functional Specification. The System Design Specification is not a Supplier Description, or Product Specification, but it will incorporate the same by reference (as relevant) in respect of the Products of which the said system is comprised;
'Variation' means any alteration of the Contract by way of addition, modification or omission, pursuant to Condition 22;
'Works' means the execution of the Civil Works and the delivery, installation and commissioning of the System by the Supplier;
'Writing' means any manuscript, type-written or printed statement and any electronically transmitted and received text, and 'Written' shall be construed accordingly.

1.2 The headings and titles in the Contract are for descriptive purposes only, and shall not control or alter the meaning of the Contract as set forth in the text thereof, and do not in any way limit or amplify the terms of the Contract.

1.3 Throughout the Contract, whenever required by context (including, without limitation, in relation to one of the aforesaid defined terms) the use of the singular number shall be construed to include the plural, and the use of any gender shall include all genders.

1.4 The Appendices to the Contract constitute an integral part thereof.

1.5 All references to Conditions or Appendices, are references to Conditions or Appendices of the Contract.

2   Purpose and scope

The Supplier agrees to supply the System and execute the Works in accordance with the Contract, and the Customer agrees to pay the Supplier therefor in accordance with the Contract.

3   Title and risk

3.1 The Supplier warrants that (except in relation to intellectual property rights of third parties as referred to in Condition 3.3) the Supplier has good title to the Equipment and the Civil Works Items, and that (pursuant to s 12(3) of the Sale of Goods Act 1979, or s 2(3) of the Supply of Goods and Services Act 1982, whichever Act applies) it will transfer such title as it may have in the

Equipment and the Civil Works Items to the Purchaser pursuant to Condition 3.4.

3.2 The Supplier warrants that it is not aware of any actual or alleged infringements of any intellectual property rights of third parties which relate to the System or the Civil Works Items [, other than those (if any) which the Seller has disclosed to the Purchaser prior to the signature of the Contract].

3.3 The Supplier shall have no liability to the Customer (other than as provided in Condition 17) in the event that the System or the Civil Works Items infringe any intellectual property rights of a third party (including without limitation by reason of possession, sale or use, whether alone or in association or combination with any other goods); the Supplier gives no warranty that the System or the Civil Works Items will not infringe as aforesaid, and all conditions, warranties, stipulations or other statements whatsoever relating to such infringement or alleged infringement (if any), whether express or implied, by statute, at common law or otherwise howsoever, are hereby excluded.

3.4 Subject and pursuant to Condition 3.1, title to and risk in the Equipment and the Civil Works Items shall vest in the Customer upon the Acceptance Date.

4 Liability for death or personal injury and damage to property

4.1 In the event of death or personal injury or damage to property occurring before the Acceptance Date the liabilities shall be apportioned as follows:

4.1.1 The Supplier shall at its own expense make good any loss or damage to any part of the System arising from any cause whatsoever other than a negligent act or omission of the Customer.

4.1.2 If the System or any part thereof is lost or damaged, from causes for which the Supplier is not responsible under Condition 4.1.1 the loss or damage shall, if required by the Customer be made good by the Supplier at the expense of the Customer.

4.1.3 In respect of loss or damage to the property of the Customer other than the System, the Supplier shall indemnify the Customer to the extent that such damage was caused by the Supplier.

4.1.4 In respect of death or personal injury, if the deceased person's estate or the injured person (as the case may be) or any other third party brings a claim against the Customer, the Supplier shall indemnify the Customer against such claim to the extent that the relevant death or personal injury was caused by the Supplier. If such claim is made against the Supplier, the Customer shall indemnify the Supplier against such claim save to the extent that, by the operation of this paragraph, the Supplier would have been liable to indemnify the Customer had the claim been brought against the Customer.

4.1.5 In respect of loss or damage to the property of third parties, the provisions of Condition 4.1.4 shall apply *mutatis mutandis*.

4.2 The respective liability of the Customer and the Supplier under this Condition shall extend to the relevant acts or omissions of their respective servants, agents or subcontractors.

4.3 In order to avail itself of its rights under Conditions 4.1.4 and 4.1.5 the party against whom a claim is made must notify the other of such claim and must permit the other or that other's insurers, if the other so wishes, to conduct all negotiations for the settlement of such claim and to act in its stead or, to the extent permitted by the law of the relevant jurisdiction, to join in such litigation.

4.4 The maximum liability of the Customer and the Supplier to each other under this Condition shall not exceed £[   ] from any one event or series of connected events, and £[   ] in the aggregate.

4.5 In this Condition the word 'Loss' shall be deemed to include 'destruction'.

4.6 Without limiting its responsibilities or obligations under this Condition each party shall insure against its liabilities hereunder and shall provide evidence (if so required by the other) of its compliance with this requirement.

4.7 The provisions of this Condition (except for Conditions 4.1.1 and 4.1.2 and the words 'other than the System' in Condition 4.1.3 which shall be deemed for the purposes of this Condition 4.7 to be deleted) shall also apply while the Supplier is on the Site in fulfilment of an obligation under Condition 13.

4.8 Each party's entire liabilities to the other party, and each party's sole and exclusive remedies against the other party, in respect of death, personal injury and loss of or damage to property, prior to the Acceptance Date and while the Supplier is on the Site after the Acceptance Date in fulfilment of an obligation under Condition 13, howsoever caused, and in respect of all loss, damages, costs and expenses caused by or relating thereto, regardless of the form of action, whether in contract, tort (including negligence and breach of statutory duty), strict liability, or otherwise howsoever, shall be as set forth in this Condition 4.

5 Price

5.1 For the purposes of the Contract, the 'Contract Price' means the sum of [   ] as adjusted from time to time pursuant to any provision of the Contract, including without limitation Condition 7 and Condition 22.

5.2 The Contract Price excludes Value Added Tax which will be charged at the rate applicable at the time of invoicing. The Supplier will provide suitable Value Added Tax invoices to enable the Customer to reclaim the relevant Value Added Tax.

5.3 The Contract Price is payable by the Customer to the Supplier in consideration of the supply of the System and the performance of the Works by the Supplier. It excludes any payment for spares or Consumable Supplies purchased by the Customer from the Supplier pursuant to Condition 14.1 and Condition 15 respectively. It also excludes the payments to be made by the Customer under the Licence Agreement referred to in Condition 17.7 and any such payments under any Maintenance or Support Agreement entered into by the Customer with the Supplier pursuant to Condition 14.2.

6 Terms of payment

6.1 Subject to condition 6.5, the Supplier shall invoice the Contract Price in the following instalments:

[25%] of the Contract Price on signature of the Contract;
[25%] of the Contract Price on commencement of delivery of Equipment to the Site;
[25%] of the Contract Price on completion of the delivery of the Equipment to the Site;
[15%] of the Contract Price on the Acceptance Date;
[10%] of the Contract Price on the expiry of the Defects Correction Period.

6.2 Whenever the Contract Price is adjusted from time to time pursuant to any provision of the Contract, including without limitation Condition 7 and Condition 22 (a 'Relevant Adjustment') and one or more instalments ('Prior Instalments') of the Contract Price have been invoiced pursuant to Condition 6.1 prior to the Relevant Adjustment and therefore without taking the same into account, the percentage of the Relevant Adjustment which would have been included in the invoices for the Prior Instalments (had the Relevant Adjustment been in effect at the time the invoices for the Prior Instalments were issued) shall be added to or (as the case may be) deducted from the invoice for the instalment of the Contract Price which is next due following the putting into effect of the Relevant Adjustment.

6.3 Payment of each invoice of the Supplier shall be made by the Customer within 30 days of its receipt by the Customer.

6.4 The Supplier's invoices shall be in the form set out in Appendix G and shall be sent to the Customer, at the address and for the attention of the person detailed in Appendix G.

7   Escalation

7.1 The Contract Price shall be increased at the times and in the manner specified in Condition 7.2 in order to take account of:
7.1.1 any rise in the cost of labour;
7.1.2 any rise in the cost of material;
7.1.3 any rise in the cost of transport, and any rise in the cost of conforming to Legislation; and
7.1.4 any costs or expenses caused by reason of delay arising from a default of, or matters within the reasonable control of, the Customer;
which increase the cost of the Supplier's performance of its obligations under the Contract, [provided that no account shall be taken of any amount by which any cost incurred by the Supplier has been increased by the default or negligence of the Supplier or by any delay or other circumstance within the reasonable control of the Supplier].

7.2 Increases in the Contract Price shall be implemented as follows:
7.2.1 In respect of any rise in the cost of labour, the Contract Price shall be increased on and with effect from the date thirty days prior to the date for Acceptance set out in the Programme (the 'Adjustment Date') at the rate of [0.40] per cent for each 1.0 percentage point of increase (if any) between the index figure for the [BEAMA Labour Cost Index for Mechanical Engineering] last published before the [date of Contract signature] and the average of the index figures for such Index published in respect of each [calendar month] [quarter] (or part thereof) which falls within the [last one-third of] the period commencing on [the date of Contract signature] and ending on the Adjustment Date.
7.2.2 In respect of any rise in the cost of material, the Contract Price shall be increased on the 'Adjustment Date' at the rate of [0.60] per cent for each 1.0 percentage point increase (if any) between the index figure for the [Price Index of Materials used in the Mechanical Engineering Industry last published in the Trade and Industry Journal] before the [date of Contract signature] and the average of the index figures for such Index published in respect of each [calendar month] [quarter] (or part thereof) which falls within the [last one-third of] the period commencing on [the date of Contract signature] and ending on the Adjustment Date.

7.2.3 In respect of any rise in the cost of transport, and any rise in the cost of conforming to Legislation, in comparison with the level of such cost prevailing at the date of signature of the Contract (the 'Relevant Rise'), the Contract Price shall be increased by the additional amount of cost (the 'Relevant Increase') incurred or to be incurred by the Supplier in the execution of the Contract by reason of such Relevant Rise; the Supplier shall (upon becoming aware of a Relevant Rise) deliver to the Customer a notice specifying the extent and nature of the Relevant Rise and the amount of the Relevant Increase; and the Contract Price shall be increased by the Relevant Increase with effect from the date when the Customer receives such notice.

7.2.4 In respect of any additional costs or expenses caused by reason of delay arising from a default of, or matters within the reasonable control of, the Customer (an 'Additional Cost') the Contract Price shall be increased by the amount of such cost (the 'Relevant Amount') incurred or to be incurred by the Supplier in the execution of the Contract by reason of the Additional Cost; the Supplier shall (upon becoming aware of an Additional Cost) deliver to the Customer a notice specifying the extent and nature of the Additional Cost and the Relevant Amount; and the Contract Price shall be increased by the Relevant Amount with effect from the date when the Customer receives such notice.

7.3 For the purposes of this Condition:

7.3.1 The phrase 'the cost of material' shall be construed as including any duty or tax (by whomsoever payable) which is payable under or by virtue of any Act of Parliament on the import, purchase, sale, appropriation, processing or use of such material.

7.3.2 The phrase 'the cost of labour' shall be construed as including wages, salary and any duty or tax or other imposition or contribution (by whomsoever payable) which is payable under or by virtue of any Act of Parliament, collective agreement or contract of employment, on or in respect of the payment of wages or salary or otherwise in respect of the supply of such labour, including without limitation employer's and employees' social security and occupational and personal pension scheme contributions.

7.3.3 For the formulae set out in Conditions 7.2.1 and 7.2.2:

7.3.3.1 where any index figure is stated to be provisional or is subsequently amended, the figure shall apply as ultimately confirmed, or amended; and

7.3.3.2 the [BEAMA Labour Cost Index figure] for each [month] is deemed to be published on [the last day of the preceding month].

8 Programme

The Contract shall be executed in accordance with the dates and time scales specified in the programme attached as Appendix H (the 'Programme').

9   Delivery and storage

The Contract Price is based on the Programme which allows progressive deliveries of Equipment direct from the Supplier's factory to the Site. If owing to circumstances outside the reasonable control of the Supplier, it becomes necessary to deliver Equipment to any temporary store the costs of such storage and movement from the temporary store to the Site shall be paid by the Customer unless the necessity arose through matters outside the reasonable control of the Customer.

10   Delay

In the event of any known or anticipated delay in the execution (in accordance with the dates and time scales specified in the Programme) by one party of its obligations under the Contract, and whatever the cause of the delay, that party shall inform the other party immediately of the reason therefor and when it expects to proceed with its obligations.

11   Liquidated damages

11.1 Subject to Conditions 21 and 26, if Acceptance is delayed beyond the date for Acceptance specified in the Programme, then the Supplier shall pay to the Customer a sum by way of liquidated damages (in full and final satisfaction of its liability in respect of such delay) calculated at [0.25 per cent] of the Contract Price for each week (or part thereof) between the date for Acceptance specified in the Programme and the Acceptance Date, up to a maximum of [5 per cent] of the Contract Price.

11.2 Subject to Conditions 21 and 26, the Supplier's entire liabilities to the Customer, and the Customer's sole and exclusive remedies against the Supplier, in respect of the Supplier's failure to comply with all or any of the dates and time scales specified in the Programme (including without limitation the date specified for Acceptance), howsoever caused, and in respect of all loss, damages, costs and expenses caused by or relating thereto, regardless of the form of action, whether in contract, tort (including negligence and breach of statutory duty), strict liability, or otherwise howsoever, shall be as set forth in Condition 11.1.

12   Acceptance

12.1 The Supplier shall give Written notice to the Customer when it is ready for the Acceptance Tests to be carried out in accordance with the relevant dates and time scales specified in the Programme. Such notice shall specify the time and date when the Acceptance Tests can commence. The Acceptance Tests shall be carried out by personnel of the Supplier in the presence of representatives of the Customer not later than 14 days from the date of receipt of the notice by the Customer.

12.2 If the Acceptance Tests show the Civil Works and the System to be in accordance with the relevant Specifications, the Customer shall forthwith issue the Acceptance Certificate to the Supplier and take over the System for commercial use.

12.3 If the Acceptance Tests show the Civil Works and/or the System not to be in accordance with the relevant Specifications the Supplier shall rectify the defect after which the Acceptance Tests or such portion of them as may be mutually agreed upon shall be repeated under the same conditions as aforesaid.

12.4 The Customer shall not use the System commercially prior to Acceptance. In the event that the Customer does use the System commercially prior to Acceptance as aforesaid, the Civil Works and the System shall thereupon be deemed to have achieved Acceptance, the Customer shall immediately issue the Acceptance Certificate, and the Supplier shall be under no further obligations in respect of Acceptance and the carrying out of the Acceptance Tests.

12.5 If after due notice the Customer does not attend at the relevant time and place for any Acceptance Tests to take place then the Supplier shall be free to carry out the relevant Acceptance Tests in the Customer's absence and the result of those Acceptance Tests shall be binding on the Customer.

13 Warranty

13.1 The Supplier warrants that (i) (subject to Condition 13.2) the System Design Specification specifies a system which performs the functions set out in the Functional Specification, (ii) the System will conform in all material respects with the System Design Specification, (iii) (subject to Condition 13.2) the Civil Works Specification specifies civil works which will prepare the Site so that delivery, installation, commissioning and Acceptance of the System can take place in accordance with the Contract, (iv) the Civil Works will conform in all material respects with the Civil Works Specification [and will be performed with reasonable care and skill], (v) all Civil Works Items will conform in all material respects to the Civil Works Specification [and will be of sound materials and workmanship], (vi) all Products will conform in all material respects to the relevant Product Description or Product Specification incorporated by reference in the System Design Specification (except where any of the same are constrained by or conflict with the System Design Specification in which case the latter shall prevail) [and will be of sound materials and workmanship] and (vii) the Works (excluding the Civil Works) will be carried out with reasonable care and skill.

13.2 The Supplier gives no warranty, under Condition 13.1(i) and Condition 13.1(iii) in respect of any design provided by the Customer which the Customer has required it to include in the System Design Specification and the Civil Works Specification respectively to the extent that the relevant Specification contains a note identifying the design and stating that no warranties are given in respect thereof pursuant to this Condition 13.2.

13.3 Except for the express warranties set out above in Condition 13.1, and except for those warranties as to title and quiet possession implied by s 12(3) of the Sale of Goods Act 1979 and s 2(3) of the Supply of Goods and Services Act 1982, whichever Act is applicable, the Supplier grants no warranties relating to defects in the design workmanship or materials of the Civil Works, Civil Works Items, the Works, Products and the System, and all other conditions, warranties, stipulations or other statements whatsoever, whether express or implied, by statute at common law or otherwise howsoever, relating to defects in the Civil Works, Civil Works Items, the Works, Products and the System, are hereby excluded; in particular (but without limitation of the foregoing) the Supplier grants no warranties (other than as provided in the aforesaid warranties set out above) regarding the fitness for purpose, performance, use, quality or merchantability of the Civil Works, Civil Works Items, the Works, Products and the System, whether express or implied, by statute at common law or otherwise howsoever, and, in particular, grants no warranty that the System, or a Program will be free from errors or will run without interruption.

13.4 Subject to other provisions of the Contract, the Supplier will make good, by rework, rectification, repair or replacement or where applicable by the supply of replacement parts, any Defects in relation to the warranties given under Condition 13.1(i) or 13.1(ii), which appear in the System within the Defects Correction Period, and have been notified by the Customer to the Supplier in Writing within thirty days of their appearance.

13.5 Subject to other provisions of the Contract, the Supplier will make good, by rework, rectification, repair or replacement or where applicable by the supply of replacement parts, any Defects in relation to the warranties given under Condition 13.1(iii) and 13.1(iv), which appear in the Civil Works within the Defects Correction Period, and have been notified by the Customer to the Supplier in Writing within thirty days of their appearance.

13.6 Subject to the other provisions of the Contract, the Supplier shall, in respect of Civil Works Items, Products and the Works (excluding the Civil Works) and to the extent that Defects occur in the same under the warranties contained in Conditions 13.1(v), 13.1(vi) and 13.1(vii) respectively, remedy such defects as follows:

13.6.1 The Supplier shall make good, by rectification, repair or replacement or at its option by the supply of replacement parts, Defects which appear in the Civil Works Items and the Equipment within the Defects Correction Period, and have been notified by the Customer to the Supplier in Writing within [14] days of their appearance.

13.6.2 For each Program (unless otherwise specifically stated in the relevant Product Description or Product Specification) the Supplier will investigate any Defect reported by the Customer in Writing and will provide appropriate remedial or avoidance information in accordance with the provisions of the relevant Software Error Correction Service set out in the Supplier's relevant Product Description or Product Specification and for so long as the Supplier is offering the service to other customers generally provided that for Programs subject to a one-time licence charge such period of service is limited to three months duration unless otherwise stated.

13.6.3 The Supplier will remedy (by rework or as it otherwise thinks appropriate) any Defect in respect of performance of the Works (excluding the Civil Works) or any part thereof which the Customer notifies to it in Writing within [three months] of the date of the performance of the relevant part of the Works.

13.7 The Supplier may remove from the Site any Civil Works Item or Product or any part thereof if the nature of the relevant Defect is such that the remedying of the Defect cannot be expeditiously carried out on the Site. When such Defect is remedied the Supplier shall return and reinstall such removed Civil Works Item or Product or part thereof. The cost and expenses of such removal, remedy and reinstallation together with the risk of any loss or damage to the removed Civil Works Item or Product or part thereof shall be borne by the Supplier.

13.8 Where a Civil Works Item or Product or part thereof is removed from the Site in accordance with Condition 13.6 the Supplier shall at its own cost and expense, provide and install a replacement to keep the System operational until the removed Civil Works Item or Product or part thereof is returned and reinstalled.

13.9 If the Supplier fails to correct a Defect in accordance with its obligations under Condition 13 within a reasonable period having regard (*inter alia*) to the nature of the Defect, the Customer may correct the Defect itself or have the Defect corrected by third parties, and the Customer may deduct from any payment due to the Supplier or recover by other means as a debt due from the

Supplier all reasonable costs and expenses incurred in so doing.

13.10 The remedies given under this Condition shall only be available provided that the Civil Works, Civil Works Items, the Works, Products and the System (as relevant) have not been modified other than by or on behalf of the Supplier, and have been used properly, and maintained and operated in accordance with the Supplier's recommendations.

13.11 The Supplier's entire liabilities to the Customer, and the Customer's sole and exclusive remedies against the Supplier, in respect of Defects, howsoever caused, and in respect of all loss, damages, costs and expenses caused by or relating thereto, regardless of the form of action, whether in contract, tort (including negligence and breach of statutory duty), strict liability, or otherwise howsoever, shall be as set forth in this Condition 13.

14   Spares and support

14.1 The Supplier shall maintain a supply of spares or replacement parts suitable for the Products comprised within the System for a period of not less than [   ] years from the Acceptance Date, such spares or replacement parts to be fully compatible with but not necessarily identical to similar items previously supplied. Each consignment of spare parts shall be supplied to the Customer at fair and reasonable market prices, and upon the Supplier's standard terms and conditions of sale prevailing at the time of such supply.

14.2 Not later than three months prior to the date for Acceptance specified in the Programme the Supplier will recommend to the Customer a complete set of spares to be held at the Site. The supply of such set of spares (if the Customer requests the Supplier to supply the same) shall take place in accordance with Condition 14.1.

14.3 At the request of the Customer, the Supplier will provide a support and/or maintenance service to the Customer in respect of the System, from the Acceptance Date, as specified in, and upon the prices terms and conditions detailed in, the Support Agreement and the Maintenance Agreement attached as Appendix I and Appendix J respectively.

15   Consumable supplies

15.1 The Customer may procure Consumable Supplies from the Supplier (upon prices, terms and conditions to be agreed) or any other source the Customer may deem appropriate. The Supplier will no later than three months prior to the date specified for Acceptance in the Programme supply a list of all potential Consumable Supplies to the Customer, together with their technical and performance specifications.

15.2 The Customer shall have no recourse against the Supplier if the use of Consumable Supplies procured by the Customer adversely affects the performance of the relevant Product or the System, unless such Consumable Supplies were supplied by the Supplier.

16   Termination

16.1 Either party may terminate the Contract at any time by serving notice of termination upon the other party if the other party defaults by failing to perform any substantial obligation upon its part to be performed pursuant to the Contract. The termination will become effective thirty days after receipt by the party in default of the aforesaid notice unless during the said period of thirty days the party in default has remedied the default (or in the case of a default which is capable of remedy but not within the said period of thirty days) is diligently proceeding to cure the default by taking active effective and continuing steps so to do and the default is in fact cured within [90 days] [a reasonable period of time].

16.2 The Contract may be terminated with immediate effect by either party giving notice of termination to the other party (the 'Insolvent Party'):
16.2.1 if the Insolvent Party shall pass a resolution for winding up (otherwise than for the purposes of a solvent amalgamation or reconstruction where the resulting entity is at least as creditworthy as the Insolvent Party and assumes all of the obligations of the Insolvent Party under the Contract) or a court shall make an order to that effect; or
16.2.2 if the Insolvent Party shall cease to carry on its business or substantially the whole of its business; or
16.2.3 if the Insolvent Party becomes or is declared insolvent, or convenes a meeting of or makes or proposes to make any arrangement or composition with its creditors; or
16.2.4 if a liquidator, receiver, administrator, manager, trustee, or similar officer is appointed over any of the assets of the Insolvent Party.

16.3 The Customer may, in addition to its rights under Condition 16.1, also terminate the Contract for convenience at any time by giving notice to the Supplier, such notice to take effect thirty days after its receipt by the Supplier.

16.4 If the Customer terminates the Contract pursuant to Condition 16.1 or 16.2 then:

16.4.1 the Customer shall itself be entitled to complete the supply of the System and the execution of the Works in accordance with the Contract to the extent that the same have not been so completed by the Supplier at the date of termination, or to enter into a contract with a third party to effect such completion, and, for the avoidance of doubt, such completion shall be taken to include the manufacture production or procurement of any Civil Works Items or Products (or reasonable equivalents thereof) which the Supplier has not delivered to the Site at the date of termination or which the Customer has rejected pursuant to Condition 16.5; and

16.4.2 the Supplier shall pay to the Customer the amount by which the reasonable cost to the Customer of completion of the Contract pursuant to Condition 16.4.1 exceeds the Contract Price, and the Customer may deduct the said amount from such amounts (if any) as are due to the Supplier (pursuant to Condition 16.5 or otherwise) or to recover such amount as a debt due from the Supplier; and

16.4.3 the Customer shall (subject to Condition 16.5 and Condition 16.6) be entitled to use or have used on its behalf all Know-how and Intellectual Property Rights owned or controlled by the Supplier free of charge for the purposes of (i) completion in accordance with Condition 16.4.1 and (ii) use of the System after such completion.

16.5 Subject to Condition 16.4.2 the Customer shall pay the Supplier for all Works properly performed and for all Civil Works Items and Products manufactured produced procured or appropriated by the Supplier for purposes of the Contract at the date of termination (whether or not at that date delivered to the Site) to the extent that the Customer has not already paid for them, provided that in respect of such Civil Works Items and Products:

16.5.1 payment shall only be made in respect of such Civil Works Items and Products which the Customer wishes to retain, and (subject to the making of any payment due after the application of Condition 16.4.2) the Supplier shall deliver to Site all of the aforesaid which have not already been so delivered; and

16.5.2 all such Civil Works Items and Products not so retained which have already been delivered to Site prior to the date of termination shall be returned by the Customer to the Supplier; and

16.5.2.1 in respect of all such Civil Works Items and Products not so retained and returned as aforesaid which have not been paid for by the Customer prior to their return, the Customer shall (subject to Condition 16.4.2) only be obliged to pay to the Supplier such amount (if any) as represents a reasonable payment for the use of such Civil Works Items and Products by the Customer prior to their return; and

16.5.2.2 in respect of all such Civil Works Items and Products not so retained and returned as aforesaid, to the extent that the same have been paid for by the Customer prior to their return, the Customer may recover an amount equal to such payment as a debt due from the Supplier less (subject to Condition 16.4.2) such amount (if any) as represents a reasonable payment for their use prior to such return; and

16.5.3 where a Product retained by the Customer is a Program payment therefor shall (subject to Condition 16.4.2) be made in accordance with Condition 16.6; and

16.5.4 ownership and risk in each of the Civil Works Items and Products (other than Programs) retained by the Customer pursuant to Condition 16.5 shall be transferred to the Customer upon termination of the Contract or (subject to Condition 16.4.2) when the same has been paid for in full (whichever event last occurs).

16.6 To the extent that the Customer cannot use Programs retained by the Customer pursuant to Condition 16.5, without a licence, under any of the Know-how and Intellectual Property Rights relating to the System, in accordance with the Licence Agreement referred to in Condition 17.7, the Customer shall enter into the Licence Agreement and be bound by the same (including without limitation, but subject to Condition 16.4.2, in respect of payments to be made thereunder to the Supplier) in so far as it relates to such Know-how and Intellectual Property Rights.

16.7 If the Supplier terminates the Contract pursuant to Condition 16.1 or 16.2, or the Customer terminates the Contract pursuant to Condition 16.3:

16.7.1 the Supplier shall be entitled to total termination charges (the 'Total Termination Charges') upon the basis of:

16.7.1.1 the direct and overhead costs (together with a reasonable profit thereon) incurred by the Supplier in the performance of the Contract; and

16.7.1.2 reasonable costs incurred by the Supplier with respect to the termination of the Contract and with respect to settlement with vendors and subcontractors as a result of such termination; and

[**16.7.1.3** an amount equal to the balance of overhead recovery and profit which would have been achieved by the Supplier if the Supplier had completed the Contract;]

16.7.2 the Total Termination Charges shall be determined in accordance with the Supplier's standard accounting practice, supported by proper vouchers and records and verified by the Supplier's auditors, who shall be an independent firm of chartered accountants, acting as experts and not as arbitrators, and whose decision shall be final and binding upon the parties;

16.7.3 the Customer shall pay the Supplier the Total Termination Charges within 60 days of submission of the claim therefor to the Customer (accompanied by a certificate issued by the Supplier's auditors verifying the same pursuant to Condition 16.7.2) less the following:

16.7.3.1 amounts, if any, previously paid by the Customer to the Supplier under the Contract; and

16.7.3.2 amounts representing the total direct costs of material and labour incurred by the Supplier in relation to all Civil Works Items and Products manufactured produced procured or appropriated by the Supplier for the purposes of the Contract at the date of termination (whether or not delivered to Site) which the Customer does not desire and which the Supplier has agreed to retain or take redelivery of for the Supplier's own use;

[and provided that in no event shall the Total Termination Charge exceed the Contract Price at the date of termination];

16.7.4 ownership and risk in all Civil Works Items and Products manufactured, produced, procured or appropriated by the Supplier for the purposes of the Contract (other than Programs), except those which the Supplier agrees to retain as mentioned in Condition 16.7.3.2, shall, upon payment of the Total Termination Charges, be transferred to the Customer, and all Civil Works Items and Products manufactured produced procured or appropriated by the Supplier for the purposes of the Contract at the date of termination if not already delivered to Site, shall thereupon be so delivered by the Supplier;

16.7.5 to the extent that the Customer cannot use Products (including in particular Programs) in the possession or ownership of the Customer pursuant to Condition 16.7.4, either separately or in combination as a system or part thereof, without a licence, under any of the Know-how and Intellectual Property Rights relating to the System, in accordance with the Licence Agreement referred to in Condition 17.7, the Customer shall (if it wishes so to use all or any of the Products aforesaid) enter into the Licence Agreement and be bound by the same (including without limitation in respect of payments to be made thereunder to the Supplier, which payments shall be made in addition to the Total Termination Charges) in so far as it relates to relevant Know-how and Intellectual Property Rights.

16.8 On termination of the Contract the Supplier shall remove its equipment and personnel from the Site, and, if so requested by the Customer, assign to the Customer any subcontract related to the Works and/or the System, or any part thereof, provided that the Supplier has the right so to assign such subcontract or the relevant subcontractor (notwithstanding the absence of such right) gives its consent to such assignment.

16.9 Each party's entire liabilities to the other party, and each party's sole and exclusive remedies against the other party, in respect of termination of the Contract howsoever caused, and in respect of all loss, damages, costs and expenses caused by or relating thereto, regardless of the form of action, whether in contract, tort (including negligence and breach of statutory duty), strict liability, or otherwise howsoever, shall be as set forth in this Condition 16.

17   Know-how and intellectual property rights

17.1 In the event that any third party claims that the System or any part thereof infringes such third party's Intellectual Property Rights or makes unauthorised use of such third party's Know-how (collectively an 'Allegation of Infringement') then:

17.1.1 the Supplier shall have the right to conduct all negotiations with such third party; and

17.1.2 the Supplier shall have the right to conduct the defence of any suit brought against the Customer by such third party; and

17.1.3 the Supplier shall (subject as provided below) pay all damages and costs awarded against the Customer in such suit provided that:

17.1.3.1 the Customer shall promptly notify the Supplier in Writing of any Allegation of Infringement of which it has notice and shall make no admissions without the Supplier's consent; and

17.1.3.2 the Customer shall give the Supplier all reasonable assistance for the purpose of this Condition; and

17.1.3.3 the Customer shall not incur any cost or expense for the Supplier's account without the Supplier's prior Written consent.

17.2 If at any time any Allegation of Infringement is made or in the Supplier's opinion is likely to be made the Supplier may (as an alternative or in addition to taking the actions set out in Condition 17.1) at its own expense:

17.2.1 procure for the Customer the right to continue using the relevant Intellectual Property Rights or the relevant Know-how on terms not restricting the Customer's use of the same as contemplated by the Contract; or

17.2.2 modify or replace any items the use or possession of which gives, or in the Supplier's opinion is likely to give, rise to the relevant Allegation of Infringement, so that the use or possession of the same ceases to give, or be likely in the Supplier's opinion to give, rise to the relevant Allegation of Infringement, provided that such modification or replacement does not materially detract from the performance or quality of the System when used as contemplated by the Contract.

17.3 This indemnity shall not apply to, and the Supplier shall have no liability to the Customer hereunder for, any Allegation of Infringement arising by reason of the Supplier having followed a design or instruction furnished or given by the Customer, and the Customer warrants and undertakes to the Supplier that any design or instruction furnished or given by the Customer shall not be such as will cause the Supplier to infringe any Intellectual Property Rights or make unauthorised use of any Know-how in the execution of the Contract.

17.4 This indemnity shall not apply to, and the Supplier shall have no liability to the Customer hereunder for, any Allegation of Infringement arising by reason of any modification of the System by the Customer or any third party, or by reason of the use of the System or of any of the Supplier's Products in combination with the Customer's equipment or other items not supplied by the Supplier, unless such modification or use has (prior to the arising of the relevant Allegation of Infringement) been approved in Writing by the Supplier specifically for the purposes of this Condition.

17.5 The Supplier's entire liabilities to the Customer, and the Customer's sole and exclusive remedies against the Supplier, in respect of infringement or alleged infringement of Intellectual Property Rights, unauthorised or alleged unauthorised use of Know-how, howsoever caused, and in respect of all loss, damages, costs and expenses caused by or relating thereto, regardless of the form of action, whether in contract, tort (including negligence and breach of statutory duty), strict liability, or otherwise howsoever, shall be as set forth in Condition 17.1 to Condition 17.4 inclusive.

17.6 The Customer acknowledges that all of the Intellectual Property Rights subsisting in or relating in any way to the Specifications, the Civil Works Items, the System and the Works, and all Know-how embodied in, or used in connection with, any of the foregoing are and shall remain (as between the Supplier and the Customer) the sole property of the Supplier or such other party as may be identified therein or thereon.

17.7 The Supplier shall upon the Acceptance Date grant to the Customer a licence for the use of certain Know-how and Intellectual Property Rights relating to the System (including without limitation Intellectual Property Rights relating to Programs) as detailed in, and for the purposes and upon the prices terms and conditions (including obligations relating to confidentiality of the relevant Know-how) set out in, the Licence Agreement attached as Appendix K.

17.8 Know-how and Intellectual Property Rights evolved, generated from or arising in the performance of, or as a result of, the Contract, shall (to the extent that they are not already vested in the Supplier) vest in and be the absolute property of the Supplier.

17.9 Each party shall keep confidential and shall not without the other's prior consent in Writing disclose to any third party any information (whether of a commercial or technical nature) concerning the business and affairs of the other which was acquired from the other pursuant to or as a result of the Contract.

18 Project management

18.1 In order to establish and maintain clear and effective communications throughout the execution of the Contract the Customer and the Supplier shall each nominate an individual (referred to in the Contract as 'Project Managers') who will be responsible for:
18.1.1 co-ordination and dissemination of all information within their own organisations, subcontractors and suppliers and between the Customer and the Supplier;
18.1.2 obtaining resolution of matters relating to work on the Site, and of any problems which could delay the execution of the Works in accordance with the Contract;
18.1.3 preparation of progress reports at monthly intervals; and
18.1.4 administration and implementation of the procedures, and resolution of the matters, detailed in Condition 7, Condition 8, Condition 10, Condition 12, Condition 19, Condition 20, Condition 21, Condition 22, Condition 24 and Condition 26.

18.2 The individuals shall be nominated within two weeks of the date of the signature of the Contract. If either party wishes to replace its Project Manager by another, that party will give two weeks' notice of its intention to the other party. During the two weeks following nomination or receipt of notice of replacement (as the case may be) the party not employing the individual concerned will have the right to accept or refuse the nomination or replacement. Acceptance shall not be withheld unreasonably.

19 Supply of contract implementation information

19.1 Where one party supplies Contract Implementation Information to the other party, the party supplying such Contract Implementation Information shall be responsible for the accuracy and completeness thereof, and the party receiving the same shall be entitled to rely upon it for the purposes of the performance of its obligations under the Contract. A party receiving Contract Implementation Information shall not be obliged to check or verify the same, but where it discovers any apparent error, omission or ambiguity therein it shall notify the other party, and give the other party a reasonable opportunity to correct the relevant Contract Implementation Information.

19.2 When the receiving party relies upon Contract Implementation Information which is inaccurate, incomplete or misleading, then, whether or not the supplying party has had the opportunity to correct the same, and/or has in fact corrected the same, and:
19.2.1 if such reliance causes the receiving party to incur extra costs and ex-

pense, then the supplying party shall reimburse such costs and expense to the receiving party upon substantiation of these to the supplying party's reasonable satisfaction; and/or

19.2.2 if such reliance causes delay or disruption to the performance of the Works or dates or time scales specified in the Programme, then, as appropriate, both parties shall consent to such extensions of time as may be reasonable to take account of such delay or disruption.

19.3 Each party's entire liabilities to the other party, and each party's sole and exclusive remedies against the other party, in respect of the supply by that party to the other party of Contract Implementation Information, and in respect of all loss, damages, costs and expenses caused by or relating thereto, regardless of the form of action, whether in contract, tort (including negligence and breach of statutory duty), strict liability, or otherwise howsoever, shall be as set forth in this Condition 19.

20   The site

20.1 The Supplier shall:

20.1.1 deliver the Civil Works Items to the Site and execute the Civil Works at the Site, in accordance with the relevant dates and time scales specified in the Programme and with the Civil Works Specification, ready for installation of the System; and

20.1.2 deliver, install and commission the System at the Site, in accordance with the relevant dates and time scales specified in the Programme.

20.2 The Supplier shall provide all plant, equipment and labour for the purposes of Condition 20.1 other than the assistance, facilities and other things to be provided by the Customer as specified in Appendix J.

20.3 The Customer shall give the Supplier access to the Site for the purpose of performance of the Works (including without limitation for purposes of Condition 20.1 and 20.2) in accordance with the relevant dates and time scales specified in the Programme, provided that (subject to any provisions to the contrary contained in the Programme) such access shall only be permitted from 8 am–5 pm Monday to Friday inclusive (other than on public and bank holidays) and none of the Works shall be carried out on the Site outside the said times and days without the consent of the Customer (which shall not be unreasonably withheld or delayed) except when necessary for the saving of life or property or for the safety of the Products the System or the Site in which case the Supplier shall be entitled to such access subject (where practicable) to giving prior notification thereof to the Customer. The Customer may request the Supplier to carry out the Works at other times and on other days than provided for in Condition 20.2, and such request shall be dealt with as a proposal for a Variation pursuant to Condition 22.

20.4 While carrying out the Works on the Site, the Supplier shall comply with all of the Customer's regulations relating to the Site of which the Supplier has notice, and with all Legislation, and all reasonable and practicable instructions issued by the Customer to the Supplier, in respect of health and safety at work, provided that if the Customer notifies the Supplier in writing that it wishes to impose regulations or instructions which were not in existence or not brought to the attention of the Supplier prior to the date of signature of the Contract, such notification shall be dealt with as a proposal for a Variation pursuant to Condition 22.

20.5 Upon Acceptance, the Supplier shall remove all of its personnel, materials, plant and equipment from the Site, and shall leave the Site clean and tidy.

20.6 Except to the extent that it impedes the execution of the Works in accordance with the Contract, the Supplier shall co-operate with and give all reasonable opportunities for carrying out their work to any other contractors engaged by the Customer, and to the Customer's personnel, who are working on or near the Site.

21 Suspension

21.1 The Customer may from time to time by notice to the Supplier suspend the Works or any part of them, specifying in such notice that part of the Works which is to be suspended, the effective date of suspension (which shall not be less than three nor more than thirty days from the date of receipt of the relevant notice by the Supplier), and such other reasonable instructions in relation to such suspension as the Customer may wish to issue.

21.2 If the Supplier considers that the cost and expense of and/or the time required to perform the Works has increased or will increase due to any suspension under Condition 21.1 the Supplier shall notify the Customer giving justification in principle and such details as the Customer shall reasonably require. Thereupon, the Customer shall make a fair and reasonable adjustment to the Contract Price and/or grant a fair and reasonable extension of the dates and time scales under the Programme.

21.3 The Supplier shall wherever possible in consultation with the Customer mitigate any additional cost and expense arising from suspension by utilising the Supplier's personnel and other resources on work other than the Works during the period of such suspension, provided always that such utilisation will not render the Supplier's personnel and other resources unavailable to the Customer immediately upon receipt by the Supplier of the Customer's notice under Condition 21.5.

21.4 The Supplier shall, during any suspension, continue to perform any of the Works not covered in the relevant notice of suspension, to the extent that it is reasonably practicable so to do. To the extent that it is not reasonably practicable so to do, the Supplier shall so inform the Customer, and the relevant part of the Works shall be deemed to have been included within the relevant notice of suspension.

21.5 The Customer may at any time by reasonable notice to the Supplier authorise resumption of all of the suspended Works and the Supplier shall, on being given such notice, resume such performance. If the Customer serves reasonable notice for the resumption of part only of the suspended Works, the Supplier shall not be obliged to comply with such notice unless it is reasonably practicable so to do.

21.6 If any suspension by the Customer pursuant to this Condition continues for more than [one hundred and eighty days], or if and when the Customer has invoked different suspensions under this Condition having effect for an aggregate of [one hundred and eighty days], the Supplier shall have the option to require the Customer either (i) to issue a notice, pursuant to Condition 21.5, authorising resumption of all of the Works then suspended, and to undertake that no more suspensions will be invoked pursuant to this Condition without the consent of the Supplier, or (ii) to terminate the Contract for convenience pursuant to Condition 16.3.

21.7 The Supplier shall incorporate similar provisions to those in this Condition in all subcontracts relating to the Works.

22   Variations

22.1 The Customer may at any time during the Contract require the Supplier to revise the dates and time scales specified in the Programme, including the date for Acceptance, and/or to undertake any reasonable alteration or addition to or omission from the Works, the Products and the Civil Works Items (a 'Variation'). In the event of a Variation being required, the Customer shall formally request the Supplier to provide a proposal in Writing setting out the effect of the proposed Variation on the Works and the System, and what adjustment if any, will be required to the Specifications, the Contract Price and/or to the dates and time scales specified in the Programme.

22.2 Similarly the Supplier may propose to the Customer a Variation and in such case shall also provide to the Customer a proposal as described in Condition 22.1.

22.3 The Supplier shall satisfy the Customer as to the reasonableness of any changes to the dates and time scales specified in the Programme and any adjustments to the Contract Price resulting from Variations under this Condition. The Supplier shall furnish such details within 14 days of receipt of the Customer's request or within such period as may be mutually agreed.

22.4 The Supplier shall not, and shall have no obligation to, implement the relevant Variation unless and until the relevant proposal or any mutually agreed amended proposal has been accepted by the Customer in Writing. Upon such acceptance, the relevant proposal, or mutually agreed amended proposal (as the case may be), as so accepted, shall constitute a Variation for all the purposes of this Condition and the Contract.

22.5 No Variation under the above shall invalidate the Contract but if such Variation involves a change in the Specifications, an increase or decrease in the cost to the Supplier for carrying out the Contract and/or a change to any of the dates and time scales specified in the Programme, an appropriate adjustment to the Specifications, the Contract Price and/or to the dates and time scales specified in the Programme (being the adjustment set out in the relevant proposal or amended proposal accepted by the Customer in Writing pursuant to the above) shall be deemed to have been made with effect from the date of the relevant acceptance by the Customer as aforesaid.

22.6 Notwithstanding the foregoing, the Supplier shall be under no obligation to implement any Variation which could in its opinion give rise to a Defect, and to the extent that the Supplier agrees to implement such Variation, but disclaims responsibility therefor in Writing, any defect in the Civil Works Items, Products, the System or the Works shall not be a Defect for any purpose of the Contract, and in particular, but without limitation of the foregoing, any change required in the Civil Works Specification or the System Design Specification by reason of the implementation of such Variation shall, for the purposes of Condition 13.2, be deemed to be a design provided by the Customer in respect of which the Supplier gives no warranties under Condition 13.1(i) and Condition 13.1(iii), and the aforesaid disclaimer shall be deemed to be the note relating thereto as referred to in that Condition 13.2.

23   Responsibility for functional specification

The Customer shall be responsible in all respects for the Functional Specification, including, without limitation, for its accuracy and its compliance with the Customer's requirements in respect of the use to which the System will be put by the Customer and the fitness of the System for such purpose.

24 Assignment and subcontracting

24.1 Neither party may assign this Contract or any part of it without the consent of the other.

24.2 The Supplier shall not subcontract the whole of the Contract.

24.3 The Supplier shall not subcontract any part of the Contract (other than those parts of the Contract for which it is normal industry practice for undertakings like the Supplier to subcontract) without prior Written consent of the Customer, which shall not be unreasonably withheld.

24.4 No subcontract shall relieve the Supplier from any obligation or liability under the Contract and the Supplier shall be liable for the acts, omissions or negligence of its subcontractors and their respective employees, servants and agents, as though they were the acts, omissions or negligence of the Supplier.

24.5 The Supplier shall ensure that every subcontract shall:
24.5.1 impose confidentiality obligations on the subcontractor similar to those imposed on the Supplier under the Contract; and
24.5.2 contain provisions relating to subcontracting to the same effect as this Condition.

25 Consequential loss

25.1 With the exception of, and subject to, Condition 25.2, notwithstanding anything expressed or implied in the Contract to the contrary, neither the Customer nor the Supplier shall be liable to the other, regardless of the form of action, whether in contract, tort (including negligence and breach of statutory duty), strict liability, or otherwise howsoever, (i) for any loss of profit, business, contracts, or revenues, or (ii) for failure to achieve anticipated savings in costs or expenses or (iii) for any special, indirect or consequential damage of any nature whatsoever.

25.2 In the event of the termination of the Contract pursuant to Condition 16.1 or Condition 16.2 by the Customer, the payments which the Supplier is expressly required to make to the Customer pursuant to Condition 16.4, and, in the event of the termination of the Contract pursuant to Condition 16.1 or

Condition 16.2 by the Supplier, or pursuant to Condition 16.3 by the Customer, the payments which the Customer is expressly required to make to the Supplier pursuant to Condition 16.7, shall be calculated without reference to the provisions of Condition 25.1, which shall have no application in respect of such payments.

26 *Force Majeure*

26.1 For the purposes of the Contract '*Force Majeure*' means (i) Acts of God, explosion, flood, lightning, tempest, fire or accident, (ii) war, hostilities (whether war be declared or not), invasion, act of foreign enemies, (iii) rebellion, revolution, insurrection, military or usurped power or civil war, (iv) riot, civil commotion or disorder, (v) acts, restrictions, regulations, byelaws, refusals to grant any licences or permissions, prohibitions or measures of any kind on the part of any local, state, national, governmental, or supra-governmental authority, (vi) import or export regulations or embargoes, (vii) strikes, lock-outs or other industrial actions or trade disputes of whatever nature (whether involving employees of the Supplier or a third party), (viii) defaults of suppliers or subcontractors [where such default is itself caused by *Force Majeure*], (ix) any failure, default, delay in performance, or any act or omission of any nature whatsoever on the part of the Customer, or its employees, agents, suppliers or subcontractors (other than in relation to those obligations of the Customer relating to Contract Implementation Information pursuant to Condition 19), or (x) any cause or circumstance whatsoever beyond the Supplier's reasonable control.

26.2 Neither the Supplier nor any of its employees agents or subcontractors shall be considered in breach of this Contract or under any liability whatsoever to the Customer for non-performance, part performance, defective performance or delay in performance (collectively a 'failure in performance') of any obligation performed or to be performed by the Supplier its employees agents or subcontractors under the Contract (collectively a 'Contract Obligation'), which is directly or indirectly caused by or is a result of an event of *Force Majeure*, and the dates and time scales specified in the Programme shall be extended by a fair and reasonable period of time which is sufficient to enable the Supplier to perform or re-perform the relevant Contract Obligation.

26.3 The Supplier shall use all reasonable endeavours in any situation where it has invoked Condition 26.2 to perform or re-perform the relevant Contract Obligation as soon as reasonably practicable, but (subject to Condition 26.6 and Condition 26.7) shall be under no obligation, in order so to do, (i) to use any means, methods or modes of working or performance other than those specified in or required under the terms of the Contract (an 'Alternative

Method') or (ii) to incur any incremental or additional costs, expenses or liabilities not compensated for by an adjustment to the Contract Price pursuant to Conditions 5 or 7. ('Additional Cost'.)

26.4 Where an event of *Force Majeure* occurs which does not necessitate an extension pursuant to Condition 26.2, but, as a direct or indirect result of such event, performance or re-performance of any Contract Obligation necessitates the use of an Alternative Method, or the incurring of Additional Cost, the Supplier shall (subject to Condition 26.6 and Condition 26.7) be under no obligation to perform or re-perform that Contract Obligation.

26.5 Upon becoming aware of the occurrence of a relevant event of *Force Majeure*, the Supplier shall promptly issue a notice in Writing (a *'Force Majeure* Notice') to the Customer detailing such event and its anticipated effect upon the performance of the Contract by the Supplier. As appropriate the *Force Majeure* Notice shall also state any extension of time to which the Supplier considers it is entitled pursuant to Condition 26.2, and details of any Alternative Method, and the amount of any Additional Cost for the purposes of Condition 26.3 or 26.4.

26.6 A *Force Majeure* Notice shall be deemed to be a proposal for a Variation proposed to the Customer by the Supplier pursuant to Condition 22.2 (to which Condition 22.3 shall consequently also apply) covering, as relevant, a proposed extension of time, proposals to use an Alternative Method and/or proposals to incur Additional Cost, and the acceptance by the Customer of such *Force Majeure* Notice (or any mutually agreed amendment thereof) shall constitute a Variation pursuant to Condition 22.4 (to which Condition 22.5 shall consequently apply).

26.7 For the avoidance of doubt:
26.7.1 in the event that no agreement is reached pursuant to Condition 26.6 between the Customer and the Supplier in relation to the use of an Alternative Method or the incurring of an Additional Cost, the Supplier shall not be obliged to use such Alternative Method or to incur such Additional Cost, but may rely for exemption from liability for its failure in performance of the relevant Contract Obligations upon Condition 26.2 (to the extent that an extension of time pursuant thereto has been agreed as a Variation pursuant to Condition 26.6) or upon Condition 26.4 (where the relevant event of *Force Majeure* did not necessitate such extension); and
26.7.2 to the extent that the Customer and the Supplier cannot agree upon an extension of time pursuant to Condition 26.2, such failure to agree shall be a Matter in Dispute to be dealt with under Condition 32.

26.8 Nothing in this Condition shall be taken to limit or prevent the exercise by the Customer of its rights of termination for convenience under Condition 16.3 or of suspension under Condition 21.

27   Order of precedence

In the event of any conflict between these Conditions and any part of the Specifications, the former shall prevail.

28   Waiver and variation

28.1 In no event shall any delay failure or omission on the part of either of the parties in enforcing exercising or pursuing any right power privilege claim or remedy, which is conferred by the Contract, or arises under the Contract, or arises from any breach by the other party of any of its obligations hereunder, be deemed to be or be construed as (i) a waiver thereof, or of any other such right power privilege claim or remedy, or (ii) operate so as to bar the enforcement or exercise thereof, or of any other such right power privilege claim or remedy, in any other instance at any time or times thereafter.

28.2 The Contract may be amended or modified in whole or in part at any time but only by means of an agreement in Writing (including without limitation by an agreement which constitutes a Variation pursuant to Condition 22.4) which is executed in the same manner and by the same persons as the Contract. Any purported amendment or modification of this Agreement in any other manner (including without limitation an oral amendment or modification) shall have no validity.

29   Severability

If any term or provision of the Contract (or any part of such a term or provision) shall be held by any court of competent jurisdiction to be illegal or unenforceable, under any enactment or rule of law, such term or provision or part shall to that extent be deemed severable and not to form part of the Contract, but the validity and enforceability of the remainder of the Contract shall not be affected.

30   Entirety

30.1 This Contract comprises the entire agreement between the parties relating to the subject matter hereof, to the exclusion of all terms and conditions, prior or collateral agreements, negotiations, notices of intention, promises, warranties, undertakings, arrangements, understandings and representations, whether written or oral (collectively 'Representations') other than those Representations expressly included in the Contract; the parties agree and warrant to each other that they have not relied upon or been induced to enter into this Contract on the basis of any Representations other than those expressly included in the Contract; and neither party shall be bound by or be liable for any Representation of any kind or nature not expressly included in the Contract.

30.2 Without prejudice to the generality of Condition 30.1, save as expressly provided in the Contract, the Supplier gives no Representations to the Customer in respect of the transactions contemplated by, and the subject matter of, the Contract, and all other Representations express or implied by law legislation or otherwise howsoever (except for those warranties as to title and quiet possession implied by s 12(3) of the Sale of Goods Act 1979 and s 2(3) of the Supply of Goods and Services Act 1982) are hereby expressly excluded.

30.3 Each party's entire liabilities to the other party, and each party's sole and exclusive remedies against the other party, in respect of the transactions contemplated by, and the subject matter of, the Contract, and in respect of any breach of the Contract, and all loss, damages, costs and expenses caused by or relating to such breach, regardless of the form of action, whether in contract, tort (including negligence and breach of statutory duty), strict liability, or otherwise howsoever, shall be as expressly set forth in the Contract, and all other liabilities and remedies express or implied by law legislation or otherwise howsoever (except in respect of those warranties as to title and quiet possession implied by s 12(3) of the Sale of Goods Act 1979 and s 2(3) of the Supply of Goods and Services Act 1982) are hereby expressly excluded.

30.4 No provision of this Contract shall operate or be construed to operate so as to exclude or restrict the liability of the Supplier for breach of the express warranties contained in Condition 3, or for breach of the applicable warranties as to title and quiet possession implied into this Contract by s 12(3) of the Sale of Goods Act 1979, or s 2(3) of the Supply of Goods and Services Act 1982.

30.5 Each party agrees and undertakes to the other that no breach of this Contract shall entitle it to rescind this Contract, and that its remedy for any breach of this Contract shall lie solely for in damages, which remedy shall be subject to and in accordance with the provisions of this Contract.

30.6 No provision of this Contract, including without limitation Condition 30.1, shall operate so as to exclude any liability of one of the parties in respect of a fraudulent misrepresentation made by that party to the other, or to restrict or exclude any remedy which the other party may have in respect of such misrepresentation.

31   Notices

31.1 Any notice, invoice or other document or communication which may be given by either party under the Contract shall be given in Writing, and shall be deemed to have been duly given if left at or sent by post (whether by letter or on magnetic tape, floppy disc or other form of electronic storage medium), telex or facsimile transmission or by electronic mail to each party's address as set out below:

31.1.1 The Customer
Address:
Telex No:
Facsimile Number:
Electronic Mail Box:
31.1.2 The Supplier
Address:
Telex No:
Facsimile Number:
Electronic Mail Box:
or to any other address notified to the other in accordance with this Condition as an address to which notices, invoices and other documents or communications may be sent.

31.2 All notices, invoices and other documents or communications sent pursuant to Condition 31.1 shall be addressed for the attention of the Project Manager appointed by the party to whom the same is sent.

31.3 Any such communication shall be deemed to have been made to the other party (if by post) [4] days from the date of posting (and in proving such service or delivery, it shall be sufficient to prove that such communication was properly addressed, stamped and put in the post), and if by telex or facsimile transmission on the day and at the time of the transmission provided that the same shall not have been received in a form which is unintelligible due to errors in transmission. Any communication by electronic mail shall be deemed to have been made on the day and at the time on which the communication is delivered to the other party's electronic mailbox, as evidenced by an advice of delivery sent back through the relevant electronic mail system to the transmitting party.

32   Law and disputes

32.1 If any question, dispute or difference (the 'Matter in Dispute') shall arise between the Supplier and the Customer in relation to the Contract which cannot be settled by agreement between the parties, within 30 days of both parties being aware of the Matter in Dispute, either party may as soon as reasonably practicable give to the other notice of the Matter in Dispute specifying its nature and specifying the steps that the party giving the notice considers need to be taken to resolve the Matter in Dispute. Failing resolution of the Matter in Dispute by the parties within thirty days after receipt of such notice, either party may commence legal proceedings in order to resolve the Matter in Dispute without further notice.

32.2 The Supplier shall continue to perform that part of the Works which are not in dispute except to the extent that such continuance would prejudice the Supplier's legal position in respect of the Matter in Dispute.

32.3 The Contract and any dispute between the parties arising under or in connection with it shall be governed by the Law of England. Any such dispute not amicably resolved shall be subject to the exclusive jurisdiction of the English courts.

Signed by the duly authorised representatives of the supplier and the customer the day and year first above mentioned

Name [   ]   Name [   ]
Title [   ]   Title [   ]
Signature   Signature
For and on behalf of the supplier   For and on behalf of the customer

Chapter 5

Standard conditions for the supply of goods and services to consumers

5.1 Introduction

The legal theory behind contracting with consumers has been discussed in Chapter 1, together with the relevant UK and EC legislation. It is, however, convenient just to summarise once again at the outset of this chapter the relevant pieces of legislation and their sphere of application.

The UCTA and the EC Directive on Unfair Contract Terms (93/13/EC) (referred to in this chapter as the 'Unfair Terms Directive') as implemented under the Unfair Terms in Consumer Contract Regulations 1994 (SI No 3159) (referred to in this chapter as the 'Unfair Terms Regulations') will apply to all consumer contracts.

The EC General Product Safety Directive (92/59/EC) and the Consumer Protection Act 1987 will apply to all consumer contracts relating to the supply of defective products, as will, in due course, when finalised and implemented, the proposed Directive on the sale of consumer goods and associated guarantees (referred to in this chapter as the 'proposed Guarantee Directive').

The Consumer Credit Act 1974 will apply to all consumer credit transactions within the particular monetary limits laid down in the Act.

The Directive to Protect the Consumer in Respect of Contracts Negotiated Away from Business Premises (85/577/EC) (referred to in this chapter as the 'Door-to-Door Directive') and implemented in the UK by The Consumer Protection (Cancellation of Contracts Concluded Away From Business Premises) Regulations 1987 (SI No 2117) (referred to in this chapter as the 'Door-to-Door Regulations') catches all consumer transactions, within its sphere of application, for either goods or services. The same situation will apply with the Directive on the Protection of Consumers in Respect of Distance Contracts (97/7/EC) (referred to in this chapter as the 'Distance Contracts Directive') once it has been implemented in the UK.

It now remains to look at the practical aspects of drafting consumer contracts, bearing in mind the impact of the above legislation on the various possible types of transactions.

There are two guiding principles in drafting for consumers. The first is to set out clearly in plain English what the supplier undertakes to do under the contract and what he does not undertake to do, rather than to promise a lot, and then attempt to exclude liability for failure to achieve it. The second is not to try to exclude liability for defective products, but to rely on the relevant legal principles of causation and remoteness of damage, together with product or public liability insurance to cover the risk. The combination of s 2 of the UCTA, the EC General Product Safety Directive and the Consumer Protection Act (and in due course the advent of the proposed Guarantee Directive) make such exclusion impossible to achieve except, perhaps, in cases of pure economic loss.

Finally, it should be noted that this chapter does not attempt to deal in detail with consumer credit transactions, although they are referred to in connection with Precedent 3. The subject of transactions governed by the Consumer Credit Act 1974, and the relevant hire purchase legislation, is complex, and outside the scope of this book. There are many excellent detailed works on the subject which should be consulted as necessary.

The precedents in this chapter cover the most common types of consumer transactions, and, in general, are compliant with the spirit of the Unfair Terms Directive and the Unfair Terms Regulations. The indicative and non-exhaustive list of terms which, according to art 3(3) of the Unfair Terms Directive may be regarded as unfair, is set out as Appendix 1 to this chapter following the precedents. It will be seen that the precedents comply with this list. However, the fact is that most large commercial concerns had moved forward in their treatment of consumer transactions, for marketing reasons, and in response to competitive pressure, to a position which approximated or even surpassed that of the Unfair Terms Directive, well before it was even published in draft form.

Appendix 2 contains a summary of the activities of the Office of Fair Trading under its powers to consider unfair terms contained in reg 8 of the Unfair Terms Regulations, which is extracted from a *Bulletin on Unfair Contract Terms* (No 4 of December 1997) which is one of a series issued regularly by the Office of Fair Trading on this subject. The full text of this and the other past and future bulletins on the subject can be obtained from the Office of Fair Trading (free of charge) either in hard copy or as an electronic document over the internet. These bulletins are vital reading for practitioners concerned with the practical application of the Unfair Terms Regulations. The bulletin includes a summary of the commoner types of potentially unfair contract terms which the Office has encountered over the last two years since the Unfair Terms Regulations came into force. The clauses detailed in the bulletin exceed 150, but they were only a sample of the clauses looked at during the two-year period. It must, however, be stressed that, just as in the case of clauses caught under the UCTA, each clause can only be determined as fair or unfair within the context of the particular transaction which is being considered. (See the discussion on this point in relation to the UCTA in Chapter 1, and the detailed comparison of the two tests under the UCTA and the Unfair Terms Directive in Appendix 1 to Chapter 1.) This means that both Appendices 1 and 2 should be used as guides only. In particular the Office of Fair Trading may build up some kind of consistent practice (for instance it has generally taken a stand against whole agreement clauses in many contracts) but it is at pains to point out in the bulletin that this is not equivalent to a ruling that such clauses are unfair *per se* in the context of all consumer contracts.

5.2   Distance Contracts Directive

The precedents discussed in the following sections of this chapter are not suitable for contracts governed by the Distance Contracts Directive. The thrust of the Distance Contracts Directive is, first, to make sure that prescribed information about the proposed contract is disclosed to the consumer during the distance communication through which the contract is negotiated and concluded, and, secondly, to ensure that this information is subsequently confirmed to the consumer in writing or other durable medium. In that sense, the problem is not in writing a relevant precedent but deciding how these communications of information should take place in practice. Thus the precedents discussed in the following sections of this chapter would be as suitable for distance contracts as for any other type of contract. However, the other requirement of the Distance Contract Directive is for a cooling-off period. The precedents, even those that already contain a cooling-off period, would have to be adjusted to comply with the precise terms of the Distance Contracts Directive, particularly in relation to the return of money or goods where the contract is cancelled. Until the regulations implementing the Distance Contracts Directive in the UK have been brought into force it would be premature to attempt to draft compliant cooling-off provisions, but in practice the final procedure is likely to be similar to that already provided by the Door-to-Door Regulations discussed in section 5.6 below. The only difference, curiously, is that the Door-to-Door Directive specifies a cooling-off period of seven days, while the Distance Contracts Directive specifies one of seven working days.

5.3   Precedent 1

Most consumer transactions are oral contracts relating to transactions which take place on the spot 'over the counter' for cash. In most cases there is no written documentation at all, except, perhaps a receipt, and the transaction is governed solely by the SGA or the SGSA. The only opportunity in such cases to provide any written term affecting the contract is some type of guarantee on a receipt or on the packaging of the goods. The former is of course a guarantee provided by the trader who enters into the transaction with the consumer, while the latter can only apply to a transaction under which goods are supplied, in packaging of some kind, and is given by the manufacturer of the goods in question.

The practice of using such guarantees to exclude liability is now no longer possible, as discussed in Chapter 1, and now such terms merely give the consumer an express remedy in addition to his statutory rights under the SGA or the SGSA and the UCTA. Precedent 1.1 is a standard guarantee that could be used upon packaging. Precedent 1.2 is a standard guarantee that could be used upon a receipt.

When the proposed Guarantee Directive is implemented the wording of express guarantees will have to be reconsidered. It currently seems from a close reading of the draft that an express guarantee given to a consumer is only permitted where it provides the consumer with rights which are more favourable than those granted by the proposed Guarantee Directive. Draft art 5(1) currently provides that 'any guarantee offered by a seller or producer shall legally bind the offerer ... and *must* place the beneficiary in a more advantageous position than that resulting from [the relevant member state's implementation of the Directive]'. These words would thus not only prohibit an express guarantee which was less favourable than the guarantee provided by the proposed Guarantee Directive. They would also appear to prohibit an express guarantee which merely reproduces the terms of the guarantee granted by the proposed Guarantee Directive. This may well be an unintended consequence of the current wording which will be remedied by the time of the final draft. It seems illogical to prohibit a guarantee which grants expressly the same terms as those granted by the proposed Guarantee Directive. Such a guarantee can do the consumer no harm, and will at least alert him to his statutory rights.

On this basis Precedent 1.1 would seem to survive the proposed Guarantee Directive since it is clearly more favourable than the rights under the proposed Guarantee Directive, while Precedent 1.2 would not survive, even if its duration were extended to two years.

It is premature to attempt to draft an express guarantee that would satisfy draft art 5(1) of the proposed Guarantee Directive, since its final form and indeed the form of its implementation in the UK, is still unknown. However, it should be noted that draft art 5(2) provides that 'the guarantee must feature in a written document which must be freely available for consultation before purchase and must clearly set out the essential particulars necessary for making claims under the guarantee, notably the duration and territorial scope of the guarantee, as well as the name and address of the guarantor.'

Thus it would seem that once the proposed Guarantee Directive is implemented it will not be sufficient to provide the terms of the guarantee on the receipt, but instead they must be provided before the transaction is concluded, either in pre-contract documentation such as advertisements, catalogues, product leaflets or quotations, or at least on a notice visible in the trading premises where the transaction is concluded. Presumably, if this requirement is satisfied there is no harm in providing a copy of the guarantee on the packaging or the receipt for the consumer's future reference. Further, a guarantee visible on packaging of a product which can be examined before purchase would seem acceptable in its own right. Again, if clearly visible on packaging which can be examined before purchase, or if included in pre-contract documentation, Precedent 1.1 would appear to satisfy draft art 5(2), since it is not limited in duration or territorial scope, and it sets out the procedure for making the claim, including the name and address of the guarantor.

It may be questioned whether express consumer guarantees will in practice survive the implementation of the proposed Guarantee Directive at all. However, the proposed Guarantee Directive only imposes mandatory obligations in relation to repair or replacement of goods and refund of the purchase price. Liability for other types of loss occasioned by defective goods will continue to be governed by the current legal rules. As discussed above, exclusion of liability for physical injury or damage to tangible property is probably almost impossible under the current legislation, but avoiding liability for economic loss may in some cases be possible. This possibility would not appear to be ruled out by the current form of the proposed Guarantee Directive.

Exclusion of liability for economic loss is best dealt with, not by excluding liability for it in a guarantee, but by describing the product in such a way that it is clear the product cannot operate free of faults all the time in every environment, so that total reliance on a product in all situations, without some form of check or back up, cannot be recommended. The liability for repair or replacement of the product, either under the current legislation or the proposed Guarantee Directive remains unaffected, but such a clause should avoid the liability for economic loss caused by the defective product. Even if such clauses are not incorporated in the contract itself (for instance because they are contained in an operating manual read only after the contract has been concluded and the product is being readied for use) they do act as warnings to the consumer as to the actions he should take to avoid or mitigate the loss in question. It may be argued that the sort of loss dealt with by such clauses is often too remote to give rise to any legal liability to the consumer in any event, but some manufacturers, rather than relying on the rules of remoteness, do find such disclaimers helpful.

Precedent 1.3 gives an example of such a disclaimer, which would not cause problems under the current legislation, and would also seem to survive the proposed Guarantee Directive for the reasons discussed above. It must be emphasised that such clauses will fall to be scrutinised under the Unfair Terms Directive and Unfair Terms Regulations for fairness. Precedent 1.3 has been drafted with this in mind, but clearly drawing its existence to the attention of the consumer in a clear way will also be a necessary prerequisite of its enforceability.

5.4   Precedent 2

Where a consumer enters into a major transaction for the purchase of some expensive item such as a car or a suite of furniture, which has to be ordered and delivered at a later date, it is not unusual to find that a short written agreement is entered into. Here the areas of concern are time and procedures for delivery, and what happens if there is a price increase between the date of order and the date of delivery. Precedent 2 is a typical set of terms to deal with such issues.

Other issues are the consumer's rights to cancel, if he later changes his mind, and whether he has to pay a deposit. The usual procedure in the past was to allow no right of cancellation except for a period at the start of the contract, when cancellation is allowed on forfeiture of the deposit. In this connection, it should be noted that it is assumed that the agreement to which these terms relate is not a credit sale, so that the legislation relating to cooling-off periods, discussed in relation to Precedent 3, has no application.

Under the Unfair Terms Regulations (see paras 1(*c*)–(*f*) inclusive and (*l*) of the Annex), automatic forfeiture of the deposit on cancellation is in most cases likely to be unfair. This is discussed below in relation to Precedent 3. It should be noted that these provisions change the common law rules on the forfeiture of deposits.

Following the implementation of the Unfair Terms Directive, for such simple types of arrangement as envisaged by Precedent 2, the best way of dealing with the issue is to take a deposit, but not to allow cancellation, except perhaps for a brief cooling-off period granted on an *ex gratia* basis (some large retailers do this now) during which the deposit is returned in full. After this the contract should be silent on cancellation and the way the deposit is dealt with. If the consumer then refuses to perform, the retailer can presumably claim from him the loss of his bargain (subject to ordinary rules on mitigation of loss), deduct this amount from the deposit and refund the balance (if any).

5.5   Precedent 3

This precedent is a more elaborate contract for the supply of goods and services relating to small building works to be carried out on the consumer's house. The purpose of this document is not so much for use as a precedent to be followed in specific situations but for illustration of the principles of drafting consumer contracts. Each consumer contract of this nature will vary according to its subject matter, and will need considerable specific drafting, and consultation with the client, to ensure that the issues relevant to the particular transaction are properly covered.

The introduction to the precedent is useful in that it draws the attention of the consumer to the importance of the terms in the document, and at least makes it more difficult for him to claim later that he never read the terms, or did not realise their importance.

The first two parts set out the positive responsibilities which the contractor and the consumer respectively are agreeing to undertake under the contract. The third part states clearly and unambiguously those things which the contractor does not undertake, and the risks the consumer will run if he does not comply with certain specific instructions as to maintenance of the contract works after completion. This part is all-important, since it replaces the traditional exclusion clauses. This part of the contract should be outside the scope of s 3 of the UCTA, since the contractor is not excluding liability for breach of an obligation, but is clearly refusing to take on certain obligations in the first place. The principle of clearly stating which obligations are not undertaken should also survive the impact of the Unfair Terms Directive.

Part 4 relates to payment of the contract price by way of a deposit with the balance on completion. The provision for payment of interest if the settlement of the balance of the price is delayed is probably fair under the terms of the Unfair Terms Directive, provided the rate of interest is not excessive. The part also warns that in the event of cancellation the consumer's deposit may be forfeit.

Part 5 sets out the consumer's rights to cancel. This part is drawn up on the assumption of three possible situations.

First, the contractor may have arranged finance for the transaction. If this is so, and the finance agreement is a regulated agreement within the definition of s 8 of the Consumer Credit Act 1974 (a personal credit agreement by which the creditor provides the debtor with credit not exceeding £25,000) then the relevant finance agreement will fall within the definition of both a 'restricted-use credit agreement' and a 'debtor-creditor-supplier agreement' under ss 11 and 12 of the Act respectively, and the actual transaction between the consumer and the contractor will be a 'linked transaction' in relation to the finance agreement pursuant to s 19 of the Act.

Where the above applies, the finance agreement must be drawn up in compliance with the strict statutory requirements of the Consumer Credit Act 1974, and relevant statutory instruments, relating to both form and content, particularly as regards method of signature, and notification of the consumer's statutory rights. Failure to comply with these formalities renders the agreement unenforceable. (s 127 of the Act). Additionally, both the contractor and the supplier of the finance under the finance agreement are jointly and severally liable to the consumer for any misrepresentation or breach of contract under the linked transaction. (s 75 of the Act). Finally, the consumer has a statutory right to cancel the relevant finance agreement, and, if he does so, the contract between the consumer and the contractor, as a linked transaction, also terminates automatically (s 69 of the Act) and his deposit must be returned (s 70 of the Act).

The second possibility presumes that no finance has been arranged, in which case the Consumer Credit Act has no application, since under the terms of part 4 of the agreement no credit is granted to the consumer by the supplier. Leaving aside the possibility that the contract in question could have been concluded in circumstances where the Door-to-Door Regulations applied, it is still very often the practice to allow an *ex gratia* cooling-off period, and that is provided for in this precedent. As it stands the precedent would not satisfy the requirements of the Door-to-Door Regulations in relation to cancellation. A discussion of these requirements and a precedent is set out in section 5.6 below.

The rights to cancel under the first two possible situations in this part of the agreement relate only to a period before work has commenced. Under these circumstances, even where the Consumer Credit Act applies to the transaction its provisions relating to repayment of credit, return of goods in the consumer's possession and of goods given in part exchange by the consumer (ss 71, 72 and 73) have no application. However, the requirement for the return of the consumer's deposit is applicable not only where the transaction is a linked transaction (s 70) but is also usually provided for as part of the provisions relating to cooling-off periods otherwise granted by suppliers.

The third possibility is that the consumer may wish to cancel after the cooling-off period, when he has lost his statutory right to do so. In this case, he will have to obtain the agreement of the contractor.

The rights of the contractor to cancel, contained in part 6 of the agreement, relate only to circumstances where technical problems arise which cannot be circumvented, or in respect of which the consumer is unwilling to pay an increased fee to enable them to be circumvented, and where the consumer cannot obtain necessary finance for the transaction.

It is a question how far parts 5 and 6 can be regarded as fair in the light of paras 1(*c*) to (*f*) inclusive and (*l*) of the Annex to the Unfair Terms Directive. These paragraphs are not entirely clear, and in some cases seem to contradict or to be inconsistent with each other (for instance para 1(*d*) and the second part of para 1(*f*)) and in any event are only indicative, and only 'may' be regarded as unfair.

On balance, the provisions of parts 5 and 6 should be regarded as fair, since the consumer's rights to cancel are largely present to comply with statute, the contractor is not able to cancel the contract under part 6 without having a good reason to do so, and the consumer is not unduly penalised in the matter of the retention of his deposit in certain circumstances of cancellation (see the last part of para 1(*f*) of the Annex.)

Paragraph 1(*d*) of the Annex is particularly important. Its provisions prevent the current practice of the forfeiture of the consumer's deposit by the contractor (if the consumer decides to cancel after any relevant cooling-off period) unless the contractor undertakes to pay the consumer an amount equal to the deposit if the contractor cancels the contract. Such a 'reverse deposit' provision is unlikely to be attractive to contractors, and, in this case, might cause problems if the contractor chooses to cancel under Part 6.

Precedent 3 is therefore drafted on the basis that when such cancellation occurs, the actual direct damage (ie expenses and the value of work in progress) can be deducted from the deposit, and any balance paid over. If such charges are more than the value of the deposit, the consumer must pay the excess. If an offer is made to deliver work in progress to the consumer, such a provision would seem to be fair, since he will then have received, or could have received if he wished, value for what he has to pay, provided, given the wording of para 1(*e*), that such charges are fair and reasonable in amount and do not represent a disguised penalty.

The last point on Precedent 3 is that what is omitted is as important as what is included. There are no exclusions of liability in the sense that these are known in commercial transactions, and the consumer's remedies for defective design materials and workmanship are unhampered by any provision of the contract. The contractor will have to cover such potential liabilities either by making provision for them out of the profit margins he makes on all of his contracts generally, or by taking out insurance cover. Most prudent contractors in fact do both.

5.6 Door-to-Door Directive

The precedents discussed in the preceding sections of this chapter are not of themselves suitable for sales governed by the Door-to-Door Directive and the Door-to-Door Regulations. The main additional requirement is the conformance with a specified procedure relating to the notification to the consumer of the right of cancellation and the way the consumer should exercise that right. Appendix 3 sets out the detailed requirements contained in the Door-to-Door Regulations. It will be seen that the requirements of the Door-to-Door Regulations may be satisfied either by providing the consumer with a separate notice of cancellation or by incorporating one in the relevant contract or other documentation. In either case, the notice must incorporate a specimen Cancellation Form that the consumer can use. However, even if the consumer fails to use this form, the notice of cancellation will still be valid provided it is in writing and indicates the intention of the consumer to cancel (see reg 5(5)). A specimen notice of cancellation is set out as Precedent 4.

Consumer guarantee

Precedent 1.1 Statement on packaging

We guarantee that if the goods contained in this pack fail to satisfy you in any way, and you return them by post to us at the address stated below, we will refund you their purchase price and the cost of postage by return.

This guarantee is in addition to and does not affect your statutory rights.

Precedent 1.2 Statement on receipt

All our goods are guaranteed for a period of 12 months against defective materials and workmanship. In the event of any such defect please return the goods to us in their original packaging, together with proof and date of purchase, and we will refund you your postage (if any) and, at our choice, refund you their purchase price, repair and return them to you, or send new goods to you as a replacement.

Goods which have become defective for any other reason, such as accidental damage or failure to use in accordance with the operating manual, are not covered by this guarantee. If you return such goods to us, we will notify you of this, and we will, according to your choice, either return the goods or repair them for you if possible, but in each case at your expense.

This guarantee is in addition to and does not affect your statutory rights.

Precedent 1.3 Clause covering economic loss

However carefully your camera is manufactured and tested, it may still have some defect or from time to time require repair or maintenance. Thus before using your camera for the first time, and whenever you intend to take photographs of any important event or for any special purpose, please check in advance that it is properly maintained and in full working order and consult us if necessary. If the camera fails to take photographs because of some defect and it is covered under our warranty (which is in addition to your statutory rights) set out above [see precedent 1.1 above] we will of course repair or replace it or refund your money as appropriate. However, we can take no responsibility (other than, in the case of a defect covered by our warranty, to replace the spoiled film) for any disappointment, loss or expense you may suffer because the camera has failed to take the photographs you wanted.

Precedent 2

Purchase order for consumer goods

1 We are pleased to accept your order as set out below, and acknowledge receipt of your deposit as detailed below. Please note that if you change your mind you may cancel your order by notifying us of this in writing within [seven] days at the address above, and we will refund your deposit in full. After this date we regret that cancellation of your order will not be possible [unless paragraph 2 (delay in delivery) or paragraph 5 (price increases) applies].

2 The goods will be ready for delivery to your address within a reasonable period of time, which we currently estimate to be approximately [six weeks], from the date of your order. If the goods are not ready for delivery within [three months] from the date of your order you may cancel the order at any time after that, even if the goods are ready for delivery at that time. If you do cancel in this case your deposit will be returned to you in full.

3 We will contact you when the goods are ready for delivery, to request payment of the balance of the price, and to arrange a time for delivery once payment of the balance has been received. There will be a delivery charge of £[   ] and this is payable together with the balance of the price.

4 We would expect you to take delivery of the goods within a reasonable time, and if you cannot accept delivery within one month of the day when the goods are ready for delivery, we reserve the right to charge a reasonable storage fee to cover the period from the end of that month until delivery actually takes place.

5 If the rate of value added tax increases between the date of your order and the date of delivery we will add the necessary additional amount of value added tax to the price of the goods. If the price of the goods increases for any other reason between the date of your order and the date of delivery we will notify you of this, and give you the choice of accepting the price increase or cancelling the order in which case your deposit will be refunded in full.

[*Note*: the second guarantee above in Precedent 1 could be added (suitably adapted) if required.]

Precedent 3

Agreement for the supply of work and material to a consumer

Statements on front of quotation:

THE CONDITIONS OVERLEAF APPLY TO THIS QUOTATION AND TO
ANY CONTRACT BETWEEN US FOR THE SUPPLY OF WORK AND
MATERIALS DETAILED IN THIS QUOTATION.

TO PROTECT YOUR OWN INTERESTS PLEASE READ THE CONDI-
TIONS CAREFULLY BEFORE SIGNING THEM. WE WANT YOU TO
KNOW THAT YOU WILL ALWAYS GET A FAIR DEAL FROM US, AND
TO UNDERSTAND EXACTLY WHAT WE ARE BOTH AGREEING TO
UNDER OUR BARGAIN. IF YOU ARE UNCERTAIN AS TO YOUR
RIGHTS UNDER THEM OR YOU WANT ANY EXPLANATION ABOUT
THEM PLEASE WRITE OR TELEPHONE TO OUR CUSTOMER QUE-
RIES DEPARTMENT, AT THE ADDRESS AND TELEPHONE NUMBER
SET OUT BELOW.

IF YOU WISH TO ACCEPT THIS QUOTATION PLEASE SIGN THE
DUPLICATE COPY WHERE INDICATED AND RETURN IT TO US TO-
GETHER WITH YOUR DEPOSIT FOR THE AMOUNT STATED BELOW.

ONCE YOU ACCEPT THIS QUOTATION WE WILL BOTH HAVE EN-
TERED INTO A LEGALLY BINDING CONTRACT. HOWEVER, FOR A
SHORT PERIOD OF TIME YOU HAVE THE RIGHT TO CANCEL THIS
CONTRACT. YOUR RIGHTS TO DO SO, AND THE PROCEDURE YOU
MUST FOLLOW, ARE EXPLAINED OVERLEAF (PLEASE SEE PART 5
OF THE CONDITIONS).

[*Note*: the front page of the Quotation will contain the price (including deposit) and specification of the works, delivery schedule, and space for the signatures of both the contractor and the consumer, and the dates on which they
each sign. Given that the conditions overleaf envisage that the transaction covered by them may be a linked transaction under the Consumer Credit Act 1974,

the statement above dealing with the consumer's rights of cancellation is designed to draw attention to his statutory rights of cancellation under that Act.]

1   Our responsibility

(*a*) We will ensure that the design of your installation complies with safe building practice, and our quotation is made only on this basis. Before starting work we will carry out a technical survey to make sure that this is the case, and also that the work as quoted for is appropriate and practicable. We will let you have a copy of the technical survey report when the technical survey is finished.

(*b*) If, after technical survey, any further work is necessary, because of alterations in design or otherwise, to complete the work quoted for, and this causes an increase in costs, we will send you, together with the copy of the technical survey report, a further quotation giving details of the extra costs; we will (at your request) discuss and explain the technical survey report and the further quotation and will, in any case, only carry out the whole job (including the further work) once your written acceptance has been received.

(*c*) Subject to paragraphs (*a*) and (*b*) above we will carry out the work in accordance with our quotation.

(*d*) We will make every effort to complete the work on time, but you will appreciate that we cannot be held responsible for delays due to weather or other circumstances beyond our control. In this case we will complete the work as soon as reasonably possible.

(*e*) In addition to your statutory rights we will provide you with a Guarantee Certificate (which is transferable to future owners of your house) once the work has been completed and payment has been made in full.

(*f*) We will make good any damage caused in the course of installation to plaster, floor, render, brickwork and so on, immediately surrounding any window or door installed, to a standard which will accept redecoration.

(*g*) We will prime all new softwood timber likely to be exposed to the weather.

(*h*) We will remove all old windows, doors and glass, and other building rubble, from the site, unless you wish us to leave them.

(*i*) We will on completion leave all surfaces clean and tidy.

2   Your responsibility

(*a*) You will permit us, during normal working hours, first to conduct a technical survey, and then to undertake the installation, according to the programme set out in the quotation.

(*b*) You will ensure, at the time of installation, that all pelmets, rails, blinds, furnishings, radiators and so on are removed so that we can carry out the installation.

(*c*) You will cover and protect from dirt and dust all fixtures and fittings not required to be removed.

(*d*) You will obtain all permissions and consents (including, if necessary, planning permission) from landlords, local authorities and so on, which are required before the job can be carried out.

(*e*) You will provide, at no cost to us, within ten metres of the installation, an electricity supply of 220/240 volts with a three-pin point.

(*f*) You will redecorate, and in particular carry out the finishing coats of paintwork or stain to any timber we have left primed.

3　Things you should know

We do not undertake structural or other types of building surveys, and therefore, if the work cannot be completed, or any damage is caused through existing structural or other defects in your property, we cannot be responsible for this.

The glass supplied by us is of standard commercial quality, and optical phenomena or minor cosmetic blemishes may occasionally occur in such glass due to the manufacturing process.

We do not undertake to provide matching ceramic or other tiles, or specialised finishes (eg pebble dash), or to avoid damage to wallpaper or paintwork immediately surrounding any window or door installed.

We do not undertake to remove intact any panes of glass or frames you may wish to keep.

Our products do not in all circumstances reduce or eliminate condensation, as this depends on prevailing conditions in and around the building where the product is installed, and these conditions are beyond our control.

If you provide us with incorrect measurements or any other incorrect information, and we rely on this in preparing our quotation, we reserve the right to increase our price to cover the cost of making good any errors or doing any additional work required because of them.

If you do not complete the finishing coats of paintwork or stain within a reasonable time, and redecorate and maintain them properly in the future, damage will result to timber frames, beads and putties, and the double glazing units, and we can take no responsibility for any loss or damage resulting.

Additionally, with certain products, special types of maintenance may be required. We will provide you with the necessary instructions for this on the Guarantee Certificate (see para 1(*e*), above), and again we can take no responsibility for damage caused because you did not carry out maintenance work as specified in those instructions.

4   Your deposit

At the time the contract is signed, a deposit of a specified amount must be paid. The balance of the contract price will be due upon satisfactory completion of the work.

If you fail to pay the balance in full within seven days of the date when it becomes due we may charge interest at a rate of [2 per cent] per month on any outstanding amounts.

Should you later cancel your order your deposit might not be repaid. You should refer to part 5 below.

5   Your right to cancel

If we have arranged for you to finance payment for the work through a finance company which we have recommended to you then we will give you a copy of the contract signed by both you and us, and the finance company will arrange in due course for you to have a copy of the credit agreement signed by the finance company and yourself. From the date on which you first have in your possession fully signed copies of both of these documents, you will then have a period of five days in which you may cancel BOTH the contract and the credit agreement by giving notice of cancellation in writing to the finance company. At the same time please send a copy of your notice of cancellation to us. If you do cancel in this way we will return your deposit to you in full.

In a case where we have not arranged for you a source of finance, then any financing arrangements will be your own responsibility, but you may cancel the order itself by notice in writing to us within five days of your receiving a copy of the order signed by you and us. Again, in this case, we will return your deposit to you in full.

Apart from the special circumstances described above, you may only cancel your order with our agreement. If we do agree such cancellation, your deposit will be returned to you, but only after we have deducted a fair and reasonable amount for our expenses incurred up to the date of cancellation. Since our products are custom made to your requirements and measurements, if we have already started work on your contract, we are unlikely to be able to use any items we have made elsewhere. In this case, we will deduct the value of these items from your deposit, and ask you to pay any additional amount if their value is more than the amount of your deposit. Where you pay for such items, we will deliver (but not install) them for you free of charge if you wish us to do so.

Any notice to cancel the contract, and any copy of a notice to cancel the credit agreement, must be given, in writing, for the attention of the Sales Manager and posted or delivered by hand to the address shown overleaf, quoting the contract number. For cancellation of the credit agreement, notice in writing will again be necessary, and you should follow the instructions contained in the credit agreement as to the procedure for giving notice.

6   Our right to cancel

We reserve the right to cancel this contract in the following three cases:

    (1)   where, after a technical survey has been carried out, it is apparent that the work as shown in our quotation cannot be carried out for safety or other technical reasons;

    (2)   where, after a technical survey has been carried out, we find it necessary to recommend design changes for safety or other technical reasons which you do not want to agree to, either because they will cost more, or for any other reason; and

    (3)   where we have arranged for you to finance payment for the work through a finance company which we have recommended to you and your application for finance is not accepted by the finance company.

In the first two cases, you will have received a copy of the technical survey report, together, in the second case, with the quotation for further work (see paragraphs 1(*a*) and (*b*) above). We will explain the report and quotation (if any) to you and discuss the situation with you to see if together we can agree a way to carry out the work subject to changes in design and price which are acceptable to both of us. If we cannot reach agreement within [a reasonable period of time] [ten days] from the date our discussions start, we will cancel this contract by giving you notice in writing, posted or delivered by hand to your address shown overleaf, to take effect immediately you receive it.

In the third case, we will notify you in writing of the rejection of your application for finance, and give you [fourteen days] to make alternative financial arrangements. If you do not wish to make alternative arrangements or you are unable to do so within the period of [fourteen days] we will cancel this contract by giving you notice in writing, posted or delivered by hand to your address shown overleaf, to take effect immediately you receive it.

In the case of cancellation under all three cases, we will return your deposit to you, but in the third case we will first deduct any fair and reasonable expenses we have incurred, up to the date of cancellation.

Specimen Cancellation Notice

XYZ Encyclopaedias Ltd
XYZ House
123 Any Road, Any Town
AB1 2CD

Dear Mr Jones

Contract reference number AB/123 dated 10 December 2000

Following the visit of our representative to your home last week, I have pleasure in enclosing a signed acceptance for your order for one copy of the *Gardener's World Encyclopaedia* in ten volumes. Our contract reference number for your order is set out above.

You have the right to cancel this contract, within the period of seven days from the date you receive this notice, by sending or taking a written notice of cancellation to the Sales Manager, XYZ Encyclopaedias Ltd, at the above address.

I attach a cancellation form which I have already filled out for you, and which you can use for your convenience if you wish.

Yours sincerely

XYZ Encyclopaedias Ltd

Cancellation Form
(Complete, detach and return this form ONLY IF YOU WISH TO CANCEL
THE CONTRACT)

To: The Sales Manager, XYZ Encyclopaedias Ltd at XYZ House, 123 Any Road, Any Town, AB1 2CD.

I, Mr A Jones of 456 Any Street, Any Town, EF3 4GH, hereby give notice that I wish to cancel my contract reference number AB/123 dated 10 December 2000 for one copy of the *Gardener's World Encyclopaedia* in ten volumes.

Signed

A Jones
Date

Appendix 1

Terms referred to in art 3(3)

1   Terms which have the object or effect of:

(*a*) excluding or limiting the legal liability of a seller or supplier in the event of the death of a customer or personal injury to the latter resulting from an act or omission of that seller or supplier;

(*b*) inappropriately excluding or limiting the legal rights of the consumer *vis-à-vis* the seller or supplier or another party in the event of total or partial non-performance or inadequate performance by the seller or supplier of any of the contractual obligations, including the option of offsetting a debt owed to the seller or supplier against any claim which the consumer may have against him;

(*c*) making an agreement binding on the consumer whereas provision of services by the seller or supplier is subject to a condition whose realisation depends on his own will alone;

(*d*) permitting the seller or supplier to retain sums paid by the consumer where the latter decides not to conclude or perform the contract, without providing for the consumer to receive compensation of an equivalent amount from the seller or supplier where the latter is the party cancelling the contract;

(*e*) requiring any consumer who fails to fulfil his obligation to pay a disproportionately high sum in compensation;

(*f*) authorising the seller or supplier to dissolve the contract on a discretionary basis where the same facility is not granted to the consumer, or permitting the seller or supplier to retain the sums paid for services not yet supplied by him where it is the seller or supplier who dissolves the contract;

(*g*) enabling the seller or supplier to terminate a contract of indeterminate duration without reasonable notice except where there are serious grounds for doing so;

(*h*) automatically extending a contract of fixed duration where the consumer does not indicate otherwise, when the deadline fixed for the consumer to express this desire not to extend the contract is unreasonably early;

(*i*) irrevocably binding the consumer to terms with which he had no real opportunity of becoming acquainted before the conclusion of the contract;

(*j*) enabling the seller or supplier to alter the terms of the contract unilaterally without a valid reason which is specified in the contract;

(*k*) enabling the seller or supplier to alter unilaterally without a valid reason any characteristics of the product or service to be provided;

(*l*) providing for the price of goods to be determined at the time of delivery or allowing a seller of goods or supplier of services to increase their price without in both cases giving the consumer the corresponding right to cancel the contract if the final price is too high in relation to the price agreed when the contract was concluded;

(*m*) giving the seller or supplier the right to determine whether the goods or services supplied are in conformity with the contract, or giving him the exclusive right to interpret any term of the contract;

(*n*) limiting the seller's or supplier's obligation to respect commitments undertaken by his agents or making his commitments subject to compliance with a particular formality;

(*o*) obliging the consumer to fulfil all his obligations where the seller or supplier does not perform his;

(*p*) giving the seller or supplier the possibility of transferring his rights and obligations under the contract, where this may serve to reduce the guarantees for the consumer, without the latter's agreement; or

(*q*) excluding or hindering the consumer's right to take legal action or exercise any other legal remedy, particularly by requiring the consumer to take disputes exclusively to arbitration not covered by legal provisions, unduly restricting the evidence available to him or imposing on him a burden of proof which, according to the applicable law, should lie with another party to the contract.

2   Scope of subparagraphs (*g*), (*j*) and (*l*)

(*a*) Subparagraph (*g*) is without hindrance to terms by which a supplier of financial services reserves the right to terminate unilaterally a contract of indeterminate duration without notice where there is a valid reason, provided that the supplier is required to inform the other contracting party or parties thereof immediately.

(*b*) Subparagraph (*j*) is without hindrance to terms under which a supplier of financial services reserves the right to alter the rate of interest payable by the consumer or due to the latter, or the amount of other charges for financial services without notice where there is a valid reason, provided that the supplier is required to inform the other contracting party or parties thereof at the earliest opportunity and that the latter are free to dissolve the contract immediately.

Subparagraph (*j*) is also without hindrance to terms under which a seller or supplier reserves the right to alter unilaterally the conditions of a contract of indeterminate duration, provided that he is required to inform the consumer with reasonable notice and that the consumer is free to dissolve the contract.

(*c*) Subparagraphs (*g*), (*j*) and (*l*) do not apply to:

      (i) transactions in transferable securities, financial instruments and other products or services where the price is linked to fluctuations in a stock exchange quotation or index or a financial market rate that the seller or supplier does not control;

     (ii) contracts for the purchase or sale of foreign currency, travellers' cheques or international money orders denominated in foreign currency.

  (*d*) Subparagraph (*l*) is without hindrance to price-indexation clauses, where lawful, provided that the method by which prices vary is explicitly described.

Appendix 2

Summary of Office of Fair Trading Bulletin No 4 on unfair terms

1 Clauses considered for unfairness:

- exclusion of liability for death or personal injury
- no liability for breaches of contract
- excluding liability for poor work or work and materials
- restricting the level and type of liability
- unreasonable time limits on notification of claims
- binding the consumer when the supplier is at fault
- assignment clauses
- restricting the consumer's remedies
- excluding rights of set-off
- excluding liability for delay
- allowing a supplier not to perform obligations at all
- binding consumer while allowing supplier to offer no service
- allowing retention of prepayments
- penalties
- unequal cancellation rights
- termination subject to conditions
- termination without notice
- automatic renewal clauses
- binding consumers to hidden terms
- general variation clauses
- allowing changes in what is supplied
- price variation clauses
- giving the supplier the right of final decision
- entire agreement clauses
- allowing the supplier to impose undue financial burdens
- inappropriate indemnification clauses
- unfair enforcement clauses
- non-assignable guarantees
- signed statements re contractual circumstances.

2 Clauses considered for plain and intelligible language:

Clauses using legal jargon, excessive cross-references, double negatives and other convoluted language rewritten. The test in most cases is can the intelligent layman understand the clause without having to take legal advice. In

particular the following terms were considered too technical in various clauses:
- indemnify
- waiver
- without prejudice
- time of the essence
- lien
- force majeure
- references to statutory rights.

Appendix 3

Cancellation procedure under the Door-to-Door Regulations

Regulation 4(1)

No contract to which these regulations apply shall be enforceable against the consumer unless the trader has delivered to the consumer notice in writing in accordance with paragraphs (3) and (4) below indicating the right of the consumer to cancel the contract within the period of seven days mentioned in paragraph (5) below containing both the information set out in Part I of the Schedule to these Regulations and a Cancellation Form in the form set out in Part II of the Schedule to these Regulations and completed in accordance with the footnotes.

Regulation 4(3)

The information to be contained in the notice under paragraph (1) shall be easily legible and if incorporated in the contract or other document shall be afforded no less prominence than that given to any other information in the document apart from the heading to the document and the names of the parties to the contract and any information inserted in handwriting.

Regulation 4(4)

The notice shall be dated and delivered to the consumer [when a contract is concluded on a consumer visit or event] at the time of the making of the contract; and [where the consumer makes an offer] at the time of the making of the offer by the consumer.

Regulation 4(5)

If within a period of 7 days following the making of the contract the consumer serves a notice in writing (a 'notice of cancellation') on the trader or any other person specified in a notice referred to in paragraph (1) above ... which, however expressed and whether or not conforming to the cancellation form set out in Part II of the Schedule ... indicates the intention of the consumer to cancel the contract, the notice of cancellation shall operate to cancel the contract.

Regulation 4(7)

Notwithstanding anything in section 7 of the Interpretation Act 1978, a notice of cancellation sent by post by a consumer shall be deemed to have been served at the time of posting whether or not it is actually received.

Part I of the Schedule

Information to be contained in Notice of Cancellation Rights

1 Name of the Trader.
2 The trader's reference number, code or other details to enable the contract or offer to be identified.
3 A statement that the consumer has a right to cancel the contract if he wishes and that this right can be exercised by sending or taking a written notice of cancellation to the person mentioned in paragraph 4 within the period of 7 days following the making of the contract.
4 The name and address of a person to whom notice of cancellation may be given.
5 A statement that the consumer can use the cancellation form provided if he wishes.

Part II of the Schedule

Cancellation Form to be included in Notice of Cancellation of Rights

(Complete, detach and return this form ONLY IF YOU WISH TO CANCEL THE CONTRACT)

To: [Trader to insert name and address of person to whom notice may be given]

I/We* hereby give notice that I/we* wish to cancel my/our* contract [Trader to insert reference number, code or other details to enable the contract or offer to be identified. He may also insert name and address of the consumer].

Signed

Date

Part II

Agency and Distribution

Chapter 6

Basic principles

6.1 Introduction

Manufacturers or importers of goods have a number of ways in which they can arrange the supply chain by which their products reach the ultimate consumer. Some of them prefer no continuing formal arrangements, and simply market their products to a number of wholesalers who place orders for such products as and when they choose, but most manufacturers or importers prefer a more orderly arrangement.

The choices open to them are either to set up a vertically integrated supply chain, where they own and control the various links in that chain, to appoint distributors or a network of distributors at various levels in the supply chain, or to deal directly with suppliers at various levels in the supply chain (perhaps wholesalers or retailers) but (in some cases) through and with the assistance of a network of agency agreements.

Vertical integration has the attraction of total control, but brings with it the assumption of all of the risk and expense associated with the supply chain. The use of distributors effectively removes the risk and expense of the supply chain from the manufacturer or importer, but this is at the price of loss of most of the control over the supply chain and a reduction in the margins received when selling to a distributor who requires remuneration himself in order to take on the risk and expense of distribution. The use of agents is a middle way in that some of the risk and expense are borne by the agent, and the specialist marketing services of the agent are available to the principal on a basis (remuneration by way of commission) which provides the maximum incentive to the agent to act efficiently and effectively. However, the principal still remains as much in control as if he were negotiating directly with the relevant level in the supply chain. If this level is a low one (eg retailers) the principal can be in almost the same position as if he had set up a vertically integrated supply chain.

Most of the issues concerned with agency and distribution revolve around the attempts of various jurisdictions to regulate the relevant relationships by law, particularly to ensure that such relationships are not used to restrict competition contrary to public policy. Thus any draftsman dealing with such agreements has to be concerned with three main issues: the commercial arrangements under which the distributor or agent will deal with third parties; the commercial arrangements between the distributor or agent and his principal, particularly in regard to remuneration and in the area of control by the principal over the other party's activities; and the impact which competition or regulatory law of the relevant jurisdiction has on the first two issues.

In this chapter, the basic principles of agency and distribution agreements will be considered, particularly in the light of EC and UK competition law. In Chapter 7 precedents for short and long form agency agreements will be analysed, and in Chapter 8 precedents for various types of distribution agreement will be considered.

6.2   Definition of agency

When the term 'agent' is used in its proper legal sense, it denotes someone who has the power to act on behalf of his principal for the purpose of concluding a legally binding relationship (often a contract) between a third party and the principal. The agent is not a party to this relationship and has no liability under it (except in the special cases of the *del credere* agent, and the agent acting for an undisclosed principal, discussed below). Further, the agent is entitled to an indemnity from his principal against any liability to the third party in respect of the relationship so created, and to be compensated for his expenses properly incurred in the discharge of his duties. Should he exceed his authority he may still bind his principal, but in that event he will be liable to both his principal and the third party for so doing.

The agency relationship is a consensual one, created by the intention of the parties, but, even in common law jurisdictions, a contract supported by consideration is not necessary. However, because it is really a relationship involving three parties (agent, principal and third party), agency should be regarded rather as a status where the network of rights and obligations between the three parties subsists and is regulated under the general law. This has always been the case in Civil Code jurisdictions, and largely so in common law jurisdictions as well, except that, in the latter, the relationship between the agent and the principal can always be regulated by an express contract based on the will of the parties which overrides the general law to the extent that it is inconsistent.

However, irrespective of the legal definition, in business circles the term 'agent' tends to be misused since most commercial agents have the power to introduce customers to their principal, some may have the power to negotiate (often within rigidly defined guidelines), but very few have the power to conclude contracts on behalf of their principal.

Commercial agents who merely introduce prospects are often called sales representatives or consultants. They normally receive an agreed commission on orders actually accepted by the principal from the prospective customers whom they introduce, and are therefore sometimes called commission agents. Commercial agents who actually go seeking orders, and then forward them to their principals are often called canvassing agents. However, they are more properly called indenting agents if they also have the power to accept the orders on behalf of their principal, and forward concluded orders merely for automatic execution. Usually this only occurs in the case of commodities, or standard manufactured items, sold to defined lead times from a set price list.

The *del credere* agent is an exception to the rule that an agent takes no liability in respect of the relationship between the principal and the third party. Here, the agent guarantees the credit of the third party introduced by him and agrees to compensate the principal if the third party fails to pay in accordance with the contract finally concluded between the principal and the third party.

Where an agent fails to disclose to the third party that he is acting as agent, then he is regarded as acting as 'agent for an undisclosed principal'. In practice this means that, although the relationship between the principal and the agent is unaffected, not only is the principal liable on the contract with the third party, but so is the agent.

There are other types of agents used in the commercial world who have little to do with commercial agency in the pure sense as described above. For instance, forwarding and clearing agents handle the formalities concerned with the transportation of goods for their principals, particularly export and import licences and customs clearance. Confirming agents have a role halfway between that of a distributor and an agent. The confirming agent acts as agent for his principal for the purpose of entering into a contract for the purchase of goods, but is himself liable on the contract with the third party seller. He pays the seller, and the goods are sent direct by the seller to his principal. He is then reimbursed by his principal for the purchase price and any expenses (under the principle of the indemnity owed by the principal to his agent) and in addition is paid an agreed remuneration (usually by way of commission). This concept is the opposite of the *del credere* agent in that the agent in effect guarantees the credit of his principal rather than that of the customer.

6.3 European Commission Notice on Exclusive Agency Agreements

In terms of EC law, the commercial agency relationship is looked upon primarily as one of status, rather than arising out of contract. The current statement of the Commission's view is the Commission Notice on Exclusive Agency

Agreements of 24 December 1962. Commercial agents are defined as those who negotiate or negotiate and conclude a commercial contract on behalf of their principal. They perform an auxiliary function rather like an employee, and thus are considered to be an extension of their principal rather than an independent entity.

They are to be distinguished from the independent trader who assumes the risk on a transaction. Carrying stock, free customer service, setting prices or terms and conditions, are some of the things that indicate an independent trader, even if he resembles an agent in other respects. A trader who clearly purchases and resells on his own account is of course outside the scope of the announcement. However, the risk assumed by a *del credere* agent is expressly stated not to put him outside the definition of a commercial agent for the purposes of the Notice.

When looking at the various types of agent mentioned above it is clear that all types of commercial agents who have full authority to negotiate and conclude contracts will be covered by the Notice, as will those who can carry out negotiations but not conclude. *A fortiori* sales representatives and consultants and commission and canvassing agents who take even less risk should be covered by the Notice, even if they have very little negotiating power in practice.

The agent who chooses to act for an undisclosed principal, or as a confirming agent, is likely to be excluded on the grounds that he takes the risk in the transaction. Forwarding and clearing agents do not fall within the definition at all.

On the basis of this reasoning, the Notice states that the provisions of art 85(1) of the Treaty of Rome cannot apply to the exclusive commercial agency contract. The agent cannot in truth be regarded as a separate undertaking from his principal, and therefore it is not possible to find two undertakings (in the terms prescribed by art 85(1) as a precondition for its application) who are parties to the arrangement between the agent and the principal. The extent to which non-exclusive agency contracts are covered by the Notice is less clear, but presumably the test still turns upon whether or not the agent is regarded as a separate undertaking from his principal. Thus, in principle, the question of exclusivity or non-exclusivity is irrelevant for the purposes of art 85. If the agent is to be regarded as one undertaking with his principal the article will not apply, whatever the terms of the agency agreement.

There is one further issue of competition law raised by the Commission under the Notice, in relation to exclusive agency agreements. Under such agreements, the agent agrees to supply his services as an agent only to the principal, and the principal agrees to use only the services of the agent, in respect of particular products or a particular territory. If one considers that the supply and use of agency services is itself a market, then an exclusive agency agreement could be said to be an agreement which affects competition in that market. A principal who is a party to such an agreement is restricted in the use of other agents, while an agent who is party to such an agreement is restricted in the supply of his services to other principals. However, in the Notice, the Commission states that it regards the restrictions in such agreements as arising from the 'special obligations' to protect each other's interests which exist between the commercial agent and his principal. Consequently, the Commission states that it did not regard such restrictions as of themselves involving any restrictions on competition.

6.4 Circumstances where agency agreements are affected by art 85

The statements made in section 6.3 have, however, to be qualified in the light of certain European Court and Commission decisions, made after the publication of the 1962 Notice, which defined certain situations where the agent is considered to be sufficiently independent of his principal that principal and agent can be looked at as two separate undertakings. In these rather rare situations, art 85 can apply to the agency relationship. The basic test to be applied is whether the agent is truly economically dependent upon his principal, or whether his activity as an agent is just one of a number of activities which go to make up his business. In the latter case he cannot be said to be so dependent upon his principal that he and the principal should be regarded as one undertaking. This economic independence can arise in two ways.

First, the agent can carry on other activities than agency, such as distribution, the manufacture and sale of his own products, or the sale of his own services. See Decision of the Commission *Re Pittsburgh Corning Europe* [1973] CMLR D2, European Court Decision *Suiker Unie et al v EC Commission* [1976] 1 CMLR 295 and *Re Eirpage* (Commission Decision (1991) OJ L306 and the European Court Decision in Case C-266/93, *Bundeskartellamt v Volkswagen AG VAG Leasing GmbH*. However, it does not automatically follow that every agent who carries on another activity will always be regarded as an independent undertaking. For instance in the Decision of the Commission *Re Austin Rover Group/Unipart* (Commission Decision [1987] 1 CMLR 446), the Commission decided that Unipart was one undertaking with Austin Rover, for whom it acted as agent for the supply of certain categories of its spare parts, even though it also acted as distributor for Austin Rover in respect of other categories. In part, the reasoning behind the case may have been influenced by the fact that Unipart was a division of Austin Rover which had been sold off, so that Unipart was still clearly very dependent upon Austin Rover for its continued survival.

Secondly, the agent can act for a number of principals. The classic example here is the travel agent who acts for very many principals and who can in truth be regarded as dependent upon no particular one of them (see the European Court of Justice decision in the *Flemish Travel Agents* case (*Vlaamse Reiseburos v EC Commission*) [1983] ECR 1241, *Re International Federation of Associa-*

tion Football (FIFA), Commission Decision (1992) OJ L326 and *Re Consilio Nazionale degli Spedizionieri Doganali/Associazione Italiana dei Corrieri Aeri Internazionali*, Commission Decision (1993) OJ L203). The test in these cases seems to be somewhat subjective and to depend upon the number of principals for which the agent acts. It cannot be assumed that an agent who made a living acting for a small number of principals would necessarily be regarded as an independent trade.

Considering all of these decision, the Commission attempted in 1990 to revise the 1962 'Christmas Message' by a new Notice on Commercial Agency Agreements. This Notice was issued in draft, and attempted to lay down principles to distinguish between agents who were to be considered as economically dependent upon their principals, and therefore one undertaking with them ('integrated agents') and those who were not. The draft was complicated, and some of the points it made were of doubtful legal validity. In any event, it aroused considerable opposition from industry, and appears to have been dropped. It appears that currently the Commission is giving some thought to revising the 1962 Notice again, but at the moment, the 1962 Notice remains in force in its original form as supplemented by the decisions set out above.

6.5   European Council Directive on Self-employed Commercial Agents

Given the Civil Code emphasis on the regulation of all aspects of the agency relationship by the general law, it is not surprising that many countries in continental Europe (for example France) have legislation regulating the terms upon which commercial agents act for their principals, setting out the rights and duties of both sides, particularly in the area of remuneration and compensation for termination. Although these concepts are wholly alien to the common law in general, and to UK practice in particular, the Council Directive 653/1986 on self-employed commercial agents chose to adopt the Civil Code approach, thus bringing about a fundamental change in the way agency agreements have to be approached both in the UK and in Ireland.

The Directive caught all new agreements made after 1 January 1990, except in the UK and Ireland (1 January 1994) and in Italy (as regards the provisions on compensation only, 1 January 1993). In any event all existing agreements were caught from 1 January 1994 throughout the EC (see art 22). Thus by 1 January 1994 the Directive had been fully implemented for both new and existing agreements in all of the then member states of the EC, and also within the EEA. So far as states which have become members of the EC after that date their relevant treaties of accession apply this legislation to agency agreements, on and from the date of accession.

Within the UK, the Directive was implemented by statutory instrument. So far as England, Wales and Scotland are concerned (Great Britain) the enabling instrument is the Commercial Agents (Council Directive) Regulations 1993 (SI No 3053) (mention should also be made of SI 1993 No 3173 which corrected an error in SI 1993 No 3503, by adding the words 'indemnity or' after the opening word of the first line of reg 17). The Directive was implemented for Northern Ireland by a separate set of regulations, the Commercial Agents (Council Directive) Regulations (Northern Ireland) 1993 (Statutory Rules for Northern Ireland 1993 No 483), with similar provisions. In this chapter, however, references to the Regulations should be understood as references to SI 1993 No 3053 as amended.

Commercial agents having the authority to negotiate, or to negotiate and conclude a transaction for their principal are covered by the Directive, and here the same considerations as in the Commission Notice would be relevant to determine who was an agent as opposed to an independent trader (see art 1(2) and (3)). However, commodity agents and unpaid agents are specifically excluded, and so-called 'secondary' agents (ie those who in general carry on the basic business of buying and selling on their own account, and only act as agents to a limited extent as a subsidiary activity) may be excluded at the option of each member state (see art 2(2)). The UK has chosen to implement this option, and the Regulations contain a Schedule which gives guidelines as to what types of agents are to be regarded as secondary for the purposes of the Regulations.[6]

The question is the extent to which canvassing agents, commission agents or mere sales representatives are covered. In practice, judging by the Civil Code provisions of the various member states upon which the Directive is based, the standard of negotiation required is not likely to be a very high one, so most of these so-called commercial agents are likely to be caught, except those whose activities fall very clearly in the area of marketing or sales consultancy. An interesting but unresolved question is whether the extent of negotiating power required to cause an 'agent' to come within the terms of the Notice is the same as that required to bring him within the terms of the Directive. Since the words are the same, logically there should be no difference, but the Notice and the Directive each have a very different status and purpose. The Commission would want to restrict the ambit of the Notice (as a statement of the limitations on the applicability of art 85(1)) while extending the Directive as wide as possible in the interests of protection of agents in general.

In any event, it should be remembered that there is no penalty for putting in a representative agreement provisions inconsistent with the Directive on the basis that it does not apply. The worst that can happen is that the representative will go to law to claim that the Directive is applicable, the court will find for him, and the inconsistent provisions will be ruled inoperative.

The Directive imposes an overall obligation on both parties to act in good faith towards each other, and to provide each other the information needed to fulfil the other's obligations under the contract. In particular, the agent must give the principal proper and regular market intelligence, and the principal must notify the agent if he anticipates that volume of business will be less than the agent would normally expect (see arts 3 and 4). The parties may not derogate from these provisions by contract (see art 5).

The Directive specifies that the level of remuneration shall be as agreed between the principal and agent, except that, if no agreement exists, remuneration shall be that customary for the trade and territory in question, or, if no customary rates can be adduced, what is reasonable in the circumstances (see art 6).

Where the agent is remunerated wholly or partly by way of commission, he is entitled to that commission both on the contracts he concludes, and on those concluded directly (or perhaps through another agent) by the principal with customers generated by the agent (see art 7(1)). In addition, if contracts are concluded (whether directly or through another agent) in a territory or customer group which has been specifically entrusted to the agent, the agent will be entitled to commission on the transaction whether it relates to a customer he has generated or not (see art 7(2)). (Here the Directive does allow each member state the option in its enabling legislation to specify that this provision will only apply in the case of exclusive agents, and the UK has adopted this approach in the Regulations.)

The agent is also entitled to continue to receive commission on contracts concluded after his appointment terminated if the order reached the principal or the agent before termination, and, for a reasonable period, on transactions entered into after termination, if they came about due to his efforts before termination (see art 8).

A new agent who has been appointed in substitution for the old agent is not entitled to post-termination commission paid to the old agent under art 8, unless 'it is equitable because of the circumstances' for the two agents to share such commission between them (see art 9).

The agent has the right to be paid when the principal executes his part of the contract, or when the third party executes his part, provided that he must be paid no later than when the third party has executed (see art 10). If the principal fails to perform on a contract through his own default, the agent is still entitled to payment of his commission on the contract, and this is due no later than when the third party would have executed the contract (if the principal had not defaulted) (see art 11). The agent is entitled to a quarterly statement of commissions due to him from his principal, and to an extract from the principal's books to determine if he is being paid the proper commission (see art 12). A combination of arts 10(4) and 11(3) and 12(3) ensures that the parties cannot contract out of the rules relating to entitlement to and payment of commission to the detriment of the agent.

If the agreement is for an indefinite period, the agent must be given at least one month's notice for each year of the duration of the agreement, up to a maximum of three years. The Directive gives member states the option to extend the scheme on the same basis up to a maximum of six months' notice for six years (see art 15). (The UK government has not taken this option, see *King v T. Tunnock Ltd* [1995] SCLR 742) If the agreement is for a fixed term, it expires automatically unless the parties continue to operate as if it were still in effect after the expiry of the fixed term, in which case it is deemed to be converted into an agreement for an indefinite period (see art 14).

Where termination or expiry by effluxion of time brings the agreement to an end without any fault on the part of the agent, or if the agent retires (due to age, infirmity or ill-health) or dies, the principal is bound to pay him equitable compensation (see arts 16, 17 and 18). This compensation can be calculated on one of two bases: indemnity (art 17(1)) or compensation (art 17(2)). The Commission originally agreed to the incorporation of alternative remedies on the basis that all of the member states could not agree on one remedy. The remedy of compensation is copied from the French law, and the remedy of indemnity from the German law. Article 17(6) required the Commission to submit a report to the Council on the operation of art 17, for the purpose of assessing the practical consequences of the two options, and to decide if one option or the other is more advantageous to the agent. If necessary, after enquiry, art 17(6) required the Commission to submit a proposal to the Council to amend the Directive in this respect. The Commission sought information from interested parties during 1995 and published its report on 23 July 1996 (COM (96) 364). This report is required reading for anyone who wishes to understand the nature and principles of the remedies for compensation or indemnity contained in art 17, and how the amounts payable are calculated under these remedies. The Commission was satisfied with the operation of art 17, and recommended no changes to it. However, it drew attention to the guidelines contained in the report for the detailed understanding and operation of the two remedies.

The remedy of compensation can basically be regarded as a payment made by the principal to the agent for the 'purchase' of the good will that the agent has created for the principal by his activities under the agency agreement. In French courts the typical level of payment seems to be about two years' average commission.

The calculation of the payment under the remedy of indemnity in Germany depends upon a formula. The court decides how much annual revenue the principal enjoys, as a result of the activities of the agent, at the moment of termination of the agency agreement. This revenue is deemed to continue to be enjoyed by the agent for a number of years into the future, but to decrease gradually to zero at a rate (called the 'decay rate') which reflects the court's judgment as to how soon the customers generated by the agent will move away from the principal to other sources of supply. The arrangements for commission set out in the agency agreement are then applied to this revenue stream to produce a commission stream for the agent. The court reduces this to its net present value, to arrive at a lump sum. The court has the power to adjust this sum up or down for reasons of equity, but rarely does so. If this sum is less than one year's commission for the agent, averaged over the last five years, or the life of the agency agreement if shorter, the agent receives the lump sum. If the lump sum is higher than the average commission, the agent receives only the average commission. In awards in German courts the lump sum seems in most cases to be calculated at about half of the average annual commission, so that the cut-off provision is rarely applied. This is because the courts are particularly severe in the application of a high decay rate to the hypothetical revenue stream.

Since the Directive provides two possible remedies, indemnity or compensation., art 17(1) states that each of the member states shall 'take measures necessary to ensure that the commercial agent ... is indemnified in accordance with paragraph 2, or compensated in accordance with paragraph 3'. Initially most commentators in the UK read this provision as meaning that, when implementing the Directive, each member state had to choose to implement either indemnity under art 17(2) or compensation under art 17(3). All of the member states except the UK have interpreted art 17(1) this way. France opted for compensation. Ireland regarded compensation as equivalent to damages at common law, and therefore made no express adoption of either remedy in its implementing legislation. All other member states, except the UK, opted for indemnity.

In the UK the DTI were inundated with representations from various interest groups as to which alternative should be chosen. The DTI finally, and to many people's surprise, chose a very elegant way of resolving the situation. They did not interpret art 17(1) as requiring (or at the least permitting) them to decide which alternative the agent should have available to him in the UK and then to implement that alternative by legislation. Instead, they interpreted art 17 as requiring (or at least permitting) them merely to ensure that the agent always had available one or the other alternative, but leaving the choice of which alternative to the parties when they negotiated the specific agency agreement in each case. The DTI's solution is implemented by reg 17(1). Regulation 17(2) then provides that, unless the parties choose otherwise, the agent shall be compensated rather than indemnified.

Recommendations as to which remedy to choose are not easy to make. Given that awards under the compensation remedy seem to be higher in France than awards under the indemnity remedy in Germany, at first sight principals are best advised to opt for indemnity and agents for compensation. This contention is strengthened by the fact that, although the remedy of indemnity is capped, there is no cap on the remedy of compensation. However, this assumes that all courts throughout the EU and the EEA, and in particular the UK courts, will make their calculations based upon the recommendations in the report and the French and German methods as appropriate. Currently, the report reveals a wide disparity of actual methods of calculation. For instance, Scandinavian courts tend to award the maximum payment under the indemnity remedy without appearing to take much notice of the precise method of calculation, while in Greece and Spain, although the remedy of indemnity has been adopted, the assessment of the amount paid appears to be made more on the basis of an assessment of damage actually suffered than on the basis of a formula.

So far as the UK courts are concerned, there have not been any very compelling decisions in the area of compensation. In interlocutory proceedings in *Graham Page v Combined Shipping and Trading Ltd* [1997] 1 WLR 327, the Court of Appeal, after hearing evidence of the methods of calculating compensation in France, accepted that the remedy of compensation was *sui generis*, created under European law and not equivalent to damages for breach of contract at common law. However, the court did not immediately accept the French method of calculation and suggested that final guidelines as to calculation could only come from a reference to the European Court of Justice.[7] The remedy of indemnity was not relevant to either case, and therefore not considered. The only other factor to take into account is that the wording of art 17(2) as reproduced in the Regulations is very clear, and one can easily see how, on the basis of the wording alone, a formula along the lines of the German calculation could be applied. The same is not true for the remedy of compensation, where the wording of art 17(3) is much vaguer. The approach of a court in the UK, which will of course in the first instance proceed by looking at the words contained in the Regulations, is therefore far more likely to be predictable if it is asked to apply the remedy of indemnity.[8]

Given this consideration, and the fact that, however interpreted, the remedy of indemnity has a cap, but the remedy of compensation does not, it still appears the best advice for a principal applying the Regulations to an agency agreement to opt for the former remedy rather than the latter.

Whether the remedy adopted is indemnity or compensation, there is a one-year limitation period for the bringing of such claims (see art 17(5)), but such claims are in addition and without prejudice to the right of the agent to claim damages at law for any other loss suffered. It should also not be forgotten that the agent also has the right to post-termination commissions under art 8.

Finally, art 19 provides that the agent cannot contract out of his rights under arts 17 and 18 before the agency contract expires. This, of course, allows the agent to negotiate a legally binding settlement with his principal after the agreement has ended, but protects the agent from pressure by the principal to give up his rights as part of the terms for the grant of the agency.

Non-competition clauses after termination may be imposed for a maximum period of two years, provided they are in writing and restricted to the geographical area, or to the group of customers and geographical area, entrusted to the agent, and to the type of goods covered by his agency agreement. However, the provision in the Directive is subject to any more stringent requirements restricting non-competition clauses contained in the local legislation of any member state (see art 20).

The Directive regulates in reasonable detail the agency relationship, and obviates the need for a written contract, although the Directive does provide that the agent has the right in all cases to ask for a written statement from the principal setting out the main terms of his appointment. However, a written contract is not prohibited and will no doubt continue to be used in most commercial situations (see art 13). Nevertheless, the mandatory provisions of the Directive will override any inconsistent contractual provisions, as set out above.

One point as to the extent of the Directive's effect should be noted. The Treaty of Rome only requires member states to implement Council Directives to the extent necessary to comply with their obligations under the Treaty. This means that, although under the enabling legislation of member states the provisions of the Directive become part of the local law of each member state, the enabling legislation need only apply the Directive to agents established in one of the member states of the EC.

The UK has taken this option. The Regulations only have application in relation to the activities of commercial agents in Great Britain (reg 1(2)), and the equivalent statutory instrument for Northern Ireland makes the same provision in relation to that territory. Further the Regulations (and the equivalent statutory instrument for Northern Ireland) do not apply even in this case where the agency agreement is to be governed by the law of some other member state. Thus the Regulations (and the equivalent statutory instrument for Northern Ireland) implement the Directive for agency agreements within the UK only. For the rest of the world the parties could still specify that an agency agreement be subject to the laws of England, Northern Ireland or Scotland on the old basis without the Directive applying.

This causes no problems for territories outside the EU and the EEA, but there is one apparent lacuna. On the basis described above the Regulations (or the equivalent statutory instrument for Northern Ireland) would have no application to an agency agreement governed by one of the systems of law in force in the UK (eg the law of England and Wales) but made with an agent carrying on his activities in a member state other than the UK. Would this leave the agent without any protection under the Directive? Some commentators in other member states have suggested this is a problem, and advised agents outside the UK never to accept a system of UK law as governing their agency agreement unless the Regulations (or the equivalent statutory instrument for Northern Ireland) are expressly stated to apply to the agreement. Probably, however, in practice, in the absence of such an express clause, a local court in the agent's jurisdiction would regard the governing law clause as an attempt to exclude the operation of the Directive in the form of its local implementation, strike it out and apply the local implementation of the Directive as an overriding provision of local law.[9]

6.6   Definition of distributor

A distributor is the converse of an agent. He is an independent trader who is entrusted by the manufacturer of a product with the right (often on an exclusive basis) to satisfy the demand for that product from customers in a particular territory. He does this by purchasing the product from the manufacturer at his own risk, and then reselling upon whatever prices, terms and conditions he decides, providing any extra benefits such as repair and servicing that his customers require, and paying for all of this out of the margin between his buying and his selling prices.

6.7   Distribution under EC competition law

In the words of the Commission Notice on Exclusive Agency Agreements, a distributor takes the risk on the transaction and is therefore regarded as a separate undertaking from his principal. In these circumstances, art 85(1) can always apply potentially to any distribution agreement, and will certainly do so where the relationship is exclusive for a particular territory within the EC.

However, the Commission has long recognised that exclusive distribution agreements are a standard practice in many businesses, and has felt forced to come to terms with them. If every exclusive distribution agreement were referred to the Commission for specific exemption under art 85(3), it would be unable to cope with the administrative burden. It therefore utilised its powers, under Council Regulation 19/1965 (to grant block exemptions under art 85(3) to certain kinds of agreements otherwise caught by art 85(1)), to exempt exclusive distribution agreements which complied with certain criteria that it had, from previous decisions, determined not to be anti-competitive.

The first such block exemption was passed in 1967, and this was updated and reissued in 1983 (Commission Regulation 83/1983). The regulation permits the principal to undertake to supply the goods into the whole of the EC, or into only a defined geographical area of the EC (the 'territory'), only to the distributor. No other restriction on the principal is permitted. The distributor may undertake not to manufacture or distribute competing goods, to obtain the contract goods only from the supplier, and not to seek customers, establish a branch or maintain a distribution depot outside the territory. No other restriction on the distributor is permitted.

The distributor may also undertake to purchase complete product lines, or minimum quantities, to sell goods under specified trademarks, or packed and presented in a certain way, to advertise, maintain a sales network, maintain a stock of goods, provide customer and guarantee services and employ specialist staff.

The exemption does not apply to competitors who grant each other reciprocal exclusive distribution arrangements, nor to situations where users cannot obtain the goods in the territory from an alternative source of supply outside the territory, nor where one of the parties exercises industrial property rights so as to prevent or hinder parallel imports, or otherwise prevents or hinders imports into the territory.

The Regulation has one annoying inconsistency. Unlike the more sophisticated block exemptions issued later (such as those relating to know-how or patent licences) it applies only to exclusive agreements. There is no provision equivalent to that in the other block exemptions which states that while they apply primarily to exclusive agreements they also apply to agreements which contain 'one or more' of the permitted restrictions (included among which is of course exclusivity) and to agreements which contain restrictions of the types listed but 'with a more limited scope' than permitted by the block exemption. The wording of art 1 of the Regulation clearly restricts the effect of the legislation to exclusive agreements only. Additionally, the Regulation does not contain the useful short-notice procedure which is a feature of the later block exemptions. Thus, if a non-exclusive distribution agreement is entered into, it seems that the question of the application of art 85(1) has to be decided purely upon the merits of each case, with an individual submission to the Commission for clearance where necessary. If the obligations contemplated by the Regulation (other than exclusivity) are imposed upon the distributor, submission may well be necessary, but exemption is virtually certain.

European Commission Regulation 84/1983 is a block exemption along similar lines to Regulation 83/1983, but relating to exclusive purchasing agreements. This Regulation, although similar to Regulation 83/1983, has several important differences of detail. It does not, in general, impact on distribution agreements, and certainly not on exclusive ones, even though it covers exclusive purchase agreements of products for resale. This is because it cannot apply to agreements where the supplier confers an exclusive right of resale on the reseller in a particular geographical territory. Instead, only a vaguer limitation, binding the principal not to supply the goods to other resellers at the same level of distribution in the reseller's 'principal sales territory' may be imposed. Additionally, the Regulation does not permit the reseller to undertake a restriction against active canvassing either outside a geographical area, or, indeed, outside his principal sales territory. Given these limitations, this Regulation is unhelpful in relation to distribution agreements, except perhaps for non-exclusive ones where the principal is totally unconcerned with territorial restrictions.

Furthermore it should be noted that Regulation 84/1983 does not, in general, apply to agreements of more than five years in length, or to agreements for an indefinite period. The former limitation is inconvenient for distribution agreements in many cases, and the latter limitation would exclude the great number of distribution agreements that have an initial fixed term, and then continue indefinitely until terminated by due notice. Regulation 83/1983 contains no such limitations.

Thus although a distribution agreement, could be worded so as to fall within Regulation 84/1983, and some of the less restrictive distribution agreements (particularly those entered into by retailers) may actually do so, it is usually more sensible to take advantage of Regulation 83/1983, except in the specific instances of tied houses for the sale of beers, wines and spirits, and tied service stations for the sale of petrol and lubricants, where Regulation 83/1983 is specifically stated to have no application, and Regulation 84/1983 contains special provisions covering those businesses.

6.8   Selective distribution and EC competition law

While the position with what are essentially two party exclusive distribution arrangements has been settled by Regulation 83/1983, the situation with regard to networks of distribution agreements, usually known as selective distribution networks, is more complicated and has been settled mostly by an evolutionary process through Commission decisions and judgments of the European Court of Justice.

It is a common business practice for manufacturers to set up co-ordinated distribution networks for their products. These are caught under art 85 (1) in two ways. Either the manufacturer exercises what are regarded as anti-competitive criteria as to whom he permits to be a distributor, or else he imposes unacceptable obligations on the free flow of goods through and outside the network.

The case law divides the types of criteria for deciding upon admission to the network as a distributor into three classes: quantitative criteria (quotas which restrict the number of distributors and keep out some of those who would otherwise qualify, in order to ensure a higher level of sales revenue, and perhaps an exclusive territory, for each distributor who is allowed to join the network); subjective qualitative criteria (particular matters that the manufacturer would like distributors to comply with, but which not all distributors who are capable of distributing his goods need or are willing to comply with, such as minimum purchase obligations or bearing sales promotion expenses); and objective qualitative criteria (particular matters that any distributor who is properly to distribute the relevant products, and serve his customers, must comply with, such as providing proper premises for sales and service, and employing technically trained staff) (see, for instance, *Re Kodak* [1970] CMLR D19, *Re Omega Watches* [1970] CMLR D49, *Re BMW* [1975] 1 CMLR D44, and *Re SABA* [1978] 1 CMLR D61).

The first two classes are always potentially caught by art 85(1) and require consideration, and possibly submission to the Commission for clearance. The last one is not. Thus a system which imposes only objective qualitative criteria and allows any applicant to join who is able to comply with them, will, *prima facie*, not be caught under art 85(1). It is, however, clear that the Commission's rules for distinguishing between subjective and objective qualitative criteria are flexible and change depending upon the trade or industry concerned. Even within the same trade or industry the rules may change with the passage of time as the industry matures. For instance, the requirement for the presence of technically trained sales staff was regarded as an objective qualitative criterion in regard to admissions to a network for the sale of personal computers, but the Commission stated that, as the industry matured, and consumers became more familiar with personal computers, they doubted if such staff would be necessary. On this basis, such a criterion would then cease to be regarded as objective in respect of the business of selling personal computers (see *Re IBM Personal Computers* [1984] 2 CMLR 42).

Finally, it should be noted that any selective distribution system which provides an exclusive territory for each of its members is automatically caught by art 85(1). Not only is this a restriction on the free flow of trade between member states, as in the case of any other exclusive distribution agreement, but it is also a sort of quota system (quantitative criteria) since no more than one distributor can be appointed in respect of each exclusive area.

However, even if the criteria imposed for qualification are acceptable in that they are only objective qualitative criteria, the Commission will still consider what restrictions if any are imposed on the free flow of goods throughout and outside the system. The most important of all such restrictions is the standard restriction on the distributor to sell only to end-users and (perhaps) authorised dealers who are members of the network. Such a restriction is obviously essential to the existence of the network as otherwise products will leak out of the network when sales are made to unauthorised dealers. Again this restriction obviously contravenes art 85(1).

Thus, a selective distribution system which grants exclusive territories and limits sales to end-users and (perhaps) members of the network will contravene art 85 (1). It will require a submission to the Commission for exemption under art 85(3) because it contains quantitative criteria for selection of members, and because the free flow of goods is limited to the network and to end-users.

The Commission's ideal system, and one to which it normally grants exemption relatively easily is one where all applicants who satisfy objective qualitative criteria are admitted (ie no exclusive territories and thus no quota system), but where any member of the system is allowed to buy from and sell to any other member of it, anywhere in the EC, and each distributor (but not necessarily the manufacturer) can also sell to end-users of the goods in question anywhere in the EC, but otherwise sales to any other person outside the system are prohibited. The Commission is prepared to accept that a free flow of goods around the system and to end-users provides sufficient competition for end-users from different sources of supply within the EC to justify an exemption under art 85(3) (see *Re IBM Personal Computers*, above; *Re SABA (No 2)* [1984] 1 CMLR 677 and *Re Yves St Laurent Parfums* (1992) OJ L12/24).

However, other restrictions on the free flow of goods within the EC, such as attempts at export bans or resale price maintenance, or prescribing an exclusive source of supply for a particular distributor or level of distribution in the network are always potentially caught under art 85(1) and almost never receive exemption (see *Re AEG-Telefunken AG* [1984] 3 CMLR 325; a fine of ECU one million).

So far as quota restrictions are concerned, the Commission is in some cases prepared to grant an exemption to networks with areas of exclusivity or other types of quota restriction. Commission Regulation 123/1985 on selective distribution in the motor vehicle trade provides a good example of the Commission's thinking in this area, and may be adapted in other areas to identify selective distribution agreements with exclusivity or quota provisions which have a fair chance of exemption. The Commission recognises arguments that a certain degree of restriction of competition in this way is permissible since it encourages serious distributors who are willing to invest in and concentrate on their business in a defined area, thus providing a better and more economical service for consumers.

Finally, it should be noted that Regulations 83/1983 and 84/1983 provide no real help in the area of selective distribution agreements. The main restriction required in such networks, as stated above, is the limitation of sales to authorised members of the network, and to end-users. Neither of the Regulations permits such a restriction. The only potential area would be a network which conferred exclusivity in particular areas, but did not limit in any way the persons to whom the members could sell. This might be possible in the area of a purely retailer network, but even here the general wording about anti-competitive activity in the event of which the Regulations do not apply, or in the event of which their benefit can be withdrawn by the Commission in any particular case, makes it dangerous to rely on them except in very special cases, when the obligations are so watered down that it is hard to call the resulting structure a selective distribution network at all (see, for instance, *Re Gas Water-Heaters* [1973] CMLR D41 and *Re AEG-Telefunken AG* [1984] 3 CMLR 325).

In recent years the Commission has grown increasingly sensitive, however, to selective distribution networks which on the surface seem to comply with its requirements for exemption under art 85(3), but in fact are operated in a way which brings pressure to bear on the members to comply with restrictions which would not be exempted if specifically included in the agreements. For instance, the principal may, in practice, operate an unwritten quota system, despite specifying only objective qualitative criteria, by failing to process applications in a timely manner. He may exercise any discretion to refuse to accept orders, granted to him by the agreement, to withhold supplies from members who sell to customers of whom he does not approve or fail to observe recommended retail prices. Finally, bearing in mind that distributors do not normally receive compensation upon expiry of their agreements, he may simply fail to renew, or give lawful notice to terminate, the agreement of any distributor of whose practices he disapproves (see *Re IBM Personal Computers*, above and *Re SABA (No 2)*, above).

In recent decisions, the Commission has attempted to counter such problems first by fining heavily principals who operate systems containing disguised restrictions (see, for instance, *Hasselblad (GB) Ltd v EC Commission* [1984] 1 CMLR 559), and, secondly, by imposing further obligations on the principal as a condition for granting exemption. In one case, for instance, the Commission insisted that all applications for membership that were not clearly rejected within a stated time for demonstrable failure to comply with objective qualitative criteria, would automatically be deemed to be accepted, that the principal would not refuse to supply a distributor as long as he had sufficient goods available to do so, and that no distributor would be terminated without cause unless the principal intended to wind up the whole of the distribution network (see *Re SABA (No 2)* and *Re IBM Personal Computers* and *Re Yves St Laurent Parfums*, above)

The Commission Decisions in *Yves St Laurent Parfums SA* (Commission Decision (1992) OJ L12), and *Parfums Givenchy SA* (Commission Decision (1992) OJ L236) set out a useful summary of the Commission's current thinking on selective distribution agreements in the area of luxury up-market goods such as high-fashion perfumes. There are summaries of the terms and conditions in the Yves St Laurent and Givenchy selective distribution agreements and a commentary upon their acceptability or otherwise. The Commission Decision in *Grundig AG* (Commission Decision (1994) OJ L20) provides an up-to-date summary of the Commission's thinking in the area of selective distribution agreements for technical products. These three Decisions are worth reading in detail for anyone who intends to draft a selective distribution agreement in these areas of the market.

6.9   The future direction of EC competition law

So far as agency is concerned the position of apparent stability that has continued for almost 30 years may undergo some change if the Commission decides to revise the 1962 Notice, but subject to this it is hard to envisage much future change, except perhaps by way of attempts to be increasingly strict as to the circumstances in which the agent can no longer be regarded as an auxiliary of his principal because he takes a share of the risk on the transaction and thus, in some fashion or other, ceases to be, in the words of the old draft Notice, a 'genuine intermediary'.

So far as distribution is concerned, Regulation 83/1983 was due to expire at the end of 1997, along with the companion Regulation on exclusive purchasing agreements (Regulation 84/1983). The Commission therefore started in 1996 a review of its position on vertical restraints (ie, those between different levels of industry, such as manufacturer/distributor, distributor/wholesaler, wholesaler/reseller, franchisor/franchisee) as embodied in distribution, purchasing or franchise agreements. It decided not to circulate new drafts of the two block exemptions which were due to expire, but to invite a general discussion as to what its new approach should be. A Green Paper was published by the Commission in January 1997, and since then the debate is still continuing. The Commission asked for comments by 31 July 1997, but has still not published the results of the consultation. Regulations 83/1983 and 84/1983 have been extended to 31 December 1999 (when the block exemption on franchise agreements, 4087/1988, is also due to expire). This will give time for a proper debate to take place. Currently the Commission is considering four possible options: maintain the current system of block exemptions, widen the scope of block exemptions so more agreements are covered, adopt more focused block exemptions which exclude agreements where the parties have market shares of more than 40 per cent, or reduce the scope of art 85(1) so that firms with market shares of less than 20 per cent could enter into any type of vertical agreement (with the exception of resale price maintenance or export bans) without breaching EC competition law.

The Department of Trade and Industry in the UK has suggested a number of possible alternatives. First, the Commission could continue with individual block exemptions for particular relationships and update the drafts of these as and when necessary. Secondly, the Commission could have a single block exemption covering all vertical restraints. The Commission is concerned about this because it does not feel that a single block exemption, covering in particular all types of selective distribution agreements, is feasible or desirable, since such arrangements need to be considered very much in the light of their own peculiar circumstances. Thirdly, the Commission could dispense with block exemptions altogether and leave undertakings to be guided by Commission Decisions and European Court case law. Fourthly, the Commission could in the longer term seek Community-wide agreement to removing non-price vertical restraints from the scope of art 85, combining this approach with amendment to art 86 to extend it to cover abusive practices by groups of undertakings.

In general, the Commission is also likely to become increasingly tougher on the level of fines it imposes for breaches of arts 85 and 86, particularly where the organisations are large undertakings which could have chosen to take proper advice, or the breach is of a kind generally known to be regarded severely by the Commission, such as export bans or price-fixing. A detailed set of guidelines on the calculation of fines was adopted by the Commission and published in the form of a press release dated 3 December 1997 (*Guidelines on the Method for the Setting of Fines in the Context of European 'Anti-Trust' Legislation* (ip/97/1075)). Using these guidelines, in March 1998, the Commission fined Volkswagen AG 102m ECU (£68m) for entering into anti-competitive arrangements with its Italian dealers to prevent them selling cars to foreign customers.

The other noticeable trend is that the Commission is becoming more concerned about the power of undertakings with large market shares to cause significant harm by breaches of competition law, while undertakings (however large their size) with smaller market shares seem to cause it less concern. This thinking can be seen in the proposals in the Green Paper discussed above to limit the operation of art 85 to undertakings with large market shares. It can also be seen in the new Notice on Agreements of Minor Importance 1997, published in the *Official Journal* (1997) OJ C372, 9 December 1997, which replaces the old 1986 Notice.

The new Notice abolishes the turnover test of the 1986 Notice, and concentrates only on the concept of market share. The Commission holds the view that agreements between undertakings engaged in the production or distribution of goods or in the provision of services do not fall under the prohibition in art 85(1) if the aggregate market shares held by all of the participating enterprises (whatever the turnover of those enterprises) do not exceed 5 per cent for horizontal agreements, and 10 per cent for vertical agreements. Where an agreement is mixed or of uncertain classification the 5 per cent threshold applies. Agreements to fix prices, share markets, control resale prices or impose export bans are regarded as so serious that art 85(1) will still apply even if the relevant threshold is not exceeded. The Commission also considers that agreements between small and medium-size enterprises are rarely capable of significantly affecting trade between member states and competition within the common market. Consequently as a general rule they are not caught by the prohibition under art 85(1). In cases where such agreements exceptionally meet the conditions for the application of that provision the Commission considers that they will not be of sufficient Community interest to justify any intervention. The Commission will therefore not institute any proceedings either on its own initiative or upon request, to apply the provisions of art 85(1) to such agreements even if the thresholds are exceeded.

Given this emphasis on the importance of market shares, both in the Green Paper and in the 1997 Notice, the Commission has also published a Notice on the definition of the relevant market for the purposes of Community competition law (OJ C372, 9 December 1997).

6.10   Distribution and UK competition law

In discussing UK competition law, it is first of all necessary to note that the current regime is due to be replaced later in 1998 by a completely new set of legislation. Details of both the current regime (embodied in the Restrictive Trade Practices Act 1976, the Resale Prices Act 1976 and the Competition Act 1980) and the new regime, currently under the Competition Bill 1997, to be known in due course as the Competition Act 1998, and the provisions for transition between the old and the new regimes, will be found in Chapter 15. At this stage it need only be said that the new regime approximates very closely to arts 85 and 86. The wording of the key provisions is almost identical, with the exception that there is no requirement for an effect on trade between member states. However, since the Competition Act is not likely to become law before September 1998, its commencement date is likely to be 12 months after this, and there will in any event be a transitional period after the commencement date of at least 12 months, it is still useful to consider the details of the old regime.

The Resale Prices Act (which can in a sense be called part of the UK 'fair trading' legislation, and which is the only part that directly concerns the area of unfair trade practices) is reasonably straightforward, forbidding resale price maintenance, and prohibiting refusal to deal with a customer on the grounds that he will not observe resale prices, unless (in certain strictly-defined cases) he sells the supplier's products as 'loss-leaders' (ie at a price below cost in order to attract other business).

The Restrictive Trade Practices Act has little application to distribution agreements since there are two specific exemptions which in combination take distribution agreements outside the Act, unless extraordinary circumstances apply.

The first (Sched 3, para 2) states that the Act does not apply to an agreement for the supply of goods between two persons, neither of whom is a trade association, provided that (i) no other person is a party and (ii) no such restrictions as are described in s 6(1) of the act are accepted other than restrictions accepted (*a*) by the party supplying the goods, in respect of the supply of goods of the same description to other persons or (*b*) by the party acquiring the goods, in respect of the sale, or acquisition for sale, of other goods of the same description.

The prohibited restrictions concern such matters as prices to be charged, quoted or paid, or recommended or suggested as the prices to be charged or quoted for goods; conditions of sale; persons to whom or from whom goods may be sold or bought; and the quantities or kinds of goods to be made, sold or bought.

The second exemption (in s 9(3)) provides that in determining whether an agreement for the supply of goods is an agreement to which the Act applies, no account is to be taken of any term which relates exclusively to the goods supplied in pursuance of the agreement. This section thus, in effect, exempts any of the prohibited restrictions which are applied to the goods which are the subject matter of the contract. The exemption is of course not just for the Act as a whole but also for the purposes of Sched 3, para 2.

The combination of these two exemptions means that a standard distribution agreement, where the principal gives the distributor an exclusive territory (ie accepts restrictions on supply of goods of the same description to other persons) and the distributor agrees not to handle competing goods (ie accepts restrictions on the sale or acquisition for sale of other goods of the same description) exempted from the operation of the Act. In addition, because of s 9(3), the distributor and the principal can accept restrictions on the goods which are actually supplied under the contract. In the context of distribution agreements the most common restrictions are of course limitation of the distributor's right to sell the goods acquired from the principal only to a certain territory, or (particularly in the case of a selective distribution agreement) only to a certain class of customers, and the imposition on the distributor of minimum purchase commitments. Other matters which relate only to the goods which are the subject matter of the contract could relate to obligations on how they are to be stored, the amount of stock to be held, or the premises from which they are to be sold. Interestingly enough, resale at a price fixed by the principal is also one such restriction relating to the goods themselves. It would appear that this is permitted by the Restrictive Trade Practices Act. Hence the need for the separate legislation in the Resale Prices Act.

From the above it can be seen that those types of distribution agreement (including selective distribution agreements) which contain what may be called the minimal restrictions necessary to operate such an agreement can be regarded as exempt under the Act. The danger arises when the distribution agreement is part of a larger framework of co-operation between two enterprises (often but not always competitors) who seek to use the distribution agreement as part of a scheme for some kind of market sharing or the imposition of controls upon what would otherwise be a free market. In the course of setting up such an arrangement, the usual pitfall is to include (either written or unwritten) restrictions which fall within the definition of registrable restrictions. If this occurs the usual result is that reliance on the specific exemption for distribution agreements is impossible, and the disregarding of restrictions relating to goods which are the subject matter of the contract no longer helps, because the restrictions concerned, by their very nature, if they are trying to control the market in general, will relate to more matters than the goods which are the subject matter of the contract.

Finally, the position of selective distribution networks needs some mention. In the UK a selective distribution system consisting of a series of agreements, each of which was between two parties only, would be lawful under both the Restrictive Trade Practices Act and the Resale Prices Act, provided there were no price controls.

Refusal to sell to dealers who did not meet the qualification criteria would be lawful provided such refusal was not a disguised means of excluding or punishing distributors who cut prices. The problem would be in the area of the Competition Act 1980, which would consider the effect on competition of the existence of the selective distribution network as a whole, rather along the lines of an investigation into the abuse of a dominant position under art 86 of the Treaty of Rome.

This Act does have a small business exclusion (Anti-Competitive Practices (Exclusion) Order 1980 (SI No 979)), which exempts the activities of any person whose market share in the relevant market does not exceed 25 per cent and whose annual turnover in the relevant market does not exceed £5m. However, this exemption is of limited value in dealing with selective distribution systems since the target here will be the manufacturer who set up the network and the turnover will be the aggregated turnover of the supplies that he makes to all the distributors appointed by him. A useful document to study for the way the Act is applied to selective distribution agreements in the UK is the report of the Monopolies and Mergers Commission on a selective distribution system for the supply of bicycles to retail outlets, *Re TI Raleigh Industries Ltd and TI Raleigh Ltd* of 16 December 1981 (published by HMSO).

It must also be noted that the new regime put forward in the Competition Bill 1997 differs very little from previous proposals to reform UK competition law and to approximate it to EC competition law. The previous government has published various green and white papers which contained suggestions along the same lines as the Competition Bill, and, while no comprehensive Bill was introduced by them, piecemeal attempts at reform of the old regime were made through the medium of statutory instruments. The present government has continued with this approach, pending the coming into law of the new regime.

The Deregulation (Restrictive Trade Practices Act 1976) (Amendment) (Time Limits) Order 1996 (SI No 347) changed the provisions of the Restrictive Trade Practices Act in regard to time limits for notification under the Act. Previously, the Act provided for notification before the restrictions took effect or within three months of signature whichever was the earlier. Now the time limit is three months from signature in any event, with no reference to the date on which the restrictions take effect. However, the Act has also been amended to provide that it is unlawful to give effect to any registrable restrictions in the agreement prior to notification. Thus the parties can operate the agreement from the date of signature (with the exception of the registrable restrictions) and still have three months in which to notify it.

The Restrictive Trade Practices (Non-Notifiable Agreements) (Turnover Threshold) Order 1996 (SI No 348) provides a small business exemption to the Restrictive Trade Practices Act, where the combined turnover of the parties to the agreement does not exceed £20,000,000. This threshold has now been increased to £50,000,000 by the Restrictive Trade Practices (Non-Notifiable Agreements) (Turnover Threshold) Amendment Order 1997 (SI No 2944).

The Restrictive Trade Practices (Non-Notifiable Agreements) (EC Block Exemptions) Order 1996 (SI No 349) provides that an agreement is not notifiable for the purposes of the Restrictive Trade Practices Act 1976 if it is exempt under an EC block exemption or if it would have been so exempt, except for the fact that it is not caught by art 85(1) in the first place, for example because the agreement has no appreciable effect on trade between member states or is of minor importance (see the Commission Notice on Agreements of Minor Importance referred to in section 6.9). This Order means that, in effect, exclusive distribution agreements between two parties in the UK, whether or not they are subject to art 85, can take advantage of the block exemption under

Regulation 83/1983 to avoid notification under the Act.

The Restrictive Trade Practices (Non-Notifiable Agreements) (Sale and Purchase, Share Subscription and Franchise Agreements) Order 1997 (SI No 2945) deals with a number of issues relating to mergers and acquisitions which will be discussed in Chapter 9. However, it also provides that most franchise agreements are now exempt from notification.

So far as the new regime and distribution agreements are concerned the situation is much simpler. First, there will in practice be no difference between agreements subject to art 85 and agreements subject to the new regime. The Competition Bill, in addition to providing for power to the Secretary of State to issue local 'block exemptions' by statutory instruments, also contains provisions equivalent to the Restrictive Trade Practices (Non-Notifiable Agreements) (EC Block Exemptions) Order 1996 (SI No 349), which in effect incorporate EC block exemptions within the operation of the new regime, even though art 85 does not apply to the agreement in question. On this basis, the competition law relating to distribution agreements in the UK should be very closely approximated to the relevant EC competition regime. The problem of overlap is solved in the Competition Bill by providing that the European regime has supremacy. Thus any actual exemption under art 85(3) (either by way of a specific exemption or a block exemption) (called in the Bill a 'parallel exemption') means that the agreement in question is excluded from the ambit of the Competition Bill.

6.11 Agency and UK competition law

So far as UK competition law is concerned in relation to agency agreements, it is once again necessary, for the reasons described in the previous section, to consider both the old and the new regimes.

Under the old regime, the relevant Act will still be the Restrictive Trade Practices Act 1976, but this time the relevant part of the Act will be that relating to the supply of services, since under the agency agreement the agent supplies the services of an agent to his principal.

Except to the extent that the principal grants him authority to do so under the terms of the agency agreement, the agent has no authority to bind the principal with regard to the contracts for the supply of goods which he negotiates and/or concludes between the principal and third parties in accordance with his mandate. Therefore, the agency agreement should be looked at not as imposing restrictions on the authority the agent would otherwise have to negotiate and/or conclude such contracts, but as conferring on him limited authority, when otherwise he would have none at all. The actual function of the agreement is not to restrict the agent by contract, but to give him a partial freedom to act which the general law would otherwise deny him. Agreements performing this function have been described in various cases as 'opening the door' for the party to whom the limited rights are granted. (For a discussion of this 'opening the door' principle see *Ravenseft Properties Ltd v Director General of Fair Trading* [1977] 1 All ER 47 RPC.) On this basis, even though the agency agreement contains apparent limitations on the scope of the agent's authority, it cannot be construed as imposing restrictions within the terms of the Act in relation to the supply of goods. Thus those provisions of the Act have no application to the agreement.

The part of the Act relating to services contains exemption provisions which are similar but not identical to Sched 3, para 2 and s 9(3), discussed above in relation to distribution agreements. These are Sched 3, para 7, and s 18(1), (2) and (3) respectively. Their combined effect is to permit exclusive or non-exclusive agency agreements of the type normally in commercial usage, but the same problems would apply, as in the case of distribution agreements, if competitors attempted to enter into reciprocal agency agreements as a part of a scheme to partition the market.

So far as the new regime is concerned, since provisions in the Competition Bill and art 85 are almost identical, the principles set out in the Commission's 1962 Notice on Exclusive Agency Agreements should apply in the UK as well, as should the line of ECJ cases and Commission Decisions discussed above which set down the test of when an agent is considered to be sufficiently independent of his principal to constitute a separate undertaking for the purposes of art 85. The Competition Bill does not include Commission Notices or ECJ case law within the operation of the new regime in the way that it does with formal block exemptions. Nevertheless, the Bill has a provision which requires the new regime to be operated upon principles which approximate so far as possible to EC competition law, so that account is taken of Commission announcements and Decisions and of ECJ decisions. It is hard to see how a UK authority would lightly diverge from the EC position on agency. This point is discussed in more detail in Chapter 15.

Chapter 7

Standard agency agreements

7.1   Precedent 1

Precedent 1 is a short form document, relatively informal, which is suitable for situations where the principal intends to appoint a considerable number of canvassing agents (probably for low value standardised consumer or commercial items which the principal produces in volume on regular production runs) without regard to territory or exclusivity, on the theory that the more agents who are engaged in canvassing the more orders are likely to result. Such agents may deal direct with consumers (visiting their houses) or they may canvass retailers or commercial establishments, depending on the nature of the products concerned. As discussed in Chapter 6 the terms of this precedent are such that the EC and UK competition law has no impact.

The precedent complies with the European Council Directive on Commercial Agency Agreements, but takes advantage of art 13, and the common law prevailing in the UK, in that it does not reproduce in contractual form all of the provisions of the Directive. It should be regarded as a basic document setting out the grant of the agency and the main issues which the parties need to agree expressly, while leaving the balance of their rights and obligations to be regulated by the general law and the provisions of the Directive. This is justified where the agency relationship is straightforward, the duties of the agent are simple, and the products uncomplicated.

For these reasons, the basic obligations of the parties to each other, contained in arts 3 and 4, are not set out, nor are the complicated arrangements relating to compensation on termination (see art 17). Paragraphs 1–4 of the Agreement set out the grant of the agency and its scope.

Because of the nature of the relationship, the grant of agency is a non-exclusive one, with no power to conclude transactions on behalf of the principal, and the definition of 'Products' is very flexible. In the first instance it is tied to a set of price lists attached to the agreement. This list also contains the commission rates for each product, and restrictions in respect of particular products as to the area in which, or the customers with whom, the agent can conduct business. By signing the agreement and the attached lists, the parties thus agree on the products to be handled by the agent, any relevant restrictions on activities, and the commission rates which apply to each product.

Amendments to this initial list are permitted, but must be agreed between the parties. In practice, where the principal merely makes changes by deleting old products and adding new ones, and any changes to commission rates or in restrictions of activity are made in good faith and reasonably, the agent is likely to accept them without a great deal of discussion. It is true that drastic changes to the agreement could well be unacceptable to the agent, but a failure to agree is not a serious matter under this agreement, since either party is always free to terminate it by due notice anyway. A prudent principal would thus, where possible, give sufficient advance notification of proposed changes so that (in the event of a failure to agree) he has sufficient time to give due notice of termination of the agreement.

Paragraphs 5, 6 and 7 relate to payment of commission. Paragraph 5 sets out the basic entitlement of the agent, and makes it clear that since the agent is only a commissioning agent, and has no power to bind the principal by concluding orders, the principal is free to reject any orders forwarded to him by the agent for acceptance. Paragraph 6 reproduces the mandatory provisions of the Directive as to the entitlement to and the timing of payments of commission (see arts 10, 11 and 12). Paragraph 7 is an attempt to deal with the issues of direct dealing by the principal and conflicts between agents, and gives rise to some particular problems of interpretation.

It will be recalled that the second part of art 7(1) of the Directive gives the agent a right to commission on transactions effected directly by the principal, or through another agent, with customers generated by the agent. The basic principle of para 7, which is used to resolve these problems, is that where the principal deals direct or two agents both have a claim on the transaction the agent receives half the usual commission. This either cuts down on the principal's costs, where he has dealt direct, or frees the principal to split the commission between the two agents concerned. Since the principal will have appointed all of the network of his agents on the same terms this effectively prevent conflicts between non-exclusive agents, and allows the principal the flexibility to deal direct.

Article 7(2) of the Directive also states that where an agent has been specifically entrusted with a customer group or territory he is entitled to commission on transactions in that group or territory effected by other agents or directly by the principal even though he has not himself generated the customer in question. However, member states have an option either to implement this provision only in respect of exclusive agency agreements, or to implement it in respect of all agency agreements which contain grants of specific customer groups or territories whether those grants are exclusive or not. The UK has adopted the option of applying art 7(2) only to exclusive agency agreements. Thus this agreement, since it is a non-exclusive one, ignores the provisions of art 7(2). However, it is important to remember that if the agent were appointed in other member states under an agreement governed by the local law of that state, the agent might have a right to commission in the circumstances described in art 7(2), even though the agreement is non-exclusive, if the relevant price list or guidelines contain a restriction as to customer group or territorial restriction and the member state concerned has not adopted the option to limit art 7(2) to exclusive agreements only.

In general, the best way to avoid art 7(2), whatever option has been adopted in any member state, is to appoint a network of non-exclusive agents, with no restrictions as to territory or customer group. The extent of the agent's operations can then be determined by the practicalities of where he finds it feasible to canvass and what types of customers are likely to buy the particular product he deals with. On this basis, the only problems that can arise are those covered by art 7(1) relating to conflicts over, or direct dealing with, a customer actually generated by the agent. These are covered by the provisions of para 7 of the Precedent.

The final problem to be resolved in relation to art 7 is the extent to which the parties can contract out of its provisions, if at all. Can different rates of commission be applied as between those transactions which the agent concludes himself, and those transactions effected directly by the principal or by another agent, where the second part of art 7(1) or art 7(2) confers a right to commission on the agent? Unless this is possible, para 7 of Precedent 1 would be unenforceable as a derogation from the rights of the agent under the Directive. Furthermore, is it possible for the parties to provide in their agreement for the entire exclusion of any of the rights which the agent would otherwise enjoy under art 7?

Articles 10, 11 and 12 of the Directive, which deal with agent's entitlement to commission, are expressly stated to be mandatory and cannot be restricted or derogated from by the terms of the agency contract. However, art 7 is not expressly stated to be mandatory in the same way as arts 10, 11 and 12, and art 6 states as the primary principle that the agent is entitled to such levels of commission as the parties agree. The question to be asked is thus whether the principal can render arts 7, 10, 11 and 12 partially impotent, either by agreeing in respect of some of the heads of art 7(1) or 7(2) a zero rate of commission, or contracting out of them altogether. If this were possible, then the whole of the provisions of art 7(1) and 7(2) relating to conflicts between agents and direct dealing by the principal could be rendered academic. Although the drafting of the Directive leaves something to be desired (and the UK statutory instrument does not resolve the issue since it simply implements the terms of the Directive), it seems contrary to common sense and the intended purpose of the Directive that most of art 7 could so easily be rendered nugatory. If this were the case, it is hard to see why the article was drafted in this form in the first place. If one accepts that, in one way or another, art 7 is mandatory, as to the entitlement to commission in respect of the various transactions specified therein, so that an attempt to contract out of a right granted under art 7 is not possible, then the only question to arise is whether the parties can reach an agreement to pay different rates of commission in respect of the same product for the various circumstances set out in art 7, provided that any difference in rates is based on fair and reasonable criteria, such as the effort expended by the agent.

If the view were to be taken that once a rate of commission has been fixed under art 6 for a particular product that this must be applied in the case of all the transactions covered by art 7, then such differences in rates would not be possible. However, the wording of art 6 does not really support such a contention. The wording refers to 'such commission as is agreed'. There is nothing here to suggest that only one rate is required. Further, suppose no agreement were reached as to commission at all. Then customary rates or, in the absence of custom, fair and reasonable rates would apply. Now, it is certainly customary in many types of commerce for an agent to receive a reduced commission where his principal deals direct, and for him to share commission with another agent involved in the same transaction. Furthermore, reduced commission could well be fair and reasonable in such circumstances, on the basis that the agent has expended less, or no, effort, in relation to the transaction. It seems unlikely that the parties should be more fettered if they make an express agreement, than if they leave the level of commission to be set by custom or standards of what is fair and reasonable.

On this basis, it is considered that setting by agreement a different rate of commission for the various classes of transactions covered by art 7 is permissible provided that a rate is not set at zero or at a level so low as to be unreasonable in all the circumstances of the case.

This conclusion seems to be borne out by the only case on the operation of art 7(2) which has come before the ECJ, *Georgios Kontogeorgas v Kartonpak AE* (Case C-104/95 [1997] 1 CMLR 1093). This was a case concerning a Greek agent who sought compensation under art 7(2) for direct sales which his principal had made into his assigned territory in certain parts of Greece. In that case, the contract itself was silent on the issue of direct sales, and the agreement was not an exclusive one. The contract merely appointed the plaintiff agent of the defendant and specified a 3 per cent commission on the sales that he negotiated in the relevant territory. There was thus no specific exclusion of art 7(2). It should be noted that in Greece, the implementation of art 7(2) confers the right to commission on the agent in respect of direct sales even where the grant of territory or customer group is not on an exclusive basis.

The case was concerned with two issues. The first was whether the provisions of art 7(2) only applied to sales generated by the agent's actions. The second was the definition of the phrase, used in art 7(2), 'customers belonging to that area' (ie the territory granted to the agent).

So far as the second point was concerned the court held that where the customer was a legal person the definition must be determined by reference to the place where the customer actually carried on its commercial activities. However, where a company carried on its commercial activity in various places, or where the agent operated in various areas, other factors had to be taken into account to determine the 'centre of gravity' of the transaction effected, in particular the place where the negotiations with the agent took place or should, in the normal course of events, have taken place, the place where the goods were delivered and the place where the establishment which placed the order was located.

The first point is by far the most interesting one. The court said that art 7(1) referred to sales generated by the agent's ongoing or previous activities. Article 7(2) simply provided that remuneration must be paid on all transactions within a certain area, no mention being made of the need for any particular act on the part of the agent. The entitlement under art 7(2) was clearly thus additional to the entitlement under art 7(1). However, if art 7(2) also required activity on the part of the agent, art 7(2) would be rendered meaningless since the right to commission would already have arisen under art 7(1). Thus art 7(1) confers a right to commission in respect of direct sales to customers generated by the activity of the agent and art 7(2) confers a right (subject to the necessary conditions of grant of territory or customer group) to commission in respect of direct sales to all other persons in the specified group or territory even though they are not customers generated by the activity of the agent.

Although, the judgment is not very clear on this point, it appears as if one of the arguments which Kartonpak put forward as a reason for not paying commission on direct sales was that art 6 allows the parties to agree the remuneration of the agent. Presumably the argument ran that, if art 6 gives the parties the power to agree, and they had not agreed any specific provision for remuneration on direct sales, art 7(2) could have no application, in the absence of an exclusive territory. This argument would go even further than claiming that the parties can contract out of art 7(2), and would amount to an argument that art 7(2) could never apply unless the right under it was included in the contract either expressly, or implicitly by way of a grant of an exclusive territory, in other words by means of agreement in respect of remuneration in terms of art 6. The ECJ did, however, proceed on the basis that art 7(2) provided the agent with a right to commission on the direct sales even though no such right had been granted under the contract, and rejected Kartonpak's argument as follows:

> 'Kartonpak considers, however, that Article 7 of the Directive must be read in conjunction with Article 6, which leaves it to the parties to the contract to specify what remuneration the commercial agent will receive. Since exclusivity is not mandatory in law, it would be incomprehensible if the agent were entitled to commission for all sales in his area. It should

be noted on this point, that Article 6 of the Directive concerns an agent's rate of remuneration and not, in contradistinction to Article 7, transactions on which the Commission is payable. The matters covered by those two provisions are consequently not the same.'

This section of the judgment would support the contentions made above. First, any argument as to the necessity for agreement as to the *level of remuneration* under art 6 has no impact on the *entitlement* to commission in respect of the *transactions* specified under art 7. Even though the case did not contain an express contracting-out clause, the way the court approached this issue is certainly consistent with regarding art 7 as having a mandatory status. Secondly, given that art 6 and art 7 deal with different issues, there would be no reason why the parties could not agree a different *level* of commission for direct sales under art 6, provided they respected the *entitlement* to commission on direct sales under art 7, by agreeing a realistic level of commission and not one which amounted to no commission at all, in order indirectly to defeat the entitlement to commission granted by art 7(2).

Paragraph 8 gives the agent the right to the necessary sales literature and other documentation needed to carry out his duties, and also imposes on him the obligation to return them to the principal upon request. Paragraphs 9, 10, 11 and 12 clarify the agent's obligations to cover his own expenses, prevent him dealing in competing products, make it clear that he is not an employee of the principal, and state his lack of authority to bind the principal. It should be noted that claiming the agent is not an employee will not be conclusive, if in fact the agent is treated in such a way that he is indistinguishable from an employee. Some employers have in the past tried to turn all of their sales force into self-employed agents by changing the terms of their contracts of employment to agency agreements. However, depending on the degree of control the employer retains over them, this measure may not be effective. (Reference should be made to the discussion on this subject in Chapter 3.)

Paragraph 13 reproduces the provisions of art 15 of the Directive relating to notice periods and art 8 relating to entitlement to commission after termination of the agency agreement. Article 8 states that commission shared with the new agent appointed in substitution of the terminated agent must be shared equitably. Paragraph 13 suggests that the easiest way to avoid arguments is to split the commission equally. The exact wording of para 7 is important here. The provision in parentheses in para 7 is sufficiently wide that it requires the agent to share his commission with another agent who has been terminated. This provision is the other side of the right to the entitlement to post-termination commission in para 13. Both provisions are obviously necessary as a standard term in all the principal's agency agreements if the principal is not to have conflicts between current and terminated agents over such commission.

Paragraph 14 confers on the principal an express right of termination for breach or non-performance. Paragraph 15 contains a governing law clause, although (in most cases) this simple type of agreement is likely to be used in domestic rather than foreign transactions. Where it is used, reference should be made to the discussion of the choice of law clause used in Precedent 2 as to optional exclusion of the Directive for areas outside the EC.

7.2   Precedent 2

Precedent 2 is a long-form agreement which in fact sets out to reproduce the provisions of the Directive as closely as possible, while incorporating all of the more usual clauses governing the agency relationship. In practice, it would also be suitable for agency relationships outside the EC where the Directive has no application, subject only to consideration of the provisions in Sched 3 relating to payment of commission. Once again the impact of UK and EC competition law can be ignored.

The precedent is for an exclusive canvassing agency, with closely defined products and territory, and this is dealt with in cll 1 and 2. Clause 2.2 specifies an initial fixed period followed by an indefinite term subject to notice of three months. This complies with art 15 of the Directive as implemented in the UK.

Clause 3 details the responsibilities of the agent. Clause 3.1 imposes a general duty to act in good faith for the benefit of the principal and the promotion of the products in the market, while cl 3.3 provides for transmission of market intelligence to the principal. These reproduce the mandatory provisions of art 3 of the Directive. Clauses 3.2 and 3.4, respectively, contain standard obligations as to the provision of suitable facilities for the agency by the agent, and impose confidentiality obligations on the agent in relation to the principal's technical and commercial information. Clauses 3.8, 3.10, 3.11 and 3.12 circumscribe the agent's sphere of activity to the contract territory. Clause 3.8 also provides for dealing in the agent's territory direct by the principal or through another agent. This issue will be discussed further below in relation to Sched 3. Clause 3.9 contains the standard non-compete clause for activities by the agent during the currency of the agreement. Clause 3.9 also imposes a two-year post-termination non-compete obligation on the agent. This is permitted under art 20 of the Directive, provided that any stricter provisions contained in relevant local law are not breached by such a restriction. There is no provision of UK law which expressly forbids a two-year period, but some other member states do have local legislation limiting such clauses to a lesser period, in many cases only one year. Clauses 3.5, 3.6 and 3.7 are an attempt to deal with the problem of ostensible authority, first by stating the limits of the agent's authority to bind the principal, and then by requiring the agent to advertise his status to third parties so that no question of ostensible authority can arise. Finally, cl 3.13 is a *del credere* provision which can be used in circumstances where the agent undertakes a *del credere* obligation.

Clause 4 sets out the reciprocal obligations of the principal. Clauses 4.1

(supply of product information), 4.6 (information about orders accepted and in progress), 4.8 (advance warning of anticipated decrease in demand for the products) and 4.9 (duty to act towards the agent in good faith), all reproduce the relevant provisions of art 4 of the Directive. Clause 4.7 imposes the obligation on the principal to pay commission in accordance with the details set out in Sched 3. The remainder of cl 4 deals with general matters usual as obligations for the principal in agency agreements: supply of samples (cl 4.2), direct dealing in the territory by the principal (cl 4.3), payment of expenses (cl 4.4), and control of advertising and sales promotion (cl 4.5).

Clause 5 contains standard provisions to protect the principal's intellectual property rights (particularly trademarks) from misuse or appropriation by the agent. Clause 6 prevents assignment of the agreement by the agent. Clause 7 contains the usual provisions for termination on breach, insolvency or change of control of the agent. Particular note should be taken of cl 7.3, which provides that the agent is not entitled to compensation on termination of the agreement for any cause (including termination by notice) unless and to the extent that the governing law provides for it. This would make the agreement suitable for use in all areas, whether or not the Directive applies. The compensation provisions in art 17 of the Directive do not have to be set out in the agency agreement and, in any event, overrule any provision in the agreement excluding the right to compensation for which they provide. Thus, a clause like 7.3 has the advantage of brevity, and makes it incumbent upon the agent to ascertain and exercise what rights he has to compensation, without particularising the agreement to an undesirable extent by setting out art 17 of the Directive in the agreement in full.

Finally, cl 8 contains a set of 'boilerplate' clauses suitable for an agency agreement. These are obviously in a short form but could be expanded if desired.

One notable omission is that there is no limitation of liability for lost profits or revenue, or any form of consequential loss, for the benefit of either party. The omission is deliberate in that, in general, such clauses are not customary in agency agreements, and, in any event, where the Directive is concerned, it is doubtful that such a clause could be relied upon by the principal as a defence against an action brought by the agent, precisely because some of the areas in which the agent would be looking for compensation would relate to lost revenue or profit—ie his commission or compensation for termination. It is true that an agent might be able to rely on such a clause in an action brought against him by the principal, but principals are unlikely to agree to such clauses if they cannot also be invoked for the benefit of the principal. Where the Directive does not apply, such a clause (on a mutual basis) could be included, and there are ample precedents for such clauses in the earlier chapters relating to conditions of sale and purchase.

Clause 8.2 imposes English law as the governing law of the agreement. In this connection, the possibility of opting out of the Directive for territories outside of the EC should be considered (see the discussion of this subject in Chapter 6, section 6.5).

Scheds 1 and 2 contain the definitions of the products and the territory respectively, while Sched 3 contains the detailed provisions relating to payment of commission, and complies with arts 6–12 inclusive of the Directive. Paragraph 1 provides for differing rates of commission depending upon whether the agent has concluded the transaction himself, or whether the principal has dealt direct or through another agent. Since this is an exclusive agreement covering a particular territory, art 7(2) of the Directive requires that commission be paid on all such transactions within the territory, even though they are with customers whom the agent has not himself generated. The problem of conflict between agents should not exist if the principal is using this type of precedent for his network, since each agent will be forbidden under the appropriate provisions of cl 3 from acting outside his territory. The problems as to the mandatory nature of art 7 and the issue of differing commission rates for transactions in the territory of the agent in which he was not personally involved arise under this precedent in the same way as under the equivalent provisions in Precedent 1, and the discussion in relation to Precedent 1 should be referred to.

Paragraph 2 deals with payment of commission. It should be noted particularly that, in the Directive, the wording of entitlement to commission under art 10(1) refers to commission becoming due 'as soon as and to the extent that' the qualifying circumstances obtain, and art 10(2) provides that commission shall become due at the latest when the third party has executed his part of the transaction (ie paid the price). Thus the combination of arts 10(1) and 10(2) permits payment of commission under para 2 to be tied to the pattern of payments by the customer of the purchase price under the relevant order.

Paragraph 3 provides for post-termination commission in accordance with art 8 of the Directive. Paragraphs 4, 5 and 6 cover usual provisions relating to commission. It is the agent's sole remuneration, out of which his expenses must be paid (see cl 4.4), and provisions relating to currency of payment and withholding taxes are included for use in international agreements. The last sentence of para 5 implements art 10(3) requiring payment of commission not later than the last day of the month following the month in which it became due.

Finally, para 7 reproduces the provisions of art 12, as to the information which the principal must give the agent about commission due to him.

Precedent 1

Short form agency agreement

THIS AGREEMENT is made this [   ] day of [   ] 19
[   ] BETWEEN [   ] of [   ] (the principal) and
[   ] of [   ] (the agent) whereby the parties agree as
follows:

1 The principal hereby appoints the agent as non-exclusive agent for the purpose of canvassing for sales of the principal's products covered by this agreement.

2 The products covered by this agreement (the 'Products') are all the principal's products for which the principal has from time to time provided the agent with a price list or pricing guidelines and in respect of which the agent has agreed to act as agent in accordance with the relevant price list or pricing guideline.

3 The initial set of such price lists and pricing guidelines (the 'Initial Set') is attached hereto and signed by the parties for the purposes of identification. The parties may from time to time by agreement add further price lists and guidelines to or amend or delete existing price lists or guidelines from the Initial Set by means of an exchange of letters.

4 The agent is free to canvass for orders for the Products in any geographical area and to any customers except in cases where the relevant price list or guidelines sets out in respect of a Product instructions from the principal restricting the operations of the agent in relation to that Product to defined geographical areas and/or to specific categories of customer.

5 The principal reserves the right to refuse any order for the Products on any grounds; but shall, if required by the agent, supply to the agent the reasons for such refusal. The principal will pay to the agent commission on orders for the Products negotiated by the agent and contracted by the principal. The rate of commission to be paid may vary according to the circumstances of the sale and the Product sold, the appropriate rate of commission being specified in the relevant price list or guidelines.

6 Commission will be paid in respect of each order accepted by the principal at the end of the month following the month in which the principal accepts that order, provided that in the event of refusal of any order by the principal, or upon subsequent cancellation of any order by either the customer or the principal, but in each case only where the same has not occurred because of default of the principal, then the principal reserves the right to vary the commission due for that order or to pay no commission at all. In the event that commission may have already been paid, then this may become refundable and the principal reserves the right to offset such commission against any other commission that may be payable to the agent. The principal will provide to the agent a quarterly statement of commission due to him (such statement to be provided not later than the end of the month following the relevant quarter) and the agent may (subject to reasonable notice) inspect the principal's accounting records to verify such statement and the commission due to him.

7 If the principal deals directly or through another agent with a customer generated by the agent, the agent shall be entitled to [half] of the normal commission on the transaction. If the agent negotiates an order from a customer generated by another agent of the principal (who is either currently appointed as such or else whose appointment has terminated, but who is entitled to commission under a provision in his agency agreement equivalent to para 13) the agent shall be entitled to [half] of the normal commission on that transaction, the balance of such commission being paid to the other agent.

8 The principal shall provide all necessary samples, order books, contract forms, leaflets and brochures and other documents relating to the Products provided by the principal (the 'Documents') and the same shall remain the property of the principal. The Documents shall be maintained in good condition and returned to the principal at any time when requested.

9 The agent shall be responsible for all his operating expenses, shall provide his own transport suitably insured for the conduct of the principal's business in the Products and shall indemnify the principal against any loss or claim arising from the use of any vehicle in the conduct of such business.

10 It is agreed that, while acting as an agent for the principal, the agent will not act as agent for or otherwise directly or indirectly deal in any items which are similar to or compete or are likely to compete with any of the Products.

11 Nothing in this agreement, or otherwise, shall make the agent an employee of the principal.

12 Nothing in this agreement or otherwise shall entitle the agent to make any representations or warranties on behalf of the principal (save to confirm or communicate any terms conditions or information contained in the Documents) or enter into any contract or agreements on behalf of the principal, or pledge the credit of the principal.

13 This agreement may be terminated by either party giving one month's notice in writing in the first year thereof, two months' notice in the second year thereof, and thereafter by three months' notice in writing. The agent shall following such termination be entitled to commission on all orders which reached him or the principal prior thereto, and on all orders concluded during a period of [three months] subsequent thereto, to the extent that they were due to his efforts prior to such termination. Where the principal has appointed a new agent after such termination, the agent shall be entitled to commission on all of the foregoing at [half] of the normal rate, balance of such commission being paid to the new agent.

14 Without prejudice to any remedy it may have against the agent for breach or non-performance of this agreement, the principal shall have the right summarily to terminate this agreement in the event of the agent committing any such breach or non-performance or neglect of his duties under this agreement or being guilty of dishonest conduct.

15 The construction, performance and validity of this agreement shall be governed by the Laws of England.

The Principal

The Agent

Date

Precedent 2

Long form agency agreement

THIS AGREEMENT is made the [   ] day of [   ] 19
[   ] BETWEEN [   ] Limited (the 'Principal') and
[   ] Limited (the 'Agent') WHEREBY the parties agree as fol-
lows:

1   Definitions

1.1 The 'Products' are as defined in Schedule One.

1.2 The 'Territory' is as defined in Schedule Two.

2   Grant and terms of agency

2.1 Subject to cl 3.8 the Principal hereby appoints the Agent to be the exclusive agent of the Principal in the Territory for the marketing and the promotion
of the sale of the Products to customers resident or carrying on business in the
Territory and for the soliciting from such customers and transmission to the
Principal of requests for quotations or orders for the Products for sale use or
consumption within the Territory.

2.2 This Agreement shall run for a period of [two] years from the date of its
signature, and thereafter unless or until terminated by either party giving to the
other not less than three months' prior notice in writing, such notice to expire
at the end of the said period of [two] years or at any time thereafter.

3   Responsibilities of the agent

3.1 During the period of this Agreement the Agent shall serve the Principal as agent on the terms of this Agreement with all due and proper diligence (acting dutifully and in good faith) observe all reasonable instructions given by the Principal as to its activities under this Agreement act in the Principal's interests and use its best endeavours to increase the sale of the Products in the Territory.

3.2 The Agent shall maintain and provide at its own expense and to the reasonable satisfaction of the Principal such offices and other premises administration facilities and marketing organisation as may be necessary for the efficient and effective performance of its obligations under this Agreement.

3.3 The Agent shall pass on promptly to the Principal all information useful for the business of the Principal including that relating to marketing sales prospects product reliability competitor activity and unauthorised use by third parties of the Principal's trademarks patents or other intellectual or industrial property rights. The Agent shall (without prejudice to the generality of the foregoing) send to the Principal a written report on the first day of each calendar month covering any items which have arisen in the previous month relevant to the matters covered by this clause. Such a report shall also include an estimate by the Agent of likely orders for the Products during the coming [two] months.

3.4 The Agent shall keep strictly confidential, not disclose to any third party and use only for the purposes of this Agreement all information relating to the Products (whether technical or commercial) and to the affairs and business of the Principal whether such information is disclosed to the Agent by the Principal or otherwise obtained by the Agent as a result of its association with the Principal.

3.5 Save as expressly authorised by the Principal in writing the Agent shall not without the Principal's prior express approval incur any liabilities on behalf of the Principal nor pledge the credit of the Principal nor make any representations nor give any warranty on behalf of the Principal.

3.6 The Agent has no authority to and shall not take part in any dispute or institute or defend any proceedings or settle or attempt to settle or make any admission concerning any dispute proceedings or other claim relating to the Products or any contract concerning the Products or relating to the affairs of the Principal generally. The Agent will immediately inform the Principal of any of the foregoing and will act in relation thereto only upon and in accordance with the instructions of the Principal but so that the Principal will indemnify the Agent against any costs expenses or liabilities incurred by the Agent by reason of the Agent so acting other than any of the same incurred by reason of the Agent's own negligence or default.

3.7 The Agent will cause to be printed an express statement that it acts only as canvassing agent for the Principal on all letterheads invoices leaflets brochures or other documents issued by it on or in which it refers to the Products or the Principal. The Agent shall also affix a clearly visible plaque containing such statement at the Agent's registered office and at any other place of business of the Agent. Such statement shall likewise appear in all advertisements published by the Agent in which the Products or the Principal are mentioned. The Agent shall not expressly or by implication in any negotiations relating to the Products or otherwise describe itself as acting in any capacity for or on behalf of or in relation to the affairs of the Principal other than in accordance with such statement.

3.8 The Principal will refer to the Agent all requests for quotations on Products intended for sale in the Territory provided that where for any reason (including without limitation a conflict of interest in which the Agent becomes involved) the Principal in its entire discretion considers it inappropriate for the Agent to act in respect of any transaction then the Principal retains the right in respect of such transaction to appoint another agent to act for the Principal and/or to negotiate with and effect relevant sales direct with customers. In all such cases the Principal will advise the Agent of the actions it has taken and will pay to the Agent his commission upon such sales in accordance with the relevant provisions of Schedule 3.

3.9 The Agent shall not during the continuance of this Agreement and for a period of two years after its termination market or promote nor assist or advise in the marketing or promotion of any products which would or could compete or in any way interfere with the sale of the Products inside the Territory.

3.10 The Agent shall not during the continuance of the Agreement market or promote the Products to customers resident or carrying on business outside the Territory nor solicit from such customers requests for quotations and orders for the Products.

3.11 The Agent shall in all cases solicit requests for quotations and orders for the Products only for sale use or consumption by persons within the Territory and only at the prices and upon the terms established and notified from time to time by the Principal to the Agent.

3.12 The Agent shall not deal with and shall promptly refer to the Principal all requests for quotations or orders for the Products by persons resident or carrying on business outside the Territory, and all requests for quotations or orders for Products intended for sale use or consumption outside the Territory.

3.13 Subject to the prior consent of the Agent either generally or in relation to any specific transaction the Agent shall guarantee to the Principal the due performance by any customer or customers of contracts that they have entered into with the Principal as a result of the Agent's activities under this Agreement. Such guarantee shall be by way of separate agreement in writing between the Principal and the Agent in a form to be agreed but which shall in any event provide that the Agent is not to be liable thereunder in the event of a refusal to perform by the customer or customers which is caused by any default of the Principal.

4   Responsibilities of principal

4.1 The Principal shall supply to the Agent free of charge a reasonable quantity of sales literature, all other necessary documentation relating to the Products and all other information (if any) which is necessary to enable the Agent to perform his duties hereunder to the Principal.

4.2 The terms and conditions for the supply of any necessary models or samples relating to the Products shall in each case be the subject of special agreement between the Principal and the Agent.

4.3 The Principal shall not submit offers or quotations nor enter into any negotiations with nor effect sales or disposals to any person in the Territory without the Agent's consent except in the circumstances provided for in cl 3.8 and subject to that exception shall refer all such offers quotations or tenders to the Agent.

4.4 The Principal shall be under no obligation to reimburse to the Agent any expenses incurred in the discharge of the Agent's duties hereunder.

4.5 The Principal may in its absolute discretion carry out advertising or publicity activities in the Territory but the Agent shall not be entitled to carry out such activities upon its own initiative without the prior consent of the Principal irrespective of whether the Principal decides to contribute towards the cost of the same or not.

4.6 The Principal shall not be obliged to accept any order tender or request submitted by the Agent in the course of its activities in the Territory and shall accept the same only at its absolute discretion and only on such terms and conditions as it may consider appropriate and shall supply all Products thereunder direct to customers in the Territory. The Principal shall at the end of each month notify the Agent of all orders for the Products procured by the Agent which it has accepted or refused during that month. The Principal shall also (within seven days of the same occurring) notify the Agent of any such order accepted by the Principal which the Principal has failed to execute in accordance with its terms. The Principal shall at the date of despatch of any Products to such customers send a copy of the relevant invoice to the Agent, by way of notification of delivery of such Products.

4.7 The Principal shall pay commission to the Agent in accordance with Schedule 3.

4.8 The Principal shall notify the Agent within a reasonable period of time once he anticipates that the volume of sales of the Products in the Territory will be significantly lower than that which the Agent could normally have expected.

4.9 In discharging his obligations to the Agent the Principal shall act dutifully and in good faith.

5 Intellectual property rights

5.1 The Agent shall not use or permit to be used by any person under its control any of the patents trademarks or trade or brand names registered designs or any other industrial or intellectual property rights owned or controlled by the Principal without the prior consent of the Principal.

5.2 The Agent shall not register any patents trademarks trade or brand names registered designs or other industrial or intellectual property rights covering products or processes owned devised or manufactured by or on behalf of the Principal without the prior written consent of the Principal.

5.3 The Agent agrees to send the Principal prior to the use of any such trademarks or trade or brand names a sample of each letterhead invoice price list label packing material sign brochure and all other advertising material displaying such trade mark or trade or brand name and only to use items of such printed materials the proofs for which have received in each case the express and specific prior approval of the Principal.

5.4 Upon termination of this Agreement for any reason the Agent shall immediately cease to describe itself as an agent of the Principal and cease to use all such trademarks or trade or brand names in any manner whatsoever (including without limitation on stationery or vehicles) for which consent was granted and shall return to the Principal or otherwise dispose of at the Principal's direction free of any charge all printed matter displaying such trademarks or trade or brand names in the Agent's possession.

6   Assignment

This Agreement shall not be assigned or transferred by the Agent without the prior consent of the Principal.

7   Termination for breach, insolvency or frustration

7.1 Notwithstanding the provisions of cl 2 the Principal may by notice to the Agent terminate this Agreement immediately upon the happening of any one of the following events:

7.1.1 if the Agent shall become bankrupt or be wound-up or make any arrangement or composition with its creditors;

7.1.2 if the Agent shall attempt or purport to assign or transfer this Agreement in breach of cl 6;

7.1.3 if the Agent's ability to carry out its obligations hereunder is prevented or substantially interfered with for any reason whatsoever (whether or not within the control of the Agent) including without limitation by reason of any regulation law decree or any act of state or other action of a government;

7.1.4 if the Agent shall commit any breach of any of its obligations hereunder (other than cl 6) and fail to remedy such breach within thirty days of receipt of the Principal's notice specifying such breach; and

7.1.5 if the Agent shall become resident outside the Territory or (being a company) shall change its place of registration or have its ownership or control altered without the prior consent of the Principal.

7.2 Termination of this Agreement shall not affect the rights and liabilities of either party subsisting at the date of termination.

7.3 Termination or expiry of this Agreement, whether under cl 7 or cl 2.2, shall not entitle the agent to any compensation or indemnity in respect of such termination or expiry except to the extent that the governing Law of this Agreement provides for such compensation or indemnity.

8   Miscellaneous

8.1 No waiver, alteration, variation or addition to the Agreement shall be effective unless made in writing on or after the date of signature of this Agreement by both parties and accepted by an authorised signatory of both parties.

8.2 The interpretation construction effect and enforceability of this Agreement shall be governed by English Law, and the parties agree to submit to the jurisdiction of the English courts.

8.3 All notices documents consents approvals or other communications (a 'Notice') to be given hereunder shall be in writing and shall be transmitted by first class registered or recorded delivery mail, or by telex, facsimile or other electronic means in a form generating a record copy to the party being served at the relevant address for that party shown at the head of this Agreement. Any Notice sent by mail shall be deemed to have been duly served three working days after the date of posting. Any Notice sent by telex facsimile or other electronic means shall be deemed to have been duly served at the time of transmission [if transmitted during normal business hours at the location of the recipient and if not so transmitted then at the start of normal business hours on the next business day commencing at such location after the time at which the transmission was made].

8.4 The headings in this Agreement shall not affect its interpretation.

8.5 Throughout this Agreement, whenever required by context, the use of the singular number shall be construed to include the plural, and the use of the plural the singular, and the use of any gender shall include all genders.

8.6 The Schedules to this Agreement constitute an integral part hereof.

8.7 Reference in this Agreement to a clause or a Schedule is to a clause or Schedule of this Agreement.

8.8 If any term or provision in this Agreement shall be held to be illegal or unenforceable, in whole or in part, under any enactment or rule of law, such term or provision or part shall to that extent be deemed not to form part of this Agreement but the validity and enforceability of the remainder of this Agreement shall not be affected.

8.9 The waiver or forbearance or failure of a party in insisting in any one or more instances upon the performance of any provisions of this Agreement shall not be construed as a waiver or relinquishment of that party's rights to future performance of such provision and the other party's obligations in respect of such future performance shall continue in full force and effect.

SCHEDULE 1
The Products

SCHEDULE 2

The Territory

SCHEDULE 3

Commission Arrangements

1 During the continuance of this Agreement the Agent shall be paid a commission at the relevant percentage or percentages set out below upon the net invoice price (Ex Works) of all Products sold to customers in the Territory under orders received from the Agent:

Product   Percentage

In the event that the Principal makes sales of the Products direct to customers in the Territory or through another agent in the Territory pursuant to cl 3.8 the Principal shall pay commission to the Agent at the following percentages:

Product   Percentage

2 Commission shall become due and payable to the Agent as soon as the Principal has received the full order price from its customers. Where the order provides for payment by instalments a proportionate part of the commission shall become due and payable to the Agent (as soon as such instalments are received by the Principal) equivalent to the proportion which such instalments form of the order price except that where the Principal is required under the terms of such order to provide bonds or other securities for such instalments no proportionate part of such commission shall become due and payable to the Agent unless and until such bonds or other securities are released to the Principal provided that notwithstanding anything contained in this Agreement the Agent shall be entitled to such commission as is provided for under this Agreement upon all such orders in respect of which the Principal has failed to execute the same for reasons within the control of the Principal and that such commission shall become due upon the date or dates upon which, but for the default of the Principal the customer who placed the relevant order would have been obliged to make the relevant payment or payments to the Principal in respect of that order.

3 After termination of this Agreement the Agent shall be entitled to commission as aforesaid on orders for the Products accepted by the Principal after such termination (*a*) if the said orders were mainly attributable to the Agent's efforts during the period covered by this Agreement and if they were accepted within a period of [six months] after the termination of this Agreement or (*b*) if the said orders reached the Principal or the Agent before the termination of this Agreement; provided that if upon the termination of this Agreement a new agent has been appointed by the Principal for the Products the Agent shall only be entitled to such proportion of the aforesaid commissions as is equitable in the circumstances, the balance being paid to the new agent.

4 Any commission paid to the Agent by the Principal hereunder shall represent the Agent's sole remuneration for its activities within the Territory and unless otherwise agreed the Agent shall not be entitled to reimbursement by the Principal in respect of any out-of-pocket or other expenses incurred by the Agent in connection with its duties hereunder all of which expenses shall be for the sole account of the Agent.

5 Unless otherwise agreed the currency of payment of commission payable to the Agent in respect of each order shall be the same currency as the currency of payment of the price of that order and payment shall (subject to the granting of any necessary exchange control or other governmental permission) be made by cheque sent to the Agent's registered office. Commission shall be payable not later than on the last day of the month following the month in which it became due.

6 The commission payable hereunder is to be paid net by the Principal after deducting all withholding taxes, levies or other deductions of any kind which may be made from the commission or required to be paid by either party in respect of such commission and all such deductions shall be for the account of the Agent.

7 The Principal shall supply the Agent with a statement of all commissions due hereunder not later than the last day of the month following the quarter in which such commissions have become due. Such statement shall set out the main components used in calculating the amount of such commission. The Agent shall, upon request, be entitled to all the information (including without limitation an extract from the Principal's books of account) which is available to the Principal and which the Agent needs in order to check the amount of such commission due to the Agent.

SIGNED the [   ] day of [   ] by the duly authorised representatives of the Principal and the Agent

Signature

Name

Title

for and on behalf of the
Principal

Signature

Name

Title

for and on behalf of the
Agent

Chapter 8

Standard distribution agreements

8.1　Introduction

Distribution agreements are much less subject to regulation under the general law than agency agreements, except in relation to those areas of competition law, particularly under art 85 of the Treaty of Rome, discussed in Chapter 6. However, certain countries (for example The Netherlands) do provide mandatory compensation for a distributor upon termination of a distribution agreement without cause which is similar in scope and principle to that provided to commercial agents under the Agency Directive.

It is thus possible to start with a general purpose distribution agreement which is largely based upon the agreement reached between the parties, with little regard for regulating law. This is contained in Precedent 1. It is possible to adapt Precedent 1 to comply with EC competition law with only the modification of a few clauses. The necessary clauses, duly adapted, are set out as Precedent 2.

Lastly, in view of the importance of selective distribution networks, Precedent 3 shows how Precedent 1 can be adapted to constitute a selective distribution agreement, and Precedent 4 shows an example of an agreement permitting a retailer to take part in a selective distribution network as an authorised retailer supplying consumers. These two precedents are modelled largely upon the applicable EC competition law, but could be used as they are even in a context where art 85 did not apply, although, in this case, a draftsman acting for a principal may wish to amend some of the provisions to provide greater control over the distributor or retailer, and to provide for more flexible rules in relation to termination.

8.2   Precedent 1

Clauses 1 and 2 describe the scope of the agreement in relation to products and territory, and permit the distributor to sell the principal's products under the principal's trademarks. It should be noted that under cl 2, the grant may be on an exclusive or non-exclusive basis. Most principals prefer, if at all possible, to make a non-exclusive grant, even if they do not intend to trade directly or appoint other distributors in the territory, since it gives them greater flexibility in the event the distributor does not perform well. Instead of resorting to termination for some breach of the agreement, the principal at least has the theoretical possibility of bypassing an incompetent distributor and trading himself directly or of appointing another, and hopefully more competent, distributor for the territory.

Clause 3 sets out a standard set of obligations to be undertaken by the distributor. Clause 3.1 contains the usual obligations of due diligence. It is very hard to terminate a distributor for breach of this type of clause, except in cases of the grossest delinquency, but its presence often provides a useful bargaining tool when the principal wishes to persuade the distributor to make greater efforts for sales. Clause 3.2 requires the distributor to act legally under the law of the territory in which he operates. Such a clause is often of greater use to enable the principal to disown a distributor who has acted illegally than it is to provide the principal with grounds of termination for its breach. Clause 3.3 provides for the imposition of minimum targets. In a situation where art 85 has no application these targets may be minimum sales or minimum purchase targets. Both types of target are more commonly, but not solely, found in exclusive distribution agreements, since, in return for exclusivity, the distributor can fairly be required to undertake minimum objectively verifiable performance standards, failure to achieve which can result in termination of the agreement. The principal may, in practice, not exercise his right of termination at once or at all, but, again, the right confers a useful bargaining tool in negotiations with delinquent distributors. For instance, in exchange for continuance of the agreement, the principal could require that the distributorship become non-exclusive. Clause 3.4 contains the usual obligation, often imposed on distributors, particularly exclusive ones, not to deal in competing goods. Clause 3.5 prevents the distributor tampering with the packaging of the products, by, for instance, removing labels giving information about the principal's intellectual property rights.

Clauses 4 and 5 deal with circumscribing the distributor's activity outside the territory. The principal must refer all enquiries arising from the territory to the distributor, and the distributor must refer all enquiries received by him from outside the territory to the principal. Similarly, the distributor is forbidden to sell outside his assigned territory. As shown in the precedent, the first sentence of cl 4 is in square brackets, and should be deleted if the grant of the distributorship is on a non-exclusive basis.

Clause 6 contains details of the way in which the distributor will obtain supplies of the products. He is obliged to obtain all supplies only from his principal (cl 6.1) and on the principal's standard terms and conditions of sale (cl 6.2). This form of clause is sometimes extended to permit the distributor to obtain supplies either from the principal or any other source of supply authorised or nominated by the principal. Clause 6.3 deals with the question of modifications to the products covered by the agreement. As it stands, the whole of the clause after the first one and a half lines is set in square brackets and can be regarded as optional. If the optional section is not included the principal can vary products, including those under order, at his discretion. However, most distributors will wish to have the sort of protection provided by the optional section, so that substantial alterations affecting the nature of the products require prior notification to the distributor, and cannot be applied automatically to current orders without his consent.

Clauses 7, 8 and 9 enable the principal to exercise some degree of control over the distributor's sales, marketing and advertising policies. This is particularly important where the principal wishes to have his products sold in a uniform manner over large geographical areas. Such provisions are also very important where the principal sells under brand names or trademarks that have a substantial reputation which he needs to protect from the disrepute that a distributor's inappropriate or unauthorised marketing, sales promotion or advertising activities might produce.

Clause 9.2 is particularly significant. In nearly all jurisdictions, resale price maintenance is nowadays illegal (it is certainly contrary to art 85 of the Treaty of Rome) and cl 9.2 makes it clear that selling prices are set by the distributor. It is, however, possible for a principal in some jurisdictions, for instance the UK and Australia, to recommend a retail price, and to put this recommendation on the package of the product in question.

Where this is the case, the combination of cl 3.5 and cl 9.3, which prevents the distributor from tampering with the products or their packaging, would make it a breach of contract for the distributor to remove any such resale price recommendation. This would prevent the distributor removing the recommendation in order to avoid consumer complaints if he charged a higher price, but would have no effect if he chose to charge a lower price, since then the recommendation would remain on the package, but would be irrelevant. Since the aim of many recommended retail prices (or, at any rate, the only legitimate aim, so far as competition law authorities are concerned) is to prevent resellers from charging higher prices which adversely affect the volume of sales for the product, and result, perhaps, in unjustifiably high margins for the reseller, competition law regimes tend to look relatively benignly on recommended resale prices, at least in comparison with their stance on resale price maintenance.

Clause 10 requires the distributor to carry a sufficient stock of the products to satisfy reasonable demands from his territory, and cl 11 requires him to maintain a proper staff and sales force. Clause 12 imposes minimum obligations on the distributor to provide information to the principal about his activities in relation to sales of the products.

Clause 13 imposes obligations for the safeguarding of the principal's intellectual property rights, including trademarks. This clause is particularly important in relation to trademarks where distributors are concerned. In many territories, if the principal has not registered, or cannot register, his trademark, the distributor, since he is the person selling the goods in the territory under the trademark, may be able to acquire rights in the trademark, either under the general law, or by registration, to the detriment of the principal. Clause 13 is, in particular, designed to prevent this.

Clause 14 makes it clear that the distributor has no authority to bind or act on behalf of the principal. Although such clauses are of no assistance against third parties in the event the distributor does make such representations to them, the clause does provide some remedy against a distributor who breaches it, and should serve to make the distributor think twice before doing so deliberately. Furthermore, the principles relating to ostensible authority mean that in many jurisdictions it is much more difficult (where a distributor is concerned rather than an agent) for a third party to claim that he reasonably believed a distributor (clearly an independent entity) had the authority to bind the principal.

Clauses 15, 16 and 17 deal with commencement and termination of the agreement in a reasonably standard fashion. Clause 15.1 provides (depending upon how the optional phrases in square brackets are used) for a fixed period agreement, an indefinite one terminable by notice or one with a fixed initial term which is thereafter to continue indefinitely until terminated by due notice. Most distribution agreements use the last option, as the distributor usually requires an initial period of certainty to justify him making a substantial investment in setting up the distribution operation.

Clause 15.4 provides for no compensation in the event the agreement is lawfully terminated or expires in accordance with its terms. This will probably hold good in most jurisdictions (it does in the UK) but enquiry should always be made in foreign jurisdictions to see if any local legislation will override this clause and provide mandatory compensation for the distributor. Where a single fixed period is provided for the phrase in square brackets in cl 15.4 must be added.

Clauses 15.2 and 15.3 provide for the distributor to obtain any necessary regulatory consents (such as product licences from health authorities) for the sale of the products in the territory, and for the termination of the agreement within six months of its commencement if he is by then unsuccessful in obtaining such consents. These clauses may not be necessary in many agreements, but where they are appropriate they should be included (particularly if the distribution agreement is an exclusive one) since otherwise the principal can be tied for long periods to a distributor who cannot obtain the necessary consents to sell, so that the products are not sold in the territory at all, when, with more diligence, or perhaps a different, better qualified distributor, consent could have been obtained and the products put on sale. The clauses at least enable the principal to put pressure on the distributor to do all he can to obtain consent, or, at worst, let the principal try again with a new distributor after a reasonable interval.

The termination clause (cl 16) contains the usual provisions for termination on breach, insolvency or change of control, and also provides for termination in the event the minimum targets imposed by cl 3.3 are not met. However, in this case, if the phrase in square brackets is included for the benefit of the distributor, the right to terminate is qualified to exclude occasions where failure to achieve the target was caused by default of the principal or *force majeure*.

Clause 17 covers the consequences of termination. (Again the phrase in square brackets in cl 17.1 should be inserted if the agreement is for a fixed term.) The clause requires the distributor to cease using the principal's trademarks, to return confidential information, to provide a list of customers and, if possible, to assign to the principal any licences required for the sale of the products in the territory. However, here the most controversial issue is what to do with the stock of the products in the hands of the distributor at termination. As drafted, cl 17.2 makes it obligatory for the distributor to sell and the principal to buy back fresh stock in good condition at predetermined price formulae (landed cost, less a discount for older stock), while old, obsolete or deteriorated stock has to be destroyed pursuant to cl 17.3. Principals would of course like only an option to buy back stock, and distributors only an option to sell it back. However, the clause as drafted gives a reasonable compromise. The principal is protected from the distributor (particularly if he has been terminated for breach) dealing with the stock in a way detrimental to the reputation of the product or in competition with a new distributor who has been appointed to succeed him. The distributor has unwanted stock taken off his hands, on a basis which should fairly recompense him for the money tied up in inventory, if he has controlled stock levels properly, and not allowed old stock to remain or build up in his warehouse. In return for these benefits each side has to give up some degree of flexibility.

It should, however, be noted that the opening wording of cll 17.2 and 17.3 places the burden of proof upon the distributor to demonstrate which categories the products in his inventory fall under. Thus, if he has not kept proper records of invoicing and purchases from the principal, he may be in considerable difficulty in recovering the full value of his stock, unless the product packaging itself contains date or other coding which yields the necessary information.

Finally, cl 18 imposes confidentiality obligations, cl 19 makes the agreement non-assignable by the distributor, and cl 20 provides a set of 'boilerplate' appropriate for a distribution agreement.

It should be noted that cl 20 contains no provisions limiting liability (eg for loss of profits or for default through *force majeure*). These provisions are more appropriately applied to individual orders by way of the principal's standard conditions of sale, and, so far as the principal is concerned, he has little exposure to such issues under the main agreement, where he would prefer for the liability of the distributor in such areas to be unlimited. This is particularly true in the case of the distributor's failure to perform because of *force majeure* (see cll 16.2. and 16.6, for instance). Nevertheless, where the parties desire it appropriate limitation and exclusion clauses can be added without any difficulty.

The contents of the Schedules is self-explanatory, but note should be taken of the provisions in Sched 3 relating to the agreement of new targets once those fixed for the initial period of the agreement have become superseded. In this case, the agreement must prescribe what happens if the parties cannot agree new targets. The only real choices are to terminate the agreement, or to forget about setting new targets and, in the case of an exclusive agreement, make it non-exclusive. The proviso for Sched 3 sets out these alternatives. It is, of course, also possible simply to provide that no further targets are to be set once the targets for the initial period have expired.

In practice, it is unlikely to be necessary to have any provisions relating to targets where the agreement is terminable by a reasonably short period of notice, since the principal has a complete discretion to terminate (or renegotiate the agreement to a non-exclusive one under threat of termination) if he is dissatisfied with the distributor's performance. Targets are thus usually only appropriate during any period when the agreement is running for a fixed period (usually of a duration of more than a year). It is sometimes argued that minimum purchase targets are always appropriate (even if the agreement is otherwise terminable by notice), as, if the distributor is forced to buy stock he cannot sell, the risk of a poor market is borne by him, rather than the principal. However, most sensible principals would feel such provisions are impractical to operate. The distributor will either deal with surplus stock by dumping it in ways the principal will not approve of, or in the end the distributor may become insolvent, in which case the principal will have to resolve the problem of surplus stock himself under the provisions of cll 17.2 and 17.3. The only real use of targets is to provide an objective measure to permit termination during a fixed period agreement if the target is not met.

8.3   Precedent 2

This set of clauses is designed to turn Precedent 1 into an exclusive distribution agreement which complies with the requirements of EC Regulation 83/1983 (the block exemption for exclusive distribution agreements) discussed in Chapter 6. Apart from the specific clauses listed in this precedent, there is, with one possible exception, no provision of Precedent 1 which is contrary to art 85 except such provisions which are exempted under the Regulation, provided that the reference in Sched 4 is to minimum purchase targets (which are the only sort of targets permitted by the Regulation) and not sales targets. The provisions in question are the buy-back provisions of cll 17.2 and 17.3. There is some argument that a provision which restricts the ability of an owner of goods which he has purchased to deal with them freely is itself in contravention of art 85 (see *Société de Vente de Ciments & Betons de l'Ouest SA v Kerpen & Kerpen GmbH & Co KG* [1985] 1 CMLR 511). In theory it could be argued that a mandatory buy-back is such a provision, because the distributor cannot sell his closing stock to any person other than the principal. The real question is whether such a restriction could be said to have an appreciable effect on trade between member states. Where there are sufficient sources for supply for the product, particularly if a new distributor has been appointed in place of the one who has been terminated, it is hard to see why a buy back provision could normally have sufficient appreciable effect to fall foul of art 85. Nevertheless the prudent draftsman will not include such a clause unless the parties specifically require it, and he has at least considered the effect on trade between member states in the particular circumstances of the case.

Clauses 2.1, 2.2 and 5.1 in Precedent 2 mirror the wording in the Regulation closely. Clause 4 is optional. It may be included since it does not have any effect on trade between member states as it requires the distributor to pass on to the principal only enquiries received by the distributor from outside the EC. Clause 5.2, forbidding the distributor to sell products outside the EC, is also optional and has a similar effect. However, it should be said that, ideally, it is safer not to include such clauses unless the parties are absolutely insistent, and quite specific about the territories over which they are to have effect. Given the considerable current and still further proposed extension of the EU, and the proliferation of bilateral treaties between the EU and Central and Eastern European countries, the exact territory in relation to which such clauses can operate without contravening art 85 is now quite unclear.[10]

Finally, cl 5.3 obliges the principal to impose on all distributors appointed by him for other territories within the EU restrictions, identical to cl 5, against active canvassing outside their respective territories. This protects the distributor from active canvassing in his territory by other distributors, and represents the only territorial regulation permitted under the Regulation.

In addition to the substituted clauses, it may be useful to add a definition of the EU, and a suggested one is included in Precedent 2.

8.4   Precedent 3

This precedent shows how Precedent 1 can be adapted for use as an authorised distributor agreement under a selective distribution network. The changes made in the precedent have been designed to comply so far as possible with the relevant Commission decisions and the principles laid down in judgments of the European Court of Justice, as discussed in Chapter 6, so that, at least in theory, and depending upon the commercial justification in each case, exemption under art 85(3) would be likely.

Clause 2.1 sets out the appointment of the distributor as an authorised distributor for the relevant selective distribution network. Since, for the purposes of avoiding contravention of art 85, it is necessary to have a free flow of goods throughout the network, the network is in a sense the territory in which each of the members is authorised to operate, and any other limitation to a geographical area is irrelevant, except for the purpose of confirming an exclusive appointment on the distributor and requiring him to confine his active selling to that area. The wording of clause 2.2 confers this sort of exclusivity on the distributor. As discussed in Chapter 6, a grant of exclusivity of this nature is in fact a quantitative or quota restriction on the number of distributors in the network.

Clause 2.3 ties the whole network together by requiring the principal to appoint all his distributors on the same terms, and not to supply the products except to such distributors.

Clause 3 follows cl 3 of Precedent 1, except that it contains no obligation in relation to minimum targets, since such obligations are, as discussed in Chapter 6, subjective qualitative criteria, which in principle contravene art 85. These clauses are normally not favoured by the Commission, so that their inclusion will mean a grant of exemption is less likely. However, in appropriate cases, the parties may wish to include either sales or purchase targets and put the clause up to the Commission seeking exemption. Additionally, the clause contains the obligation to observe and comply with the necessary requirements for qualification as an authorised distributor which are set out in Sched 4 of the precedent.

Clause 4 goes as far in limiting the activities of the distributor as is compatible with the need for a free flow of goods around the network, again a key requirement of the Commission for exemption under art 85(3). Clauses 4.1 and 4.2 restrict the distributor to selling only to retailers and distributors who are members of the network, and to end users. Clause 4.3 merely affirms the freedom of the distributor in respect of pricing matters. Clause 4.4 (restricting active canvassing outside the territory) should be inserted when cl 2.2 is used.

Clause 5 relating to the supply of products to the distributor contains the same provisions as cl 6 of Precedent 1, except that clause 5.1 affirms the freedom of the distributor to obtain supplies of the products not only from the principal but also from any other member of the selective distribution network.

Clause 6 requires the distributor to retain records of both his sales and purchases of the products. The purpose of this is to enable him to supply information to the principal which will prove that he is buying only from the principal or other sources within the selective distribution network and that he is selling only to end-users or other members of the network. Ultimately, the principal has a right of audit of these records to check the information given. Since the European Commission is very concerned that principals do not monitor their distributors in selective distribution networks for improper reasons (such as to detect price cutting or cross-border trade), cl 6.4 removes any such suspicion from the principal by requiring the audit to be carried out by an independent third party who will merely certify to the truth or otherwise of the matters which the principal is entitled to monitor pursuant to cll 4 and 5 of the agreement.

Clauses 7–9 (advertising, sales and marketing policies and monthly reports), 10 (protection of principal's intellectual property rights), 11 (no joint venture or partnership between the parties), 15 (confidentiality), 16 (no assignment) and 18 ('boilerplate') are the same as the equivalent provisions of Precedent 1 and reference should be made to the commentary on the relevant clauses in that precedent. Additionally, because of the special provisions of cl 13.4 discussed below, cl 19 includes an arbitration clause.

Clauses 12, 13 and 14, relating to commencement, term and termination of the agreement are based on cll 15, 16 and 17 of Precedent 1, but there are some important differences in the case of their adaptation to a selective distribution agreement.

Clause 12.2 sets out the restrictions on the principal's rights to terminate other than for cause, which the Commission normally now requires in order to grant an exemption in the area of selective distribution agreements, so that the agreement cannot be terminated without cause unless the principal is winding up the whole of the network, and has served notice of termination on all of its members. On the other hand, cl 12.3 permits the distributor to terminate without cause and withdraw from the network very easily, by giving only six months' notice.

The rights of summary termination under cl 13 are the same as those provided in cl 16 of Precedent 1, except that additional safeguards have to be built in to satisfy the Commission that any right of summary termination for cause is not being exercised by the principal unfairly or arbitrarily, or for the purpose of discriminating against distributors who cut prices. Clause 13.2 permits termination of distributors who do not comply with the distributor requirements, but cl 13.4 provides that such termination can be contested by an aggrieved distributor who can appeal the matter to independent arbitration. Clause 13.3 permits termination if the distributor trades in breach of local fair trading regulations (the most common example is using the products as loss leaders, or indulging in predatory pricing policies) but cl 13.5 provides, if the distributor contests the issue, that termination cannot take place until a competent court has in fact adjudged the distributor guilty of the relevant unfair trading practice.

Clause 13.1.6 (change of control) requires special mention. The equivalent provisions in Precedent 1 extended to all persons of whom the principal might disapprove at his complete discretion. This seems unreasonable since in many cases such persons could fulfil the objective qualitative criteria set out in Sched 4, and as such the principal would have no justifiable reason for refusing to admit them as successors to the existing distributor. The limitation in this precedent to coming under the control of a competitor seems more reasonable, as this is something the principal could legitimately object to.

Clause 14, relating to the consequences of termination is the same as cl 17 of Precedent 1, except that it does not contain the buy-back provisions of cll 17.2 and 17.3. The arguments against including such provisions because of possible problems with art 85 are stronger in the case of selective distribution agreements, than in the case of ordinary distribution agreements subject to art 85 as discussed with reference to Precedent 2, and make it less likely the Commission will exempt the whole agreement under art 85(3). However, it can of course be argued that since the relevant distribution arrangements will be submitted to the Commission anyway, there is no harm in inserting such provisions (if the parties agree upon them) since they can always be revised if, in any particular case, the Commission requires this as a condition of exemption. In any event, cl 14.2 prevents the distributor from any longer describing himself as an authorised distributor or making use of the trademark in the sale of the products, and this should probably provide sufficient safeguards for the principal's reputation in most cases, where buy-back provisions are not included.

Finally, cl 17 deals with the training of the distributor by the principal in the technical information relating to the products that he is required to know if he is to do a good job as a distributor. This type of clause is common to most selective distribution agreements, and is essential for all but the simplest types of products.

The only schedule which requires special comment is Sched 4. The distributor requirements contained in this schedule are intended to be objective qualitative criteria with which any distributor who was willing to devote himself properly to the sale and marketing of the products could be expected to comply. On this basis, the criteria do not contravene art 85, and the only limitation on the appointment of distributors who can qualify will be the effective quota restriction if cl 2.2 is included. It will be recalled that the boundary line between objective qualitative criteria and subjective qualitative criteria (the latter contravening art 85 and requiring a submission for exemption under art 85(3)) fluctuates depending upon the type of products concerned and the maturity of the particular industry under which they are distributed.

8.5   Precedent 4

Precedent 4 sets out the agreement for the authorised retailer corresponding to that of the authorised distributor set out in Precedent 3. Again the purpose of this precedent is to build on the principles set out in Chapter 6 to provide a selective distribution retailer agreement which would achieve exemption under art 85(3).

The term 'appointor' is used rather than 'principal', since it may well be the case in the selective distribution network that retailers are appointed not only by the principal but also by authorised distributors.

The terms of Precedent 4 correspond very closely with those of Precedent 3 but are less formal. They are suitable for small retailers who would operate one or two outlets. If a retailer agreement were being struck with a large retailer, perhaps operating a chain of department stores, or a large number of outlets, then it would be preferable to use a combination of Precedent 3, somewhat adapted, probably on a non-exclusive basis, together with the retailer requirements set out in App 2 of this Precedent.

The body of Precedent 4 contains first the appointment of the retailer as an authorised retailer within the network and then ties the retailer to obtain products only from members of the network and sell products only to members of the network and to end users.

The appointor then binds himself only to sell within the network. The reference in square brackets undertaking that he will not sell to end-users is usually only granted exemption by the Commission where the appointor is the manufacturer of the products and not an authorised distributor. There is then a provision, equivalent to cl 2.3 of Precedent 3, requiring the appointor to appoint all authorised retailers on the same terms.

The retailer is then obliged to keep records of all his sales and purchases of the products. However, unlike Precedent 3, cl 6, the appointor is entitled to inspect these records directly rather than through an agent, although a provision stating that the appointor is not entitled to monitor pricing is included as a precaution. The agreement then moves on to deal with the assistance the appointor is to give the retailer by way of sales and technical training, and publicity and promotional material. The agreement assumes that the retailer will support sales promotion campaigns of the appointor, and will carry out simple adjustments and maintenance to products on the retailer's premises.

The agreement then sets out provisions preventing assignment, and deals with termination as a result of the insolvency of the retailer, or, in the case of a natural person or partnership, of death.

The provisions for termination without cause by due notice are the same as those in Precedent 3, but in the case of termination for breach, no appeals or arbitration procedure is included, since this is regarded as impractical when dealing with a large number of retailers. The appointor should simply be scrupulously fair in his termination of retailers, in the knowledge that the legality of any termination could always be challenged, if not at law, then, in practice, by a complaint to the European Commission. The consequences of termination do not address stock or buy back provisions, but simply require the retailer to cease to describe himself as authorised and to cease using the appointor's trademarks.

The retailer requirements set out in App 2 are designed to fall within the definition of objective qualitative criteria as laid down for retailers in the various cases discussed in Chapter 6. They are examples designed to suit the types of products most commonly handled by retailers under selective distribution agreements, but will have to be tailored extensively to suit individual product ranges. Again the fluctuating boundary between objective and subjective qualitative criteria has to be kept very much in mind.

Standard long-form distribution agreement

This Agreement is made on the [   ] day of [   ]
19[   ] between [   ] Limited whose registered office is at
[   ] (the 'Principal') and [   ] Limited whose registered office is at [   ] (the 'Distributor').

1   Definitions

1.1 The 'Products' means those products listed in Schedule 1.

1.2 The 'Territory' means those areas listed in Schedule 2.

1.3 The 'Trademark' means those trademarks and trade names listed in Schedule 3.

2   Grant and terms of distributorship

The Principal hereby grants the Distributor [an exclusive] [a non-exclusive]
licence to distribute and sell the Products under the Trademark in the Territory
during the continuance of this Agreement.

3   Responsibilities

3.1 The Distributor shall during the continuance of this Agreement diligently
and faithfully serve the Principal as its distributor in the Territory and shall use
its best endeavours to improve the goodwill of the Principal in the Territory

and to further and increase the sale of the Products in the Territory.

3.2 The Distributor will ensure that it conforms with all legislation rules regulations and statutory requirements existing in the Territory from time to time in relation to the Products.

3.3 The Distributor undertakes to achieve targets in relation to the Products in accordance with Schedule 4.

3.4 The Distributor undertakes during the continuance of this Agreement not to manufacture or sell in or import into the Territory any goods competitive with the Products and not to be interested directly or indirectly in any such manufacture sale or importation.

3.5 The Distributor shall leave in position and not cover or erase any notices or other marks (including without limitation details of patents or notices that a trademark design or copyright relating to the Products is owned by the Principal or a third party) which the Principal may place on or affix to the Products.

4   Enquiries

4.1 [The Principal shall during the continuance of this Agreement refer all enquiries received by it for sale of the Products in the Territory to the Distributor.] The Distributor shall during the continuance of this Agreement refer to the Principal all enquiries it receives for the Products for sale outside or export from the Territory.

5   Extra-territorial activities

During the continuance of this Agreement the Distributor shall not sell outside or export or assist in or be a party to the export of the Products from the Territory unless the prior consent of the Principal has been obtained.

6   Supply of the products

6.1 The Distributor shall purchase all its requirements for the Products ready packaged from the Principal.

6.2 The parties hereto agree that orders placed by the Distributor with the Principal under cl 6.1 or for any other items shall be on the terms set out in Schedule 5.

6.3 The Principal reserves the right to improve or modify the Products without prior notice [provided that details of any modification affecting [form fit function or maintenance] [or] [any permissions consents or licences obtained by the Distributor pursuant to cl 15.2] shall be notified to the Distributor in which event the Distributor may vary or cancel any orders placed for the Products prior to the receipt of such notification except to the extent that these orders can be met by the supply of Products which do not incorporate the improvement or modification notified hereunder. Variation or cancellation hereunder shall be effected by the Distributor notifying the Principal thereof within fourteen days of receipt by the Distributor of the relevant notification of the relevant improvement or modification. The Distributor's rights of cancellation under this clause shall be its sole remedy in the event of any improvement or modification being made to a Product, and in particular, but without limitation, no compensation or damages for breach of contract shall be payable to the Distributor by reason of such improvement or modification].

7 Advertising

7.1 The costs of all advertising and sales promotion activities shall unless otherwise decided be borne by the Distributor.

7.2 All advertisements point of sale promotion merchandising and publicity material for the Products issued by the Distributor shall be subject before issue to the prior approval of the Principal.

7.3 All sales promotion activities carried on by the Distributor for the Products of whatever nature must receive the prior approval of the Principal.

8 Merchandising

The cost of all merchandising returns from customers relating to the Products shall (except in respect of Products which the Principal is obliged to replace as defective in accordance with its warranty obligations under Schedule 5), be borne by the Distributor.

9 Sales and marketing policies

9.1 The Distributor shall conform to the general sales and marketing policies of the Principal and the Principal reserves the right to issue directions from time to time to the Distributor to ensure such conformity.

9.2 Selling prices for the sale of the Products in the Territory by the Distributor shall be established and revised from time to time by the Distributor.

9.3 The Distributor undertakes not to alter treat or otherwise deal with any of the Products (or their packaging) or to present any such Products for sale in a group package without in both cases obtaining the prior written consent of the Principal.

10   Stocks of the products

The Distributor shall at all times during the continuance of this Agreement carry at least [three months'] stock of the Products so that all orders received by the Distributor can be supplied without undue delay. The Distributor shall supply such reports as to stock levels and movements as the Principal may from time to time request.

11   Staff

The Distributor shall maintain during the continuance of this Agreement sufficient staff to sell distribute and promote the sale of the Products throughout the Territory and perform in a timely and satisfactory manner the Distributor's obligations under this Agreement and in particular shall create and maintain a sales force of sufficient size from time to time to fulfil the Distributor's obligations under this Agreement in relation to the sale and marketing of the Products.

12   Monthly reports

The Distributor shall send to the Principal by the thirtieth day following the end of each calendar month during the continuance of this Agreement a report of sales made of the Products in the Territory during that month together with such other marketing and other information in relation to the operation of the Agreement as the Principal may reasonably require.

13   Intellectual property rights

13.1 It is agreed that all rights to the Trademark (and all other intellectual property rights relating to or subsisting in the Products) are and shall remain the exclusive property of the Principal. The Distributor shall at the expense of the Principal enter into such agreements with the Principal (including without limitation registered user agreements) and shall execute such documents and carry out such actions as may be necessary to protect such rights of the Principal in the Territory.

13.2 The Trademark shall not be used in any manner liable to invalidate the registration thereof and the right to use the Trademark in connection with the appropriate Products is only granted to the extent that the Principal is able to do so without endangering the validity of the registration.

13.3 The Distributor shall (in so far as it becomes aware thereof) notify the Principal of any unauthorised use in the Territory of the Trademark. At the request and cost of the Principal the Distributor shall take part in or give assistance in respect of any legal proceedings and execute any documents and do any things reasonably necessary to protect the Trademark in the Territory.

14   No joint venture or partnership

Nothing in this Agreement shall create a partnership or joint venture between the parties hereto and save as expressly provided in this Agreement neither party shall enter into or have authority to enter into any engagement or make any representation or warranty on behalf of or pledge the credit of or otherwise bind or oblige the other party hereto.

15   Commencement and term of agreement

15.1 This Agreement shall (subject to earlier termination as herein provided) commence upon [the date of signature hereof] and continue in force [for [a] [an initial]] period of [three years] [and thereafter shall continue] [unless and until terminated by not less than [six months'] notice given by one party to the other] [such notice not to be given prior to the expiry of the said period].

15.2 The Distributor shall obtain at its own expense all necessary permissions consents and licences (including but without limitation those required to be given by any government department or any body constituted under the law of the Territory for licensing or other regulatory purposes relating to the Products) to enable the Distributor to market distribute and sell the Products in the Territory and to ensure the full and legal operation of this Agreement.

15.3 If the said permissions consents and licences are not obtained and fully operative within a period of [six months] from the aforesaid date of commencement the Principal shall thereafter have the option to terminate this Agreement immediately by notice to the Distributor. The said option shall cease if (prior to its exercise) the aforesaid permissions consents and licences have in fact been obtained and are fully operative even though this has been achieved outside the said period of [six months].

15.4 The Distributor shall not be entitled to any compensation on the termination of this Agreement under cll 15 or 16 for any cause whatsoever [including but without limitation expiry by effluxion of time].

16   Termination

16.1 Without prejudice to any right or remedy the Principal may have against the Distributor for breach or non-performance of this Agreement the Principal shall have the right summarily to terminate this Agreement:

16.2 On the Distributor committing a material breach of this Agreement other than a breach of cl 3.3 providing the Distributor has been advised in writing of the breach and has not rectified it within twenty-one days of receipt of such advice.

16.3 On the Distributor failing to achieve a target under cl 3.3 [unless such failure was caused by a default of the Principal or by reason of act of God, fire explosion war riot civil commotion or governmental decree or legislation].

16.4 If the Distributor shall have any distress or execution levied upon its goods or effects.

16.5 On the commencement of the winding up or bankruptcy of the Distributor or on the appointment of a receiver or administrator of the distributor's assets or on the Distributor ceasing to do business at any time for 30 consecutive days (other than for annual holidays).

16.6 On the Distributor for any reason of whatsoever nature being substantially prevented from performing or becoming unable to perform its obligations hereunder.

16.7 On the Distributor assigning or attempting to assign this Agreement without the prior written consent of the Principal.

16.8 If control of the Distributor shall pass from the present shareholders or owners or controllers to other persons whom the Principal shall in its absolute discretion regard as unsuitable.

17 Effect of termination

17.1 Upon termination of this Agreement from any cause whatsoever pursuant to cl 15 or 16 [(or by reason of expiry by effluxion of time)] the Distributor shall at the request of the Principal promptly return to the Principal all documentation of any nature whatsoever in his possession or control relating to the Products or to the Principal and to the activities of the Distributor in relation to the Products or the Principal (other than correspondence between the Distributor and the Principal which does not relate to technical matters).

17.2 Upon such termination the Distributor shall sell back to the Principal, and the Principal shall buy back from the Distributor, at the prices set out below, all Products falling within the following classes (but in all cases excluding Products covered by cl 17.3) purchased by the Distributor from the Principal hereunder and remaining unsold at the date of such termination:

17.2.1 Products which the Distributor can demonstrate were invoiced within 12 months of the termination date of this Agreement—landed cost (including customs duties if any) into Distributor's warehouse; and

17.2.2 Products which the Distributor can demonstrate were invoiced more than 12 months but less than 24 months from the termination date of this Agreement—60 per cent of landed cost (including customs duties if any) into the Distributor's warehouse.

17.3 Upon such termination Products which the Distributor cannot demonstrate were invoiced within the periods referred to in cll 17.2.1 or 17.2.2, Products invoiced more than 24 months before the said termination date and Products (irrespective of when invoiced) which are unmerchantable obsolete illegal damaged deteriorated defective or otherwise unfit for sale or (where any Product has a shelf-life) with more than half of their shelf-life expired shall be destroyed forthwith by the Distributor in the presence of the Principal or the authorised representative of the Principal at the expense of the Distributor and without making any charge upon the Principal.

17.4 Upon such termination the Distributor shall have no further rights to use the Trademark in any way whatsoever and in particular but without prejudice to the generality of the foregoing shall cease to use the Trademark on its letterheads packaging vehicle liveries or elsewhere and shall at the request of the Principal sell any stocks of the Products not disposed of under cll 17.2 or 17.3 in packaging which bears neither the Trademark nor the name of the Principal.

17.5 Upon such termination the Distributor shall (if so required) supply the Principal with a list of the Distributor's customers for the Products.

17.6 Upon such termination the Distributor shall (if legally possible) assign to the Principal free of charge all permissions consents and licences (if any) relating to the marketing and or distribution and or sale of the Products and execute all documents and do all things necessary to ensure that the Principal shall enjoy the benefit of the said permissions consents and licences after the said termination to the entire exclusion of the Distributor.

18   Confidentiality

The Distributor shall keep strictly confidential not disclose to any third party and use only for the purposes of this Agreement all information relating to the Products (whether technical or commercial) and to the affairs and business of the Principal and its subsidiary or associated companies, whether such information is disclosed to the Distributor by the Principal or otherwise obtained by the Distributor as a result of its association with the Principal.

19   Assignment

This Agreement and the benefit of the rights granted to the Distributor by this Agreement shall be personal to the Distributor who shall not without the prior consent of the Principal mortgage or charge the same to any third party nor subcontract nor assign the same nor part with any of its rights or obligations hereunder save that the foregoing shall not prevent the Distributor from factoring or mortgaging or in any way creating a charge or security over Products the title in which shall have passed to it or over book-debts created by the sale of such Products.

20   Miscellaneous

20.1 No waiver, alteration, variation or addition to this Agreement shall be effective unless made in writing on or after the date of signature of this Agreement by both parties and accepted by an authorised signatory of both parties.

20.2 The interpretation construction effect and enforceability of this Agreement shall be governed by the laws of England, and the parties agree to submit to the [non-exclusive] jurisdiction of the English courts.

20.3 All notices documents consents approvals or other communications (a 'Notice') to be given hereunder shall be in writing and shall be transmitted by first class registered or recorded delivery mail, or by telex, facsimile or other electronic means in a form generating a record copy to the party being served at the relevant address for that party shown at the head of this Agreement. Any Notice sent by mail shall be deemed to have been duly served three working days after the date of posting. Any Notice sent by telex facsimile or other electronic means shall be deemed to have been duly served at the time of transmission [if transmitted during normal business hours at the location of the recipient and if not so transmitted then at the start of normal business hours on the next business day commencing at such location after the time at which the transmission was made].

20.4 The headings in this Agreement shall not affect its interpretation.

20.5 Throughout this Agreement, whenever required by context, the use of the singular number shall be construed to include the plural, and the use of the plural the singular, and the use of any gender shall include all genders.

20.6 The Schedules to this Agreement constitute an integral part hereof.

20.7 Reference in this Agreement to a clause or a Schedule is to a clause or Schedule of this Agreement.

20.8 If any term or provision in this Agreement shall be held to be illegal or unenforceable, in whole or in part, under any enactment or rule of law, such term or provision or part shall to that extent be deemed not to form part of this Agreement but the validity and enforceability of the remainder of this Agreement shall not be affected.

20.9 The waiver or forbearance or failure of a party in insisting in any one or more instances upon the performance of any provisions of this Agreement shall not be construed as a waiver or relinquishment of that party's rights to future performance of such provision and the other party's obligations in respect of such future performance shall continue in full force and effect.

SCHEDULE 1
Details of the Products

SCHEDULE 2
Details of the Territory

SCHEDULE 3
Details of the Trademarks

SCHEDULE 4
[Sales] [Purchase] Targets

The Distributor undertakes (subject to prior termination in accordance with cl 15) to achieve [during the following periods set out below] [during each consecutive period of twelve months of the currency of this Agreement (the first such period to commence upon the date of commencement of this Agreement)] the following minimum targets for purchases from the Principal for the Products during the relevant period as follows:

Period   Target

[Provided that the quantity for all periods thereafter shall be set by the mutual agreement of the parties hereto as a result of review to be completed not later than three calendar months prior to the commencement of the relevant period; and that if the parties are unable to reach mutual agreements to the fixing of any minimum quantity as aforesaid [then no further target shall be set and the Principal shall have the right to amend cl 2.1 to a non-exclusive licence, but the Distributor shall not be regarded as in any way in breach of this Agreement nor shall any of its rights hereunder be prejudiced or removed save as provided in relation to cl 2.1] [then the Distributor shall be regarded as in breach of this Agreement under cl 16.2]].

SCHEDULE 5
Terms of Supply of Principal

Signed the day and year first above written by the duly authorised representatives of the Principal and the Distributor.

For and on behalf of the   For and on behalf of the
Principal   Distributor

Precedent 2

Clauses for use in EC distribution agreements

A Grant of licence [to replace cl 2 of Precedent 1]

2.1 The Principal hereby grants the Distributor a licence to distribute and sell the Products under the Trademark in the Territory during the continuance of this Agreement.

2.2 The Principal undertakes that during the continuance of this Agreement it will not appoint in the Territory any other distributor or reseller of the Products nor directly supply any of the Products to distributors, resellers or users located within the Territory.

B Enquiries [to replace cl 4 of Precedent 1]

4.1 The Distributor shall during the continuance of this Agreement refer to the Principal all enquiries it receives for the Products for sale or ultimate delivery outside the EC.

C Extra-territorial activities [to replace cl 5 of Precedent 1]

5.1 The Distributor shall not during the continuance of this Agreement outside the Territory:
5.1.1 advertise the Products or canvass or solicit for orders for the Products; or
5.1.2 open branches for the sale of the Products; or
5.1.3 maintain distribution depots for the Products.

5.2 The Distributor shall not sell the Products outside the EC except into areas from which it is reasonably likely that reimportation of the Products into the EC would occur.

5.3 The Principal shall impose on any other distributor or agent appointed by it for areas of the EC outside the Territory obligations identical to those imposed upon the Distributor under cll 4 and 5, including cl 5.3.

D   Definition of EC

The EC shall mean the member states that from time to time constitute the European Community. For the avoidance of doubt if a state shall cease to be a member state or shall become a member state of the European Community it shall thereupon cease to be or become, respectively, part of the European Community for the purposes of this definition.

Selective distribution agreement

This Agreement is made on the [   ] day of [   ]
19[   ] between [   ] Limited whose registered office is at
[   ] (the 'Principal') and [   ] Limited whose registered office is at [   ] (the 'Distributor').

1   Definitions

1.1 The 'Products' means those products listed in Schedule 1.

[**1.2** The 'Territory' means those territories listed in Schedule 2.]

1.3 The 'Trademark' means those trademarks and trade names listed in Schedule 3.

1.4 The 'EC' means the member states that from time to time constitute the
European Community. For the avoidance of doubt if a state shall cease to be a
member state or shall become a member state of the European Community it
shall thereupon cease to be or become, respectively, part of the European Community for the purposes of this definition.

2   Grant and terms of distributorship

2.1 The Principal hereby appoints the Distributor as an Authorised Distributor
of the Products and hereby grants the Distributor (pursuant to such appointment) a licence to market distribute and sell the Products under the Trademark
in accordance with and subject to the terms of this Agreement.

[**2.2** The Principal undertakes that during the continuance of this Agreement it will not appoint in the Territory any other distributor or reseller of the Products nor directly supply any of the Products to distributors, resellers or users located within the Territory.]

2.3 The Principal also undertakes not to supply the Products to any distributor within the EC [outside the Territory] (at the same level of distribution as the Distributor) except subject to the conclusion of a distribution agreement with such distributor in identical terms to this Agreement and appointing such distributor an Authorised Distributor for the Products.

3   Responsibilities of distributor

3.1 The Distributor shall during the continuance of this Agreement diligently and faithfully serve the Principal as its distributor and shall use its best endeavours to improve the goodwill of the Principal and to further and increase the sale of the Products.

3.2 The Distributor will ensure that it conforms with all applicable legislation rules regulations and statutory requirements from time to time in relation to the Products.

[**3.3** The Distributor undertakes during the continuance of this Agreement not to manufacture or sell any goods competitive with the Products and not to be interested directly or indirectly in any such manufacture, sale.]

3.4 The Distributor shall leave in position and not cover or erase any notices or other marks (including without limitation details of patents or notices that a trademark design or copyright relating to the Products is owned by the Principal or a third party) which the Principal may place on or affix to the Products.

3.5 The Distributor will (for so long as this Agreement continues in force) comply with and satisfy the Distributor Requirements set out in Schedule 4.

4   Sales activities

4.1 The Distributor shall be free to sell the Products to any retailer or distributor who has been appointed in respect of any part of the EC as an Authorised Retailer or Authorised Distributor for the Products and shall also be free to sell the Products to any consumer or end-user anywhere in the EC [whether inside or outside the Territory.]

4.2 The Distributor shall not sell the Products outside or inside the EC except as provided in cl 4.1.

4.3 The Distributor shall at its own entire discretion determine the prices at which and (except as specifically provided in this Agreement) the terms and conditions on which it sells the Products.

[**4.4** The Distributor shall not during the continuance of this Agreement outside the Territory:
4.4.1 advertise the Products or canvass or solicit for orders for the Products; or
4.4.2 open branches for the sale of the Products; or
4.4.3 maintain distribution depots for the Products.]

5   Supply of the products

5.1 The Distributor shall purchase all its requirements for the Products (ready packaged) either from the Principal or from any other Authorised Distributor or Authorised Retailer for the Products within the EC.

5.2 The parties hereto agree that orders placed by the Distributor with the Principal under cl 5.1 or for any other items shall be on the terms set out in Schedule 5.

5.3 The Principal reserves the right to improve or modify the Products without prior notice [provided that details of any modification affecting [form fit function or maintenance] [or] [any permissions consents or licences obtained by the Distributor pursuant to cl 12.4] shall be notified to the Distributor in which event the Distributor may vary or cancel any orders placed for the Products prior to the receipt of such notification except to the extent that these orders can be met by the supply of Products which do not incorporate the improvement or modification notified hereunder. Variation or cancellation hereunder shall be effected by the Distributor notifying the Principal thereof within fourteen days of receipt by the Distributor of the relevant notification of the relevant improvement or modification. The Distributor's rights of cancellation under this clause shall be its sole remedy in the event of any improvement or modification being made to a Product, and in particular, but without limitation, no compensation or damages for breach of contract shall be payable to the Distributor by reason of such improvement or modification].

6   Distribution records

6.1 The Distributor shall retain for at least one year duplicate copies of all invoices relating to sales of the Products by it, recording the date of sale and the name and address of the purchaser, and details of the relevant Products.

6.2 The Distributor shall retain for at least one year duplicate copies of all purchase orders for the Products placed by it on the Principal or any other person, recording the date of purchase and the name and address of the seller, and details of the relevant Products.

6.3 The Distributor shall in addition to the specific requirements of cll 6.1 and 6.2 keep all relevant accounts together with supporting vouchers (including without limitation copies of invoices) and other relevant papers relating to the business carried on by it in the Products under this Agreement.

6.4 The Distributor shall upon reasonable notice supply at any time to the Principal, upon request, details of persons who have sold to it and bought from it Products during the preceding 12 months, including names and addresses and the details of the relevant Products for each transaction.

6.5 The Principal shall have the right at any time upon reasonable notice to appoint an independent firm of chartered accountants (the 'auditor') to audit and inspect all of the records referred to in this clause for the purpose of verifying the accuracy of any information given to it by the Distributor under cl 6.4 and otherwise for verifying that the Distributor is in compliance with its obligations under this Agreement provided that the auditor shall not disclose to the Principal details of the records concerned which shall remain confidential between the auditor and the Distributor and the auditor shall issue a certificate either stating that the information given under cl 6.4 is correct or that the Distributor is in compliance with its obligations under this Agreement as aforesaid, or stating that this is not the case and specifying details of the inaccuracies or the lack of compliance as the case may be.

6.6 Nothing in this clause or elsewhere in this Agreement shall entitle the Principal to pay regard to or monitor the prices at which the Distributor sells the Products.

7   Advertising and merchandising

7.1 The costs of all advertising and sales promotion activities shall unless otherwise decided be borne by the Distributor.

7.2 All advertisements point of sale promotion merchandising and publicity material for the Products issued by the Distributor shall be subject before issue to the prior approval of the Principal.

7.3 All sales promotion activities carried on by the Distributor for the Products of whatever nature must receive the prior approvals of the Principal which reserves the right to veto the same entirely at its discretion.

7.4 The cost of all merchandising returns from customers relating to the Products shall (unless otherwise agreed in writing or in respect of Products which the Principal is obliged to replace as defective in accordance with its warranty obligations under Schedule 5) be borne by the Distributor.

8 Sales and marketing policies

8.1 The Distributor shall conform to the general sales and marketing policies philosophies and principles of the Principal and the Principal reserves the right to issue directions from time to time to the Distributor to ensure such conformity.

8.2 Selling prices for the sale of the Products by the Distributor shall be established and revised from time to time by the Distributor.

8.3 The Distributor undertakes not to alter treat or otherwise deal with any of the Products (or their packaging) or to present any such Products for sale in a group package without in both cases obtaining the prior written consent of the Principal.

9 Monthly reports

The Distributor shall send to the Principal by the thirtieth day following the end of each calendar month during the continuance of this Agreement a report of sales made of the Products during that month together with such other marketing and other information in relation to the operation of the Agreement as the Principal may reasonably require. Forms for these reports will be supplied by the Principal.

10 Intellectual property rights

10.1 It is agreed that all rights to the Trademark (and all other intellectual property rights relating to or subsisting in the Products) are and shall remain the exclusive property of the Principal. The Distributor shall at the expense of the Principal enter into such agreements with the Principal (including not without limitation registered user agreements) and shall execute such documents and carry out such actions as may be necessary to protect such rights of the Principal.

10.2 The Trademark shall not be used in any manner liable to invalidate the registration thereof and the right to use the Trademark in connection with the appropriate Products is only granted to the extent that the Principal is able to do so without endangering the validity of the registration.

10.3 The Distributor shall (in so far as it becomes aware thereof) notify the Principal of any unauthorised use of the Trademark. At the request and cost of the Principal the Distributor shall take part in or give assistance in respect of any legal proceedings and execute any documents and do any things reasonably necessary to protect the Trademark.

11   No joint venture or partnership

Nothing in this Agreement shall create a partnership or joint venture between the parties hereto and save as expressly provided in this Agreement neither party shall enter into or have authority to enter into any engagement or make any representation or warranty on behalf of or pledge the credit of or otherwise bind or oblige the other party hereto.

12   Commencement and term of agreement

12.1 This Agreement shall commence on [the date of signature hereof] and shall continue unless and until terminated in accordance with cl 12 or 13.

12.2 The Principal may terminate this Agreement at any time by not less than [12] months' notice provided that at the same time the Principal serves notice of the same length upon all its Authorised Distributors and Authorised Retailers for the Products in order to terminate all Authorised Distributor Agreements and all Authorised Retailer Agreements with the intention of disbanding and terminating the activities of its selective distribution network for the Products.

12.3 The Distributor may terminate this Agreement at any time by six months' notice to the Principal.

12.4 The Distributor shall obtain at its own expense all necessary permissions consents and licences (including but without limitation those required to be given by any government department or any body constituted for licensing or other regulatory purposes relating to the products) to enable the Distributor to market distribute and sell the Products and to ensure the full and legal operation of this Agreement.

12.5 If the said permissions consents and licences are not obtained and fully operative within a period of [six] months from the aforesaid date of commencement the Principal shall thereafter have the option to terminate this Agreement immediately by notice to the Distributor. The said option shall cease if (prior to its exercise) the aforesaid permissions consents and licences have in fact been obtained and are fully operative even though this has been achieved outside the said period of [six] months.

12.6 The Distributor shall not be entitled to any compensation on the termination of this Agreement under cl 12 or 13 for any cause whatsoever.

13   Summary termination

13.1 Without prejudice to any right or remedy the Principal may have against the Distributor for breach or non-performance of this Agreement the Principal shall (subject to cll 13.4 and 13.5) have the right summarily to terminate this Agreement:

13.1.1 on the Distributor committing a material breach of this Agreement providing the Distributor has been advised in writing of the breach and has not rectified it within 21 days of receipt of such advice or;

13.1.2 If the Distributor shall have any distress or execution levied upon its goods or effects or;

13.1.3 On the commencement of the winding up or bankruptcy of the Distributor or on the appointment of a receiver of the distributor's assets or on the Distributor ceasing to do business at any time for thirty consecutive days (other than for annual holidays); or

13.1.4 On the Distributor for any reason of whatsoever nature being substantially prevented from performing or becoming unable to perform its obligations hereunder; or

13.1.5 On the Distributor assigning or attempting to assign this Agreement without the prior written consent of the Principal; or

13.1.6 If control of the Distributor shall pass from the present shareholders or owners or controllers to a competitor of the Principal in respect of the Products.

13.2 On the Distributor ceasing to comply with any of the Distributor Requirements provided that (where the relevant breach is remediable) the Principal shall have given to the Distributor notice of such failure and the Distributor shall have failed to remedy the breach complained of within [30] days of the receipt of such notice.

13.3 On the Distributor committing any breach or failing to comply with any legislation prohibiting or regulating unfair trading practices which may from time to time be in force any area in which the Distributor sells the Products provided that the Principal shall have served notice requiring the Distributor to cease such practice and the Distributor shall have failed to do so within [30] days of receipt of such notice.

13.4 If the Distributor contends that termination has been effected under cl 13.2 in bad faith or that the Distributor has not in fact ceased to comply with the relevant Distributor Requirement as alleged the Distributor shall have the right to appeal the termination of this Agreement by submitting the matter for resolution by an arbitrator in accordance with cl 19. In the event of such an appeal the notice shall be suspended pending its outcome and immediately upon the giving of the decision by the arbitrator the notice shall thereupon be cancelled or have immediate effect depending upon whether the appeal is allowed or disallowed respectively.

13.5 No termination shall take effect under cl 13.3 if the Distributor contests the same unless, and until a court of competent jurisdiction rules (upon the application of the Principal or otherwise) that the Distributor has in fact carried on the unfair trading practice in question and upon the giving of a ruling to this effect this Agreement shall thereupon automatically terminate.

14   Effect of termination

14.1 Upon termination of this Agreement from any cause whatsoever pursuant to cl 12 or 13 the Distributor shall at the request of the Principal promptly return to the Principal all documentation of any nature whatsoever in his possession or control relating to the Products or to the Principal and to the activities of the Distributor in relation to the Products or the Principal (other than correspondence between the Distributor and the Principal which does not relate to technical matters).

14.2 Upon such termination the Distributor shall cease to describe or refer to itself in any way as an Authorised Distributor for the Products, shall have no further rights to use the Trademark in any way whatsoever and in particular but without prejudice to the generality of the foregoing shall cease to use the Trademark on its letterheads packaging vehicle liveries or elsewhere and shall at the request of the Principal sell any stocks of the Products remaining in its ownership at the date of termination in packaging which bears neither the Trademark nor the name of the Principal.

14.3 Upon such termination the Distributor shall (if so required) supply the Principal with a list of the Distributor's customers for the Products.

14.4 Upon such termination the Distributor shall (if legally possible) assign to the Principal free of charge all permissions consents and licences (if any) relating to the marketing and or distribution and or sale of the Products and execute all documents and do all things necessary to ensure that the Principal shall enjoy the benefit of the said permissions consents and licences after the said termination to the entire exclusion of the Distributor.

15 Confidentiality

The Distributor shall keep strictly confidential not disclose to any third party and use only for the purposes of this Agreement all information relating to the Products (whether technical or commercial) and to the affairs and business of the Principal and its subsidiary or associated companies, whether such information is disclosed to the Distributor by the Principal or otherwise obtained by the Distributor as a result of its association with the Principal.

16 Assignment

This Agreement and the benefit of the rights granted to the Distributor by this Agreement shall be personal to the Distributor who shall not without the prior consent of the Principal mortgage or charge the same to any third party nor subcontract or assign the same or part with any of its rights or obligations hereunder save that the foregoing shall not prevent the Distributor from factoring or mortgaging or in any way creating a charge or security over Products the title in which shall have passed to it or over book-debts created by the sale of such Products.

17 Technical support for distributor

The Principal undertakes to provide the know-how and technical support and training in accordance with Schedule 6 to the Distributor to enable it to market sell service and maintain the Products and the Distributor undertakes to accept implement and make full use of the same in order to market sell service and maintain the Products in accordance with its obligations under this Agreement.

18 Miscellaneous

18.1 No waiver, alteration, variation or addition to the Agreement shall be effective unless made in writing on or after the date of signature of this Agreement by both parties and accepted by an authorised signatory of both parties.

18.2 The interpretation construction effect and enforceability of this Agreement shall be governed by English Law, and the parties agree to submit to the non-exclusive jurisdiction of the English courts.

18.3 All notices documents consents approvals or other communications (a 'Notice') to be given hereunder shall be in writing and shall be transmitted by first class registered or recorded delivery mail, or by telex, facsimile or other electronic means in a form generating a record copy to the party being served at the relevant address for that party shown at the head of this Agreement. Any Notice sent by mail shall be deemed to have been duly served three working days after the date of posting. Any Notice sent by telex facsimile or other electronic means shall be deemed to have been duly served at the time of transmission [if transmitted during normal business hours at the location of the recipient and if not so transmitted then at the start of normal business hours on the next business day commencing at such location after the time at which the transmission was made].

18.4 The headings in this Agreement shall not affect its interpretation.

18.5 Throughout this Agreement, whenever required by context, the use of the singular number shall be construed to include the plural, and the use of the plural the singular, and the use of any gender shall include all genders.

18.6 The Schedules to this Agreement constitute an integral part hereof.

18.7 Reference in this Agreement to a clause or a Schedule is to a clause or Schedule of this Agreement.

18.8 If any term or provision in this Agreement shall be held to be illegal or unenforceable, in whole or in part, under any enactment or rule of law, such term or provision or part shall to that extent be deemed not to form part of this Agreement but the validity and enforceability of the remainder of this Agreement shall not be affected.

18.9 The waiver or forbearance or failure of a party in insisting in any one or more instances upon the performance of any provisions of this Agreement shall not be construed as a waiver or relinquishment of that party's rights to future performance of such provision and the other party's obligations in respect of such future performance shall continue in full force and effect.

19   Arbitration

Any question or difference which may arise concerning the construction meaning or effect of cll 13.2 and 13.4 or concerning the rights and liabilities of the parties thereunder or any other matter arising out of or in connection therewith shall be referred to a single arbitrator in London to be agreed between the parties. Failing such agreement within thirty days of the request by one party to the other that a matter be referred to arbitration in accordance with this clause such reference shall be to an arbitrator appointed by [the President for the time being of the London Chamber of Commerce]. The decision of such arbitrator shall be final and binding upon the parties. Any reference under this clause shall be deemed to be a reference to arbitration within the meaning of the Arbitration Act 1996.

SCHEDULE 1
Details of the Products

SCHEDULE 2
Details of the Territory

SCHEDULE 3
Details of the Trademarks

SCHEDULE 4
Distributor requirements

1 The Distributor shall carry on business as [an electrical and electronic equipment wholesaler] [motor vehicle distributor] or have a separate and substantial division of its operations carrying on such business and such business shall be carried on from separate premises having suitable facilities for the storage, handling and sale of the Products on a wholesale basis.

2 The Distributor will employ and establish and maintain suitable technically trained staff service facilities plant and equipment so as to provide a service for the maintenance and repair of the Products (whether or not under warranty) of a sufficient capacity to satisfy the requirements of end users of the Products in the Territory for such service.

3 The Principal will provide advice to the Distributor on special tools and special test equipment recommended to support the Products. The Principal will upon request sell to the Distributor all such tools and equipment at reasonable prices and in reasonable quantities, and the Distributor undertakes to purchase a sufficient quantity thereof (either from the Principal or any other suitable source) to enable him to carry out his obligations under para 2.

4 The Distributor shall at all times during the continuance of this Agreement carry at least [three] months' stock of the Products so that all orders received by the Distributor can be supplied without undue delay. The Distributor shall supply such reports as to stock levels and movements as the Principal may from time to time request.

5 The Distributor shall maintain during the continuance of this Agreement sufficient staff (with appropriate marketing, commercial and technical training) to sell distribute promote and administer the sale of the Products throughout the Territory and in particular shall create and maintain a sales force of sufficient size from time to time to fulfil the Distributor's obligations under this Agreement in relation to the sale and marketing of the Products.

SCHEDULE 5
Terms of supply of Principal

SCHEDULE 6
Technical support for Distributor

In witness whereof the duly authorised representatives of the Principal and the Distributor have set their hands the day and year first above written

Name

for and on behalf of the
Principal

Name

for and on behalf of the
Distributor

Precedent 4

Authorised retailer agreement

This Agreement is made between [   ] Limited of [   ] (the 'Appointor') and [   ] of [   ] (the 'Retailer') and commences on [   ] 19[   ].

The Appointer hereby appoints the Retailer as one of its authorised retailers for the sale of the products listed in Appendix 1 (the 'Products') and the Retailer hereby accepts such appointment and agrees to comply with the requirements set out in Appendix 2 (the 'Retailer Requirements') and to permit the Appointer to verify such compliance by inspection of its relevant premises and records.

The Retailer may obtain supplies of the Products from the Appointor or from any other retailer or distributor who has been appointed anywhere in the EC as an Authorised Retailer or Authorised Distributor for the Products. The Retailer shall not purchase the Products from any other source.

The Retailer undertakes to the Appointor not to sell Products to any persons other than Authorised Distributors and Authorised Retailers for the Products and end-users of the Products.

The Appointor undertakes to the Retailer not to supply the Products to any persons other than [end-users of the products and] Authorised Distributors and Authorised Retailers for the Products [and further undertakes not to supply to end-users of the Products].

The Appointor undertakes to the Retailer that all retailers appointed by it as Authorised Retailers for the Products will be appointed upon terms identical to this Agreement.

The Appointor will accept orders for the Products placed with it by the Retailer provided it has sufficient stock of the Products to do so and will make all reasonable efforts to execute such orders in accordance with the terms of the relevant order.

All orders for the Products placed by the Retailer upon the Appointor shall be upon the current standard terms and conditions of sale of the Appointor.
The Retailer shall retain for at least one year duplicate copies of invoices relating to all purchases of the Products and the Appointor shall have the right to inspect the said invoices on demand.

The Retailer shall retain for at least one year duplicate copies of invoices or other supporting vouchers relating to sales of the Products by it and the Appointor shall have the right to inspect the same on demand.

Nothing in this Agreement shall entitle the Appointor to pay regard to or monitor the prices at which the Retailer sells the Products.

The Appointor will supply to the Retailer reasonable quantities of available publicity, sales promotion and technical literature, catalogues and maintenance manuals and data appropriate to the Products free of charge.

The Appointor will train the Retailer's service and technical sales staff in accordance with an agreed training programme, free of charge to the Retailer, and in particular will explain and assist the Retailer to implement a system of warranty service for the Products in accordance with the policy laid down from time to time by the Appointor. The Retailer undertakes to observe the technical instructions and operate the system of warranty service for the Products as communicated to it by the Appointor.

Technical channels of communication will be established so that the Retailer's staff can obtain technical advice and support from the Appointor. Such advice and support will be promptly provided by the Appointor to the Retailer free of charge.

The Retailer shall not assign this Agreement. This Agreement shall terminate automatically upon the bankruptcy, liquidation or other insolvency of the Retailer, and upon the death of the Retailer (where the Retailer is a natural person) or upon the death of one of the partners in the Retailer (where the Retailer is a partnership). A surviving partner or spouse or adult child of the Retailer carrying on the Retailer's business shall, however, have the right to enter into an Agreement with the Appointor upon terms identical to this Agreement.

The Appointor may terminate this Agreement at any time by not less than [12] months' notice provided that at the same time notice of the same length has been served upon all Authorised Distributors and Authorised Retailers for the Products in order to terminate all Authorised Distributor Agreements and all Authorised Retailer Agreements with the intention of disbanding and terminating the activities of the selective distribution network for the Products.

The Retailer may terminate this Agreement at any time by [six] months' notice to the Appointor.

The Appointor shall have the right summarily to terminate this Agreement if the Retailer commits a material breach of this Agreement, or if the Retailer persists (after a written request to cease) in selling the Products, or any of them, as loss leaders [within the meaning of the Resale Prices Act 1976].

Upon termination of this Agreement from any cause whatsoever the Retailer shall cease to describe himself as an Authorised Retailer for the Products and at the request of the Appointor promptly return to the Appointor all documentation of any nature whatsoever in his possession or control relating to the Products or to the Appointor and to the activities of the Retailer in relation to the Products or the Appointor (other than correspondence between the Retailer and the Appointor which does not relate to technical matters). Upon such termination the Retailer shall also (if so required) supply the Appointor with a list of the Retailer's customers for the Products.

APPENDIX 1
The products

APPENDIX 2
Retailer requirements

1 The Retailer shall have premises suitable for the retail sale of [perfume toiletry and beauty products] [electrical and electronic equipment] and where the premises are not solely dedicated to the sale of such or related [products] [equipment] the retailer shall sell such [products] [equipment] in a specialised department if carrying on business as a department store or other outlet carrying and selling different types of products.

2 The Retailer shall not carry on business from a dwelling house unless from a part thereof set up as a retail shop with a separate customer entrance and with its own sales area and display windows looking out onto the street.

3 The Retailer shall not exhibit or sell any item whose trademark or brand name might give rise to confusion with the trademarks under which the Products are sold by the Appointor.

4 The Retailer shall carry stocks of all of the Products so that he shall at all times have a full range of the Products from which customers may satisfy their needs for any of the Products.

5 The Retailer will employ a sufficient number of the technically trained sales staff on duty at all times during business hours while the retailer's outlet is open for business to enable all demand for the Products to be satisfied and shall provide at its retail outlet facilities tools and test equipment for routine adjustment commissioning and first-line maintenance and repair of the Products.

6 The Retailer shall at reasonably frequent intervals mount exhibits of the Products in the most prominent positions in both external shop windows and interior show cases and shall in general at all times display the Products in such a way that their sale appears an essential part of the retailer's commercial activities.

7 The Retailer shall use best endeavours to assist all publicity campaigns applicable to the retailer in relation to the Products.

8 The Retailer shall not use any trademark applied to any of the Products except to identify such Products and to describe itself as an Authorised Retailer for those Products. Prior to any such use of such trademarks, the Retailer shall obtain the consent of the Appointor or (through the Appointor) of the owner of that trademark to such use.

Signed by
the Appointor

Signed by
the Retailer

Part III

Mergers and Acquisitions

Chapter 9

Basic principles

9.1 Introduction

Whether one is dealing with the acquisition of one business or undertaking by another, or the merger of two businesses in such a way that the two previous owners continue to have an interest in the merged entity, there are two basic methods by which such transactions can be implemented.

First, a business can be sold by transferring the shares of the legal entity carrying on that business (the 'owner'). Since control of the owner and not the business itself is transferred it is unnecessary to define closely the business and its assets and liabilities. The business continues uninterrupted by the transaction, and, absent contractual provisions to the contrary, all of the owner's contracts with employees, customers and suppliers continue unaffected by the transfer. This is also, however, the case with the owner's liabilities to third parties, such as debts or litigation. Share sales are thus quick and easy to implement, but carry with them the danger of taking on unforeseen and unknown liabilities along with the business.

Secondly, a business can also be sold by the transfer of its assets and liabilities. These must therefore be listed and the business defined in detail, or else the purchaser may not get the assets he needs to run the business, and the seller may be left with liabilities (like creditors or litigation) which properly belong to the business. Further, except in the case of employment contracts, which transfer automatically by operation of law under the Transfer of Undertakings (Protection of Employment) Regulations 1981 (SI No 1794), contracts with and liabilities owed to third parties cannot be transferred without obtaining their consent. Thus asset transactions are laborious, time consuming and complicated to implement. However, unlike a share sale, the risk of taking on unwanted liabilities is very much smaller. The purchaser's main concern is not to guard against unforeseen liabilities but to ensure that he has good title to all the relevant assets and that these assets are sufficient to carry on the business.

There are in fact two types of asset transactions. The first is the true sale of a business by means of the transfer of its individual assets and liabilities, often called a 'business transfer'. The second is the sale of selected assets and liabilities, which are used by the seller in an existing business, and which the purchaser will use in his own business, but which is not accompanied by a transfer of any business as a going concern from the seller to the purchaser. This second type of transaction is often called an 'asset sale'.

The line between the business transfer and the asset sale is not always easy to draw. Drawing this distinction, however, becomes more than an academic exercise in the context of the application of the Transfer of Undertakings (Protection of Employment) Regulations 1981, which apply to a business transfer but not to an asset sale. This issue will be considered in more detail in Chapter 11 but at this stage the general effect of the Regulations must be noted. As originally drafted the Regulations only applied to the transfer of commercial undertakings, but following the European Court decision in *Dr Sophie Redmond Stichting v Bartol* [1992] IRLR 366 ECJ, it became clear that reg 2 did not comply with the EEC Acquired Rights Directive (187/1977) which it was supposed to implement. Section 33 of the Trade Union Reform and Employment Rights Act 1993 amended the Regulations so that they applied to transfers of non-commercial undertakings. The most obvious effect of this was that the practice of transfers of various functions of central or local government bodies (often called out-sourcing) to private contractors is, in appropriate circumstances, caught by the Regulations, even if the transfer is of a non-commercial venture (eg a facilities-management contract whereby a private contractor acquires the data-processing department of a local authority and in return provides data processing services to the local authority for its internal purposes).

The situation with outsourcing contracts and the Regulations has to be approached with some care.

A merger can be effected either by a share sale or a business transfer, or indeed by a combination of both. Where the merger is implemented by one undertaking acquiring the other, in consideration of the issue of shares, the sellers of the undertaking that has been acquired become partners in the acquiring business by virtue of the consideration shares issued to them. Alternatively, the merger can be implemented by the transfer of both undertakings (again in exchange for the issue of shares) to a new legal entity that will operate the merged businesses, and in which the owners of the transferred businesses will both become shareholders.

The implementation of a merger or acquisition by a share sale or a business transfer is usually determined by tax considerations rather than commercial considerations. The particular considerations relating to tax are outside the scope of this book, and will obviously vary depending upon the particular facts of each case, and the jurisdiction involved, but no decisions as to the form of the transaction should be taken without a thorough exploration and understanding of the effect on the tax position of both parties. This is particularly significant in that what results in a favourable tax position for one party may result in an unfavourable position for the other. For instance, a business transfer often enables the purchaser to ascribe a high value (and hence a larger part of the consideration) to assets which attract an accelerated rate of write-down for the purposes of depreciation allowances, but the consequence of enabling the purchaser to avoid tax by setting off depreciation allowances against income could well be that the seller will have to pay a greater amount of capital gains tax if the price at which he disposes of the asset is greater than its written down value in his books of account.

The financial consequences of optimising the transaction from the point of view of taxation are usually so significant as to outweigh any commercial issues. However, it can be said that, where the taxation consequences are neutral, a share sale is probably simpler for both parties, unless the purchaser is particularly concerned about the liabilities he knows or fears he may acquire with the legal entity carrying on the business.

9.2 The phases in the implementation of a merger or acquisition

All mergers and acquisitions fall into a number of distinct phases and in most cases these phases are the same and occur in approximately the same order. As a rule of thumb, the earlier a phase the more important it is in structuring and influencing the outcome of the whole transaction, and, unfortunately, the less likely it is to have the benefit of input from legally trained experts. Nevertheless, in all cases, a legally oriented contribution to the relevant decision making is both useful and necessary, and, where the legal adviser is sufficiently close to his client that it is practical for him to make such an early contribution, he should certainly strive to persuade his client of the wisdom of putting him in a position to do so.

The first phase is the identification of the target. Although this appears to be primarily a task for the businessman, who will evolve the strategy leading to the need for merger or acquisition and identify the best possible fit out of the available targets, the lawyer can be useful even here, since various aspects of regulatory law will impact the transaction, making a target more or less desirable, or even impossible. Will the transaction need competition law clearance in some jurisdiction? Is it likely to receive it? Will this cause an unacceptable delay? The lawyer can also advise on the difficulties caused by particular local laws, such as restrictions on foreign investment, ownership or control, the need to get exchange control permission for repatriation of dividends or capital, the need for shareholder approval where a public company is concerned, special taxation legislation, the need to obtain permission under local law to transfer technology, and so on. A legal input is thus a vital part of identifying the best possible target.

Once the target has been identified, the parties will enter into preliminary negotiation. At this stage, the parties have got to get to know each other, and to decide whether a transaction is in principle desirable in a price range that the seller is prepared to accept and the purchaser to pay. In this early phase, discussions tend to be vague and both sides often gloss over points of real difference in the interests of keeping the discussions going. Sometimes these differences remain submerged until final negotiation of detailed agreements, when it is often too late to reconcile them, and the deal collapses. In other cases, the parties agree on certain matters, perhaps the outline structure of the deal (eg a share sale), which turn out to have undesirable legal or tax implications for one party that are not discovered until much later, when negotiations have gone too far to change direction, and again the deal falls through.

A legal input at this stage can help to bring precision to the discussions, so that difficult points are resolved rather than ignored, and can also identify early on legal pitfalls in the way the deal is being structured, in order to ensure that both parties understand the legal consequences of their agreements before it is too late to negotiate an acceptable compromise. Last but not least, the time spent by the lawyer in listening to and participating in these discussions makes drafting definitive documents which reflect the true intentions of the parties much easier and more efficient.

A purely legal task which also occurs at this stage is the drafting of a preliminary confidentiality agreement, which both parties will want to sign to keep the fact of their negotiations, and any information exchanged between them (particularly about the target), confidential.

As an aid to the smooth implementation of these preliminary phases, both parties will need to collect general information about the other side, although the acquirer's need to collect information about the target is probably greatest. This information may be obtained from the other side (in which case the lawyer will again be concerned to draw up or approve a confidentiality agreement protecting it) or else from public sources, such as databases or registries. The lawyer is well placed to conduct such a search on behalf of his client, and to understand and interpret the information received.

Once the preliminary phases have been completed, and the parties are still talking, the deal will not progress unless agreement in principle upon all the important points has been reached, and recorded in writing in some form of 'Heads of Agreement' or 'Memorandum of Understanding'. Basically, this document should cover the structure of the deal (eg asset or share transaction), identification of what is being purchased, price (either an absolute amount or a formula for determining this), non-competition clauses, basic warranties and undertakings, how employees and their accrued rights under current pension and benefit plans are to be dealt with, problems of change of control clauses in the target's supply or customer contracts and its licences to use third party intellectual property rights, and, finally, in the case of a joint venture, main shareholder rights and protections. Agreement will also be reached at this stage on the timetable for the remaining phases of the transaction, whether there should be exclusive negotiating rights for the acquirer, and if compensation should be paid in the event the target is eventually acquired by a third party.

In many transactions, the lawyer's first appearance will be when Heads of Agreement have been signed, and he is asked to proceed to definitive agreements with the other side's lawyers. However, it is a hard fact that in most transactions all of the important elements are decided by the time Heads of Agreement are signed. After this, the remaining phases of the transaction (important though they are) are really only concerned with implementing this agreement. Later attempts to change the principles in Heads of Agreement for the benefit of one of the parties are normally either unsuccessful or result in the failure of the transaction. In any event, the idea that negotiations at the stage of the definitive legal agreements can turn things around at best wastes time, and at worst loses the deal.

Unfortunately, too many Heads of Agreement are drafted by lay businessmen, who cannot put down on paper, clearly and unambiguously, what has been agreed, so that the parties have a proper meeting of minds. In some cases, ambiguity is still used at this stage to keep alive a deal which, if both parties had properly expressed their views to each other, would not have continued. In other cases, the principles that have been agreed give rise to insoluble legal problems, so that the deal has to be restructured before it can proceed.

The lawyer's role, having provided relevant input in the preceding phases, should now be to assist the negotiators to achieve proper and mutually satisfactory agreement on a set of principles which serve their legal and commercial ends, and then to ensure that these are embodied in clear and unambiguous Heads of Agreement. He will also advise at this stage to what extent such a document should be legally binding and on the need to disclose it to third parties, such as shareholders or regulatory authorities (depending upon local jurisdiction); to the extent permitted by law, he will then adjust the wording to achieve the degree of commitment and disclosure the parties require.

Following the signature of Heads of Agreement, and whether the transaction is to be implemented by means of a share sale or a business transfer, the prudent purchaser should investigate the financial, commercial and legal condition of the business before purchase. This investigation is often known, but for no very obvious reason, as 'due diligence'. Due diligence should cover corporate records, employees and pensions, verification and analysis of accounts (particularly debtors and creditors) and of title to and existence of major assets, checking of current supply and customer contracts (are their prices, terms and conditions right, are there any breaches, are there change of control clauses which could lead to termination on transfer of the business?) and discovery of any third party liabilities such as lawsuits or tax claims. Due diligence is usually carried on by auditors, lawyers, and the purchaser's commercial and technical staff.

Since due diligence is usually carried out to ascertain as objectively as possible the value of the assets and the extent of the liabilities of the target, the results will have an impact upon the price that has been set down in the Heads of Agreement and upon the extent and nature of the warranties and indemnities that the acquirer will seek in the definitive agreement. Additionally, where the seller is not deemed to be entirely credit-worthy, the existence of extensive contingent liabilities will not only be covered through warranties and indemnities but also by some sort of retention or escrow arrangement to hold back part of the purchase price.

Since the results of an unsatisfactory due diligence will either impact upon the price, or require more stringent indemnities and, perhaps, a retention, there is something to be said for carrying out due diligence before the Heads of Agreement stage while the deal can still be renegotiated easily. Thus, the ideal situation is to finalise due diligence as part of the preliminary negotiations. Unfortunately, most sellers' desire for confidentiality, and fear of wasting their time, lead them to insist upon at least signature of Heads of Agreement, and sometimes even of definitive documents (which should in both cases then be expressly stated to be subject to due diligence), before they will permit full due diligence to take place.

The lawyer will be involved in carrying out parts of the due diligence, usually in co-operation with accountants (who will carry out the usual financial audits to ensure the accuracy of the target's books of account and financial statements). He will be particularly concerned with investigating title to real and intellectual property, assessing the extent of legal liability in relation to third party claims, the target's compliance with relevant laws, and the contractual terms and conditions, and state of performance, of the target's customer and supplier contracts. Additionally, he will be involved in assessing the risks posed by contingent liabilities and advising upon the best way to cover against them.

If the preceding phases have gone according to plan, the lawyer's task is now to turn the Heads of Agreement, as modified if necessary by the results of the due diligence, into a definitive acquisition agreement. In practice, unless there have been serious problems found in the due diligence exercise, or the Heads of Agreement have not been properly prepared, the main negotiations will centre around the extent of the warranties and indemnities to be given.

In most cases, the known risks and problems are relatively easily dealt with, on the basis that losses arising out of pre-closing matters are for the seller, and out of post-closing for the buyer. The problem arises in areas where there are no known liabilities, but the buyer requires the seller to act as absolute insurer for all liabilities (particularly in relation to third party claims) arising in relation to pre-closing events. Here the discussion is about risk allocation in the light of the agreed purchase price. The lawyer is probably the best qualified adviser upon the subject of risk allocation, given his blend of legal expertise, and experience in past transactions of a similar nature.

The definitive agreement is normally drafted as being legally binding subject to the granting of any necessary regulatory and other consents. Regulatory consents are usually necessary in transactions where competition law or exchange or foreign investment control considerations arise. The other most common type of consent required is that of the shareholders in large transactions relating to public companies either as acquirers, sellers or targets.

The consent of boards of directors, or private shareholders, is not usually a matter to which a definitive agreement is made subject, although it is not uncommon to make Heads of Agreement subject to such conditions. The reason for this is that the imposition of such a condition effectively turns a legally binding definitive agreement into a voluntary one from which the party concerned can resile at will.

The primary task of the lawyer is to ensure that the definitive agreement is made subject only to those consents that are properly required, and that termination for failure to obtain such consents is restricted to situations where it is justified. At all costs the definitive agreement must provide certainty as to the conditions to be fulfilled, and the criteria by which failure will be judged.

Whether the agreement should also be subject to due diligence, giving the purchaser the right to withdraw if he is dissatisfied with the results of his enquiry, is a different matter, which is discussed in detail in Chapter 10.

Once the definitive agreement has been signed, the lawyer will have the main responsibility, in most cases, for filing the necessary documents and requests, and negotiating with the relevant authorities to obtain any relevant consents, particularly in the area of competition law. In most jurisdictions he is also responsible for drawing up circulars to shareholders and dealing with the other procedures necessary to obtain their consent.

The penultimate phase of the transaction is the completion or closing, when instruments of title to the target and its assets are handed over in exchange for the purchase price, and any other relevant legal formalities, such as the holding of board meetings to appoint new directors and secretary of the target, or to change its bank mandates, take place. Closings sometimes take place simultaneously with signature of the definitive agreement (in which case any necessary consents will have been obtained prior to signature) but it is more usual to allow a period of time between signature and closing in which consents are obtained, and the parties perhaps finish due diligence and investigations of title. Closing is above all the province of the lawyer, because it is here that he ensures the implementation of the transaction for his client in its agreed-upon form.

Following closing, the lawyer's task is in most cases completed, except for the need to provide a comprehensive set of all documents relating to the transaction, often known as a 'bible'. Price adjustments are sometimes made after closing, usually in asset transactions, on the basis of values shown in financial statements drawn up as of the closing date. This is necessarily a post-closing event, but is the province of the lawyer rather than the accountant. The lawyer will only be required again if warranty or indemnity claims are made. In this event, he will be required not only to advise upon the strict legalities of the claims in the light of their nature and the drafting of the agreement, but, more often, to assist the parties in reaching a negotiated settlement rather than resorting to protracted litigation in accordance with the strict terms of the agreement.

It can thus be seen that the task of the lawyer in a merger or acquisition is not that of a scribe, nor purely that of a legal adviser. A lawyer expert in this field has the advantage of having seen many similar transactions, whereas for each of his clients the particular transaction they are concerned with may be the only one they ever encounter. This breadth of practical experience should enable the lawyer to act as a business counsellor, working from his special legal perspective. A client who properly engages his legal adviser in the transaction will increase the chances of its successful conclusion, and, in addition to achieving the proper completion of the essentially mechanical task of the legal implementation of a predetermined agreement, will also achieve a far better business transaction.

9.3   The balance between warranties, disclosures and due diligence

The legal formalities of a merger or acquisition have become increasingly standardised, although not to the same extent as transactions relating to the conveyancing of real property, and it is tempting for the lawyer to feel that he has discharged his duty to his client by providing an adequate acquisition agreement, with a set of warranties which covers the major potential areas of exposure. However, since warranty claims are in effect a mechanism for reducing the price of the acquisition after closing, it is important for the lawyer to take account of the dynamics of negotiating the particular warranties to be included in the acquisition agreement and to attempt to produce the best possible position for his client. In order to achieve this, and whether he is acting for the seller or the purchaser, he must understand the balance between the exercise of due diligence, the extent and timing of the disclosures the seller makes about the business, and the scope of the warranties actually included in the definitive agreement.

In both share sale and business transfer agreements, the seller warrants to the purchaser the truth of certain facts about the business. Warranties normally cover the same areas as those dealt with in the due diligence exercise. Sellers usually stipulate that warranties do not apply to matters (eg defects in title) disclosed to the purchaser prior to signature of the sale agreement. Such disclosures are usually summarised and recorded in a formal document called a disclosure letter, which is handed to the purchaser on signature of the agreement, and lists the specific exceptions to each warranty. Such letters are often written and signed by the seller's solicitors.

Most purchasers audit the affairs of the target before committing to acquisition. Such investigations often include requests for detailed disclosures from the seller. However, a seller tries to qualify his warranties by excluding everything which the purchaser learns through his investigations, so the more the purchaser knows the less the warranties are worth. Purchasers usually respond by refusing to accept that knowledge acquired through investigations is automatically excluded from the warranties, and require the seller to list in a formal disclosure letter those matters that are to be so excluded.

The most common trap for a purchaser is to insist upon voluminous disclosures. For instance, a request for a copy of all customer contracts may result in thousands of documents. Any warranty about enforceability of the target's contracts, or the legality of their terms, presence of change of control clauses, and so on, will not be given in respect of those contracts disclosed to the purchaser since he is deemed to be aware of their terms. The purchaser will find it hard to resist this, but is practically speaking unlikely to be able to read and assess all the contracts in the time available before closing. He will thus end up by taking on an unknown liability.

A further trap is to continue negotiating the terms of the warranties right up until just before signature. Since it can be argued that the seller cannot prepare the disclosure letter until he knows what warranties he is disclosing against, the letter will come very late. The purchaser will then either have to close without time to assess it properly, or put off closing while he does so. In many cases, because of commercial pressures to complete the deal quickly, purchasers do not assess disclosure letters properly, and often accept liability for disclosed matters which, if they had more time to consider, they would reject. On the other hand, time pressure can work to the disadvantage of the seller, in that his desire to complete the deal may be greater than the purchaser's, so that he prepares the disclosure letter sketchily in order to meet the time scales for closing, and leaves out, or does not discover, significant liabilities, for which he will now have to take liability under a warranty.

Timing is vital. The ideal scenario is a focused due diligence, the results of which are quickly used in finalising warranty negotiations and preparing a short and meaningful disclosure letter, with enough time between finalisation of the letter and closing to enable the parties to assess the implications of the exercise on the purchase price.

A purchaser who is sure of his seller's financial stability, or can retain a sufficient amount of the purchase price until the expiry of the warranty period, could in theory forego all investigations, and thus be in a stronger position to resist a significant disclosure letter. However, in practice, a balance between reliance on warranties and assessment of exposure in advance of closing (together with acceptance of a disclosure letter) is usually struck, with an investigation which focuses on key areas and a disclosure letter limited to significant items, normally indexed to specific warranties.

9.4   Competition law considerations

Competition law considerations in relation to a merger or acquisition have two aspects:

The first aspect relates to the question of dominant or significant market shares. An enterprise may already have such a market share before it enters into the relevant merger or acquisition (and this may have been obtained by organic growth or earlier mergers and acquisitions). The completion of the relevant merger or acquisition will therefore increase and strengthen that enterprise's existing (and already dominant or significant) market share. Alternatively none of the parties to the relevant merger or acquisition may by itself have a dominant or significant market share, but the completion of the relevant transaction will give the acquiring entity, or create a merged entity with, such a dominant or significant market share. The strengthening or creation of such a dominant or significant market share has obvious impacts on competition in the relevant market, and may or may not be in the public interest. Competition law authorities are thus concerned to regulate this aspect of mergers and acquisitions and to forbid those which strengthen or create a dominant or significant market share where this weakens competition and is otherwise not in the public interest.

The second aspect relates to the question of ancillary restrictions such as non-competition clauses or exclusive supply contracts or licences of intellectual property which are entered into as part of the relevant transaction. The most obvious examples are covenants entered into by the vendor of a business not to compete with that business once the transaction has been completed and it is being run by the purchaser (vendor non-compete covenants), and similar covenants which the shareholders in a joint venture company enter into undertaking not to compete with the joint venture. Such ancillary restrictions again have an obvious, but less direct, effect on competition.

In the UK, so far as the first aspect is concerned, under the Fair Trading Act 1973, the Office of Fair Trading ('OFT') has a duty to consider all mergers and acquisitions which are made by an enterprise with a significant share in the market to which its business activities relate (normally over 25 per cent), or which, upon completion of the transactions, would result in the creation of such an enterprise. There is no duty to refer potential mergers and acquisitions to the OFT in advance of their completion, and no penalty for not doing so, although there are procedures in existence by which clearance can formally be obtained in advance, or by which advance, informal, confidential but non-binding guidance can be obtained as to the view which the OFT is likely to take of the transaction.

If no advance clearance is obtained, the OFT has the right to investigate the transaction once the parties have made it public, either because they have signed a binding agreement subject to various matters including regulatory consents, or because they ignored the issue and completed the transaction anyway. The

OFT can, and often does, decide to investigate, even if it has given confidential guidance that the transaction is unlikely to be of interest to it, although, in this case, if it has been given the full story when confidential guidance was sought, it is unlikely to change its decision.

It should be said that it is courteous, as well as prudent, where the parties do not intend to seek advance clearance or advice, but feel that the OFT are likely to be interested in the transaction (even if they themselves feel that the 25 per cent market share threshold will not be exceeded) for them to notify the OFT, just prior to the transaction being made public, of the existence and broad details of the transaction, and to offer to provide any information that the OFT requires should it decide to make an investigation. This starts things off on a better footing, should there be an investigation, than if the first the OFT learns of the matter is through the newspapers. In any event, the OFT has the legal right to compel the parties to produce information relevant for its investigation, so there is nothing to be gained by being reticent.

If the OFT feels it appropriate, because it believes that one or more of the parties to the transaction has a market share exceeding 25 per cent, or that the transaction will create an undertaking with a market share in excess of 25 per cent, it will refer the transaction to the Monopolies and Mergers Commission ('MMC'). If the MMC rules that the transaction is generally in the public interest, that is an end of the matter, but if it takes an adverse view then the transaction cannot proceed, and, if the parties have implemented it before the MMC has made its decision, the transaction can be unwound on the direction of the Secretary of State, although such directions are given only rarely.

When the Competition Bill 1997 becomes law the MMC will be dissolved. The Bill creates a new body called the Competition Commission which discharges a variety of functions under the new competition regime. However, it will also take over the functions of the MMC. Any reference to the MMC in any legislation (in particular the Fair Trading Act 1973) will be deemed to be a reference to the Competition Commission. In a statement introducing the Bill, made in August 1997, the President of the Board of Trade said:

> 'I see value in the investigatory approach of the Monopolies and Mergers Commission, and I intend that the current framework for considering mergers should continue, essentially unchanged, within the Competition Commission. References to the Commission should be made largely on competition grounds. If the Commission finds that a merger could operate contrary to the public interest then the decision on whether or not to block the merger and whether to permit it subject to conditions should continue to be the responsibility of Ministers. Within this framework of impartial investigation by the Commission I see no need to change the burden of proof in assessing the public interest. There is a case, however, for some procedural streamlining changes to the current regime.'

Schedule 1 of the Competition Bill therefore excludes from its operation any transaction which results in 'any two enterprises ceasing to be distinct enterprises for the purposes of Part V of the Fair Trading Act 1973'. It should be noted that, despite the intention of the Bill to harmonise as much as possible with EC competition law, this exclusion is likely to mean that more joint ventures will be subjected to the scrutiny of the Competition Bill than would be the case if an exclusion based upon the EC concept of a 'full function joint venture' (discussed below) had been applied.

Under European law the first aspect is governed by the EC Merger Regulation (Council Regulation 4064/1989). The Merger Regulation (referred to in this chapter as the 'Regulation') has lately been the subject of some amendment by Council Regulation 1310/1997, which came into effect on 1 March 1998. References in this discussion to the Regulation are to the Regulation as amended.

The Regulation applies in three circumstances. The first is where two independent undertakings merge. The second is where one or more persons or undertakings acquire control of the whole or parts of one or more other undertakings. The third is the creation of a joint venture performing on a lasting basis all the functions of an autonomous economic entity (this type of joint venture is often generally referred to as a 'full function joint venture'). These three circumstances are all referred to in the Regulation as a 'concentration'. Prior to the passing of the amending Regulation a full function joint venture could only be regarded as a concentration, controlled by the Regulation, if it did not give rise to co-ordination of competitive behaviour of the parties among themselves or between them and the joint venture. Thus, prior to the passing of the amending Regulation, joint ventures which were merely horizontal co-operation arrangements but did not amount to the creation of a full function joint venture (co-operative operations) and full function joint ventures giving rise to co-ordination of competitive behaviour were both outside the Regulation, and were both regarded merely as horizontal co-operation agreements to be considered under art 85. Following the passing of the amending Regulation all full function joint ventures are now considered to be concentrations falling with the Regulation so that only the co-operative operations will continue to be dealt with under art 85.

In 1994 the Commission published a Notice on the distinction between concentrative and co-operative joint ventures and a Notice on the notion of a concentration. These Notices are useful guides to the application of the Regulation, but the first has to be read with some caution in the light of the changes to the way full function joint ventures are now dealt with after the passing of the amending Regulation. The Commission may well see the need to update these Notices in due course.

However, the amending Regulation introduced one additional distinction. In general all concentrations are appraised under the Regulation as to whether they 'create or strengthen a dominant position as a result of which effective competition would be substantially impeded in the common market or a substantial part of it' (art 2(2)). Thus all full function joint ventures will now be appraised on this basis. However, where a joint venture 'has as its object or effect the co-ordination of the competitive behaviour of undertakings that remain independent', the Commission must use two criteria for appraisal. The first, under art 2(2), is the creation or strengthening of a dominant position and the second, under art 2(3), is the relevant co-ordination of competitive behaviour 'which shall be appraised in accordance with the criteria of art 85(1) and (3) of the Treaty with a view to establishing whether or not the operation is compatible with the common market'. It is important to realise that this second appraisal does not take place under art 85. It is merely that the criteria which would have been used under art 85 are to apply to the appraisal made under the Regulation. Thus, with the one addition of the second set of criteria, the Regulation now applies to the full function joint venture which has as its object or effect the co-ordination of competitive behaviour.

This widening of the scope of the Regulation to include all full function joint ventures is desirable for two reasons. First, clearance under the Regulation is given on a once-and-for-all basis, while under art 85(3) exemption can only be granted for a defined period of time, after which the parties, if they wish to continue to operate the arrangement, must apply for a further period of exemption. It is obviously highly desirable for a full function joint venture (which by definition will last for an indefinite period of time) to receive clearance once and for all, rather than have to keep reapplying, with the prospect that, as has happened in some cases previously, the Commission will, on re-examining the case, refuse the extension, so that the joint venture has to be discontinued. Secondly, once a concentration falls to be dealt with under the Regulation, local competition authorities in individual member states cease to have jurisdiction, and a clearance under the Regulation is all that is required. This is not the case with an application under art 85, where local authorities can also have parallel jurisdiction. This 'one-stop shop' approach is clearly easier for businessmen and their advisers to deal with, so that the extension of this approach to more joint ventures must be welcome.

Any concentration is, however, only subject to the Regulation (with all the benefits of the 'one-stop shop') if it has what the Regulation calls a 'community dimension'. Following the amending Regulation, there are now two sets of criteria which are used to decide this. Satisfaction of either set is sufficient to give rise to the community dimension.

The first set of criteria provides that the community dimension will exist where the combined aggregate worldwide turnover of all the parties to the transaction (measured on a group basis, where a relevant party is part of a group of companies) exceeds ECU 5,000m, and the aggregate European Community turnover of at least two of the parties (taken individually) exceeds ECU 250m. However, even in this case, the Regulation does not apply if two thirds of the European Community turnover of each party arises in the same member state.

The second provides that the community dimension will exist where:

(*a*) the combined aggregate worldwide turnover of all the parties to the transaction (measured on a group basis, where a relevant party is part of a group of companies) exceeds ECU 2,500m;

(*b*) in each of at least three member states, the aggregate turnover of all the undertakings concerned is more than ECU 100m;

(*c*) in each of at least three of the member states included for the purpose of point (*b*), the aggregate turnover of each of at least two of the undertakings is more than ECU 25m; and

(*d*) the aggregate community wide turnover of each of at least two of the undertakings concerned is more than ECU 100m.

Again, even if these criteria are satisfied, the Regulation does not apply if two thirds of the European Community turnover of each party arises in the same member state.

Article 5 of the Regulation contains rules for the calculation of turnover, and the Commission published two Notices in 1994, one dealing with the notion of undertakings concerned and the other with calculation of turnover, which are helpful explanations of these rules.

Where the Regulation applies, approval to the transaction must be sought in advance from the Commission (on pain of large fines for failure to do so) in accordance with the Regulation and with Commission Regulation 447/98 which lays down procedural rules for applications and the way they are to be dealt with, including tight time limits by which the Commission must give its decision. No concentration caught by the Regulation can be implemented prior to Commission clearance under the Regulation. Where the Commission decides that, on the application of the criteria discussed above, the concentration is not compatible with the common market, it will either refuse clearance or, in cases where this is practicable, it will discuss with the parties variations to the terms of the transaction which would satisfy its concerns. It will then clear the transaction on the basis that the agreed variations are implemented. If a merger or acquisition is regarded as a concentration, but it does not have a community dimension, then the Regulation cannot apply. In these circumstances, it is questionable whether the European Commission has any jurisdiction at all. Article 85 does not apply to a concentrative merger or acquisition. The only possible ground of jurisdiction is the old principle in *European Commission v Continental Can* which states that where an enterprise already has a dominant position in a market, a transaction which strengthens that dominant position (eg an acquisition which will give that enterprise a still larger market share) is itself an abuse of a dominant position under art 86.

If these special circumstances do not apply, then the Commission will have no jurisdiction over the concentrative acquisition or merger, and the relevant competition law authorities of the member states involved will have jurisdiction instead. There is no possibility of overlap between the Commission and the competition law authorities in the member states, because where the Regulation applies the local authorities have no jurisdiction, although where the interests of one member state are particularly affected, the Commission can, under the Regulation, refer aspects of the transaction to the relevant authority for consultation and comment.

The case of the full function joint venture is different. If it falls outside the Regulation, it will nevertheless be subject to art 85 since there will be some kind of continuing agreement or arrangement between the shareholders or partners in the joint venture entity that will survive the transaction creating the entity, have a continuing effect and therefore be subject to scrutiny under art 85. So far as co-operative joint ventures are concerned, these can only be the subject of consideration by the Commission under art 85, since by definition they are not concentrations and cannot fall within the ambit of the Regulation in any event.

In both cases, the competition law considerations usual for exemption under art 85(3) will all apply, as will any applicable block exemptions applying either to joint ventures which are small in size (see the 1997 Notice on Agreements of Minor Importance), or which are in areas, such as research and development, which are generally understood by the Commission not to affect competition (see Commission Regulation 417/1985 (specialisation agreements), Regulation 418/1985 (research and development agreements), both as amended by Regulation 151/1993, and Regulation 240/1996 (technology transfer block exemption)). In 1993 the Commission published a Notice on Assessment of Co-operative Joint Ventures under Article 85, which contains some helpful guidelines.

However, even if a joint venture transaction is caught by art 85, the Office of Fair Trading may still have jurisdiction under the Fair Trading Act 1973, over certain joint ventures, if the transaction involves the creation of an enterprise with a market share of greater than 25 per cent in the UK. This would still be the case under the new regime, given the exclusion for mergers and concentrations under Sched 1 of the Competition Bill. However, where a joint venture can be examined under art 85, but does not fall to be dealt with under the Fair Trading Act, there would clearly be a possibility that it could also be scrutinised under the provisions of the Competition Bill equivalent to art 85, but, in most cases, the provisions of the Competition Bill, as discussed in Chapter 15, would give the priority to the EC scrutiny in order to avoid the need for parallel references. So far as the second aspect, ancillary restrictions, is concerned, in the UK such restrictions currently fall to be treated under normal competition law considerations, as part of the transaction, usually under the Restrictive Trade Practices Act 1976. By and large, unless the agreement contains unusual provisions an acquisition agreement, even if it contains a vendor non-compete clause, is not likely to be caught by the Act, although some joint venture agreements may well be caught, particularly where there are a number of non-competition covenants or exclusive supply or licensing agreements, binding between the various partners in the joint venture and the joint venture company. The relevance of the Restrictive Trade Practices Act has been much reduced by the Restrictive Trade Practices (Non-Notifiable Agreements) (Sale and Purchase, Share Subscription and Franchise Agreements) Order 1997 (SI No 2945). Where an ancillary restriction is for a period of not more than five years, and is contained in a sale and purchase agreement for the sale of a company or of an unincorporated business, or in a share subscription agreement, it is declared non-notifiable under the Act. The only proviso is that in the case of a sale and purchase of shares, the purchaser must buy at least 25 per cent of the equity of the target and finish by owning more than 50 per cent, and in the case of the sale and purchase of an unincorporated business the vendor must retain no interest in the business after the sale.

Under the new regime in the UK, Sched 1 of the Competition Bill, discussed above, currently excludes from its operation not only 'mergers and concentrations' caught by the Fair Trading Act 1973 but also *'any provision directly related and necessary to the implementation'* of the merger or concentration (Sched 1). On this basis, as is the case with equivalent provisions under EC competition law, where the Fair Trading Act 1973 applies, ancillary restrictions would be dealt with as part of the clearance process under that Act, and not under the Competition Bill. However, any ancillary restrictions in a joint venture which is not caught by the 1973 Act will not be excluded under Sched 1 and will fall to be dealt with under the Competition Bill. Since the regime under the Bill is closely aligned to the EC competition law regime, as discussed in Chapter 15, the practice of the Commission in dealing with such restrictions, as discussed below, is likely to be closely followed by the Office of Fair Trading and the Competition Commission.

So far as the European Commission is concerned, ancillary restrictions in any type of joint venture which is not caught by the Regulation (either because it is not a full function joint venture or because it does not have a Community dimension) fall to be considered under art 85, but ancillary restrictions in a concentration (including a joint venture) caught by the Regulation are treated differently.

Where the transaction is subject to the Regulation, ancillary restrictions on competition, such as non-compete clauses, are considered as part of the procedure of clearing the merger under the Regulation, and not dealt with separately under art 85. The Commission published in July 1990 a Notice 'regarding restrictions ancillary to concentrations' which sets out the guidelines the Commission will use in deciding whether or not to clear such restrictions. Broadly, they must be restrictions which are directly linked to the concentration (ie not dealing with matters which have nothing to do with the particular transaction) and be necessary to the implementation of the concentration. If alternatives are available which fulfil these criteria the parties must choose the alternative which is least restrictive of competition.

In the case of a pure acquisition, a vendor non-competition clause is generally acceptable for a five-year period if goodwill and know-how have been sold, but for two years if only goodwill has been sold. The clause should be limited to the geographic area and the economic activity covered by the business concerned. Where a concentrative joint venture is concerned, this guideline would presumably not affect a non-compete clause for the benefit of the joint venture company which was given by a joint venture partner. Presumably this should last for the duration of the participation in the joint venture of the relevant partner, and then bind him after withdrawal, as if he were a vendor, for the periods applicable to a vendor non-compete clause as discussed above.

Licences of intellectual property rights and know-how, and purchase and supply agreements between seller and purchaser are also classed as ancillary restrictions. Where an outright acquisition is concerned, the Notice prescribes time limits on their duration, the life of the patent or similar right or the 'economic life' of the know-how, in respect of licences, and a period sufficient to enable the purchaser to make the transition away from dependence on the seller, in the case of purchase and supply agreements. Similar provisions apply in the case of a concentrative joint venture, except that here the licences may be exclusive and not limited as to duration or territory.

Where a concentrative transaction (other than a full function joint venture, as discussed above) is not subject to the Regulation, not only does the Commission usually not have jurisdiction to consider it at all, but it will also, arguably, have no jurisdiction to consider any ancillary restrictions, which, if the transaction had been subject to the Regulation would have fallen to be dealt with under the Regulation as part of the general clearance procedure and otherwise complied with the definition of ancillary restrictions.

9.5   Acquisitions where the seller retains a minority stake

These acquisitions usually occur either because the purchaser does not have enough money to buy the whole of the business at once, or because the parties cannot entirely agree on the purchase price, and therefore choose to ascertain it by reference to the future performance of the business. Earnouts are also sometimes used where the purchaser desires to give the seller an incentive to remain connected with the business, for a period of time, because of special technical expertise or customer connections. On the seller's part the desire to retain a stake often arises because of a wish to participate in the further growth of the business. None of these reasons is a foundation for a true long-term joint venture based upon a merger of equals each of whom has a unique and valuable contribution, and, in these cases, the interests of the parties will diverge after a period of time, and friction will arise. The purchaser will want to run the business as he sees fit, and will only be hampered by the presence of the seller, which he will see as increasingly irrelevant.

The simplest solution is to leave the seller a minority shareholder with no more than the rights accorded to him by law, but in the long term even these rights will become a hindrance to the purchaser if he wants to develop and change the target's operations, particularly by integration with other operations of which he owns 100 per cent, or the injection of further capital.

The starting point for all such transactions should be a defined exit route for the seller after a predetermined period of time. The period can be defined either by when the purchaser can raise sufficient money to buy out the remaining minority interest, or the time when the presence of the seller is likely to become irrelevant.

The simplest route is a deferred purchase, whereby the purchaser will take successive tranches of the shares at fixed dates until he owns a 100 per cent. An alternative, which is sometimes more palatable to a seller, because it appears to give more of an element of choice is to take out the tranches after the initial purchase by means of a combination of a call option in favour of the purchaser and a corresponding put option in favour of the seller. Thus, at each successive date, the purchaser can compel the seller to sell the relevant tranche, and, if he fails to do so, the seller can, if he wishes, force him to buy it.

Once the seller has a defined exit route for all of his holding, his arguments for requiring a say in the long-term running of the business are nullified. However, persuading him to accept only those rights enjoyed at law by a minority shareholder, so that the purchaser has maximum possible freedom of action while the seller is a shareholder, will depend upon the way the exit price for the minority shareholding is calculated. A price fixed initially, perhaps the price per share of the initial purchase (but after deducting the premium paid upon the initial tranche for obtaining control) plus interest at a defined rate, removes all objections by the seller that he is sharing in the risk of the business and therefore should have a say in how it is run. As long as the purchaser (not the target) remains solvent he will eventually be paid the agreed price.

However, a fixed price removes the possibility of the seller taking any of the reward of the growth of the business. While this is acceptable if the purchaser simply wanted to leave a minority stake until he could afford to buy it, it will not serve if the purchaser requires the seller's active co-operation in the business for a period of time. This co-operation requires participation in the reward, but also of course in the risk, of the business, and if the formula for the price is not carefully chosen will again make the seller want a say in running the business so that he can not only maximise the reward but also reduce the risk. Most formulae which are based upon a share in the profits of the business are open to this objection. At the very least a disgruntled seller will accuse the purchaser of bad management, or even of favouring other businesses, of which he owns 100 per cent, over that of the target, to the detriment of the seller's minority interest. Underpinning the profit formula with a guaranteed minimum is unlikely to work. Either the underpin will be so high as to remove the seller's incentive or so low as to fail to remove the risk.

The better solution is to base the formula upon turnover. The seller's participation in the affairs of the target is most often in the area of helping to obtain customers, and thus it is fair that he be measured and incentivised on turnover. The purchaser can manage as he sees fit, and the risk and reward of profit made as a result of that management is for him alone. The seller thus has no interest in the running of the business, beyond perhaps a non-competition clause from the purchaser to ensure that he puts available turnover through the target and does not set up another business to compete. The only safeguard required by the purchaser here is a cap (perhaps based upon something in excess of an optimistic business plan for the period in question) so that the seller cannot benefit by a windfall to a totally unexpected extent. This arrangement is not a good idea, however, if the seller continues to run the business, for instance as a managing director under a contract of employment, after he has sold control of the company to the buyer. In this situation, the temptation to increase turnover to the prejudice of profit may well be too great, and the safest course is to use an earnout based on net profit before tax. Here the seller has less cause to complain since he is running the business and should be responsible for the profits produced in any event.

However, it must be stated that nearly all earnout arrangements, whatever their basis, tend sooner or later to lead to friction between the buyer and the seller, and that, if at all possible, it is best to avoid them.

9.6   Use of the precedents

In conclusion, a word should be said about the contents of Chapters 10, 11 and 12, and the precedents in them. The subject of acquisitions and mergers is so wide, and the types of individual transaction so various, that it is not possible, certainly in the space available in this book, to provide standard precedents covering every aspect with, in each case, the inclusion of every possible clause which might be used. Instead the precedents have been chosen to deal with the most common issues which arise in the various transactions, but the clauses in many of the precedents are often suitable for use in precedents relating to other transactions if the commercial details of the transaction require it. For instance, the share sale agreement— Precedent 2 of Chapter 10— contains no vendor non-compete clause, but cl 6 of Precedent 2 in Chapter 12 can be included with suitable adaptation to make it binding only upon one party. In particular many of the clauses and legal concepts set out in Precedent 2 of Chapter 10 in relation to sale of shares (such as two-stage completion, the impact of due diligence, and ascertainment and adjustment of the purchase price) can all be used in appropriate types of business transfers and grafted on to the relevant business transfer precedent (Precedent 1 of Chapter 11).

It is therefore recommended that before drafting in the area of mergers and acquisition commences, the user of this book should, at least for the first time of use, scan the whole of this part, and the precedents contained in it, so as to get a grasp of the scope of the subject as a whole.

Chapter 10

Share acquisitions

10.1 Introduction

This chapter concentrates on share sale agreements. Precedent 1 is a 'Heads of Agreement', or 'Memorandum of Understanding', adapted to cover a typical share sale transaction. It can be used as a basis for drafting heads of agreement to cover any of the transactions relating to acquisitions, by retaining its framework, and incorporating the relevant details of the particular transaction. Precedent 2 is a reasonably long form of share sale agreement. Not all of its provisions are likely to be appropriate to every share sale transaction, and certain other clauses (for instance a vendor non-competition clause) could be inserted, but it gives a good idea of the way in which a more complicated transaction would be covered and, for simpler transactions, the agreement can be shortened and streamlined as required. Finally, Precedent 3 provides a short form specimen disclosure letter.

10.2 Precedent 1

Clauses 1, 2 and 3 set out the parties and the general transaction into which they intend to enter. Clause 4 sets out the conditions precedent to which completion of the proposed transaction is subject: satisfactory audit report (cl 4.1), granting of regulatory consents (cl 4.2) and conclusion of a definitive agreement (cl 4.3).

In connection with cl 4.3, it is important to note that the heads of agreement are the place to spell out the particular issues that the parties agree should be covered in the definitive agreement. In this precedent, by way of example, the purchaser has asked for a guarantee that the net assets of the company to be purchased will, on a specified date, not be less than a specified amount (cl 4.3.1).

Such a net asset 'underpin' is a common safeguard requested by purchasers even if they have struck a price on some basis other than net asset value of the target company, since it effectively imposes on the seller the risk of deterioration in the performance of the business, between the date of the heads of agreement and the specified reference date. This is because the net asset value of a business is affected by virtually any sort of deterioration in the business for any reason, whether in the course of trading or outside the ordinary course of business. Either liabilities will increase (for instance, because of increased bank borrowings if the business is trading poorly or making a loss, or if a third party makes a well-founded claim against the company, for which a provision has to be made in its accounts) or the value of assets will decrease (for instance, because stock has become unsaleable due to changes in market conditions and has to be written off, or because debtors have defaulted, resulting in an increased write-off for bad debts).

Clauses 4.3.2 and 4.3.3 set out the ground rules relating to warranties. Clause 4.3.2 provides an additional safeguard by requiring the seller to warrant, in the definitive agreement, the accuracy of the balance sheet of the target company as at a specified date, and to take the risk of any deterioration in the business between that balance sheet date, and the closing of the transaction. This is usually the balance sheet on the basis of which the parties have commenced their negotiations on the value of the target company, and it is often the last balance sheet prepared and audited before their discussions commenced. It is therefore fair that the seller should stand by the accuracy of what is the base line for the purchaser's assessment of the value of the target company. Clause 4.3.3 gives the purchaser the opportunity to make his initial statement as to the sort of warranties he will be requiring, and to include any specific warranties (usually at this stage only one or two) that he is particularly concerned about. One of the most contentious areas is the warranting of receivables. It is always a good idea to put a marker in the ground at the time of the heads of agreement if the purchaser intends to seek this warranty from the seller, and this is the position cl 4.3.3 takes.

The question of the right of the purchaser to retain part of the purchase price (either directly or through an escrow agent) for a period after completion, against which to set off any warranty claims, is also a controversial one best dealt with up front in the heads of agreement, and, again, this is covered by cl 4.3.3.

Clause 5 deals with confidentiality of the transaction. By and large it is not sensible to announce a transaction of this nature until the signature of the definitive agreement, or, often preferably, until the time of closing. Announcement of a transaction prematurely, when either of the parties can still withdraw, could well damage the target company's business, particularly if the deal collapses, and, often, when such an announcement has been made, one side or the other is forced to make concessions in the negotiations (which it would otherwise have withheld) purely to keep the transaction alive in order to avoid such damage. Care has to be taken, however, where companies whose shares are quoted on a stock exchange are concerned. Most stock exchanges require the disclosure of price sensitive information (including of course the existence of negotiations relating to a merger or acquisition) whether the company involved is the seller, the purchaser or the target. There are strict rules, which vary with the relevant stock exchange, as to the stage which negotiations must reach before an announcement has to be made, and as to the amount of detail that the announcement has to contain. As a general rule, subject to any rules which exempt transactions of a certain size from the necessity of an announcement, the signature of a heads of agreement would normally require that an announcement be made. In some cases the parties prefer, in order to avoid the need for an announcement, not to enter into heads of agreement, but to go straight to a definitive agreement, and to make the announcement on its signature. However, even here, if the negotiations have reached a sufficient stage of detail and agreement, an announcement may still have to be made prior to the signature of the definitive agreement. This whole question is one for an experienced practitioner well-versed in the securities laws and stock exchange practice of the relevant jurisdiction.

Clause 6 makes reference to the fact that the original structure, and indeed some of the commercial details of the transaction, may have to be rethought, and renegotiated, once detailed consideration of the form of the transaction has taken place. The most likely areas which will cause such changes are the subsequent deliberations of the parties' taxation advisers, or difficulties with the obtaining of regulatory consents.

Clause 7 deals with the most difficult issue surrounding heads of agreement both from a legal and a commercial point of view: the extent to which the purchaser can obtain an exclusive negotiating position with the seller.

During the course of negotiations, purchasers often ask for an undertaking from the seller that for a period of time he will not negotiate with anyone else. The obligation can range from one merely not to solicit third party offers (often called a 'no-shop' clause) to one which in addition contains an undertaking not to negotiate with third parties even if they make an unsolicited offer (a 'lock- out' clause).

Because of fiduciary duties to shareholders, boards of directors of publicly-quoted companies often find it difficult to accept full lock-out clauses, when negotiating with a purchaser for the sale of their company, since they have a duty to consider all potential purchasers, and to choose the best offer available. In these cases, most purchasers settle for a no-shop clause.

The reason for such clauses is not just the desire to avoid loss of a bargain. The purchaser will now undertake a significant commitment of time and money in carrying out due diligence and arriving at a definitive agreement; he may also be foregoing other business opportunities to concentrate on the target.

Besides such 'lock-out' or 'no-shop' clauses, purchasers sometimes demand what are known as 'break-up fees'. These are an amount, often of about 1–1.5 per cent of the proposed purchase price, which is payable by way of compensation for wasted expenditure if the transaction does not go through. Break-up fees originated in agreed public tender offers in the USA, and were payable if the target's shareholders rejected the relevant tender in favour of a higher tender from a third party. They have since spread to some public offers in the UK, and also into private deals, where the trigger is usually the failure of the transaction by reason of refusal of regulatory approval (eg from the European Commission) or the withdrawal of the seller in favour of a competing offer from a third party.

Although lock-out or no-shop clauses and break-up fee clauses address the same areas of concern, they are not mutually exclusive, and often a purchaser will ask for both. Lawyers advising the purchaser should always consider whether any of these clauses is appropriate at relevant stages of the transaction. Failure to advise a client of the possibility of their inclusion might well give rise to allegations of negligence in the event of a transaction which fails through the intervention of a third party.

The legal status of lock-out clauses was considered in the case of *Walford v Miles* [1992] 1 All ER 453. The case concerned a lock-out agreement whereby the vendor of a photographic business undertook to continue negotiations with the vendor, and not to negotiate with third parties for the sale of his business, during a fixed period of time in return for the provision by the prospective purchaser of a comfort letter from his bankers confirming that he was good for the price. The comfort letter was provided but the vendor sold to a third party in breach of the alleged agreement. The Court of Appeal held that an agreement to negotiate was void for uncertainty, but did not make clear whether an agreement not to negotiate could be legally binding if properly supported by consideration. In a dissenting judgment Bingham LJ held that although he accepted that an agreement to continue negotiations was unenforceable, he felt that the arrangement was in substance an agreement not to negotiate with a third party and that this was enforceable.

The matter was laid to rest by the judgment of the House of Lords on 23 January 1992. The House of Lords agreed with Bingham LJ, although they found on the facts that the arrangement in the case amounted to a positive agreement to continue negotiations and therefore dismissed the appeal. On the basis of *Walford v Miles* it can therefore now be said with confidence that it is possible to enforce an agreement not to negotiate with third parties for a defined period of time, if the agreement is supported by consideration.

Walford v Miles was followed in *Pitt v PHH Asset Management Ltd* [1993] 4 All ER 961, CA, in which a lock-out agreement (preventing the defendant from negotiating, for a fixed period, with persons other than the plaintiff, for the sale of a house) was held to be enforceable, as it had been given for good consideration, and damages were awarded for its breach.

However, this agreement is obviously of limited value if it cannot be coupled with some kind of enforceable positive obligation to negotiate. Nevertheless the House of Lords refused to accept that an obligation to negotiate in good faith can exist under English Law.

'An obligation to negotiate in good faith is as unworkable in practice as it is inherently inconsistent with the position of a negotiating party ... In my judgment while negotiations are in existence either party is entitled to withdraw from those negotiations at any time and for any reason.' (*per* Lord Ackner)

Walford v Miles has subsequently been followed and applied in over 20 decisions, the latest being *Laceys Footwear (Wholesale) Ltd v Bowler International Freight Ltd* [1997] 2 Lloyd's Rep 369, where the Court of Appeal referred to 'the magisterial rejection of any general concept of a duty to carry on negotiations in good faith by Lord Ackner'. It should be said that there are jurisdictions (France is one) where certain limited obligations of good faith negotiation are recognised and considered enforceable. Also, following one strand of the judgment of Bates J, at first instance, in *Walford v Miles* it would seem that an undertaking to negotiate in good faith could be regarded as a representation that one will negotiate in good faith. There would thus seem no reason why, under the right conditions, an action would not lie for breach of such a representation. The House of Lords did not consider this point, but there is nothing in their judgment which would seem to prevent this.

The final question to be answered with regard to lock-out clauses is how the court will enforce them. It is entirely possible that, if the clause is considered enforceable in principle, not only damages, but, in appropriate cases, an injunction to enforce the obligations contained in the clause might be forthcoming.

However, coupling the lock-out clause with a break-up fee could cause some problems. Care must be taken not to draft the break-up fee clause as if it were a payment of damages related to the breach of the lock-out clause. In such a case, the break-up fee would either be a genuine pre-estimate of the damage suffered by the purchaser because the transaction has not been completed, or else it is a penalty. In the former case, damages would appear an adequate remedy for breach of the lock-out clause, so that no injunction to enforce the lock-out clause should be granted, and, in the latter case, the break-up fee clause would be unenforceable as a penalty, and the status of the injunction would still be problematic, because the actual damages suffered would presumably be less than the amount of the break-up fee.

The best way to handle the drafting where both a lock-out and a break-up fee clause are required is to make the break-up fee clause an obligation to pay a sum of money, upon the happening of a certain event (ie a sale to a third party) which is expressed as totally independent from the lock-out clause. This should have the desired result of avoiding the construction of the clause as either a liquidated damages or a penalty clause. However, in common law jurisdictions, which recognise the concept of consideration, such an obligation will only be enforceable if the seller grants it in return for good consideration from the purchaser, or if it is granted by way of a deed.

Clause 7 combines a lock-out clause and a break-up fee clause, by prohibiting negotiations, and the conclusion of transactions, with third parties during the time the heads of agreement are in force, and providing for a break-up fee if such a prohibited transaction is in fact concluded. As discussed above the obligations are undertaken by the seller in consideration of the purchaser agreeing to enter into negotiations for the purchase of the company and to put in hand the due diligence investigation. The break-up fee clause is a separate obligation from the lock-out clause, and not drafted as if it were a liquidated damages clause providing compensation for breach of the lock-out clause.

Clause 8 provides for termination of the heads of agreement either because they have been superseded by a definitive agreement (cl 8.1) or because the purchaser has decided to withdraw (cl 8.2) or by expiry by effluxion of time (cl 8.3). Clause 7.2 provides that cl 7.1 terminates along with the rest of the heads of agreement in the event of termination under cl 8.1 (the lock-out is no longer relevant) or cl 8.2 (the purchaser cannot insist on compensation if he withdraws) but retains the obligation to pay a break-up fee (cl 7.1.4) if the seller sells to a third party within a defined period of time after the heads of agreement expire by effluxion of time pursuant to cl 8.3

This is to prevent the seller prolonging the negotiations with the purchaser until the heads of agreement expire, and then bringing out into the open a third party with whom he has perhaps been negotiating in secret, and with whom, in any event, he now prefers to conclude the transaction. It may be argued that if the heads of agreement have expired by effluxion of time because the parties have tried, pursuant to cl 4.2, but been unable, to obtain a necessary regulatory consent before the expiry date, that the seller should thereafter be free to sell to any third party without the need to pay a break-up fee. If this argument prevails the appropriate exceptions can be written into cll 7 and 8, but it should be stated that even in these situations, the purchaser may still require, and it is usually fair to grant him, some level of break-up fee. As Precedent 1 stands, it provides that the break-up fee is payable for a period after the expiry of the heads of agreement by effluxion of time, whatever the reason for the delay which caused such expiry, even failure to obtain regulatory consent.

Clause 9 addresses the issue of the extent to which the heads of agreement are to be legally binding. It has already been stated that an agreement to negotiate is not enforceable in most jurisdictions, so even if the parties desired it, the heads of agreement as a whole could not be legally enforceable. In any event, cl 9 takes the position which is usual in such documents. As a whole the document is not, and is not intended to be, legally enforceable, but cll 5 (confidentiality) and 7 (lock-out and break-up fee clauses) as well as the choice of law clause (cl 10) are expressed to be legally enforceable. This position safeguards the ability of the parties to negotiate their bargain freely with the right to withdraw if they cannot do so, while ensuring that those obligations which are intended to be legally enforceable can be so enforced.

10.3   **Precedent 2**

Precedent 2 is a reasonably long form share sale agreement. Following the definition and interpretations clause (cl 1), cl 2 sets out the details of the transaction, and it is here that the problems start to arise. The structure of the transaction in this precedent is one where the parties sign a binding agreement, but one which is subject to obtaining the necessary regulatory consents and also subject to the carrying out by the purchaser of satisfactory due diligence. Thus completion cannot take place until consents have been obtained and the purchaser is satisfied with the results of the due diligence exercise. Clause 2.1 outlines the basic transaction, cl 2.2 imposes the obligation to obtain regulatory consents, and cl 2.3 permits the purchaser to carry out the due diligence exercise for a period ending 60 days after the signature of the agreement or seven days after the grant of all regulatory consents, whichever last occurs. If the necessary consents are not obtained within six months then (unless the parties agree to an extension) the agreement is terminated without liability on either side (cl 13.1).

However, the position with regard to due diligence is much more complicated. One approach would be to give the purchaser unfettered discretion to withdraw from the transaction without liability if he is in any way dissatisfied with the results of his due diligence. Such a provision is unlikely to be acceptable to the seller in what is intended to be a legally binding sale agreement. If the seller were minded to accept such an arrangement it would only have been at the stage of heads of agreement which were not legally binding in any event. It is now too late for the purchaser to withdraw upon what the seller would no doubt claim could amount to a whim.

Nevertheless, the main reason for entering into a sale agreement with a delayed completion date (apart from obtaining regulatory consents) is to enable the purchaser to have time to complete a detailed due diligence exercise which he would have been reluctant to undertake (because of the commitment in time and money such an exercise entails) unless he knew that, subject to the exercise being satisfactory, both he and the seller were bound to complete the transaction.

The remainder of cl 2 is designed to offer an equitable compromise to solve these problems. Clause 2.4 first provides that, on the expiry of the due diligence exercise, the purchaser must either tell the seller that he is satisfied, in which case he will then be bound, after a short period, to complete, or that he is not satisfied, in which case he must provide the seller with a 'Due Diligence Report' detailing his complaints. There are a number of necessary ground rules as to the matter which can constitute such complaints.

First, it should be noted that cl 2.4 only permits the purchaser to complain of matters which are breaches of the warranties that he has negotiated with the seller and included in the sale agreement (see cl 4 and Sched 2), and that cl 2.6 contains special provisions restricting further the rights of the purchaser to complain of such breaches. The most important of such provisions relates of course to matters disclosed in the disclosure letter (cl 2.6.1). The other provisions of cl 2.6 relate to standard exclusions from liability for breach of warranty. Clause 2.6 excludes matters covered by insurance and claims below a certain monetary threshold unless in the aggregate they exceed a specified amount. In this latter case, however, the proviso to cl 2.6 provides that minor claims which are ignored because they have not reached in aggregate the specified amount may be carried forward for the purposes of the equivalent provision dealing with minor claims after completion (see Sched 3, paras 7(*a*) and (*b*)). Clause 2.6 also excludes matters giving rise to claims which occur either because of the actions of the purchaser, or as a result of actions of the seller carried out at the request of the purchaser, or merely because of the implementation of the agreement in accordance with its terms.

Secondly, the question of timing of the delivery of the disclosure letter is vital. In this connection, care should be taken with the definition of 'Disclosure Letter' contained in cl 1. This provides for the disclosure letter to be delivered on signature of the agreement, not on completion. While the disclosure letter is delivered on completion, where completion takes place simultaneously with the signature of the share sale agreement, obviously it would defeat the purpose of due diligence, and throw all of the risk of the business onto the purchaser for the period between signature and completion if the seller could, in a two-stage transaction, deliver the disclosure letter on completion and thus avoid liability for any breaches of warranty arising between signature and completion which are discovered during due diligence.

Thirdly, it would be inappropriate, in a two-stage transaction of the sort set out in this precedent, for the seller to state that the purchaser was aware of a breach by reason of his due diligence exercise and therefore should not be able to claim for it as a breach of warranty whether before or after completion. (Such a provision is only arguably appropriate if the purchaser has the unfettered right to withdraw if not satisfied with the results of his due diligence exercise.) Clause 4.1 makes this situation clear.

Fourthly, cl 2.4 provides that the seller cannot escape being fixed with liabilities which are qualified by being given only as to the best of his knowledge and belief, if he is unaware of the matter which would otherwise give rise to the breach at the date of signature, but later becomes aware of the matter in question prior to completion. In fact cl 2.4 provides that the seller is to be deemed to be aware, for the purposes of such qualified warranties, of all the matters which the purchaser discloses to him in the due diligence report.

Given that cll 2.4 and 2.6 have established the types of matters for which the purchaser can complain in his due diligence report, what are the consequences of that complaint? Clause 2.5 sets out a detailed procedure to deal with the issue in accordance with a set timetable.

First, the seller must be given a chance to cure the breaches complained of. If he succeeds, that is the end of the matter and completion takes place (cl

2.5.1). If he does not or cannot cure the breaches, then the purchaser must either be allowed to withdraw from the transaction or be given appropriate compensation by way of a reduction in the purchase price.

Even in a transaction where the purchaser is normally bound (subject to receiving appropriate compensation) to complete whatever the breaches uncovered by his due diligence, there must come a point at which the breaches discovered are so severe that, even if the seller were prepared to pay the necessary amount by way of compensation, the purchaser would wish to withdraw in any event, since the transaction he was now being asked to enter into had become fundamentally different from that which he had initially agreed to conclude. The only realistic benchmark for deciding when this right to withdraw arises is by reference to the sum of money necessary to compensate the purchaser for the breaches in question. The parties therefore first agree what the amount of compensation should be (cl 2.5.2). When this amount is agreed to be above a pre-determined level (defined in the agreement as the 'threshold') then the agreement automatically terminates without liability on either side (cl 2.5.2.2). However, if the amount agreed on is less than the threshold, then the price is reduced by the appropriate amount and completion takes place. The threshold will obviously vary depending upon the size of the transaction, but it should be a large portion of the proposed purchase price, probably between one third and a half.

If the parties cannot agree on the amount of compensation, then unless they can at least agree that it is higher than the threshold (in which case the agreement automatically terminates—cl 2.5.3), the matter can only be submitted to arbitration. Arbitration takes place in two stages if necessary. First, if there is total disagreement, the arbitrator is asked to decide if the amount is likely to be more or less than the threshold (cl 2.5.5). If he determines that it is likely to be more, the agreement terminates without liability on either side (cl 2.5.5.2). If he determines that it is not (cl 2.5.5.3) or if the parties themselves can agree, without resort to arbitration, that it is not (cl 2.5.4), then the parties must make one more attempt to settle their dispute by exchanging offers of the amount at which each of them would be willing to settle for payment of compensation (cl 2.5.6). If no agreement is reached at this stage, the purchaser can then either reduce the purchase price by the average of the two offers and submit the dispute to arbitration (cl 2.5.7) or reject the seller's offer, and complete, leaving the matters in issue to be settled as post-completion warranty claims and/ or as part of the settling of the completion accounts referred to in cl 3.5. It should be noted that the procedure in cll 2.5.6 and 2.5.7 is designed to force the parties to a reasonable compromise if at all possible since the submission to arbitration is to so-called 'pendulum arbitration' in which the arbitrator must award either the amount offered by the purchaser or that offered by the seller. This is a very significant deterrent to excessive claims from the purchaser and unreasonably low offers of compensation from the seller.

Clauses 2.5.9 and 2.5.10 provide that any award by the arbitrator resulting from a reference pursuant to cl 2.5.7 shall be treated as an adjustment to the purchase price. For a variety of reasons relating to taxation issues, this is nearly always the correct way to deal with such matters, and does, indeed, describe the real effect of the arbitrator's award.

The only remaining problem is what happens if the arbitrator takes an unduly long time to come to a decision on the question put to him under cl 2.5.5 as to whether the amount payable by way of compensation exceeds the threshold. This will delay completion, unlike a reference pursuant to cl 2.5.7. One possibility is to keep matters pending and the agreement in force, until his award is made, but putting off completion indefinitely is often commercially impossible. This precedent attempts to solve the problem in two ways. First, cll 2.11 and 2.12 provide expressly, what is in any event always implicit, that the parties can at any time short circuit any of the procedures and agree mutually on the amount to be paid as compensation (whether below or above the threshold) and complete accordingly. Failing such agreement, if the arbitrator's award under cl 2.5.5 is still outstanding six months after the purchaser submitted his due diligence report, then cl 13.2 provides that the agreement thereupon terminates automatically. However, when the arbitrator's award is finally published, if it states that the compensation payable was not likely to have exceeded the threshold, then termination is not wholly without liability, in that the party who contended that it would exceed the threshold (and who was therefore responsible for the collapse of the transaction) is liable to the other in damages on a full indemnity basis for all losses suffered as a result. The consequences of an adverse award are thus so great (they will certainly include compensation for loss of the bargain, if the seller is at fault, for instance) that neither party will lightly contend that the threshold is likely to be exceeded purely as a device for avoiding completion of the transaction.

Clause 3 deals in a standard way with the actual completion of the transaction, and various matters consequent upon it, and requires little comment, except in regard to ascertainment and payment of the purchase price. This precedent proceeds upon the assumption that the purchase price of the target company is to be its net asset value as shown on its balance sheet, plus a predetermined sum of money which is in effect the price the purchaser is willing to pay for goodwill and other intangible assets not reflected on the balance sheet. If cl 3.2.5 is included, then the purchaser will pay the first instalment of the purchase price (probably equal to the pre-determined sum for goodwill and other intangible assets referred to above) on completion, leaving the balance of the purchase price to be paid, together with interest from the 'Completion Date' to the date of payment (see cl 3.7) when the net asset value is determined through the preparation of the 'Completion Accounts' pursuant to cl 3.5 and Sched 1. If cl 3.2.5 is not included, then cl 3.7, suitably adapted, would provide for the payment of the whole of the purchase price upon ascertainment of the net asset value. Even in the absence of a formal retention provision, this method of payment of the purchase price gives the purchaser a retention of all or a significant part of the purchase price for the period of time it takes to draw up and finalise the completion accounts. Therefore, as a practical matter, he will, before payment, be able to set off any post-completion warranty claims that he has discovered in the meantime. His right to do this is strengthened by the inclusion, as cl 14, of a general set off clause.

The procedure for preparation and agreement of the completion accounts set out in Sched 1 is self-explanatory. The purchaser, as the person now in control of the company prepares the accounts, and passes them to his auditors and the seller's auditors for auditing. If the two sets of auditors agree, that is the end of the matter. If not, the purchaser and the seller attempt to resolve the dispute, and, if they fail to do so, the matter is submitted to an independent auditor who determines the matter conclusively acting as an expert (from whose decision there is no appeal) and not as an arbitrator.

The most important part of the schedule is para 2. This directs that in the preparation of the accounts provision should be made for all liabilities, and prescribes the accounting policies upon the basis of which the accounts should be drawn up. The negotiation and agreement of these accounting policies is absolutely vital, since they will determine the way in which the net asset value, and hence the purchase price, is calculated, and should only be agreed in conjunction with the auditors of the client for whom the lawyer concerned is acting. The use of the accounting policies of the purchaser or the seller will normally favour the purchaser and the seller respectively, whereas the agreement of a special set may be a compromise which is acceptable to both parties.

However, it is worth noting, if acting for the purchaser, that the consequence of not adopting the purchaser's accounting policies, if they are stricter than the ones actually adopted in the agreement, can be very adverse for the purchaser. For instance, if the purchaser's policy on ageing and writing-off of debts is stricter than that adopted in the agreement, the purchaser, on the completion of the acquisition, will normally be required to change the target company's accounting policies to match his own. This will result in the write-off of debts that were counted as good for the purpose of calculating the net asset value. The purchaser will show this write-off as an expense to be set off against the target company's on-going profits, but he will not have been compensated for this by a decrease in the purchase price of the company, nor will he normally be able to make a post-completion warranty claim, even if he can find an appropriate warranty under which to do so (which is unlikely), because one of the exclusions of liability under warranties routinely included by the seller's advisers is one excluding claims which arise because of a change made by the purchaser in the accounting policies of the target company—see Sched 3, para 7(*f*).

Another area where application of the right accounting policies is vital is the valuation of inventory (or stock) and work in progress. The writing off or writing down of obsolete or excessive amounts of these items depends upon the accounting policies adopted and the view taken of the future demand in the

370 Drafting Commercial Agreements

market for the various items comprised within the inventory and work in progress at the date of completion.

The accounting treatment of receivables, inventory and work in progress can result in very large changes to the net asset value, and hence the purchase price, and one of the most significant contributions to the transaction that can be made by the lawyer is to assist his client and his client's auditors to negotiate accounting policies which favour his client's position.

The proviso at the end of the paragraph requires some comment. Its effect is to avoid double recovery and double jeopardy. If the purchaser has agreed on a pre-completion price reduction for some matter which is a liability of the company, then he should not receive double compensation. Since the liability still exists unaltered for the company despite the compensation given to the purchaser, it must be reflected in the completion accounts and create a reduction in the net asset value. The provision in square brackets in the proviso, by disallowing the liability only to the extent that it has been satisfied by the agreed price reduction, mean that double recovery is avoided, but that double jeopardy remains, since the agreement of the price reduction is not in full and final settlement of the matter. The purchaser can reopen the issue, if he thinks that the price reduction did not fully satisfy the loss, by seeking to reflect the balance in the completion accounts. Such a provision is obviously unpopular with sellers who would argue that if the purchaser has agreed a price reduction that should be the end of the dispute. As a practical matter, where such a provision is included, when the parties agree a price reduction it should be broken out into individual reductions covering each head of claim, if the purchaser is to be able to rely on this provision. A global figure covering all claims raised by the purchaser would make it almost impossible for him to rely on this provision, even if the seller has initially agreed to its inclusion, since he could never show whether a particular issue had been wholly or partially satisfied by the global price reduction.

Similarly, the proviso provides that, if there is a pre-completion dispute about the amount of a price reduction in respect of a liability, then the dispute must either be dealt with by a unilateral price reduction and a submission to arbitration pursuant to cl 2.5.7, or be reflected in the completion accounts and/or as a warranty claim pursuant to cl 2.5.8; the parties must choose one method or the other of dealing with the issue and then stick to it. In any event, problems of timing (the arbitration award will not be known until after completion, and quite likely after the time when the completion accounts must be finalised) make it difficult to see how the parties could change between remedies or take the result of the arbitration into account in preparing the completion accounts.

The treatment of completion accounts in the precedent tends to favour the purchaser, but not unduly. This method of calculating the purchase price does not provide the net asset value underpin as discussed in relation to cl 4.3.1 of Precedent 1, with all of the consequent advantages for the purchaser, but, in effect, adjusts the purchase price up or down, depending on the net asset value, which seems a fair compromise for both sides.

There are, obviously, other ways of dealing with the purchase price. It would probably be the desire of the seller to avoid completion accounts altogether, and to settle on a figure for the purchase price which is paid in full without retention upon completion. In most cases the seller is unlikely to prevail on this issue. However, possible compromises are to provide for as large a down payment on the purchase price upon completion as the purchaser can be prevailed upon to accept.

One further, and more usual, method is to fix the purchase price in the agreement at an absolute figure, and then introduce a post-completion adjustment to this figure, based upon completion accounts struck in the manner described in this precedent. If one intends to favour the purchaser one can then introduce a net asset underpin, whereby the price is retrospectively adjusted downward, pound for pound, if the net asset figure is below a certain figure. (A provision along these lines is included as cl 4.10 of Precedent 1 in Chapter 11.) Alternatively, the provision could operate only to adjust the purchase price upward if the net asset value exceeded a given amount, with no net asset underpin, although such a provision is very uncommon. However, a compromise with an adjustment up or down depending upon whether the specified net asset value is respectively above or below a particular figure is often used instead. Such a provision has almost the same effect as that contained in this precedent, but, unless it is coupled with a specific retention provision, does not give the purchaser the added advantage of holding back part of the purchase price.

Clause 4 and Sched 2 deal with the warranties given by the seller to the purchaser. Clause 4.1 contains the actual representations by which the seller makes the warranties in Sched 2 to the purchaser, and includes the important provision whereby the warranties are made as of the date of signature of the agreement and are remade as of the completion date, in order to catch any change in the position of the company between signature and completion. Clause 4.1 also contains the important provision ensuring that the purchaser is not barred from making a claim because of actual or constructive knowledge (except actual knowledge through the disclosure letter) of any matter giving rise to a claim, including knowledge arising through the due diligence exercise. Without this latter provision, the procedure relating to due diligence and pre-completion claims for breach of warranty set out in cl 2 would be unworkable.

Schedule 2 contains a general short set of warranties that are appropriate for most transactions, although those who require longer sets of warranties, or warranties specially tailored to a particular transaction, can and should consult the many specialist works on this subject. It should, however, be said that the copying of long sets of warranties without thought as to their applicability to the particular transaction is to be deprecated, since it does not serve the purchaser's interests adequately, and can well be counter-productive in prolonging negotiations over matters which have little real importance in the context of the transaction.

The warranties contained in Sched 2 are designed to focus attention on the key issues relating to a share acquisition, but, again, should not be used blindly, without consideration of their suitability for a particular transaction, and the need to include other warranties tailored to suit particular circumstances.

In general, it should be noted that phrases qualifying various warranties to the best of the seller's knowledge and belief (there is a definition of the relevant phrase in cl 1, which makes this a reasonably serious qualification by imposing a high standard of constructive knowledge) appear throughout the warranties in square brackets. Inclusion of this phrase in the case of any warranty will cut down the seller's liability considerably, particularly since he will have disclosed anything he knows prior to signature in the disclosure letter.

Warranty 1 is a standard representation as to the truth of matters set out in the agreement and the disclosure letter. Warranty 2 contains the standard representations as to the capacity of the seller to enter into the transaction, and of the good standing of the company and its compliance with all applicable legislation. This last warranty is a very wide-ranging one, and can stand in for pages of warranties which represent that particular statutes have been complied with.

Warranty 3 represents that the company will have no indebtedness to the seller on completion, except ordinary trade debts, and thus obliges the seller to clear off or forgive such indebtedness. Such indebtedness has to be dealt with very carefully, since its presence at completion is in effect an increase in the purchase price, and its discharge prior to completion results in a reduction of the net asset value (either by an outflow of cash or an increase in bank borrowings). If the agreement contains, as does this precedent, a purchase price adjustment by reference to net asset value, the matter is self-adjusting, and the warranty deals sufficiently with the duty to discharge the debts. In the absence of such a purchase price adjustment clause, a specific provision dealing with inter-company indebtedness, and the requirement to capitalise (before completion) any amount whose discharge would cause the company to exceed a permitted level of bank borrowings should be included in the agreement.

Warranty 4 is arguably the most important warranty in the schedule. First, the seller warrants the set of accounts against which the purchaser assessed the initial price for the transaction and on the basis of which he presumably largely decided to go ahead with the acquisition. To the extent that these accounts failed properly to provide for any liabilities of the target company that should have been reflected in such accounts, the purchaser will have a claim for breach of warranty. The seller then warrants that from the date of these accounts until the completion date the business will not deteriorate, and will be carried on in the ordinary course. This warranty puts the risk of the business, and the obligations to carry it on properly, upon the seller. Warranty 4 then turns to specific issues not covered by the general balance sheet warranties. First, the solvency of the target company's pension fund is warranted. Then the collectability of the target company's accounts receivable, the suitability and value of its fixed assets, and the level and saleability of its inventory are also warranted. It should be noted that these specific warranties cover issues which should be dealt with in the completion accounts prepared pursuant to cl 3.5 and Sched 1. However, the difference here is that the completion accounts look forward from the completion date to project what is likely to happen on the basis of agreed accounting policies. These warranties look backwards to see what has actually happened, and provide the purchaser with an additional remedy if the projections in the completion accounts were too optimistic.

Warranty 5 contains a number of standard warranties relating to employment matters.

Warranty 6 in effect warrants the good standing and profitability of the business of the company as it is currently being carried on through its customer contracts. This warranty is again very wide-ranging, and if warranty 4 provides protection to the purchaser against prior undisclosed liabilities, this warranty provides protection in relation to the future well being of the business that is being acquired.

Warranty 7, relating to litigation and other claims against the target company is arguably unnecessary, since any failure to reflect a claim (whether or not it was known at the time) on the balance sheet is certainly a breach of warranty 4, and all claims discovered prior to completion will either be dealt with as part of the pre-completion procedure, or will be reflected in the completion accounts. Pre-completion liabilities for such claims discovered post-completion will also be reflected in the completion accounts, if they are discovered while these accounts are still being prepared. However, although the wording of warranty 4, and the accounting procedures, may catch some claims it is unlikely to be wholly effective for contingent claims, particularly those for which the relevant accounting policies would prescribe not a provision but only a note to the accounts. Thus a specific warranty like warranty 7 is usually included to cover all possibilities. A particularly contentious point here is the liability for claims arising out of pre-completion issues which were not known to the seller and not discovered by the purchaser prior to completion. The wording of the last part of warranty 7 imposes liability for these claims on the seller, but the inclusion of the reference in square brackets to the seller's knowledge and belief would, in effect, remove this liability in most cases.

Warranty 8 covers the condition of the target company's fixed assets and real property, and the adequacy of its title. With the inclusion of such a warranty it is not normally necessary for the purchaser to investigate the target company's title to its real property, although, of course, he may choose to do so for significant items as part of the due diligence exercise.

Warranty 9 deals with the intellectual property of the target company. The seller warrants that the target company owns all, or is licensed to use all, the intellectual property it needs to carry on its business, that its title to such intellectual property is valid, and that it is not infringing the intellectual property rights of third parties.

Warranty 10 covers a number of specific financial and tax issues, many of which are included in the broad warranties of warranty 4, or will be covered when drawing up the completion accounts, but which it is useful or prudent to deal with expressly. The matters covered relate principally to the absence of undisclosed encumbrances over the assets of the target company; to the validity of, and the seller's good title to, and right to transfer free of encumbrances, the shares which are to be transferred pursuant to the acquisition agreement; to proper payment of all taxes that are due; to the proper keeping of books of account; to the absence of any previous extraordinary transactions involving the share capital of the target company; and to the absence of any obligations to issue more shares in the company or to enter into extraordinary capital investments.

Clause 4.2 imposes a duty on the seller to disclose to the purchaser any breach of warranty of which he becomes aware. This duty operates not only for the purposes of the due diligence exercise, but also after completion. Clause 4.3 stops up one possible way for the seller to avoid a warranty claim, by preventing him from seeking compensation either from the target company, or an employee of the target company, for any wrongful act by the company or employee which gave rise to the matter in respect of which the purchaser makes his warranty claim.

Clause 4.4 provides an indemnity to the purchaser from the seller in respect of each breach of warranty for which a claim is made, either pursuant to cll 2.4 and 2.5 (for pre-completion claims dealt with under those clauses prior to completion or by submission to an arbitrator) or pursuant to Sched 3 (for pre-completion claims not dealt with in this way and for all post-completion claims). Clause 4.5 restricts the right of the purchaser to repudiate or rescind the agreement solely to the express remedies to this effect contained in cll 2.4 and 2.5 and further provides, in exchange for the granting by the seller of the indemnity in cl 4.4, that that indemnity is the purchaser's sole and exclusive remedy for all breaches of warranty.

Purchasers normally prefer the inclusion of provisions like cll 4.4 and 4.5 as they provide them with the certainty of a remedy. In the case of this precedent, since, by and large, the purchaser can either choose to accept a negotiated settlement under cl 2.5 for pre-completion claims, or leave them to be dealt with as post-completion claims under the indemnity in Sched 3, he has at his disposal a full indemnity provision which (subject to the limitations contained in it) provides a full recovery for all loss suffered which he can prove was a result of any warranty claim, without reference to questions of remoteness of damage.

Sellers often prefer not to include any such indemnity provision at all, and to leave the purchaser to pursue his common law remedies for breach of warranty by proving to the court not only the breach of warranty but also that the damages claimed are recoverable under the relevant common law rules on the remoteness of damage. Even here sellers will attempt provisions limiting warranty claims along the lines of those contained in para 7 of Sched 3, and also to impose time limits, shorter than the normal statutory limitation periods, during which warranty claims can be brought. However, in this latter case, purchasers often advance with success that, if they are to be required to bring claims in accordance with the common law rules relating to breach of contract, they should also be entitled to rely on the usual statutory periods of limitation during which such claims can be brought, and that the seller should not have the protection of specific exclusions (except perhaps an overall cap on liability) but rely on the common law rules relating to remoteness and the duty to mitigate.

One area where, in any event, indemnity is customarily given by the seller, even if he refuses to give it elsewhere, is in relation to pre-completion liabilities for taxation. Where a general indemnity provision is not included, such an indemnity is often given by a separate tax indemnity deed.

Schedule 3 sets out the procedure which is to be followed by the purchaser in bringing claims for indemnity for breach of warranty.

Paragraph 1 provides the basic time periods in which claims must be brought. Most warranty claims are usually limited to a period of one or two years after completion. A good rule of thumb is to allow sufficient time for two sets of audited accounts of the company to have been issued in addition to the completion accounts. If warranty claims have not been thrown up by then, in most cases they never will be. The particular warranties which are most likely to require longer periods of time are those relating to tax (usually six years, or by reference to the applicable periods specified in the relevant statutes during which taxation authorities can bring and reopen claims) and warranties relating to environmental matters, which, in order to cover the liabilities now being imposed in some jurisdictions, should even, if possible, be perpetual!

Paragraph 2 contains the basic obligation to indemnify the purchaser and deems for this purpose that losses suffered by the target company are losses suffered by the purchaser. Coupled with para 9, which treats indemnity payments as a reduction of the purchase price, this paragraph provides the most tax efficient way of dealing with payment of warranty claims. It is extremely hard to provide for a direct compensation to be paid to the target company, as opposed to the purchaser, without this payment being treated as income in the hands of the target company which is subject to tax. If this happens, the seller either has to gross up the payment (if legally possible) or the company has to suffer tax on the compensation received. Incidentally, where a provision deeming the losses of the company to be the losses of the purchaser is not included, either for the purposes of the indemnity provisions, or generally in relation to the purchaser's rights to bring warranty claims at common law, the purchaser is in a very difficult position, because it by no means follows that the loss suffered by the company and by the purchaser in respect of the same event is of the same amount. In these situations the purchaser is faced with two hurdles: first he has to prove the loss suffered by the company, and then to show what damage he himself has suffered as a result of the company suffering this loss.

Paragraphs 3 and 4 of Sched 3 deal respectively with the procedures for bringing claims, for direct loss suffered by the purchaser, and for loss suffered by the purchaser through claims brought by third parties.

The latter part of para 4, together with para 5, contains the mechanism by which the seller can take over, defend and settle third party claims in respect of which he agrees he is liable to provide indemnification to the purchaser. This is a valuable provision for the seller, and is usually not available to him if there is no indemnity provision in the agreement relating to third party claims. If the purchaser has to rely on his common law remedies of breach of warranty when such claims are brought against him, then, subject to common law rules on mitigation of damage, he can handle them as he thinks fit, without consultation with the seller, and then sue the seller for the relevant damage suffered. In the precedent the purchaser can only deal with third party claims in this way if the seller has refused to indemnify him against them (see paras 5 and 6).

Paragraph 7 contains a selection of the standard limitations on indemnification. Paragraphs 7(*a*) and (*b*) deal with the questions of *de minimis* claims, while 7(*c*) imposes an overall limitation on the seller's liability, taking into account any price reduction relating to pre-completion claims. Paragraph 7(*d*) prevents the purchaser being compensated for contingent claims, but preserves his right to be so compensated when they become actual. Paragraph 7(*e*) excludes any losses which have already been reflected in the completion accounts. This paragraph, coupled with para 7(*h*), excluding losses already compensated for prior to completion under cll 2.4 and 2.5, prevents double or triple recovery of any loss. Paragraphs 7(*f*), 7(*j*) and 7(*k*) exclude liability for losses arising through acts of the purchaser, acts of the seller carried out at the request of the purchaser, and matters arising by reason of the implementation of the agreement in accordance with its terms. Paragraph 7(*g*) excludes losses covered by insurance and para 7(*i*) excludes losses relating to matters raised in the disclosure letter.

The above exclusions are relatively non-controversial, but the remaining two are more problematic. Paragraph 7(*l*) excludes liability for claims relating to breaches of warranty which arise because of new legislation after the completion date or any change in law or administrative practice which takes effect after the completion date with retroactive effect. While the purchaser seeks to resist this provision as a rule, it is hard to see why the seller should be liable for matters of this nature which are totally outside his control, and, in most cases, completely unforeseen by both parties at the time of completion.

Paragraph 7(*m*) is more difficult. Here the seller requires credit to be given for any tax relief obtained by the purchaser or the company in respect of the loss which gives rise to the claim, or which would have been obtained if the purchaser or the company had taken reasonable steps to pursue the claim for relief. This provision is fiercely resisted by purchasers, first because the obtaining of such relief is often uncertain, and long-delayed in relation to the time at which the loss is suffered, and, secondly, because, since the compensation under the indemnity payment is treated as a reduction in the purchase price (ie a capital transaction), the loss itself must be suffered as a trading loss affecting the profits of the company or the purchaser, with no offset against the indemnity payment. In these circumstances, the reduction of the indemnity payment by the 'benefit' of the tax relief relating to the trading loss affecting the ongoing profitability of the company seems to be adding insult to injury.

It should be noted that (as is the case with cl 2.6 and the proviso to para 2 of Sched 1) care has to be taken with the exact drafting which excludes double recovery and double jeopardy. All of the provisions of para 7 except paras 7(*a*), (*b*), (*d*) and (*i*) (where the concept is irrelevant) prevent a claim being brought 'only to the extent that' the exception applies. For the exceptions where this is a straightforward and uncontroversial concept (see paras 7(*c*), (*f*), (*g*), (*j*), (*k*), (*l*) and (*m*)) the wording is not put in square brackets. Paragraphs 7(*e*) and 7(*h*) require more discussion.

If the wording in square brackets is included in para 7(*e*), then, although double recovery is avoided, double jeopardy remains, since despite the provision made in the completion accounts, the purchaser can raise again any additional loss in respect of the relevant matter that later comes to light within the relevant warranty period. Similar concepts apply in the case of the inclusion of the words in square brackets in relation to an agreed price reduction in para 7(*h*)(i). There are two possibilities given under para 7(*h*)(ii) in relation to pre-completion claims put to arbitration. The first set of words in square brackets excludes totally the possibility of making a post-completion warranty claim in respect of any such matter, whereas the second permits double jeopardy by allowing the purchaser to make a post-completion warranty claim once the outcome of the arbitration is known if he feels that the award has not fully compensated for all relevant losses.

The inclusion of double jeopardy in para 7(*e*) is probably more likely to be acceptable to a seller, but is likely to be resisted in the case of para 7(*h*), particularly for 7(*h*)(ii). The same considerations apply to these paragraphs as to the proviso to para 2 of Sched 1, which deals with double recovery and double jeopardy in relation to preparation of the completion accounts, and reference should be made to the commentary on that paragraph set out earlier in this chapter.

Finally, para 8 provides the usual provisions, analogous to those in insurance contracts, for payment over to the seller of any sums subsequently recovered from third parties in respect of claims paid by the seller, and for the seller to be subrogated to the purchaser's rights against such third parties to the extent that the seller has already made a relevant indemnity payment to the purchaser.

Care should be taken with para 8(*b*), where a warranty concerning collectability of receivables has been included. If the seller pays out on a claim under the warranty, he will, under para 8(*b*) be entitled to sue the defaulting debtor to recover the outstanding debt. The purchaser may not wish this to occur if the debtor in question is an existing customer. In the absence of an exclusion in para 8(*b*) relating to debtors, he would not be able to prevent this, and, in appropriate cases, would therefore be dissuaded from relying on the warranty. Of course the seller will resist the exclusion of defaulting debtors from para 8(*b*). The purchaser, at least, needs to understand that where the exception is not included, he will have to make the choice between collecting a payment under the warranty (and risking the displeasure of his customer if sued by the seller) or foregoing the claim over the bad debt, in the interest of good relations and possible future business with the customer.

The remaining clauses of the precedent deal with a variety of subsidiary matters. Clause 5 and Sched 4 make provision for pension transfer arrangements. In this precedent the details have been left blank, but a fuller precedent and a discussion of the issues involved are included in Chapter 11. Clause 6 makes it clear that insurances relating to the target company cease to be the responsibility of the seller, and become the responsibility of the purchaser, on the completion date. Clause 7 prevents assignment of the agreement by either party without the other's consent. Clause 8 deals with co-ordination and mutual approval of press releases. To the lawyer this may not seem a very important provision, but to the commercial persons involved on both sides of the transaction it often assumes great importance, with press releases being negotiated as fiercely as the acquisition agreement. The draftsman who omits such a clause usually does so at his peril. Clause 9 provides that each side shall bear their own costs and expenses of the transaction, and that, in particular, the purchaser shall pay stamp duty on the transfer of shares.

Clause 10, which provides that the relevant provisions of the agreement, particularly the warranties and indemnities, will survive completion, is included because of the peculiar common law doctrine of merger, which states, at least in some cases, that where an agreement for the transfer of property is completed by its actual legal conveyance, in this case the share transfer, the purpose of the agreement is fulfilled, it is said to have 'merged' with the conveyance, and thereupon ceases to have effect. It is doubtful if this doctrine really applies to share transfers (it originated in relation to the conveyance of real property), particularly where the express words of the agreement clearly provide for provisions to survive completion, and to operate after it, but most draftsmen put in this type of provision out of an abundance of caution.

Clause 11 provides the framework for references to arbitration pursuant to cl 2.5. Clause 12 provides detailed provisions for the service of notices, which is particularly necessary given the numerous types of notices and communications which have to pass between the parties, particularly pursuant to cll 2.4 and 2.5 and Scheds 1 and 3.

Clause 13, dealing with termination of the agreement, and cl 14, dealing with the purchaser's general right of set off, have been discussed earlier, while cl 15 provides a governing law clause.

One final word needs to be said about the structure of this precedent. As it stands, it provides the parties, but particularly the purchaser with four separate opportunities to negotiate the purchase price. The first is when the initial figure is struck on signature of the agreement, the second when the due diligence exercise is carried out, the third through the preparation of completion accounts, and the fourth through post-completion warranty claims. The parties to an acquisition agreement are not usually concerned with a long-term relationship, and are therefore each concerned to optimise their position in relation to the transaction in question. In the case of the purchaser this is achieved by building in successive and cumulative opportunities to reduce the purchase price as is done in this precedent, while in the case of the seller it is achieved by obtaining the highest possible initial purchase price, with the greatest possible cash payment upon completion, preferably the whole of the purchase price, and limiting or excluding wherever possible subsequent procedures for purchase price adjustment or warranty claims. The legal adviser who is alive to these issues, and assists his client in protecting his position and achieving the desired result in these areas will have performed a more valuable and useful task than one who has confined himself to drafting an impeccable document in accordance with the transaction negotiated by his client without the benefit of his advice.

10.4 Precedent 3

Precedent 3 provides for a skeleton form of a disclosure letter which it would be appropriate for a seller to use in either a share sale or a business transfer. The form proposed is a standard one, and its provisions are neither particularly favourable to the seller or the purchaser, but strike a fair balance, and aim for clarity and certainty, although para 1(*d*), where included, tends to favour the seller. Provisions deeming matters to be disclosed which can be ascertained by inspection of public registers (eg the Companies Registry) are sometimes also included, but such provisions are disliked and often resisted by purchasers, because of the lack of certainty they create.

Eurocopy v Teesdale [1992] BCLC 1067, CA, raises some potential problems with the interaction between whole agreement clauses and disclosure letters. This was an interlocutory hearing, which went to the Court of Appeal, over whether a particular part of a defence should be struck out. The case concerned a share sale agreement, under which the plaintiff bought and the defendant sold the company concerned. The defendant delivered a disclosure letter, and warranted that the disclosure letter disclosed all material facts and circumstances which might reasonably be expected to affect the decision of a purchaser entering into the agreement. The agreement further provided that no other information of which the purchaser had actual, constructive or imputed knowledge should prevent the purchaser from bringing a claim for breach of warranty. The purchaser made warranty claims after completion in respect of matters which had not been disclosed. The seller raised as a defence the fact that the purchaser had in fact been aware of those matters prior to conclusion of the agreement with the consequence that neither party intended the facts to be material for the purposes of the agreement, that it was unconscionable for the purchaser to complain of facts already within his actual knowledge, that his complaint was fraudulent, and that the price which he had paid for the shares must have reflected the facts known to the purchaser at the time of conclusion of the agreement. The purchaser applied to have the defence struck out on the grounds that the terms of the agreement precluded any reliance by the seller, on the fact that the purchaser knew of the matters in question, in order to defeat a warranty claim. The Court of Appeal dismissed the application and held that the defences raised by the seller could not be regarded as unarguable for the purposes of striking them out.

The case was never heard on the merits, so the decision remains, at least arguably, good law, and, in the absence of contrary ruling on similar facts in a decision on the merits, the case continues to raise two problems for purchasers.

First, purchasers may well, as a result of preliminary investigations, or even due diligence, carried out before the agreement is signed, have actual or constructive knowledge of matters in respect of which they may well wish to raise a claim for breach of warranty later. If this is so, and *Eurocopy* when heard on the merits upholds the seller's defence, then only a plain listing of these facts in the agreement, and the granting by the seller of an express indemnity in respect of them, is likely to provide a remedy to the purchaser. The problem is likely to be at its greatest where the agreement is signed and completion takes place on the same day, because then any investigations or due diligence will have been carried out before conclusion of the agreement and before delivery of the disclosure letter. Where (as in Precedent 2) there is an interval between signature and completion, due diligence takes place in that interval, and the disclosure letter is delivered on signature, there is in practice likely to be less of a problem, because the purchaser will know less about the target company before the agreement is concluded. On this basis the procedure for dealing with claims arising as a result of due diligence investigations between signature and completion, as set out in Precedent Two, would remain unaffected.

The other issue is that in many cases it is usual to 'negotiate' the contents of a disclosure letter. If the purchaser is unwilling to accept the risk of a particular matter shown in a draft disclosure letter, then he will demand that it be deleted from the final document. If the seller agrees to this, a decision on the merits, in favour of the defendant, in *Eurocopy*, would make this practice of doubtful efficacy. Again express listing of the matter in question, and the granting of an indemnity by the purchaser, would be the most prudent way to proceed.

Heads of agreement for share sale

---

1 These Heads of Agreement are entered into on [   ] by:

1.1 [   ] Limited (the 'Purchaser') and

1.2[   ] (the 'Shareholders') of [   ] Limited (the 'Company').

2 The Shareholders have agreed in principle and subject to contract to sell with full title guarantee and the Purchaser has agreed in principle and subject to contract to purchase the whole of the issued share capital of the Company for the sum of £[   ], completion to take place during the month of [   ].

[**3** The undertaking, assets and liabilities of the branch of the Company which is situated at [   ] and carries on the business of [   ] in the county of [   ] are excluded from and shall form no part of the transaction.]

4 These Heads of Agreement are subject to:

4.1 a full investigation and audit report on the affairs and business of the Company satisfactory to the Purchaser by the Purchaser's auditors Messrs [   ] being received not later than [   ], which investigation shall be commenced forthwith upon the signature hereof and in respect of which the Shareholders shall extend all necessary co-operation to the Purchaser and the Purchaser's auditors;

[**4.2** the granting of all necessary governmental and other consents including without limitation a determination by the Office of Fair Trading that no reference in relation to this transaction shall be made to the [Monopolies and Mergers Commission] [Competition Commission] and any necessary grant of exemptions or consents by the Commission of the European Community pursuant to art 85(3) of the Treaty of Rome or the EC Merger Control Regulation (4064/1989). In the event any such consents or authorities are not obtained within a reasonable period following the date of signature hereof, the parties shall assess the situation and determine jointly a suitable course of action;]

4.3 the negotiation, agreement and signature of a suitable definitive agreement appropriate to the transaction detailed herein with the following special matters to be included:

4.3.1 if the net assets of the Company as shown by the audited accounts of the Company for its financial year ending on [   ] (to be prepared by the Purchaser no later than [60] days after completion on the same basis as the audited accounts of the Company for its financial year ending on [   ]), are less than [   ], then an amount equal to such shortfall shall forthwith be paid over to the Purchaser by the Shareholders *pro rata* to their shareholdings;

4.3.2 the balance sheet of the Company as at [   ] shall be warranted and the financial affairs of the Company on the completion date shall be in no way worse than the position disclosed in that balance sheet; and

4.3.3 warranties appropriate to the transaction shall be given by the Shareholders to the Purchaser (including without limitation a general warranty of the collectability of all receivables of the Company after making allowance for bad debt reserves) and a retention out of the purchase price of the Company shall be retained [by the Purchaser] [deposited in escrow in an interest bearing account] for periods to be agreed to cover possible claims for breaches of such warranties.

5 Save as required by law [or stock exchange regulations] each party shall keep confidential and shall not make a public announcement or other disclosure in respect of these Heads of Agreement or the transaction contemplated herein, without the consent of the other party.

6 The parties shall agree upon the most efficient and cost-effective method of structuring the transactions detailed above, and the parties further undertake to review and, if necessary, to renegotiate any materially affected terms and conditions of these Heads of Agreement if for valid and substantial reasons the transactions are structured so as to cause serious deviations from the original intent.

7 In consideration of the Purchaser (*a*) agreeing to enter into these Heads of Agreement and to negotiate in good faith with the Shareholders concerning the transaction detailed herein, and (*b*) putting in hand the investigation and audit report referred to in cl 4.1, the Shareholders hereby jointly and severally agree with and undertake to the Purchaser the following obligations, each of which shall be a separate obligation, legally binding upon the Shareholders and separately enforceable by the Purchaser as follows:

7.1 the Shareholders shall not, directly or indirectly, knowingly encourage, solicit or initiate, nor engage in or participate in, discussions or negotiations with, nor provide any information to, any company, partnership, person or other entity or group other than the Purchaser (a 'Third Party') concerning any sale, merger, business combination, acquisition or other similar transaction involving the Company or all or any part of the business or undertaking of the Company (whatever the form or nature of such transaction, including without limitation a transaction effected by the sale and purchase or the issue of shares, and/or by the sale and purchase or assignment of any of the assets of the Company) (a 'Prohibited Transaction');

7.2 the Shareholders shall use their best endeavours to have collected up and returned to them all copies of all non-public information they or any person acting on their behalf has distributed to other potential acquirers of the Company or its assets or of any interest therein;

7.3 the Shareholders shall immediately notify the Purchaser, and will disclose to the Purchaser all details, of (i) any proposals they receive to enter into or take any other action in relation to a Prohibited Transaction ('Acquisition Proposal'), (ii) any indications that any person is potentially interested in an Acquisition Proposal or (iii) the initiation and status of discussions or negotiations relating to an Acquisition Proposal;

7.4 if the Shareholders conclude any Prohibited Transaction with a Third Party or an affiliate, associate or subsidiary of such Third Party, then the Shareholders shall pay to the Purchaser the sum of £[   ];

7.5 if these Heads of Agreement terminate pursuant to cll 8.1 or 8.2 the obligations contained in cll 7.1 to 7.4 shall also thereupon terminate and be of no effect *provided that* if these Heads of Agreement terminate pursuant to cl 8.3 the obligations contained in cll 7.3 and 7.4 shall survive such termination and remain in full force and effect for a period of [12 months] after such termination, and shall thereupon terminate automatically upon the expiry of the said period;

7.6 each of the obligations contained in cll 7.1–7.4 inclusive shall be construed as a separate obligation, and if any such obligation shall be held by any court of competent jurisdiction to be illegal or unenforceable, in whole or in part, under any enactment or rule of law, such obligation or part thereof shall to that extent be deemed not to form part of cl 7 but the validity and enforceability of the remainder of cl 7 shall not be affected and the remaining obligations contained therein shall continue to bind the parties.

8 These Heads of Agreement and the understandings herein set forth shall come into effect immediately upon signature by both parties and unless otherwise mutually agreed shall terminate:

8.1 on the execution of a definitive agreement pursuant to cl 4.3 expressly superseding this Memorandum;

8.2 on the date (if any) that the Purchaser notifies the Shareholders in writing that it is no longer interested in effecting the transactions contemplated hereby; or

8.3 on [   ];
whichever first occurs.

9 Except for cll 5, 7 and 10 of these Heads of Agreement, which are intended to be legally binding, and shall so bind the parties, these Heads of Agreement are not intended to be legally binding nor do they represent a complete summary of the contractual or commercial aims of the parties, but express their current desires and understandings subject to obtaining legal and other professional advice. These Heads of Agreement will form the basis of negotiation for the definitive agreement referred to in cl 4.3, but, save in respect of cll 5, 7 and 10 as aforesaid, neither party is legally obligated to the other unless and until such an agreement is signed by both parties and has become effective in accordance with its terms.

10 The construction validity and performance of these Heads of Agreement shall be governed by the laws of England.

Signed:

For the Purchaser   For the Shareholders

Precedent 2

Share sale agreement

THIS AGREEMENT is made the [   ] day of [   ]
19[   ] between (1) [   ] Limited whose registered office is at
[   ] and [   ] Limited whose registered office is at
[   ] (the 'Vendors') and (2) [   ] Limited whose registered office is at [   ] (the 'Purchaser')

WHEREAS the Vendors have agreed with the Purchaser for the sale of
[   ] Limited (the 'Company') being a company registered in England, with registered number [   ], the entire issued share capital
of which is at the date of this Agreement beneficially owned by the Vendors;

NOW, THEREFORE, IT IS HEREBY AGREED AS FOLLOWS:

1   Definitions

For the purposes of this Agreement:
'Agreed Price Reduction' is defined in cl 2.5.2.1;
'Arbitrator's Price Reduction' is defined in cl 2.5.9;
'Arbitrator's Price Increase' is defined in cl 2.5.10;
'Balance Sheet' means the balance sheet and profit and loss statement for the
Company for the [12] month period ending on the Balance Sheet Date;
'Balance Sheet Date' means [   ] 19[   ];
'Business Day' means any day on which [clearing] banks are open for busi-
ness in [London, England];
'Business Hours' means [9am–5pm inclusive on any Business Day] [those
hours on the Business Day in question during which clearing banks are open
for business in London, England];
'Compensation Amount' is defined in cl 2.5.2;

'Completion' means the process of completing the sale and purchase of the Shares in accordance with cl 3;

'Completion Accounts' means the balance sheet and profit and loss statement for the Company for the [12] month period ending on the [Completion Date];

'Completion Certificate' is defined in cl 2.4;

'Completion Date' means the applicable date determined pursuant to the provisions of cl 2.5 (or such other date as the parties shall agree) on which Completion takes place;

'Cure Period' is defined in cl 2.5.1;

'Disclosure Letter' means the disclosure letter of even date herewith (including all the annexes and exhibits thereto) signed by the Vendor, delivered to the Purchasers upon the date of signature hereof, and signed upon such delivery by the Purchaser to signify acceptance of its contents and acknowledgment of receipt thereof;

'Due Diligence Period' is defined in cl 2.3;

'Due Diligence Report' is defined in cl 2.4;

'Existing Commitments' means all contracts of the Company on the Completion Date and all bids by the Company outstanding on the Completion Date which subsequently become binding contracts upon the terms contained in those bids;

'Loss' or 'Losses' means any and all liabilities, losses, costs, claims, damage (including special, indirect and consequential damage), penalties and expenses (including reasonable legal fees and expenses and reasonable costs of investigation and litigation). In the event any of the foregoing are indemnifiable pursuant to Schedule Three, the terms 'Loss' and 'Losses' shall also include any and all reasonable legal fees and expenses and reasonable costs of investigation and litigation incurred by the Purchaser in enforcing such indemnity;

'Net Asset Value' means the value of the net assets of the Company as shown in the Completion Accounts as prepared and audited pursuant to cl 3.5 and Schedule 1;

'Pension Schemes' is defined in para 5.5 of Schedule 2;

'Person' means an individual, corporation, government or governmental subdivision or agency, business trust, estate, trust, partnership, or association, two or more of any of the foregoing having a joint or common interest, or any other legal or commercial entity or undertaking; and 'Persons' shall be construed accordingly;

'Purchase Price' is defined in cl 3.6;

'Requisite Consents' is defined in cl 2.2;

'Shares' means the [   ] ordinary shares of [   ] each of the Company;

'Sub-Contracts' means the subcontracts entered into in order to enable the performance of, or otherwise in connection with, the Existing Commitments;

'Tax' includes (but is not limited to) income tax, corporation tax, advance corporation tax, capital gains tax, development land tax, development gains tax, social security and earnings related contributions, income tax payable by way of Pay-As-You-Earn ('PAYE') deductions, estate duty, inheritance tax, capital transfer tax, stamp duty and value added tax, and all costs, charges, interest, penalties, surcharges and expenses related to any disallowance of relief or claim for taxation;

'Threshold' is defined in cl 2.5.2.1;

'Unilateral Price Reduction' is defined in cl 2.5.7;

'Warranties' means the warranties set forth in Sched 2; and 'Warranty' shall be construed accordingly;

in this agreement reference to a 'day' means a period of twenty-four hours ending at twelve midnight, reference to a 'month' means a calendar month, and reference to a 'year' means any period of twelve consecutive months;

all references to a statutory provision shall be construed as including references to:

(*a*)   any statutory modification, consolidation or re-enactment (whether before or after the date of this Agreement) for the time being in force;

(*b*)   all statutory instruments or orders made pursuant to a statutory provision;

(*c*)   any statutory provisions of which a statutory provision is a consolidation, re-enactment or modification;

unless otherwise stated, a reference to a clause or a schedule is a reference to a clause of or a schedule to this Agreement;

the schedules and appendices to this Agreement constitute an integral part thereof;

the Headings in this Agreement are for convenience only and shall not constrain or affect its construction or interpretation in any way whatsoever;

references to days or dates (including without limitation the Completion Date) which do not fall on a Business Day shall be construed as references to the day or date falling on the immediately subsequent Business Day;

wherever in this Agreement a period of time is referred to, the day upon which that period commences shall be the day after the day from which the period is expressed to run, or the day after the day upon which the event occurs which causes the period to start running;

as used in this Agreement, the term 'to the best of the knowledge, information and belief' when used in relation to the Vendors shall mean (*a*) within the actual knowledge, information and belief of any director, officer, employee, agent or representative of the Vendors or of the Company, and (*b*) within the knowledge, information and belief that any of the same would have gained after making due and careful enquiry into the matter in question;

where the context so admits, any reference to the singular includes the plural, any reference to the plural includes the singular, and any reference to one gender includes all genders; and

any reference to a 'party' means the Vendors or the Purchaser and references to the 'parties' shall be construed accordingly.

2   Sale and purchase of the shares

2.1 In consideration of the Purchase Price to be paid by the Purchaser to the Vendor and subject to the terms and conditions hereof the Vendors shall sell (with full title guarantee s), and the Purchaser shall purchase, the Shares, free from all claims, liens, charges, encumbrances and equities together with all rights attached or accruing thereto (including without limitation accrued dividends if any).

2.2 The Vendors and the Purchasers shall (immediately upon the signature hereof) seek the grant of all governmental and other consents necessary to enable Completion lawfully to take place (the 'Requisite Consents') including without limitation a determination by the Office of Fair Trading that no reference in relation to this transaction shall be made to the [Monopolies and Mergers Commission] [Competition Commission] and/or any necessary grant of exemptions or consents by the Commission of the European Community pursuant to art 85(3) of the Treaty of Rome or the EEC Merger Control Regulation (4064/1989).

2.3 For a period (the 'Due Diligence Period') commencing on the day after the date of signature hereof and ending either [60] days thereafter or [seven] days after the date upon which the last of the Requisite Consents was granted (whichever last occurs) the Vendors will ensure that the directors, officers, employees, representatives and agents of the Company (including the Company's auditors) afford the Purchaser and its representatives, including its lawyers and auditors, such access to the Company's records, premises, accounts and management personnel, during Business Hours, as the Purchaser and its representatives may reasonably require so that the Purchaser may perform a purchase investigation of the Company's business, financial and legal condition. [The Purchaser will conduct such purchase investigation in co-operation with the Company so as to minimise any disruption to the Company's business.]

2.4 Upon the last day of the Due Diligence Period, the Purchaser shall deliver to the Vendors either (*a*) a written report (the 'Due Diligence Report') detailing breaches of the Warranties (or any event, fact or circumstance which, if not cured, would constitute a breach of the Warranties on the Completion Date) of which the Purchaser has become aware during the Due Diligence Period or (*b*) a certificate (the 'Completion Certificate') stating that there are no such breaches events facts or circumstances and that the Purchaser is ready for Completion. (For the avoidance of doubt, the Vendors shall be deemed to be aware of any event, fact or circumstance of which they are notified by the Purchaser in accordance with the preceding sentence, and, accordingly, the Vendors shall be in breach of any relevant Warranty qualified by their awareness (when such Warranty is remade on the Completion Date) if such event, fact or circumstance would constitute a breach of such Warranty if it were not so qualified and such breach is not cured prior to the Completion Date.) If the Purchaser delivers a Completion Certificate, Completion shall take place on the day following the day on which the Completion Certificate was delivered.

2.5 If the Purchaser delivers a Due Diligence Report the following procedure shall apply:

2.5.1 the Vendors shall within a period of fifteen days from the date of delivery of the Due Diligence Report (the 'Cure Period') exercise their [best] [all reasonable] efforts to cure all of the breaches detailed in the Due Diligence Report. If the Vendors cure all of the aforesaid breaches within the Cure Period, Completion shall take place upon the day following the expiry of the Cure Period;

2.5.2 if, and to the extent that, the Vendors are unable to cure all of the aforesaid breaches within the Cure Period, the Vendors shall (also within the Cure Period) negotiate in good faith with the Purchaser (who shall likewise negotiate in good faith) the amount (the 'Compensation Amount') necessary to compensate the Purchaser for such uncured breaches. If the parties agree on the Compensation Amount prior to the expiry of the Cure Period, then:

2.5.2.1 if the Compensation Amount is less than £[   ] (the 'Threshold') the Purchase Price shall be reduced by the Compensation Amount (an 'Agreed Price Reduction') and Completion shall occur upon the day following that on which such agreement is reached; but

2.5.2.2 if the Compensation Amount is equal to or greater than the Threshold, neither the Purchaser nor the Vendors shall be obligated to agree to a reduction in the Purchase Price of the Compensation Amount, neither the Vendors nor the Purchaser shall be obliged to complete the purchase and sale of the Shares, this Agreement shall automatically terminate upon the expiry of the Cure Period and neither party shall be under any liability to the other by reason of such termination;

2.5.3 if the parties are unable to agree on the Compensation Amount but agree prior to the expiry of the Cure Period that it is equal to or greater than the Threshold, neither the Vendors nor the Purchaser shall be obliged to complete the purchase and sale of the Shares, this Agreement shall automatically terminate upon the expiry of the Cure Period and neither party shall be under any liability to the other by reason of such termination;

2.5.4 if the parties are unable to agree on the Compensation Amount, but, prior to the expiry of the Cure Period, agree that it is (or is reasonably likely to be) less than the Threshold, the procedure detailed in cl 2.5.6 shall apply;

2.5.5 if the parties are unable, prior to the expiry of the Cure Period, to agree on the Compensation Amount, and also as to whether it is equal to, greater than or less than the Threshold, then the following procedure shall apply:

2.5.5.1 the parties shall jointly submit the dispute to arbitration pursuant to cl 11, with instructions to the arbitrator to determine the single issue of whether the Compensation Amount is reasonably likely to be equal to, greater than or less than the Threshold; and

2.5.5.2 if the arbitrator determines that the Compensation Amount is reasonably likely to be equal to or greater than the Threshold neither the Vendors nor the Purchaser shall be obliged to complete the purchase and sale of the Shares, this Agreement shall automatically terminate upon the publication by the arbitrator of his determination and neither party shall be under any liability to the other by reason of such termination; and

2.5.5.3 if the arbitrator determines that the Compensation Amount is reasonably likely to be less than the Threshold, then, the procedure detailed in cl 2.5.6 shall apply;

2.5.6 within three days from the day on which the determination of the arbitrator pursuant to cl 2.5.5.3 is made or the agreement of the parties pursuant to cl 2.5.4 (as the case may be) occurs, the Purchaser shall make an offer to the Vendors of the amount the Purchaser is willing to accept, and the Vendors shall make an offer to the Purchaser of the amount the Vendors are willing to pay, in settlement as the Compensation Amount;

2.5.7 within seven days from the day on which the exchange of offers described in cl 2.5.6, takes place, the Purchaser may exercise an option to reduce the Purchase Price by the average of the amount offered by the Purchaser and the amount offered by the Vendors (a 'Unilateral Price Reduction'). If the Purchaser exercises such option, Completion shall take place three days from the day on which the exercise of such option occurs, and the amount in dispute shall be submitted to arbitration on or after the Completion Date in accordance with cl 11, and the parties shall jointly instruct the arbitrator to award one of the Purchaser, on the one hand, or the Vendors, on the other hand, fifty per cent (50 per cent) of the difference between the amount set out in the Purchaser's offer and the amount set out in the Vendors' offer and not to make an award in any other amount (except for fees and expenses);

2.5.8 if the Purchaser does not exercise its option described in cl 2.5.6, then Completion shall take place on the tenth day from the day on which the exchange of offers described in cl 2.5.6 takes place. In such event the Purchaser shall be compensated for the Losses arising from the breaches of the Warranties identified pursuant to cl 2.4 and not cured by the Purchaser pursuant to cl 2.5.1 by (i) indemnification in respect of such Losses after the Completion Date in accordance with but subject to Schedule 3 and/or (ii) the reflecting of such Losses as liabilities in the Completion Accounts to the extent required by cl 3.5 and Schedule 1; and Completion shall be without prejudice to the Purchaser's rights to seek indemnification for such Losses after the Completion Date in accordance with cl 4 and Schedule 3, and without prejudice to the rights of the Vendors to assert that such Losses are not subject to indemnification in accordance with cl 4 and Schedule 3;

2.5.9 the amount of any award made by the arbitrator in favour of the Purchaser pursuant to cl 2.5.7 (an 'Arbitrator's Price Reduction') shall be treated

392 *Drafting Commercial Agreements*

as a reduction in the Purchase Price, the Purchase Price shall be reduced by the amount of such award, and the Vendors shall pay such amount to the Purchaser in cash within 30 days from the making of the relevant award by the arbitrator;

2.5.10 the amount of any award made by the arbitrator in favour of the Vendor pursuant to cl 2.5.7 (an 'Arbitrator's Price Increase') shall be treated as an increase in the Purchase Price, the Purchase Price shall be increased by the amount of such award, and the Purchaser shall pay such amount to the Vendors in cash within 30 days from the making of the relevant award by the arbitrator;

2.5.11 nothing contained in cll 2.5.4–2.5.11 inclusive shall prevent the parties from reaching a mutual agreement at any time before or after the expiry of the Cure Period (i) on the termination of any of the procedures described in the said clauses which are then in progress, (ii) on the fixing of an amount as the Compensation Amount (irrespective of whether such amount is greater than, equal to or less than the Threshold), and (iii) on a reduction of the Purchase Price by the relevant Agreed Price Reduction; and

2.5.12 if the parties reach an agreement pursuant to cl 2.5.11, Completion shall take place three days from the day on which such agreement was finalised.

2.6 Notwithstanding anything contained in cll 2.4 or 2.5 no account shall be taken of any breach of the Warranties for the purposes of cll 2.4 and 2.5, and the Vendors shall not be obliged to compensate the Purchaser prior to Completion pursuant to cll 2.4 and 2.5 for the Loss claimed by the Purchaser in respect of such breach:

2.6.1 if such Loss arises from any matter truly and fairly disclosed in the Disclosure Letter;

2.6.2 unless the amount of such Loss exceeds [£10,000]; provided, however, that if the aggregate amount of all such Losses less than or equal to [£10,000] exceeds [£500,000], the Vendors shall, subject to subsection (*b*), be liable for all such Losses less than or equal to [£10,000];

2.6.3 in respect of any Loss if but only to the extent that it would not have occurred but for any voluntary act, omission or transaction of the Purchaser after the date of signature hereof and prior to the Completion Date (including a change in any accounting policy or practice of the Purchaser) done or omitted to be done other than in the ordinary course of business;

2.6.4 if but only to the extent that such Loss is covered by a policy of insurance covering the Company and payment is made under such policy to the Company by the insurer prior to the expiry of the Due Diligence Period;

2.6.5 if but only to the extent that such Loss relates to any matter or thing done or omitted to be done by the Vendors or caused by the Vendors to be done or omitted to be done by the Company (being a matter or thing which the Vendors are not obliged to do or omit to do or cause the Company to do or omit to do pursuant to the terms of this Agreement) at the written request of or with the written approval of the Purchaser provided that this cl 2.6.5 shall only apply in the case where the Purchaser makes such request or gives such approval with knowledge that it would give rise to a Loss;

2.6.6 if but only to the extent that such Loss arises in relation to any matter required to be done or performed under the terms of this Agreement or required to be carried out in the implementation thereof;

provided that (and for the avoidance of doubt) all claims for Loss in respect of breaches of the Warranties which are less than or equal to [£10,000] but of which no account was taken for the purposes of cll 2.4 and 2.5 by reason of cl 2.6.1 shall be taken account of for the purposes of paras 7(*a*) and (*b*) of Schedule 3.

3 Completion

3.1 Completion shall take place on the Completion Date at [10 am] at [the offices of the Vendors' solicitors, Messrs [   ] at[   ]] [the registered office of the Company].

3.2 At Completion:

3.2.1 the Vendors shall deliver to the Purchaser duly executed transfers in favour of the Purchaser or, if the Purchaser so directs, in favour of a nominee of the Purchaser, in respect of the Shares together with the current share certificates relating to the Shares;

3.2.2 the Vendors shall deliver to the Purchaser or to any person whom the Purchaser may nominate such of the following as the Purchaser may require:

3.2.2.1 the statutory books of the Company (which shall be written up to but not including the Completion Date), its certificate of incorporation and any certificates of incorporation on change of name, and its common seal (if any);

3.2.2.2 all books of account, cheque books, paying in books and unused cheques of the Company;

3.2.2.3 resignations of the Directors and the Secretary from their respective offices in the Company confirming that they have no outstanding claims of any kind against the Company;

3.2.2.4 resignation of the existing auditors of the Company confirming that they have no outstanding claims of any kind against the Company;

3.2.2.5 appropriate forms to amend the mandates given by the Company to its bankers;

3.2.3 the Vendors shall procure that a meeting of the Board of Directors of the Company shall be held at which:

3.2.3.1 such persons as the Purchaser may nominate shall be appointed as additional directors of the Company with immediate effect;

3.2.3.2 the existing directors of the Company shall resign and acknowledge that they have no claims against the Company and such resignations shall be accepted;

3.2.3.3 the Secretary of the Company shall resign and acknowledge that he has no claims against the Company, such resignation shall be accepted, and a person nominated by the Purchaser shall be appointed as Secretary, with immediate effect;

3.2.3.4 the registered office of the Company shall be changed to[   ];

3.2.3.5 the share transfers referred to in cl 3.2.1 shall be approved for registration (subject to stamping);

3.2.3.6 all existing mandates to banks shall be revoked and new instructions shall be given to such banks in such form as the Purchaser may direct; and

3.2.3.7 the resignation of the Company's auditors shall be accepted in favour of Messrs [   ] who shall thereupon be appointed as auditors of the Company with immediate effect;

3.2.4 the Purchaser shall procure that the additional directors to be appointed pursuant to cl 3.2.3.1 attend the said meeting of the Board of Directors and accept office;

[**3.2.5** the Purchaser shall deliver to the Vendors a [cheque] [bankers draft] drawn on a [London bank] in the sum of £[   ] by way of payment of the first instalment of the Purchase Price.]

3.3 Should any Person whose resignation from office the Vendors are obliged to procure in order to comply with cl 3.2.2.3 or 3.2.2.4 bring a claim against the Company by reason of that Person's resignation from office the Vendors shall indemnify the Company against such claim and against all Losses incurred by the Company in connection with such claim.

3.4 To the extent that they shall not already have done so on Completion, and to the extent that the same is within the possession and/or control of the Vendors, the Vendors shall (for a period of [12 months] after the Completion Date) make available to the Company copies of such information, records and data as are necessary for the operations of the Company as are requested by the Purchaser by notice in writing to the Vendors.

3.5 The Completion Accounts shall be prepared and audited in accordance with the provisions of Schedule 1.

3.6 The Purchase Price shall be an amount equal to the aggregate of £[   ] and the Net Asset Value.

3.7 Upon the completion of the preparation and audit of the Completion Accounts pursuant to cl 3.5 the Purchaser shall forthwith deliver to the Vendors a [cheque] [bank draft] drawn on a [London bank] in an amount equal to [the balance of] the Purchase Price [after deduction of the first instalment thereof paid pursuant to cl 3.2.5] plus interest at [   ] per cent on [the balance of] the Purchase Price on and from the Completion Date up to and including the day on which the [cheque] [bank draft] is delivered to the Vendors pursuant to this clause.

4   Warranties

4.1 The Vendors hereby jointly and severally warrant to the Purchaser, in terms of the Warranties, as of the date of this Agreement and as of the Completion Date (as if the Warranties were remade on the Completion Date), and acknowledge that the Purchaser has entered into this Agreement in reliance [only] upon the Warranties and the undertakings contained in this Agreement. Each of the Warranties shall be separate and independent and (subject to cl 2.6.1 and para 7(*i*) of Schedule 3) claims may be made whether or not the Purchaser knew or could have discovered (whether by any investigation made by it or on its behalf into the affairs of the Company or otherwise) that any of the Warranties has not been complied with or carried out or is otherwise untrue or misleading.

4.2 The Vendors jointly and severally undertake to disclose to the Purchaser promptly anything which comes to their notice which is to the knowledge of the Vendors or either of them materially inconsistent with any of the Warranties.

4.3 The Vendors jointly and severally undertake (in the event of any claim being made against either or both of them pursuant to cll 2.4 and 2.5 and/or cl 4.4 and Schedule 3) not to make any claim against the Company or its employees in respect of the matter giving rise to such claim.

4.4 In the event any Warranty given by the Vendors herein is shown to be incorrect or inaccurate, the Vendors shall jointly and severally indemnify the Purchaser in respect thereof in accordance with and subject to cll 2.4 and 2.5 and/or Schedule 3 as applicable.

4.5 The Purchaser shall, after the date of signature hereof (but subject to the provisions of cll 2.4 and 2.5), have no right to claim that any breach of any Warranty constitutes a repudiation of this Agreement, or to rescind or terminate this Agreement for breach of any of the Warranties. The Purchaser's sole and exclusive remedies in respect of all such breaches shall be pursuant to, in accordance with and subject to the provisions of cll 2.4 and 2.5 and/or Schedule 3 as applicable.

4.6 This Agreement (including the documents and instruments referred to herein) supersedes all prior representations, arrangements, understandings and agreements between the Parties (whether written or oral) relating to the subject matter hereof and sets forth the entire complete and exclusive agreement and understanding between the parties hereto relating to the subject matter hereof.

4.7 No provision contained in this clause, or elsewhere in this Agreement, shall operate so as to exclude any liability of one of the parties in respect of a fraudulent misrepresentation made by that party to the other, or to restrict or exclude any remedy which the other party may have in respect of such misrepresentation.

5   Pension arrangements

The provisions of Schedule 4 shall apply in relation to pensions.

6   Insurance

6.1 With effect from the day after the Completion Date, the Company shall cease to have the benefit of any insurance policy held by the Vendors except in respect of any act or omission (for which insurance was maintained prior to the Completion Date), which occurred prior to the Completion Date and which is notified in writing by the Purchaser to the Vendor within a time sufficient to enable a claim to be made against the relevant insurance policy after the same has come to the notice of the Purchaser.

6.2 The Vendors will, at their own cost, at the request of the Purchaser, pursue any claim which the Company is entitled to make under any insurance policy in respect of any loss suffered by the Company as a result of any act or omission for which insurance is maintained and which occurred prior to completion and will account to the Company or, as the case may be, the Purchaser, for the proceeds (if any) recovered in respect of any such claim.

7   Assignment

This Agreement shall not be assignable by either of the parties hereto without the prior written consent of the other party hereto.

8 Press release

No press release, notice or other public announcement concerning the transactions set out herein shall be made or issued (other than to the extent required by law [or stock exchange regulations]) by one party hereto without the prior written approval of the other.

9 Costs and expenses

9.1 Each party shall pay its own costs in relation to the negotiations leading up to the sale of the Shares and to the preparation, execution and carrying into effect of this Agreement and of all other documents referred to in it.

9.2 Without prejudice to the generality of cl 9.1 the Purchaser shall be responsible for the stamping of the transfers of the Shares delivered by the Vendors pursuant to cl 3.2.1 and for the payment of the relevant stamp duty.

10 Survival of warranties

The Warranties, and all undertakings or representations contained in, or obligations imposed by, this Agreement, shall survive Completion and continue in full force and effect notwithstanding Completion, except for those obligations to be performed on or prior to Completion but only to the extent that they have been so performed.

11 Arbitration

Any question or difference which is to be referred to arbitration pursuant to any provision of this Agreement shall be referred to a single arbitrator in London to be agreed between the parties. Failing such agreement within [seven] days of the request by one party to the other that such a question or difference be referred to arbitration in accordance with this clause such reference shall be to an arbitrator appointed by the President for the time being of the Law Society of England and Wales. The decision of such arbitrator shall be final and binding upon the parties. Any reference under this clause shall be deemed to be a reference to arbitration within the meaning of the Arbitration Act 1996.

12 Service of notice

12.1 Any notice and any certificate permission consent licence approval or other communication or authorisation to be served upon or delivered or given or communicated to one party hereto by the other (in this clause called a 'communication') shall be in the form of a document in writing including without limitation a telex or telegram but not a facsimile or an electronic mail message.

12.2 All communication shall be made to the Vendors at the following address or to the following telex number:
Address:
Telex No:
For the attention of: [the Company Secretary]
and to the Purchaser at the following address or to the following telex number:
Address:
Telex Number
For the attention of: [the Company Secretary]

12.3 All communications shall be delivered by hand during Business Hours or sent by telegram or telex or sent by registered post (where possible by airmail).

12.4 A communication shall have effect for the purposes of this Agreement and shall be deemed to have been delivered to and received by the party to whom it was addressed:
12.4.1 if delivered by hand upon receipt by the relevant person for whose attention it should be addressed as provided above, or upon receipt by any other person then upon the premises at the relevant address who reasonably appears to be authorised to receive post or other messages on behalf of the relevant party;
12.4.2 if sent by telex upon the transmission of the communication to the relevant telex number and the receipt by the transmitting telex machine of an answer-back code showing that the telex message has been received properly by the telex machine to which it was transmitted; and
12.4.3 if sent by telegram [twenty four hours] after the text of the cable has been given to the relevant telegraph company or other authority for transmission unless before the expiry of that period an advice of inability to deliver is received by the party making the communication;
12.4.4 if sent by registered post [seven days] from the date upon the registration receipt provided by the relevant postal authority.

12.5 Each party shall be obliged to send a communication to the other in accordance with this clause notifying any changes in the relevant details set out in the second paragraph of this clause, which details shall then be deemed to have been amended accordingly.

13   Termination

13.1 If the Requisite Consents are not obtained within a period of six months from the date hereof, then (unless the parties otherwise agree) neither the Vendors nor the Purchaser shall be obliged to complete the purchase and sale of the Shares, this Agreement shall automatically terminate upon the expiry of the said period and neither party shall be under any liability to the other by reason of such termination.

13.2 If Completion has not taken place within a period of six months from the date upon which the Cure Period has expired because the parties have submitted to arbitration pursuant to cl 2.5.5 a dispute as to whether the Compensation Amount is greater than equal to or less than the Threshold, and the arbitrator has not yet made an award in respect of such dispute, then (unless the parties otherwise agree) neither the Vendors nor the Purchaser shall be obliged to complete the purchase and sale of the Shares, this Agreement shall automatically terminate upon the expiry of the said period and neither party shall be under any liability to the other by reason of such termination, [save that, if the arbitrator subsequently makes a determination that the Compensation Amount was reasonably likely to have been less than the Threshold, then the party who contended that it was greater than or equal to the Threshold shall be liable to compensate the other party for all Losses suffered by the other party as a result of such termination and the failure of the transaction contemplated by this Agreement].

14   Set-off

Whenever under this Agreement or any other agreement or contract binding upon the parties any sum of money shall be recoverable from or payable by one party hereto (the 'paying party') to the other party (the 'receiving party'), the same may be deducted from any sum then due or which at any time thereafter may become due to the paying party from the receiving party under this Agreement or any other agreement or contract between the paying party and the receiving party.

15   Governing law

The construction, validity and performance of this Agreement shall be governed by the laws of England.

IN WITNESS WHEREOF, the Parties hereto have signed and executed this Agreement on the date first above mentioned.

SCHEDULE 1
Preparation and audit of Completion Accounts

1 Not later than the expiry of a period of [60] days from the Completion Date, the Purchaser shall cause the appropriate employees of the Company to prepare the Completion Accounts, and to deliver them to the auditors of the Purchaser, Messrs [   ] (the 'Purchaser Auditors') and to the auditors of the Vendors, Messrs [   ] (the 'Vendor Auditors').

2 The Completion Accounts shall be prepared in accordance with the requirements of the relevant statutes and [the Purchaser's accounting policies] [the Vendor's accounting policies] [the accounting policies set out in the Appendix to this Schedule], to show a true and fair view of the state of affairs of the Company as at the Completion Date and of its operations for the [12 month] period ending on the Completion Date, provision to be made in the Completion Accounts to the extent required by good accounting practice for all liabilities (actual or contingent), all financial commitments in existence at the Completion Date and all unusual or non-recurring items; and the Completion Accounts will reserve or provide in full for all Tax or other sums imposed, charged, assessed, levied or payable for which the Company was liable at the Completion Date and for any contingent or possible deferred liability for Tax *provided that* no account shall be taken in the preparation of the Completion Accounts of any liability or contingent liability of the Company in respect of which [but only to the extent that] the Purchaser has received an Agreed Price Reduction pursuant to cl 2.5.2.1, or in respect of which a Unilateral Price Reduction coupled with a submission to arbitration has been made pursuant to cl 2.5.7.

3 The Purchaser Auditors and the Vendor Auditors shall, after receipt thereof, conduct an audit of the Completion Accounts and shall complete such audit within thirty (30) days. As part of such audit, the Purchaser Auditors and the Vendor Auditors shall determine the Net Asset Value.

4 If the Purchaser Auditors and the Vendor Auditors agree on the Completion Accounts and the determination of the Net Asset Value, they shall jointly sign an auditor's certificate (in the form set out in Appendix A to this Schedule) as to the preparation of the Completion Accounts and the determination of the Net Asset Value. The Purchaser Auditors and the Vendor Auditors shall deliver the original Completion Accounts, together with the original of their signed auditors' certificate, to the Purchaser, and shall deliver copies of the same to the Vendors.

5 If the Vendor Auditors and the Purchaser Auditors cannot agree jointly to sign such a certificate, they shall, within forty-five (45) days after their receipt of the Completion Accounts, deliver to the Purchaser and the Vendors a list of disputed adjustments (the 'Disputed Adjustments'), together with a statement setting forth the effect of the Disputed Adjustments on the determination of the Net Asset Value. The Purchaser and the Vendors shall use their best endeavours to resolve the Disputed Adjustments. If the Purchaser and the Vendors are able to reach an agreement on the Disputed Adjustments and their effect, the Completion Accounts shall, if necessary, be amended to reflect such agreement and the Purchaser Auditors and the Vendor Auditors shall thereupon issue their auditors' certificate on the basis of the Completion Accounts as so adjusted.

6 If the Purchaser and the Vendors are unable to reach an agreement on all Disputed Adjustments within fifteen (15) days after their receipt of the Disputed Adjustments, the Purchaser and the Vendors shall appoint an independent accounting firm [with significant international experience] [of repute] or, if they fail to agree on such a firm within seven (7) days after the expiry of such fifteen (15) day period, they shall submit the still Disputed Adjustments to an independent accounting firm appointed, upon application of either party, by the President for the time being of the Institute of Chartered Accountants in England and Wales (in either case, the 'Independent Accountant'). The Purchaser and the Vendor shall deliver a list of the still Disputed Adjustments to the Independent Accountant who shall act as expert and not as an arbitrator. The Purchaser and the Vendor shall instruct the Independent Accountant to review the still Disputed Adjustments and determine the final value of each still Disputed Adjustment promptly and, in any event, within thirty (30) days after the Independent Accountant's receipt of the list of still Disputed Adjustments. In making such determination, the Independent Accountants shall consider only the still Disputed Adjustments (and any other items or amounts necessary to derive the still Disputed Adjustments). The Completion Accounts shall then be amended and signed by the Purchaser Auditors and the Vendor Auditors to reflect the Independent Accountant's determination of the final value of each Disputed Adjustment and shall thereupon issue their auditors' certificate on the basis of the Completion Accounts as so adjusted.

7 The fees, costs and expenses of the Vendor Auditors in conducting the audit of the Completion Accounts shall be borne by the Vendors, and the fees, costs and expenses of the Purchaser Auditors in conducting the audit of the Completion Accounts shall be borne by the Purchaser. The fees, costs and expenses of the Independent Accountant in conducting its review of the Disputed Adjustments shall be borne equally by the Purchaser and the Vendors.

8 The parties shall procure that the Purchaser Auditors, the Vendor Auditors and, if applicable, the Independent Accountant, shall have full access to all books, information and records and reasonable access to facilities, employees, consultants and professional advisers (including the Purchaser Auditors and the Vendor Auditors) relating to the Company in order to make any determination required by this Schedule.

[APPENDIX ONE
Accounting Policies]

APPENDIX TWO
Auditors' Certificate

The attached balance sheet and profit and loss account of [   ] Limited (the 'Company') are the Completion Accounts of the Company, as defined in the Agreement for the sale of all of the issued share capital of the Company, made between [   ] and [   ] on [   ] (the 'Agreement').

The Completion Accounts have been prepared in accordance with the provisions of the Agreement (including without limitation Schedule One thereof) and show a true and fair view of the state of affairs of the Company as at [   ] (the 'Completion Date' as defined in the Agreement).

The Net Asset Value (as defined in the Agreement) derived from the Completion Accounts for the purposes of the Agreement (including without limitation cl 3.6) is £[   ].

Signed etc

SCHEDULE TWO
Warranties

The Vendors jointly and severally warrant to the Purchaser as follows:

1   Information

The information contained in this Agreement and the Schedules hereto and in the Disclosure Letter and the exhibits and annexes thereto is true and accurate in all material respects.

2   Corporate authority and standing

2.1 The Vendors have full power and authority to enter into and perform this Agreement and this Agreement when executed will constitute a valid binding obligation on the Vendors, in accordance with its terms.

2.2 The Company is a corporation in good standing, duly organised and validly existing under the [laws of England], and has all corporate power and legal authority to carry on its business as now being conducted.

2.3 [To the best of the Vendors' knowledge, information and belief] the business of the Company has at all times been conducted in accordance with all applicable laws, regulations and bye-laws in the United Kingdom and in any relevant foreign country and [to the best of their knowledge, information and belief] there is no investigation or enquiry, order, decree or judgment of any court or any governmental agency or regulatory body outstanding or anticipated against the Vendors or the Company which may have a [material] adverse effect upon the business of the Company.

3 Inter-company indebtedness

At completion the Company will have no indebtedness of any amount or nature whatsoever to the Vendors or to any subsidiary or holding company of the Vendors or to any subsidiary of such holding company other than accruals in the ordinary course of trading.

4 Company accounts

4.1 The Balance Sheet has been prepared in accordance with the requirements of the relevant statutes and the accounting policies set out in the notes to the accounts (which policies have been applied consistently in each case with the previous accounting period, except as stated in such notes) and shows a true and fair view of the state of affairs of the Company as at the Balance Sheet Date and of its operations for the [12] months ended on the Balance Sheet Date and provision is made in the Balance Sheet (and/or disclosure is made in the notes thereto) to the extent required by good accounting practice of all liabilities (actual or contingent), all financial commitments and all unusual or non-recurring items.

4.2 The Balance Sheet reserves or provides in full for all Tax of any nature whatsoever or other sums imposed, charged, assessed, levied or payable for which the Company was liable at the Balance Sheet Date and to the extent required by good accounting practice the Balance Sheet reserves (and/or disclosure is made in the notes thereto) in full for any contingent or possible deferred liability for Tax.

4.3 Since the Balance Sheet Date and until the Completion Date there has not been any [material] adverse change in the financial or trading position of the Company and no dividend or other distribution has or will at Completion have been declared, paid or made by the Company.

4.4 Since the Balance Sheet Date and until the Completion Date:

4.4.1 the Company has carried on business in the ordinary course;

4.4.2 the Company has not entered into any contract, obligation or commitment except in the ordinary course of business;

4.4.3 there has not been any change in the assets or liabilities or contingent liabilities (including Tax) of the Company except for changes arising in the ordinary course of business.

4.4 The assets, investments or policies held by the trustees of the pension plans of the Company are sufficient as at the Completion Date to satisfy the liabilities and obligations (both current and contingent) which the said pension plans have to their members at the Completion Date, it being understood that between the date of signature hereof and the Completion Date the Company shall continue to deduct and pay over to the said pension plans the relevant employee contributions and (if any) employer contributions.

4.5 Accounts receivable of the Company as at the Completion Date will be recoverable in full in the ordinary course of business within a period of [90 days] from the Completion Date (less any provision for bad debts made in the Completion Accounts) and (except as otherwise provided for) none of such accounts receivable is subject to any counterclaim or set off or has been written off or has proved to any extent to be irrecoverable or is now regarded by the Company as irrecoverable in whole or in part.

4.6 The plant, machinery, equipment, vehicles and other equipment and fixed assets (other than leasehold improvements) used in connection with the business of the Company are necessary, appropriate and, in so far as not required for the business of the Company, can be disposed of at not less than net book value within [12 months] from the Completion Date.

4.7 All of the Company's inventory is at an appropriate level for its business, and will be sold within the ordinary course of business within [12 months] from the Completion Date.

5 Employment

5.1 No trade union is recognised or bound to be recognised by the Vendors as representing any of the employees of the Company.

5.2 The basis of the remuneration payable to the directors and employees of the Company at the Completion Date is the same as that in force at the Balance Sheet Date and the Company is under no contractual or other obligation to make a material increase in the rates of remuneration of or to make any bonus or incentive or other similar payment to any of its directors or employees at any future date.

5.3 All agreements for service or contracts of employment with the directors or employees of the Company may be terminated by not more than three months' notice without payment of compensation or damages other than pursuant to statutory provisions.

5.4 No moneys other than in respect of emoluments are payable to any director or senior employee of the Company, no director or employee has the benefit of any unusual terms of employment and the Company is not under any present, future or contingent liability to pay compensation for loss of office or employment to any ex-officer or ex-employee of the Company.

5.5 There have been disclosed to the Purchaser full details of all legal [and moral] liabilities of the Company to pay or contribute towards the provision of retirement and death benefits, pensions, lump sums, and/or gratuities to or for the benefit of all past and present employees of the Company including without limitation all ex gratia or unfunded promises and any unapproved arrangements (collectively the 'Pension Schemes') and the Vendors have delivered to the Purchaser a complete copy of all trust deeds, rules and explanatory literature (including members' booklets) relating to each of the Pension Schemes.

6 Contracts

6.1 All Existing Commitments and all Sub-Contracts are being performed by all the parties thereto substantially on time, substantially within budget and in accordance with all of the material terms and conditions thereof. None of the Existing Commitments or the Sub-Contracts has given rise to any claim by any of the parties thereto, or by any subcontractor or by any third party, for payment of damages or for any other demand, or is the subject of any dispute or allegation of breach or of any disagreement on invoicing or payment, and no performance bond or guarantee in respect thereof has been called. None of the Existing Commitments or Sub-Contracts has been the subject of any dispute, allegation of breach or disagreement on invoicing or payment, which in any such case is of a material nature, during the period of [two years] immediately preceding the date hereof.

6.2 Each of the Existing Commitments are or are capable of being entered into on prices terms and conditions which provide a reasonable profit, and there has been no [material] adverse change in the level of profitability of any of the Existing Commitments between the Balance Sheet Date and the Completion Date.

6.3 [To the best of the Vendors' knowledge, information and belief] none of the Existing Commitments is invalid, unenforceable, or can be cancelled or repudiated or is in material breach, or can be rescinded, avoided or terminated, and the Vendors have received no notice of any intention to terminate, cancel, repudiate or disclaim any of the Existing Commitments and [to the best of the Vendors' knowledge, information and belief] neither this Agreement nor the consummation, performance or completion of any of its provisions would give rise to any of the foregoing.

6.4 Neither this Agreement nor the consummation, performance or completion of any of its provisions will entitle any person who is a party to any contract, rental agreement, lease, licence or other agreement (which in any such case has a value to the Company of £[   ] or more and to which the Company is a party) to terminate the same. [To the best of the Vendor's know-ledge information and belief] neither this Agreement nor the consummation performance or completion of any of its provisions will or is likely to cause any person who is a party to one or more of the Existing Commitments not to continue to do business on materially the same basis with the relevant Company.

7   Litigation

7.1 Neither the Company nor any Person for whose acts or defaults the Company may be vicariously liable is a party in any civil, criminal or arbitration proceedings or any administrative or investigative proceedings or enquiries, and no written representation or intimation of any breach of contract or other duty has been received, which has threatened, or is likely to give rise to, any such proceedings, nor [to the best of the Vendors' knowledge, information and belief] are there any circumstances which [are likely to] [will] give rise to any such violation or proceedings.

8   Properties, plant and equipment

8.1 The properties listed in Schedule Five comprise all the land and premises owned, controlled or occupied by the Company. The Company is the beneficial and legal owner in possession of all of the relevant properties listed, free from any encumbrances or any provisions in any leases or licences materially adverse to the Company's use and enjoyment and right to dispose of the properties, and there is no defect in its title to, or any outstanding material breaches of covenant as regards, any of the said properties and there are no circumstances:
  (*a*) which would entitle any landlord:
      (i) to exercise any powers of entry or taking of possession of any lease, agreement or licence under which the Company occupies any of the

said premises; or

(ii) to refrain from fulfilling any obligation to accept a surrender or other termination of any such lease or licence; or

(*b*) which would otherwise restrict the continued possession and enjoyment of the said properties or any part thereof.

8.2 The Company is in actual occupation of each of the said properties and no lease, tenancy or licence has been granted or agreed to be granted to any third party in respect of the said properties or any part thereof.

8.3 There are no outstanding notices, complaints or requirements issued by any local, county or other competent authority in respect of any of the said properties and no proposals, orders, acts or things made or done or, [to the best of the knowledge, information and belief of the Vendors] intended to be made or done by any local, county or any other competent authority concerning the compulsory acquisition of all or any part of the said properties or which would adversely affect the value of the same or any part thereof.

8.4 All deeds and documents necessary to prove such title as the Company has to each of the said properties are in the possession of the Company or its solicitors Messrs [   ].

8.5 The said properties and all buildings and erections and all fixtures and fittings thereon and all plant, machinery, equipment, vehicles and other equipment and fixed assets owned or used by the Company have been [adequately] [properly and fully] maintained [in accordance with industry standards] and [to the best of the Vendors' knowledge, information and belief] are in [reasonably] satisfactory operating condition and repair [having regard to their age and the use to which they are being put].

8.6 All of the tangible and intangible assets used by the Company, including without limitation, all buildings and erections on the said properties, all fixtures and fittings thereon, all stock and work in progress, and all plant, machinery, equipment, vehicles and other equipment and fixed assets are the absolute property of the Company and none is the subject of any option, right to acquire, assignment, mortgage, charge, lien or hypothecation or other encumbrance whatsoever (excepting only liens arising by operation of law in the normal course of trading) or the subject of any factoring arrangement, hire-purchase, conditional sale or credit sale agreement.

9 Intellectual property rights

9.1 The Company owns or is validly licensed to use all intellectual property rights necessary for the carrying on of its business including without limitation for the discharge of the Existing Commitments.

9.2 All agreements and licences (and all provisions thereof) for the use by the Company of the intellectual property rights referred to in warranty 9.1 are valid and subsisting and the Company has not received notice of breach by it of any of the provisions thereof nor [to the best of the Vendors' knowledge, information and belief] is any licensor in material breach of any of the provisions thereof.

9.3 [To the best of the Vendors' knowledge, information and belief,] the processes employed and products and services dealt with in the business of the Company do not infringe any intellectual property rights and [to the best of the Vendor's knowledge, information and belief] no claims of such infringement have been made or are the subject of litigation actual or threatened.

10   Financial, corporate and tax matters

10.1 Except as disclosed in the Balance Sheet there are not any loans, guarantees, material undertakings, commitments on capital account or unusual liabilities which have been made, given, entered into or incurred by or on behalf of the Company nor are there any options, rights to acquire, mortgages, charges, pledges, liens or other forms of security or encumbrance or equity on, over or affecting the whole or any part of the share capital, undertaking or assets of the Company, nor is there any agreement to give or create any of the foregoing and no claim has been made by any Persons to be entitled to any of the foregoing.

10.2 The Company has made or caused to be made all proper returns in relation to Tax, duties, levies or statutory contributions, and all information required to be supplied to any relevant revenue or other competent authority has been supplied to the appropriate authority, and there is no dispute or disagreement outstanding, nor is any such dispute or disagreement contemplated, with such authorities regarding liability or potential liability to any Tax, duty, levy or statutory contribution recoverable from the Company or regarding the availability to the Company of any relief from Tax, duties, levies or statutory contributions.

10.3 The Company has within the time limits specified by the competent authorities made all due and appropriate payment of Tax, duties, levies and statutory contributions of whatever nature.

10.4 All the accounts, books, ledgers and financial and other material records of whatsoever kind of the Company have been fully and properly kept and been completed up to date in all material respects and all necessary returns and filings with applicable government bodies or departments have been duly made.

10.5 There are no agreements in force which call either at the date of signature hereof or in the future for the issue of, or accord to any Person the right to call for the issue of, any shares or loan capital of the Company.

10.6 The Company has not at any time:
  (*a*) repaid or agreed to repay or redeem any shares of any class of its share capital or otherwise reduced or agreed to reduce its issued share capital or any class thereof; or
  (*b*) capitalised or agreed to capitalise, in the form of shares or debentures or other securities, or by means of paying up any amounts unpaid on any shares, debentures or other securities, any profits or reserves of any class or description or passed or agreed to pass any resolution to do so.

10.7 The Company is not subject to or the beneficiary of any obligation or requirement to provide funds to any person, or to make any investment, of an amount in excess of £[   ] (whether in the form of a loan, capital contribution or otherwise) under a loan agreement or otherwise.

10.8 All the shares comprising the share capital of the Company have been validly issued and allotted in accordance with the Memorandum and Articles of Association of the Company and the [laws of England] and are fully paid up. All such shares are freely transferable by the Vendors with full title guarantee free of any encumbrances, pre-emption or similar rights or any agreement, pledge, lien, option, charge over or affecting any of the shares, or any arrangement to create such, and no claim has been made by any Person to be entitled to any of the foregoing.

SCHEDULE 3
Indemnification

1 All rights and obligations in respect of the Warranties, except the Warranties contained in [   ] shall survive the Completion for a period of [two] years from the Completion Date. The rights and obligations in respect of the Warranties contained in [   ] shall survive the Completion for a period of [six] years from the Completion Date.

2 The Vendors hereby agree, jointly and severally, to indemnify the Purchaser against, and agree to hold the Purchaser harmless from, any and all Losses incurred or suffered by the Purchaser (it being understood that, if the Completion occurs, Losses incurred or suffered by the Company shall be deemed for purposes of this Agreement to have been incurred or suffered by the Purchaser) relating to or arising out of or in connection with any breach of or any inaccuracy in any of the Warranties, provided, however, that:

(a) a notice of a claim in respect of a breach of or inaccuracy in any of the Warranties (other than the Warranties contained in [   ]) shall have been given to the Vendors in accordance with paragraph 3 or 4 not later than the [second] anniversary of the Completion Date; and

(b) a notice of a claim in respect of a breach of or inaccuracy in any of the Warranties contained in [   ] shall have been given to the Vendors in accordance with para 3 or 4 not later than the [sixth] anniversary of the Completion Date; and

(c) a claim by the Purchaser in respect of a breach of or inaccuracy in any of the Warranties shall cease to be subject to indemnification hereunder (notwithstanding that notice of such claim shall have been timely given by the Purchaser in accordance with para 3 or 4), if the Purchaser shall not have commenced legal proceedings against the Vendors in respect thereof by the later of (a) the [first] anniversary of the date such claim ceases to be contingent and becomes an actual liability of the Purchaser or the Company and is due and payable and (b) the [first] anniversary of the latest date notice of such claim is required to be given pursuant to para 2(a) or para 2(b), as the case may be.

3 The Purchaser shall give written notice as promptly as is reasonably practicable to the Vendors of any claim for indemnification hereunder (other than a claim for indemnification described in para 4 which shall be governed by that paragraph) setting out in reasonable detail the nature of the claim, the provisions of this Agreement on which such claim is based, and the amount the Purchaser will be entitled to receive hereunder from the Vendors and attaching all relevant documents not in the Vendors' possession; provided, however, that the failure of the Purchaser to give notice shall not relieve the Vendors of their obligations under this Schedule except to the extent (if any) that the Vendors shall have been prejudiced thereby. If the Vendors do not object in writing to such indemnification claim within [90] days from the day on which they received notice thereof, the Purchaser shall be entitled to recover promptly from the Vendors the amount of such claim (but such recovery shall not limit the amount of any additional indemnification to which the Purchaser may be entitled pursuant to para 2, and no later objection by the Vendors shall be permitted). If the Vendors agree that they have an indemnification obligation but object that they are obligated to pay only a lesser amount, the Purchaser shall be entitled to recover promptly from the Vendors the lesser amount, without prejudice to the Purchaser's claim for the difference.

4 The Purchaser shall give written notice as promptly as is reasonably practicable to the Vendors of the assertion of any claim, or the commencement of any suit, action or proceeding, by any Person not a party hereto in respect of which indemnity is claimed by the Purchaser under this Agreement setting out in reasonable detail the nature of the claim, suit, action or proceeding, the provisions of this Agreement on which the Purchaser's claim for indemnification hereunder is based and the amount (if ascertainable) of such claim and attaching all relevant documents not in the Vendors' possession; provided, however, that the failure of the Purchaser to give notice shall not relieve the Vendors of their obligations under this Schedule except to the extent (if any) that the Vendors shall have been prejudiced thereby. The Vendors may, at their own expense:

(*a*) participate in the defence of any claim, suit, action or proceeding; and

(*b*) at any time during the course of any such claim, suit, action or proceeding, assume the defence thereof, upon written notice to the Purchaser, together with delivery of a written agreement, that the Purchaser is entitled to indemnification pursuant to para 2 for all or the major part of the Losses arising out the such claim, suit, action or proceeding, and that the Vendors shall be liable for all or such major part, as applicable, of such Losses; and *provided that*

(i) the Vendors' counsel is reasonably satisfactory to the Purchaser; and

(ii) the Vendors shall thereafter consult with the Purchaser, upon the Purchaser's reasonable request for such consultation from time to time, with respect to such claim, suit, action or proceeding.

If the Vendors assume such defence, the Purchaser shall have the right (but not the duty) to participate in the defence thereof and to employ counsel, at its own expense, separate from the counsel employed by the Purchaser. If, however, the Purchaser reasonably determines in its judgment that representation by the Vendors' counsel of both the Vendors and the Purchaser would present such counsel with a conflict of interest or if the Vendors have agreed to indemnify the Purchaser for less than all Losses arising out of such claim, suit, action or proceeding, then the Purchaser may employ separate counsel to represent or defend it in any such claim, action, suit or proceeding and the Vendors shall pay the fees and disbursements of such separate counsel. Whether or not the Vendors choose to defend or prosecute any such claim, suit, action or proceeding, the parties hereto shall co-operate in the defence or prosecution thereof. In furtherance thereof, the Purchaser shall, and shall procure that the Company shall, provide the Vendors all assistance reasonably necessary to enable the Vendors to participate in or conduct the defence of such claim, suit, action or proceeding, including providing reasonable access for the Vendors and their professional advisors to the relevant books, files, and records of the Purchaser and the Company.

5 Any settlement or compromise made or caused to be made by the Purchaser or the Vendors, as the case may be, of any such claim, suit, action or proceeding of the kind referred to in para 4 shall also be binding upon the Vendors or the Purchaser, as the case may be, in the same manner as if a final judgment or decree had been entered by a court of competent jurisdiction in the amount of such settlement or compromise; provided, however, that no obligation, restriction or Loss shall be imposed on the Purchaser as a result of such settlement without its prior written consent. The Purchaser will give the Vendors at least [60] days' notice of any proposed settlement or compromise of any claim, suit, action or proceeding it is defending, unless there is a material likelihood that such notice would jeopardise such settlement or compromise, in which case such notice shall be as long as practicable under the circumstances. During such time, the Vendors may reject such proposed settlement or compromise; provided, however, that from and after such rejection, the Vendors shall be obligated to assume the defence of and shall have full and complete liability and responsibility for such claim, suit, action or proceeding and any and all Losses in connection therewith in excess of the amount of unindemnifiable Losses which the Purchaser would have been obligated to pay under the proposed settlement or compromise.

6 In the event that the Vendors do not elect to assume the defence of any claim, suit, action or proceeding, then any failure of the Purchaser to defend or to participate in the defence of any such claim, suit, action or proceeding or to cause the same to be done, or any settlement or compromise made or caused to be made by the Purchaser, shall not relieve the Vendors of their obligations hereunder.

7 Notwithstanding anything to the contrary in para 2, the Vendors shall not be liable for any claim for a Loss arising out of or in connection with any matter described in para 2 whether discovered before or after the Completion Date:
  (*a*) unless the amount of such claim exceeds [£10,000]; provided, however, that if the aggregate amount of all such claims less than or equal to [£10,000] exceeds [£500,000], the Vendors shall, subject to subsection (*b*), be liable for all such claims;
  (*b*) unless and until the aggregate amount of all such claims for which the Parent and the Vendors would otherwise be liable pursuant to this Paragraph 7 exceeds [£1,000,000] in the aggregate, [in which event the liability of the Vendors shall be limited to the amount of such excess];
  (*c*) to the extent but only to the extent that the aggregate amount of:
    (i)   any Agreed Price Reduction;
    (ii) any Unilateral Price Reduction which has not been reversed by the award of an Arbitrator's Price Increase pursuant to cl 2.5.10;
    (iii) any Arbitrator's Price Reduction; and
    (iv) any Losses paid by the Vendors pursuant to this Schedule would thereby exceed [£50,000,000];

(*d*) in respect of any such claim that is contingent, unless and until such contingent claim becomes an actual liability and is due and payable; provided, however, that this subsection shall not operate to avoid a claim with respect to which notice has been given in accordance with para 4 or 5 to the Vendors within the applicable time period set forth in para 2, and which, if relevant, has become the subject of legal proceedings within the applicable time period, if relevant, set forth in para 2;

(*e*) in respect of any Loss if [but only to the extent that] such Loss is re-served against or reflected in the Completion Accounts;

(*f*) in respect of any Loss if but only to the extent that it would not have occurred but for any voluntary act, omission or transaction of the Purchaser after the Completion Date (including a change in the nature of, or in the manner of conducting, the business of the Company or a change in any accounting policy or practice of the Purchaser or the Company after Completion but excluding the Purchaser's exercise of its right not to defend pursuant to para 6) done or omitted to be done other than in the ordinary course of business;

(*g*) if but only to the extent that such Loss is covered by a policy of insur-ance covering the Company and payment is made under such policy to the Company by the insurer;

(*h*) in respect of any Loss:

    (i) for which the Purchaser has received an Agreed Price Reduction pursuant to cl 2.5.2.1 [but only to the extent to which such Loss was satisfied by such Agreed Price Reduction], or

    (ii) in relation to which [a Unilateral Price Reduction coupled with a submission to arbitration has been made pursuant to cl 2.5.7] [a Unilateral Price Reduction coupled with an Arbitrator's Price Re-duction has been made but only to the extent that such Loss was satisfied by such Unilateral Price Reduction and Arbitrator's Price Reduction];

(*i*) if such claim relates to any matter truly and fairly disclosed in the Dis-closure Letter;

(*j*) if but only to the extent that such claim relates to any matter or thing done or omitted to be done by the Vendors or caused by the Vendors (prior to Completion) to be done or omitted to be done by the Company (being a matter or thing which the Vendors are not obliged to do or omit to do or cause the Company to do or omit to do pursuant to the terms of this Agreement) at the written request of or with the written approval of the Purchaser provided that this cl 2.6.5 shall only apply in the case where the Purchaser makes such request or gives such approval with knowledge that it would give rise to a Loss;

(*k*) if but only to the extent that such claim arises in relation to any matter required to be done or performed under the terms of this Agreement or required to be carried out in the implementation hereof;

(*l*) if but only to the extent that such claim arises from (or is increased by virtue of) any legislation (primary or subordinate) not in force at or prior to the Completion Date or any change of law or administrative practice after Completion (including any change of practice in relation to, or any withdrawal of, any extra-statutory concessions) which takes effect retroactively, or any decision of the courts of any jurisdiction altering the accepted interpretation of the law (including the interpretation of any legislation) as at or prior to the Completion Date, or any increase in the rates or change in the scope or practice of any Tax in force at the Completion Date (in either case whether retrospective or otherwise);

[(*m*) if but only to the extent that any such claim gives rise to any Tax relief allowance or other benefit actually obtained by the Purchaser or the Company (or which would have been obtained had the Purchaser or the Company, as appropriate, acted reasonably).]

8(*a*) If the Vendors shall have made payment to the Purchaser of an amount in respect to a claim under this Schedule, and subsequent to the making of such payment, the Purchaser or the Company shall recover from a third Person, including any Tax authority or insurance company, any sum or benefit which is referable to the circumstances giving rise to such payment, then the Purchaser shall pay, or procure that the Company pays, to the Vendors, the amount so recovered.

(*b*) If a third Person, including any Tax authority or insurance company, may be liable (including any liability to make a refund of Tax or to agree any relief in respect of Tax) for any claim in respect of which the Vendors shall have made payment to the Purchaser under this Schedule, the Purchaser shall provide all reasonable assistance (including executing transfer documentation) to the Vendors, at their expense, to enable them to pursue such claim against such Person and, to the extent the Vendors shall have made payment to the Purchaser in respect of such claim, the Vendors shall be entitled to full subrogation to the rights of the Purchaser and the Company to the extent of such payment.

9 All claims payable to the Purchaser under this Schedule shall be paid in cash to the Purchaser within 30 days of their becoming due, and shall be treated as a reduction in the Purchase Price.

SCHEDULE 4
Pension Arrangements

SCHEDULE 5
Details of Properties

Signed by	Signed by
For and on behalf of	For and on behalf of
the Vendors	the Purchaser

Short form disclosure letter

This Disclosure Letter is delivered to the Purchaser pursuant to the Share Acquisition Agreement dated [   ] between [   ] and [   ] (the 'Agreement'). Capitalised terms used but not defined herein have the meanings given them in the Agreement.

1   General disclosures

The following preliminary matters are recorded in relation to this Disclosure Schedule:

   (*a*) although every effort has been made to relate the matters herein to the specific portion of the Agreement or to the relevant representation or warranty contained in Schedule [   ] to the Agreement, any information contained herein and, subject to paragraph (*e*) below, in any document attached hereto or listed herein, shall be treated and deemed to be treated as a disclosure in respect of all representations and warranties contained in Schedule [   ] to the Agreement;

   (*b*) the disclosure of any matter or document hereby shall not imply any representation, warranty or undertaking as to that matter or document or as to any statement or reference contained in that matter or document that is not expressly included in the Agreement, nor shall such disclosure be taken as extending the scope of any representation or warranty contained in Schedule [   ] to the Agreement or of any undertaking contained in the Agreement;

   (*c*) the headings and numbering are used merely for convenience and shall not affect the interpretation of this Disclosure letter;

   [(*d*) there is deemed to be disclosed any matter or information contained in any statutory book, minute book, register or record of the Company to the extent they have been made available for inspection by or on behalf of the Purchaser prior to the date hereof:]

(*e*) the listing of any document herein or the attachment of any document hereto shall constitute disclosure only of the provisions contained in such document:

(*f*) there shall be deemed to be disclosed all matters described in this Disclosure letter:

[(*g*)in respect of real property, there shall be deemed to be disclosed all matters contained or described in the Certificates of Title attached hereto together with all other information contained in Replies to Enquiries (copies herewith):]

(*h*) there shall be deemed to be disclosed all or any information described in the accounts and other financial statements of the Company attached hereto.

2   Specific disclosures

The following specific disclosures are made (subject to para 1(*a*), above) in relation to the various representations and warranties contained in Schedule [   ] to the Agreement, as detailed below.

For and on behalf of
the Vendors   Date

We acknowledge receipt of the above letter on [   ] on the basis that it is the Disclosure Letter as defined in and for the purposes of the Agreement.

For and on behalf of
the Purchaser   Date

Chapter 11

Asset acquisitions

11.1 Introduction

This chapter is concerned with the analysis of one precedent only, a long form business transfer agreement. The precedent intentionally deals with a complex business transfer, under which the seller is carrying on more than one business from a single location, and wishes to sell only one of those businesses to the purchaser. This situation, which is not uncommon, highlights the particular problems of definition and carve-out of the business to be transferred, which are the concern of business transfer transactions as opposed to share sale transactions.

The agreement has been simplified in other areas to enable attention to be focused upon these particular issues. First, completion takes place upon signature of the agreement, and, secondly, the purchase price is fixed and payable in large part on completion. This means that no provision need be made to deal with the complications discussed in Chapter 10, in connection with a share sale, relating to ascertainment of the purchase price and post-completion price adjustments by way of completion accounts, nor to the problems surrounding a two-stage transaction with due diligence carried out after signature of the acquisition agreement and before completion.

In any case, the considerations discussed in Chapter 10 in relation to these issues would be relevant for a two-stage business transfer transaction with a requirement for price ascertainment and adjustment, and the relevant provisions of Precedent 2 of Chapter 10 could be amended accordingly. The greatest practical issue here is that the completion accounts could not relate to a legal entity, since the business is being transferred without the legal entity carrying it on. More accounting work has to take place to construct divisional or management accounts of the business, particularly if the seller has never accounted separately for the business in previous years, but this is in practice not insuperable. It should be remembered that if a balance sheet cannot be constructed for the business being transferred it will probably be impossible to define the business with sufficient precision to enable a true business transfer, as opposed to the transfer of a collection of assets and liabilities, to take place at all.

11.2   Clause 1

Following details of the parties, cl 1 sets out the various definitions and interpretations to be used in the agreement. The most important definitions are those which define the business itself, and the information, assets and liabilities and employees relating to the business, which are to be transferred to the purchaser or retained by the seller. It should be noted that such definitions are either all-encompassing (see for instance 'Business Information') or relate to lists in Schedules attached to the agreement (see for instance 'Relevant Employees'). Although it is tempting for the purchaser to require the seller to define each item by reference to complete lists this is often not practical. For the purchaser who wants to achieve some certainty plus the protection of the all-encompassing definition, the best course is to insert in a global definition a statement that the definition includes but is not limited to items of major significance which are listed in a schedule (see for instance 'Chattels').

11.3   Clause 2

This clause deals with the segregation of the assets of the business which are to be transferred to the purchaser (those listed in cl 2.1) and those which are to remain with the seller (those listed in cl 2.2). It will be seen that the transaction depends totally upon the definitions set out in cl 1. The division in the precedent between assets to be transferred and assets to be retained is a common one. The items in cl 2.1 are what the purchaser needs to carry on the business as a going concern, while there is no point in transferring cash or the benefit of insurance claims (cl 2.2(*a*) and (*b*)) since the seller would be required to be compensated on a pound for pound basis in the purchase price for the value of any such items transferred. So far as debtors and creditors are concerned (cl 2.2(*c*) and (*d*)) these may or may not be transferred, although it is very common to retain them. Their transfer will also result in a pound for pound change in the purchase price to compensate the seller for giving up the debtors and the purchaser for taking on the creditors. In addition the assignment of debtors and creditors to the seller is legally complicated (normally requiring the consent of the debtor or creditor) and, in the case of debtors, the seller will probably be required to give a warranty of collectability. All in all, there seems little point in transferring these items.

Special provisions relating to the real property which is being transferred along with the business are provided in Sched 5 (see cl 2.3). The conveyancing aspects of business transfers are more complicated than those under a share sale, because, since no legal entity which holds the title to the real property is being transferred, individual conveyances of freeholds or assignments of leaseholds (with the need to get landlord's consent) are required. These issues then become the province of the specialist real property lawyer who will deal with the necessary provisions to be inserted in the schedule in accordance with the particular facts of each transaction. In particular the schedule will contain any warranties relating to title to the properties which the parties negotiate, although it should be said that it is usual, since a true transfer of title is effected here, for the purchaser to make full title searches as he would in any other real property transaction. In the event that warranties are to be included, the warranties relating to real property in Sched 2 of Precedent 2 in Chapter 10 provide a good starting point.

Finally it should be noted that one of the commonest reasons for delay in completion of business transfers is failure to obtain in time the necessary landlord's consents to the assignment to the purchaser of leasehold property from which the business is carried on. Most leases not only forbid assignment without consent, but also forbid subletting or licensing to or sharing occupation with an unconnected third party without the landlord's consent. In these cases, the need for formal consent cannot be circumvented by some informal permission given to the purchaser by the seller to occupy the premises on a temporary basis, until formal consent is obtained, even if the purchaser were willing to accept this.

11.4 Clause 3

Clause 3.1 sets out the purchase consideration as a total cash sum, and cl 3.2 allocates it between the various classes of assets to be transferred. Tax considerations are of paramount importance here. First, in so far as consideration is allocated to assets which pass by delivery, the payment of stamp duty is avoided. Secondly, the purchaser will wish to allocate as much consideration as legitimately possible to those assets which he can write off most quickly, so as to pull forward his depreciation allowances as much as possible; and also to allocate a high consideration to those assets for which he would be liable to capital gains tax on disposal, so as to ensure a high base value for them. The seller on the other hand will be concerned to allocate the consideration in such a way as to minimise his exposure to capital gains tax. As usual, the interests of the seller and purchaser in taxation matters are unlikely to coincide, and the allocation of consideration tends to turn into a commercial negotiation.

Clause 3.3 deals with the issue of Value Added Tax. If properly dealt with the transfer of a business is exempt from Value Added Tax, and the correct way of dealing with the matter is set out in this clause.

Clause 3.4 provides that the allocation of the purchase price is not to affect the concept that the price paid for the business as a whole is the aggregate sum specified in cl 3.1. This is important to prevent any future claims under the agreement, arising in relation to a particular asset, being restricted to the value ascribed to that asset pursuant to cl 3.2 instead of being assessed upon the basis of the effect of the matter in question on the business as a whole. For instance, in the event of a claim relating to a fixed asset used in carrying on the business, such as production machinery, which is missing or defective, the amount of the claim should not be based solely on the part of the consideration allocated to that machinery, but also include the damage suffered through the resultant lost production.

11.5   Clause 4

This clause deals with the mechanics of completion, which revolve around the transfer of title to the assets either by delivery or conveyance, and the need to obtain the consent of third parties in the case of customer and supplier contracts. The board meetings and other formalities which are a feature of share sales are of course unnecessary in a business transfer. In so far as the transfer of assets needs the consent of third parties, and such consent has not been obtained by completion, cl 4.6 provides that the seller will continue efforts to obtain the necessary consent after completion, and hold the relevant assets on trust for the purchaser until it is obtained. Clause 4.7 provides that the purchaser is not obliged to complete the transaction unless all of the assets can be transferred to him, but, of course, he can waive his right not to complete if the omissions are not significant. Clause 4.8 provides a mutual indemnity in the event either party delivers to the other an invalid document of transfer or consent pursuant to the previous provisions of the clause.

Clause 4.9 provides for payment of the purchase price in two instalments, the majority on completion, with the remainder to be kept back as a retention until a valuation of the stock transferred at the completion has taken place. Clause 4.10 deals with the method of the valuation of the stock, cl 4.11 provides for a pound for pound adjustment if the stock is less than a specified valuation, while cl 4.12 provides a value underpin in respect of the stock to be transferred. It would be useless to the purchaser if he received no stock at all, even if the purchase price were fully adjusted to compensate him for this, since he would have at least temporary difficulty in carrying on business. By including in cl 4.12 a warranty as to the minimum stock level to be transferred the purchaser can sue for breach of this warranty to recover not only the value of the stock, but also compensation for interruption to his business. The amount to be filled in in the square brackets in cll 4.11 and 4.12 should in each case be the same if the clauses are to inter-work properly.

Finally cl 4.13 envisages that since the parties will still be sharing occupation of a common site, there will be certain services that they will use in common, and for which they will share the cost. Access to these services and payment for them will be regulated by a shared service agreement drawn up in advance to fit the particular circumstances of the case, and signed and delivered on completion.

11.6 Clause 5

This clause deals with the future performance by the purchaser of the customer contracts assigned to him as part of the business transfer. The purchaser is to be solely responsible for their performance after completion, and undertakes to indemnify the seller against any failure so to do (cl 5.1). This indemnity is given on condition that the seller allows the purchaser to have the conduct of any relevant claim (cl 5.2).

Clause 5.3 deals with the question of warranty claims that arise after completion but relate to defective products put into circulation prior to completion. Although the purchaser will attempt to leave liability for all such claims with the seller, this is not a commercially realistic position, when the seller has transferred to the purchaser the benefit and burden of the business as a going concern together with goodwill. On the one hand any settlement of warranty claims by the seller will in fact increase the goodwill of the purchaser for the benefit of his future business, and, on the other hand, any failure to satisfy claims (and the seller will be motivated to satisfy as few claims as possible) will affect the purchaser's ongoing business and reputation adversely.

Additionally, where warranty claims are to be satisfied by repair or replacement, only the purchaser can actually satisfy them, since he now carries on the business producing the goods to which the claims relate. Clause 5.3 takes a practical compromise. The purchaser deals with all claims, but only bears the expense of so doing for a reasonable period of time and up to a reasonable amount. The seller has to indemnify the purchaser for his costs and expenses in dealing with claims outside the specified time period or in excess of the specified monthly amount.

Clause 5.4 merely reinforces the point contained in cl 4.6, that until customer and supplier contracts are properly assigned to the purchaser the seller receives any benefits under them as agent for the purchaser.

11.7 Clause 6

This clause deals with the transfer of employees. Under cll 6.1 and 6.2, the parties have accepted that this is a business transfer to which the Transfer of Undertakings (Protection of Employment) Regulations 1981 (SI No 1794) (implementing the EEC Acquired Rights Directive No 187/1977) apply. Accordingly, the contracts of employment of all employees employed in the business are automatically transferred (except with regard to pension rights) to the purchaser and all of these employees move over to continue their employment with the business.

The Directive and the Regulations (as now amended by the Collective Redundancies and Transfer of Undertakings (Protection of Employment) (Amendment) Regulations 1995) also require the seller and the purchaser to consult either with any trade unions recognised in respect of the 'affected employees', or, if there is no such trade union, with their elected employee representatives. Consultation must take place in a meaningful way 'with a view to seeking their agreement', although there is no absolute obligation on the parties to the transaction to obtain such agreement. Where there is both a recognised trade union and elected employee representatives, the employer may consult with either the trade union or the representatives at his option. The DTI has just issued a consultation document on 'Employees' Information and Consultation Rights on Transfers of Undertakings and Collective Redundancies' which proposes changes to the 1995 regime. In the case where there are both representatives and a trade union, the proposals would require the employer to consult with the trade union. Consultation with elected employee representatives would be permitted only where there was no trade union. The employer would be required to show that any such employee representatives were independent and held a proper mandate to represent the affected employees. The characteristics of independence and being properly mandated are collectively described in the proposals as being 'capable'.

It should be noted that whether or not the Regulations apply to a transaction is a question of fact to be determined by the appropriate tribunal (which may include the European Court of Justice), and that neither the parties to the transfer nor the employees concerned can contract out of their rights and duties under the Regulations. There has been, however, and continues to be considerable doubt about the precise definition of a transfer of an undertaking.

Clearly, a transaction whereby a business is expressed to be transferred as a going concern, together with goodwill, and the right for the purchaser to describe himself as carrying on the business as a successor to the seller, will be a business transfer (see *Premier Motors (Medway) Ltd v Total Oil (Great Britain) Ltd* [1984] ICR 58, EAT and *Spijkers v Gebroeders Benedik Abattoir CV* [1986] 2 CMLR 296, ECJ) while the sale of a few assets and contracts will be an asset sale (see *Gibson v Motortune Ltd* [1990] ICR 740, EAT) not subject to the Regulations. However, there are many variations between these two extremes where the distinction becomes blurred.

According to (*Watson Rask & Christensen v ISS Kantineservice A/S* ECJ No 209/91,) the main question to be determined is whether there is a transfer of a 'business activity' as a going concern, and that this can best be decided by looking at the type of undertaking, what assets and liabilities were being transferred, whether employees and/or customers were being taken on by the new owner, and the degree of similarity between activities before and after the transfer. However, the fact that no tangible property has been transferred as part of the transaction is not by itself fatal to the application of the Directive, and, hence, in the UK, the Regulations.

In *Curling v Securicor Ltd* [1992] IRLR 549, the EAT took a narrower view than the ECJ, in that it concentrated on whether there had been a transfer of the 'economic unit' carrying on the business activity concerned, which would in most cases include the tangible property, both real and personal, controlled by that economic unit.

Some clarification of the conflict between the approach of the ECJ and the EAT was provided by the Trade Union Reform and Employment Rights Act 1993. The Act followed the decisions of the ECJ in *Spijkers* and *Rask* by making it clear that the absence of transfer of tangible property does not automatically mean that no business has been transferred and that therefore the Regulations cannot apply. The tribunal must look at all of the facts of the case, no one of which, by itself, is conclusive, and the transfer of property is just one of the facts to be taken into account reaching a decision.

In recent years the lack of emphasis upon transfer of property increased until the ECJ restored the balance in the landmark decision of *Ayse Suzen v Zehnacker Gebaudereinigung GmbH Krankenhausservice* [1997] IRLR 255.

In *Dines v Initial Healthcare Services Ltd* [1994] IRLR 366, there was held to have been a transfer of undertaking where a hospital ceased to use one cleaning contractor and arranged for a new one to take over the cleaning of the hospital under a new contract. In the ECJ case *Christel Schmidt* [1994] 1 ECR 1311, the court held that a transfer of undertaking could take place even if there was no transfer of assets or other physical materials between the transferor and the transferee. The EAT followed this approach in *Kelman v Contract Case Services* [1995] ICR 260 when it held that an undertaking may simply comprise an activity and employees, so long as the identity of activity is the same before and after the transfer. Finally, in *Merck v Ford Motors Co Belgium SA* [1996] IRLR 467 the ECJ held that a transfer of undertaking can take place even when there is no contract between the transferee and the transferor.

The European Commission was not happy with this situation and attempted to amend the Acquired Rights Directive, to make it clear that transfers of the kind in *Christel Schmidt* should be outside the Directive, but the European Parliament would not accept the amendment. In *Ayse Suzen*, the ECJ in effect clarified the situation by holding that (in a situation very similar to *Christel Schmidt*) there was no transfer of an undertaking. The court said that an entity could not be reduced to the activity entrusted to it, and that the mere loss of a service contract to a competitor cannot by itself indicate the existence of a transfer within the meaning of the Directive. The court went on to say that every case depended upon its own facts and that the correct test for whether there had been a transfer of undertaking was set out in *Spijkers*. The Court of

Appeal has subsequently followed *Suzen* in an unreported case *Betts v (1) Brintel Helicopters Ltd (2) KLM ERA Helicopters (UK) Ltd* (1997) unreported, 26 March, CA.

Suzen is clearly of importance in the context of outsourcing, either when an outsourcing contract is placed by the customer for the first time, or when, later on, the contract terminates either because the customer has taken the activity concerned back in-house, or appointed a new outsourcer when retendering of the service takes place. Previously it was assumed (relying on *Christel Schmidt*) that in all of these circumstances there would be a transfer of undertaking. The assumption was that the employees used by the departing outsourcer on his contract (often taken over from the customer) would transfer automatically to the new outsourcer or back to the customer (as the case might be) when the contract terminated. After *Suzen* this is not necessarily the case. Each situation would be decided upon its own merits, after *Spijkers* and *Rask*. Certainly the mere replacement of one outsourcing contract by another would be insufficient alone to create a transfer of undertaking. This has practical consequences for outsourcers who may well be left with substantial redundancy payments on the termination of their contracts, which they have not provided for in their costing of the contract, since they assumed that the employees would always transfer to the new contractor or back to the customer. Clearly these issues can be dealt with as a matter of contract. In the original outsource contract the customer can require the outsourcer to implement a transfer of undertaking (ie employees and perhaps assets) to any succeeding contractor, and undertake to mandate as part of tendering process that any new contractor accept that transfer as a condition of being awarded the contract. Alternatively the outsourcer might negotiate a termination payment to cover any liabilities. Outsourcers in future will be wise to cover these issues with their customers as part of the contract for the outsource.

In January 1998 the DTI published a consultation paper on possible changes to the Directive and the Regulations, and the government announced that it would use the UK presidency of the EU to push for changes in the Directive.[11]

Under the Regulations (regs 5(2) and (4)) liability is transferred to the purchaser not only for the relevant contracts of employment for the future, but also for any past civil liabilities of the seller to the transferred employees under their contracts of employment, to the extent that the seller has not discharged these prior to the transfer. This transfer under the Regulations thus puts the purchaser in the shoes of the seller, as if the purchaser had always been the employer of the transferred employees from the day they started work with the seller. Further, this transfer of liability under the Regulations relieves the seller of any of his past civil liabilities as a previous employer of the transferred employees.

This is not a satisfactory basis for a negotiated commercial transfer of a business (although it is eminently suitable where an insolvent business is sold by a receiver or liquidator). Thus cll 6.1 and 6.2 provide that, as between the seller and the purchaser (although this cannot affect the rights of the employees against the purchaser under the Regulations) the transfer is on the basis that the seller accepts liability for pre-completion issues relating to the employees, and will indemnify the seller against such claims made by the transferred employees, while the purchaser agrees to employ them upon substantially the same terms and conditions as the seller, and to take responsibility for all post-completion liabilities relating to the employees.

It should be noted that the seller should not take on liability to compensate the purchaser for accrued holiday rights subsisting at transfer in respect of the transferred employees, and that cl 6 so provides (see also cl 8.2).

Many employers do not accrue in their accounts for such holiday entitlement, simply recording holiday pay as an expense when the relevant employee takes his holiday. In this case, it is clearly unfair for the seller to recognise now a liability which he never recognised previously. In any event, even if there are accruals in the books of the seller to reflect his liability for accrued holiday pay, if he undertakes to continue to accept that liability after transfer, he is, in effect, transferring the benefit of those accruals to the purchaser. In this case, he will want a pound for pound adjustment in the purchase price. The whole matter is better left the responsibility of the purchaser, and the parties should take into account any liability of the purchaser, to the extent that this is agreed and felt necessary, when they negotiate the purchase price.

Problems arise as to the treatment of employees whom the purchaser does not wish to continue to employ in the business after the transfer. Prior to the House of Lords decision in *Litster v Forth Dry Dock and Engineering Co Ltd* [1989] IRLR 161, the seller could have dismissed the unwanted employees prior to the completion of the transaction, and the purchaser would have been entirely unconcerned with such employees or their treatment. This was because the Regulations only apply to employees who are employed in the business 'immediately before the transfer' (reg 5(3)) and previous authorities interpreted this phrase as meaning that the Regulations only applied to those employees whose contracts of employment were subsisting at time of transfer (see *Secretary of State for Employment v Spence* [1986] ICR 248, in the Court of Appeal).

However, *Litster* restricted this decision by an ingenious argument relying on reg 8(1), which provides that a dismissal which took place by reason of the transfer is to be regarded as unfair. The House of Lords took this provision to mean in effect that the transfer was not to constitute a ground for dismissal. Once this was assumed, it was logical to imply into reg 5(3) as a gloss on the phrase 'employed immediately before the transfer' the phrase 'or would have been so employed if he had not been unfairly dismissed in the circumstances described in reg 8(1)' (*per* Lord Oliver). However, the court distinguished

Spence, which was said to be correct upon its facts, since the dismissals in that case did not take place because of the transfer, but for another reason. From this decision it follows that dismissals by reason of the transfer will be ineffective to avoid the liabilities imposed on the purchaser by reg 5, but that dismissals for other reasons will fall outside of the Regulations.

The general opinion of the effect of *Litster* is not that, despite the dismissal, the contract of employment still subsists, and is transferred, but that the rights of the employee against the seller in respect of the unfair dismissal are transferred to the purchaser who then becomes liable to compensate the dismissed employee to the exclusion of the seller. Following the above reasoning, in relation to the effect of reg 5(2), this transfer of liability not only imposes the liability to compensate the dismissed employees upon the purchaser, but removes it from the seller. There has been some refinement of this proposition, and some further confusion, as a result of two recent decisions in the Court of Appeal.

In *Wilson v St Helens Borough Council*, Lancashire County Council decided to close down a school which it could no longer afford to run, and St Helens Borough Council agreed to take it over, provided it could make changes to the way the school was run. Lancashire CC made the school employees redundant and St Helens BC offered them employment on new, but less favourable, terms. The employees started work but some months later claimed that there had been a transfer of undertaking and that consequently their old terms of employment should still apply. They sued under the Wages Act for the loss of earnings they had suffered as a result of the change in their terms of employment. The EAT (see [1996] IRLR 320) (following the ECJ Decision in *Forenigen af Arbejdsledere i Danmark v Daddy's Dance Hall a/s* [1988] ECR 739) decided that, since an employee cannot waive his rights under the Directive (see reg 12 of the Regulations), it is not open to an employee subject to a transfer of undertaking to agree to a change in his terms of employment where the change is made by reason of the transfer. Consequently the old terms still applied.

In *Meade and Baxendale v British Fuels Ltd*, the facts were similar in that there was once again a transfer of undertaking, and the employees were dismissed for redundancy by the old employer and then employed by the new employer upon less favourable terms. The EAT here ([1996] IRLR 54) said that since the employees had been dismissed and then re-employed, although the dismissal might be unfair under reg 8, it was sufficient to change the terms of employment for the future.

There was appeal in both cases from the EAT to the Court of Appeal which heard the appeals together (see [1997] IRLR 505). The two EAT decisions appeared to be contradictory, but the Court of Appeal explained this when it found that the EAT, in *Wilson*, had not given any weight to the question of the dismissal. The court thus found that the facts in *Wilson* and *Meade* were similar, in that there had been a dismissal in both cases. Therefore the only question to be answered was whether the dismissal and subsequent engagement could render the variation in terms valid under the Regulations. The decision in *Daddy's Dance Hall* was irrelevant for this purpose, since there had been no dismissal in that case. The court then considered reg 8 which provides that a dismissal in connection with a transfer of undertaking is prohibited and must be treated as ineffective unless (reg 8(2)) it is for an 'economic, technical or organisational reason' entailing changes within the workforce. Regulation 8(2) thus requires either a redundancy situation or a significant change in the work which is to be performed after the transfer. In *Wilson*, the court found that there was a proper reason within reg 8(2), so that the dismissals were valid as was the employment upon the new terms and conditions. In *Meade*, the court found no such reason. It therefore held that, since the Regulations prohibited a dismissal by reason of the transfer, the dismissal was not only unfair but also ineffective. Thus the employees could claim that they had continued to be employed all along on their old terms and conditions and were entitled to be compensated for their loss of earnings.

Both Cases have been appealed to House of Lords so that a final decision on all of these matters is still to come. However, the current decisions in these cases cause considerable problems. First, if the EAT in *Wilson* is right then, relying on *Daddy's Dance Hall*, a change to transferring employees' terms and conditions by reason of the transfer will be invalid even if the employees agree to it. Since the basis for this finding is reg 12, which does not contain provisions equivalent to reg 8(2), it seems unlikely that even if the new employer has an economic, technical or organisational reason which would justify the change, that he will be able to rely on it. Because of the findings of fact, the court of Appeal never had to decide this point, but there are passages in the judgments which approve the EAT's approach. Secondly, the finding in *Meade* that a dismissal contrary to reg 8 is not only unfair but also invalid breaks new ground and appears to go beyond *Litster*. Presumably the transferee employer is not forced to employ an employee who has been dismissed contrary to reg 8. If he chooses not to, then, under *Litster*, he is liable for the consequences only of the unfair dismissal. However, if *Meade* is correct then, if he does employ such a dismissed employee, he can only do so on the terms of the old contract, even if the employee is willing to agree otherwise.

The Employment Appeal Tribunal commented on the difficulties raised by these two cases in *Cornwall County Care Ltd v Brightman* (1998) IRLR 228. In this case a county council ran a number of care homes which proved too expensive. The council transferred the homes to a company which it created and funded but which had independent charitable status. Both parties agreed that this constituted a transfer of undertakings. The company tried to renegotiate the contracts of employment of the staff, but, failing to agree on this, dismissed the staff concerned, and offered re-employment on less favourable terms which the employees accepted under protest. They then brought proceedings before a tribunal for unfair dismissal and sought a declaration that they were entitled to their old conditions of employment. Both the tribunal and the EAT agreed that the dismissal was unfair. However, the EAT discussed the difficulties that arose because of the decisions in *Meade* and *Wilson*, and said that it was 'unreal' to hold that the dismissal was ineffective, so that the old terms and conditions of employment still applied. The thrust of *Brightman*, coupled with the Court of Appeal decisions in *Meade* and *Wilson*, which are of course binding on the EAT, would thus be that an employer who dismisses and offers re-engagement on less favourable terms which the employees accept only under protest has proceeded incorrectly, and has only two ways to set matters right. The first is to insist on the dismissal, accept that it is unfair and pay compensation. The second is to withdraw the dismissal and offer of re-engagement, and take the employees back on their original terms and conditions.

In its consultation paper on the Directive and the Regulations mentioned above, the government sought views as to whether agreed variations to the contract of employment by reason of the transfer should become permitted provided that they have been properly negotiated between the transferee employer and a recognised union representing the affected workers, or, if none, duly elected employee representatives.[12] Given the current situation in this area of the law, cl 6.4 now approaches the dismissal of employees whom the purchaser wishes to make redundant (and who are therefore regarded as dismissed by reason of the transfer) in a different fashion. All of these employees remain in employment at completion and are transferred with the business. However, prior to completion the parties have agreed a list of the employees who are to be made redundant. If the purchaser makes these employees redundant after the transfer (within a specified period of time) then the seller will reimburse the purchaser for their severance payments. The basis of the reimbursement as set out in cl 6.3 is the amount due under statute and at common law, plus (the phrase in square brackets) an *ex gratia* payment which is assumed to coincide with the provisions of the seller's severance scheme that would have applied to the employees if the business had not been transferred and the seller had made them redundant. This is a reasonable basis for the indemnity, and if the purchaser chooses to be more generous he must bear the extra cost himself. Finally, if the purchaser rehires any of the redundant employees within a further specified period, then he must repay the amounts the seller has paid to him by way of indemnity for the relevant severance payments. These provisions should still be capable of application following *Wilson* and *Meade* since the reasons for the dismissal are ones which fall within reg 8(2), and the question of the invalidity of the dismissal does not arise.

The Directive itself provides that member states may, if they choose, but do not have to, provide in their implementing legislation that the transferor and the transferee should be jointly and severally liable to employees under the Directive. In its consultation paper the government has indicated that it will oppose any suggestion to make joint and several liability mandatory.[13]

Lastly, it should be noted that (following the ECJ decision in *Katsikas v Konstantinidis* [1993] IRLR 179, which decided that employees have the right to object to the transfer to a new employer if they so wish, but that it was a matter for the local law of each member state to provide for the consequences of such refusal) the Trade Union Reform and Employment Rights Act 1993 provided that such a refusal to transfer will result in the immediate termination of the relevant contract of employment, but that such termination will not be regarded as a dismissal by either the transferor or the transferee of the business. On this basis, an employee who refuses to transfer is free to do so, but loses his statutory rights to compensation for unfair dismissal and redundancy, and his common law right to pay in lieu of notice. Thus, even the employees who know that they will be made redundant after the transfer would be foolish to object to the transfer, since such refusal will extinguish their rights to the redundancy payments the transferee will otherwise be obliged to give them, either under *Litster* or under a provision similar to cl 6.3.

Clause 6.4 ensures that if the transferee later hires back employees, in respect of whom he has received reimbursement for their termination payments, those payments must be refunded to the transferor.

Clause 6.5 deals first with the problem of other claims made by the transferred employees who are made redundant. Since they have transferred to the purchaser they will have the same rights against the purchaser in respect of pre-completion matters as the transferred employees who continue in employment, so again an indemnity against such claims should be given by the seller to the purchaser.

Clause 6.5 also deals with the problems of employees who do not transfer with the business. It is a question of fact whether any particular employee is employed in the transferred business or not. Thus, the seller and the purchaser cannot arbitrarily decide that some employees should be retained by the seller, against their will, even if they are not to be made redundant. They have the right to transfer if they wish to. The best that the parties can do is to decide as objectively as possible which employees are not employed in the business (even if they provide some services to the business (eg security guard, switchboard operator or maintenance man who looks after the whole of a common site)) and provide that these employees shall not transfer. If any of the employees in question objects then his status can only be decided by a court or tribunal as a question of fact, but cl 6.5 provides that the seller is solely responsible for dealing with, and will indemnify the purchaser against, all claims that such an employee may make, whether they relate to periods before or after completion.

11.8   Clause 7 and Schedule 7

These clauses deal with matters relating to occupational pension schemes. It may be possible to avoid going into great detail about occupational pension schemes when a share sale is involved if the legal entity concerned has its own self-contained scheme, but in a business transfer provision has to be made as to what happens to the accrued rights of transferred employees in any occupational pension scheme run by the seller.

In theory, the business transfer agreement could be silent upon the issue, since the Transfer of Undertakings (Protection of Employment) Regulations 1981 do not apply to pension rights.

The Trade Union Reform and Employee Rights Act 1993 amended the Regulations to make it clear that they do not exclude any benefits provided under an occupational pension scheme other than benefits for old age, invalidity and survivors. This provision is designed to cover the situation where the pension scheme also provides benefits which are not traditionally regarded as pension benefits (perhaps accident insurance, or some form of severance payment on termination of employment for redundancy) but normally provided under the contract of employment. However, the Act makes it clear that the traditional view on the subject, that neither the Directive nor the Regulations applied to transfer true pension benefits under an occupational pension scheme, is indeed the correct one. (See also *Adams v Lancashire County Council* (1997) *The Times*, 19 May, CA.)

If it is decided that the business transfer agreement should be silent on the subject, the transferred employees would cease to be members of the seller's pension scheme upon completion, just like any other employee who left the employment of the seller, and their rights would be whatever are the prescribed rights for leavers contained in the seller's pension plan; in most cases the choice between a deferred pension payable on retirement, and the right to take a transfer payment to another occupational pension scheme or a personal pension scheme.

Each of the transferred employees would then have to decide whether they wished to join the purchaser's occupational pension scheme (if he had one) or to rely on the state scheme or take out a personal pension. Under current legislation relating to pension schemes the choice of the employee is a free one, and it is not possible, as it was in the past, for the purchaser to compel employees, as a condition of employment, to join the purchaser's occupational scheme. If an employee does decide to join the purchaser's scheme, or set up a personal pension, he can either transfer his entitlement under the seller's scheme into the new arrangement, or leave that entitlement where it is as a deferred pension, and start afresh.

This simple picture has one large flaw. Even under the current legislation which has improved the rights which any occupational pension scheme must grant to leavers both in relation to deferred pensions and transfer payments, the position of leavers from most schemes (particularly schemes where pension and benefits for retiring employees are calculated on the basis of salary levels prevailing at or near to retirement) is worse than that of continuing members. It is thus possible for employees who are transferred without their true consent, as a result of a business transfer subject to the Transfer of Undertakings (Protection of Employment) Regulations 1981, to suffer a significant diminution of their pension rights, even though every other aspect of their employment remains the same. Even after *Katsikas*, above, the position of such employees has not improved, since the only result of their refusal, under the Trade Union Reform and Employee Rights Act 1993, is that they lose all their other rights, and their jobs, as well as their pension position.

This situation usually creates industrial relations problems which in extreme cases can jeopardise the transaction, and which, in any event, both the seller and the purchaser usually wish to avoid in the interests of a smooth transaction.

The normal solution adopted is for the seller to offer to make a bulk transfer from his pension fund either to the pension scheme of the purchaser or (in some cases) to a new scheme to be set up specially by the purchaser, in respect of all those transferred employees who wish to join the relevant scheme and take advantage of the offer. The attraction for them to do so is that the transfer is made upon more favourable terms than usually granted to individual leavers. The seller undertakes to the purchaser to provide an amount by way of a bulk transfer which is sufficient to fund accrued benefits in the new scheme of a level substantially (often exactly) the same as the accrued rights which each transferred employee enjoyed at the completion date in the seller's scheme. The purchaser undertakes, in return for the transfer to procure that the relevant benefits are provided to the transferred employees by the scheme of the purchaser that receives the transfer.

The exact provisions required to deal with these matters are complex, and should not be drafted without a thorough knowledge of relevant pensions legislation and actuarial issues. Further, any lawyer dealing with such matters, should do so in close co-operation with his client's actuary.

Schedule 7 sets out by way of illustration one way in which this bulk transfer can be achieved. The transferred employees who wish to take advantage of the offer remain temporarily after completion as members of the seller's scheme on the basis that the purchaser pays any employer contributions in respect of them and collects and pays over any employee contributions that they are required to make under the rules of the scheme. In the meantime the purchaser sets up the new scheme (often called a 'mirror-image' scheme) to provide equivalent benefits to the transferring employees, and the actuaries calculate the amount of the transfer value required to fund those benefits as at the completion date. When everything is ready a date for the transfer is set, and on that date the transferred employees become members of the new scheme and the bulk transfer payment is paid into it, but adjusted by the actuaries to take account of changes in its value between the completion date and the transfer date.

There is one point of detail that needs great emphasis. This is the question of agreement of the actuarial assumptions on which the calculation of the transfer amount is based. The actuarial assumptions must be fixed, as provided in

Sched 7, before the signature of the agreement, and attached to the agreement for reference. If the determination of the actuarial assumptions is left for subsequent agreement the whole schedule will become inoperable if no agreement is reached; leaving a third party to decide the assumptions is too uncertain. In practice, the only assumptions which the seller can safely use are those already used by the actuary to the seller's scheme for the general purposes of that scheme. The seller can only request the trustees of the scheme to make a bulk transfer. He cannot compel them, unless the power to do so has been expressly included in the trust deed. In either event, he will not be able to use a different set of assumptions to the one already in use for the scheme. A more favourable set will penalise the remaining employees, and a less favourable set will penalise the transferring employees. The trustees would be in breach of their duties if they agreed to either, and the employer would be answerable to the employees who suffered loss if he were to attempt to use any of his powers under the deed to force the trustees to comply. A seller who agrees to procure the trustees to make a bulk transfer calculated on the basis of actuarial assumptions more favourable than those used by the actuary to the seller's scheme, puts himself in an impossible position. The trustees will presumably agree only to transfer on the basis of the assumptions their actuary normally applies, and the seller, as a result of the breach of his obligation to procure, will have to make up the shortfall out of his own pocket.

Given the above skeleton outline the somewhat complex provisions of the pension schedule easily fall into place when handled by practitioners who are familiar with the relevant law and practice. However, one commercial issue must be faced. What is the situation if the seller's fund, despite the adoption of the actuarial assumptions of the actuary to the seller's scheme, does not have sufficient assets to fund the transfer payment at the required level? Two solutions are possible: one is that the transfer amount is reduced to that proportion of the fund which is attributable to the transferred employees ('share of the fund basis'), and the benefits provided by the purchaser are reduced accordingly. This will be the preferred solution for the seller. The purchaser will prefer that the seller makes up the shortfall himself, and this is what is provided in para 5(*d*) of the Schedule.

The opposite problem occurs if the seller's fund has a surplus. Should transferred employees receive a transfer payment which is just high enough to fund their benefits, or should the transfer be made on a share of the fund basis, this time thus carrying with it a share of the surplus? Although the purchaser and the employees will press for a share of the surplus (it makes the new fund stronger and possibly can provide increased benefits or a reduction in contributions) the seller will obviously wish to retain the surplus in his own fund, and despite considerable discussion and litigation in recent years over who owns the surplus in a pension fund, the employer or the employees, in the current state of the law it is not obligatory for the seller to transfer any part of the surplus with the transferring employees.

It should, however, be understood that the issues of who bears any shortfall and who receives the benefit of any surplus are not concerned, in the last analysis, with safeguarding the rights of employees, whatever the rhetoric the parties may employ in their negotiations. These issues have a bearing on the purchase price paid for the business, and sometimes a very great bearing, given the current sizes of the pension surpluses in many occupational pension schemes.

Finally, in its consultation paper, the government sought views as to whether the Regulations should be amended to end the exclusion of occupational pension schemes and to require transferee employers to provide comparable pension benefits. As a result of this initiative it appears amendments to the Directive will make it possible for member states to extend the Directive to cover pension benefits, if they so wish. Clearly this proposal may well become law in the UK. If so, something along the lines of the provisions of Sched 7 would presumably be acceptable.

11.9 Clause 8

Clauses 8.1 and 8.2 provide for apportionment between the seller and the purchaser of periodic payments, such as utilities charges, remuneration, PAYE and social security, made before completion but which relate to periods after completion. Clause 8.3 provides that pre-completion VAT liabilities (including any refunds) are the responsibility of the seller, and cl 8.4 that any deposits or prepayments received by the seller before completion in respect of goods or services to be supplied by the purchaser after completion shall be accounted for to the purchaser by the seller. Clause 8.5 provides that all of the above issues will be calculated in, and the relevant payments made on the basis of, a completion statement.

11.10 Clause 9

This clause imposes on the purchaser the obligation to take on and discharge existing contracts for the service and maintenance of acquired assets, and to assist the seller in collecting the debts relating to the transferred business that he has retained.

11.11 Clause 10

This clause deals with the general obligations of the seller. He is to discharge all pre-completion creditors retained by him pursuant to cl 2.2 and to indemnify the purchaser for any claims such creditors may make against the purchaser for his failure so to do (cl 10.1). Additionally, cl 10.2 contains further assurance provisions and a vendor non-compete clause.

Reference should be made to the discussion on non-compete clauses contained in Chapter 14, but in general care should always be taken that they are reasonable in extent of area and time, and go no further than really necessary to protect the goodwill of the business transferred. Even though the courts are more lenient towards such clauses than in the case of employee non-compete clauses, the draftsman should always have in the forefront of his mind the need to ensure that the clause imposes no more than a reasonable restraint on competition if it is not to run the risk of it being declared void when any attempt is made to invoke it in court.

11.12   Clause 11

This clause deals with the making of the warranties and the regulation of claims to be made for breach of them. Unlike Precedent 2 of Chapter 10, there are no indemnity provisions so that the purchaser must claim and prove damage for breach of warranty at common law, and the various provisions limiting liability under the warranties and regulating matters relating to third party claims are all contained in cl 11.

The issues surrounding the provisions in this clause are the same as those relating to the equivalent provisions in Precedent 2 of Chapter 10, and reference should be made to the commentary and specimen clauses in that chapter as necessary.

The two approaches to warranty claims taken in Chapter 10 and Chapter 11 could each be applied in relation to a business transfer and a share sale. The real difference between them is that the approach and drafting in Chapter 10 favours the purchaser while that in Chapter 11 favours the seller.

11.13   Clause 12

Clause 12 makes the obvious point that risk in the business and the assets acquired by the purchaser pass to the purchaser on completion.

11.14   Clause 13

This clause contains a set of miscellaneous provisions relating to various aspects of the transaction: regulation of publicity, prohibitions on assignment of the agreement, a whole agreement clause, a clause making time of the essence in implementing the agreement, provision for disputes over stock valuation (cl 4.10) or the completion statement (cl 8.5) to be submitted to an expert for resolution, a provision apportioning the costs of the transaction between the parties, a clause providing for payment of interest on overdue sums, a notice clause, a severance clause, and a confidentiality clause.

11.15 Clause 14

Given the nature of a business transfer both parties may have possession of records relating to the transferred business or to the business retained by the seller. Clause 14 provides for each party to have access to relevant records needed by it for its own business purposes but which are in the possession of the other.[14]

11.16 Clause 15

This clause permits the purchaser to carry on the transferred business for a transition period under the name and style previously used by the seller. This is a very important provision where the business is not carried on under a separate name and style which is transferred with the business, but simply under the name and style under which the seller did business generally before completion and under which he will continue to do business after completion. In such cases the seller needs to be sure that he will not appear to be connected with the business once the transition period has passed, while the purchaser needs a transition period to enable him to sell off stock in old packaging, to use up or overprint sales literature and stationery, and to change building signs, vehicle livery and so on.

11.17 The Schedules

Most of the schedules to this precedent are vacant since they are intended to be filled with definitions or lists to suit the details of the particular transaction. The two exceptions are Sched 7, relating to pensions, which has already been discussed, and Sched 11 which contains the warranties.

The warranties in Sched 11 concentrate on the title to and condition of the assets to be transferred, and information about the business and the way in which it has been conducted prior to completion, and have little to do with liabilities, taxation or balance sheets, given that no legal entity is to be transferred. The set of warranties contained in this schedule is intentionally short, and fairly neutral as to favouring either the seller or the purchaser, although, as in the case of warranties for a share sale, specialist works on the subject can be consulted for those who require long form detailed warranties which, depending upon bargaining power, favour one side rather than the other. Consideration should also be given to the warranties contained in Sched 2 of Precedent 2 in Chapter 10, to see if any are relevant. Warranty 6 of Precedent 2, for instance, relating to the current contracts of the business could, after some adaptation, be included with advantage.[15]

Appendix 1

Business transfer agreement

THIS AGREEMENT is made on [   ]
BETWEEN:
(1) [   ] LIMITED whose registered office is at [   ]
(the 'Vendor'); and
(2) [   ] LIMITED whose registered office is at [   ]
(the 'Purchaser').
IT IS AGREED as follows:

1   Interpretation

In this Agreement, including its Schedules, the headings shall not affect its
interpretation and, unless the context otherwise requires:
1.1 Definitions:
'Agreed Terms' means in relation to any document such document in the terms
agreed between the parties and for the purposes of identification signed by the
Purchaser and the Vendor;
'Assets' shall have the meaning ascribed thereto in cl 2.1;
'Business' means the business described in Schedule 1 hereto, and including
the rights and assets agreed to be sold hereunder;
'Business Information' means all books and records embodying Know-how
and embodying other information relating to the Business (whether or not confidential and no matter in what form held) including, without limitation, all
designs, specifications, data, manuals and instructions and all lists of customers, suppliers, agents and distributors, business plans and forecasts and all notices, correspondence, orders and enquiries and other documents, and all computer discs or tapes or other machine readable or other records owned by the
Vendor and used in connection with the Business, *provided that* in the case of
embodiments of computer programs no such embodiments shall form part of
this definition unless such computer programs are used exclusively for the

purposes of the Business and *provided further* that where any book or record as aforesaid embodies information or Know-how which does not relate to the Business ('extraneous data') the Vendor shall be entitled to delete or remove all extraneous data from the said book or record;

'Chattels' means all assets currently used principally by the Business including without limitation those assets detailed in Schedule 2 hereto;

'Claims' means the benefit of all rights and claims of the Vendor arising out of or in connection with the Business under any agreements, licences, warranties, conditions, guarantees, indemnities or other rights subsisting at the Completion Date (whether express or implied) in favour of the Vendor in relation to any of the Assets included in the sale under this Agreement or previously sold or let on hire by the Vendor in the course of carrying on the Business (including without limitation the benefit of any claim for grants from any government, local or public authority relating to the Business);

'Completion' means the completion of the sale and purchase of the Business pursuant to cl 4;

'Completion Date' means close of business on [   ] or on such later date as the Purchaser and the Vendor may agree or as may be applicable pursuant to cl 4.1;

'Completion Date Statement' means the statement to be produced and agreed by the Vendor and the Purchaser pursuant to cl 8;

'Creditors' means all the obligations of the Vendor (other than those provided for in the Completion Date Statement) at the Completion Date to pay moneys to third parties (whether or not then due and payable) in respect of goods or services or other benefits sold or supplied or provided to or by the Vendor in connection with the Business prior to Completion including, without limitation, all moneys due to any other divisions of the Vendor and any liability for Taxation and VAT and all moneys which may be due to Relevant Employees at Completion;

'Customer Contracts' means all contracts entered into prior to the Completion Date by or on behalf of the Vendor with third parties for the design, manufacture or sale of goods or provision of services by the Vendor in connection with the Business *provided that* nothing contained in this definition shall be construed so as to prevent the Vendor having the full benefit of the Debts (as hereinafter defined);

'Debts' means the book and other debts owing to the Vendor in connection with the Business (whether or not then due and payable) at the Completion Date (including, without limitation, from other divisions of the Vendor and all recoveries of Taxation and VAT) other than Employee Loans;

'Distributorship Agreements' means the agreements listed in Schedule 3;

'Disclosure Letter' means the letter dated [   ] from the Vendor to the Purchaser disclosing information relating to the Warranties;

'Employee Loans' means those loans made by the Vendor to Relevant Employees as shown in Schedule 4 the benefit of which are to be acquired by the Purchaser;

'Encumbrance' means any mortgage, charge, lien, pledge, option, right to acquire, security interest, equity, and any other like claims;

'Goodwill' means the goodwill of the Business as a going concern and of the Vendor in connection with the Business together with the exclusive right (so far as the Vendor can grant the same) for the Purchaser and its assignees to represent themselves as carrying on the Business in succession to the Vendor;

'Intellectual Property' means patents, trademarks and service marks, designs, trade names, copyrights, including (without prejudice to the generality of the foregoing) those subsisting in Know-how and inventions (whether or not any of these is registered and including applications for registration of any such thing) and all rights or forms of protection of a similar nature or having equivalent or similar effect to any of these which may subsist anywhere in the world;

'Know-how' means all industrial and commercial information and techniques including (without prejudice to the generality of the foregoing) drawings, formulae, test reports, operating and testing procedures, shop practices, instruction manuals, lists and particulars of customers, marketing methods and procedures, advertising copy and computer programs;

'Leasehold Property' means the property of which short particulars are set out in Part I of Schedule 5;

'Literature' means all existing stocks of promotional and advertising material and information leaflets produced by the Vendor for distribution to customers or potential customers of the Business;

'the Order' means the Value Added Tax (Special Provisions) Order 1995 (SI No 1268);

'Parking Spaces' means the parking spaces of which short particulars are set out in Part V of Schedule 5;

'Properties' means the Leasehold Property and the Sub-leasehold Property;

'Purchaser's Scheme' is defined in Schedule 7;

'Purchaser's Solicitors' means Messrs [   ] of [   ];

'Relevant Employees' means those employees, details of which are set out in Schedule 4, of the Vendor;

'Shared Services Agreement' means the agreement between the parties hereto in the form set out in Schedule 15;

'Stock' has the meaning ascribed thereto in para 16 of Part 2 of SSAP 9 but excluding the Debts;

'Sub-leasehold Property' means the property of which short particulars are set out in Part III of Schedule 5;

'Supplier Contracts' means all contracts entered into prior to the Completion Date by or on behalf of the Vendor with third parties for the sale or provision of goods or services in connection with the Business (including without limitation the agreements brief details of which are contained in Schedule 12 and the leased services provided to the Properties brief details of all such leased services being set out in Schedule 13) which then remain to be performed in whole or in part and for this purpose contracts for the supply of goods shall be deemed to be performed when the relevant items have been delivered to the Vendor pursuant thereto *provided that* nothing contained in this definition shall be construed so as to relieve the Vendor of its obligations in relation to the Creditors;

'Taxation' includes all forms of taxation and statutory, governmental, state, provincial, local governmental or municipal impositions, duties, contributions and levies, in each case whether of the United Kingdom or elsewhere, whenever imposed and all penalties, charges, costs and interest relating thereto;

'Transfer Regulations' means the Transfer of Undertakings (Protection of Employment) Regulations 1981 (SI No 1794);

'VAT' means UK Value Added Tax;

'Vendor's Employees' means those employees of the Vendor who provide general services for the whole of the Vendor's site at [   ] and who indirectly have provided services in connection with the Business;

'Vendor's Intellectual Property' means the Intellectual Property specified in Schedule 8;

'Vendor's Know-how' means the Know-how specified in Schedule 9;

'Vendor's Licensed Intellectual Property' means the Intellectual Property specified in Schedule 10;

'Vendor's Plan' is defined in Schedule 7;

'Warranties' means the warranties, representations and undertakings set out in cll 4.12 and 11 and Schedules 7 and 11;

1.2 any reference to a statutory provision shall include any subordinate legislation made from time to time under that provision;

1.3 any reference to a statutory provision shall include that provision as from time to time modified or re-enacted whether before or after the date of this Agreement so far as such modification or re-enactment applies or is capable of applying to any transactions entered into prior to Completion and (so far as any liability thereunder may exist or can arise) shall include also any past statutory provision (as from time to time modified or re-enacted) which such provision has directly or indirectly replaced;

1.4 the words 'company', 'subsidiary' 'wholly-owned subsidiary', 'holding company' and 'fellow subsidiary' shall have the same meanings in this Agreement as their respective definitions in the Companies Act 1985;

1.5 the Interpretation Act 1978 shall apply in the same way as it applies to an enactment;

1.6 A reference to an SSAP means a Statement of Standard Accounting Practice published by the Institute of Chartered Accountants, in England and Wales.

2   Agreement to sell the business

2.1 The Vendor shall sell as beneficial owner and the Purchaser shall purchase free from all Encumbrances the following (hereinafter collectively referred to as the 'Assets'):

2.1.1 the Stock;

2.1.2 the benefit of the Customer Contracts, the Supplier Contracts and the Distributorship Agreements in so far as such Distributorship Agreements relate to the Business;

2.1.3 the Business as a going concern and the Goodwill;

2.1.4 the Chattels;

2.1.5 the Vendor's Intellectual Property;

2.1.6 the right to receive monies owing under the Employee Loans;

2.1.7 the benefit (so far as the same can lawfully be assigned or transferred to or held in trust for the Purchaser) of the Claims;

2.1.8 the Business Information and the Literature;

2.1.9 the Leasehold Property, the Sub-leasehold Property and the Parking Spaces; and

2.1.10 the non-exclusive right to use the Vendor's Know-how and the Vendor's Licensed Intellectual Property.

2.2 No assets other than as expressly provided in cl 2.1 shall be sold or transferred to the Purchaser under this Agreement. Without prejudice to the generality of the foregoing the following are excluded from the sale under this Agreement:

2.2.1 all cash in hand or in a bank or credited in any account with a bank;

2.2.2 the benefit of any insurance claims made by the Vendor in respect of costs, expenses and/or liabilities incurred by the Vendor and arising prior to the Completion Date;

2.2.3 the Debts; and

2.2.4 the Creditors.

2.3 The provisions of Part II of Schedule 5 shall apply to the sale of the Leasehold Property, the provisions of Part IV of Schedule 5 shall apply to the sale of the Sub-leasehold Property and the provisions of Part VI of Schedule 5 shall apply to the sale of the Parking Spaces.

3   Consideration

3.1 The consideration for the purchase of the Business shall, subject as provided in cll 4.9, 4.10 and 4.11, be the cash sum of [   ].

3.2 The total consideration shall be allocated as follows:

	Item	Amount
3.2.1	The Stock:	£
3.2.2	Properties:	£
3.2.3	Goodwill including the value of the Customer Contracts:	£
3.2.4	Know-how and Intellectual Property:	£
3.2.5	The Chattels:	£
3.2.6	Other assets:	£
	Total	£

3.3 The parties hereto intend that art 12 of the Order shall apply to the transfer of the Business under this Agreement and accordingly:

3.3.1 the Vendor shall give notice of such transfer to HM Customs and Excise as required by para 11 of Schedule 1 to the Value Added Tax Act 1994 or by para 6 of the Value Added Tax Regulations 1995 (SI No 2518) or as otherwise required by law;

3.3.2 where records are to be maintained by the Vendor, the Vendor shall apply to HM Customs and Excise for and obtain a direction that all records referred to in s 49 of the Value Added Tax Act 1994 may be retained and the Vendor undertakes to preserve those records in such a manner and for such periods as may be required by law;

3.3.3 the Vendor and the Purchaser shall use all reasonable endeavours to secure that the sale of the Business is treated under the Order as neither a supply of goods nor a supply of services and the Vendor and the Purchaser shall agree the form of a letter to be sent by the Vendor to HM Customs and Excise as soon as practicable after Completion seeking confirmation that the sale is to be so treated;

3.3.4 if such confirmation is expressly refused before Completion the Purchaser shall (against production of tax invoices in respect thereof) pay the amount of any VAT which may be chargeable on the sale of the Business hereunder. If such confirmation shall not have been expressly refused before Completion no amount in respect of VAT shall be paid by the Purchaser on Completion but, if VAT shall be finally determined to be payable on the sale, the Purchaser shall pay to the Vendor such VAT; such payment by the Purchaser to be made within seven days against delivery of a copy of the relevant tax invoice and evidence of payment thereof by the Vendor to HM Customs and Excise or if later against delivery by the Vendor to the Purchaser of the appropriate tax invoice.

3.4 While the total consideration is to be allocated as provided in cl 3.2 above, it is nevertheless agreed between the parties hereto that the consideration for the purchase of the Assets and the Business is a single price and that, in the event of there being any claim arising under or in connection with this Agreement, the compensation payable by the Vendor to the Purchaser shall be determined accordingly.

4   Conditions and completion

4.1 Subject as hereinafter provided, Completion shall take place at the registered office of the Vendor immediately upon the execution of this Agreement:

4.1.1 if any licences, authorisations, orders, grants, confirmations, consents, permissions and approvals from third parties (hereinafter collectively referred to as 'Consents') are necessary or required for the transfer of any Assets to the Purchaser or for the conduct by the Purchaser of the Business the Vendor shall use its [reasonable] [best] endeavours to procure that the same are issued or, as the case may be, transferred to the Purchaser prior to Completion at the expense of the Vendor;

4.1.2 the Vendor shall ensure that prior to Completion all bolts and fastenings attaching plant, machinery or fittings to land or buildings (insofar as included in the sale under this Agreement) which can safely be undone shall be undone so that the same shall be severed at the Completion Date and title shall pass by delivery pursuant to cl 4.2.2.

4.2 On Completion the Vendor shall deliver to the Purchaser:

4.2.1 together with the relevant documents of title and any requisite consent or licence, such executed conveyances, transfers and assignments (if practicable, in a form previously approved by the Purchaser's Solicitors) as may be required or necessary to complete the sale and purchase of the Business and the Assets and to vest in the Purchaser or as it may direct title and the full benefit of the Business and the Assets and shall permit the Purchaser or its nominee to enter into and take possession of the Business and the Assets;

4.2.2 all the Assets which are capable of transfer by delivery, whereupon the title thereto shall pass to the Purchaser by such delivery;

4.2.3 duly executed licences in the forms set out in Schedule 6 Parts I and II granting the Purchaser the non-exclusive right to use respectively the Vendor's Know-how and the Vendor's Licensed Intellectual Property;

4.2.4 all the records of the Business for VAT purposes that are required under s 49(1)(*b*) of the Value Added Tax Act 1994 to be preserved by the Purchaser in place of the Vendor;

4.2.5 a duly executed power of attorney together with a certified copy of the minute of a meeting of the board of directors of the Vendor authorising the execution by a nominated representative of the Vendor of this Agreement and the documents to be delivered pursuant hereto.

4.3 On Completion the Purchaser shall deliver to the Vendor:

4.3.1 a duly executed power of attorney together with a certified copy of the minute of a meeting of the board of directors of the Purchaser authorising the execution by a nominated representative of the Purchaser of this Agreement and the documents to be delivered pursuant thereto;

4.3.2 satisfactory evidence of the deposit and subsequent release of the monies referred to in cl 4.9.1.

4.4 Without prejudice to the obligations of the Vendor under the provisions of this cl 4, the Vendor shall immediately assign to the order of the Purchaser, or procure the assignment to the order of the Purchaser of, all Customer Contracts and Supplier Contracts and all other Assets which are capable of assignment without the consent of other parties and in the case of any such agreements or contracts not so capable of assignment shall use its reasonable endeavours to immediately procure all necessary consents for the assignment or novation of the same and, pending such assignment or novation, the Vendor shall subcontract to the Purchaser on the same terms, *mutatis mutandis*, and for the same remuneration as therein specified, the performance of any such agreements or contracts.

4.5 The Vendor shall use its reasonable or, in the case of distributorships held in respect of the Business by other divisions or subsidiaries of the Vendor, its best efforts to procure that parties to the Distributorship Agreements consent to the substitution of the Purchaser as a party thereto as regards the Business and shall take such actions as the Purchaser may reasonably request to transfer to the Purchaser the benefit of the Distributorship Agreements in so far as they relate to the Business and in any case where such consent is refused or otherwise not obtained the Vendor shall hold such benefit of the relevant Distributorship Agreement in trust for the Purchaser absolutely subject to being indemnified by the Purchaser against the performance thereof only. The Purchaser undertakes and the Vendor undertakes to procure (without prejudice to the generality of the foregoing) the continuance upon fair and reasonable arm's length terms and conditions of the distributorships held in respect of the Business by other divisions or subsidiaries of the Vendor. The Vendor will for a period of six months after the Completion Date give to the Purchaser reasonable assistance to renegotiate the terms and conditions of any Distributorship Agreement in so far as the same relates to the Business, provided always that nothing in this subclause shall oblige the Vendor to take any action which may reasonably damage its commercial interests.

4.6 Until the Consents mentioned in cl 4.1.1 have been obtained the Vendor shall use its reasonable endeavours to ensure that all such Consents are issued, obtained or, as the case may be, transferred to the Purchaser and, until such time, the Vendor shall hold the Assets in question in trust for the Purchaser absolutely as from the Completion Date, shall grant to the Purchaser such powers of attorney as the Purchaser may require to enable the Purchaser to vest in itself or otherwise to deal with such Assets, and shall deliver to the Purchaser forthwith upon receipt any benefit, information or any notice or other document concerning or relating to such Assets.

4.7 The Purchaser shall not be obliged to complete the purchase of any of the Assets unless all of the requirements set out in cl 4 above have been complied with and all of the Assets are included in the sale. However, the Purchaser may at its discretion (and without prejudice to any claim for breach of this agreement and without waiving any of its rights) complete this Agreement even though all of the requirements set out in cl 4 above have not been complied with.

4.8 The Vendor, or, as the case may be, the Purchaser, shall indemnify the Purchaser and the Vendor, respectively, against any document delivered by the Vendor, or, as the case may be, the Purchaser, pursuant to this clause being unauthorised, invalid or for any other reason ineffective for its purpose or against failure by the Vendor, or, as the case may be, the Purchaser, to satisfy all of its obligations under this clause.

4.9 Against compliance with the foregoing provisions the Purchaser shall satisfy the purchase consideration specified in cl 3 as follows:
4.9.1 £[   ] together with interest, if any, accrued thereon from the Completion Date shall be released to the Vendor on Completion; and
4.9.2 subject to cl 4.11, £[   ] on the sixtieth day after Completion, or (if that day shall not be a business day) on the next business day immediately succeeding that day or, if the provisions of cl 13.5 apply, within seven days from the notification to the parties of the decision thereunder.

4.10 In order to determine the value of the Stock, the Vendor and the Purchaser shall jointly carry out an audit of the Stock as follows:
4.10.1 immediately after Completion the Vendor and the Purchaser shall jointly undertake or shall procure the making of a physical stock-take;
4.10.2 within 30 days after the Completion Date the Purchaser and Vendor shall propose and agree jointly a valuation of the Stock based upon the accounting principles laid down in SSAP 9 using the following formulae in the determination of 'net realisable value' in s 16 of Appendix 1 of SSAP 9:
4.10.2.1 'Annual Usage' shall be defined as Customer Contracts on hand as at the Completion Date, including unscheduled contracts or agreements, plus the historical usage for the [six months] prior to the Completion Date. Where a specific stock item has superseded a previous stock item then the usage of the previous item will be added to that of the current term for the purposes of defining the Annual Usage. All superseded stock referred to above shall be valued at nil;
4.10.2.2 stock awaiting rework will be valued taking into account appropriate historical scrap rates experienced in such circumstances;
4.10.2.3 all inventory holdings equating to half of the relevant Annual Usage or less shall be costed at [100] per centum of their book value;
4.10.2.4 all inventory holdings equating to more than half and up to the whole of

the relevant Annual Usage shall be costed at [75] per centum of their book value;
4.10.2.5 that portion of an inventory holding in excess of the relevant Annual Usage is deemed to be an 'Excess Stock Holding';
4.10.2.6 an Excess Stock Holding of up to [100] per centum of the relevant Annual Usage shall be costed at [25] per centum of its book value; and
4.10.2.7 that portion of an Excess Stock Holding of more than 100 per centum of the relevant Annual Usage shall be deemed to have no value.

4.11 In the event that the value of the Stock as determined in accordance with cl 4.10 is less than [   ] the instalment of the purchase consideration payable under cl 4.9.2 shall be reduced on a pound for pound basis by an amount equal to the amount by which the value of the Stock is less than [   ].

4.12 The Vendor hereby warrants and undertakes to the Purchaser that the value of the Stock will not be less than [   ].

4.13 On Completion the Vendor and the parties hereto shall enter into the Shared Services Agreement.

5   The supplier contracts and customer contracts

5.1 The Purchaser shall after the Completion Date carry out and complete for its own account the Supplier Contracts and the Customer Contracts to the extent that the same have not been previously performed. In so doing the Purchaser shall complete the same in timely and efficient manner and hereby indemnifies and agrees to keep indemnified the Vendor from and against all customer, supplier and third party claims and actions, damages and costs arising solely from the Purchaser's acts or omissions in performing the same. [Without prejudice to the generality of the foregoing the Purchaser undertakes to continue to supply the Vendor, its divisions and subsidiaries with the products manufactured in the Business at fair and reasonable market prices and the Vendor undertakes to procure that its divisions and subsidiaries shall continue to purchase products manufactured by the Business on the basis that the Business is treated as a preferred supplier *provided that* price, quality and delivery terms are competitive [and] satisfactory otherwise to the Vendor. In the event the Purchaser wishes to discontinue manufacture of any such product, it shall give the Vendor not less than three months' notice thereof and the opportunity to make a lifetime buy of such product].

5.2 In the event of any such claim or action being threatened or brought against the Vendor, the Vendor shall not compromise or settle the same but shall notify the Purchaser thereof and, subject to being indemnified to its reasonable satisfaction, the Vendor will at the request of the Purchaser take such action in respect thereof (including lending its name to any legal action) as the Purchaser may require, provided always however that nothing in this subclause shall oblige the Vendor to take any action which may reasonably damage its commercial interests.

5.3 Subject always as provided below, the Purchaser shall indemnify the Vendor from costs and expenses incurred as a result of any claim from customers for repair or replacement under any warranties, representations or guarantees given expressly by the Vendor and disclosed in the Disclosure Letter or, as the case may be, given by implication of law in respect of goods or services of the Business supplied by the Vendor prior to Completion, and the Purchaser shall likewise indemnify the Vendor from costs and expenses incurred as a result of any claim by third parties arising under any such warranties, representations or guarantees, provided always that:

5.3.1 the Vendor shall notify the Purchaser as soon as practicable after the receipt of any such claim;

5.3.2 the Purchaser shall deal with such claims in the ordinary course, by repair or (if repair is not practical or economic) by replacement, but shall if appropriate resist such claims if not in accordance with the relevant warranty, representation or guarantee;

5.3.3 the Vendor shall not be entitled to be indemnified against such costs and expenses incurred as a result of any claim arising more than [24] months after the Completion Date;

5.3.4 the liability of the Purchaser under this clause shall be limited to an amount of £[   ] per month in respect of all costs and expenses to the Purchaser (calculated where relevant at the Purchaser's standard rates for the time being current) of effecting such repair or replacement as is referred to in (*b*) above, and where the said costs and expenses exceed £[   ] in any one month, the Purchaser shall not be liable for such excess. The Purchaser shall give the Vendor a monthly statement with details of each claim settled as aforesaid and of the costs and expenses of the Purchaser in respect thereof.

Subject as provided above, the Vendor shall indemnify and keep the Purchaser indemnified from any claims, costs, expenses or losses arising in respect of any warranties, representations and guarantees given expressly or by implication of law in respect of goods or services of the Business supplied by the Vendor prior to Completion.

5.4 Prior to the assignment or novation of the Supplier Contracts and the Customer Contracts in accordance with cl 4 and in respect of the Distributorship Agreements in so far as they relate to the Business the Vendor shall receive any benefits, goods or Business Information delivered to it as agent for the Purchaser and taking all reasonable care shall deliver the same to such address of the Purchaser as the Purchaser may specify.

6 The relevant employees

6.1 The parties agree that the transfer of the Business to be effected by this Agreement is governed by the provisions of the Transfer Regulations and the following provisions shall apply in connection therewith:

6.1.1 the contract of employment of each of the Relevant Employees (save insofar as such contract relates to any occupational pension scheme) shall be transferred to the Purchaser with effect from the Completion Date which shall be the 'time of transfer' under the Transfer Regulations;

6.1.2 the Vendor shall discharge all wages and salaries, excluding accrued holiday remuneration (if any), of the Relevant Employees and all other costs and expenses relating to the Relevant Employees up to and including the Completion Date and shall indemnify the Purchaser against each and every liability, cost, claim, expense or demand arising from the Vendor's failure so to discharge;

6.1.3 the Vendor shall indemnify the Purchaser against each and every cost, claim, liability, expense, or demand which relates to or arises out of any act or omission by or in relation to the Vendor or any other event or occurrence prior to the Completion Date and which the Purchaser may incur in relation to any contracts of employment or collective agreements concerning the Relevant Employees pursuant to the Transfer Regulations or otherwise but including without limitation any matter relating to or arising out of:

6.1.3.1 the Vendor's rights, powers, duties and/or liabilities under or in connection with any such contract of employment (which rights, powers, duties and/or liabilities are or will be transferred to the Purchaser expressly under cl 6.1 and/or in accordance with the Transfer Regulations); or

6.1.3.2 anything done or omitted to be done before the Completion Date by or in relation to the Vendor in respect of any such contract of employment or any such collective agreements of any person employed in the Business, which is deemed to have been done or omitted to be done by or in relation to the Purchaser in accordance with the Transfer Regulations;

6.1.4 the Vendor and the Purchaser shall deliver to each of the Relevant Employees a letter in the agreed terms.

6.1.5 Nothing in this cl 6.1.4 shall render the Vendor liable to the Purchaser in relation to accrued holiday rights or accrued holiday remuneration in respect of the Relevant Employees.

6.2 Subject always as provided in cl 6.3, the Purchaser undertakes that it shall employ each of the Relevant Employees after the Completion Date upon terms and conditions of employment which are such that they do not amount to a substantial change to such employees' working conditions (as referred to in para 5 of reg 5 of the Transfer Regulations) provided (for the avoidance of doubt) that (subject to cl 7 and Schedule 7) the Purchaser shall not be obliged to assume any liability for any pension or insurance benefits or any other benefit provided under an occupational pension scheme provided or made available to the Relevant Employees prior to the Completion Date or to offer to the Relevant Employees terms in respect of such benefits which relate to a period or give credit for service or deemed service, before the Completion Date and provided also (for the avoidance of doubt) that cl 6.2 shall place the Purchaser under no obligation whatsoever to either the Vendor or the Relevant Employees with regard to their pension entitlement.

6.3 After Completion the Purchaser will declare redundant and terminate with effect from a date as soon as possible after and in any event within 15 days following Completion, subject to consultation and any other requirements of law, the contracts of employment of those Relevant Employees whose names are listed in Schedule 14 (hereinafter the 'Schedule 14 Employees'). Upon such termination, the Purchaser will pay no more than, and the Vendor will reimburse the Purchaser for, the following costs in respect of each Schedule 14 Employee:

6.3.1 statutory redundancy pay; and

[**6.3.2** half a week's actual pay per complete year of service; and]

6.3.3 pay in lieu of notice, whether statutory, contractual, or under common law, whichever is the greater. In addition, the Vendor shall reimburse the Purchaser for the payment of all wages and salaries paid to each Schedule 14 Employee from the Completion Date up to and including the date that employee ceases to be employed in the Business.

6.4 If the Purchaser shall re-employ any Schedule 14 Employee or any such employee shall otherwise be employed in connection with the Business or on the Properties within a period of 12 months following Completion, the Purchaser shall refund to the Vendor any moneys paid by the Vendor to the Purchaser in respect of that Employee pursuant to this subclause. The Purchaser further undertakes to the Vendor not to solicit the Vendor's Employees for the purpose of employing them in connection with the Business or on the Properties for a period of 12 months following Completion.

6.5 The Vendor shall indemnify and keep the Purchaser indemnified from and against any claims, payments, costs, expenses and other liabilities arising in connection with or relating to any of the Schedule 14 Employees and/or the Vendor's Employees, including without limitation, relating to the contract of employment of any such employee or the termination of such contract *provided always that* such indemnity shall not extend to any such claim, payment, cost, expense or other liability to the extent that it is covered, or should have been covered by law, by employer's liability insurance, *and provided further that* the indemnity provided under this cl 6.5 shall not apply to any claim, suit or proceeding by a Schedule 14 Employee relating to redundancy, unfair dismissal or wrongful dismissal or in respect of accrued holiday remuneration or accrued holiday rights ('transfer claims') on the basis that the payments to be made to the Purchaser by the Vendor pursuant to cl 6.3 are in full and final satisfaction of all liability the Vendor owes to the Purchaser (whether pursuant to this Agreement or otherwise) in respect of transfer claims.

7 Pensions

The provisions of Schedule 7 shall have effect in relation to pensions.

8 Apportionments

8.1 All rents, rent charges, rates, gas, water, electricity and telephone charges, royalties and other periodical payments relating to or payable to or accruing in respect of the Business (including without limitation the Properties and those Supplier Contracts under which periodical payments are made) down to and including the Completion Date shall be borne by or, as the case may be, accounted for to, the Vendor, and thereafter borne by, or accounted for to, the Purchaser and shall be apportioned accordingly.

8.2 Subject as provided in cl 6.3, all salaries, wages and other emoluments and all Taxation and National Insurance relating to them for which an employer is accountable, all employer's contributions to the Vendor's Plan and all other normal employment costs (including without limitation, personal expense accounts, but excluding accrued holiday remuneration) in respect of the Relevant Employees shall be borne by the Vendor down to the Completion Date and shall be apportioned accordingly.

8.3 VAT payable in respect of all goods and services supplied or deemed to be supplied by the Vendor prior to the Completion Date and all interest payable thereon and penalties attributable thereto shall be paid to HM Customs and Excise by the Vendor and the Vendor shall be entitled to receive and retain all reimbursement or credit from HM Customs and Excise for VAT borne by the Vendor on goods and services supplied to the Vendor prior thereto and any payments received in respect of VAT overpaid to HM Customs and Excise prior thereto.

8.4 If and to the extent that the Vendor has prior to the Completion Date received any deposit or payment in advance in respect of any Customer Contract then the Vendor shall account to the Purchaser for the same. Such amounts shall be included in the Completion Date Statement.

8.5 The Vendor shall prepare and deliver to the Purchaser for review by the Purchaser a statement showing the apportionments and pre-payments referred to in cll 8.1, 8.2, 8.3 and 8.4 as soon as practicable and in any event within 90 days after the Completion Date. Subject to the Purchaser agreeing the amounts and the calculations in such statement, such payment as is necessary shall be made to the Vendor or the Purchaser, as the case may be, in cash seven days after the delivery of the Completion Date Statement. Any dispute arising in connection with the Completion Date Statement shall be governed by the provisions of cl 13.5 hereof.

9   Obligations of purchaser

9.1 With effect from the Completion Date the Purchaser shall take over and shall be responsible for all the Supplier Contracts relating to the maintenance and service of the Properties and the Chattels.

9.2 The Purchaser shall, at the request and at the expense of the Vendor, provide the Vendor with all reasonable information and other assistance to enable the Vendor to collect the Debts. In the event that a payment is received by the Purchaser which is in respect of any of the Debts, the Purchaser shall receive the same as trustee and agent for the Vendor, and shall immediately remit the same to the Vendor.

10   General obligations of vendor

10.1 Except as otherwise expressly provided in this Agreement, the Vendor shall be responsible for and shall duly and punctually pay and discharge all Creditors, and other liabilities in connection with the Business existing at the Completion Date, or arising, accruing or assessed in respect of any period or in consequence of any transaction carried out prior thereto, subject as provided in cl 8, and shall indemnify and keep the Purchaser indemnified from and against all claims and actions, damages, costs, expenses and other liabilities arising from the Vendor's acts or omissions in performing the obligations under this cl 10.1.

10.2 Notwithstanding Completion the Vendor hereby undertakes in addition to its obligations under cll 4 and 10.1 and at its own expense:
10.2.1 from time to time to execute such further assurances and afford to the Purchaser such assistance as the Purchaser may reasonably require for the purpose of vesting in the Purchaser or its nominee the full benefit of the Business and the Assets (including, so far as consistent with the terms of this Agreement, the benefit of any rights accruing against third parties, whether such rights have or have not accrued or become enforceable at the Completion Date);

10.2.2 from time to time to supply to the Purchaser such information and assistance as the Purchaser may reasonably require for the purpose of implementing cll 4.10, 7, 8, 9 and 10;

10.2.3 wholly to discontinue carrying on the whole or any part of the Business and save as so provided not thereafter for a period of [two] years from the Completion Date to make or have made or sell products manufactured and sold in connection with the Business at Completion [anywhere in the United Kingdom], provided however that nothing in this subclause shall restrict the Vendor from: acquiring a business, a company or a group of companies part of whose business is the manufacture and/or sale of such products provided always that with regards to any such acquisition:

(a) such part of the business does not, according to the latest audited accounts available, have net assets in excess of 10 per centum of the net assets of the business, company or group of companies being acquired; and

(b) such part of the business shall be disposed of as soon as commercially practicable and in any event within 12 months of its acquisition by the Vendor; and

(c) the Vendor shall offer to the Purchaser, in advance of other potential purchasers, the opportunity to purchase such part of the business.

10.3 The Vendor shall not at any time make a request to HM Customs and Excise for the records delivered to the Purchaser pursuant to cl 4.2.4 to be taken out of the custody of the Purchaser.

11   Warranties

11.1 The Vendor hereby warrants and represents to and undertakes with the Purchaser and its successors in title in the terms set out in the Warranties provided that the Purchaser shall not be entitled to claim that any fact renders any of the Warranties untrue or misleading or causes any of the Warranties to be breached if it has been fully and fairly disclosed to the Purchaser in the Disclosure Letter.

11.2 The Vendor hereby:

11.2.1 undertakes (in the event of any claim being made against it in connection with the sale of the Business or the Assets to the Purchaser) not to make any claim (in the absence of fraud, dishonesty or deliberate misstatement or concealment) against any Relevant Employee (other than those to whom cl 6.3 applies) on whom it may have relied before agreeing to any term of this Agreement or authorising any statement in the Disclosure Letter; and

11.2.2 agrees to consent to the grant of injunctive relief to restrain a breach of the undertaking contained in this subparagraph if requested by the Purchaser so to do.

452 Drafting Commercial Agreements

11.3 Notwithstanding the provisions of cl 11.1, the Vendor shall not be liable under the Warranties in respect of any claim:

11.3.1 subject as provided in cl 11.8, unless notice of it is given in writing by the Purchaser to the Vendor setting out particulars of the grounds on which such claim is based within [12 months] following Completion;

11.3.2 unless it exceeds [£10,000] provided always that in the case of any number of claims arising out of similar circumstances, such claims shall be deemed to form a part or parts of a claim and the amounts of such claims shall be aggregated in order to calculate the amounts of the claim for the purposes of this subclause;

11.3.3 unless the aggregate amount of all claims for which the Vendor would otherwise be liable under this Agreement exceeds [£100,000];

11.3.4 to the extent that the claim is attributable to any voluntary act, omission or transaction of the Purchaser, or its directors, employees or agents or their successors in title after Completion; or

11.3.5 to the extent that the claim arises from an act or at the written request of or with the written consent of the Purchaser or from any matter done or omitted to be done in accordance with the terms of this Agreement.

11.4 The aggregate maximum liability of the Vendor under the Warranties and in respect of any breach of this agreement is limited to [£1,000,000].

11.5 Any amount paid by the Vendor to the Purchaser in respect of a breach of the Warranties and in respect of any other breach of this agreement shall be treated primarily as a reduction in the purchase price attributable to goodwill unless agreement is reached otherwise between the parties hereto.

11.6 The Purchaser shall reimburse to the Vendor an amount equal to any sum paid by the Vendor under any breach of this Agreement which is subsequently recovered by or paid to the Purchaser by any third party, save to the extent that such sum ultimately recovered or paid was taken into account by the Purchaser in its claim against the Vendor under this clause and in all cases less the Purchaser's costs and disbursements in connection with the recovery or payment of such sum on an indemnity basis.

11.7 In respect of claims under the Warranties or any of them the Vendor shall not be liable to the extent that a claim arises as a result of the passing of any enactment or other regulation having the force of law having retrospective effect.

11.8 If any claim under the Warranties or any of them is based upon matters or circumstances which may, contingent on the happening of certain events, give rise to a claim (a 'potential claim') the Vendor shall not be liable to make any payment hereunder unless and until such potential claim becomes an actual liability provided always that this provision shall not preclude the Purchaser from notifying the Vendor of any potential claims for the purposes of cl 11.3.1 if not to do so would mean that the Purchaser would otherwise be precluded from making such claims and the Purchaser shall have a valid claim if notice of the potential claim is given to the Vendor within 12 months following Completion.

11.9 Without prejudice to the liability of the Vendor under the warranties:
11.9.1 the Purchaser shall notify the Vendor of any claim or of any matter which may give rise to a claim against the Purchaser in respect of which (if valid) a claim would lie against the Vendor under any of the Warranties as soon as practicable upon the Purchaser receiving notice of the same;
11.9.2 the Vendor shall be provided with or have made available to it all relevant information and documents of the Purchaser reasonably required by it in connection with any such claim and while the conduct of any action to resist such claim shall be solely in the hands of the Purchaser it is agreed that:
11.9.2.1 the Vendor shall be kept informed on a timely basis of all matters pertaining to any such claim;
11.9.2.2 the appointment of solicitors and other professional advisers shall be subject to the approval of the Vendor (such approval not to be unreasonably withheld or delayed); and
11.9.2.3 the Purchaser shall not make any settlement or compromise of the claim which is the subject of the dispute nor agree any matter in the conduct of such dispute which may affect the amount of liability in connection therewith without the prior approval of the Vendor such approval not to be unreasonably withheld or delayed provided that, in the event of the Vendor refusing such approval to the settlement or compromise of a claim and the Purchaser subsequently becoming liable for a higher amount than the figure at which it would have so settled or compromised the claim, the Vendor shall, notwithstanding the financial limit set out in this cl 11.14, be liable for the additional amount of the liability and any costs properly incurred since the proposed date of settlement or compromise.

11.10 The Warranties and all other provisions of this Agreement in so far as the same shall not have been performed at Completion shall not be extinguished or affected by Completion.

11.11 Each of the remedies conferred on the Purchaser by this Agreement for any breach hereof (including the breach of any Warranty) shall be cumulative and without prejudice to all other remedies and the exercise of or failure to exercise any such remedy shall not constitute a waiver by the Purchaser of any other such remedy so conferred hereunder.

11.12 For the purposes of this clause, references to liabilities include contingent liabilities.

12   Insurance

12.1 The Purchaser shall acquire the Business and the Assets with effect from the Completion Date, from which moment, subject to the provisions in cl 5, the Purchaser shall in all respects be at risk in respect thereof.

13   Other provisions

13.1 The Vendor and the Purchaser shall consult together as to the terms of, the timetable for and manner of publication of any announcement (unless specified by law [or The Stock Exchange]) to shareholders, employees, customers and suppliers or to [The Stock Exchange or] other authorities or to the media or otherwise which either may desire or be obliged to make regarding this Agreement.

13.2 The Purchaser shall not be entitled to assign the benefit of this Agreement to other parties without the prior written consent of the Vendor.

13.3 This Agreement (including all documents to be executed pursuant to cl 4) and the Disclosure Letter and its attachments supersedes all prior representations, arrangements, understandings and agreements between the Parties (whether written or oral) relating to the subject matter hereof (other than a document to be executed pursuant to cl 4 as aforesaid) and sets forth the entire complete and exclusive agreement and understanding between the parties hereto relating to the subject matter hereof. Each party warrants to the other that it has not relied on any representation, arrangement, understanding or agreement (whether written or oral) not expressly set out or referred to in this Agreement (including all documents to be executed pursuant to cl 4). Without prejudice to the generality of the foregoing, save as expressly provided in this Agreement (including all documents to be executed pursuant to cl 4) and the Disclosure Letter and its attachments, (*a*) the Vendor gives no promise, warranty, undertaking or representation to the Purchaser, and (*b*) the Vendor shall be under no liability in respect of the transactions contemplated by, and the subject matter of, this Agreement. [Each party further agrees and undertakes to the other that no breach of this Agreement (including all documents to be executed pursuant to cl 4) shall entitle it to rescind this Agreement, and that its remedies for any breach of this Agreement shall be solely for breach of contract, which remedies shall be subject to and in accordance with the provisions of this Agreement.] No variation of this Agreement shall be effective unless in writing and signed by or on be-half of the parties. Without prejudice to the generality of the foregoing, all promises, representations, warranties and undertakings express or implied by law or legislation are hereby expressly excluded. In the case of any in-consistency between the provisions of the Shared Services Agreement and this Agreement, the provisions of this Agreement shall prevail unless ex-pressly provided otherwise therein. No provision contained in this clause, or elsewhere in this Agreement (including all documents to be executed pursu-ant to cl 4), shall operate so as to exclude any liability of one of the parties in respect of a fraudulent misrepresentation made by that party to the other, or to restrict or exclude any remedy which the other party may have in respect of such misrepresentation.

13.4 Time shall be of the essence of this Agreement, both as regards the dates and periods mentioned and as regards any dates and periods which may be substituted for them in accordance with this Agreement or by agreement in writing between the parties.

13.5 In the event of dispute between the parties in relation to the matters con-tained in cll 4.10.1, 4.10.2 or 8.5 such dispute shall be determined by an inde-pendent firm of Chartered Accountants situated in the UK appointed at the request of either party hereto by the President for the time being of the Insti-tute of Chartered Accountants in England and Wales who shall act as experts and not as arbitrators and whose decision in respect of the reference, and as to who shall pay the costs of the reference to him, or how such costs shall be apportioned, shall be final and binding save in the event of bad faith or mani-fest error.

13.6 The Vendor shall bear all legal, accountancy and other costs and expenses incurred by it in connection with this Agreement and the sale and delivery of the Business and the Assets. The Purchaser shall bear all such costs and ex-penses incurred by it in relation to the registration, preparation and execution of this Agreement and bear all stamp duties and VAT arising out of or in conse-quence of this agreement.

13.7 If the Vendor or the Purchaser defaults in the payment when due of any sum payable under this Agreement (whether determined by agreement or pur-suant to an order of a court or otherwise) the liability of the Vendor or the Purchaser (as the case may be) shall be increased to include interest on such sum from the date when such payment is due until the date of actual payment (as well after as before judgment) at a rate per annum of [1] per centum above the base rate from time to time of [[   ] Bank plc]. Such interest shall accrue from day to day and shall be paid subject to any with-holding tax.

13.8 Any notice, claim or demand requiring to be served under or in connection with this Agreement or with any arbitration or intended arbitration hereunder shall be in writing and shall be sufficiently given or served if delivered in the case of the Vendor to its secretary at its registered office and in the case of the Purchaser to its secretary at its registered office. Any such notice delivered by hand or cable, telegram, telex or facsimile shall conclusively be deemed to have been given or served at the time of despatch in the case of service in the UK or 48 hours thereafter in the case of international service and if sent by post shall conclusively be deemed to have been received 48 hours from the time of posting.

13.9 If any term or provision in this Agreement shall be held to be illegal or unenforceable, in whole or in part, under any enactment or rule of law, such term or provision or part thereof shall to that extent be deemed not to form part of this Agreement but the enforceability of the remainder of this Agreement shall not be affected.

13.10 Except as provided in and for the purpose of this Agreement, the Vendor shall keep confidential and not disclose any part of the Business Information and each party hereto shall keep confidential and shall not disclose any part of the Vendor's Licensed Intellectual Property and Vendor's Know-how (except any part thereof required or used by such party in the conduct of its business in the ordinary course).

14   Access to documents and records

14.1 Without prejudice to the provisions of this cl 14, for the purposes of future audits and Taxation assessments only, the Vendor and Purchaser hereby agree that they will each give the other reasonable access to documents pertaining to the Business which may be reasonably requested in connection with such audits and Taxation assessments for inspection or copying (at the expense of the relevant party) regardless of whether those documents are situated at the Properties or elsewhere.

14.2 Subject as provided in cll 2 and 4, the Vendor shall be under no obligation to deliver to the Purchaser any records which do not relate exclusively to the Business but shall preserve any such records ('retained records') which it retains for a period of not less than seven years.

14.3 The Purchaser shall preserve all records which may be delivered to it by the Vendor at Completion pursuant to cl 4 and relevant or necessary for the purposes of cl 14.1 ('transferred records') for a period of not less than seven years.

14.4 The Vendor agrees that subject to the provisions of subcl 14.5 below it shall, upon reasonable notice and at reasonable cost, grant to the Purchaser access during normal business hours whether by itself or by its professional advisers, to the retained records.

14.5 To the extent that any information to which the Purchaser may gain access as a result of this clause is not publicly available, and does not relate to the Business, such information and records are personal to, and the confidential property of, the Vendor, and the Purchaser undertakes that it shall take all reasonable precautions to keep secret, and not without the prior written consent of the Vendor disclose, such information to any person or body except as may be required by law, or use the same for any purpose other than for the purpose of the Business for which access was authorised by the Vendor.

14.6 The provisions of subcll 14.4 and 14.5 shall apply *mutatis mutandis* to the Vendor, as if the references to the Purchaser were replaced by references to the Vendor, references to the retained records were replaced by references to the transferred records, and references to the Business were replaced by references to the business of the Vendor.

14.7 Each of the parties undertakes that insofar as the VAT records and the retained or transferred records shall comprise personal data as defined by s 1(3) of the Data Protection Act 1983 it will at all times before and after Completion observe the data protection principles and the Purchaser will use all reasonable endeavours to obtain registration in respect of the transferred records as soon as practicable.

15   Use of name

15.1 Subject as provided below, the Purchaser undertakes with the Vendor that after Completion the Business shall not be conducted under the style or name [   ] and that the Purchaser shall not, at any time following 30 days after Completion, whether alone or jointly with another, or as employee or agent of any other person, firm or company, trade under or by reference to or do or conduct business under or use in any way whatsoever the style or name [   ] or any colourable imitation thereof or hold itself out or allow itself to be held out as being connected with the Vendor other than as successor to the Vendor in respect of the Business. *Provided always that* the above shall be without prejudice to the Purchaser's right to sell the Stock in the form in which it was delivered to the Purchaser at Completion. The name [   ] shall be removed from all business stationery and so far as practicable from all premises and Chattels occupied or used by the Purchaser in connection with the Business provided that, in the case of any Chattels where any tooling changes are required to comply with this clause, the Purchaser shall effect such changes as soon as practicable and in any event within a period of six months from Completion but shall be entitled to use such Chattels and the products thereof pending such compliance.

15.2 The Vendor hereby licences the Purchaser for a period of three months following Completion to continue to use the Literature and the Purchaser shall procure that each item of the materials bears a sticker indicating the change of ownership of the Business. Without prejudice to cl 15.1 above, the Vendor hereby grants to the Purchaser the right to reproduce and adapt the Literature in whole or in part for use in the Business, so far as the Vendor is able to do so.

IN WITNESS whereof this Agreement has been entered into on the above date.

SCHEDULE 1
Definition of the Business

SCHEDULE 2
Chattels

SCHEDULE 3
Distributorship Agreements

SCHEDULE 4
Relevant Employess

SCHEDULE 5
Part I: Leasehold Property
Part II:Sale of leasehold Property
Part III:Sub-leasehold Property
Part IV:Sale of Sub-leasehold
Part V:Parking Spaces
Part VI:Sale of Parking Spaces

SCHEDULE 6
Part I: Licence of Vendor's Know-How
Part II: Licence of Vendor's Intellectual Property

SCHEDULE 7
Pension Arrangements

1   Definitions

In this schedule the following expressions shall unless the context otherwise requires have the following meanings:

'Actuarial Assumptions' means the actuarial methods and assumptions which are for time being applied by the Vendor's Actuary for the purpose of funding the Vendor's Plan as set out the Actuary's Letter;

'Actuary's Letter' means the letter dated [   ] from the Vendor's Actuary to the Purchaser's Actuary (a copy of which letter, signed for the purposes of identification by the Vendor and the Purchaser, is contained in Appendix A to this schedule);

'Asset Adjustment' means the adjustment or adjustments to be made in respect of the period from the Completion Date up to but excluding the Payment Date (or in respect of such other period or periods as may be specified in this Schedule) as set out in the Actuary's Letter;

'guaranteed minimum pension' has the meaning given by s 8 of the Pension Schemes Act 1993;

'Interim Period' means the period from the Completion Date up to and including the Partition Date;

'Interest' means interest equal to the base rate from time to time prescribed by [[   ] Bank plc] [compounded with quarterly rests];

'Interim Period Pension Contributions' means an amount equal to the contributions (excluding any additional voluntary contributions) due after the Completion Date to the Vendor's Plan by and in respect of the Transferring Employees pursuant to para 2(*b*) hereof plus the Asset Adjustment on such contributions from the date of payment of each such contribution to the Vendor's Plan up to but excluding the Payment Date;

'Partition Date' means [   ] or such earlier date as the Purchaser and the Vendor shall agree in writing or the Inland Revenue shall require for the cessation of the Purchaser's participation in the Vendor's Plan;

'Payment Date' means such date as shall be agreed between the Vendor and the Purchaser falling on or after the Partition Date or, in default of agreement, the date which is one month after the Transfer Amount is determined;

'Purchaser's Actuary' means [   ] or such other actuary as the Purchaser may for the time being appoint for the purposes of this Schedule;

'Purchaser's Scheme' means the retirement benefits scheme nominated, established or to be established by or at the instance of the Purchaser in accordance with para 3 of this schedule;

'Purchaser's Interim Period Costs' means the amount equal to the aggregate of:

(*a*) the total risk premium cost of the following benefits contingently payable under the Vendor's Plan in respect of the Transferring Employees during the Interim Period calculated in accordance with the Actuarial Assumptions:

    (i)   salary related lump sums on death in service;

    (ii)   the future service element of ill-health retirement pensions; and

    (iii) the future service element of spouses' pensions on death in service;

(*b*) the cost of any benefits (other than those referred to in (*a*) above) paid or payable under the Vendor's Plan to or in respect of the Transferring Employees during the Interim period calculated in accordance with the Actuarial Assumptions; and

(*c*) five per cent of the Interim Period Pension Contributions towards the administrative costs and expenses arising out of or in connection with the participation of the Purchaser in the Vendor's Plan;

together with a sum equal to the Asset Adjustment on each such cost and amount from the date on which such cost is incurred or amount becomes payable as the case may be up to but excluding the Payment Date and for this purpose such costs and amounts shall be deemed to have been incurred or to have become payable as the case may be at the end of each calendar month in respect of the preceding calendar month;

'Relevant Employees' means those employees of the Business who are members of the Vendor's Plan on or before the Completion Date and who become employed by the Purchaser immediately after the Completion Date;

'Section 9(2B) rights' means such rights as are given pursuant to s 9(2B) of the Pension Schemes Act 1993;

'Transfer Amount' means such amount as shall be calculated by the Vendor's Actuary and agreed by the Purchaser's Actuary in accordance with para 4 of this schedule as being equal to the aggregate of:

(*a*) the Vendor's Pension Liabilities; plus

(*b*) the Interim Period Pension Contributions; less

(*c*) the Purchaser's Interim Period Costs increased by the total of all sums referred to in para 2(*b*) below which are due but unpaid at the Partition Date;

'Transferring Employees' means those of the Relevant Employees:

(*a*) who have not opted out of the Vendor's Plan during the Interim Period; and

(*b*) who become members of the Purchaser's Scheme with effect from the Partition Date pursuant to the offer of membership referred to in para 3(*a*) below; and

(*c*) who consent to a payment or transfer from the Vendor's Plan to the Purchaser's Scheme in respect of the benefits under the Vendor's Plan for and in respect of them; and

(*d*) in respect of whom the appropriate amount has been paid to the Purchaser's Scheme as part of the Transfer Amount;

'Vendor's Actuary' means [   ] or such other actuary as the Vendor may for the time being appoint for the purposes of this Schedule;

'Vendor's Pension Liabilities' means an amount equal to the higher of (i) the actuarial value (calculated as at the Completion Date in accordance with the Actuarial Assumptions and adjusted thereafter in respect of the period from the Completion Date up to but excluding the Payment Date by applying the Asset Adjustment thereto) of the benefits prospectively and contingently payable under the rules of the Vendor's Plan in force at the Completion Date to and in respect of the Transferring Employees and their dependants (excluding for the avoidance of doubt any salary-related lump sum death in service benefits other than refunds of contributions, the prospective future service element of any ill-health retirement pensions and the prospective future service element of spouses' pensions payable on death in service and any benefit arising from the payment of additional voluntary contributions pursuant to the provisions of the Vendor's Plan) calculated by reference to Pensionable Service (as defined in the rules of the Vendor's Plan) completed by and Pensionable Pay (as so defined) at the Completion Date, but, for the avoidance of doubt, making proper allowance (on the basis of the Actuarial Assumptions) for projected increases in the rate of Pensionable Pay of each Transferring Employee after the Completion Date; and (ii) the 'cash equivalent' (as that term is used in Chapter IV of the Pension Schemes Act 1993) calculated as at the Partition Date in the same manner and using the same assumptions as the trustees of the Vendor's plan use for determining the cash equivalent for members leaving the Vendor's employment in the normal course of events; and 'Vendor's Plan' means [   ].

2   Interim period

It is hereby agreed that:
   (*a*) subject to the approval of the Commissioners of Inland Revenue and to the Vendor the trustees of the Vendor's Plan and the Purchaser executing a Deed of Adherence in the form contained in Appendix B to this Schedule, the Purchaser shall participate in the Vendor's Plan in respect of the Relevant Employees up to the Partition Date subject to exempt approval of the Vendor's Plan not being adversely affected thereby;
   (*b*) irrespective of any change in the contribution arrangements which may be declared in respect of the Vendor's Plan after the Completion Date the Purchaser shall (i) promptly pay to the trustees of the Vendor's Plan (A) the contributions payable by the Purchaser as a participating company during the Interim Period pursuant to the rules of the Vendor's Plan in force at the Completion Date at the rate of [12] per cent of Pensionable Pay (as defined in the rules of the Vendor's Plan) and (B) the contributions under such rules during the Interim Period at the rate of [five] per cent of the said Pensionable Pay of the Relevant Employees who have not opted out of the Vendor's Plan and who are from time

to time in the purchaser's employ and (ii) comply in all other respects with the trust deed and rules of the Vendor's Plan during the Interim Period; in the event that the said contributions are received by the trustees of the Vendor's Plan more than 14 days after the date on which the same became due the Purchaser shall in addition and at the same time pay to the trustees of the Vendor's Plan Interest thereon from the said due date to the actual date of payment. The Purchaser shall ensure that all such contributions are correctly calculated and shall make available to the Vendor such information as it may reasonably request in order to verify the said contributions from time to time;

(c) the Purchaser and the Vendor shall use their respective reasonable endeavours to procure that the Relevant Employees who are members of the Vendor's Plan and have not opted out of the Vendor's Plan shall continue to be in contracted-out employment (within the meaning of s 38 of the Pension Schemes Act 1993) by reference to the Vendor's Plan during the Interim Period while they are employed by the Purchaser;

(d) during the Interim Period the Vendor will not amend or terminate or consent to the amendment or termination of the Vendor's Plan in respect of the Relevant Employees without approval of the Purchaser which will not be unreasonably withheld *provided that* nothing contained in this para 2(d) shall prevent such alterations and modifications as the Vendor may from time to time require to be made to the Vendor's Plan in so far as the same (i) are necessary to maintain approval of the Vendor's Plan under Chapter I of Part XIV of the Income and Corporation Taxes Act 1988, or (ii) to give effect to any changes required by or under statute or applicable law, or (iii) do not affect the rights and duties of Relevant Employees thereunder as at the Completion Date; and

(e) the Vendor and the Purchaser shall give all such consents and execute all such documents in their power as may be required to give effect to this para 2.

3   Purchaser's scheme

(a) The Purchaser shall procure that with effect from a date no later than the Partition Date the Purchaser will have nominated or established a retirement benefits scheme: (i) which is approved or capable of approval under Chapter I or Chapter IV of Part XIV of the Income and Corporation Taxes Act 1988; (ii) which is a contracted-out scheme (as defined in s 9 of the Pension Schemes Act 1993); (iii) to which the trustees of the Vendor's Plan can make a transfer of cash and/or assets without prejudicing approval of the Vendor's Plan as an exempt approved scheme; and (iv) to which the trustees of the Vendor's Plan can transfer guaranteed minimum pensions and Section 9(2B) rights under the Vendor's Plan in accordance with the Contracting-Out (Transfer and Transfer Payment) Regulations 1996. Such of the Relevant Employees as have not ceased to be in the employment of the Purchaser or opted out of the Vendor's Plan or attained the normal pension age in the Purchaser's Scheme or the Vendor's Participation Plan at the Partition Date will be offered membership of the Purchaser's Scheme with effect from the Partition Date.

(*b*) The Purchaser undertakes that:
(i) membership of the Purchaser's Scheme shall be first open to the Relevant Employees on the Partition Date; and
(ii) service with the Vendor prior to the Completion Date shall count towards the period of service qualifying for admission to the Purchaser's Scheme.

4   Determination of transfer amount

(*a*) Immediately after the Partition Date, the Vendor shall instruct the Vendor's Actuary to calculate the amount of the Transfer Amount and to submit his findings to the Purchaser's Actuary for verification by him. If the Purchaser's Actuary is unable to verify the Transfer Amount as aforesaid within [30 days] of such submission the matter shall be referred to an independent actuary pursuant to para 8 below.

(*b*) Each party shall use its best endeavours to procure that all such information as the other party's actuary may reasonably request for the purpose of calculating or verifying the Transfer Amount (as the case may be) shall be made available to the other party's actuary and that all such information shall be true and complete to the best of the knowledge and belief of the party who procures its availability.

5   Payment of transfer amount

(*a*) The Vendor shall cause the trustees of the Vendor's Plan to have the Transfer Amount paid or transferred to the trustees of the Purchaser's Scheme on the Payment Date in full and final satisfaction of the interests of and in respect of the Transferring Employees in the Vendor's Plan.

(*b*) Such payment shall be made in such cash and assets as the trustees of the Vendor's Plan shall determine. For this purpose there shall not be transferred any investment consisting of shares which cannot be bought or sold through the [London] Stock Exchange.

(*c*) If the Transfer Amount is not transferred on the Payment Date pursuant to para 5(*a*) above the Vendor shall procure that there is paid to the trustees of the Purchaser's Scheme in addition to the Transfer Amount an amount in cash equal to Interest on the Transfer Amount from the Payment Date to the date of actual payment.

(*d*) If the value of the cash and assets actually transferred by the Payment Date from the Vendor's Plan to the Purchaser's Scheme pursuant to this Schedule is either nil or an amount which is less than the Transfer Amount (the amount of such difference being referred to in this paragraph as 'the shortfall') then the Vendor shall pay to the trustees of the Purchaser's Scheme within seven days after the Payment Date a sum in cash equal to the shortfall together with Interest thereon in respect of the period from and including the Payment Date up to but excluding the date of actual payment.

6   The purchaser shall procure that:

(*a*) the Purchaser's Scheme will provide for and in respect of each Transferring Employee who becomes a member of the Purchaser's Scheme on the Partition Date benefits in relation to his service with the Purchaser on and after the Partition Date on a basis no less favourable overall than the Vendor's Plan presently provides;

(*b*) the Purchaser's Scheme will additionally provide for and in respect of each Transferring Employee:

(i) such benefits on a final salary basis in relation to his service before the Completion Date which was pensionable under the Vendor's Plan and thereafter with the Purchaser up to the Partition Date as would have been provided for and in respect of him had he remained in membership of the Vendor's Plan upon the terms in force at the Completion Date and as if such terms had continued to apply in an unamended form until the date of termination of such Transferring Employee's pensionable service under the Purchaser's Scheme; and

(ii) the Purchaser's Scheme will accept liability for (i) the accrued rights to guaranteed minimum pensions and (ii) the Section 9(2B) rights of each Transferring Employee in respect of whom an amount is included in the Transfer Amount; and

(*c*) a relevant Employee who does not agree to become a Transferring Employee by the Partition Date shall on and after the Partition Date be eligible for membership of the Purchaser's Scheme but otherwise in accordance with the rules thereof as are generally applicable to employees of the Purchaser.

7 Additional voluntary contributions

Any additional voluntary contributions made by the Transferring Employees together with the accrued investment return thereon shall be disregarded for the purposes of determining the Transfer Amount.

The Vendor shall use its best endeavours to procure that on the Payment Date the trustees of the Vendor's Plan shall pay or transfer to the trustees of the Purchaser's Scheme in addition to the Transfer Amount any sums or policies which the Vendor's Actuary determines as at the Payment Date to relate to additional voluntary contributions paid to the Vendor's Plan by the Transferring Employees.

8 Disputes

Any dispute between the Vendor and the Purchaser or the Vendor's Actuary and the Purchaser's Actuary concerning the calculation of the Transfer Amount or any other matter of an actuarial nature (except the determination of the Actuarial Assumptions which shall not be open to dispute) shall, in the absence of agreement between them, be referred to an independent actuary agreed by the Vendor and the Purchaser or, failing such agreement within 14 days of one party calling upon the other in writing so to agree, appointed by the President for the time being of the Institute of Actuaries. Any such independent actuary shall determine the dispute in accordance with the provisions of this Schedule and in accordance with the Actuarial Assumptions, and shall act as an expert and not as an arbitrator and his decision shall (in the absence of manifest error) be final and binding upon the Vendor and the Purchaser. The charges and expenses of the independent actuary in respect of any such reference shall be borne equally by the Vendor and the Purchaser.

9 Debt on the Employer

The Vendor shall procure that no action is taken that gives rise to any liability on the part of the Purchaser under s 75 of the Pensions Act 1995 and the Occupational Pension Schemes (Deficiency on Winding Up etc) Regulations 1996 on account of the Purchaser's participation, or the cessation of its participation, in the Vendor's Plan (save where such liability is due to an act or omission of the Purchaser) failing which the Vendor shall pay to the Purchaser a sum equal to the amount of such liability incurred by the Purchaser, such payment to be made to the Purchaser seven days [before the date upon which the Purchaser is obliged to make] [after the date on which the Purchaser has actually made] the payment in discharge of such liability, and such payment by the Vendor shall be in full and final discharge of the Vendor's obligations to the Purchaser under this clause.

APPENDIX A TO SCHEDULE [   ]
Actuarial Assumptions

APPENDIX B TO SCHEDULE [   ]
Deed of Adherence

MADE the [   ] day of [   ] BETWEEN:

(1) [   ] Limited whose registered office at [   ]
(hereinafter called the 'Principal Company')

(2) [   ] Limited whose registered office is at [   ]
(hereinafter called the 'New Participating Company') and

(3) [   ] Pension Trust Limited whose registered office is at
[   ] (hereinafter called the 'Trustees')

SUPPLEMENTAL to the Deeds (short particulars of which are set out in the Schedule hereto) which together establish and constitute a retirement benefits scheme known as the [   ] Pension Plan (hereinafter called the 'Plan') for the purpose of providing pensions on retirement at a specified age and other benefits for certain employees of the Principal Company and of any Group Company.

1   Recitals

(*a*) The Trustees are the present trustees of the Plan.

(*b*) By clause [   ] of the deed numbered [   ] in the said Schedule (hereinafter called the 'Trust Deed') the Principal Company may extend the benefits of the Plan to such employees of any Group Company as are eligible for membership of the Plan *provided* that:

(i) any such Group Company shall enter into a deed by which it covenants with the Trustees and the Principal Company to comply with and observe the provisions of the Trust Deed so far as they are applicable to it in relation to its Employees; and

(ii) the participation of any such Group Company will not prejudice the exempt approved status of the Plan nor contravene any statutory or other provision or any requirement of the Commissioners of Inland Revenue or of the Occupational Pensions Board.

(*c*) By r [   ] of the rules annexed to the Trust Deed 'Group Company' is defined as any company which is controlled by controlling or in common control with the Principal Company and any other company acceptable to the Commissioners of Inland Revenue as a Group Company and shall with the consent of the Principal Company include a company which has acquired the whole or part of the business or undertaking of any of the Employers and the Employees engaged therein and which intends to maintain such Employees in Pensionable

Service under the Plan for a period not exceeding [one] year (pursuant to [clause [   ] of Part [   ] of the [Second] Schedule to] the Trust Deed).

(*d*) The New Participating Company is a Group Company having been accepted as such by the Commissioners of Inland Revenue.

(*e*) The Principal Company and the New Participating Company desire that such former employees of the Principal Company should continue in membership of the Plan on a temporary basis and the New Participating Company has agreed with the Principal Company and the Trustees to enter into the covenant in this deed.

2   Operative provisions

2.1 Subject to the provision of clause [   ] of the Trust Deed the Principal Company HEREBY EXTENDS the benefits of the Plan during a period of [12] months from [   ] (hereinafter called the 'Temporary Period') to such former employees of the Principal Company who become employees of the New Participating Company during the Temporary Period and who are otherwise eligible for membership of the Plan and the New Participating Company HEREBY COVENANTS with the Trustees and the Principal Company that it will duly comply with and observe the provisions of the Plan (as from time to time amended) so far as they are applicable to it in relation to such employees with effect on and from [   ] until the earliest of (*a*) the date of the determination of the trusts of the Plan and the winding-up thereof or (*b*) the end of the Temporary Period or (*c*) the date on which the New Participating Company ceases to be included in the Plan whether upon the happening of one or more of the events set out in clause [   ] of the Trust Deed or otherwise.

2.2 Words and expressions used in this deed and not defined herein shall have the meaning given to them in the Trust Deed.

IN WITNESS whereof the Principal Company the New Participating Company and the Trustees have caused their respective Common Seals to be hereunto affixed the day and year first before written.

THE SCHEDULE above referred to

Number   Date   Document

SCHEDULE 8
VENDOR'S INTELLECTUAL PROPERTY

SCHEDULE 9
VENDOR'S KNOWHOW

SCHEDULE 10
VENDOR'S LICENSED INTELLECTUAL PROPERTY

SCHEDULE 11
WARRANTIES

1   The vendor

1.1 *Authority and capacity of the Vendor*
1.1.1 The Vendor has full power and authority to enter into and perform this Agreement and this Agreement when executed will constitute a binding obligation on the Vendor, in accordance with its terms.
1.1.2 The execution and delivery of, and the performance by the Vendor of its obligations under this Agreement will not:

   (*a*) result in a breach of any provision of the memorandum or articles of association of the Vendor; or
   (*b*) result in a breach of any order, judgment or decree of any court or governmental agency to which the Vendor is a party or by which the Vendor is bound.

1.2 *Vendor's other interests*
[To the best of the Vendor's knowledge, information and belief] the Vendor has no right or interest, direct or indirect, in any business other than the Business which is, or is likely to become, competitive with the Business save as registered holder or beneficial owner of any class of securities of any company which is listed on [The Stock Exchange], or dealt in on the Unlisted Securities Market and in respect of which the Vendor together with any person connected with it holds, and is beneficially interested in, less than [five per cent] of any single class of the securities in that company.

2   Supply of information

Accuracy and adequacy of information disclosed to the purchaser
All information contained in this Agreement and the Disclosure Letter was when given [to the best of the knowledge, information and belief of the Vendor] true, complete and accurate in all material respects.

3   Legal matters

3.1 *Compliance with laws*
[To the best of the Vendor's knowledge and belief] the Business has at all

times been conducted in accordance with applicable laws, regulations and byelaws in the UK and in any relevant foreign country and there is no investigation or enquiry order, decree or judgment of any court or any governmental agency or regulatory body outstanding or anticipated against the Vendor which may have a [material] adverse effect upon the Business.

3.2 *Litigation*
3.2.1 The Vendor is not involved whether as plaintiff or defendant or otherwise in any legal action, proceedings or arbitration in connection with the Business or its assets (other than as plaintiff in the collection of debts arising in the ordinary course of business) or is involved in any proceedings of a criminal nature and there are no such legal actions, proceedings or arbitrations pending or threatened against the Vendor in connection therewith.

3.2.2 There are no investigations disciplinary proceedings or other circumstances [known to the Vendor] [after making due and careful enquiries] [likely to] [which will] lead to any such claim or legal action, proceedings or arbitration (other than as aforesaid) or prosecution.

3.4 *Fair trading and restrictive practices*
So far as the Vendor is aware in connection with the Business, the Vendor is not a party to any agreement, arrangement or concerted practice or is carrying on any practice which in whole or in part:

(*a*) is or requires to be registered under the Restrictive Trade Practices Acts;

(*b*) contravenes arts 85(1) or 86 of the Treaty of Rome or which has been notified to the Commission of the European Communities for an exemption or in respect of which an application has been made to the said Commission for a negative clearance;

(c) contravenes or is invalidated by (i) the Consumer Credit Act 1974; (ii) the Resale Prices Act 1976 (iii) the Competition Act 1980; or (iv) any anti-trust legislation in any other jurisdiction in which there are assets of the Business of the Business is carried on;

(d) contravenes the Chapter I or the Chapter II Prohibition of the Competition Act 1988 or which has been notified to the Competition Commission for an exemption or in respect of which an application has been made to the said Commission for clearance.

The Vendor has not received any notification that proceedings under any applicable anti-trust law have been initiated nor are any such proceedings contemplated by the Vendor in connection with the Business, nor has any claim been made or threatened alleging any anti-trust law contravention.

4   Employees and terms of employment

4.1.1 The Relevant Employees will be the only employees transferred to the

Purchaser by reason of the Purchaser acquiring the Business.

4.1.2 All the terms and conditions upon which the Relevant Employees are employed at the Completion Date and all amounts owing or promised to Relevant Employees have been delivered to the Purchaser prior to the date hereof and are summarised in Schedule 4.

4.1.3 No changes to the contracts or agreements with any of the Relevant Employees have been proposed whether by the Vendor or the employee in the six months preceding this Agreement.

4.2 *Liabilities to and for employees*
[So far as the Vendor is aware] in respect of the Relevant Employees no liability has been incurred by the Vendor and not yet discharged for breach of any contract of service or employment or for the actual or proposed termination or suspension of employment or variation of any contract of employment of any such Relevant Employee.

4.3 *Compliance with statutes*
[So far as the Vendor is aware] the Vendor has in relation to each Relevant Employee complied with:

(*a*) all obligations imposed upon it by art 119 of the Treaty of Rome and all statutes, regulations and codes of conduct and practice relevant to the relations between it and any Relevant Employee or any relevant trade union;

(*b*) all collective agreements and customs and practices for the time being dealing with such relations or the terms and conditions of service of any of the Relevant Employees; and

(*c*) all relevant orders, declarations and awards made under any relevant statute, regulation or codes of conduct and practice affecting the conditions of service of any of the Relevant Employees.

The Vendor has maintained current, adequate and suitable records regarding the service of each of the Relevant Employees and these will be delivered to the Purchaser upon Completion.

4.4 *Industrial disputes and negotiations*
The Vendor is not in connection with the Business involved in any dispute or negotiation [regarding a claim of material importance] with any trade union or association of trade unions or organisation or body of employees and there are no facts known [or which would on reasonable enquiry be known] to the Vendor which might indicate that there may now or in the future be any such dispute.

4.5 *Pensions*
4.5.1 The Vendor's Plan is the only Plan to which the Vendor makes or could become liable to make payments for providing retirement, death or life assurance benefits in respect of Relevant Employees. No proposal has been

announced to establish any other plan for providing such benefits, and the Vendor does not provide and has not promised to provide any such benefits in respect of any Relevant Employees except under the Vendor's Plan.

4.5.2 The Vendor's Plan is an exempt approved scheme within the meaning of Chapter I Part XIV of the Income and Corporation Taxes Act 1988. The Relevant Employees who are members thereof are contracted-out of the State Earnings Related Pension Scheme by reference to the Vendor's Plan. The Vendor's Plan complies with, and has been managed in accordance with all applicable laws, regulations and requirements.

4.5.3 The Vendor has given the Purchaser copies of:

(*a*) all trust deeds and rules of the Vendor's Plan;

(*b*) all explanatory booklets and announcements relating to the Vendor's Plan.

These documents contain full details of all benefits payable under the Vendor's Plan in respect of the Relevant Employees who are members thereof and no power to increase those benefits or to provide different benefits has been exercised.

4.5.4 The Vendor has notified the Purchaser of the rate at which contributions to the Vendor's Plan are paid, the basis on which they are calculated and that they are paid [monthly in arrears]. All contributions due to the Vendor's Plan in respect of the Relevant Employees have been paid.

4.5.5 The Vendor has no notice of any dispute about the benefits payable under the Vendor's plan in respect of any Relevant Employee, and has no knowledge [after making reasonable enquiry] of any circumstances which might give rise to any such dispute.

5   Taxation matters

5.1 None of the assets agreed to be sold under this Agreement is the subject of any charge power of sale or mortgage in favour of a Taxation Authority for the purposes of any Taxation nor are there any circumstances which may give rise to the same.

5.2 All proper records have been kept and all proper returns and payments have been made as required by law for the purposes of VAT in connection with the Business.

5.3 None of the assets agreed to be sold under this Agreement is the subject of any security in favour of HM Customs and Excise pursuant to any provision of the Value Added Tax Act 1994.

5.4 The person selling the Vendor's Intellectual Property Rights is resident in the UK for the purposes of UK Taxation.

6 Assets (other than the properties)

6.1 *Title*
The Chattels and the Useful Stock are the absolute property of the Vendor and none is the subject of any option, right to acquire, assignment, mortgage, charge, lien or hypothecation or other encumbrance whatsoever (excepting only liens arising by operation of law in the normal course of trading) or the subject of any factoring arrangement, hire-purchase, conditional sale or credit sale agreement.

6.2 *Sufficiency of chattels*
The Chattels comprise [substantially] all those used by the Vendor in the carrying on of the Business in the manner in which it is presently conducted.

6.3 *Insurance*
The Chattels and the Stock have at all material times been and are at the date of this Agreement insured to the full replacement value thereof against fire and other risks normally insured against by persons carrying on similar businesses or owning assets of a similar nature and the Vendor has at all material times been and is at the date of this Agreement adequately covered against accident, third party injury, damage and other risks normally covered by insurance by persons carrying on such businesses. In respect of all such insurances:
  (a) all premiums have been duly paid to date;
  (b) all the policies are in force and are not voidable on account of any act, omission or non-disclosure on the part of the Vendor;
  (c) there are no special or unusual terms or restrictions and the premiums currently payable are not in excess of the normal rates [and no circumstances exist which are likely to give rise to any increase in premiums];
  (d) no claim is outstanding and [so far as the Vendor is aware] no circumstances exist which are likely to give rise to any claim; and
  (e) full particulars are contained in the Disclosure Letter.

6.4 *Grants*
There are no investment or other grants, loan subsidies or financial assistance received by virtue of any statute by the Vendor in connection with the Business.

6.5 *Plant and machinery*
The Chattels are [in good repair and condition and] in satisfactory working order for carrying on the Business.

6.6 *Intellectual property*

6.6.1 All the Vendor's Intellectual Property is in the legal and beneficial ownership of the Vendor, and, where registrable, is registered in the name of the Vendor, or in that of its wholly-owned subsidiary and there are no adverse liens, charges or encumbrances over it and it is not subject to any licence or authority or other permission in favour of another (save only for such licences as are disclosed).

6.6.2 [So far as the Vendor is aware] the processes employed and products and services dealt in the Business in the manner in which they are so employed and dealt by the Vendor in the Business do not infringe any Intellectual Property or Know-how of third parties and [so far as the Vendor is aware] in relation to the Intellectual Property and Know-how of third parties no claims have been made and they are not the subject of litigation actual or threatened and no applications are pending which if pursued or granted might be material thereto.

6.6.3 All inventions made by persons employed by the Vendor in connection with the Business were made in the course of the normal duties of the employee concerned and [the Vendor is not aware of any] [there is no] claim for compensation under s 40 of the Patents Act 1977 made or pending.

6.6.4 The Vendor will use all reasonable endeavours to obtain permission for the Purchaser to use the computer programs comprising part of the Vendor's Know-how.

SCHEDULE 12
Supplier Contracts

SCHEDULE 13
Service Contracts
relating to the Properties

SCHEDULE 14
Relevant Employees to be selected for Redundancy

SCHEDULE 15
Shared Services Agreement

SIGNED for and on behalf
of the Vendor in the
presence of:

SIGNED for and on behalf
of the Purchaser in the
presence of:

Chapter 12

Joint ventures

12.1 Introduction

Joint ventures can take a number of forms, but this chapter is concerned only with a joint venture which is implemented through a legal entity in which the joint venture partners both take shareholdings, the purpose of which is to run a business on a commercial basis. All references to joint ventures in this chapter should be construed accordingly, and, for the sake of brevity, the legal entity through which the joint venture is to be implemented will be referred to as the 'joint venture company'.

Partnerships and other types of contractual joint ventures are outside the scope of this chapter. It should be noted that, although many joint ventures relate to co-operation or collaboration in research and development, marketing, or joint purchasing clubs, these are rarely carried on other than as limited contractual joint ventures. In the event that a company is set up to run the joint venture its operation and constitution is usually not controversial. Although the precedents in this chapter could be adapted for such a company they are not really intended for this purpose, and are in most cases likely to contain too much detail relating to the administration of the company, and to focus too much on the resolution of disputes. Once again, such 'non-commercial' joint venture companies are not dealt with in this chapter.

Although the actual purpose for which joint ventures are formed, and the actual details of the rights and obligations of the parties, are capable of wide variation depending upon the commercial objectives to be achieved, all joint ventures have to deal with the same basic issues.

The first relates to decision making. How will the joint venture company be run? What decisions should be left to its chief executive and his staff? What decisions should be referred to its board of directors; and what should the composition of that board be—solely executive directors, solely appointees of the shareholders, or a mixture of both, perhaps with the addition of outsiders acting as independent non-executive directors? Finally, what decisions should be reserved for the shareholders alone?

The second relates to the protection of the rights of individual shareholders of the joint venture company, often referred to as 'minority protection rights'. Whatever the procedures allocated for decision-making, should a shareholder be entitled to veto any decision, or certain types of decisions, with which he does not agree, even if the shareholders holding the majority of the shares wish to implement it?

The third relates to the deadlock situation which arises either because the shareholders in the joint venture company cannot agree on a course of action, and one of them exercises a veto granted to him as part of his minority protection rights, or because the relevant decision makers have split into two blocks with opposing ideas each holding 50 per cent of the votes. When deadlock occurs how is it to be resolved? Deadlocks at lower levels of decision making may be resolved by passing the problem up to higher levels, but if the deadlock occurs either initially, or, after referral upwards, at the shareholder level, there is nowhere else to go. The agreement must contain some method of resolving such ultimate deadlocks or the joint venture company will be paralysed.

The fourth relates to termination or break up of the joint venture company. How does one of the shareholders exit if he wishes to do so? Must he sell his shares to the other shareholders, or can he sell to a third party? Alternatively can one of the shareholders force the dissolution of the joint venture company, or its sale as a going concern on the open market? Finally, if one of the shareholders becomes unpopular or undesirable as partner in the eyes of the other shareholders can they force him out of the joint venture company, and, if so, upon what terms?

It will be seen that each of these issues is interlinked. Once one considers decision making mechanisms, one is forced to legislate for minority protection rights, which inevitably brings the draftsman face to face with the problem of deadlock, which in most cases can only be resolved in practice by the break up of the joint venture company or the voluntary or forcible exit of the dissenting shareholders. Not only are the issues interlinked, but they are all potentially divisive ones, concerned with disagreement or with the termination of the joint venture company in unpleasant circumstances.

Many prospective partners, who are excited about the potential of their proposed venture, and planning for the future, react to their adviser's suggestions that such matters should be considered and negotiated in detail at an early stage in their discussions, even before the joint venture company is set up, in much the same way that a couple who have just got engaged would react to their family solicitor's suggestion that they should start planning the terms of their divorce settlement at once!

Nevertheless, the truth is that when a joint venture is going well the businessmen concerned will make pragmatic decisions in the interest of the business without worrying too much about the formalities laid down in the joint venture agreement. For instance, it is very rare at meetings of partners in joint ventures for matters actually to be put to a formal vote or for business to be done except by unanimous agreement after discussion of all aspects of the problem, so that the concerns of initial or potential dissenters are taken into account and a compromise position is reached with which all the partners agree. However, this pre-supposes goodwill and trust between all the partners, and a large measure of identity of interests. It is only when the relationship between the partners breaks down or their interests seriously diverge that they, and their lawyers, start studying the joint venture agreement.

It is for this reason that the draftsman of the joint venture agreement should always concentrate on the above issues, force his client to concentrate on them as well, and draft with the possibility of disagreement and dissolution always on his mind. Disagreement may never arise, dissolution may never occur, and the agreement may be left to gather dust in the archives, but it is the unfortunate task of the lawyer to play the role of the skeleton at the feast, and to remind his client to prepare for the worst.

Before considering each of these issues in detail in relation to precedents, there are a number of preliminary matters that have to be considered. The first matter is the way in which the joint venture company is created.

Where the joint venture is already a going concern, operated through an existing legal entity, and the desire is simply to bring in another partner, perhaps because of the need for more capital, or because of that partner's expertise or business connections, the transaction is effected simply by the sale of part of the existing shareholders' shares to the new partner, or the issue of new share capital to the new partner in return for a capital contribution paid into what has now become the joint venture company.

As a variation on this, if the existing business is only a part of the undertaking of the existing shareholders, it may first be necessary to hive it off, by means of a business transfer, into a separate legal entity which will itself become the joint venture company.

Where the future partners in the joint venture company intend to merge existing businesses, this can be done by means of either share sales or asset or business transfers as appropriate, with the joint venture company being either a new company specially set up to hold the merged businesses, or merely an existing company running one of the businesses, which then acquires and merges into its undertaking the businesses of the other partners.

All of these transactions can be effected by the use of the share sale or business transfer agreements discussed in Chapters 10 and 11, using the precedents contained in those chapters as a basis, with the difference that the consideration for the transfers is likely to be shares in the joint venture company (although sometimes a balancing payment in cash also needs to be made). It should not be forgotten that in most cases, the participants in the joint venture will want to have the same safeguards by way of warranties, due diligence and price adjustment for each transfer of a business or the acquisition of shares which takes place in the course of setting up the joint venture, as they would if that transaction were an isolated one standing upon its own commercial merits. The only point of difference is that, since the parties are contemplating an ongoing relationship, neither side should attempt to negotiate an agreement which gives it too great a commercial advantage over the other.

Even if this tactic prevails in the heat of the initial discussion surrounding the setting up of the joint venture, attempts to enforce that advantage in the future will lead to disputes between the partners which are not likely to be conducive to the smooth running of the joint venture. The better course is to negotiate transfer and acquisition agreements which are transparently even-handed, with, if possible, most disputes being referred to an arbitrator or expert for summary resolution, to avoid a great deal of wrangling between the partners, who should, instead, be concentrating on the success of the joint venture company.

Once the joint venture company has been properly constituted, the joint venture agreement proper should be entered into, to regulate the future rights and obligations of the partners and the operation of the joint venture company. Although the acquisition agreements and the joint venture agreement are negotiated and entered into contemporaneously, it is a good idea to keep all of the various agreements separate rather than run them into one omnibus agreement, since this not only makes drafting easier but also assists clarity and focus in the case of each document. However, some transactions are so complicated that it is useful to have a master agreement or heads of agreement which sets out all of the steps of the transaction, and the various agreements needed to implement them, and to which, in the case of a legally binding agreement (but probably not a preliminary heads of agreement) the subsidiary agreements would be attached in draft form. In some cases, the master agreement is the joint venture agreement itself, but again this is not particularly recommended in the case of complex transactions.

The second matter concerns the bearing of competition law upon the creation and operation of the joint venture. First, the very creation of the joint venture can lead to restrictions on competition so that the transaction may require approval from the Office of Fair Trading, or, in appropriate cases the European Commission.

Secondly, most joint venture agreements contain elaborate clauses regulating the extent to which the partners in the joint venture can compete with the joint venture company, and also, in many cases, restricting the areas in which the joint venture company can operate, so as to avoid competition with the partners in areas where they have not pooled their interests in the joint venture company. Such clauses are subject to the scrutiny of either national competition law (in the UK the Restrictive Trade Practices Act 1976 and the common law principles relating to covenants in restraint of trade) or, in appropriate cases, the European Commission under art 85 of the Treaty of Rome, or the Merger Regulation in the case where the merger is a concentrative one and they fall within the definition of 'ancillary restrictions'.

For more detail on these issues, reference should be made to the discussion on competition law aspects of mergers and acquisitions in Chapter 9, and to the detailed discussion of the law surrounding non-compete clauses which will be found in Chapter 14.

Finally a checklist of the required documentation and other issues to be considered when setting up a joint venture is set out in Appendix 1 to this chapter.

12.2   Entrenchment of minority protection rights

A general word needs to be said regarding the enforceability of minority protection rights in the light of the important House of Lords decision on the subject in *Russell v Northern Bank Development Corporation Ltd* [1992] 1 WLR 588. This case concerned a shareholders agreement, to which both shareholders and the joint venture company concerned were parties, which provided (*inter alia*) that the creation of new share capital required the unanimous written consent of the shareholders, and of the joint venture company. The clause thus, *inter alia*, bound the company not to increase its capital without the consent of all the shareholders.

The House held that such a clause amounted, so far as the joint venture company was concerned, to 'an unlawful and invalid fetter on the statutory power of [the company] to increase its share capital'. However, the clause was capable of being a valid and binding obligation between the shareholders themselves as to the manner in which they would jointly exercise the voting rights conferred upon them by their shareholdings in the joint venture company in order to bring about the desired effect. The following dictum of Lord Davey in *Welton v Saffery* [1897] AC 299 at 331 was quoted with approval:

> 'individual shareholders may deal with their own interests by contract in such a way as they may think fit. But such contracts, whether made by all or some only of the shareholders, would create personal obligations, or an *exceptio personalis* against themselves only, and would not become a regulation of the company.'

Lord Jauncey of Tullichettle commented:

> 'I understand Lord Davey there to be accepting that shareholders may lawfully agree inter se to exercise their voting rights in a manner which, if it were dictated by the articles, and were thereby binding on the company, would be unlawful.'

The judgment drew a distinction between a clause of the type under consideration, and a provision in the articles of a company which provided for weighted voting rights. Lord Jauncey here quoted with approval *dicta* from *Bushell v Faith* [1969] 2 Ch 438, which considered a provision in the articles of a private company which laid down that, in the event a resolution was proposed at a general meeting for the removal of a director who was also a shareholder, that director would be granted, in respect of the shares held by him, additional voting rights, namely three votes per share. In that case Russell LJ said:

> 'a company cannot by its articles or otherwise deprive itself of the power by special resolution to alter its articles or any of them ... An article purporting to do this is ineffective. But a provision as to voting rights which has the effect of making a special resolution incapable of being passed, if a particular shareholder or group of shareholders exercises his or their voting rights against a proposed alteration, is not such a provision. An article in terms providing that no alteration shall be made without the consent of X is ... ineffective. But the provision as to voting rights ... is wholly different, and it does not serve to say that it can have the same result.'

Lord Jauncey thus affirmed that *Bushell v Faith* would support the view that the clause in question was ineffective against the company, but has left intact the possibility of achieving substantially the same effect by providing in the articles of the company for weighted voting rights in respect of the issue concerned.

Applying the above principles, Lord Jauncey found that the clause was void as against the company, but amounted to a binding agreement as between the shareholders since the clause was drafted in such a way that the obnoxious provision relating to the company could be severed, and the provisions binding the shareholders preserved in force.

Finally, Lord Jauncey considered the relief that would be available to the plaintiff, who had sought to enforce the clause. In the particular circumstances of the case, the plaintiff had no objection to the increase of capital proposed at that time. He was simply concerned to ensure that his right under the clause to object to future issues was preserved in case he wished to exercise it. He was therefore refused an injunction, and the case was resubmitted to the Court of Appeal for a declaration on the validity of the clause as between the shareholders. It was not possible for the House of Lords to give such a declaration itself, because the parties' minds had not been addressed to this issue, they had not sought such a declaration, and no argument on the subject had been addressed to the court.

The conclusion to be drawn from this case for the draftsman of minority protection rights in joint venture agreements (in respect of issues which must be dealt with at several meetings of the company) is that the joint venture company should not be a party to the joint venture agreement for the purpose of making minority protection rights enforceable against the joint venture company. This is at best ineffective, and at worst will render the whole of the minority protection provisions void as against the shareholders as well, unless the doctrine of severance can be prayed in aid to save the balance of the clause. If there are clauses in respect of which the joint venture company needs to be bound or to enforce directly against all or some of its shareholders, these provisions should be hived off into a separate agreement to which the joint venture company and all the shareholders are parties. Alternatively, the joint venture company can be made a party to the joint venture agreement, and the minority protection rights be hived off into a separate agreement to which only the shareholders are parties. This is a more difficult drafting exercise, and, in most cases, there is little need for the joint venture to be a party to the whole agreement, since the clauses in respect of which it is to be bound, or to take the benefit of direct enforcement, are usually few in number and normally relate to discrete matters such as non-competition covenants, supply agreements and licences of intellectual property rights, which can conveniently be dealt with in separate agreements.

Contractual agreements between shareholders as to minority protection rights are worth having for two reasons. The first is that they are directly enforceable between the parties, and, presumably, either by injunction or by damages. The fact that no injunction was granted in *Russell* is not relevant since here the court in the exercise of its discretion decided that an injunction was not an appropriate remedy. This does not mean that the court will not grant an injunction in suitable circumstances. The second is that, by and large, businessmen tend to honour the agreements that they come to, if these are clearly spelt out. It is therefore of great use for the smooth running of the joint venture if the minority protection rights are spelt out in clear simple language as contractual obligations in the joint venture agreement. In practical terms, the parties will usually honour the agreement that they have come to, without thinking about the technical question of whether or not the joint venture company is also bound by it.

As to the correct way of drafting minority protection rights, it would seem from *Russell* that the best way is to set up an agreement to vote the shares of all the parties together in the way necessary to achieve the desired effect. This can either be by way of a simple agreement to vote all of the shareholdings together at general meetings, or through the more elaborate device of setting up a shareholders' committee which will decide the way in which the parties will cast the votes of all their shareholdings collectively in the case of certain matters being put to a resolution at a general meeting. The committee route is more elaborate, but is well suited to situations where the minority protection rights are elaborate, and the draftsman would like to phrase them as matters which should not be implemented without the consent of certain of the parties. It is then possible to provide, as a matter of contract, that the shareholders' committee shall first consider one of the relevant issues, on the motion of one of its members, and that each member will undertake not to propose as a general resolution to a general meeting any issue which has not first been discussed and approved at the shareholders' committee. Once the issue has been raised, if it is approved in the prescribed way (majority, supermajority or unanimity), all the members will be obliged to exercise their votes together to obtain the result agreed upon in the committee.

So far as entrenchment of these rights within the articles of the company is concerned, the best way seems to be to provide for weighted voting in the case of the proposal of a resolution affecting any of the relevant rights, along the lines of the provision approved in *Bushell*, although depending upon the nature of some rights it may not always be possible to draft an article in such a way that the desired result is achieved.

It also appears possible to specify certain agreed conditions in the company's memorandum, but not its articles, including that such conditions may not be altered, or only altered in a specified way, by relying upon s 17 of the Companies Act 1985. However, this is of limited assistance, since most of the issues surrounding minority protection rights are bound up in the articles.

The third possibility is to express the relevant rights as class rights, relying upon *Cumbrian Newspapers Ltd v Cumberland and Westmoreland Herald Newspaper and Printing Co Ltd* [1987] Ch 1. However, the problem with this is that it is not always easy to express many minority protection rights in the terms of class rights.

The final drafting issue, which comes out of *Russell*, is the use of clauses which either provide that in the event of conflict between the joint venture agreement and the articles, the agreement will prevail, and/or provide that, in the event of such conflict, or at the request of one of the parties, the articles will be altered to conform to the relevant minority protection right contained in the agreement.

Such a clause, if contained in an agreement binding upon the joint venture company, will be open to the same objections as clauses binding upon the company which relate to the direct protection of minority rights. A clause which merely states that the agreement will prevail over the articles as between the shareholders themselves, without reference to the company, is unobjectionable and useful. A clause which goes on to commit the shareholders to vote to amend the articles in case of conflict is unobjectionable as a voting agreement, but useless if the provision which it is sought to embody in the articles is one which would be void if stated to be binding upon the company, as opposed to binding between the shareholders.

The correct course for the draftsman is to start by drafting the joint venture agreement and inserting the minority protection rights which the parties agree should be binding as between themselves, and without reference to the company. He should then consider which of those rights can lawfully be entrenched in the memorandum and articles of the joint venture company, and the means of achieving this result. He should also consult the wishes of the parties, bearing in mind that the memorandum and articles are public documents, and the

parties may not want the outside world to be aware of certain minority protection rights, even if they can lawfully be entrenched. Once this exercise has
been accomplished he can produce a set of amendments, or a new memorandum and articles, which can be annexed to the joint venture agreement, and
which the parties can undertake, in that agreement, to vote to adopt in general
meeting upon the establishment of the joint venture company.

This will leave the only use of the conflicts clause to provide that the agreement will prevail over the memorandum and articles so far as the parties to the
agreement alone are concerned. This is a very necessary provision in the event
that one of the parties decides to take legal steps to enforce his rights under the
agreement. It is possible to add a provision that, in the event of such conflict,
the parties will vote to include an appropriate amendment in the memorandum
or articles to bring them into line with the agreement to the extent, and in a
manner, which such amendment can lawfully be included in the memorandum
or articles. However, such a provision, while probably harmless, may well be
too vague to be enforceable. If the draftsman has done his work properly with
the draft memorandum and articles in the first place, it should, in any event, be
unnecessary to include this further provision.

The above discussion, and, indeed *Russell*, focuses on the extent to which
shareholders can impose minority protection rights in respect of issues which
are dealt with at general meetings of the company. So far as there is a need to
impose minority protection rights upon issues which are dealt with at a board
meeting different issues arise. The board derives its rights to manage the company by delegation from the shareholders. Thus, as a first principle, the shareholders can decide (subject to the provisions of company law which provide
that some matters can only be decided by the shareholders of the company in
general meeting and cannot be delegated to the board) which issues relating to
the company's affairs should be reserved exclusively to them for decision, and
which should be delegated to the board, and embody the relevant division of
powers in the articles.

Once they have decided upon the issues which the board should be competent to deal with, there is no provision of company law which prevents them
adopting procedures at meetings of the directors which entrench minority protection rights, so far as matters dealt with by the board are concerned, by requiring in the articles that certain resolutions should only pass on the basis of
a supermajority, or unanimity, or if certain directors vote in favour of them.

Clauses which oblige the shareholders to exercise voting powers to ensure
the implementation of a resolution of the shareholder's committee, or otherwise to exercise them so as to ensure that minority protection rights should be
preserved, should have little application to board matters, for the reasons discussed, but a clause should be included to bind shareholders to procure, so far
as possible, that matters which are reserved for the shareholders should not be
raised at board meetings, and that, so far as applicable, they will use their
powers as shareholders, including voting at general meetings, to ensure that

decisions of the board, carried out in accordance with whatever procedure is laid down in the articles, are properly put into effect.

A simple way of achieving entrenchment of minority protection rights in the articles, in relation to issues discussed at board meetings, is the creation of classes of ordinary shares (otherwise ranking *pari passu*) normally designated A, B, C and so on, which carry with them for each shareholder holding a class the right to appoint a number of directors, normally entitled 'A Directors', 'B Directors', 'C Directors' and so on. The articles can then provide that certain resolutions put before the board shall only pass if one or more of the designated classes of director vote in favour of it. Another method, which requires some calculation, is to provide for appointment of a number of directors by certain shareholders such that a majority vote cannot be obtained unless those directors vote in favour of it. This enables a number of shareholders effectively to control the board, but presupposes that there is a shareholders' agreement, or at least some unity of purpose, in the background.

The only problem with providing such entrenchment in the articles relating to board matters is that any director is supposed to act in the interests of, and to owe a fiduciary duty to, the company and the shareholders as a whole. What if a director exercises his vote to block or to ensure the passing of, a resolution, not because he believes that he is acting in the best interests of his company, but because the shareholder who appointed him wished him to vote that way to further that shareholder's interests? This would, in strict legal terms, amount to an improper exercise of his powers as a director, and to a breach of fiduciary duty which would render him personally liable to the company, and perhaps to the other shareholders as well.

In practice, where joint venture companies are concerned, if there are only a few participants in the arrangement, each of whom is taking advantage of minority protection rights, the parties tend to ignore this issue, on the basis that all of them have an interest in not raising it.

In any event, such conflicts should not arise if the draftsman of the joint venture company's memorandum and articles has done his job properly, by ensuring that matters which really concern the personal interests of the shareholders are removed from the jurisdiction of the board, and reserved for the shareholders to decide in general meeting as discussed above. If this drafting exercise has been carried out properly, the matters the board will deal with will relate to operational (and perhaps strategic) matters concerning the running of the company. Where these matters are concerned, the real issue for a director is in truth to decide what he believes is in the best interests of the company and to vote accordingly.

In a joint venture company situation, all shareholders naturally have as their objective the appointment of a board of directors which will run the company properly and make decisions which are in the best interests of the company. Directors appointed by shareholders are thus chosen because the appointor believes that his appointee is a suitable person, from the point of view of his common sense and commercial ability, to achieve this objective. In particular, the shareholder who appointed that director will expect that, in appropriate cases, where that director has a power of veto (through the existence of minority protection rights) he will use that power to stop the other directors making decisions which the director (and/or the shareholder appointing him) genuinely feels are not in the best interests of the company.

It is not true to say that a director appointed by a shareholder will never be in a position where his fiduciary duty to the company and the interests of his appointor come into conflict. However, the above analysis shows that, at least where the parties are all acting in good faith, and the draftsman has done a proper job of reserving matters for the shareholders' decision alone, such conflicts should not arise. Such conflicts as there are should not be about protecting the personal interests of any individual shareholder. They should only arise where one individual shareholder requires his appointed director to impose his view, or prevent another shareholder from imposing his view, of what is the best way for the company to be run. If the quarrel is about this, and providing all the parties concerned are acting in good faith, there should be no conflict between a director's fiduciary duty to the company and his representation of the interests of the shareholder who appointed him, whatever the outcome of the conflict.

12.3 Drafting the memorandum and articles of a joint venture company

Finally, it should be said that space does not permit the inclusion in this chapter of precedents covering the memorandum and articles of association of a joint venture company, but Precedent 7 is an example of an article providing for weighted voting rights, and Precedent 8 is an example of an article dealing with the appointment of classes of directors.

Although many joint venture agreements provide for the adoption of full draft articles, by and large Table A from the Companies Acts provides a very good starting point, with the addition of the articles along the lines of Precedent 7 and 8 as appropriate.

Apart from entrenchment of minority rights, the only other special issue which normally requires consideration is the extent to which the special provisions covering restrictions on disposal of shares, and the pre-emption rights of the other shareholders, should be reflected in the articles as well as (or instead of) being set out in the joint venture agreement. Company law does not prevent provisions regarding restrictions on transfer from being entrenched in the articles, and thus the legal considerations relating to the entrenchment of minority protection rights have no application in this case.

While in theory, it might be possible merely to bind the joint venture company by way of contract not to register transfers in breach of provisions in a joint venture agreement, it is in most cases advisable not to attempt to do this, but simply to entrench the relevant parts of these rights in the articles. This ensures that a transfer of shares to a third party in breach of the terms of the joint venture agreement is not just actionable as between the parties to the agreement, but is also ineffective so far as the third party is concerned, since the board of the company will have no power to register it.

Further, the fact that such restrictions are contained in the articles will be a matter of public record, and will be seen by any third party who is a prospective purchaser of shares in the company if he makes company searches when assessing the possibility of entering into the transaction. He will then obviously raise objections if the transferring shareholder has not told him the whole story. This will make it less likely that any transaction in breach of the transfer provisions will ever occur.

Finally, it should be noted that instances have occurred in England where the Registrar of Companies has required that, where articles of association cross-refer to a joint venture agreement, not only the articles but also the agreement be put on the public register. This possibility should be borne in mind by the draftsman where the parties are concerned to keep the contents of the agreement confidential.

12.4   Taxation issues

Although the detailed impact of taxation in relation to joint ventures is outside the scope of this book, two issues do need to be raised, concerning the impact of withdrawal arrangements on group or consortium relief and on capital gains tax.

Certain provisions of the Income and Corporation Taxes Act 1988 apply special provisions which disallow various types of group or consortium relief by deeming there to have been a breaking of the relevant group if there are certain 'arrangements' or 'option arrangements' in existence which involve a future change in the ownership of shares or securities in a group company (s 240(11)(*a*)—surrender of Advance Corporation Tax to a subsidiary, s 247(1A)(*b*)—group income elections in certain consortium cases, s 410(1) and (2)—group and consortium relief, and para 5B(1) of Sched 18, which applies to 'option arrangements').

However, in practice the Revenue does not apply these rules in relation to the withdrawal provisions usually found in joint venture agreements, or the articles of jv companies, which have the potential to change the ownership of the shares, but do not actually do so until the happening of certain triggering events (broadly, voluntary withdrawal, change of control, or breach of the party whose shares change ownership as a result of the triggering event). Further, the use of shares as securtiy by way of legal or equitable mortgage is regarded as not constituting an 'arrangement' or 'option arrangement' until the mortgagee is permitted to exercise his rights.

Details of the conditions which the Revenue require in order to permit the operation of this extra-statutory concession can be found in their Extra-Statutory Concession (ESC 10), revised and republished on 22 January 1993, and Statement of Practice SP3/93 published on the same date. Broadly the conditions cover the normal types of withdrawal and pre-emption provisions found in many joint venture agreements, such as those in Precedents 1, 4 and 5. They would probably not apply to the option arrangements in Precedent 2 because there is an irrevocable and unconditional obligation (see cl 5.3) on the majority shareholder to exercise his call option at the end of the option period, if the minority shareholder has not by then exercised his put option.

Whenever the above issues are important to the partners in the joint venture, the details of the extra-statutory concession should be considered, and, if they do not exactly meet the withdrawal provisions proposed for the joint venture agreement, then specific advice, guidance and clearance should be sought from the Revenue.

So far as capital gains tax is concerned, the fettering of the right to dispose of the shares in a joint venture company by pre-emption rights and withdrawal provisions does not amount to a disposal, since there is at the stage of entering into the joint venture agreement no irrevocable and unconditional obligation to dispose of the shares. Thus, in these cases, capital gains tax is payable when the triggering event occurs, and the shares are actually disposed of. This would apply to the arrangements in Precedents 1, 4 and 5, but not, for the reasons stated above, to Precedent 2.

12.5 Precedent 1

Precedent 1 is a heads of agreement for a joint venture where two groups of companies have decided to merge their operations in a particular territory. Although joints ventures vary so much that it is hard to produce a standard heads of agreement which will cover all cases, this precedent gives a useful example of how some of the common issues in joint ventures can be worked out in practice, and also provides a checklist of the main items that need to be considered in most types of joint ventures.

Paragraph 1 provides details of the entities and businesses that are going to be merged, and refers to a more detailed description in Apps 1 and 2, while para 2 sets out the way in which the merger will take place, how the parties will value their relative contributions to the merged entity (by reference to Apps 3 and 4), and how that value will be adjusted to ensure that ultimately the parties' shareholdings in the merged entity are maintained initially in the desired proportions.

Once the joint venture has been set up, it is desirable to avoid continued disputes over warranty claims concerning liabilities prior to the closing. Such disputes are not only time-consuming but damage the goodwill between the parties, and hinder the smooth running of the joint venture. Paragraph 2.5 provides a simple way of avoiding this. First of all, most liabilities will have been taken into account in striking the balance sheets for the valuation of the two businesses pursuant to paras 2.1 and 2.4. All that is left is pre-closing liabilities which could not be taken into account because the parties did not know about them. At the time of closing neither party knows whether such liabilities, if any, that arise after the merger will relate to its business, or that of the other partner. It therefore makes sense, on the basis of rough justice, that the joint venture should bear those unknown liabilities, whichever party was responsible for them initially. Thus, in effect, both parties bear them in proportion to their shareholdings in the joint venture, and take the rough with the smooth.

The only exception to this rule should be really significant liabilities which would seriously damage the joint venture if it had to bear them. The intention of the precedent is that such liabilities would be very much the exception, and probably outside the normal sort of business risks involved in carrying on the merged business. Paragraph 2.5 does not attempt to define the two types of liabilities, but provides that the parties shall only bear liabilities for which they are responsible if the amount of the liability exceeds a certain figure. The figure is left blank in the precedent, but the intention is that the amount would be a very large one in relation to the annual turnover and net profit of the business.

Paragraph 3 then sets out the basic principles of the joint venture operations, including business mission, financing, trading relations between the joint venture company and its shareholders, treatment of employees, and non-competition clauses.

Paragraph 4 sets out the way in which the joint venture company will operate through its board of directors, what role the shareholders will play in determining the strategic direction and policy of the joint venture company, gives a list of minority protection rights and sets out a dividend policy. The matters in this paragraph of course require consideration in the light of the discussion earlier in this chapter on the enforcement of minority protection rights, in particular as affected by the decision in *Russell v Northern Bank Development Corporation Ltd*, above. However, at this stage the precedent is only concerned to set out the broad principles to be adopted in this area, leaving the technicalities to be dealt with at the stage of drafting the definitive agreement.

Paragraphs 5 and 6 give examples of the way in which the needs of the joint venture company can be provided for in the area of licences of intellectual property rights and supply of products and services from its shareholders. It must be remembered that this precedent is dealing with the merger of two existing businesses which will already have depended, before the merger, upon their parent organisations for such licences and supply agreements in order to carry on their operations. Thus, in this case, the arrangements are more elaborate than they would have to be if the joint venture were for the start of a new business in virgin territory.

It should be noted that the licences and supply agreements continue throughout the term of the joint venture, and, as was mentioned in the discussion on competition law clearance in Chapter 9, this would some cause difficulties if the parties were seeking approval of the merger from the European Commission pursuant to the Merger Regulation. Given the changes made to the Regulation by Regulation 1310/1997, with effect from 1 March 1998, as discussed in Chapter 9, this joint venture, as a full function joint venture, would now be classed as a concentration for the purposes of the Regulation. However, given that it clearly gives rise to a co-ordination of the competitive activity of the two partners who will still remain independent, the concentration would fall to be judged not only under the dominant position criteria, under art 2(2), but also as to their effect on competition under the art 85 criteria as well, under art 2(3) of the Regulation. The ancillary restrictions would therefore have to be considered on the basis of both sets of criteria.

Paragraph 7 sets out the way the parties will plan and implement the integration. Most mergers fail because the parties do not do sufficient advance planning as to the way in which the actual integration of the businesses concerned would be implemented, and, in particular, are not sufficiently sensitive to the differences between the cultures of the two businesses which are to be merged. Paragraph 7 at least sets up the procedure by which the parties can, if they are sensible, avoid some of these problems.

Paragraph 8 deals with the question of the term of the joint venture and sketches out the relevant rights of the parties in relation to withdrawal and restrictions upon the transfer of shares. It should be noted that para 8.1 provides for a fixed initial period during which neither party can withdraw. Not all joint venture agreements have this provision, but in nearly all cases it is a good idea to include it. The joint venture company needs an initial period of stability during which it can develop its business free from the need to consider what happens if it undergoes a change of shareholders. Similarly, in order to go to the trouble of setting up a joint venture at all, most shareholders will want to be reassured that their partners will be entering the transaction for a reasonable period, and not just for short term expediency.

Finally, para 9 deals with the question of announcements, para 10 provides that the whole arrangement (except for para 9) is subject to the drawing up of a definitive agreement, and is, therefore, not legally binding at this stage, while para 11 deals with the obtaining of the necessary regulatory consents if the arrangement is to be implemented at all.

12.6   Precedent 2

This precedent is an agreement combining a simple joint venture agreement and an earnout agreement. It is, as it stands, appropriate for the situation where one party has acquired the whole business and undertaking of the other party, but requires that the other party remain as a minority shareholder for a period of time after the merger.

However, this precedent can also be used as a skeleton on which to hang the more complicated provisions of the rest of the precedents in this chapter so as to provide for a long term joint venture agreement rather than an earnout arrangement.

Clauses 1 and 2 set out the way in which the merger has been brought about, and explain the reasons for the retention by the seller of the interest in the merged businesses.

Clause 3 sets out a simple shareholders' committee structure, which complies with the guidelines set out in *Russell v Northern Bank Development Corporation Ltd*, above. The minority protection rights set out in Sched 2 are short and simple given that the arrangement is an earnout agreement where the minority party should not seek a veto of decisions concerning the business except in extreme cases. Following this principle, cl 4 provides merely that the minority party will have board representation, but, other than the guarantee of the right to appoint directors, who can cast their votes, and be heard at board meetings, it is not generally appropriate for the minority shareholder in an earnout arrangement to seek a veto over matters discussed at board meetings.

Clause 5 provides the way in which the minority partner will exit from the joint venture at the end of the earnout period. Cross put and call options are provided over his shareholding, so that, if the majority partner does not exercise the call, the minority partner can exercise the put. Note should be taken of the special provisions to protect the majority shareholder's call option from the event of the minority shareholder's insolvency, first by accelerating the option in the event of such insolvency, and, secondly, by requiring that the share certificates be deposited as security with the majority shareholder and appointing the majority shareholder the attorney of the minority shareholder. This is for the purposes of executing the necessary share transfer in the event of the triggering of the accelerated call option in an insolvency situation. These provisions, which create an equitable mortgage, by way of deposit, over the relevant shares, in favour of the majority shareholder, are generally considered better protection against a receiver or liquidator of the minority shareholder than attempting to entrench the accelerated option in the articles of the company, or providing that the minority shareholder's shares become forfeit or are cancelled on his insolvency. Where the minority shareholder is a company this equitable mortgage should be registered as a charge (over the assets of the minority shareholder) under a s 395 of the Companies Act 1985 by the majority shareholder—see Chapter 16.

The restrictions on disposal of shares contained in cl 7 are a necessary part of the provisions to ensure that cl 5 is properly effective, and should be read in this context.

Clause 6 contains a long form non-competition covenant. In this case, since an earnout is in existence, both partners have to agree not to compete with the joint venture company. On the part of the minority shareholder this is in effect a vendor's non-competition covenant, so that it continues to bind him for a period after he has withdrawn from the company on the exercise of the put or call option. On the part of the majority shareholder the covenant is present to protect the earnout, and thus it terminates so far as the majority shareholder is concerned once the minority shareholder has exited from the joint venture company at the end of the earnout. Although this clause appears in an earnout context, it can be suitably adapted for use in any type of joint venture or acquisition agreement.

Clause 8 concerns the resolution of conflict between the memorandum and articles of the joint venture company and the joint venture agreements, and is drafted so as to comply with the guidelines discussed earlier in this chapter. In this particular case the parties have not opted for any entrenchment of rights, except the right of the minority shareholder to appoint directors to the board of the joint venture company pursuant to cl 4.1.

Clause 10 sets out necessary definitions and interpretations, cl 11 contains a set of 'boilerplate' clauses suitable for this type of agreement, and cl 12 provides for payment of interest on late payments (in practice of late payments under the earnout arrangements).

Special note should be taken of the set-off clause in cl 11.11. One of the agreements between the parties will be the acquisition agreement whereby the minority shareholder sold his business to the subsidiary of the majority shareholder which now acts as the joint venture company. One of the classes of claims between the parties which can be set off against sums payable under the joint venture agreement will be warranty claims under the acquisition agreement. Thus, the inclusion of this set-off clause effectively makes the whole of the earnout sum a retention upon which the majority shareholder can rely for satisfaction of warranty claims.

Care must be taken with such set-off clauses to ensure that the acquisition agreement is between the same parties as the joint venture agreement. For instance, the clause as drafted would not work if the acquisition agreement had been concluded not between ABC and CDE, but between ABC's wholly-owned subsidiary IJK Ltd and CDE. In such a case, the set-off clause must be amended to a group set-off clause (see Chapter 16).

Finally, Sched 1 provides for a description of the business. This is an important schedule, because it forms the basis of the non-competition covenant in cl 6. Schedule 2 contains examples of the simple minority protection rights that might be appropriate to this type of agreement. Schedule 3 provides an earnout formula based on turnover. However, it should be stressed that this formula is by way of example only. The precise details of every earnout must be considered not only by the legal and financial advisers of the clients, but also by the clients themselves, because they are the only people who understand enough of the businesses concerned to decide what is a fair and practical formula in all the circumstances of the case.

12.7   Precedent 3

This precedent is largely self-explanatory. It is a long form set of provisions designed to prescribe for the split of decision making in a joint venture company between the shareholders and the board of directors, to set up the necessary mechanisms and bodies to implement the decision making procedure agreed upon, and to provide the necessary set of minority protection rights. It is designed, once again, to take account of the guidelines set out earlier in this chapter in relation to the decision in *Russell v Northern Bank Development Corporation Ltd*, above, and in relation to the way in which conflicts may be minimised between the fiduciary duty of a director to his company and the interests of the shareholder who appointed him.

It is supposed that this precedent relates to a shareholders' agreement between the two major shareholders in a joint venture company who intend to invite a number of small investors to participate, but with no minority protection rights. However, it can easily be adapted to cover situations where all the shareholders are parties to the agreement.

The issues dealt with in the precedent are long and detailed, and it is unlikely that all joint ventures will include all of them. However, the provisions provide examples which can be adapted as required, and serve as a useful checklist of the sort of issues which can be included. Once again, it must be emphasised that the draftsman should not decide on a theoretical basis what sort of minority protection rights should be included in the joint venture agreement, and then persuade his clients of the wisdom of their inclusion. Instead, he should focus his client's minds on the issue, fortified with suitable examples, since only the people who are concerned with running the business can really understand what minority protection rights are necessary and practical to implement in the particular circumstances of the case.

It will be seen that there are three levels of decision making: the shareholders, the whole board, and the chief executive. Some issues are reserved only to the shareholders or only to the whole board. Decisions on other issues are reserved to the shareholders when they have a sufficient financial impact on the business. The board is required to take decisions in relation to these latter matters at full board meetings, when the financial impact on the business is not so great, but may only delegate authority to take such decisions to the chief executive when a still lesser financial impact is involved. The cut-off between the levels of decision making in relation to these matters is based either on a specific financial amount, or upon the period of time for the commitment.

When apportioning the cut-offs between the different levels in relation to these types of decisions, as a practical matter it is best to give the board the largest possible area of authority, so that it not only does not have to take such matters to the shareholders too often for decision, but also so that it can delegate as large a measure of this authority to the chief executive as it sees fit. The theory behind this is that the shareholders have the freedom to choose the composition of the board, and, once they have done so, it is normally in the best interests of the joint venture to allow that board to get on with running the business by and large in the way that it sees fit. If the shareholders need to second-guess or approve too many decisions of the directors, they should not have been appointed in the first place.

One final point on the drafting. It will be seen that a lot of the split of decision making is by reference to monetary amounts. These amounts are by way of example only, to show how the levels of approval dovetail at each stage in the hierarchy of decision making. When altering the figures care should be taken to ensure that this dovetailing between the different levels is maintained and that no gaps are left. The same is true for those provisions where the split is by reference to periods of years.

12.8   Precedent 4

This precedent sets out a simple set of procedures for exit from a joint venture.

After the initial period, any party who wishes to withdraw must first offer his shares to the other shareholders who may purchase them *pro rata* to their existing shareholdings, or in such other proportions as they agree. The withdrawing party must state the price at which he is prepared to sell, and, if he has in mind a sale to a third party, he must state this fact, and the identity of the prospective purchaser if one has been found at this stage.

If the whole of his shareholding is not taken up by the other shareholders he then has a period of time in which he can sell to a third party, provided he does so at not less than the offer price he gave to the existing shareholders. If such a third party does take up the whole of the withdrawing shareholder's shareholding then that third party must be accepted as a joint venture partner and shareholder by the existing shareholders, provided he enters into the joint venture agreement upon the same basis as the withdrawing shareholder.

The withdrawing shareholder ceases to be bound by the joint venture agreement upon the sale of his shares, either to the other shareholders or to a third party, except for those obligations which are expressed to be binding upon him after withdrawal, usually non-competition (for some specific period, often one or two years) and confidentiality.

This precedent renders the investment of the withdrawing shareholder relatively liquid. If the existing shareholders do not choose to take up his shareholding he is free to sell to whom he likes. The only possibly contentious issue is the level of price at which he can sell. This precedent prevents him asking too high a price from the existing shareholders, for fear that they will turn him down, and then he will be unable to find a third party who will accept the price he offered. It is true he may be unrealistic in his expectations at the first time of asking, and find this out by testing the market with third parties, when the existing shareholders turn him down. However, in this case, if he does find a third party willing to buy at a lower price, the wording of the precedent requires him to go back to the existing shareholders, and offer to sell at the lower price before he can sell to the interested third party. If they turn him down again, he can then sell to the prospective third party purchaser.

This lack of flexibility is only fair, because, in the absence of a formula at which the existing shareholders may buy out the withdrawing shareholder, the mechanism provided in the precedent imposes a market discipline for striking the price that is paid for the withdrawing shareholder's shares.

The requirement to name any third party prospective purchaser may seem too onerous, but, in fact, it is a fair exchange for the right of the withdrawing shareholder to sell to that third party irrespective of whether the existing shareholders approve of him or not. If they do not approve, their remedy is to buy the offered shares themselves, and, if they wish, later sell on to a third party more to their liking.

Provisions which can be included in this type of clause, but which shareholders who are interested in keeping their investment as liquid as possible should try to avoid, are the requirement that the existing shareholders can buy part, but not all, of the withdrawing shareholder's shareholding (thus leaving him with a rump which he may find it more difficult to dispose of to a third party) or the requirement that he should sell only to a third party of whom the existing shareholders approve.

Paragraph 4 is particularly important for a withdrawing shareholder and should always be included. He should have the right, despite confidentiality provisions in the joint venture agreement, to disclose sufficient information to third parties about the joint venture company and its business to enable them to assess the company and strike a price for the purchase of his shares. If he is prevented in disclosing this information because of such obligations he will find it almost impossible to deal properly with a third party, and be confined to bargaining with the existing shareholders from a position of extreme weakness, so that he is unlikely to realise the best price for his shares.

From the above it should be clear that this precedent has been written from the point of view of a withdrawing rather than an existing shareholder. However, it is a mistake to assume that it is in the interests of existing shareholders to make withdrawal unnecessarily difficult or penalise a withdrawing shareholder so that he stays with the joint venture under duress. Unless the parties to a joint venture wish to stay together nothing is served by forcing them to remain as partners, and the business can only suffer if they do. Flexible withdrawal provisions are probably the best way of ensuring that disputes between the partners are resolved swiftly and amicably, because, if they are not, one of the parties will withdraw.

12.9 Precedent 5

This precedent is a much more complicated withdrawal provision. It is designed to deal with the situation where the joint venture company has only two
shareholders, both of whose shareholdings are approximately equal. It is particularly suitable for deadlock companies where the parties hold 50 per cent of
the voting rights each, decisions have to be made unanimously, and the arrangement is in effect a partnership.

The difficulty with a partnership type of joint venture company is that it is
not easy to impose a market discipline on the agreement of the price for the
withdrawing shareholder's shareholding, since, in practice, it will in general
be hard to find a third party who would be willing to purchase the shares and
enter into the 'partnership' unless, whatever the provisions of the agreement,
the existing shareholder approves of and is willing to work with the prospective third party. Given this, in most cases, the only realistic purchaser of the
withdrawing shareholder's participation is the remaining shareholder, and the
difficulty is how to strike a fair price.

The procedure is triggered by the withdrawing shareholder offering to sell
all but not part of his shareholding at a specified price, and revealing any prospective third party purchaser, if one exists at that time. The problem is then to
balance the threats and opportunities in the procedure which follows to ensure
that the withdrawing shareholder is motivated to ask a fair price and the remaining shareholder is motivated to accept it.

First, the remaining shareholder has to decide whether he wants to buy. If
he does not want to buy, then the withdrawing shareholder is free to attempt to
sell his shareholding to anyone who will buy at whatever price he can obtain.
If he does want to buy, then he can either agree at once to buy at the offer price,
or else opt to go through the procedure set out in para 3.

The first stage of the procedure under para 3 is for the parties to attempt to
agree a price (which may be higher or lower than the initial offer price). If no
agreement is reached, the provisions of para 3 provide for the price to be calculated on the basis of various formulae, the result will be final and binding
upon the parties, and they will be obliged to sell and buy the shares at the
formula price.

This type of procedure puts considerable pressure on the parties to agree a
fair price as soon as possible, and, preferably, on the basis of the initial offer
price.

The withdrawing shareholder knows that if he does not make his initial
offer to sell at a realistic offer price, he runs great risks. On the one hand, the
remaining shareholder may turn him down, leaving him the choice of trying to
make what will probably be a distress sale to a third party, or of stopping in the
joint venture company against his wishes. On the other hand, the remaining
shareholder may want to buy, but, because he finds the offer unattractive, will
prefer to trigger the procedure in para 3. In this case, the withdrawing share-

holder has to attempt to negotiate a price (which he knows is hardly likely to be higher than the offer price) under threat, if the negotiations fail, of having to go through the long and expensive procedure of the formula valuation. The results of the formula valuation are not certain, and, if the result is lower than his original offer price (which will be likely if he has been unreasonable), he will not only end up with a lower price, but have wasted time and money into the bargain.

So far as the remaining shareholder is concerned, he faces as many risks and uncertainties. If he chooses not to accept the offer price, he will either have to gamble on the results of the formula valuation (which he will be loathe to do if he knows that he has really rejected a reasonable offer price) or reject the offer and risk being saddled with a third party purchaser of whom he may not approve, and with whom he may not be able to work. In these circumstances, even if the withdrawing shareholder's search for third party purchasers fails, the remaining shareholder knows he will still have to suffer the presence of his current disgruntled partner.

So far as the formulae are concerned, they are fairly traditional in approach. The first is designed to realise a value based on what the investment of the withdrawing shareholder would have earned if he had invested the amount that he put into the joint venture company at its inception in some other form of investment. The form in effect depends upon the rate of interest inserted in the formula. Normally it would be a conservative figure to recognise investment in gilts or some form of bank deposit. The next formula is valuation by merchant bankers, and the third a cross-check by assessing the market value of other companies in the same type of industry which are quoted on a stock exchange. Once again there are many variations on these formulae, and other formulae which can be used.

If the highest of three results is picked, the first formula provides an underpin, the third provides a market price check, while the second modifies the first two by taking into account any special factors that the merchant bankers can discover. The dynamics of the situation can be altered by choosing the lowest of the three, in which case the first formula acts as a cap rather than an underpin.

Where both parties want to withdraw, the situation is different. Paragraph 6 provides a modified form of the procedure sometimes known as 'Russian Roulette' or a 'Texan Shoot-Out'. Again the dynamics behind the procedure are to force the parties to agree on a commercially realistic price, in the absence of a free market for the shares, and to raise the stakes every time they refuse to do so, thus giving them the maximum incentive to reach agreement at an early stage in the proceedings.

The process is triggered if, when one party gives notice of withdrawal, the other chooses not to negotiate with him but in turn to give notice of withdrawal himself. In this case, the parties' first attempt to agree who will buy the other out, and the price at which this will take place. If they cannot reach agreement, then they are obliged to try to sell the whole of the joint venture company to a third party at a mutually agreeable price.

If this does not occur within a set period, then a price is determined pursuant to the valuation formulae discussed above, and the parties have a further opportunity, in the light of that valuation, and, of course of their testing of the market, to see if they can agree a price at which one will buy the other's shareholding.

If they cannot agree at this stage, then an auction between the two parties is held by a merchant banker, with the higher bidder buying out the other party at the bid price, and the other party being obliged to sell to him at the bid price. The pressure point which keeps the bids at a realistic level is that each party has to submit a sealed bid to the merchant banker, who determines which party has made the higher bid, and rules that the higher bidder must purchase the other party's shares, and the other party sell his shares, at that bid price. Obviously each party will have to bid a price at which he is equally happy to buy or to sell, and this will prevent unrealistically low bids, since the other may then be able to buy at a bargain price, and unrealistically high bids, since then the party making such a bid may be forced to buy at an inflated price.

It is possible to go straight to an auction with the sealed bid procedure, and leave out the intervening stages, but generally, the purpose of the threat of the auction is to compel the parties to come to a commercially realistic settlement, and the procedure as drafted provides them with an opportunity to do so.

It is also of course true that a withdrawing party who gives notice of withdrawal with the aim of triggering the procedure in para 3 faces the danger that the other party will also give notice, and thus trigger the 'Texan Shoot-Out'. This is one more pressure on a withdrawing party to make an offer of a reasonable price when stating his intention to withdraw. On the other hand, the remaining shareholder is unlikely to give such notice, and let himself in for all the uncertainties it entails, unless he really feels unhappy with the price asked by the withdrawing shareholder, or wishes himself to buy the whole of the joint venture company, and is prepared to pay a higher price.

12.10 Precedent 6

This precedent sets out provisions covering forcible withdrawal of a shareholder from the joint venture agreement for default, insolvency, change of control and deadlock. It is self-explanatory, and clearly the consequences of termination can be any number of variations on the theme of withdrawal, using the formulae and procedures in the previous precedents.

Two issues arise. First, there is sometimes a temptation where forcible withdrawal is on the basis of a price fixed by a formula for the price to be at a discount compared to the formula used in the case of voluntary withdrawal. In the case of insolvency this seems unreasonable, and, in the case of breach, there seems no reason to penalise the withdrawing shareholder by a reduction in his realised shareholder value unless that reduction is in full and final satisfaction of all claims against him for breach by the remaining shareholders. Even here the remaining shareholders may run the risk that the reduction is unenforceable as a penalty. The best course is to ensure that the shareholder withdraws on a neutral basis and that he is sued for any breaches he has committed as a separate matter. So far as change of control is concerned, it is sometimes said that such a reduction acts as a poison pill, but this is open to the objection of all poison pills, that it reduces the value shareholders of the withdrawing shareholder can obtain if they sell their shares to a third party, and in most cases it is not sensible to agree such a reduction for this reason.

So far as deadlock is concerned, the situation is different. The very purpose of minority protection rights is to protect a shareholder who exercises them. If the first time he exercises them the result is that he is deemed to have withdrawn from the company, that protection is illusory. The precedent provides for such withdrawal to be deemed to have occurred if one shareholder objects consistently over a period of time to different issues, but even such provisions should be approached with caution. Another alternative is to provide that in the event of deadlock the company should be wound up, and that all parties must agree in the joint venture agreement to vote for such winding up in that event. Again such a provision makes the existence of the minority protection rights somewhat illusory. The idea of submitting what are essentially differences of commercial judgment to the binding determination of a third party is also in most cases impractical.

It is of course possible not to provide for any mechanism to resolve deadlocks, except perhaps an escalation for further discussion to higher levels of management, and final resolution by the shareholders (if possible), but to provide also for a flexible withdrawal procedure. In this case the only feasible solution to continuing differences of opinion between joint venture partners is simply the withdrawal of one of them.

12.11   Precedent 7

This precedent provides a specimen provision in the articles of a joint venture company for entrenching minority protection rights by means of weighted voting rights.

12.12   Precedent 8

This precedent shows how minority protection rights can be entrenched in the articles of a joint venture company in relation to procedures at a board meeting.

Precedent 1

Heads of agreement for a joint venture

THIS MEMORANDUM OF UNDERSTANDING between [   ]
LIMITED whose registered office is at [   ] ('ABC') and
[   ] LIMITED whose registered office is at [   ]
('DEF') records the basis upon which certain businesses carried on by ABC in
[   ] (collectively the 'ABC Territory') will be merged with cer-
tain businesses carried on by DEF in [   ] (collectively the 'DEF
Territory') to form a joint venture company:

1   Description of existing businesses

1.1 ABC Subsidiary Ltd ('ABC Subsidiary') is a wholly-owned subsidiary of
ABC which (together with certain subsidiaries of ABC Subsidiary) carries on
the businesses of [the marketing sale and distribution of] in the ABC Territory. Details of ABC Subsidiary and ABC Subsidiary's subsidiaries and a description in more detail of the said businesses is contained in Appendix 1 hereto.
The businesses carried on by ABC in the ABC Territory are referred to collectively as the 'ABC Business'.

1.2 DEF Subsidiary Ltd ('DEF Subsidiary') is a wholly-owned subsidiary of
DEF which (together with certain subsidiaries of DEF Subsidiary) carries on
the businesses of [the marketing sale and distribution of] in the DEF Territory.
Details of DEF Subsidiary and DEF Subsidiary's subsidiaries and a description in more detail of the said businesses is contained in Appendix 2 hereto.
The businesses carried on by DEF in the DEF Territory are referred to collectively as the 'DEF Business'.

2   Establishment of joint venture

2.1 The parties shall establish and agree valuations to the time schedule detailed in para 2.4 below, for the ABC Business and the DEF Business, based principally upon the value of net assets. The detailed principles and procedures for such valuations are set out in Appendix 3 to this Memorandum.

2.2 On [   ] (the 'Closing Date'), the parties will cause DEF Subsidiary to purchase the whole of the issued share capital of ABC Subsidiary, and thus to acquire the ABC business as a going concern. DEF Subsidiary shall within 12 months of the Closing Date change the names of ABC Subsidiary and all of its subsidiaries as relevant to remove from such names the word 'ABC'.

2.3 As consideration for the said acquisition, DEF Subsidiary will, on the Closing Date, allot [20] per cent of its issued share capital to ABC. The parties intend that on the Closing Date DEF will own [80] per cent of the share capital of DEF Subsidiary, and ABC [20] per cent and will therefore (on the basis of forecast pro forma balance sheets attached as Appendix 4) exercise their best endeavours to ensure that the proportion which the values of the DEF Business and the ABC Business respectively bear to each other is [80 to 20]. The parties consider that this will be most easily achieved by taking the valuation of the DEF Business on the basis of the aforesaid forecast balance sheets as a bench mark, and then ensuring that the forecast net value of the assets and liabilities of the ABC Business acquired by DEF Subsidiary through its acquisition of ABC Subsidiary is one quarter of that of the DEF Business, with any necessary adjustment being made by the following method (the 'Adjustment Method') namely by [a balancing adjustment to the DEF intercompany receivable or payable between DEF and DEF Subsidiary] [payment into or removal of a balancing amount from the assets of DEF Subsidiary by respectively either the subscription for cash at par plus a suitable premium of one new [non-voting ordinary A] share in DEF Subsidiary or the payment by DEF Subsidiary to DEF of a dividend].

2.4 The parties recognise that the basis of the valuation and the use of the Adjustment Method referred to in para 2.3 can only be based on forecasts at the Closing Date. Final valuations (as of the Closing Date) of the ABC Business and the DEF Business will therefore be prepared and agreed between the parties by no later than 60 days after the Closing Date. If the proportion that the valuations of the DEF Business and the ABC Business bear to each other is not [80 to 20] respectively, then the parties shall again use the Adjustment Method upon the DEF Business to achieve the said proportion.

2.5 The parties will effect the said acquisition by means of simple agreements with no warranties (other than as to good title to shares and assets, corporate good standing of the legal entities concerned, and authority and competence to execute), on the basis that all liabilities which are known to the parties prior to the Closing Date are properly provided for as part of the valuation process referred to in paras 2.1, 2.3 and 2.4 above. The parties agree that if claims or liabilities arise or are discovered after the Closing Date which by reason of the said acquisition have become the responsibility of DEF Subsidiary but were unknown at the Closing Date (so that no provision as aforesaid was made for them) then such claims and liabilities shall be borne by DEF Subsidiary *provided that* if such an unknown liability is discovered or arises within [two years] after the Closing Date and is either for a fixed sum in excess of £[   ] or is a contingent liability which can reasonably be estimated to exceed £[   ] if it becomes actual, then if the said claim or liability relates to the ABC Business ABC shall take responsibility for the conduct handling and settlement thereof and indemnify DEF and DEF Subsidiary against it, while if the claim relates to the DEF Business DEF shall take responsibility therefor and indemnify DEF Subsidiary and ABC against it. In both cases DEF shall procure that DEF Subsidiary renders all reasonable assistance to the indemnifying party in dealing with the said claim or liability, but at the indemnifying party's expense.

3   Basic principles of joint venture

3.1 Subject to para 3.2 below, DEF Subsidiary's business mission shall be (*a*) to combine and merge the ABC Business and the DEF Business into a single business (the 'Merged Business'); (*b*) to exploit to the full the synergistic benefits of such a combination and merger; (*c*) to develop the Merged Business vigorously throughout the DEF Territory and the ABC Territory (collectively the 'Territory').

3.2 DEF Subsidiary shall operate on an arms-length basis with the parties hereto and any other companies within their respective groups.

3.3 The parties' intention is that DEF Subsidiary shall be self-financing to the greatest possible extent.

3.4 The parties are agreed that DEF Subsidiary's accounting year shall continue to be the same as DEF's accounting year, that is ending on [   ] in each year.

3.5 Employees of the ABC Business will continue after the purchases referred to in para 2.2 initially on the same terms and conditions of employment, as the share transfers to DEF Subsidiary of the legal entities which employ them do not affect the continuity of their contracts of employment. In particular, the pension, benefit and welfare plans set up by the ABC Business will pass unaffected into the control of DEF Subsidiary, and initially continue on the same basis as before. In due course, terms and conditions of employment of the employees of the DEF Business and the ABC Business must be harmonised. As part of such harmonisation, the pension, benefit and welfare plans of the DEF Business and the ABC Business will (to the extent reasonably practicable) be merged into common plans for all employees of DEF Subsidiary and its subsidiaries.

3.6 ABC and DEF will on the Closing Date enter into suitable covenants not to compete with the DEF Subsidiary in respect of the Merged Business, in the Territory. Such covenants shall bind the party making them for the period during which that party remains a shareholder of DEF Subsidiary, and for a period of [two] years after it ceases so to be.

4 Operation of joint venture

4.1 DEF Subsidiary will have a board of directors, two of whom shall be appointed by ABC and the remainder of whom (but not less than three) shall be appointed by DEF (the 'Board'). DEF shall appoint the Chairman and Managing Director.

4.2 Representatives of the parties who are shareholders of DEF Subsidiary (the 'Shareholders') shall meet not less than three times a year in order to discuss and consult upon important aspects of running the operations of DEF Subsidiary, including the setting of its business plan and budgets, and the creation of its product, procurement and marketing strategies. The representatives of ABC shall be not more than two in number and those of DEF not less than three in number. Any decisions taken at such meetings shall be by majority vote.

4.3 DEF Subsidiary shall not act in respect of the following matters, unless both the shareholders have (after consultation together and with DEF Subsidiary) given their joint approval thereto:

4.3.1 any acquisitions or joint ventures involving an equity stake;

4.3.2 the provision of additional funding by way of loans, guarantees for loans, issue of shares debentures or bonds, or capital contributions from one or both of the shareholders;

4.3.3 acquisitions or disposals of capital assets (including real property but excluding sales of receivables for financing purposes) over £[   ];

4.3.4 any major change in DEF Subsidiary's business;

4.3.5 any extension of the business of DEF Subsidiary to areas outside the Territory;

4.3.6 any material transaction between DEF Subsidiary and one of the parties hereto which is not on an arms-length basis or which is not in the ordinary course of business, including without limitation all licence agreements granted after the Closing Date pursuant to para 5.2 below and modifications to supply agreements pursuant to para 6.3 below.

4.4 With regard to dividend policy, unless otherwise agreed by the Shareholders (after mutual consultation), DEF Subsidiary shall pay a yearly dividend to its shareholders of not less than [20] per cent of the current year's profits legally available for distribution, [*provided that* payment of such dividend can be funded either out of cash held by DEF Subsidiary or through its existing lines of credit without exceeding the Board's delegated authority in respect of borrowing limits in force at the relevant time].

5   Intellectual property rights

5.1 On the Closing Date, ABC and DEF (each, individually, a 'Licensor'; together 'the Licensors') will (to the extent that they have not already granted the same by a formal document) grant DEF Subsidiary a non-exclusive non-transferable licence or sub-licence (as relevant) within the Territory under all Intellectual Property Rights which are in existence on the Closing Date or (except in the case of subpara (*d*) below) thereafter come into existence which the Licensors own or have the unrestricted power to licence without payment:

    (*a*) to resell products acquired from any Licensor ('Acquired Products') under the trademark(s) to be applied thereto by the supplier;

    (*b*) to modify, adapt or enhance those Acquired Products for the purposes of (i) customisation (ii) enhancement (iii) adaptation to local country requirements and/or (iv) system integration but only to the extent that such rights were granted, by ABC and DEF for the ABC Business and the DEF Business respectively, in respect of any such Acquired Product prior to the Closing Date and were in existence on the Closing Date;

    (*c*) directly or indirectly to sub-licence customers to use software in object-code form to the extent necessary to permit the use of Acquired Products;

    (*d*) to continue using, in the same manner as previously, any software used immediately prior to the Closing Date for the internal purposes of the

ABC Business or the DEF Business, including without limitation for business data processing purposes or as a tool to assist in the development of software.

The licence granted in subpara (*a*) above shall be free of payment but subject to DEF Subsidiary's compliance with the reasonable directions (if any) of the Licensor concerned with respect to use of its trademarks (whether or not registered). DEF Subsidiary shall not acquire any right of ownership in respect of any Licensor's trademark used by it.

The licence granted in subpara (*b*) shall be subject to such restrictions and payment obligations (if any) as applied immediately prior to the Closing Date and any further such licence in respect of further such application software shall be granted upon a case by case basis upon such terms and conditions (which may or may not include a payment obligation) as DEF Subsidiary and ABC or DEF, as the case may be, shall agree.

The licence granted pursuant to subpara (*c*) may be granted by inclusion in a product supply agreement entered into pursuant to and on the prices, terms and conditions specified in para 6.1 hereof. DEF Subsidiary shall not disclose or sub-licence source code obtained from any Licensor without its prior written agreement. The parties acknowledge that there are in existence at the Closing Date sub-licences of the kind described in this paragraph which have been granted pursuant to a licence by DEF or ABC granted prior to the Closing Date. Such licences and sub-licences shall continue upon their current terms, including the payment of any royalty by DEF Subsidiary or ABC Subsidiary to DEF or ABC as the case may be under such licences.

The licence granted in para (*d*) above shall be subject to such restrictions and payment obligations (if any) as applied immediately prior to the Closing Date.

Unless otherwise specifically provided DEF Subsidiary shall not be entitled to any right or licence under any Licensor's Intellectual Property Right to manufacture any product or reproduce any software for commercial exploitation.

5.2 Any further licences or sub-licences of Intellectual Property Rights from the Licensors to DEF Subsidiary shall be entered into on terms and conditions to be agreed upon an arms-length basis, and all such licences shall be granted in consideration of the payment of lump sum charges and/or an ongoing royalty, and shall not be free of charge, [*provided that* where at any time after the Closing Date, a Licensor makes software generally available to its wholly owned subsidiaries for their internal purposes, DEF Subsidiary shall be entitled to be supplied with and use such software for such purposes on the basis applied by that Licensor to such subsidiaries].

5.3 Insofar as the ABC Business and the DEF Business currently make use under licence of Intellectual Property Rights owned or controlled by third parties, and by the terms of any such licence DEF Subsidiary is unable to continue such use following the merger referred to in para 2.3 above, DEF and ABC will to the extent that they have the right to do so (subject to any restrictions in the licences) make reasonable efforts to sub-licence, share or assist DEF Subsidiary in negotiating for the right to continue using such Intellectual Property Rights. DEF Subsidiary will be responsible for all costs or charges imposed by any third party in connection with the sub-licensing sharing or licensing of such rights acquired for the benefit of DEF Subsidiary.

5.4 The licences referred to in paras 5.1, 5.2 and 5.3 shall continue throughout the term of the joint venture and shall survive its termination (and ABC, DEF and DEF Subsidiary shall continue to be bound by such licences) for a period of two years after such termination.

6 Supply of products and services

6.1 On the Closing Date, DEF and ABC will (to the extent that they have not already been entered into in a formal document) each enter into an agreement with DEF Subsidiary for the supply of their respective products (the 'Supplied Products') relating to the Merged Business to DEF Subsidiary in respect of the Territory. Prices, terms and conditions of supply shall be a fair and reasonable arms-length price based on market list prices less a mutually agreed discount. The supply prices for all major Supplied Products to be supplied by DEF and ABC to DEF Subsidiary on the Closing Date, and the general formulae for the calculation of such prices thereafter, and payment terms thereafter, shall be agreed between the parties and detailed in the aforesaid supply agreements. [As part of such agreements DEF Subsidiary shall enter into covenants with DEF and ABC not to market, sell or distribute, directly or indirectly, in the territory products which compete with the Supplied Products.]

6.2 On the Closing Date, DEF and ABC will each enter into an agreement with DEF Subsidiary for the supply to DEF Subsidiary of any services previously provided to the DEF Business and the ABC Business respectively, which DEF Subsidiary wishes to continue to receive. The terms conditions and prices for the supply of such services will be agreed by the parties prior to the Closing Date.

6.3 Unless otherwise agreed, the agreements referred to in paras 6.1 and 6.2 (as modified in writing by the parties from time to time to meet the then current needs of the parties) shall continue throughout the term of the joint venture and shall survive its termination, and DEF, ABC and DEF Subsidiary shall continue to be bound by such agreements for a period of two years after such termination.

7   Integration activity

7.1 Immediately upon the signature of this Memorandum the parties shall establish teams who will consult together as to the best way to achieve the merger and combination of the ABC Business and the DEF Business.

7.2 However, the parties are agreed that no actual merger or combination shall take place prior to the Closing Date, and that prior to the Closing Date DEF and ABC shall run the DEF Business and the ABC Business respectively in the ordinary course, including in particular without any implementation of acquisitions or divestments.

7.3 Subsequent to the Closing Date the total responsibility for the implementation of integration of the DEF Business and the ABC Business shall be vested in DEF Subsidiary. However, DEF Subsidiary shall take due regard of the recommendations resulting from the work of the teams referred to in para 7.1 above.

7.4 All costs of restructuring as a result of the implementation of the integration shall be borne by DEF Subsidiary. All other costs and expenses (including without limitation legal and accountancy fees, taxes and stamp duty) in relation to this Memorandum of Understanding, the Definitive Agreements referred to in para 10, and its and their subject matter (including any of the foregoing incurred prior to the Closing Date), shall be borne by the party incurring the same.

8   Term of joint venture

8.1 The joint venture shall last for an initial term of [three] years during which neither party may withdraw or sell its shares unless the other party agrees.

8.2 after the expiry of the initial period either party shall be able to withdraw upon nine months' notice in writing in accordance with the following procedure:

8.2.1 the withdrawing party must first offer its shares at a stated price to the other party;

8.2.2 if the other party wishes to purchase the withdrawing party's shares at the stated price, it shall thereupon do so, but if it wishes to make such purchase, but disputes the fairness of the stated price, the parties shall then negotiate in good faith to determine a fair and reasonable price;

8.2.3 if the other party does not wish to purchase the withdrawing party's shares, the other party shall permit the withdrawing party to sell the withdrawing party's shares to any third party (provided that the other party shall be entitled to prohibit/obliged to consent to a sale to a competitor of the other party);

8.2.4 if the parties are unable to agree a fair and reasonable price in good faith before the expiry of the aforesaid notice period, both parties shall submit the determination of such price to an independent third party to be agreed between them, or, in default of agreement, to such firm of chartered accountants of international repute who shall be appointed on the request of either party by [the President of the Institute of Chartered Accountants in England and Wales]. Such third party shall in coming to his decision (which shall be final and binding upon the parties) act as an expert and not as an arbitrator.

9 Announcements

The parties agree that no announcement shall be made concerning the matters covered by this memorandum (unless required by law or competent regulatory authority) until a mutually agreed joint announcement can be prepared and released. The parties intend that such announcement shall be made no later than [   ].

10 Definitive agreements

This Memorandum of Understanding is not intended to be legally binding (except for para 9, which is and is intended to be legally binding) but simply expresses the intentions and understandings of the parties. It will form the basis of a set of detailed legally binding agreements to be drafted and executed by [   ]. Immediately upon the signature of this Memorandum of Understanding ABC and DEF will each arrange for the other to be provided with all necessary financial, commercial and legal information relating to the ABC Business and the DEF Business, to the extent not already provided, so that the parties can agree the valuation of the respective businesses as contemplated in and for the purposes of paras 2.1 and 2.4 above.

11 Regulatory consent

The transactions contemplated herein are subject to all necessary governmental and other regulatory consents, and the parties shall co-operate to ensure so far as possible that the necessary applications for such consents are submitted in a timely fashion to enable all such consents to be obtained before the Closing Date.

APPENDIX 1
Details of ABC Subsidiary, and its Subsidiaries, and of the ABC Business.

APPENDIX 2
Details of DEF Subsidiary, and its Subsidiaries, and of the DEF Business.

APPENDIX 3
Valuation Procedure

APPENDIX 4
Pro Forma Balance Sheet and Estimated Valuation

ABC LIMITED
By
Its
Date:

DEF LIMITED
By
Its
Date:

Precedent 2

Joint venture and earnout agreement

---

1   Parties

1.1 ABC LIMITED whose registered office is at [   ] ('ABC')
1.2 CDE LIMITED whose registered office is at [   ] ('CDE')

2   Preamble

2.1 As a result of the closing on [   ] (the 'Closing Date') of the transactions contemplated by the Share Acquisition Agreement made between the parties on [   ]:
2.1.1 ABC now holds 60 per cent of the issued ordinary share capital of FGH Limited whose registered office is at [   ] ('FGH') through ABC's wholly-owned subsidiary IJK Limited;
2.1.2 CDE now holds directly 40 per cent of the issued ordinary share capital of FGH (the 'CDE Shares'); and
2.1.3 ABC has merged the business carried on by its division known as LMN ('LMN') with the business of FGH by means of a transfer of all the contracts, assets and liabilities of LMN to FGH.

2.2 Both FGH and LMN are engaged in businesses of the type and nature detailed in Schedule 1 (hereinafter referred to as the 'Relevant Type of Business').

2.3 ABC and CDE have entered into this Shareholders' Agreement to define and regulate the nature of CDE's continuing interest in FGH and to state how the parties will work together for the successful growth of the combined businesses of LMN and FGH.

3   Shareholders' committee

3.1 As long as CDE holds the CDE Shares, FGH shall have a shareholders' committee (the 'Committee') consisting of two members. One member shall be appointed by CDE. One member shall be appointed by ABC. Each member of the Committee may from time to time be removed and replaced by the shareholder who has appointed him. If a member resigns or is removed by the shareholder who appointed such member, that shareholder shall appoint a new member within one month after the resignation or removal of the withdrawing member. The first such members shall be [   ] and [   ].

3.2 The Chairman (who shall be the member of the Committee appointed by ABC pursuant to cl 3.1) and the Secretary of the Committee (who shall not be a member thereof) shall be appointed removed and replaced from time to time by ABC. Such appointments, removals and replacements shall be notified to CDE in writing prior to the date upon which they are stated to come into effect. The first Chairman and Secretary shall be [   ] and [   ] respectively.

3.3 The Committee shall meet at least once every three months, but a meeting shall be called at any time by the Secretary upon the request of either shareholder.

3.4 The Secretary shall give both shareholders seven clear days' notice in writing of the place, date, time and agenda of each meeting of the Committee. However, if both shareholders agree all or any of these formalities may be waived.

3.5 Each member of the Committee shall have one vote. Decisions of the Committee shall be made on the basis of unanimity. In the event of an equality of votes the Chairman shall not have a second or casting vote.

3.6 Each member of the Committee may from time to time appoint remove and replace an alternate to represent him and to exercise his vote in his absence. Such appointments, removals and replacements shall be notified to the Secretary in writing prior to the date upon which they are stated to come into effect. Each member or his alternate may be accompanied by other employees of the relevant shareholder who shall act as observers and advisers as necessary but shall not be entitled to vote.

3.7 The Secretary shall keep minutes of every Committee meeting and any resolutions passed at such meeting. These minutes shall be signed by the Chairman and distributed to the other members of the Committee without delay.

These minutes shall be deemed to be accepted by the members unless an objection has been raised in writing with the Chairman within two weeks after receipt of the minutes. In case of such objection the matter shall be discussed and resolved at the next meeting of the Committee.

3.8 Meetings of the Committee shall take place at the registered office of FGH, unless the members in individual cases unanimously resolve otherwise.

3.9 There shall be a quorum at any meeting of the Committee if the representatives for each of the shareholders is present or represented by an alternate. If there is no quorum present at a meeting, the meeting shall be adjourned to the same day and time in the following week and upon its resumption a quorum shall be deemed present without regard to the actual number of members present or represented.

3.10 The Committee may discuss any matters in relation to FGH and its affairs and business that it sees fit, but shall only make decisions and pass resolutions pursuant to cl 3.3 in respect of the matters set out in Schedule 2 ('Reserved Matter(s)'). ABC and CDE each undertake to the other to use all their powers as shareholders of FGH, including voting at any general meeting of FGH to procure the implementation by FGH of any such resolutions in respect of Reserved Matters passed by the Committee; and not to propose a resolution at a shareholder meeting in respect of a Reserved Matter unless the Committee has first reached a decision and passed a resolution concerning it. Upon any of the Reserved Matters coming to vote at a shareholder meeting of FGH, all the shares held by the parties shall be voted together and in accordance with the relevant resolution of the Committee, *provided that* if, in respect of any Reserved Matter, neither party shall propose a resolution at a shareholders meeting in respect of that Reserved Matter, and (in the event that, for any reason, the foregoing of such a resolution has been so proposed) the Committee could reach no decision and pass no resolution because of a deadlock, the parties shall vote together all of the shares held by them against the said resolution at the relevant shareholder meeting in order to preserve the *status quo*. The parties further undertake to use all their powers as aforesaid to ensure that the Reserved Matters are reserved as shareholder matters which cannot be finally decided upon by the Board of Directors of FGH, although such Board may discuss and make recommendations in respect of Reserved Matters to the shareholders.

4   Board of directors of FGH

4.1 As long as CDE holds the CDE Shares, it shall have the right to appoint remove and replace from time to time two non-executive directors to the Board of Directors of FGH who shall be reasonably acceptable to ABC and of a status suitable to hold such office and to discharge the duties thereof.

4.2 Upon CDE ceasing to be a shareholder in FGH it shall remove or procure the resignation from the Board of Directors of FGH of any Director then appointed by it.

5   Purchase and sale of option shares

5.1 Subject to the terms and conditions of this Agreement:

5.1.1 CDE shall have the option, which it may exercise at any time on or after [   ], and prior to [   ] (the 'Option Period') by the delivery to ABC of written notice of its election to do so (the 'Put Notice'), to require ABC to purchase all (but not less than all) of the CDE Shares. The Put Notice, if and when delivered, shall be irrevocable. Not later than thirty (30) days following the delivery of the Put Notice (the 'Put Option Closing Date'), CDE shall sell to ABC, and ABC shall acquire from CDE, all the CDE Shares for an aggregate purchase price calculated in accordance with the relevant formula set out in Schedule 3 (the 'Option Price'). The Option Price shall be payable in cash on the Put Option Closing Date in consideration of the transfer of CDE Shares to the Purchaser;

5.1.2 ABC shall have the option, which it may exercise at any time during the Option Period by the delivery to CDE of written notice of its election to do so (the 'Call Notice') to require CDE to sell all (but not less than all) of the CDE Shares. The Call Notice, if and when delivered, shall be irrevocable. Not later than thirty (30) days following the delivery of the Call Notice (the 'Call Option Closing Date'), CDE shall sell to ABC, and ABC shall acquire from CDE, all the CDE Shares for the Option Price (references in cl 5.1.1 to the Put Option Closing Date being deemed to refer to the Call Option Closing Date). The Option Price shall be payable in cash on the Call Option Closing Date in consideration of the transfer of the CDE Shares to ABC.

5.2 If, at any time after the Closing Date and prior to the date (the 'Expiry Date') on which the Option Period expires;

5.2.1 CDE shall attempt to sell, assign, transfer, pledge, mortgage or charge or otherwise dispose of or encumber the CDE Shares or any beneficial interest in them to any Person other than ABC, or if CDE shall pass a resolution for winding-up (otherwise than for the purpose of a solvent amalgamation or reconstruction where the resulting entity assumes all of the obligations of CDE under this Agreement) or a court shall make an order to that effect, or if CDE shall cease to carry on its business or substantially the whole of its business, or convenes a meeting of or makes or proposes to make any arrangement or composition with its creditors or if a receiver administrator manager administrative receiver or similar officer is appointed of any assets of CDE or any analogous step is taken in connection with the other's insolvency or dissolution; or **5.2.2** ABC shall reduce its shareholding in FGH below 51 per cent of the issued ordinary share capital, or pass a resolution for the winding-up of FGH (provided that cl 5.2.2 shall have no application or effect in the event of ABC transferring all or part of such shareholding to a credit-worthy wholly-owned subsidiary which undertakes to be bound by the terms of this Agreement); (the events in cll 5.2.1 and 5.2.2 being hereinafter collectively referred to as 'Disposal Events') then, notwithstanding anything to the contrary in cll 5.1.1 and 5.1.2, ABC shall have the option, which it may exercise at any time within thirty (30) days after it receives notice (from CDE or otherwise) of one of the Disposal Events referred to in cl 5.2.1 (which notice shall be given promptly by CDE upon the occurrence of such Disposal Event) to require CDE to sell to it all (but not less than all) of the CDE Shares, and CDE shall have the option, which it may exercise at any time within thirty (30) days after it receives notice (from ABC or otherwise) of one of the Disposal Events referred to in cl 5.2.2 (which notice shall be given promptly by ABC upon the occurrence of such Disposal Event) to require ABC to purchase from it all (but not less than all) of the CDE Shares. Such options shall be exercised by the delivery by ABC to CDE or CDE to ABC (as the case may be) of written notice of the delivering party's election to exercise such option (the 'Acceleration Notice'). The Acceleration Notice, if and when delivered, shall be irrevocable. Not later than five (5) days following the delivery of the Acceleration Notice (the 'Accelerated Option Closing Date'), CDE shall sell to ABC, and ABC shall acquire from CDE, all the Option Shares then owned by CDE for an aggregate purchase price calculated in accordance with the relevant formula set out in Schedule 3 (the 'Accelerated Purchase Price').

5.3 In the event that neither party has exercised an option pursuant to cl 5.1 or 5.2 prior to the Expiry Date, then ABC shall be deemed to have served a Call Notice on that date pursuant to cl 5.1.2 and the provisions of that clause shall (subject to and in accordance with the remainder of this Agreement) have effect accordingly.

5.4 CDE warrants and undertakes to ABC: (i) that on the date of signature hereof it holds full clear and unencumbered title in and to all of the CDE Shares; (ii) that it will on the Put Option Closing Date, Call Option Closing Date, or Accelerated Option Closing Date as the case may be hold full clear and unencumbered title in and to all of the CDE Shares; and (iii) that it will on the Put Option Closing Date, Call Option Closing Date, or Accelerated Option Closing Date as the case may be have the full and unrestricted right power and authority to sell transfer and deliver all of the CDE Shares to ABC hereunder whereupon ABC will acquire valid and unencumbered title thereto.

5.5 On the Put Option Closing Date, the Call Option Closing Date, or the Accelerated Option Closing Date as the case may be, CDE shall deliver to ABC share transfers duly executed by CDE in favour of ABC, and CDE shall take such other actions, and deliver such other transfer documents or instruments, reasonably necessary to convey good and marketable title to all of the CDE Shares to be transferred at such Closing free and clear of all Encumbrances. On such Put Option Closing Date, Call Option Closing Date, or Accelerated Option Closing Date upon receipt of such deeds and other transfer documents or instruments, ABC shall pay to CDE the Option Price or the Accelerated Purchase Price, in accordance with this Agreement.

5.6 Payment of the Option Price or the Accelerated Purchase Price shall be made by telegraphic transfer of immediately available funds to the account of CDE, in accordance with written instructions given to ABC at least five (5) business days prior to the date such payment is due.

5.7 By way of security for its obligations under this clause, CDE hereby agrees to deposit with ABC on the closing date the share certificates relative to the CDE Shares. If CDE defaults in transferring the CDE Shares on the Put Option Closing Date, the Call Option Closing Date or the Accelerated Option Closing Date, as the case may be, the directors of FGH shall be entitled to receive, and give a good discharge for, the Option Price or the Accelerated Purchase Price, as the case may be, in trust for CDE (and to be held pending payment over to CDE in a deposit account bearing interest at a reasonable commercial rate) and CDE hereby irrevocably appoints [   ] as CDE's attorney to execute on its behalf a transfer or transfers of the CDE Shares in favour of ABC (or as it may direct) and such other documents as may be necessary to transfer title to the CDE Shares to ABC (or as ABC may direct) CDE hereby likewise agrees so to appoint as its attorney any other person or persons in future nominated by FGH in writing in substitution for [   ] and hereby authorises the directors of FGH to approve registration of such transfer or transfers or other documents executed by [   ] or any person or persons nominated in substitution for [   ] as aforesaid.

6   Non-competition agreements

6.1 CDE for itself and on behalf of [all other companies controlled by it] ('CDE Affiliates'), and on behalf of the directors and employees of itself and of CDE Affiliates, shall not in [the UK], and shall procure that each CDE Affiliate and each such director (while holding office) and each such employee (while employed) shall not in [the UK] (except with the prior written consent of ABC and except through and in relation to the combined businesses of FGH and LMN the 'Combined Business') directly or indirectly, so long as CDE owns the CDE Shares, and for a period of [one] year after CDE ceases to own the CDE Shares:

6.1.1 engage in the Relevant Type of Business; or

6.1.2 own, manage, operate, finance, join, control or participate in the ownership, management, operation, financing or control of, or be connected as a principal, agent, affiliate, representative, consultant or otherwise with, or use or permit its name or any derivations thereof to be used in connection with the Relevant Type of Business; or

6.1.3 induce or attempt to influence in any manner any employee of FGH or any employee of CDE to compete with the Combined Business with respect to the Relevant Type of Business or (in respect of an employee of FGH) to terminate such employment; or

6.1.4 solicit or serve with respect to the Relevant Type of Business any Persons that were customers of the Combined Business at any time during the one year period preceding the Closing Date with respect to the Relevant Type of Business; or

6.1.5 influence or attempt to influence such customers to divert their patronage with respect to the Relevant Type of Business from the Combined Business to any other Person; or

6.1.6 at any time disclose to any other Person any proprietary or confidential information relating to the Combined Business.

6.2 ABC for itself and on behalf of [its subsidiaries, its holding company and the subsidiaries of its holding company] ('ABC Affiliates'), and on behalf of the directors (while holding office) and the employees (while employed) of itself and of ABC Affiliates, shall not in [the United Kingdom], and shall procure that each ABC Affiliate and each such director and employee shall not in [the United Kingdom] (except with the prior written consent of CDE and except through and in relation to the Combined Businesses directly or indirectly, so long as CDE owns the CDE Shares):

6.2.1 engage in the Relevant Type of Business; or

6.2.2 own, manage, operate, finance, join, control or participate in the ownership, management, operation, financing or control of, or be connected as a principal, agent, affiliate, representative, consultant or otherwise with, or use or permit its name or any derivations thereof to be used in connection with the Relevant Type of Business; or

6.2.3 induce or attempt to influence in any manner any employee of FGH or any employee of ABC to compete with the Combined Business with respect to the Relevant Type of Business or (in respect of an employee of FGH) to terminate any such employment; or

6.2.4 solicit, serve or cater to any Persons that were customers of the Combined Business at any time during the one year period preceding the Closing Date with respect to the Relevant Type of Business; or

6.2.5 influence or attempt to influence such customers to divert their patronage with respect to the Relevant Type of Business from the Combined Business to any other Person; or

6.2.6 at any time disclose to any other Person any proprietary or confidential information relating to the Combined Business.

6.3 CDE and ABC shall exercise all reasonable endeavours to maintain develop and assist the Combined Business and in particular to assist in the identification and procuring of contracts for the Relevant Type of Business to be undertaken by FGH. The parties however agree that CDE shall be under no obligation to provide working capital for FGH. It is ABC's intention to provide for FGH's requirements for working capital on a basis no less favourable than that applied to ABC's wholly-owned subsidiaries.

6.4 ABC undertakes, in addition to its obligations contained in cl 6.2 that it will ensure that any contracts for the Relevant Type of Business identified or procured by ABC or an ABC Affiliate in the UK (other than FGH) shall be performed by and in the name of FGH so that, in particular, for the purposes of Schedule 3, the turnover generated by such contracts shall be part of the turnover of FGH.

6.5 In so far as necessary to discharge the obligations entered into under cll 6.1 and 6.2 in relation to directors and employees each party undertakes to the other that it will exercise all reasonable endeavours to enforce any relevant non-competition covenants given to it by any of its directors or employees.

[**6.6** Where through the activities of FGH business opportunities are identified by ABC which are not the Relevant Type of Business, and which ABC does not wish to take up itself, it shall refer the same to CDE. Where such opportunities are in respect of subcontracts to be let by FGH, ABC shall permit CDE to tender for the same, and shall award such subcontracts to CDE provided that its relevant tender is competitive in terms of price quality and delivery.]

7   Restrictions on disposal of FGH shares

7.1 CDE shall not after the date hereof, and until the elapse of 30 days after the Expiry Date, sell, assign, transfer, pledge, mortgage or charge or otherwise dispose of or encumber the CDE Shares or any beneficial interest in them to or in favour of any Person other than ABC.

7.2 As long as CDE holds the CDE Shares, ABC shall not reduce its shareholding in FGH below 51 per cent of the issued ordinary share capital, nor pass a resolution for the winding-up of FGH, provided that this clause shall not prevent ABC transferring all or part of such shareholding to a creditworthy wholly-owned subsidiary which undertakes to be bound by the terms of this Agreement.

8 Memorandum and articles of association of FGH

8.1 Within thirty days of the Closing Date, ABC shall alter the Articles of Association of FGH to include the provisions of cl 4.1 of this Agreement.

8.2 Should there be any inconsistency or conflict between the terms of this Agreement and the Memorandum and Articles of Association of FGH then the terms of this Agreement shall (as between the parties hereto, but not so as to bind FGH) prevail.

8.3 Within thirty days of the Closing Date ABC shall alter the name of FGH to some other name acceptable to ABC which does not contain the words 'FGH'.

9 Definitions and interpretation

9.1 Any undertaking by either party not to do any act or thing shall be deemed to include an undertaking not to permit or suffer the doing of that act or thing.

9.2 The headings in this Agreement shall not affect its interpretation.

9.3 'Person' shall mean an individual, corporation, government or governmental subdivision or agency, business trust, estate, trust, partnership, or association, two or more of the foregoing having a joint or common interest, or any other legal or commercial entity or undertaking.

9.4 The singular includes the plural and *vice versa* and any gender includes any other gender.

9.5 All of the Schedules to this Agreement constitute an integral part hereof.

9.6 References in this Agreement to clauses and Schedules are to clauses and Schedules of this Agreement.

9.7 References in this Agreement to the parties shall include references to their successors and permitted assigns.

10 Miscellaneous

10.1 Any notice, invoice or other document which may be given by either party under this Agreement to the other shall be deemed to have been duly given if left at or sent by post, telex or facsimile transmission or by electronic mail to each party's registered office or any other address notified to each other in writing in accordance with this clause as an address to which notices, invoices and other documents may be sent. Any such communication shall be deemed to have been made to the other party (if by post) four days from the date of posting (and in proving such service or delivery, it shall be sufficient to prove that such communication was properly addressed, stamped and put in the post), and, if by telex or facsimile transmission, at the time of the transmission provided that the same shall not have been received in a garbled form. Any communication by electronic mail shall be deemed to have been made on the day on which the communication is first stored in the other party's electronic mailbox.

10.2 This Agreement may not be released discharged supplemented interpreted amended varied or modified in any manner except by an instrument in writing signed by a duly authorised officer or representative of each of the parties hereto. This Agreement contains the whole agreement between the parties relating to the subject matter of this Agreement, and shall supersede any and all promises, representations, warranties, undertakings, statements, whether written or oral made by or on behalf of one party to the other of any nature whatsoever, prior to the date of signature of this Agreement. Each party warrants to the other that it has not relied on any representation, arrangement, understanding or agreement (whether written or oral) not expressly set out or referred to in this Agreement. [Each party further agrees and undertakes to the other that no breach of this Agreement shall entitle it to rescind this Agreement, and that its remedies for any breach of this Agreement shall be solely for breach of contract, which remedies shall be subject to and in accordance with the provisions of this Agreement.] No provision contained in this clause, or elsewhere in this Agreement, shall operate so as to exclude any liability of one of the parties in respect of a fraudulent misrepresentation made by that party to the other, or to restrict or exclude any remedy which the other party may have in respect of such misrepresentation.

10.3 Nothing contained in this Agreement shall be so construed as to constitute either party to be the agent of the other.

10.4 This Agreement shall not operate so as to create a partnership or joint venture of any kind between the parties hereto.

10.5 This Agreement shall not be assigned or transferred (nor the performance of any obligations hereunder subcontracted) by either party except with the prior written consent of the other.

10.6 No attempted assignment shall relieve the assignor of any of its obligations hereunder without the written consent of the other party.

10.7 Each party shall from time to time upon the request of the other party execute any additional documents and do any other acts or things which may reasonably be required to effectuate the purposes of this Agreement.

10.8 If any covenant clause or provision or any part thereof contained in this Agreement (a 'term') shall be held to be illegal or unenforceable, in whole or in part, under any enactment or rule of law, such covenant clause or provision or the relevant part thereof shall to that extent be deemed not to form part of this Agreement but the validity and enforceability of the remainder of this Agreement shall not be affected.

10.9 In no event shall any delay failure or omission on the part of either of the parties in enforcing exercising or pursuing any right power privilege claim or remedy, which is conferred by this Agreement, or arises under this Agreement, or arises from any breach by the other party to this Agreement of any of its obligations hereunder, be deemed to be or be construed as (i) a waiver thereof, or of any other such right power privilege claim or remedy, or (ii) operate so as to bar the enforcement or exercise thereof, or of any other such right power privilege claim or remedy, in any other instance at any time or times thereafter.

10.10 The parties acknowledge and agree that in the event of a default by either party in the performance of their respective obligations under this Agreement, the loss or damage incurred by the non-defaulting party by reason of such default will be such that damages alone will not be an adequate remedy. Accordingly, the non-defaulting party shall have the right to specific performance of the defaulting party's obligations.

10.11 Whenever under this Agreement or any other agreement or contract binding upon the parties any sum of money shall be recoverable from or payable by one party hereto (the 'paying party') to the other party (the 'receiving party'), the same may be deducted from any sum then due or which at any time thereafter may become due to the paying party from the receiving party under this Agreement or any other agreement or contract between the paying party and the receiving party.

10.12 The provisions of this agreement, and the rights and remedies of the parties under this Agreement are cumulative and are without prejudice and in addition to any rights or remedies a party may have at law or in equity; no exercise by a party of any one right or remedy under this agreement, or at law or in equity, shall operate so as to hinder or prevent the exercise by it of any other such right or remedy.

11   Interest

If either party defaults in the payment when due of any sum payable under this Agreement (whether determined by agreement or pursuant to an order of a court or otherwise) the liability of that party shall be increased to include interest on such sum from the date when such payment is due until the date of actual payment (as well after as before judgment) at a rate per annum of [three] per cent above the base rate from time to time of [[   ] Bank plc]. Such interest shall accrue from day to day and shall be paid subject to any withholding tax.

SCHEDULE 1
Description of the Business

SCHEDULE 2
Shareholders' Committee

The Shareholders' Committee shall only pass resolutions in respect of:
any alteration to the Memorandum and Articles of FGH;
any acquisitions or joint ventures by FGH involving an equity stake of a value grater than £[   ];
any major change in the Combined Business; or
any disposal of all or a material part of the Combined Business.

SCHEDULE 3
Option Price

For the purposes of cl 5 the Option Price and the Accelerated Purchase Price shall be calculated as:
$(A + B) - C$
where:
$A = £ [\quad]$;
B = an amount equal to [   ] per cent of the Combined Turnover (as defined below) or £[   ] whichever is the lesser [provided that where an Acceleration Notice is served pursuant to cl 5.2.2 'B' shall equal £[   ] or [   ] per cent of the Combined turnover (as defined below)], whichever is greater; and
C = the gross amount of any dividends paid by FGH to CDE in respect of periods after the Closing Date.

For the purposes of this Schedule 'Combined Turnover' shall mean an amount equal to the total amount excluding VAT receivable by FGH (including but not limited to in respect of the Combined Business) for services provided by FGH to customers other than ABC or companies (including but not limited to ABC Affiliates) in which ABC holds not less than 20 per cent of the issued ordinary share capital during (*a*) in the case when a Call Notice or Put Notice is served the period of [24 months] ending on the date of service of the Call Notice or the Put Notice as the case may be; and (*b*) in the case when an Acceleration Notice is served the period commencing on the Closing Date and ending on the date five days prior to the Accelerated Option Closing Date.

In the event of any disagreement between the parties as to the amount of Combined Turnover as defined above, an independent firm of Chartered Accountants (to be appointed by agreement between the parties, and, in default of such agreement, by the President for the time being of the Institute of Chartered Accountants, upon the application of either party) shall decide the said amount, acting as experts not arbitrators, and such decision shall be final and binding upon the parties.

Detailed decision-making process and minority rights protection in a joint venture company as set out in agreement between the two major shareholders in the joint venture company

Note 1: In this Precedent references to the 'parties' means SHAREHOLDER 1 *and* SHAREHOLDER 2, and references to a 'party' means either SHARE-HOLDER 1 *or* SHAREHOLDER 2.

Note 2: This Precedent is based on the assumption that SHAREHOLDER 1 and SHAREHOLDER 2 each hold 40 per cent in JV COMPANY, and that there will be a number of smaller shareholders each holding around 3 per cent to 5 per cent.

Article 1 Constitution of the shareholders' committee

1 JV COMPANY shall have a Shareholders' Committee ('Shareholders' Committee') consisting of two duly authorised representatives of SHAREHOLDER 1 and two duly authorised representatives of SHAREHOLDER 2. The Chairman of the Shareholders' Committee shall be one of its members and be appointed to hold office for a period of one year at a time alternately by SHARE-HOLDER 1 and SHAREHOLDER 2, commencing with SHAREHOLDER 1. The first such Chairman shall be [   ].

2 The quorum for meetings of the Shareholders' Committee shall be equal to the number of the representatives of SHAREHOLDER 1 and SHAREHOLDER 2 in the Shareholders' Committee and decisions of the Shareholders' Committee shall be taken by simple majority vote. In case of a tied vote, the Chairman shall not have a second or casting vote.

3 If either or both of the parties intend to propose a resolution at a shareholders' meeting of JV COMPANY relating to one of the matters listed in art 4 para 4 (the 'Reserved Matter(s)'), the parties shall hold a meeting of the Shareholders' Committee at a place and time to be mutually agreed (unless the parties mutually agree to substitute such meeting with an exchange of written documentation) but in any event such meeting shall be held or such exchange take place before the shareholders of JV COMPANY are served with notice of the relevant shareholders' meeting.

4 If the parties receive notice of a meeting of the shareholders of JV COMPANY which contains a proposal for a resolution in respect of one of the Reserved Matters, being a proposal which has been put forward by one of the shareholders of JV COMPANY other than the parties hereto, and whether or not with their prior knowledge, the parties shall hold a meeting of the Shareholders' Committee at a place and time to be mutually agreed (unless the parties mutually agree to substitute such meeting with an exchange of written documentation) but in any event such meeting shall be held or such exchange take place prior to the holding of the relevant meeting of the shareholders of JV COMPANY.

5 The meeting of the Shareholders' Committee pursuant to para 3 shall decide whether the relevant proposed resolution shall be put forward at the relevant shareholders' meeting, and what directions shall be given to the parties in respect of voting the shares held by them in JV COMPANY in relation to that proposed resolution, if so put forward.

6 The meeting of the Shareholders' Committee pursuant to para 4 shall decide what directions shall be given to the parties in respect of voting the shares held by them in JV COMPANY in relation to the relevant proposed resolution contained in the said notice of shareholders' meeting.

7 The parties agree and undertake to each other not to put a resolution in respect of a Reserved Matter to a shareholders' meeting of JV COMPANY unless the Shareholders' Committee has first approved the same pursuant to para 5.

8 The parties agree and undertake to each other that upon a resolution being proposed in respect of a Reserved Matter at a shareholders' meeting of JV COMPANY, all the shares held by SHAREHOLDER 1 and all the shares held by SHAREHOLDER 2 in JV COMPANY shall be voted together and in accordance with the relevant direction of the Shareholders' Committee pursuant to para 5 or 6.

9 If a resolution to implement, progress or proceed with any Reserved Matter is proposed at a shareholders' meeting of JV COMPANY and the Shareholders' Committee has made no decision as to what directions should be given to the parties in respect of voting the shares held by them in JV COMPANY in relation to that resolution, either because the Shareholders' Committee could reach no decision because of a tied vote, or for any other reason (including without limitation because no meeting of the Shareholders' Committee took place, or no quorum was present at the relevant meeting) then the direction of the Shareholders' Committee shall be deemed to be against the said resolution to implement, progress or proceed with the said Reserved Matter, and the parties agree and undertake to each other that all of the shares held by the parties shall be voted together against the said resolution in order to preserve the *status quo*.

Article 2 Constitution of the board of directors

1 The Board of Directors of JV COMPANY (the 'Board') will consist of ten directors as follows:
three non-executive directors appointed removed and replaced from time to time by SHAREHOLDER 1;
three non-executive directors appointed removed and replaced from time to time by SHAREHOLDER 2;
two executive directors from the management of JV COMPANY appointed removed and replaced from time to time in accordance with arts 2.2 and 2.3 respectively;
two non-executive directors to be elected by all of the shareholders of JV COMPANY (other than SHAREHOLDER 1 and SHAREHOLDER 2) in general meeting.

2 One of the executive directors aforesaid shall be the Chief Executive of JV COMPANY and shall be appointed, removed and replaced from time to time by SHAREHOLDER 2 both as a director of JV COMPANY and as Chief Executive. The first such director and Chief Executive shall be [   ].

3 The other of the executive directors aforesaid shall be the Finance Director of JV COMPANY and shall be appointed, removed and replaced from time to time by SHAREHOLDER 1 both as a director of JV COMPANY and as Finance Director; in addition to his duties as a director of JV COMPANY he shall be responsible for the financial, treasury and accounting aspects of JV COMPANY and shall report to the Chief Executive on a day to day basis. The first such Finance Director shall be [   ].

4 The Chief Executive and the Finance Director shall be committed full time to the JV COMPANY management team and shall not hold any responsibility outside JV COMPANY on behalf of SHAREHOLDER 1 or SHAREHOLDER 2.

5 The Company Secretary of JV COMPANY shall be nominated by SHARE-HOLDER 2. The first such Company Secretary shall be [   ].

Article 3 Management of JV company

1 The JV COMPANY Board of Directors (the 'Board') has the responsibility to define the JV COMPANY strategy, profitability and growth objectives taking into consideration the interests of all JV COMPANY shareholders. The Chief Executive will have the responsibility to execute the strategy and the plans decided by the JV COMPANY Board.

2 The first line of management of JV COMPANY will be approved by the Board, on the basis of proposals submitted by the Chief Executive of JV COMPANY.

3 Subject as provided in arts 4 and 5, all decisions related to the operations of JV COMPANY, including (subject as provided in arts 4 and 5) their delegation by the Board to the Chief Executive pursuant to art 3.1, and the approvals of the related documents (strategic plans, budget, quarterly or yearly reports etc), will be taken by simple majority at a meeting of the Board.

Article 4 JV company shareholders' meetings

1 An annual general meeting of JV COMPANY shall be held each year within three months of the end of the preceding financial year at JV COMPANY's registered office or at such other place as shall be designated by the Board. This meeting shall be called by the Board and its agenda and the matters that the meeting shall deal with shall be established in accordance with JV COMPANY's Articles of Association.

2 Extraordinary general meetings of JV COMPANY may be convened at any time by the Board, or if requested by a shareholder or group of shareholders with at least ten per cent (10 per cent) of JV COMPANY voting ordinary share capital.

3 The quorum for all shareholder meetings shall consist of any two shareholders, who between them hold not less than [80] per cent of the shares in JV COMPANY. If a quorum is not present at the time fixed for any such meeting, the meeting shall be adjourned for a period of fifteen working days. Upon reconvening the said meeting those shareholders present shall constitute a quorum. Except as provided in art 4.4 all resolutions proposed at a shareholders' meeting shall require, if they are to pass, a simple majority vote in favour thereof, or such other majority as may be specified by JV COMPANY's Articles of Association.

4 The parties agree and undertake to each other to procure that the following matters shall be decided upon only by the shareholders of JV COMPANY in general meeting to the entire exclusion of the Board and further agree and undertake to each other to procure that provisions to achieve this effect shall be inserted in the Articles of Association of JV COMPANY pursuant to art 7:

4.1 the issuing of any unissued shares or the creation or issuing of any new shares of JV COMPANY;

4.2 the altering of any rights attaching to any class of shares in the share capital of JV COMPANY;

4.3 the consolidation, subdividing or converting of any of JV COMPANY share capital or the alteration in any way of the rights attaching thereto;

4.4 the granting to any person of any right to acquire or subscribe for shares in JV COMPANY including options or instruments convertible into, or warrants giving the right to subscribe for, shares in JV COMPANY (and the amendment of any agreement relating thereto or release of any liability thereunder) and the allotment transfer or purchase by JV COMPANY of any shares, instruments convertible into, or warrants giving the right to subscribe for, shares in JV COMPANY (and the amendment of any agreement relating thereto or release from any liability thereunder);

4.5 the winding up or amalgamation of JV COMPANY or the doing of anything the natural consequence of which would (without further resolution of the shareholders) be to cause JV COMPANY to be wound up or amalgamated;

4.6 the issuing by JV COMPANY of any debentures or other securities convertible into shares or debentures or any share warrants or any options in respect of shares;

4.7 the acquisition, purchase or subscription by JV COMPANY for any shares, debentures, mortgages or securities (or any interest therein) in any company, trust or other body;

4.8 any modification, alteration or changes to JV COMPANY's Memorandum and/or Articles of Association;

4.9 approval of any of the transactions referred to in art 5 paras 2.1, 2.2, 2.3 and 2.4 where the amount of the transaction exceeds [£1,000,000] or the number of years exceeds [five] as the case may be;

4.10 any matters referred to in art 5 para 3 in respect of which the Board has been unable to pass a resolution because the directors appointed by SHAREHOLDER 1 and SHAREHOLDER 2 have not voted in favour thereof.

Article 5 Meetings of the board of directors of JV company

1 The quorum for meetings of the Board shall consist of five directors (or their alternates). The first such director shall be one of the directors appointed by SHAREHOLDER 1 (other than the executive director appointed as the Revenue Director). The second such director shall be one of the directors appointed by SHAREHOLDER 2 (other than the executive director appointed as the Chief Executive). The third such director shall be the executive director appointed as Chief Executive. The fourth such director shall be the executive director appointed as Finance Director. The fifth such director shall be one of the directors appointed by all of the shareholders (other than SHAREHOLDER 1 and SHAREHOLDER 2) in general meeting. If a quorum is not present at the time fixed for any such meeting, that meeting shall be adjourned for seven working days and all of the directors of JV COMPANY shall immediately be notified by hand, telex, facsimile or electronic mail of such adjournment and those directors (or their alternates) present at the resumed meeting shall constitute a quorum.

2 The following matters shall be decided upon only by the Board (to the entire exclusion of the shareholders of JV COMPANY) at a duly convened meeting and may not be delegated to the Chief Executive:

2.1 any investment in or acquisition or disposal of capital assets by JV COMPANY in an amount exceeding the sum of [£250,000] and not exceeding the sum of [£500,000] or such other limits as the Board shall from time to time determine in advance, pursuant to art 3.1;

2.2 any agreement for sale or purchase of products or services consumed, used or supplied by JV COMPANY, in which the aggregate amount of the consideration exceeds the sum of [£250,000] but does not exceed the sum of [£500,000] or such other limit as the Board shall from time to time determine in advance, pursuant to art 3.1;

2.3 the entering into of any distribution agreement, licensing agreement, agency agreement, or operating lease of real or personal property, for a period in excess of [two] years but not in excess of [three] years or a sum exceeding [£250,000] but not in excess of [£500,000] or such other limit of value or period as the Board shall from time to time determine in advance, pursuant to art 3.1;

2.4 the negotiation of any borrowing facility (including leasing except as provided in para 2.3 above) or any debt factoring facility and the charging of any assets, in each case in excess of the sum of [£250,000], but not in excess of the sum of [£500,000] or such other limit as the Board shall from time to time determine in advance, pursuant to art 3.1.

3 The following matters shall be decided upon only by the Board (to the entire exclusion of the shareholders of JV COMPANY) at a duly convened meeting and may not be delegated to the Chief Executive provided that resolutions on these subjects may only be passed if all of the directors appointed by SHARE-HOLDER 1 and SHAREHOLDER 2 present at the relevant meeting vote in favour thereof:

3.1 any changes to the limits referred to in paras 2.1, 2.2, 2.3, and 2.4 above provided that the revised upper limit shall not exceed [£750,000] or [four] years as applicable;

3.2 approval of any of the transactions referred to in paras 2.1, 2.2, 2.3 and 2.4, in an amount exceeding the relevant upper limit then prevailing in respect of paras 2.1, 2.2, 2.3 and 2.4, but not exceeding in respect of any such transaction the amount of [£1,000,000] or the period of [five] years as the case may be; (for the avoidance of doubt the Board shall have no power to approve any of the aforesaid transactions where the relevant upper limit exceeds [£1,000,000] or [five] years as the case may be, such approval being reserved to the shareholders of JV COMPANY pursuant to art 4 para 4.9);

3.3 the entering into of any contract or transaction with or any loan from any shareholder of JV COMPANY, or any company, firm or entity in whom any shareholder of JV COMPANY has directly or indirectly not less than 20 per cent of the voting rights;

3.4 the granting to any person of any loans other than in the ordinary course of business;

3.5 the issue of any guarantee or indemnity or provision of credit other than in the ordinary course of business;

3.6 any material change in the nature or conduct of JV COMPANY's business, or of any material part of such business;

3.7 any discontinuance of, or disinvestment from existing lines of business, which in either case constitutes a material part of JV COMPANY;

3.8 any recommendation to be given to the shareholders of JV COMPANY as to the course of action which should in the opinion of the Board be pursued in relation to any matter referred to in art 4 para 4.

4 Meetings of the Board shall be held monthly (unless the Board otherwise decides) and shall normally be held in [London], but such meetings may be held anywhere in the [UK]. Any director shall have the right to require the Company Secretary of JV COMPANY to convene a Board meeting at any time upon due notice given in accordance with the Articles of Association of JV COMPANY.

5 The Company Secretary for the time being of JV COMPANY shall circulate minutes of each meeting of the Board to all directors of JV COMPANY within fourteen (14) days after the date of each such meeting.

6 All directors shall upon appointment give written details to the Company Secretary of their respective addresses in the [UK] for service of all not es.

7 The parties agree and undertake to each other (i) not to propose a resolution at a shareholders' meeting of JV COMPANY on any of the matters listed in para 3 above (except in the circumstances set out in art 4 para 4.10 and with the prior approval of the Shareholders Committee pursuant to art 1 para 3) and (ii) that neither of them will procure that any of the matters referred to in para 3 be considered at a meeting of the Board without at least 15 days' prior notice to the other that such matter will be so raised.

8 The parties agree and undertake to each other to procure that provisions to achieve the effect of paras 1–6 inclusive of this article shall be inserted in the Articles of Association of JV COMPANY pursuant to art 7.

Article 6 Dividend policy

Unless otherwise agreed, the Parties shall procure (including without limitation by voting together all of the votes in respect of their shareholdings in JV COMPANY) that JV COMPANY declares and pays in respect of each of its financial years a dividend of not less than [one-third] of its consolidated net profits after tax for the relevant financial year available for distribution as a dividend.

Article 7 Memorandum and articles of association

The Parties shall procure that JV COMPANY shall adopt within ninety days after the date of the signature of this Agreement the Memorandum, and Articles of Association set out as Schedule [   ] hereto. As between the parties hereto, in the event of any conflict between the provisions of this Agreement and the provisions of the said Memorandum and Articles of Association, the provisions of this Agreement shall prevail. The parties undertake to each other that they will at all times exercise all of the votes in respect of their shareholdings in JV COMPANY, and do all other things within their power, so as to support, maintain and implement the provisions of this Agreement and, in particular, the appointment and maintenance in office (or removal or replacement, as the case may be) of the directors of the Board of JV COMPANY as provided in art 2, and the conduct of business both at general meetings of JV COMPANY pursuant to art 4 and at meetings of the Board pursuant to art 5.

Precedent 4

Withdrawal in joint venture company with more than two shareholders

---

1 Any party hereto (in this Schedule called 'the withdrawing party') shall not be entitled to sell, mortgage, charge, or otherwise dispose of all or any part of its shareholding in JV COMPANY (its 'participation'), nor all or any part of its beneficial interest in such participation for a period of [five years] after the Completion Date; and thereafter shall be entitled to give to each of the other parties hereto not less than two months' notice in writing expiring at or at any time after the end of the [five year] period referred to above to the effect that the withdrawing party wishes to sell its participation, and stating the price at which it wishes to do so (the offer price'), and, if relevant, the identity of any third party to whom it wishes, subject to the provisions of this Schedule, to sell its participation.

2 If and whenever para 1 shall become applicable each of the other parties (a 'purchasing party') hereto shall have an option (exercisable by giving notice in writing to the withdrawing party during the currency of the withdrawing party's notice) to purchase that percentage of the withdrawing party's participation which that purchasing party's own participation bears to the aggregate of all of the purchasing parties' own participations, at the relevant percentage of the offer price, for cash payable against delivery of executed forms of transfer of the shares in question together with the relevant share certificates. In the event all of the other parties hereto exercise the said options the withdrawing party shall be deemed to have become obliged to sell its participation on the date upon which the withdrawing party gave the notice mentioned in para 1 hereof and shall be obliged to execute and deliver the relevant transfers not later than seven business days following the date upon which the last of the said options was exercised. *Provided* that if none of the other parties hereto have exercised their respective options during the currency of the withdrawing party's notice, then upon expiry of the said period the provisions of para 3 shall apply, and *provided further* that if only some but not all of the other parties hereto have exercised their respective options during the currency of the withdrawing party's notice and as a consequence any part of the withdrawing party's participation remains unpurchased then all prior acceptances shall fall away and the period of such notice shall be extended for 30 days and during such extended period any party or parties which previously exercised their aforesaid options shall collectively have an option to purchase the whole (but not part only) of the withdrawing party's participation at the offer price *pro rata* to their own participations, or in such other proportions as they may agree, and if on expiry of such extended period of 30 days, the entire participation of the withdrawing party shall not then have been so purchased, then the provisions of para 3 shall apply.

3 If the withdrawing party's participation shall not be purchased by the other parties pursuant to para 2 hereof, the withdrawing party shall be entitled within three months after the end of the period of the notice mentioned in para 1 (as extended by the proviso to that paragraph if appropriate) to sell the withdrawing party's participation (in whole but not in part only) to any third party or parties, at a price no less than the offer price, and in that event the other parties hereto shall procure that the relative transfer or transfers shall be registered by the Board. Failing a sale in terms of this para 3, any such withdrawing party shall not at any time or times thereafter sell the whole or any part of its participation without first having again followed the procedures set out in paras 1 and 2.

4 Notwithstanding any obligations of confidentiality imposed upon the withdrawing party by any of the other parties, whether under this Agreement or otherwise howsoever, the withdrawing party shall be entitled at any time (whether before or after the giving of notice pursuant to para 1) to disclose to any prospective third party purchaser and its advisers (subject to their entering into a confidentiality undertaking) any information relating to JV COMPANY which that third party and its advisers deem necessary in order to assess the proposed purchase.

5 Any sale to a third party pursuant to para 3 shall be upon the basis that the third party takes the place of the withdrawing party as a party to this Agreement upon the same terms and conditions as apply to the withdrawing party.

6 Upon transfer of the withdrawing party's participation in terms of the aforegoing, it shall (except for the provisions of Articles [   ] [Non-competition Following Withdrawal] and [   ] [Confidentiality] which shall continue to bind it in accordance with their terms) *ipso facto* cease to be bound by this Agreement, without prejudice to any antecedent breach.

Precedent 5

Withdrawal in joint venture company with only two shareholders

1 Either party hereto (in this Schedule called 'the withdrawing party') shall not be entitled to sell, mortgage, charge, hypothecate or otherwise dispose of all or any part of its shareholding in JV COMPANY (its 'participation'), nor all or any part of its beneficial interest in such participation for a period of [five years] after the Completion Date; and thereafter shall be entitled to give to the other party hereto (the 'remaining party') not less than two months' notice in writing expiring at or at any time after the end of the [five year] period referred to above to the effect that the withdrawing party wishes to sell its participation, stating the price at which it is prepared to sell (the 'offer price') and, if relevant, the identity of any third party to whom it wishes, subject to the provisions of this Schedule, to sell its participation.

2 If and whenever para 1 shall become applicable the remaining party shall have the option (exercisable by giving notice in writing to the withdrawing party during the currency of the withdrawing party's notice) to purchase the whole (but not part only) of the withdrawing party's participation for cash payable against delivery of executed forms of transfer of the shares in question together with the relevant share certificates either at the offer price or at a price to be determined in terms of para 3, in which case the withdrawing party shall be deemed to have become obliged to sell that participation on the date upon which the withdrawing party gave the notice mentioned in para 1 hereof, and shall be obliged to execute and deliver the relevant transfers not later than seven business days following the date of the exercise of the option (if it is exercised at the offer price) or the date upon which the relevant price is determined pursuant to para 3 hereof as the case may be. If the remaining party does not exercise its said option within the aforesaid period, then the said option shall lapse and the provisions of para 4 shall apply.

3 The purchase price of a party's participation for the purposes of para 2 shall be that price which is agreed or failing agreement (within 30 days of the expiry of the withdrawing party's notice served pursuant to para 1) that price which shall be determined by the application of that one of the following procedures which produces the [highest][lowest] result:

3.1 a calculation of the value of the participation using the following formula:

$$q(z(x - y))$$

where:

$x =$ the value per share ascribed to the shares of JV COMPANY at the Completion Date increased by [compound interest] at the rate of [[   ] per cent] with [quarterly rests] for the period between the Completion Date and the Application Date;

$y =$ the aggregate of all dividends per share of JV COMPANY (increased as provided below) received by the withdrawing party in the period between the Closing Date and the Application Date provided that the amount of each such dividend shall be increased by [compound interest] at the rate of [[   ] per cent] with [quarterly rests] for the period between the date of its receipt and the Application Datet

$z =$ the number of shares in the withdrawing party's participation; and

$q =$ [1.5], being a premium payable for the acquisition of full control of JV COMPANY;

3.2 the determination of the purchase price of the participation by two merchant banks (the one being appointed by the withdrawing party and the other by the remaining party) on the basis of JV COMPANY as a going concern and, as such merchant bankers may consider appropriate, having regard to net asset value, the price earnings ratio considered to be appropriate with reference to the price earnings ratios of similar companies to JV COMPANY then applicable to the valuation of shares of such companies listed on the [London] Stock Exchange, and to such other factors as may in such merchant bankers' opinions be relevant or appropriate, including without limitation an appropriate premium (of not less than [50 per cent]) for the control of JV COMPANY conferred by the purchase of the withdrawing party's participation. If such merchant bankers are unable to so agree then the determination shall be effected by a third merchant bank appointed by the President for the time being of the Institute of Chartered Accountants in England and Wales, which merchant bank, in making such determination shall be entitled to take all relevant factors into account, including the valuations prepared by the other two merchant banks;

3.3 a calculation of the value of the participation made by taking the average middle market price per share over the period of 30 days prior to the Application Date at which the shares of the companies listed in Appendix [   ] were traded on the [London] Stock Exchange, and multiplying such price by the number of shares in the relevant participation.

All calculations and valuations under this para 3 shall be made in pounds sterling and payment of the purchase price pursuant to para 2 shall be made in pounds sterling.

For the purposes of this para 3 the 'Application Date' shall be the date 30 days after the expiry of the withdrawing party's notice served pursuant to para 1.

4 If the withdrawing party's participation shall not be purchased by the other party pursuant to para 2 hereof, the withdrawing party shall be entitled within three months after the end of the period of the notice mentioned in para 1 to sell the withdrawing party's participation (in whole but not in part only) to any third party or parties, at whatever price it can obtain, and in that event the party remaining shall procure that the relative transfer or transfers shall be registered by the Board. Failing a sale in terms of this para 4, any such withdrawing party shall not at any time or times thereafter sell the whole or any part of its participation without first having again followed the procedures set out in paras 1 and 2.

5 Notwithstanding any obligations of confidentiality imposed upon the withdrawing party by the other party, whether under this Agreement, or otherwise howsoever, the withdrawing party shall be entitled at any time (whether before or after the giving of notice pursuant to para 1) to disclose to any prospective third party purchaser and its advisers (subject to their entering into a confidentiality undertaking) any information relating to JV COMPANY which that third party and its advisers deem necessary in order to assess the proposed purchase.

6 In the event that one party has given notice of withdrawal pursuant to para 1 and prior to the expiry of such notice the other party also gives notice of withdrawal pursuant to para 1 the provisions of para 3 shall not apply, and the matter shall be resolved as follows:

6.1 both parties shall attempt to reach agreement upon which one shall buy the other's participation, and at what price;

6.2 in the event of failure to reach agreement pursuant to para 6.1, within 30 days after the service of notice pursuant to para 1 by whichever of the parties was the last to serve such notice, both parties shall first seek a third party or parties who will purchase both of their participations at an acceptable price;

6.3 in the event that no such purchase is completed with six months (or such longer period as may be agreed by the parties) of the expiry of the period of the notice served pursuant to para 1 by whichever of the parties was the last to serve such notice, the procedure in the following subparagraphs shall apply:

6.3.1 the purchase prices for the participations of both of the parties shall each be determined in accordance with para 3, save that the Application Date shall be the date of the expiry of the period permitted to achieve completion of purchase by a third party pursuant to para 6.2 above. Such determination shall be completed within 30 days of the Application Date. Each such purchase price is hereinafter referred to as the Base Value of the participation of the relevant party;

6.3.2 each party shall then consult with the other to decide if one of them is willing to sell its participation to the other at that participation's Base Value, or at some other price mutually agreed;

6.3.3 if no agreement is reached pursuant to para 6.3.2 within 15 days then the parties shall resolve the matter by submitting to the following auction procedure within seven days thereafter:

6.3.3.1 the parties shall (through duly authorised representatives) convene a meeting in the presence of a merchant banker appointed by mutual agreement (or failing agreement by the [President of the Institute of Chartered Accountants in England and Wales]). Each party shall deliver to the merchant banker as stakeholder duly executed transfers of the whole of its participation in favour of the other party;

6.3.3.2 the merchant banker shall thereupon conduct an auction in which each party shall bid for the right to purchase the other's participation by thereupon submitting his bid in a sealed envelope to the merchant banker, who shall thereupon open both envelopes in the presence of both parties, declare the bid prices to both parties, and declare that the party who has made the bid with the higher bid price shall be deemed to be the winner of the auction (the 'winner') at the bid price at which the winner made his bid (the 'higher bid price');

6.3.3.3 the winner shall have the right and the obligation to purchase the other party's participation within seven days at the higher bid price, and the merchant banker shall deliver to the winner both duly executed transfers aforesaid subject to payment of the higher bid price to the other party by the winner;

6.4 each party shall bear its own costs and any tax imposed upon it on the disposal of its participation other than stamp duty or other transfer taxes upon the transfer of a participation which shall be borne by the transferee. All third party expenses of valuation and/or auction pursuant to paras 3 or 6 shall be shared equally between the parties.

7 Upon transfer of the withdrawing party's participation in terms of the aforegoing, it shall (except for the provisions of Articles [   ] [Non-competition Following Withdrawal] and [   ] [Confidentiality] which shall continue to bind it) *ipso facto* cease to be bound by this Agreement, without prejudice to any antecedent breach.

Precedent 6

Termination for change of control and other material defaults and resolution of deadlock

---

1 In the event any party (the 'first party') shall be in breach of this Agreement or fail to perform one or more of its material obligations under this Agreement, any one of the other parties (the 'second party') may, by written notice to the first party, require the remedy of the breach or the performance of the obligation and, if the first party fails to take active effective and continuing actions to remedy or perform within sixty (60) days of the receipt of a notice so to do, the second party may serve upon the first party (within thirty (30) days of the second party's receipt of the first party's notice) a further written notice to take effect immediately on receipt (a 'Default Notice').

2 In the event a third party acquires or controls [fifty per cent (50 per cent)], or more, of the issued voting shares of one party (the 'first party'), it shall so notify the other parties, promptly in writing and any one or more of the other parties (the 'second party') may serve a Default Notice on the first party to be served within ninety (90) days of the second party's receipt of the first party's notice. If none of the other parties elects to serve a Default Notice in such circumstances, all of the other parties shall nonetheless retain the right to do so in future (and the provision of the preceding sentence shall apply, *mutandis mutatis*) if such third party increases its ownership or control at any time or from time to time by an increment of at least [five (5) per cent].

3 In the event a party becomes insolvent or is the object of bankruptcy or insolvency proceedings, or makes an assignment for the benefit of its creditors, or is placed in receivership or liquidation, then any other party may immediately serve a Default Notice on that party.

4 In the event a party exercises its rights of veto pursuant to cl [   ] [Minority Protection Rights] more than [three times] in any consecutive period of 12 months [and in respect of more than three separate and unconnected matters] any other party may immediately serve a Default Notice on that party.

5 Upon service of a Default Notice pursuant to paras 1, 2, 3 or 4, the party upon whom the Default Notice has been served shall be deemed itself immediately to have served a withdrawal notice pursuant to para [   ] of Schedule [   ], and thereupon the withdrawal procedure set out in that Schedule shall be implemented in respect of that party.

Precedent 7

Variation of memorandum and articles

On a resolution put to any general meeting of the Company or any meeting of a class of members to vary the memorandum of association of the company or the articles in any manner whatsoever, for the purposes of voting against any such resolution, the voting rights attaching to the Ordinary Shares held by each Shareholder shall be increased so that the votes that may be cast by such Shareholder exceed by one vote one third of all the votes that may be cast by all the other Shareholders in respect of that resolution, such additional votes to be divided as determined by the board as nearly as practicable (without creating fractions of votes) equally between the Ordinary Shares held by that Shareholder.

Precedent 8

Power of Class A shareholder to appoint directors

The Class A Shareholder shall have the right to appoint, remove and replace from time to time two directors to the board of the Company, the first two such directors being [   ] and [   ].

Any appointment, removal or replacement of a director pursuant to this Article shall be effected by written notice to the Company signed by or on behalf of the Class A Shareholder and left at or sent by post to the registered office of the Company, for the attention of the Company Secretary, and such notice shall take effect immediately upon deposit of the notice or on such later date (if any) as may be specified in the notice.

On any resolution put to any general meeting of the Company to remove any director appointed pursuant to this Article, for the purposes of voting against such resolution, the voting rights attaching to the 'A' Ordinary Shares held by the Class A Shareholder shall be increased so that the votes that may be cast by him equal a simple majority of all the votes that may be cast in respect of that resolution, such additional votes to be divided as determined by the board as near as practicable (without creating fractions of votes) equally between the 'A' Ordinary Shares held by the Class A Shareholder.

Joint venture checklist

1 Type of joint venture

1.1 Equity joint venture.
1.2 Contractual joint venture.
1.3 European Economic Interest Grouping (see Chapter 15).

2 Documentation

2.1 Heads of agreement.

Then:

2.2 for a merger/acquisition resulting in a joint venture company:
2.2.1 merger/acquisition agreement;
2.2.2 shareholders agreement; and
2.2.3 legal entity byelaws (eg memorandum and articles).

Or:

2.3. for a contractual joint venture:
2.3.1. definitive agreement setting up joint venture (eg partnership or consortium agreement).

Together with in both cases:

2.4.1 IPR licences between JV and partners;
2.4.2 know-how transfer from partners to JV – technical assistance agreement;
2.4.3 general training for JV personnel – training or consultancy agreement;

2.4.4 management assistance for JV personnel – management agreement;
2.4.5 product supply between JV and partners – sale and/or purchasing agreements;
2.4.6 secondment of staff to JV – secondment agreement;
2.4.7 provision to JV by partner of services (eg payroll) - services agreement and;
2.4.8 sharing of partners' facilities and premises by JV - shared facilities agreement.

3 Major issues to be determined

3.1 Name of joint venture.
3.2 Purpose and scope of joint venture.
3.3 Total investment and/or registered capital:
3.3.1 parties' contributions in cash or in kind;
3.3.2 valuation of tangible contributions.
3.3.3 valuation of intangible contributions (eg IPR); and
3.3.4 liability to make future contributions (if any).
3.4 Responsibilities of each party to the JV.
3.5 Scale of products/markets/territories.
3.6 Management committee or board directors:
3.6.1 numbers;
3.6.2 quorum;
3.6.3 voting rights;
3.6.4 decision making and resolution; and
3.6.5 appointment.
3.7 Operation and management organisation.
3.8. Purchase of equipment.
3.9 Labour management.
3.10 Acquisition of premises (lease or purchase).
3.11 Term of joint venture, including any initial fixed period.
3.12 Disposal of joint venture or its assets upon expiration of the joint venture term.
3.13 Insurance.
3.14 Internal procedures for settlement of disputes.
3.15 Resolution of deadlocks.
3.16 Pre-emption rights.
3.17 Exit provisions.
3.18 Governing law.
3.19 Use of mediation, ADR or submission to expert where appropriate.
3.20 Use of court or arbitration.

Chapter 13

Confidentiality agreements

13.1 Introduction

This chapter is concerned with the protection of confidential information in a commercial context by means of express undertakings and confidentiality agreements.

Before proceeding, a distinction must be drawn between the confidentiality undertakings and agreements that will be discussed in this chapter, and know-how licences. The former cover the disclosure of technical and commercial information for strictly limited purposes such as business discussions, pre-contract negotiations, or evaluation of a product, and are usually free of charge, and certainly without the obligation to pay a royalty. The latter are contracts which grant the recipient the right to exploit confidential information for commercial purposes in return for a lump sum and/or a royalty.

The information usually covered by the latter type of agreement relates to technical information which is to be exploited for the purposes of the manufacture and sale of products or the provision of commercial services, and is normally termed know-how, although no precise legal definition of this term exists. Similarly the agreements, by analogy with licences of intellectual property rights, are usually called know-how licences.

Know-how licences are outside the scope of this chapter, although some of the basic law relating to confidentiality is applicable to them, and care should be taken not to use the precedents in this chapter in situations where a know-how licence is appropriate, as their terms are not intended, and are completely unsuitable, for this purpose.

13.2   Basic principles of confidentiality

The law governing the protection of confidential information arises independently of contract from a principle of equity. This provides that, where information, which is of a secret or confidential nature, is given by one person (the 'donor') to another (the 'recipient'), and the recipient is either expressly told by the donor, or ought reasonably to understand from the circumstances surrounding the communication, that the donor wishes the recipient to keep the information confidential, then equity acts on the conscience of the recipient to prevent him from making an unauthorised use or disclosure of the information.

In the course of this chapter, for the sake of brevity, the obligations imposed upon the recipient will be referred to as 'confidentiality obligations', although, of course, they consist both of the obligation not to disclose and of the obligation not to misuse.

This principle was originally applied to information which was of a personal nature (see *Prince Albert v Strange* (1849) 1 H&TW 1, *Argyll v Argyll* [1967] Ch 302 and *Creation Record Ltd, Sony Music Entertainment (UK) and Noel Gallagher v News Group Newspaper Ltd* (1997) *The Times*, 29 April, discussed below).

It also covers information which while not exactly personal can at least be described as non-commercial in nature, for instance political secrets (see *Attorney-General v Guardian Newspapers* (No 2) [1990] AC 109).

The principle has, however, been extended by the courts to cover confidential commercial information and trade secrets (see *Saltman Engineering Co Ltd v Campbell Engineering Co Ltd* (1963) 65 RPC 203 and *Kitechnology BV v Unicor GmbH Plastmashinen* [1995] FSR 765). In the commercial world, the cases have been concerned either with information which has passed between two independent commercial parties (see *Seager v Copydex Ltd* [1967] RPC 349 and *Coco v AN Clark (Engineers) Ltd* [1969] RPC 41) or cases where an employer seeks to restrain an employee or ex-employee from disclosing or using (for the benefit of himself or a third party) confidential information that he has generated or acquired in the course of his employment (see *Hivac Ltd v Park Royal Scientific Instruments Ltd* [1946] All ER 350 and *Faccenda Chicken Ltd v Fowler* [1986] ICR 297, CA).

In general it can be said that it is in the public interest that confidences be respected, even if the discloser of the information can point to no specific damage which he would suffer as a result of unauthorised disclosure (see *Attorney-General v Guardian Newspapers* (No 2), above). Thus, the only defence to an action for breach of confidentiality is to show that the public interest requires disclosure of the information, for instance if the information related to some wrongdoing on the part of the donor (see *Weld-Blundell v Stephens* [1919] 1 KB 520, CA).

The Law Commission in Breach of Confidence (Working Paper No 58,

1974) and in its Report on Breach of Confidence (No 110, 1981) made proposals for reform in the area of protection of confidential information. Unfortunately its proposals have never been taken up. However, the question of the creation of a legal right to privacy has been aired recently in the second Calcutt Report (Review of Press Self-Regulation, Cm 2135, 1993). A Green Paper, was published in the Summer of 1993, proposing the creation of such a right, but did not result in legislation. The current government has now proposed legislation (the Human Rights Bill 1997) which would incorporate the European Convention on Human Rights as part of the law in the UK. The Convention contains a right to privacy. This would not, however, deal, except incidentally, with most of the issues surrounding obligations of confidentiality, particularly in the area of commercial and technical information.

The issue of the extension of obligations of confidentiality to create something approaching a right of privacy was discussed in interlocutory proceedings in *Creation Record Ltd, Sony Music Entertainment (UK) and Noel Gallagher v News Group Newspaper Ltd (1997) The Times*, 29 April. Here a pop group (Oasis) were being photographed in a hotel garden, on a set with various objects placed so as to construct a special scene for the illustration on the front cover of their new album. A freelance photographer commissioned by the Sun newspaper also took photographs of Oasis on the set which were substantially similar to the picture which finally appeared on the album. The Sun intended to use its photograph to create an Oasis poster which it would then sell to its readers, the proceeds being donated to charity. The plaintiffs contended that such publication, without their consent, by the Sun of its photograph either constituted an infringement of copyright, or a breach of confidence. They sought an interlocutory injunction.

The court held there was no infringement of copyright as the Sun had not copied the plaintiff's photograph, merely taken a substantially similar one of the same scene, and the plaintiffs had no copyright (for various technical reasons under copyright law) in the set which they had constructed for the purposes of shooting the photograph. However, the court held that there had been a breach of confidentiality.

The plaintiffs had roped off the area and instituted security measures to ensure that any photographs taken by members of the public who were present should only be of the members of the group Oasis themselves, not of them on the set. The defendant stated that, although it was true these measures were in place, no attempt was made to stop the public getting access to the set and members of the public were taking photographs. The court found that the measures taken by the plaintiffs made the shooting of the pictures on the set an occasion of confidentiality, even though the event as a whole was not confidential, and that the Sun photographer, like other members of the public, must have known he was allowed to be there only on condition he did not photograph Oasis on the set. This knowledge was sufficient to impose an obligation of confidentiality on any photographs of the set taken in breach of this condition. On the particular facts of the case the court then decided to grant the plaintiffs an interlocutory injunction restraining the Sun from publishing the poster until the matter should come to trial.

This finding does not impose a general right of privacy in the guise of confidentiality. It appears to have been crucial to the decision that the plaintiffs had instituted security measures and only allowed members of the public to remain on condition they complied with instructions not to take photographs of the set. However, if it is upheld if and when the case finally comes to trial on the merits, it will go some way towards this, since anybody who in some way evades security measures surrounding a person in order to take a photograph (or, indeed, arguably, to discover any other information) should be fixed with an obligation of confidentiality in relation to the photograph or information obtained.

Finally, it should be noted that the Law Commission have recently published (November 1997) a consultation paper (No 150) on the question of making misuse of trade secrets a criminal offence. This is discussed in section 13.9 of this chapter. Should these proposals become law they will have a radical effect on the law of confidentiality.

Following this general statement of the principles relating to confidentiality obligations, it is now necessary to consider some particular problems which arise in relating to confidentiality obligations in the commercial world.

13.3   The concept of public domain

It is generally said that information cannot be confidential if it is in the 'public domain', and that information which was originally confidential ceases to be so if, at some time after its communication, it comes into the 'public domain'. The use of the term 'public domain' thus requires some definition and discussion.

It can be seen from the cases that the real test to be applied is whether or not the information in question is common knowledge. Lord Greene MR, in *Saltman Engineering Co Ltd v Campbell Engineering Co Ltd*, above, said that information cannot be subject to confidentiality obligations if it is 'public property and public knowledge' at the time that it was disclosed, since then it will lack the necessary quality of confidence. Similarly, Megarry J in *Coco v AN Clark (Engineers) Ltd* [1969] RPC 41, said 'there can be no breach of confidence in revealing to others something which is already common knowledge'.

It is also true to say that information which was confidential at the time it was first disclosed will cease to be the subject of confidentiality obligations if it becomes 'common knowledge' at some time after its original disclosure in confidence. Of course if the confidential information becomes common knowledge because of wrongful disclosure by the party who received it in confidence, that party will not be able to raise the fact that the information in question is now common knowledge in order to defeat a claim made against him by the donor for wrongful disclosure. The recipient cannot in such circumstances benefit by his own wrongdoing. However, in such cases, the court is unlikely to grant an injunction to prevent further disclosure, as this would be the equivalent of shutting the stable door after the horse had left, and the donor will be left to his remedies in damages (*Attorney-General v Guardian Newspapers (No 2)* [1990] 1 AC 109, HL).

There was a useful discussion of the concept of 'public domain' in various of the judgments in *Attorney-General v Guardian Newspapers (No 2)*, above. Scott J said (at 149):

'The public accessibility of the information sought to be protected by the duty of confidence is another factor of relevance. In general, a duty of confidence will not extend to protect information which is in the public domain, but here, too, there are and can be no absolutes. In *O Mustad & Son v Dosen* (Note) [1964] 1 WLR 109 the plaintiff sought to restrain the defendant from making use of a confidential manufacturing process [but subsequently patented the process]. It was held by the House of Lords that the specification had published the process to the world and that the plaintiff could not restrain the defendant from disclosing or using what had become common knowledge. In *Exchange Telegraph Co Ltd v Central News Ltd* [1897] 2 Ch 48 the plaintiff was a news agency which disseminated to subscribers information about the results of horse races. The subscribers were contractually bound to use the information for their private purposes only ... The race meetings in question were public race meetings ... Nonetheless, the information was confidential in the hands of the subscribers, and misused by the defendant ... *Schering Chemicals Ltd v Falkman Ltd* [1982] QB 1 was a more recent case where the confidential information sought to be protected was in the public domain in the sense that it could have been gleaned by a diligent and painstaking search through scientific literature. Nonetheless the defendant, who had not made that search, was restrained from misusing the information ... The question, therefore, whether the public accessibility of the information sought to be protected is fatal to an attempt to restrain the use or disclosure of the information by enforcing a duty of confidence, cannot be answered in any absolute terms. The answer will depend upon the circumstances of the particular case. It will depend upon the nature of the information, the nature of the interest sought to be protected, the relationship between the plaintiff and the defendant, the manner in which the defendant has come into possession of the information, and the circumstances in which and the extent to which the information has been made public.'

In the Court of Appeal, Lord Donaldson MR said (at 177):

'As a general proposition, that which has no character of confidentiality because it has already been communicated to the world, ie, made generally available to the relevant public, cannot thereafter be subjected to a right of confidentiality: *O Mustad & Son v Dosen* (Note) [1964] 1 WLR 109. However, this will not necessarily be the case if the information has previously only been disclosed to a limited part of that public. It is a question of degree ... Furthermore, if the confidant could by great exertion have acquired the information for himself, but the confider is in fact the source of the confidant's knowledge, the law may confer a right of confidentiality unless and until the information is acquired by the confidant from other sources ... The right will also be lost if the information, which is subject to a right of confidentiality, is published to the world by or with the consent of the confider, but it will not necessarily be lost if such publication is by or with the consent of the confidant: *Speed Seal Products Ltd v Paddington* [1985] 1 WLR 1327.'

Bingham LJ said (at 215):

'The information must not be "public knowledge" ... To be confidential information must have ... the base attribute of inaccessibility ... However confidential the circumstances of communication, there can be no breach of confidence in revealing to others something which is already common knowledge ... The duty of confidence ceases to apply to information which, although originally confidential, has ceased to be so otherwise than through the agency of the confidant.'

In the House of Lords, Lord Griffiths said (at 268):

'The first of these elements will not normally be present if the information is in the public domain ... it must not be something that is public property and public knowledge ... If the confider publishes the information this releases the confidant from his duty of confidence: see *O Mustad and Son v Dosen* (Note) [1964] 1 WLR 109. The courts have, however, so far refused to extend this principle where the confidential information is published by a third party: see *Cranleigh Precision Engineering Ltd v Bryant* [1965] 1 WLR 1293, or to the case of publication of the information by the confidant: see *Speed Seal Products Ltd v Paddington* [1985] 1 WLR 1327 ... The duty of confidence is, as a general rule, also imposed on a third party who is in possession of information which he knows is subject to an obligation of confidence ... The court have, however, always refused to uphold the right to confidence when to do so would be to cover up wrongdoing.'

Lord Goff of Chieveley gave the best definition of 'public domain'. He said (at 282):

'The first limiting principle (which is rather an expression of the scope of the duty) is highly relevant to this appeal. It is that the principle of confidentiality only applies to information to the extent that it is confidential. In particular, once it has entered what is usually called the public domain (which means no more than that the information in question is so generally accessible, that in all the circumstances, it cannot be regarded as confidential) then, as a general rule, the principle of confidentiality can have no application to it … The second limiting principle is that the duty of confidence applies neither to useless information, nor to trivia.'

It can thus be stated as a general principle that information is not, and will cease to be, confidential if, as a matter of fact, it is/or becomes common knowledge, without any restriction of confidentiality, either among the public at large, or, at least, among that section of the public which is interested in the particular field to which this information relates, for instance engineers who are concerned with a particular discipline. The courts tend in many cases, as can be seen from the above discussion, to use the phrase 'public domain', but in practice this seems either synonymous with, or to amount in effect to the same thing as, 'common knowledge'. If, in the words of Lord Goff, the information has to be 'so generally accessible that … it cannot be regarded as confidential' then, in truth, it must also be common knowledge.

A good example of this can be found in *Harrison v Project & Design Co (Redcar) Ltd* [1978] FSR 81, where information about a particular feature of an invention ceased to be confidential because it could be said that the product in which that feature was embodied had been 'widely distributed throughout the United Kingdom', and it was 'safe to assume that … a number of engineers and others who might be interested were aware of the major features of construction and particularly of those features which were originally confidential'. Graham J further stated: 'The date upon which it is clear that something that was once confidential ceases to be so … must … always be a question of fact to be inferred by the court from all the circumstances of the case.'

It is now necessary to understand what effect publication of confidential information has upon confidentiality obligations. For the purposes of this discussion 'publication' is to be taken as it is understood in terms of patent law. In this sense 'publication' includes dissemination of information in a literary form (for instance, in a book, newspaper or periodical for sale to the public), oral dissemination (for instance by broadcasting over a public network, or in a public lecture), and would include publishing information in a patent specification. However, as will be described in the next section, putting a product on the market is not an act of publication of information relating to that product.

Publication must be looked at in two ways. First, it is a means, but not the only means, by which information can become common knowledge. Secondly, where the publication is made by the donor of the confidential information, there is a question as to whether there are circumstances in which publication can amount to a waiver by the donor of confidentiality in the information which is published, even if the publication is not of such an extent that the relevant information becomes common knowledge.

Leaving aside the question of publication by the donor, the cases show that publication of confidential information does not of itself cause that information to cease to be confidential. The real question which always has to be asked is whether the publication has actually been on such a scale that it causes the information to become common knowledge.

Where the item of information has been published within the relevant jurisdiction in a widely available periodical, book or newspaper (for instance the daily press) or broadcast over a public radio or television station, the publication of the item of information would in most cases create, as a matter of fact, an actual state of common knowledge.

However, publication may not in fact make the information common knowledge. For instance, the information may be published in an obscure book or magazine, with a restricted circulation, or simply by the deposit of a manuscript in a single public library (as often happens with university theses), and not necessarily even within the jurisdiction. In such circumstances the information cannot be said to be common knowledge just because it would be available to any member of the public who chooses to expend the time, expense and effort necessary to conduct a search for it (see *Schering Chemicals Ltd v Falkman Ltd*).

For instance, in *Yates Circuit Foil Company v Electrofoil Ltd* [1976] FSR 345, certain information was held not to be confidential because evidence was adduced to show it was published in magazines or in patent specifications which formed 'part of the literature normally read by those interested in the field'. Thus it was not the publication of the information which caused it no longer to be confidential, but the fact that it was published in a way which meant that following its publication it could be proved that it had actually come to the attention of, and therefore become common knowledge among, the relevant interested section of the public.

The same approach can be seen from *Attorney-General v Guardian Newspapers (No 2)* above. Here it was held that it was possible to restrain the publication of information, on the grounds that it was still secret within the jurisdiction, even though it was publicly available abroad.

Lord Keith of Kinkel said (at 260):

'It is possible, I think, to envisage cases where, even in the light of widespread publication abroad of certain information, a person whom that information concerned might be entitled to restrain publication by a third party in this country. For example, if in the Argyll case the Duke had secured the revelation of the marital secrets in an American newspaper, the Duchess could reasonably claim that publication of the same material in England would bring it to the attention of people who would otherwise be unlikely to hear of it and who were more closely interested in her activities than American readers. The publication in England would be more harmful to her than publication in America. Similar considerations would apply to, say, a publication in America by the medical adviser to an English pop group about diseases for which he had treated them.'

Another comment on partial publication can be found in *Lancashire Fires Ltd v SA Lyons & Co Ltd* [1996] FSR 629 at 654 *per* Carnwath J:

'Certainly the basis processes ... are well documented. However, there was no evidence that the refinements which [the plaintiffs] had introduced into the system, and which impressed [the defendant] are so documented or widely known. It is possible they have been replicated in individual companies here or abroad, but that does not put them in the "public domain" in the sense that it is used in the cases.'

The concept of partial publication was an important issue in *Creation Record Ltd, Sony Music Entertainment (UK) and Noel Gallagher v News Group Newspaper Ltd*, discussed above. Although the court found that the photograph taken by the *Sun* was subject to obligations of confidentiality, the *Sun* had already published the photograph in their newspaper together with the offer for the poster. The court held that this publication in the newspaper, even though it put the photograph in the public domain was not a sufficient reason to prevent the making of the interlocutory injunction to restrain the publication of the image in the form of the poster, since this was an entirely different kind of publication.

Finally, *Yates Circuit Foil Company v Electrofoil Ltd*, above, makes it clear that putting a product on the market does not amount to publication of, nor does it put into the public domain knowledge of that product (eg its chemical formula or technical specifications) which is only available to a member of the public who cares to expend expense, time and effort in order to 'recreate' it by analysis.

The particular facts of the case related to ascertainment of the formula of a product by chemical analysis. The product was freely available on the open market, so any member of the public who cared to go to the trouble and expense could purchase it and analyse it. However, the principle of this case should also apply to disassembly or other types of reverse engineering of a product (other than in respect of software products for which special rules arising under copyright law apply).

Whitford J said:

'There remains the question of the effect of publication ... The defendants assert that the plaintiffs cannot restrain the use of any published information. They say that [the relevant information] is available because it can be discovered by analyses of materials sold ... The defendants rely on the principle established in relation to patents ... that, if on analysis of an article on sale you will get a disclosure of what is alleged to be an invention and would have got such a disclosure before the date of application for the patent in question, then the patent is prior used. This to my mind cannot necessarily affect the question of information in a secrets case such as I am here concerned with. Although as Lord Greene [in *Saltman Engineering Co Ltd v Campbell Engineering Co Ltd*, above] and Megarry J [in *Coco v AN Clark (Engineers) Ltd* [1969] RPC 41] pointed out there can be no confidentiality in information which is public knowledge and public property, the way in which it was put was that 'there can be no breach of confidence in revealing to others something which is already common knowledge'. The fact that the means of ascertaining the ingredients is publicly available does not, to my mind, make the information relating to those ingredients common knowledge. Someone who has taken the trouble, by analysis, to acquire specific knowledge ... may in fact have acquired information of value which, until it becomes a matter of common knowledge, in my view he is entitled to protect.'

The same points were made in the more recent case of *Alfa Laval Cheese Systems Ltd v Wincanton Engineering Ltd* [1990] FSR 583.

The question which now must be determined is the effect of publication by the donor of his confidential information. If the same rules apply as to publication by a third party, then the only issue is, again, whether the publication is of such an extent that the information has become common knowledge. If, however, publication by the donor always destroys the confidentiality in the information published then this must be on a different principle, amounting to a waiver by the donor of his right to insist on the confidentiality of the information.

The effect of publication of confidential information by the donor of that information was first considered in *Mustad v Dosen* [1963] RPC 41, where the plaintiffs published all of the information which they alleged was confidential, in a patent specification. Lord Buckmaster said 'after the disclosure had been made by the plaintiffs to the world, it was impossible for them to get an injunction restraining the defendants from disclosing what was common knowledge'.

Mustad v Dosen, above, was first discussed in detail in *Cranleigh Precision Engineering Ltd v Bryant* [1966] RPC 81, where part of the decision concerned third party publication of a patent specification relating to swimming pool construction (referred to in the case as the 'Bischoff patent'). Counsel for the defendants relied upon the fact that 'publication of the complete specification is, by s 13(2) of the Patents Act 1949, deemed to be publication to the world at large', and that 'the evidence was a visitor to the Patent Office looking generally for patents relating to swimming pools would find the Bischoff patent in twenty-five minutes'. He then relied on *Mustad v Dosen* as authority for the proposition that any publication of the secret by way of a patent specification (whether by the plaintiff or by a third party) destroyed the confidentiality of the information so disclosed.

The judgment of the court distinguished *Mustad v Dosen* as authority for the proposition that 'if the master had published his secret to the whole world (as had the appellants in that case) the servant is no longer bound by his promise to the master not to publish that same secret, but it is important to observe that the publication in that case was publication by the master. In the present case, the publication was by Bischoff ... the plaintiffs have never published anything, even their own specification'.

The treatment of the Bischoff patent in this case really turns on other issues, but, at the least, it shows that publication of the patent specification by the originator of the information has to be treated differently from publication of a patent specification by an independent third party. Here, it is clear from *Yates Circuit Foil Company v Electrofoil Ltd*, above, that where the publication is by an unconnected third party the test should be whether interested members of the public actually accessed the specification so that its existence and the information contained in it in fact became common knowledge.

The dicta in *Yates Circuit Foil Company v Electrofoil Ltd*, above, and *Attorney-General v Guardian Newspapers* (No 2), above, follow *Cranleigh Precision Engineering Ltd v Bryant*, above, in treating *Mustad v Dosen*, above, as authority for the proposition that any publication by the donor of confidential information amounts to a waiver of the confidential status of that information.

The difficulty is that Mustad v Dosen can be taken as authority for a number of different propositions. The first is that there was in fact in that case a publication of such an extent that the relevant information became common knowledge. The second is that publication of a patent specification, no matter by whom, is deemed, by virtue of special provisions of patent law, to be publication which amounts to common knowledge (whether the relevant information does in fact become common knowledge or not). The third is that publication of information in a patent specification by the donor of that information amounts to a waiver of the donor's rights of confidentiality in that information by virtue of special provisions of patent law. The fourth is that any publication by a donor of information amounts to a waiver of his rights of confidentiality in that information, and that publication by way of a patent specification is just one method of publication which creates such a waiver.

The first proposition does not seem supported by the facts in *Mustad v Dosen*, above, and the second proposition is contradicted by both *Cranleigh Precision Engineering Ltd v Bryant*, above, and *Yates Circuit Foil Company v Electrofoil Ltd*, above. There is no direct supporting evidence for the third proposition in *Mustad v Dosen*, above, nor in any later case. However, *Cranleigh Precision Engineering Ltd v Bryant, Yates Circuit Foil Company v Electrofoil Ltd*, above, *Seager v Copydex Ltd*, above and *Attorney-General v Guardian Newspapers* (No 2), above, all contain dicta supporting the fourth proposition.

Clearly, if the fourth proposition is correct in law, then the third proposition is included within it, as no more than a special case of waiver by publication. However, the difficulty is that, apart from *Mustad v Dosen*, above, all of the cases discussed above did not turn upon the loss of confidentiality because of publication by the donor of all of the information which he claimed as confidential. In all of those cases what was important was that part of a body of information remained confidential, and nothing turned on the fact that another part had, or was alleged to have, been published by the donor and/or become common knowledge.

Thus the interpretations in these cases of *Mustad v Dosen*, above, are all obiter dicta, and, to this extent persuasive rather than authoritative. There has not yet been a case which turned on the question of whether publication by the donor (other than by way of a patent specification), in circumstances which did not make that information common knowledge, was in truth a waiver of rights of confidentiality in that information.

It is submitted that, in the last analysis, the suggestion that any publication by the donor of information amounts to a waiver is not correct. Giving this interpretation to *Mustad v Dosen* goes beyond the facts, which related only to the question of publication by way of patent specification, and moreover, a publication which was stated to be to 'all the world'. Further, it was not necessary for the decision in *Cranleigh Precision Engineering Ltd v Bryant*, above, and in *Yates Circuit Foil Company v Electrofoil Ltd*, above, to decide whether any publication by the donor, other than by way of a patent specification, would amount to such a waiver. *Attorney-General v Guardian Newspapers* (No 2), above, appears to have assumed this was the case, as can be seen from the various statements of law quoted above, but again it was not necessary for the court to rule on this point as part of the judgment in that case. It is hard to see that any publication at all by the donor, however limited, would overcome the general principles relating to public domain as stated in that case, particularly in the judgments of Scott J and Lord Goff.

The best way of reconciling *Mustad v Dosen*, above, with the general principles of law on public domain or common knowledge, is to look at it as an authority for the third proposition mentioned above, namely that publication of information in a patent specification by the donor of that information amounts to a waiver of the donor's rights of confidentiality in that information by virtue of special provisions of patent law. However, until a decision is made directly on facts relating to publication by the donor other than in the circumstances of a patent specification, the matter must remain one of some doubt and conjecture.

In any event, to the extent that it can be argued that any publication by the donor waives confidentiality it is important to distinguish between publication and putting a product on the market. It is clear that putting a product on the market does not of itself amount to a publication of, or put into the public domain, information about the product or the processes of its manufacture which can only be ascertained by some form of analysis, disassembly or reverse engineering (see *Mustad v Dosen*, above, *Cranleigh Precision Engineering Ltd v Bryant* and *Yates Circuit Foil Company v Electrofoil Ltd*, above).

On this basis, whatever the analysis of law relating to publication, the donor cannot be taken to have waived confidentiality in information about a product which he puts on the market if such information can only be ascertained by analysis, disassembly or reverse engineering, because that information is neither published by him nor has it become common knowledge. There may be aspects of relevant confidential information which come into the public domain when, and simply because, a product is put on the market, but this concept will be discussed below in relation to the 'springboard' doctrine, and is not linked to the question of publication.

In conclusion, it can be said that in the use of the concept 'public domain' the first and foremost question is always whether the information was or later becomes common knowledge. The question of publication (as discussed above) is always a subordinate one. Publication (except perhaps publication by the donor of the confidential information in some circumstances) does not of itself create common knowledge, although it may do. Whether, and, if so, when, it does, can only be decided as a question of fact in each individual situation taking all of the circumstances of the case into account.

13.4   The springboard doctrine

Having clarified the principles surrounding the relationship between common knowledge and the publication of confidential information, it is now possible to consider the so-called 'springboard' doctrine, which affects the obligations of confidentiality covering technical information, particularly where a product to which that information relates has been put on the market.

First, it is necessary to consider three cases, *Mustad v Dosen*, above, *Saltman Engineering Co Ltd v Campbell Engineering Co Ltd*, above, and *Terrapin Ltd v Builders' Supply Co (Hayes) Ltd* [1967] RPC 375.

In *Mustad v Dosen*, above, Lord Buckmaster said:

> 'the important point about the patent ... was what it was that it disclosed ... The secret as a secret has ceased to exist. But the plaintiffs say—and I think with considerable force—that it might well have been that ... the defendant ... obtained knowledge of ancillary secrets connected with the patented invention which were not in fact included in the invention but which would be of very great service to any person who proceeded to make the machine.'

The plaintiffs' case failed not because of disclosure of the invention through the patent, but because they had not shown the existence and subsequent misuse by the defendant of any 'ancillary secrets'.

In *Saltman Engineering Co Ltd v Campbell Engineering Co Ltd*, above, certain drawings of tools for the manufacture of leather punches were used by a contract manufacturer to make a new set of tools which he then used to manufacture leather punches for his own account.

Lord Greene MR said:

> ' I am satisfied that in manufacturing the second set of tools or some of them use was made of the confidential information contained in the original draw-ings, or in the set of tools made from them under the original contract. They made a second set of drawings and, in order to make those drawings, they had recourse to some material derived from the original drawings.
>
> 'I think that I shall not be stating the principle wrongly if I say this with regard to the use of confidential information. The information, to be confidential, must, I apprehend, apart from contract, have the neces-sary quality of confidence about it, namely, it must be something which is not public property and public knowledge. On the other hand, it is perfectly possible to have a confidential document, be it a formula, a plan, a sketch, or something of that kind, which is the result of work done by the maker upon materials which may be available for the use of anybody; but what makes it confidential is the fact that the maker of the document has used his brain and thus produced a result which can only be produced by somebody who goes through the same process.
>
> 'What the defendants did in this case was to dispense in certain mate-rial respects with the necessity of going through the process which had been gone through in compiling these drawings, and thereby to save themselves a great deal of labour and calculation and careful draughts-manship. No doubt, if they had taken the finished article, namely, the leather punch, which they might have bought in a shop, and given it to an expert draughtsman, that draughtsman could have produced the nec-essary drawings for the manufacture of machine tools required for mak-ing that particular finished article. In at any rate a very material respect they saved themselves that trouble by obtaining the necessary informa-tion either from the original drawings or from the tools made in accord-ance with them. That, in my opinion, was a breach of confidence.'

Terrapin Ltd v Builders Supply Co (Hayes) Ltd, above, concerned portable buildings. The defendants had acted as contract manufacturers for the plain-tiffs in respect of a portable building, designed and developed by the plaintiffs and known as the 'Mark 24'. The plaintiffs had communicated to the defend-ants 'all drawings and technical information associated with its various types of buildings for the sole purpose of enabling the [defendants] to manufacture them in accordance with the [plaintiff's] designs ... and for no other purpose'. Subsequently, the plaintiffs revealed to the defendants that they were planning a new design of building, to be known as the 'Mark 36' which was of a much improved design, the improvement consisting of 'a new design with flat roof-ing and of stressed skin construction'. The defendants produced a portable building in competition with the Mark 36, called the Swiftplan, also with a flat ceiling and of stressed skin construction.

Roxburgh J enunciated the springboard doctrine as follows:

> 'When, therefore, Mr Chambers was instructed on behalf of the [defendants] to design a new building unit … he could not have avoided starting his dive into the future from the springboard of the confidential information acquired by the [defendants] and by Mr Chambers as their servant … information is nonetheless used, if it serves as a starting point for a new design, even if in the end the design wholly or partially discards the information from which it was originally built up.'

Roxburgh J thus found that there had been a misuse of the confidential know-how relating to the Mark 24 and the Mark 36, and relied upon the general principles relating to the protection of confidential information in a technical context as set out in *Saltman Engineering Co Ltd v Campbell Engineering Co Ltd*, above. He observed: 'So far I have found the case proved … against the [defendants] … without regard to the question of the flat ceiling.'

He then stated that the plaintiff's counsel had put forward the proposition that information about the flat ceiling and stressed skin construction was no longer to be treated as confidential once the Mark 24 and the Mark 36 were put on the market, as these features, and all the other general features of the buildings, and their method of construction, could be determined by reading the plaintiff's product literature, or by dismantling the building to see how it was constructed, so that in this sense there had been a publication which discharged the obligation of confidentiality.

Roxburgh J rejected this argument as inconsistent with the principles in *Saltman Engineering Co Ltd v Campbell Engineering Co Ltd*, above, and his basis for doing so was to draw a distinction between the know-how and the general features.

The key to his judgment lies in the distinction that he draws between 'features' and know-how:

> 'All patent experts are always talking about 'features', but the real point of the thing is that the feature, at least in my view, was the flat roof or ceiling. The stressed skin technique was a development in structural design which enabled that estimable result to be achieved; so that in truth it is one feature achieved by the application of a new method of construction. That is why I sometimes call it a feature and sometimes I call it two. It is the same thing.'

He observed:

> 'As I understand it the essence of this branch of the law, whatever its origin may be, is that a person who has obtained information in confidence is not allowed to use it as a springboard for activities detrimental

to the person who made the confidential communication, and spring-board it remains even when all the features have been published or can be ascertained by actual inspection by any member of the public. The brochures are certainly not equivalent to the publication of the plans, specifications, other technical information and know-how. The disman-tling of a unit might enable a person to proceed without plans or specifi-cations or other technical information, but not, I think without some of the know-how, and certainly not without taking the trouble to dismantle. I think it is broadly true to say that a member of the public to whom the confidential information had not been imparted would still have to pre-pare plans and specifications. He would probably have to construct a prototype, and he would certainly have to conduct tests. Therefore the possessor of the confidential information still has a long start over any member of the public. The design may be as important as the features. It is in my view inherent in the principle upon which the *Saltman* case rests that the possessor of such information must be placed under a spe-cial disability in the field of competition in order to ensure that he does not get an unfair start.'

Roxburgh J's judgment was quoted with approval in *Cranleigh Precision Engineering Ltd v Bryant* [1966] RPC 81, by Roskill J, who had a full tran-script of the judgment specially provided to him by counsel. He made the point that when *Terrapin Ltd v Builders' Supply Co (Hayes) Ltd*, above, was heard on appeal, the Court of Appeal did not criticise the learned judge's rul-ing on points of law, despite forceful arguments by counsel for the appellants, criticising that judgment. In Roskill J's view, Roxburgh J's judgment did in-deed follow logically from the principles in *Saltman Engineering Co Ltd v Campbell Engineering Co Ltd*, above, was a correct statement of the law, and was not (as counsel for the defendant contended) in conflict with *Mustad v Dosen*, above. The case was also quoted with approval, by Megarry J in *Coco v AN Clark (Engineers) Ltd*, above, and by Lord Denning in *Seager v Copydex Ltd* [1967] RPC 349.

In *Seager v Copydex Ltd* Lord Denning said:

'The law on this subject ... depends on the broad principle of equity that he who has received information in confidence shall not take unfair ad-vantage of it. He must not make use of it to the prejudice of him who gave it without obtaining his consent. The principle is clear enough when the whole of the information is private. The difficulty arises when the information is in part public and in part private. As for instance in this case. A good deal of the information which Mr Seager gave to Copydex Ltd was available to the public ... [Seager had published a patent speci-fication, described one of his inventions on television, and put a product embodying that invention on the market] ... If that was the only infor-mation he gave them he could not complain ... On the facts ... he told

Copydex Ltd a lot about the making of a satisfactory carpet grip which was not in the public domain … [this information] was the springboard which enabled them to go on and devise the INVISIGRIP and to apply for a patent for it.'

The 'springboard' cases show that it is a misuse of confidential technical information not only to use it to reproduce an existing product marketed by the donor of that confidential information but also to use such information as a springboard, that is 'as a starting point for a new design', even if 'in the end the design wholly or partially discards the information from which it was originally built up' (*Terrapin Ltd v Builders' Supply Co (Hayes) Ltd*, above).

This concept is simple enough when the whole of the information used as a springboard is confidential. Its use as a springboard by a person who received it in confidence is a breach of his obligations of confidentiality relating to that information. This is the ratio in *Terrapin Ltd v Builders Supply Co (Hayes) Ltd*, above. Roxburgh J, as he said himself, found for the plaintiff on the misuse of the confidential information, without having to consider the question of the 'features' which may or may not on the facts have been common knowledge.

However, two further questions arise. First, what happens where only part of the information used as a springboard is or remains confidential. Secondly, what is the effect of the putting on the market of a product which has been developed and/or manufactured and/or embodies all or part of the relevant body of information which was used as a springboard.

The answer to the first question is simple. Where part of the information only is or remains confidential, that part of the information remains subject to the obligations of confidentiality, and the fact that another part of the information has ceased so to be subject is irrelevant. This can happen in a number of ways. The originator of the information can disclose part of it in a patent specification, but still retain confidentiality in 'ancillary secrets' (*Mustad v Dosen*, above, *Seager v Copydex Ltd*, above) or he can publish part of the information in a way which makes it common knowledge, for instance by producing a description in a product brochure (*Terrapin Ltd v Builders' Supply Co (Hayes) Ltd*, above, and *Cranleigh Precision Engineering Ltd v Bryant*, above) or broadcasting it on television (*Seager v Copydex Ltd*, above).

The question of putting the product on the market is more complex. By combining the principles in *Terrapin Ltd v Builders' Supply Co (Hayes) Ltd*, above, *Yates Circuit Foil Company v Electrofoil Ltd*, above, and *Seager v Copydex Ltd*, above, it seems that putting a product on the market not only does not amount to publication of information which can only be obtained by reverse engineering of that product, but it also does not amount to publication of what Roxburgh J in *Terrapin Ltd v Builders' Supply Co (Hayes) Ltd*, above, called its 'features'. The *dicta* suggest that these are made available to the public (rather than published) by the putting on the market to the extent that anyone buying, using or even seeing the product displayed for sale, would perceive what these 'features' were. It thus would be a question of whether and when the marketing of the product was so extensive that such 'features' become common knowledge, but the question of publication would be irrelevant.

Thus, putting the product on the market may, but does not necessarily, mean that all or some of the confidential information relating to that product becomes either contemporaneously, or at some later date, common knowledge. Combining this with the first principle above, it can thus be stated that only that part of the confidential information relating to the product which, either at once or at some later date, becomes common knowledge as a result of the putting of the product on the market, will, at the time that it does become common know-ledge, cease to be confidential. This is the basis for the *dicta* in *Lancashire Fires v Lyons* (at 654, *per* Carnwath J): 'it might be possible for an expert ... to infer from the finished product [when put on the market] the general nature of the processes used to produce it, this is a far cry from detailed knowledge of the processes such as would enable them to be replicated.'

The key is to decide at what point in time information becomes common knowledge once a product is put on the market. At any rate initially, and perhaps after some lapse of time, if the product is not marketed very widely, then only the 'features' of the product which are ascertainable by visual inspection (which is almost to say nothing more than its appearance) and the information about it published in product brochures, will become common knowledge once enough people have bought or seen the product or read the brochures (*Terrapin Ltd v Builders' Supply Co (Hayes) Ltd*, above and *Seager v Copydex Ltd*, above). (Although it could be argued, as discussed above, that, where the donor of the information publishes it in a product brochure, he has waived confidentiality in that information, irrespective of the extent of the publication.) The fact that more knowledge is potentially available to anyone who is prepared to take the time and trouble to dismantle or analyse the product does not mean that this information is in fact common knowledge, unless and until either a large number of people actually carry out the process, or one person does so, and publishes the information so that it becomes common knowledge in some other way (eg by writing an article about it in the professional journal covering the relevant field). (*Yates Circuit Foil Company v Electrofoil Ltd*, above and *Harrison v Project & Design (Redcar) Ltd*, above)

At the stage when the product has just been put on the market, like the punches in *Saltman Engineering Co Ltd v Campbell Engineering Co Ltd*, above, or the 'Mark 36' in *Terrapin Ltd v Builders' Supply Co (Hayes) Ltd*, above, there is obviously still a great deal of information which remains confidential, and which can be misused as a springboard to give the person who received that information in confidence a head start in designing or manufacturing a competing product. At this stage he is thus suffering under a 'special disability'. This information that he has received is not common knowledge, and even if some people start to analyse or dismantle the product to reproduce this information by independent development, that will still not make that information common knowledge, and thus release him from his obligations of confidentiality. Therefore, on general principles of confidentiality law he would have to wait until the confidential information had become so widely disseminated as a result of various attempts at independent analysis that it could be said to be common knowledge, and therefore no longer subject to confidentiality obligations in his hands.

This is what is meant by Lord Denning in *Potters-Ballotini Ltd v Weston-Baker* [1977] RPC 20, when he said 'a time may come when so much has happened that [the recipient of confidential information] can no longer be restrained'. It is also the best way of making sense of *Harrison v Project & Design Co (Redcar) Ltd*, above. In that case, the particular idea used as a springboard was not obvious to visual inspection, but once a sufficient number of lifts had been sold it could be assumed that most interested parties would have studied them and ascertained the particular idea used, so that at that time, but not before, the springboard doctrine ceased to apply to that idea, and the defendant was free thereafter to use it without payment.

There are two basic principles of law which appear to come out of the springboard cases. The first is that use of confidential information as a 'springboard' (in the terms discussed above) is a misuse of that information, amounting to a breach of the relevant confidentiality obligations. The second is that where part of a body of confidential information relating to a product becomes common knowledge, the recipient in confidence of that body of information remains bound by his obligations of confidentiality in regard to the part that has remained confidential, and cannot use it as a 'springboard', even if a third party could recreate such part by independent analysis of the relevant product once it has been put on the market.

As Lord Denning stated in *Seager v Copydex Ltd*, above, the real problem is not the springboard doctrine itself, but the difficulties caused when the attempt is made to apply it in relation to a body of information which is partly common knowledge and partly private, even though in theory the recipient becomes free to use that part of the information which is common knowledge. This is because, as a practical matter, the person who has initially received the whole body of information in confidence may well be restrained from using the information that is common knowledge because he cannot do so without using the information which remains confidential as well. He is thus in a doubly-worse position than an unconnected third party who could not only make use of that part of the information which was common knowledge, but also recreate by independent analysis that part of the information which was confidential information.

This problem can only be solved by considering the precise nature of the confidentiality obligations that the recipient of mixed information is to be fixed with. This is discussed below when considering the remedies available for the breach of confidentiality obligations. First, however, it is necessary to consider confidentiality obligations in the light of the principles relating to restraint of trade and competition law, since the remedies available for breach of confidentiality obligations in a commercial context are significantly affected by these principles.

13.5   Commercial confidentiality obligations and restraint of trade

The public interest in restraining the breach of confidentiality obligations relating to personal information, or state secrets, is obvious enough. However, in the area of commercial confidentiality obligations, it is necessary to balance the public interest requirement that confidences be respected against the public interest requirement that business affairs should be carried on without unjustifiable restraint of trade.

The issue was summarised succinctly by Whitford J in *Yates Circuit Foil Co v Electrofoils Ltd*, above:

> 'The decisions which I have above referred to indicate quite clearly that there are limits to a proceeding in which an attempt is made to restrain the use of what might be alleged to be confidential information. An action of this kind could very easily be misused if in truth what the plaintiff is really seeking to do is to restrain competition rather than to restrain the use of information in which he can reasonably assert a proprietary right. The action for breach of confidence is a restraint which can very properly be enforced in appropriate circumstances. Like all restraints, it can however, in my judgment, only be justified if the exercise of the restraint is necessary to safeguard an interest for which protection can properly be claimed. It must not be used as a cover for a mere restraint against competition.'

The problem is at its most extreme where an employer seeks to restrain an ex-employee from using confidential information to compete with him. This issue is discussed in Chapter 14, but it is clear from *Faccenda Chicken Ltd v Fowler*, above, that once employment has ceased the only class of confidential information which the courts are prepared to invoke the equitable doctrine to protect is that which amounts to a trade secret (ie a 'proprietary interest' in the terminology of Whitford J in *Yates Circuit Foil Co v Electrofoils Ltd*, above).

Faccenda Chicken Ltd v Fowler is most often quoted as authority for the proposition that there are, in the context of employer and employee, two classes of confidential information, trade secrets and other information which is still confidential but of a lesser status and therefore only worthy of protection while the contract of employment subsists. However, it is at least arguable, based on the above *dicta* of Whitford J, and the judgments of the Court of Appeal in

Faccenda, that, at any rate in the context of the commercial world, the only information which the equitable principle can protect is trade secrets or proprietary information, and that this is so whether the two parties are independent businessmen, or stand in the relation of employer and employee. Any other attempt to protect information would amount to an unjustified restraint of trade.

The guidelines for the definition of what is a trade secret in the context of the relationship of employer and employee are discussed in detail in Chapter 14, and that discussion is also of some use in the wider commercial context. Nevertheless, most of the commercial cases are simpler because the claim is normally based on information which was disclosed or discovered as a result of a particular transaction or negotiation between the parties, rather than in a somewhat less defined way as a result of the proximity of employer and employee throughout the relationship created by the contract of employment. The conclusion of the discussion in Chapter 14 is that the term does cover more than a secret formula or manufacturing process. Sensitive commercial information can be protected as a trade secret as well. This is also true in the more general commercial context. For instance, in *Indata Equipment Supplies Ltd v ACL Ltd* [1998] FSR 248, the plaintiff's profit margin in relation to a proposed transaction, and to a lesser degree the invoice price between the plaintiff and the defendant, were held to be items of confidential information. However, whatever the nature of the information, it must have a certain level of specificity if it is to be accorded protection.

An analysis of this issue can be found in *De Maudsley v Palumbo* [1996] FSR 447, which reaches a similar conclusion. The plaintiff shared with the defendant, one night over supper, his ideas on what factors made an ideal night club. These related to opening hours, decor, the use of separate areas for dancing, resting, socialising and a VIP lounge, using an enclosed dance floor of acoustic design, and employing top disc jockeys. The plaintiff and the defendant originally intended to go into business together to operate a night club incorporating all of these factors. However, subsequently the defendant went ahead on his own and opened a night club which the plaintiff claimed was based upon his ideas. The plaintiff sued the defendant for misuse of these ideas on the basis that it was a breach of confidence. The plaintiff submitted that his ideas in combination for the ideal night club were original and sufficiently defined to qualify as confidential information.

The court held that, although oral information can be protected by obligations of confidentiality, not just information recorded in writing or another permanent form, if an idea is to be protected it must contain some significant element of originality, be clearly identifiable as the idea of the person disclosing the information and be sufficiently well developed to be capable of actual realisation. This last requirement meant that the idea in question had to have a 'considerable degree of particularity'. The court found on the facts that the factors disclosed by the plaintiff were not particularly new or original, and that nothing new had been created by their combination. The factors were, both individually and in combination, too vague to amount to confidential information. In other words, the ideas put forward by the defendant did not amount to a trade secret as to how to set up the perfect night club.

On this basis, the only instance when any other information, which might be called confidential, could be protected would be as between employer and employee while the contract of employment subsisted. However, this protection would not be afforded by the principles of equity protecting confidential information, but indirectly by the application of the equitable and common law principles which impose a general duty of loyalty on the employee and thus prevent him using any information or know-how obtained in the course of his employment, without regard as to whether it was a trade secret, either for his own personal gain or to assist a competitor (see *Hivac Ltd v Park Royal Scientific Instruments Ltd* [1946] All ER 350; and *Faccenda per* Sir Thomas Bingham MR in the Court of Appeal judgment (at page 135): 'the obligations are included in the implied term which imposes a duty of good faith or fidelity on the employee'). These principles obviously could have no application between two independent businessmen.

If the above analysis is correct, leaving aside the special case of the relationship between employer and employee while the contract of employment still subsists, the conclusion seems to be that the courts will not grant protection to commercial information unless it amounts to a trade secret or proprietary information. This can be looked at from the two points of view.

The *dicta* in *Yates Circuit Foil Co v Electrofoils Ltd*, above, can be taken to mean either that commercial information may be confidential, even if not of the nature and importance of a trade secret, but that as a matter of public policy it is not sufficiently worthy, of the extension to it of the law on confidentiality, to justify a restraint of trade, or that any attempt to invoke the protection of confidentiality for information which is not a trade secret is only a disguised means of restraining competition, because the information is not confidential in the first place. The *dicta* in *Saltman Engineering Co Ltd v Campbell Engineering Co Ltd* above, would support the second view that such information does not in truth have the necessary 'quality of confidentiality' to enable the equitable principle to be invoked for its protection, because it is public property and public knowledge. This also appears to be the basis of the decision in *De Maudsley v Palumbo* discussed above.

13.6   Commercial confidentiality obligations and other competition law considerations

So far as competition law, other than the common law doctrines of restraint of trade, is concerned, it is necessary to distinguish between the ordinary confidentiality undertaking or contract which is the subject of the precedents in this chapter, and know-how licences.

Know-how licences are the subject of considerable interest to competition law authorities, particularly the European Commission, while the confidentiality undertaking or agreement with which this chapter is concerned is largely untouched by competition law. This is because the confidentiality undertaking or agreement is not concerned with the commercial exploitation of information for the purposes of providing products or services. On the other hand, know-how licences are not only concerned with this, but usually also impose some restrictions upon such exploitation. It is these restrictions which may affect or distort competition, and which arouse the particular concern of competition law authorities.

In the UK, at present, the Restrictive Trade Practices Act 1976 governs the situation. Since nothing obliges the donor to disclose his own confidential information to third parties, restrictions imposed by him on its use and disclosure by the recipient are not registrable restrictions under the Act, but merely derogations from his right to prevent disclosure to and use by third parties at all. (The so-called 'opening the door' principle, see *Ravenseft Properties Ltd v Director General of Fair Trading* [1977] 1 All ER 47 RPC.)

However, on the same basis, restrictions undertaken by the originator of information on his own use and disclosure of it would be registrable if they are restrictions to which the Act applies. Here, for instance, the donor could undertake not to disclose the information to any person other than the recipient, or not to use the information himself in a particular territory in order to grant exclusivity of exploitation to the recipient. However, such restrictions are most usually found in know-how licences not ordinary confidentiality agreements or undertakings and certain exemptions exist under the Act anyway.

So far as UK competition law after the passing of the Competition Bill 1997 is concerned, the position is likely to be approximated to that under EC competition law (see the discussion in Chapter 15). In relation to EC competition law, confidentiality undertakings and agreements, as opposed to know-how licences, are, again, largely unaffected. In general, there appears, at least on the current state of EC competition law, to exist no obligation to require an enterprise to disclose confidential information to a third party (except, arguably where such failure to disclose relates to an abuse of a dominant position under art 86: see Case T-76/89, *Independent Television Publications Ltd v Commission (Magill TV Guide Ltd intervening)* [1991] 4 CMLR 745, Court of First Instance, which was confirmed on appeal by the ECJ on 6 April 1995: see [1995] FSR 530). This is particularly the case, where the disclosure is not for purposes of commercial exploitation.

Where confidentiality obligations merge into areas of non-competition clauses, as between employer and employee, or vendor and purchaser of a business, then there is a possibility of an infringement of art 85, if the arrangement affects trade between member states, and is not '*de minimis*'. There is some discussion of this in Chapters 9 and 12 in relation to the sale of a business and to joint ventures, but, in general, all such confidentiality undertakings which can survive the common law principles on restraint of trade have little to fear from art 85.

13.7   The enforcement of commercial confidentiality obligations

Once the confidentiality obligations have been established, and a breach of them has been proved, then the available remedies are either a permanent injunction restraining further breaches and/or damages or an account of profits in respect of past or anticipated future breaches. The court will also in appropriate cases order the recipient to destroy or return to the donor documents or other items in his possession containing or embodying the confidential information in question. The remedy of an interlocutory injunction to restrain the misuse or disclosure of confidential information pending a full trial on the merits of the case is also available, subject to the principles laid down in *American Cyanamid Co v Ethicon Ltd* [1975] AC 396.

Where confidentiality obligations relate to personal information or state secrets, the main concern of the plaintiff is usually to prevent disclosure of the information, even if the disclosure is incidental to commercial exploitation, by way, for instance, of publication of an article in a newspaper. In these cases, an interlocutory injunction is likely to be granted fairly easily, since publication is likely to cause prejudice to the plaintiff which could not be compensated for by way of damages, and the considerations of public interest lean toward preventing the disclosure. A final injunction restraining disclosure is thus the most appropriate remedy, after a trial on the merits, where the court has found in favour of the donor of the information. Thus, in most of these cases, consideration of damages will only occur where the unauthorised disclosure has already taken place, and the information has become common knowledge so that the donor has no other remedy available to him.

However, in the case of commercial information, the public interest in preserving the confidentiality obligations has to be weighed against the public interest in not restraining trade and commerce unduly. Here, the question of the grant of both interlocutory and final injunctions becomes thus much more difficult. Additionally, since most cases surrounding the breach of confidentiality obligations in a commercial context are concerned not with preventing disclosure, but with preventing a recipient of commercial information from misusing it by exploiting it for his own profit, the questions of damages and an account of profits become much more relevant.

In this discussion, it is useful to distinguish two types of confidential commercial information. The first type is what may be called general commercial information. This would cover the business affairs of the donor in general— financial data, methods of marketing or selling products or services, details of customers or suppliers, commercial agreements of all kinds, future business strategies and plans, and so on. In a sense this general commercial information is rather like personal information relating to the affairs of an individual. Secondly, there is technical information, which relates to the design, development or manufacture of a product.

So far as general commercial information is concerned, there seems no reason why, just as in the case of personal or politically sensitive information, the court should not grant both an interlocutory injunction and a final injunction (without limit of time) to prevent its misuse or disclosure. The recipient of such information is normally likely to use it for his own benefit, and, even if this involves some limited disclosure to a third party, he is unlikely to disclose the information to such an extent that it becomes common knowledge, and thus renders the grant of an injunction inappropriate.

Further, here, whether one is dealing with employer and employee or two independent business undertakings, there seems no public policy issue in relation to restraint of trade which would prevent such an injunction.

So far as technical information is concerned, and whether or not one is dealing with the relationship of employer and employee, the issues are more complicated, because it is here that considerations of restraint of trade are most important. The courts have to balance the public interest that confidential information be respected against the public interest that business affairs should be carried on without undue restraint of trade. Since the courts are here involved in a value judgment, and, moreover, a judgment in relation to the grant of an injunction which is a discretionary remedy, it is not surprising that most of the decisions turn on their own particular facts, and it is hard to draw consistent general principles from them. (Even in *Saltman Engineering Co Ltd v Campbell Engineering Co Ltd*, above, it was said, 'You therefore have a unanimous decision of this court on questions of fact involving, as it fortunately turns out, matters of no real importance and depending entirely on the particular facts of this case'.)

This problem becomes particularly acute when dealing with the use of information as a springboard, particularly where the body of information is partly public and partly private.

Further, the law has certainly developed and changed over the last 30 years or so, partly because of the landmark decision in *American Cyanamid Corp v Ethicon Ltd*, above, in relation to interlocutory injunctions in general, but also because of the many important judgments given by Lord Denning in this area, which have developed, extended and refined the basic principles of equitable protection in so far as they are applicable in a commercial context to technical information.

The best course is to survey the leading cases, and to see what general principles, if any, may be drawn from them.

In 1948, no injunction was awarded in *Saltman Engineering Co Ltd v Campbell Engineering Co Ltd*, above, since the court was reluctant to destroy the offending tools. Here the confidential information was not of great value, could have been easily recreated by an independent consultant, and the defendants had not behaved dishonestly. They were thus only obliged to pay damages (calculated on the basis of a royalty) for product already manufactured, and to be manufactured in the future, with the aid of the confidential information.

However, in *Terrapin Ltd v Builders' Supply Co (Hayes) Ltd*, above, *Peter Pan Manufacturing Corporation v Corsets Silhouette Ltd* [1963] RPC 45 and *Cranleigh Precision Engineering Ltd v Bryant*, above, the court, in judgments given in 1959, 1962 and 1964 respectively, awarded injunctions to prevent the misuse of confidential technical information to produce a rival product. Indeed in the last two cases, the injunctions were final ones without limit of time.

By 1966, Megarry J in *Coco v AN Clark (Engineers) Ltd*, above was concerned that there was a broad issue, revolving around the true nature of the duty of the recipient of confidential technical information in a commercial situation, which was particularly acute where one was dealing with a mixed body of information, part of which was confidential and part of which was not, which was used as a springboard. It will be recalled that Lord Denning also felt that this caused particular problems in *Seager v Copydex Ltd*, above.

Megarry J observed:

'I am not clear how it [the springboard doctrine] is to be put into practical effect in every case. Suppose a case where there is a confidential communication of information which is partly public and partly private; suppose that the recipient of the information adds in confidence ideas of his own? ... Suppose that the only confidential information communicated is that some important component should be made of aluminium instead of steel, and with significant variations in its design and dimensions. The recipient knows that this change will transform a failure into a success. He knows that if he had persevered himself he might have come upon the solution in a week or a year. Yet he is under a duty not to use the confidential information as a springboard or as giving him a start.

'What puzzles me is how, as a law abiding citizen, he is to perform that duty. He could commission someone else to make the discovery anew ... but that seems to me artificial in the extreme ... I also recognise that a conscientious and law abiding citizen having received confidential information in confidence, may accept that when negotiations break down the only honourable course is to withdraw altogether from the field in question until his informant or someone else has put the information into the public domain and he can no longer be said to have any start. Communication imposes on him a unique disability. He alone of all men must for an uncertain time abjure this field of endeavour, however great his interest. I find this scarcely more reasonable than the artificiality of postponing the use of the information until others would have discovered it. The relevance of the point, I think, is this: If the duty is a duty not to use the information without consent, then it may be the proper subject of an injunction, restraining its use, even if there is an offer to pay a reasonable sum. If, on the other hand, the duty is merely a duty not to use the information without paying a reasonable sum for it, then no injunction should be granted. Despite the assistance of counsel, I feel far from assured that I have got to the bottom of this matter. But I do feel considerable difficulty in expressing a doctrine of equity which law abiding citizens cannot reasonably be expected to perform. In other words the essence of the duty seems more likely to be that of not using without paying, rather than of not using at all. It may be that in fields other than industry and commerce the duty may exist in more stringent form; but in the circumstances present in this case I think that the less stringent form is the more reasonable.'

Megarry J did not grant an interlocutory injunction, in large part because he appeared satisfied that the defendant had made an offer to pay royalties at a reasonable rate into a suspense account pending the outcome of the trial on the merits.

The distinction between *Saltman Engineering Co Ltd v Campbell Engineering Co Ltd*, above, and *Peter Pan Manufacturing Corporation v Corsets Silhouette Ltd*, above, seems to arise not because the first case might be called a springboard case, and the latter was not, but because of the relative worth of the information concerned and the way it was used. The first case concerned the use of relatively simple ancillary secrets to save a relatively small sum of money and some time and effort, with no particular evidence of moral turpitude or serious breach of trust. The second case turned on the fact the defendant had deliberately, and almost completely, copied the confidential designs, and used the confidential patterns, which the plaintiff had entrusted to it (indeed, in that case, Pennycuick J refused to rule on the broader issue of 'where one trader has given to another in confidence particulars of a process for the manufacture of a given article [as in *Saltman Engineering Co Ltd v Campbell Engineering Co Ltd*, above] in what circumstances, if any, is the second trader thereafter entitled to manufacture that article in competition with the first trader?').

The same could well be said in *Cranleigh Precision Engineering Ltd v Bryant*, where the information concerned was valuable and there was also the added element of a serious breach of duty by the plaintiff's ex-managing director, Bryant. In this case, the court said that not to grant an injunction 'would involve putting a premium upon dishonesty by managing directors'.

In *Terrapin Ltd v Builders' Supply Co (Hayes) Ltd* itself, although this was the case which enunciated the concept of the springboard, it must be said that the Swift was again largely a copy of the Mark 24 and the Mark 36, and that, in part, the injunction, which was only an interlocutory one, for a relatively short period, was awarded because Roxburgh J was concerned to avoid irreparable harm to the plaintiffs, and because, after hearing oral evidence, he was not satisfied with the accuracy of the recollections of the defendant's chief witnesses, the engineer who developed the Swift, and his managing director.

However, *Coco v AN Clark (Engineers) Ltd*, above and *Seager v Copydex Ltd*, above, concerned the use of an inventive idea as a springboard to develop a new product, which entailed considerable work on the part of the defendant, and, in any event, could not be said to be a copy of the plaintiff's product, since, in both cases, the plaintiff was an inventor with good ideas who had not turned those ideas into a commercial product of his own.

In *Seager v Copydex Ltd (No 2)* [1969] RPC 250, Lord Denning looked at the matter in the context of giving guidelines for the assessment of damages for the wrongful use of the technical information, which he had found earlier in *Seager v Copydex Ltd*, above. He seemed satisfied that, however the value of the information was assessed, if the defendant had paid that value, then he could use the information freely as of right. This seems very like Megarry J's 'duty to' pay.

> 'The value of the confidential information depends upon the nature of it. If there was nothing very special about it, that is if it involved no particular inventive step, but was the sort of information which could be obtained by employing any competent consultant then the value of it was the fee which a consultant would charge for it, because in that case the defendants, by taking the information would only have saved themselves the time and trouble of employing a consultant. But ... if the information was something special, as for instance if it involved an inventive step or something so unusual that it could not be obtained by just going to a consultant, then the value of it is much higher ... It is the value between a willing buyer and a willing seller ... then it may well be right for the value to be assessed on the footing that in the usual way it would be remunerated by a royalty ... The court ... could [award a lump sum] by a calculation based on a capitalisation of a royalty ... Once a lump sum is assessed and paid then the confidential information would belong to the defendants in the same way as if they had bought and paid for it by an agreement of sale. The property, so far as there is property in it, would vest in them. They would have the right to use that confidential information.'

Lord Denning commented again on this principle in *Potters-Ballotini Ltd v Weston-Baker* [1977] RPC 20. He said 'a servant or any other person who has got confidential information ought not to save himself the time of working it out for himself or getting it from other people without paying for it. I need not go through the cases, they are all well summarised by Megarry J in his valuable judgment in *Coco v AN Clark (Engineers) Ltd*. Although a man must not use such information as a springboard to get a start over others, nevertheless that springboard does not last forever. If he does use it a time may come when so much has happened that he can no longer be restrained.'

In *Harrison v Project & Design Co (Redcar) Ltd*, above, the court took the view that the defendants should pay for the head start they had gained by the use of an idea disclosed to them by the plaintiff, which amounted to an inventive step as a springboard in their development of a new type of a lift. By the time the case came to court the defendants had already marketed a lift, embodying that idea, to such an extent that the court regarded the idea as common knowledge, and therefore an injunction restraining use or disclosure was no longer appropriate.

In that case, Graham J said: 'It would, in my judgment, clearly be right that the defendants should pay for the privilege of using the plaintiff's idea ... and for the "springboard" advantage which they obtained from information which he gave them, although they undoubtedly later improved on his ideas ... [The defendants are] liable to pay an appropriate award of damages for the use of the plaintiff's confidential information prior to [the date on which it became common knowledge].'

Going on the above analysis, it is now possible to lay down some tentative rules in relation to remedies for misuse of technical information.

The first is that, where the misuse of the technical information is not accompanied by any independent development, so that in substance it amounts to a mere copying, a final injunction will lie to prevent the continued marketing of the 'copied' product, even though the confidential information in question has become common knowledge (whether or not because of the wrongful act of the defendant). Here the duty is 'not to use at all', even if third parties are free to use the information.

The second is that where the technical information has been used as a 'springboard' to develop a new product, or even to assist in the manufacture of an existing product, particularly where the whole body of information is partly public and partly private, the correct remedy is not an injunction, but damages based upon the worth of the information used as a springboard. Here the duty is 'not to use without paying', although a duty not to further disclose might in appropriate cases also be imposed by injunction.

The third is that it is easier for the court to classify the use of information as a springboard, rather than copying, where the plaintiff has not himself put a product on the market utilising the relevant information. In borderline cases, the existence of two rival products can tip the balance towards a finding of 'copying'.

The fourth is that evidence of fraud, or serious breach of duty, will incline the court to grant an injunction rather than damages whether or not dealing with a 'spring-board' case. Given that 'equity acts on the conscience' and that an injunction is a discretionary remedy, it is quite clear that the decisive factor in many of the cases has been the degree of disapproval which the court held for the activities of the defendant.

This analysis provides a way of balancing the two facets of public interest. It is not right to ignore the public interest that confidentiality be respected in order to permit a recipient who is a mere copier, particularly one who is in serious breach of duty, to compete unfairly with his donor. However, where the recipient has expended substantial effort of his own (particularly if the donor is not currently exploiting the information himself) the public interest that confidences be respected takes second place to the public interest in the promotion of free trade. Finally, as is appropriate for an equitable remedy, where there has been some moral turpitude on the part of the recipient (whatever the extent of his independent development activity), the public interest in protecting confidentiality is more likely to prevail.

The leading cases and the issues discussed above were looked at recently in *Lancashire Fires v Lyons*, above, and *Ocular Sciences Ltd v Aspect Vision Care Ltd* (reported in (1997) *Intellectual Property Decisions*, March issue, 2). The approach of these cases to the issues in question would seem to further confirm the cases upon which the first and second principles set out above are based.

13.8   Express documentation

Given the far-reaching nature of the equitable principles relating to confidentiality, it may well be asked why any express documentation is necessary at all. There are, however, a number of good reasons for providing express documentation in commercial transactions.

Express documentation can take the form of either a confidentiality undertaking or a confidentiality agreement.

An undertaking is not a contract, and therefore need not be supported by consideration. Its purpose is to provide evidence as to what information the recipient has received, the purpose for which he has received it, and to show that it was communicated to the recipient in confidence. The undertaking thus provides the necessary evidence to trigger the operation of the general principles of equity protecting confidential information, but does not of itself offer any protection.

Where a confidentiality agreement is used, the situation is somewhat different. The first question is whether the protection afforded to the information covered by the agreement arises solely under contract, so that the protection in equity is displaced by the express terms of the contract, or whether the equitable protection subsists in addition to the contractual protection. In the view of Megarry J in *Coco v AN Clark (Engineers) Ltd*, above, 'the obligation of confidence may exist where, as in this case, there is no contractual relationship between the parties. In cases of contract, the primary question is no doubt that of construing the contract and any terms implied in it.'

Where the express terms of the contract cut down on the protection which might otherwise be granted by equity, then it seems clear from the authorities, that to this extent the equitable principles are displaced. For instance, an obligation not to disclose confidential information for a fixed period of time will free the recipient from any obligation not to disclose once that period has expired, even if, in the absence of a contract, equity might have restrained him for longer (see *Potters-Ballotini Ltd v Weston-Baker and Others*, above).

The real question to be asked, however, is can a confidentiality agreement impose, under contract, confidentiality obligations that are greater than those afforded under the general law? For instance, is it possible to restrain a recipient from using or disclosing confidential information after it has become common knowledge, because of publication by the donor or an unconnected third party—a situation where the general law would no longer impose a restraint? There is admittedly some doubt about this (see the comments of the Law Commission in their report on confidentiality mentioned earlier) but in general terms, in a commercial context, any imposition of confidentiality obligations of this nature could well be struck down as unjustifiable restraints of trade. On this point reference should be made to the discussion above concerning the impact of doctrines of restraint of trade on the protection of confidential information in a commercial context. The *dicta* in *Yates Circuit Foil Co v Electrofoils Ltd* [1976] FSR 345 at 384, mentioned in that section would equally apply to express contracts, as would the judgment in *Faccenda Chicken Ltd v Fowler*, above.

A similar question that can be asked is whether a confidentiality agreement could bind the recipient in regard to information which would be (at least arguably) of too trivial a nature to be subject to the general equitable protection afforded to secret information as described in *Saltman Engineering Co Ltd v Campbell Engineering Co Ltd* above.

Although such matters are not free from doubt, it is normally better not to produce general commercial confidentiality agreements that impose obligations greater than those which could be enforced under the general equitable principles. Such a course is not only likely to cause problems of restraint of trade, but it is also likely to raise commercial difficulties with the other party. Furthermore, it has to be asked whether there are any legitimate interests that are, in practical terms, really worth protecting, once one goes beyond the protection afforded by the general law.

The particular problems in relation to confidentiality clauses in employment contracts are discussed in detail in Chapter 14. Know-how licences also cause considerable problems in this area, particularly under European competition law, but such issues are outside the scope of this book.

Leaving aside questions of restraint of trade, the use of an agreement as opposed to an undertaking serves two clear purposes.

The first is to enable the parties to agree (in a legally enforceable document) a more circumscribed or clearly defined protection for confidential information than that afforded under the general law. Precise wording defining when information is to be regarded as common knowledge can solve the problems associated with the concepts of 'public domain' and 'publication', and the springboard doctrine discussed above. Further the parties can agree that no information shall be regarded as confidential after the expiry of a period of time, or that no protection will be granted to confidential information which is imparted orally. Such agreements are often more practical from a commercial point of view for both parties, who can define precisely what confidentiality obligations they wish to accept rather than relying on the broader and perhaps more imprecise doctrines of the general law.

The second is to impose upon a party (usually the recipient) legally enforceable obligations which are ancillary to the central obligations of confidentiality and not implied under the general law. An obligation to return documents containing confidential information upon demand, or the duty to maintain a system for recording the transmission and receipt of confidential information, can be imposed in this way. Another common instance is the imposition of an obligation to inform the donor if the recipient is requested to disclose confidential information to a court or to a government authority that has a legal right to require him to disclose it despite the obligations imposed on him. A contractual document is also useful in dealing with the issue of negligent or inadvertent disclosure. It has been said that the general law probably forbids both, but the situation is not entirely clear. Thus the best course is to insert express obligations on the recipient as to the procedures and level of care he must take to safeguard the confidential information and the documentation or other items in which it is embodied. Such obligations can also include a duty to enforce any duties of confidentiality owed to the recipient by his employees, in so far as this is necessary to prevent them disclosing the donor's information.

13.9   Special considerations relating to commercial information

Finally, so far as protection of information in the commercial world is concerned, there are a number of specific issues which need to be considered.

First, in enforcing obligations of confidentiality the most important issues are evidentiary ones. Was there an obligation of confidentiality at all? If there was, to what information did it relate, and has the recipient actually misused or disclosed the relevant information? Express confidentiality undertakings or agreements should always be used (leaving the general principles of law as a backstop in case things go wrong) and, wherever possible, details of the information disclosed, and an acknowledgment of its receipt, should be part of the undertaking or agreement, or set out in subsequent documentation recording the transmission of information in reliance upon the undertaking or agreement.

Secondly, two areas where special care should be taken are pre-contract negotiations, where the parties often exchange confidential information without any formal protection, and the receipt of unsolicited inventions and advice. In the first case, the circumstances may be such as to give rise to an obligation of confidentiality, but it is still better to formalise the situation with proper confidentiality obligations. In the second case, the circumstances may again give rise to an obligation of confidence which, this time, in the case of the recipient, will be entirely unintended and unwelcome; here, it is best to avoid accepting unsolicited advice and inventions unless the offeror signs a waiver disclaiming his rights in respect of confidentiality over the information offered.

The dangers of informal disclosure were highlighted in *De Maudsley v Palumbo*, discussed above. Here the information which was claimed to be confidential was imparted orally while the plaintiff and defendant (two business acquaintances) were having supper on a social occasion. The court stated that, where there is no express declaration that the information is being disclosed in confidence, the test of whether the information was imparted in circumstances which by implication gave rise to a duty of confidence was an objective one. The issue was not what the parties' themselves thought about the situation, but what a reasonable third party would have thought under the circumstances. However, evidence of the parties' intentions, as well as trade or industry practice, could well be relevant factors. On the facts of the case, the plaintiff never made any express statement as to the confidential nature of the ideas he was disclosing and the defendants gave evidence, which was accepted, that they did not regard the ideas disclosed as being in any way unique or confidential. Finally, the court said that the disclosure of the ideas at a social gathering rather than a business meeting was, in their view, an 'insuperable' objection to the existence of any obligation of confidence. Clearly each case will turn on its own facts, and there must be circumstances where even on social occasions an obligation of confidentiality in relation to commercial or technical information may arise by implication on the basis of the objective test. However, it is better on such occasions either to make an express statement, or, if the relationship continues over some period of time in relation to a particular project, to execute a formal confidentiality agreement.

Thirdly, there is the problem of industrial espionage. The extent to which industrial espionage can be prevented by the application of the law relating to the protection of confidential information is a vexed question. Clearly, here, express documentation is irrelevant, unless the 'spy' happens to be an employee or consultant who has signed a confidentiality agreement or undertaking which can be invoked to cover the particular piece of espionage.

Mere unauthorised accessing of confidential information is not of itself a criminal offence (see s 1 of the Theft Act 1968 and *Oxford v Moss* (1979) 68 Cr App R 183). However, a criminal offence may be committed if the item containing the relevant information (such as a file, or a floppy disk onto which information from a computer has been downloaded) is stolen, an ancillary offence like trespass, or breaking and entering, is committed in order to gain access to the information, or if information stored on a computer is obtained by accessing the computer in breach of the Computer Misuse Act 1990.

Further, where the information concerned has been copied (for instance, photocopying documents in a file), copyright law may provide a civil remedy.

In their Consultation Paper No 150 (published November 1997) the Law Commission have proposed that a new criminal offence should be created covering the misuse of trade secrets. This would be committed when any person used or disclosed a trade secret belonging to another without the other's consent. In the use of the phrase 'belonging to another', the Commission refers to the person who is entitled to the benefit of that secret. Consent to the use or disclosure of a trade secret should not amount to a defence if it was obtained by deception. However, one of the essential elements of the new offence would be that the defendant knew that the information was a trade secret belonging to another, and was aware that the other did (or might) not consent to its use or disclosure. However, no offence would be committed if the defendant believed that the person (or persons) to whom the information belonged would consent to the use or disclosure if such person or persons knew of the use or disclosure and the circumstances surrounding it.

The Commission proposes a public interest defence, and a defence where disclosure takes place under an obligation imposed by legislation, under a court order or in the course of legal proceedings, or in the lawful exercise of any official function relating to national security or the prevention, investigation or prosecution of crime.

The Commission proposes that innocent third parties, whether or not they receive the trade secret in return for payment, and whether or not they subsequently discover that is a trade secret belonging to another, should not be guilty of an offence if they use or disclose the relevant information provided that at the time they acquired the information they did not know it was a trade secret belonging to another, or were not aware that the other did (or might) not consent to its use or disclosure, or believed that the person or persons to whom the information belonged would consent to its use or disclosure if such person or persons knew of the use or disclosure and the circumstances surrounding it. The Commission also adds the proviso that, notwithstanding the foregoing, such third parties would still be liable for misuse under the offence, if they knew that the acquisition of the information by any other person from who they obtained it, either directly or indirectly, involved the commission of an indictable offence or an offence contrary to s 1 of the Computer Misuse Act 1990 (ie 'hacking').

If the new offence passes into law, it is clearly possible that concurrent civil proceedings and criminal proceedings could occur in relation to the same misuse. This will not happen in all cases, since the Commission proposes that no criminal proceedings should brought without the consent of the Director of

Public Prosecutions. However, the Commission proposes that where concurrent proceedings are brought the power of the court to stay civil proceedings, if criminal proceedings for the same matter are expected or have actually been commenced, should be extended to cover the new offence.

Finally the Commission has asked for views as to whether the law should be extended by making it an offence to acquire trade secrets, perhaps with the intention of using or disclosing them, or perhaps merely because they were acquired by wrongful means. Here the Commission has not made a firm proposal, but simply invited views.

The Commission's proposals would deal with most forms of industrial espionage, since the spy will in most cases either have acquired secrets so that he can use them himself or so that he can disclose them to a third party in return for payment. So far as the recipient of 'stolen' trade secrets is concerned, he will clearly wish to use or disclose them, and the only issue will be whether he is an innocent acquirer or not, in the terms discussed above.

The Commission have also very helpfully considered the question of the current civil remedies in relation to industrial espionage. Where the 'recipient' has obtained the confidential information through his own espionage, it seems fairly obvious that he has obtained it in circumstances where he knows that it was confidential and that the 'donor' did not intend him to disclose it or, indeed, to use it for any purpose whatsoever. In these circumstances, the general principles of law protecting confidential information should apply to bind the recipient.

The position is not so clear where a recipient of confidential information passes on that information to a third party (whether the information was obtained by industrial espionage, or disclosed to the recipient under a confidentiality obligation which he has subsequently breached).

Where the third party knows or ought to know that he is receiving information which is impressed with a duty of confidence then he too will be bound by that duty (see *Mustad v Dosen*, above, *Union Carbide Corporation v Naturin Ltd* [1987] FSR 538, and *Attorney-General v Guardian Newspapers (No 2)*, above). However, the authorities differ as to the situation where the third party is an innocent recipient.

Where the innocent third party has received the information without giving value for it, he is free to use it so long as he does not know it is confidential (see *Malone v Metropolitan Commissioner of Police* [1979] Ch 344 at 361B *per* Megarry VC), but when he later gets to know that the information is impressed with an obligation of confidentiality it appears that he can be restrained from its use or disclosure (*Fraser v Evans* [1969] 1 QB 349 and *British Steel Corporation v Granada Television Ltd* [1981] AC 1069) ('equity will not aid a volunteer').

However, where the innocent third party has given value, so that he is in a position of a *bona fide* purchaser for value without notice, there is some doubt on the position. Some commentators feel, on the analogy of the cases relating to equitable tracing of trust property disposed of in breach of trust, that he should be free to use or further disclose the information that he has innocently purchased (see *Phipps v Boardman* [1965] 2 WLR 839). Others disagree. There are *dicta* in various decisions to support both views, but no decision exactly on the point. The Law Commission, in their *Report on Breach of Confidence* (No 110, 1981), referred to above, felt that there was no certain authority on the point, but, as a matter of principle, such a third party should not be permitted to use or disclose the information, although he should be entitled to compensation from the original recipient who wrongfully disclosed it to him.

This approach seems logical in relation to commercial trade secrets, but perhaps not so desirable where technical information is concerned. In this case, perhaps the best solution would be to regard the innocent recipient of technical confidential information for value, as a general rule, to be subject to Megarry J's duty not to use without paying, rather than to the duty not to use at all (see *Coco v AN Clark (Engineers) Ltd*, above).

13.10 Precedent 1

Precedent 1 is long form comprehensive confidentiality agreement, which deals exhaustively with the matters normally covered in such agreements, including some which could well be implied into the agreement by the general law on confidentiality in any event. As will be seen from the recitals and cl 1(*a*), this precedent deals with a mutual exchange of confidential information for the purposes of the parties deciding whether to enter into a business relationship. The definition of the purpose can be replaced as required; for instance, for the purposes of negotiating an acquisition, or deciding whether to enter into a joint venture, or for the purposes of evaluating a product for purchase, or for manufacture under licence, and so on.

The definition of 'Confidential Information' in cl 1(*b*) is crucial. It will be seen that the definition is all encompassing, and covers any information disclosed to one party by the other, whether in writing, orally or visually (eg by means of manufacturing drawings) or by any other means (eg transmission of data electronically to a computer). In order to cover most of the possibilities, the definition goes on to specify certain classes of information, but these are merely examples within the all-inclusive definition. The definition then provides a series of exceptions covering information which is not to be regarded as falling within the definition of confidential information.

The definition is subject to a number of exceptions, which, mindful of the discussion above in relation to restraint of trade, are restatements of the general law imposed for clarity, but others are exclusions of information which the general law would or might arguably regard as confidential, but, which, for commercial reasons, the parties have elected not to treat as confidential at all. The primary aim of the latter exceptions is to remove the difficulties surrounding the cases on the general law relating to when information ceases to be confidential.

The first exception is a statement of the general law. It should be noted that the words often used in such an exception are 'public domain', but the use of either 'public knowledge and public property' or 'common knowledge' or 'public knowledge' is also common. Out of the possibilities, 'common knowledge' is probably better, since it covers the situation where the practitioners in a particular field are aware of the information, but the general public is not.

However, the definition leaves aside the question of what happens if the information becomes common knowledge through the wrongful act of the recipient. This at least enables the donor to keep his options open in terms of remedies. He may be able to get an injunction on the principles in *Peter Pan Manufacturing Corporation v Corsets Silhouette Ltd*, above, or only damages if the information has been used as a springboard on the principles in *Seager v Copydex Ltd (No 2)*, above.

The second exception has two purposes. First, it covers information which the receiving party already knew (unless he acquired it from the disclosing party subject to some previous confidentiality restriction). Secondly, it covers information which the recipient subsequently recreates by independent development. It is important to note that the wording of this exception throws the burden of proof on the recipient, and that this burden of proof is hard to discharge, particularly in the case of independent development. Here, realistically, the recipient can only show independent development if he has taken care that the development was carried out by personnel who had no access to the relevant information, and he gave them no hints based on his knowledge of that information. Some precedents actually go on to require that independent development, if it is to be a valid exception, must, in fact, have been carried on by such personnel, although in theory the additional condition is not strictly necessary, since the recipient will never be able to discharge the burden of proof if he uses personnel already 'contaminated' by contact with the information.

The combination of this exception with the first exception produces a way out of the dilemma posed for a recipient of a body of information which is partly public and partly private, particularly where he wants to use the private information as a springboard. The first exception permits him to use the public information, and the second exception at least permits him to use the so-called 'clean room' technique referred to in *Coco v AN Clark (Engineers) Ltd*, above, to recreate the private information independently, so that he is then free to use it.

The third and fourth exceptions concern information which is, to some degree, publicly available, but not yet common knowledge. The presence of these exceptions releases the recipient from confidentiality obligations in circumstances where the general law would not do so (see *Yates Circuit Foil Co v Electrofoils Ltd*, above). However, most draftsman include these exceptions as well as the 'common knowledge' exception as a matter of course, since, in general commercial terms, it is not fair for the recipient to continue to be bound in the circumstances covered by these exceptions.

Since many of the instances covered by these exceptions relate to disclosure by the donor himself, they provide a practical way of resolving the problem of whether publication by the donor, which does not make the information concerned common knowledge, nevertheless amounts to a waiver of confidentiality in respect of that information. However, they resolve it in favour of the recipient rather than the donor. Their absence would make it hard for the recipient to claim that a publication or disclosure by the donor, which did not make the information in question common knowledge, would release that information from the express obligations of confidentiality imposed under the agreement, unless it could fall within one of the other express exceptions set out in the agreement.

It should be noted that the first part of the third exception raises the question of whether the recipient is covered by the exception in respect of information which he actively searches for and eventually obtains from some publicly available source (such as a library or database, or even a third party patent specification). Since the recipient knows what the confidential information disclosed to him consists of, he will find it much easier to decide where to search with the best chance of finding the information from some publicly available but obscure source. Such use of the confidential information entrusted to him would probably be regarded as a misuse, and therefore a breach of his confidentiality obligations, but, for the avoidance of doubt, where this exception is included at all the prohibition in square brackets in cl 2(*a*)(iii) can be inserted.

It should be noted that the inclusion of the phrase in square brackets in the fourth exception provides a significant cutting down of the 'springboard' doctrine when the donor of confidential information puts a product embodying, or manufactured with the aid of that information, on the market. To the extent that such information is ascertainable by independent analysis or disassembly it will not (unless and until it becomes common knowledge) cease to be confidential, but to the extent that it is so ascertainable it can be argued that it is accessible to the public, and therefore will be released from the confidentiality obligations by the operation of this exception. In such case, the recipient of the information would be able to use it as a springboard without having to go to the expense of recreating it by independent analysis with the 'clean room' technique. In most cases, the phrases in square brackets should thus not be used, and reliance placed on the first exception above.

The fifth exception excludes information which was transmitted orally unless, within 30 days it is reduced to writing by the disclosing party and the relevant document is transmitted to the recipient with a statement confirming its confidential status. This is a common exception. In practice parties usually omit to confirm most disclosures of oral information in this way (except for very important and obvious situations) so that its inclusion means that oral information by and large will not be covered by the agreement. This provision is clearly a cutting down of the general equitable principles, which make no distinction between information disclosed orally or in writing or by any other means.

Many draftsmen regard this as desirable, because the evidentiary difficulties surrounding the transmission of oral information are such that it is in practice very difficult to enforce confidentiality obligations in respect of it, and, in any event, such an inclusion tends to prevent the free exchange of ideas between the parties.

The other view is that the inclusion of oral information within the protection of the agreement acts as a safeguard, and a backstop, in those cases where transmission can be proved, and that, in any case, there is nothing to stop the parties voluntarily reducing such oral information to writing and recording its transmission for evidentiary purposes if they so wish.

Finally, it should be noted that, if oral information is not covered, this tends to work against a party who has most confidential information to disclose (since there is a greater risk that he will disclose some vital piece of information orally) and in favour of the recipient (since he may receive the vital piece of information orally and thus not be bound by any confidentiality obligations).

The sixth exception covers information which is disclosed by the recipient with the consent of the disclosing party. This is probably no more than a truism, since the donor can hardly complain of breach of an obligation that has occurred with his permission, but is inserted out of an abundance of caution. Where there are two or more donors who are jointly entitled to deal with the information by disclosure or use as if they were co-owners of an asset, one 'co-owner' cannot prevent the other 'co-owner' from doing as he likes with the information, including disclosing it to a person to whom the first co-owner does not wish it to be disclosed (*Murray v Yorkshire Fund Managers Ltd* (1977) *The Times*, 18 December).

The seventh and final exception covers information which is disclosed without approval after the expiry of a stated period of time (often between three and five years) from the date of receipt.

This displaces the more general obligations in relation to the period for which information must be kept confidential at law. Equity does not impose a time limit beyond which information ceases to be subject to the obligations of confidentiality, but waits until the information has become public knowledge, or some other event has occurred which makes the continued imposition of the obligation no longer appropriate (see *Potters-Ballotini Ltd v Weston-Baker* and *Harrison v Project & Design Co (Redcar) Ltd*, above).

However, although in principle confidentiality obligations can last without limit of time (so that many draftsmen do not include the last part of this exception), in practice, after a period of time, which may vary depending on the circumstances, the information disclosed will become outdated or irrelevant, and the continued imposition of confidentiality obligations on the recipient becomes burdensome and unnecessary. In the interests of commercial efficiency, the parties should always consider whether the release of all obligations after a period of time is appropriate.

One difficulty with such provisions is the date from which the period in question should run. Some clauses start the period from the date of the agreement. This is satisfactory only if the information is disclosed within a relatively short period after the date of the agreement. If the information is disclosed over a long period of time, information disclosed later will be protected for an appreciably shorter period than that disclosed earlier. A period running from the date of receipt avoids this problem, but it does require that the date of receipt be ascertainable and recorded in respect of each item of information, and is most often impractical in respect of information orally disclosed. A compromise which is sometimes used (as in Precedent 2) is to estimate the length of time over which information will be disclosed, and to provide a period, running from the date of signature, which may be rather too long for information disclosed early, but satisfactory for information disclosed later.

Lastly, there is one circumstance, specified in the final proviso to cl 1, which restricts the operation of the exceptions themselves.

It is possible to combine different pieces of information and come up with a novel concept. Information relating to this combination should itself be protectable as confidential information, even if the underlying pieces of information are not. 'Something that has been constructed from materials in the public domain may possess the necessary quality of confidentiality: for something new and confidential may have been brought into being by the application of the skill and ingenuity of the human brain. Novelty depends upon the thing itself and not upon the quality of its constituent parts. Indeed, often the more striking the novelty the more commonplace its components' (*per* Megarry J, in *Coco v AN Clark (Engineers) Ltd*, above) (see also *Mustad v Dosen* and *Terrapin Ltd v Builders' Supply Co (Hayes) Ltd*, above, in particular as to the distinction between features and ancillary secrets, although here the information relating to the combination would more likely be a feature or features of another product than ancillary secrets).

For instance, the manufacturer of certain components could disclose confidential information about those components, and about a way of putting them together to achieve a particular purpose. If he later markets some or all of those components then the features of those components will presumably become common knowledge once the components are marketed on a reasonably wide scale to the extent that they can be ascertained by visual inspection. However, even though the features of all of the components become common knowledge, he should not thereby be freed from the restrictions relating to information on the way to combine them for the relevant purpose, if this still remains secret, and this is what the final proviso to the exceptions provides.

It is arguable that this proviso is unnecessary, since, by definition, if the information relating to the combination remains secret, it should still be protected by the agreement, even if the underlying items of information are not. However, in cases where the issue is of particular relevance this proviso should be included to put the matter beyond all doubt.

Clause 2 establishes the document as a contract rather than an undertaking providing consideration based on the mutual exchange of information between the parties. The clause then goes on to impose the standard confidentiality obligations, to use only for the permitted purpose and not to disclose to third parties, other than employees who have a need to know in connection with the permitted purpose, provided that they, in turn, are required by their contracts of employment to keep such information confidential.

Since this is a contract rather than an undertaking, cl 2(*b*) also imposes restrictions on copying or reproducing disclosed information, and cll 2(*c*) and (*d*) require the recipient to be responsible for any unauthorised disclosure of information by its employees and to enforce the obligations of confidentiality contained in their contracts of employment in order to prevent this. For the same reason, cl 2(*e*) imposes an express standard of care for safeguarding disclosed information.

Finally, the clause ends with a proviso permitting disclosure of information to the extent required by law, but imposing a duty to consult with the donor before disclosure.

Clause 3, again because the document is a contract, imposes obligations on the recipient of information to return it when the permitted purpose has been completed.

Clause 4(*a*) makes it clear that the disclosure of confidential information does not by implication confer the grant of a licence either to use the information other than for the permitted purpose or to use any intellectual property rights relating to the information. Clause 4(*b*) gives a warranty that each party has the right to disclose the relevant information to the other and to authorise the other to use it for the permitted purpose. Again it is arguable that this clause is not strictly necessary, but where one is dealing with confidential information which can be exploited commercially (eg a disclosure of know-how for preliminary evaluation so that the recipient can decide whether to take a licence for commercial exploitation) it is good practice to include this clause to avoid any misunderstandings.

The remaining clauses cover the requirement to keep the fact of the agreement itself confidential (cl 5); make provision for the service of notices (cl 6), and for termination, but subject to survival of the obligations of confidentiality imposed on information already disclosed (cl 7); prohibit assignment, which is vital in such agreements, since permission to assign would be equivalent to a grant to disclose information to third parties without restriction (cl 8); and set out a whole agreement and governing law and jurisdiction clause (cl 9).

It should be noted that if the wording in square brackets is included in cl 9 this would make clear that the agreement displaced the general principles of equity. This should cause no problems in relation to restraint of trade since, as discussed above, the agreement in fact either mirrors the equitable principles or is more restrictive than they are.

Finally, this precedent contemplates the possibility that the parties will (as is not uncommon) have started the exchange of confidential information before they have thought to sign an agreement. Information exchanged before signature is protected to the extent that it is listed in the Schedule.

13.11 Precedent 2

Precedent 2 is a shorter form of confidentiality agreement, which shows a slightly different way of dealing with the issues covered in more detail by Precedent 1. It should be read in the light of the commentary on Precedent 1, and the following points noted.

The precedent protects oral information. The exceptions to the definition of confidential information are shorter and simpler, and there is no provision specifically protecting secret information relating to combinations of items of unprotected information.

There is no obligation to enforce obligations of confidentiality which bind employees of the recipient under their contracts of employment. There is no disclaimer clause.

A whole agreement, jurisdiction and choice of law clause has been omitted, on the basis that this is not necessary where both the parties are resident in the same jurisdiction, and that it can be added where required.

The omission of the whole agreement clause and any language expressly excluding the operation of the general equitable principles makes it theoretically possible, although unlikely, that a donor under this agreement could claim not only the protection of the contract but also that of the general principles in appropriate cases. Clearly such ambiguity favours the donor rather than the recipient, and is probably to be avoided if one is acting for the recipient. In appropriate cases, the relevant language from cl 9 of Precedent 1 could be added.

Finally, the agreement makes no provision for the protection of information disclosed prior to its signature.

It is of course possible to combine clauses from Precedents 1 and 2 to make a hybrid agreement of the required degree of complexity and completeness if desired.

13.12 Precedent 3

Precedent 3 is a confidentiality undertaking, as opposed to an agreement, on a mutual basis. It can be seen that this is a much shorter and simpler document, in keeping with the need to produce evidence of the receipt of information on a basis of confidentiality so as to trigger the relevant general equitable principles to protect that information. However, the general principles upon which the documents have been drawn up are no different from those upon which Precedents 1 and 2 are based.

It should be noted that Precedent 3 covers oral information, and protects information disclosed both before and after the date of its signature.

Given that the document is not a contract, the provisions relating to delivery up and safeguarding of the information have to be dealt with somewhat differently. The approach is to focus on the concept of bailment. The recipient of the information is regarded as the bailee of the documents and other items in which information is embodied. He acknowledges this fact, and that, as bailee, he must keep them safely, and return them on demand. So far as copying the information is concerned, this is covered at the beginning of the precedent (para 2(1)) by a blanket prohibition. It is probably unnecessary to include this, since, so far as the law of copyright protects the information, the recipient will have no permission to copy the information unless the disclosing party specifically gives it to him, but it does no harm to include the provision to avoid inadvertent copying.

13.13 Precedent 4

Precedent 4 is a unilateral confidentiality undertaking. It is based on Precedent 3, but it is even simpler since it ignores the concept of bailment. It is purely a document which provides evidence of the disclosure of information in confidence, in order to satisfy the test in *Coco v AN Clark (Engineers) Ltd*, above.

Precedent 1

Long form confidentiality agreement

THIS AGREEMENT is made the [   ] day of [   ]
19[   ] by and between [   ] of [   ] of the one part
and [   ] of [   ] of the other part.

WHEREAS:

(A) The parties, for their mutual benefit, may have exchanged and wish further to exchange certain information (including but not limited to trade secrets and proprietary know-how) in order that [each of them may evaluate such information for the purpose of determining their respective interest in establishing a business relationship between them].

(B) The parties wish to define their rights with respect to the said information and to protect the confidentiality thereof and proprietary features contained therein.

NOW IT IS HEREBY AGREED AS FOLLOWS:

1 Definitions

In this Agreement the following expressions shall have the following meanings:

    (*a*) 'Purpose' shall mean any discussions and negotiations between or within the parties concerning or in connection with [the establishment of a business relationship between the parties];

    (*b*) 'Confidential Information' shall mean all information or data disclosed (whether in writing, orally or by any other means) to one party by the other party or by a third party on behalf of the other party and shall include but not be limited to (A) any information ascertainable by the inspection or analysis of samples, (B) the information described in the Schedule hereto as having been disclosed prior to the date hereof and

(C) any information relating to that party's business, operations, processes, plans, intentions, product information, know-how, design rights, trade secrets, software, market opportunities, customers and business affairs, but shall exclude any part of such disclosed information or data which:

(i) which is or becomes [in the public domain] [public knowledge and public property] [common knowledge] in any way without breach of this Agreement by the receiving party; or

(ii) which the receiving party can show (A) was in its possession or known to it by being in its use or being recorded in its files or computers or other recording media prior to receipt from the disclosing party and was not previously acquired by the receiving party from the disclosing party under an obligation of confidence; or (B) to have been developed by or for the receiving party at any time independently of the information disclosed to it by the disclosing party; or

(iii) which is hereafter disclosed or made available to the receiving party from a source other than the disclosing party without breach by the receiving party or such source of any obligation of confidentiality or non-use towards the disclosing party; or

(iv) which is hereafter [made generally available by the disclosing party or a third party or is] disclosed by the disclosing party to a third party without restriction on disclosure or use, including, without limitation, by way of the publication of a patent specification; or

(v) which is disclosed orally unless it is identified as confidential at the time of disclosure and confirmed as such in writing by the disclosing party within 30 days of disclosure; or

(vi) which is disclosed by the receiving party [   ] with the prior written approval of the disclosing party; or

(vii) in respect of which a period of [   ] years has elapsed from the date of [receipt thereof] [signature of this agreement];

provided however that the foregoing exceptions shall not apply to information relating to any combination of features or any combination of items of information merely because information relating to one or more of the relevant individual features or one or more of the relevant items (but not the combination itself) falls within any one or more of such exceptions.

2 Handling of confidential information

In consideration of the mutual exchange and disclosure of Confidential Information, each party undertakes in relation to the other party's Confidential Information:

(*a*) to maintain the same in confidence and to use it only for the Purpose and for no other purpose and in particular, but without prejudice to the generality of the foregoing, (i) not to make any commercial use thereof

(ii) not to use the same for the benefit of itself or of any third party other than pursuant to a further agreement with the other party [and (iii) not to use the same for the purpose of guiding or conducting a search of any information, materials or sources, whether or not available to the public, for any purpose whatsoever, including, without limitation, for the purpose of demonstrating that any information falls within one of the exceptions in cl 1];

(b) not to copy reproduce or reduce to writing any part thereof except as may be reasonably necessary for the Purpose and that any copies reproductions or reductions to writing so made shall be the property of the disclosing party;

(c) not to disclose the same whether to its employees or to third parties except in confidence to such of its employees or directors who need to know the same for the Purpose and that (i) such employees and directors are obliged by their contracts of employment or service not to disclose the same, and (ii) the receiving party shall enforce such obligations at its expense and at the request of the disclosing party in so far as breach thereof relates to the disclosing party's Confidential Information;

(d) to be responsible for the performance of subcll (a), (b) and (c) above on the part of its employees or directors to whom the same is disclosed pursuant to subcl (c) above; and

(e) to apply thereto no lesser security measures and degree of care than those which the receiving party applies to its own confidential or proprietary information and which the receiving party warrants as providing adequate protection of such information from unauthorised disclosure, copying or use.

Notwithstanding the foregoing, the receiving party shall be entitled to make any disclosure required by law of the other party's Confidential Information, but shall give the other party not less than two business days' notice of such disclosure and shall consult with the disclosing party prior to such disclosure [with a view to avoiding such disclosure [if reasonably practicable] [if legally possible]].

3 Return of confidential information
Each party shall:

(a) within one month of completion of the Purpose or receipt of a written request from the other party, return to the other party all documents and materials (and all copies thereof) containing the other party's Confidential Information and certify in writing to the other party that it has complied with the requirements of this subclause; and

(b) notwithstanding completion of the Purpose or return of documents and materials as aforesaid, continue to be bound by the undertakings set out in cl 2.

4 Disclaimer and warranty

(*a*) Each party reserves all rights in its Confidential Information and no rights or obligations other than those expressly recited herein are granted or to be implied from this Agreement. In particular, no licence is hereby granted directly or indirectly under any patent, invention, discovery, copyright or other industrial property right now or in the future held, made, obtained or licensable by either party.

(*b*) Each party warrants its right to disclose its Confidential Information to the other party and to authorise the other party to use the same for the Purpose.

5 Confidentiality

Each party agrees to keep the existence and nature of this Agreement confidential and not to use the same or the name of the other party (or of any other company in the Group of Companies of which the other party forms part) in any publicity, advertisement or other disclosure with regard to this Agreement without the prior written consent of the other party.

6 Notices

All notices under this Agreement shall be in writing and shall be sent by telex, facsimile or first-class registered or recorded delivery post to the party being served at its address specified above or at such other address of which such party shall have given notice as aforesaid, and marked for the attention of that party's signatory of this Agreement. The date of service shall be deemed to be the day following the day on which the notice was transmitted or posted as the case may be.

7 Termination

This Agreement shall continue in force from the date hereof until terminated by mutual consent or by either party by giving to the other not less than one month's prior notice. The provisions of cll 1, 2 and 3 shall survive any such termination.

8 Non-assignment

This Agreement is personal to the parties and shall not be assigned or otherwise transferred in whole or in part by either party without the prior written consent of the other party.

9 Entire agreement, governing law and jurisdiction

This Agreement constitutes the entire Agreement and understanding between the parties in respect of Confidential Information and supersedes all previous agreements, understandings and undertakings in such respect [and all obligations implied by law to the extent that they conflict with the express provisions of this Agreement]. This Agreement cannot be changed except by written agreement between the parties. The interpretation construction and effect of this Agreement shall be governed and construed in all respects in accordance with the laws of England and the parties hereby submit to the non-exclusive jurisdiction of the English courts.

SCHEDULE
Confidential Information disclosed prior to the date of this Agreement
Description and Disclosing Party

AS WITNESS this Agreement has been signed on behalf of each party by its duly authorised representative the day and year first above written.

SIGNED for and on behalf of

Authorised Signatory

Title

SIGNED for and on behalf of

Authorised Signatory

Title

Short form confidentiality agreement

THIS AGREEMENT is made the [   ] day of [   ]
19[   ]
BETWEEN [   ] of [   ] of the one part and
[   ] of [   ] of the other part.

WHEREAS the parties, for their mutual benefit, may have exchanged and wish further to exchange certain information of a confidential nature and wish to protect such information in the manner set out in this Agreement.

NOW IT IS HEREBY AGREED AS FOLLOWS:

1 Definitions

1.1 'Purpose' shall mean any discussions and negotiations between or within the parties concerning or in connection with the establishment of a business relationship between the parties.

1.2 'Confidential Information' shall mean any information or data relating to [   ] or to a party's business or affairs (including but not limited to software and information ascertainable by the inspection or analysis of samples) disclosed whether in writing, orally or by any other means to one party by the other party or by a third party on behalf of the other party, whether before or after the date of this Agreement, but shall exclude any part of such disclosed information or data which:
1.2.1 is or becomes common knowledge without breach of this Agreement by the receiving party;
1.2.2 the receiving party can show (*a*) was in its possession or known to it by being in its use or being recorded in its files or computers or other recording media prior to receipt from the disclosing party and was not previously ac-

quired by the receiving party from the disclosing party under an obligation of confidence, or (*b*) to have been developed by or for the receiving party at any time independently of any information disclosed to it by the disclosing party; or

1.2.3 the receiving party obtains or has available from a source other than the disclosing party without breach by the receiving party or such source of any obligation of confidentiality or non-use towards the disclosing party; or

1.2.4 is hereafter disclosed by the disclosing party to a third party without restriction on disclosure or use; or

1.2.5 is disclosed by the receiving party (*a*) with the prior written approval of the disclosing party [, or (*b*) without such approval, after a period of [seven] years from the date of signature of this agreement].

2 Handling of confidential information

The receiving party shall maintain the other party's Confidential Information in confidence and shall exercise in relation thereto no lesser security measures and degree of care than those which the receiving party applies to its own confidential information which the receiving party warrants as providing adequate protection against unauthorised disclosure, copying or use. The receiving party shall ensure that disclosure of such Confidential Information is restricted to those employees or directors of the receiving party having the need to know the same for the Purpose. Copies or reproductions shall not be made except to the extent reasonably necessary for the Purpose and all copies made shall be the property of the disclosing party. All Confidential Information and copies thereof shall be returned to the disclosing party within 30 days of receipt of a written request from the disclosing party.

3 Limitations and warranty

3.1 The receiving party shall (i) not divulge the other party's Confidential Information, in whole or in part, to any third party, (ii) use the same only for the Purpose, and (iii) make no commercial use of the same or any part thereof without the prior written consent of the disclosing party. Notwithstanding the foregoing, the receiving party shall be entitled to make any disclosure required by law of the other party's Confidential Information provided that it gives the other party not less than two business days' notice of such disclosure.

3.2 Each party warrants its right to disclose its Confidential Information to the other party and to authorise the other party to use the same for the Purpose.

4 Notices

All notices under this Agreement shall be in writing, sent by telex, facsimile or first-class registered or recorded delivery post to the party being served at its address specified above or at such other address of which such party shall have given notice as aforesaid, and marked for the attention of that party's signatory of this Agreement. The date of service shall be deemed to be the day following the day on which the notice was transmitted or posted as the case may be.

5 Termination

This Agreement shall continue in force from the date hereof until terminated by mutual consent or by either party by giving to the other not less than one month's prior notice. The provisions of cll 1, 2 and 3 shall survive any such termination.

6 Non-assignment

This Agreement is personal to the parties and shall not be assigned or otherwise transferred in whole or in part by either party without the prior written consent of the other party.

AS WITNESS this Agreement has been signed on behalf of each party by its duly authorised representative as of the day and year first above written.

SIGNED for and on behalf of

Authorised Signatory

Title

SIGNED for and on behalf of

Authorised Signatory

Title

Precedent 3

Mutual confidentiality undertaking

---

1 We [   ] of [   ] and [   ] of
[   ] each hereby respectively acknowledge that the other party
has provided, and has agreed to provide in future, to us information of a confidential or proprietary nature relating to [   ] for the purpose of
[   ].

2 We each agree that in respect of the information as detailed in para (1) received from the other party we will:
  (i)   treat it as confidential and make no copies thereof;
  (ii) not disclose it to any third party without the prior written consent of the
        other party; and
  (iii) use it solely for the purpose set out above.

3 We each further acknowledge that:-
  (*a*) the requirements of para (2) shall not apply to any part of the informa-
       tion supplied by the other party which:
       (i) is or becomes common knowledge without breach of this undertak-
            ing by us; or
       (ii) can be shown to have been in our lawful possession prior to receipt
            from the other party or to have been developed by or for us at any
            time independently of any disclosure by the other party;
  (*b*) all documents and other material things embodying any of the informa-
       tion as detailed in para (1) which are received from the other party shall
       remain the property of the other party (or other owner thereof) and the
       party receiving the same shall hold them as bailee for the other party,
       exercising reasonable care to keep them safe from access by unauthor-
       ised persons, and shall return them to the other party within one month
       of receipt of a written request from the other party.

SIGNED for and on behalf of

Authorised Signatory

Title

Date

SIGNED for and on behalf of

Authorised Signatory

Title

Date

Precedent 4

Unilateral confidentiality undertaking

---

1 We [   ] of [   ] hereby acknowledge that
[   ] of [   ] ('the Company') has agreed to provide
to us confidential or proprietary information relating to [   ] for
the purpose of [   ].

2 We agree that, in respect of all such information we will:
    (i) treat it as confidential;
    (ii) not disclose it to any third party without the prior written consent of the
       Company; and
    (iii) use it solely for the purpose set out in (1).

3 The requirements of para (2) shall not apply to any part of the information
supplied by the Company which:
    (i) is or becomes common knowledge without breach of this undertaking
      by us;
    (ii) was in our lawful possession prior to receipt from the Company or de-
      veloped by or for us at any time independently of any disclosure by the
      Company.

SIGNED for and
on behalf of

                     Authorised Signatory

                     Title

Chapter 14

Employment contracts

14.1 Introduction

This chapter deals with some of the issues surrounding contracts of employment which are of particular interest to the draftsman of commercial contracts. It cannot, however, deal in any depth with the specialised subject of industrial relations and employment law, which has grown to such an extent of complexity over the last 25 years that it is now regarded as a branch of the law in its own right, rather than, as used to be the case, a small part of commercial law in general, often known under the term of 'master and servant'.

There is also in this chapter no discussion of two other important issues surrounding employment—the definition of an employee as opposed to an independent contractor (for a discussion on this issue reference should be made to Chapter 3); and the question of transfer of employment upon the sale of a business (for a discussion on this subject reference should be made to Chapters 9 and 11).

14.2 The contract of employment

The relation between employer and employee has been likened to one of status, rather than one based on contract, in that, although the decision to enter into the contract of employment is obviously a voluntary one on both sides, once the decision is taken the relationship is governed not purely by the terms of the contract, but also by complex legislation which in many cases overrides the contract irrespective of the intention of the parties. The truth in fact lies somewhere between the two extremes, and the relevance of the actual terms of the contract of employment, whether express or implied, is clearly of vital importance.

So far as the contract of employment itself is concerned, most employees do not have formal written documents which are in the fullest sense contracts of employment containing exhaustively all of the terms and conditions relating to their employment, nor is there any statutory requirement that a contract of employment must be in writing in order to be enforceable.

In these cases, the contract will be made up from a variety of sources, such as an offer letter from the employer, an acceptance letter from the employee; terms to be implied by statute or the common law; custom and practice which has the effect of creating an implied term in a particular type of employment or industry; and collective agreements, codes of practice, and the employer's own standing instructions and procedures (such as works or office rules, disciplinary or grievance procedures and so on), which are, in some way or other, incorporated into the contract of employment so as to become part of its terms.

Such employees, who are employed for periods of more than one month, have, however, under s 1 of the Employment Rights Act 1996, the right to be provided with a written statement from their employer setting out the major terms of their employment, within two months of the commencement of that employment.

The employees most likely to have such full and formal contracts of employment are senior or key employees, particularly at board level, where it is of importance to both parties to specify clearly the rights and obligations of the relationship, particularly in the areas of competition, confidentiality and rights in inventions, and to rely as little as possible on terms implied by law. Such contracts are often entered into for fixed terms (at least an initial fixed term) because again both parties are interested in securing the stability of a long-term relationship.

Since the contract should deal in more detail with all of the matters which would otherwise be dealt with in a written statement of terms of employment, the contract of itself provides all of the information required under ss 1–7 of the Employment Rights Act 1996, and in effect constitutes the statement required under the Act, so that an additional statement is unnecessary, provided that the employee is given a copy of the contract within two months of the commencement of his employment, which will of course normally be the case in any event.

14.3   Confidential information and intellectual property rights

One of the areas in which employers need to take special care is the protection of intellectual property rights and confidential information which are either obtained by employees from their employers in the course of their employment, or generated by employees for their employers in the course of their employment.

As discussed in Chapter 13, where an employer discloses trade secrets or confidential information to an employee, so that the employee can make use of them in discharging the duties of his employment, or where the employee generates trade secrets or confidential information in the course of his employment, the circumstances imply an obligation of confidentiality, even if nothing is expressly stated to this effect.

So long as the employee is in employment he owes a duty to his employer (which may be based in some instances partly on the equitable principles protecting confidentiality, but in all cases arises out of the duty of loyalty or fidelity owed to the employer, which is implied in the contract of employment both in equity and under the common law) not to disclose any of his employer's confidential information to third parties or to use it for his own private gain (*Hivac Ltd v Park Royal Scientific Instruments Ltd* [1946] Ch 169).

However, the situation appears to change once the employee leaves employment. The leading case (*Faccenda Chicken Ltd v Fowler* [1986] ICR 297, CA) classifies information obtained by an employee during his employment into three classes. The first is information which is so obviously public, or of such a trivial nature, that no one could reasonably consider that the parties meant to treat it as confidential. The second is confidential information which, although acquired in the course of employment and protected while the employment subsists, is not deserving of such protection after its termination. It is clear that, both in this and subsequent cases, protection of confidential information of the second class is not based on the law relating to confidentiality. Instead protection is granted indirectly through the application of the duty of loyalty or fidelity under the principles in and therefore protected under *Hivac Ltd v Park Royal Scientific Instruments Ltd*, above. This is why such confidential information ceases to be 'protected' when employment ceases. The third class is information generated or acquired in the course of employment which can be said to be the 'property' of the employer, which *Faccenda* termed 'trade secrets' ('information of a sufficiently high degree of confidentiality as to amount to a trade secret') and which the employee is not entitled to use for his own account or to disclose either during his employment or after it has terminated. In this case, the law relating to confidential information gives protection to these trade secrets both during the employment and after its termination. It is, however, also true that, during employment such trade secrets are also granted overlapping protection under the duty of loyalty or fidelity.

The reason why the court in *Faccenda* refused to protect confidential information falling within the second class after the termination of employment can be found in the fact that the courts are generally against situations which prevent free trading, and do not favour restrictions which prevent employees moving freely from job to job. They will thus not prevent an employee from using the know-how and expertise, the experience, that he has acquired while working with one employer when he leaves to work for someone else. Thus, they will not extend the protection of the law of confidentiality to such information as a matter of public policy.

The distinction between the two classes of confidential information is thus largely irrelevant during the subsistence of employment, but is vital once employment has terminated. In *Faccenda* itself, Neill LJ said: 'It is clearly impossible to provide a list of matters which will qualify as trade secrets or their equivalent. Secret processes of manufacture provide obvious examples, but innumerable other pieces of information are *capable* of being trade secrets.' A number of cases since *Faccenda* have been useful in providing some guidelines as to this distinction.

In *Lansing Linde Ltd v Kerr* [1991] 1 WLR 251, Staughton LJ discussed the definition of trade secret in *Faccenda* and said 'This is my preferred view of the meaning of trade secret in this context. It must be information used in the trade or business, and, secondly, the owner must limit the dissemination of it or at least not encourage or permit widespread publication ... It can thus include not only secret formulae for the manufacture of products but also, in an appropriate case, the names of customers and the goods which they buy.'

An approach similar to *Faccenda* was recently taken in Scotland in the Court of Session in *Oil Technics Ltd v Thistle Chemicals Ltd* 1997 [SLT] 416, which related to the protection by obligations of confidentiality of a chemical formula.

A most illuminating discussion of this distinction can be found in *Lancashire Fires Ltd v Lyons* [1996] FSR 629, by contrasting the different approaches at first instance and in the Court of Appeal. At first instance, Carnwath J found that the defendant employee was not in breach of any obligation of confidentiality after the termination of his employment with the plaintiff because the relevant confidential information fell within the second class of *Faccenda* not the third class. He found that the plaintiff believed his information to be confidential, but then continued:

> 'However, such a subjective approach cannot in my view be conclusive ... There must be something which is not only objectively a trade secret, but which was known, or ought to have been known, to both parties to be so. The normal presumption is that information which the employee has obtained in the ordinary course of employment, without specific steps such as memorising particular documents, is information which he is free to take away and use in alternative employment ... [The plaintiff's] concern was direct competition [by the defendant] in the precise field in which he was engaged, but in the absence of a covenant against competition he had no power to restrain him.'

Although the Court of Appeal in large measure agreed with Carnwath J's explanation of the law of confidentiality between employer and employee, they disagreed on one important point, which made them find for the plaintiff. Sir Thomas Bingham MR said: 'The basic reason why we disagree is that we think the judge took too strict a view of the degree of precision required of an employer in defining and pointing out what he seeks to protect as a trade secret.' Earlier in his judgment he set out some guidelines as to the definition of the distinction between the two classes of confidential information:

> 'In [*Faccenda*] the court drew attention to some of the matters which must be considered ... the nature of the employment; the nature of the information itself; the steps (if any) taken by the employer to impress on the employee the confidentiality of the information; and the ease or difficulty of isolating the information in question from other information which the employee is free to use or disclose ... these are all very relevant matters ... the nearer an employee is to the inner councils of the employer, the more likely he is to gain access to truly confidential information.
>
> The nature of the information itself is also important: to be capable of protection, information must be defined with some degree of precision; and an employer will have great difficulty in obtaining protection for his business methods and practices. If an employer impresses the confidentiality of certain information on his employee that is an indication of the employer's belief that the information is confidential, a fact which is not irrelevant ... But much will depend on the circumstances. These may be such as to show that information is. or is being treated as, confidential; and it would be unrealistic to expect a small and informal organisation to adopt the same business disciplines as a larger and more bureaucratic concern. It is plain that if an employer is to succeed in protecting information as confidential he must succeed in showing that it does not form part of an employee's own stock of knowledge, skill and experience. The distinction [in *Faccenda*] between information in ... class 2 and information in ... class 3 may often on the facts be very hard to draw, but ultimately the court must judge whether an ex-employee has illegitimately used the confidential information which forms part of the stock-in-trade of his former employer ... or whether he has simply used his own professional expertise, gained in whole or in part during his former employment.
>
> In our view [on the facts of this case, the defendant] must have known the central processing unit comprising the mould technology and use was confidential to the plaintiff and not to be divulged to competitors. We do not accept that it is incumbent upon an employer to point out to his employee the precise limits of that which he seeks to protect as confidential. The limits are not easy to draw even with the assistance of expert witnesses. But we have no doubt that all the employees, [the defendant] more than most, knew that the central processing unit embodied a process which might fairly be regarded as a trade secret which belonged to the plaintiff and not to each of them as part of their respective personal knowledge and skill.'

Although *Faccenda* concerned a case where there was no express term restricting the use and disclosure of confidential information after the termination of employment, the inference to be drawn from the principles on which the decision was based is that, even if there had been an express term, it would not have been enforceable in respect of any information other than that falling within the first category of trade secrets.

This point was discussed further in *Lancashire Fires*. At first instance, Goulding J had suggested that the second class of information could be protected after employment had terminated if the employer had inserted an express confidentiality undertaking to this effect. The Court of Appeal disagreed with this suggestion and drew attention to the principle stated in *Herbert Morris v Saxelby* [1961] AC 688 that a restrictive covenant is not enforceable 'unless the protection sought is reasonably necessary to protect a trade secret or to prevent some personal influence over customers being abused in order to entice them away'. Thus, imposing an express confidentiality undertaking on information of the second class (in respect of which the court is not willing to imply an obligation under the law of confidentiality) in fact amounts to a disguised covenant not to compete. Clearly there may be circumstances where a bare covenant binding an employee not to compete after the termination of employment may be enforceable, and, if this is so, then in a sense confidential information of the second class in *Faccenda* will indirectly be protected for the duration of the covenant. However, in this case the covenant will stand or fall on considerations relating to restraint of trade (see section 14.4 below) and the law relating to the protection of confidential information will be irrelevant.

Given that the law of confidentiality does not always provide the desired solution, employers should not neglect other areas of the law in trying to protect their interests. Even items of information which are publicly available can be reserved for the exclusive use of the employer through the operation of the law on patents, copyright and registered designs. In the areas where these branches of the law operate, they can overlap the law of confidentiality, and help to provide greater protection.

The Patents Act 1977 provides that when an employee is specifically employed to create inventions, or he is of such a high status within the employing organisation (eg executive director or general manager) that he should be considered as responsible for the well-being of the organisation as a whole, then any invention he makes in the course of his employment will belong to his employer. If such an employee makes an invention, outside the course of his employment, or any other employee makes an invention, whether inside or outside the course of his employment, then that invention belongs to the employee.

Employees cannot give up their rights under the Act, and, in any situation where an employer takes advantage of an invention of 'outstanding importance' made by an employee, irrespective of to whom it belongs, the employee has a right under the Act to fair and reasonable compensation from the employer.

The Copyright Designs and Patents Act 1988 protects copyright works and designs to which the Patents Act does not apply. All such works and designs created by an employee in the course of his employment belong to the employer.

Although the general law can be invoked to protect the employer's rights, he should not simply rely on calling the law in aid when a problem arises. He should try to ensure protection in advance, by providing relevant clauses in the contract of employment.

First of all the contract of employment should spell out the obligation of the employee to keep confidential his employer's confidential information, whether commercial or technical, both during the course of employment, and (subject to *Faccenda Chicken Ltd v Fowler*, above) afterwards. The obligations should cover not only prohibitions on unauthorised disclosure, but also on the employee turning the information to his own or a third party's use or benefit. Although such provisions are no more than a statement of the general law they do serve to show beyond any doubt that the employee has accepted obligations of confidentiality when taking employment, and also to bring the need to observe confidentiality to the employee's attention.

Where an invention covered by the Patents Act 1977 is concerned, if it belongs to the employer, then all relevant patents, copyright and designs throughout the world also belong to the employer. If the invention belongs to the employee, such rights also belong to the employee. The contract of employment cannot change the situation by its provisions, and to this extent is irrelevant. However, where dealing with inventions owned by the employer, some foreign laws may not recognise the provisions of the Patents Act, and it is then useful to be able to show a specific provision in the contract of employment giving the ownership of worldwide rights in the invention to the employer. The contract of employment will also contain the obligation for the employee to sign or seal all further documents necessary to enable the employer to register his rights worldwide.

The same arguments for putting provisions in the contract of employment apply to copyright works and designs created in the course of employment, which are not inventions, and are caught only by the Copyright Designs and Patents Act 1988.

It is also important that the employee discloses the existence of inventions and other information which properly belong to his employer, so that patents can be taken out and the information otherwise protected. Although such an obligation to disclose is probably implied into the contract of employment as part of the employee's obligations of loyalty, it is wise to include an express provision to this effect in the employee's contract.

The position of consultants or independent contractors under a contract for the supply of services is somewhat different from that of employees, and requires some mention. Unlike employees they are untouched by the legislation (except for designs—s 215(1) of the 1988 Act provides that designs created in the course of a commission vest in the person commissioning the design), nor does the common law impose obligations in favour of the customer for whom they supply their services. Thus absent a special agreement to the contrary, they will own the intellectual property rights in inventions and copyright works created in the course of their assignments. However, the 1988 Act permits the customer to provide in the contract that all rights in inventions, copyright works and designs, created during the course of the assignment, should belong to him rather than the consultant or independent contractor. It is therefore up to the customer to impose obligations under the contract for the supply of services, in relation to ownership of intellectual property rights and the protection of confidential information, on a basis to be agreed between the parties.

It is important to note that the law of confidentiality will not automatically impose obligations of confidentiality on the consultant in respect of all information he generates or receives from the hirer, although it may do so. Therefore the contract for the supply of services must take care to provide for this aspect as well.

A further area which causes problems is that of suggestion schemes and unsolicited suggestions. The rules of a suggestion scheme must make very clear that any ideas or inventions that employees put forward will become the property of the employer, to be used by him as he sees fit, provided he pays out to the employee the various rewards in accordance with the scheme. Otherwise, the employer may well find himself bound not to use suggestions without first paying substantial compensation.

Where the suggestion covers something which the employer has already been working on, so that he is already in possession of the information to which the suggestion relates, the rules should provide that the employer is not bound to provide a reward. The provisions of the Patents Act on inventions by employees are not inconsistent with suggestion schemes, since even where an employee owns an invention made in the course of his employment, the Act permits him to come to an arrangement with his employer, once the invention has been made, to allow the employer to exploit the invention, in return for some reward. By putting forward his invention under the suggestion scheme, he signifies that he is satisfied to take only the rewards under the scheme.

Once the employer accepts unsolicited inventions or suggestions from an employee, he may find, if he later exploits some similar idea, that he will not be able to escape paying compensation to the employee, unless he can show that he has originated his idea independently, and, if possible, before he received the unsolicited suggestions. In most cases unsolicited suggestions should be returned immediately, preferably unopened and unread, unless their originator is willing to sign a disclaimer.

14.4   Covenants restricting an employee's right to compete

Equity imposes on an employee a general duty of loyalty and honesty towards his employer, and the common law implies a general term in the term of the contract of employment that the employee will perform his duties under the contract honestly.

The impact of this on his obligations in relation to his employer's confidential information has been discussed earlier (see *Hivac Ltd v Park Royal Scientific Instruments Ltd*, above). However, the principles are of much wider application. The employee must behave honestly (*Bell v Lever Bros Ltd* [1932] AC 161, HL), he must not take bribes or make secret profits (*Boston Deep Sea Fishing and Ice Co v Ansell* (1888) 39 Ch D 339), and he must account to his employer for them if he does (*Reading v Attorney-General* [1951] AC 507).

An employee who works for a competitor or sets up in business on his own, in competition with his employer, is in breach of this duty of loyalty, irrespective of misuse or disclosure of confidential information or trade secrets (*Hivac Ltd v Park Royal Scientific Instruments Ltd*, above, and *Thomas Marshall (Exports) Ltd v Guinle* [1978] 3 All ER 190). Such actions can be restrained by injunction and entitle the employer to dismiss the employee summarily for breach of contract. Such a dismissal, at least if the proper procedures are used, is also normally regarded as a fair dismissal for the purposes of the employment protection legislation relating to unfair dismissal.

Furthermore, some cases suggest that if an employee resigns in breach of contract without giving due notice, or if his employer chooses to let him 'work' out his notice by remaining idle at home (sometimes called 'garden leave'), this duty continues to subsist, so that the employer can restrain the employee during the relevant period of notice from setting up in competition or working for a competitor (*Evening Standard Co Ltd v Henderson* [1987] IRLR 64, *Provident Financial Group plc and Whitegates Estate Agency v Hayward* [1989] IRLR 84).

It should be noted that in the absence of an express term in the contract requiring the employee to devote his whole time and attention to the employer's affairs, and not to take a second job, or indulge in self-employed activities, the employee is under no duty to refrain from indulging in such 'moonlighting' activities, provided he does not compete with his employer, assist a competitor of his employer, or misuse his employer's confidential information or trade secrets (see *Laughton and Hawley v BAPP Industrial Supplies Ltd* [1986] IRLR 245 EAT).

Once the contract of employment has come to an end the position of the employer is much more difficult and considerations of restraint of trade become relevant.

The traditional approach to any covenant in restraint of trade is that it is *prima facie* void, and to be enforced only if it can be justified as reasonable in the circumstances, by reference both to the public interest and the interest of the parties. There are, however, some important differences in the approach of the courts in deciding the question of such reasonableness depending upon whether the covenant has been given in the context of a commercial transaction or as part of a contract of employment.

So far as the question of the public interest is concerned, where the covenant is part of a commercial bargain between two independent parties, with at least presumably equal bargaining power, the courts find it easier to hold that the covenant is reasonable so far as the public interest is concerned. The most common instances of such covenants are the non-compete covenant given by a vendor on the sale of his business (*Nordenfelt v Maxim Nordenfelt Guns and Ammunition Co* [1894] AC 535, HL) or the tying arrangements relating to breweries and petrol stations (*Esso Petroleum Ltd v Harper's Garage (Stourport) Ltd* [1968] AC 269). A further instance, already discussed in Chapter 12, is the non-compete covenants given by the members of a joint venture in favour of the joint venture itself. The courts recognise that such covenants as the foregoing are necessary to give commercial efficacy to the transactions to which they relate, and that, as a matter of standard commercial practice, they are a usual and customary part of such transactions.

So far as covenants restricting the ability of an employee to compete after the termination of his employment is concerned, the courts tend to impose a much stricter standard when deciding the question of the reasonableness of the restraint in the light of the public interest. It is not sufficient for the employer merely to say he does not wish his employee to compete. This is nothing more than a bare restraint of trade. It is not in the public interest that the employer should be able to restrict the number of his competitors, and restrict the ability of his employees to earn their living, merely because it is to his benefit to do so.

The employer must show that he wishes to impose the ban on competition to protect some personal property rights, in relation to his business, which the courts would consider it was in the public interest to protect. There are two possible bases for the grant of such protection. The first is that the law exists (*inter alia*) to protect personal property rights, and that it is in the public interest that such rights should in general be upheld. The second is that, without such protection, the employer's business could be materially prejudiced, which would result in a less efficient business or, in extreme cases, in insolvency; this would clearly not increase competition and could reduce the number of business concerns serving the community, which would not be in the public interest.

In practice, the only such interests which the courts are prepared to permit the employer to protect are the goodwill in his business, which can be defined as his trade connections (relations with suppliers and customers), and his trade secrets (see *Faccenda Chicken Ltd v Fowler*, above). If he genuinely has such interests, he can protect them directly, by imposing a restriction on disclosure of the relevant trade secrets (*Mason v Provident Clothing and Supply Co Ltd* [1913] AC 724, HL), or a restriction against soliciting customers or suppliers (*Herbert Morris Ltd v Saxelby* [1916] 1 AC 688, HL). In the latter case, such a restriction can, of course, only be valid if any restraint imposed upon an employee relates strictly to the customers or suppliers with whom he had dealings during the course of his employment.

The imposition of a blanket covenant preventing any competition at all with the employer, in the relevant trade or business, is thus not justifiable *per se*, but it can be justifiable in the case of senior employees who can be shown to have such an intimate knowledge of the business, and such a close relationship with the trade connection, that, in practice, there is no way in which they can set up in competition at all without infringing the legitimate interests of the employer in these areas (*Littlewoods Organisation Ltd v Harris* [1978] 1 All ER 1026, *Ixora Trading Incorporated v Jones* [1990] FSR 251 and *Berkeley Administration Ltd v McClelland* [1990] FSR 505).

Once the covenantee, whether he is dealing in a commercial context or as an employer, has shown that it is in principle reasonable that the covenant be enforced as in the public interest, he has another hurdle to get over. Covenants in restraint of trade usually have three parameters, the restricted activity, the geographic area in which it is restricted, and the period of time for which it is restricted. The interaction of these three parameters produces what can be regarded as the 'extent' of the covenant. The covenantee has to demonstrate that the extent of the covenant is such that it produces a reasonable balance between the interests of the covenantee in restricting competition and the interests of the covenantor in conducting his affairs freely without restraint of trade.

In the case of a covenant in a commercial transaction, the courts tend to accept a balance of the parties' interests which results in covenants with a greater extent than would be acceptable in the case of covenants in a contract of employment. This is because, in a commercial transaction, the party accepting the restraint has been given value for it by the other party. For instance, the consideration for the sale of a business will be determined in part by the existence and the extent of a vendor non-compete covenant (see *Systems Reliability Holdings plc v Smith* [1990] IRLR 377 Ch D).

So far as an employer is concerned, he has to show that the extent of the covenant is, on the particular facts of the case, adequate to protect his proprietary rights in the goodwill or trade secrets of his business, but not greater than what is required for this purpose. The court also has to be satisfied that, whether or not the extent is adequate, but no more than adequate for this purpose, it is not, in any event, of an unreasonable extent in the light of the employee's requirement to be free to earn a living in his chosen trade or profession. (*Dowden and Pook Ltd v Pook* [1904] 1 KB 45, CA and *Dairy Crest Ltd v Pigott* [1989] ICR 92, CA).

Whether dealing with covenants in commercial transactions or contracts of employment, it is not possible to turn to case law to decide what covenants are of an acceptable extent, since each case turns on its own facts. However, six general rules can be set down.

The first is that the smaller the extent of the covenant the more likely it is to be enforceable. This means that, where possible all three parameters should be restricted in scope, and that if the scope of one is increased, that of the others should be decreased to compensate. This is particularly true in the case of area and time. The longer the time, the smaller the area should be, and *vice versa*.

The second is that the scope of the restricted activity must be tightly defined so as to cover activities which have a proper connection with the transaction in which the covenantor and the covenantee are involved. For instance, the scope of the restricted activity in a vendor non-compete clause must not extend beyond the activities carried on as part of the business being sold, and, in a clause preventing an ex-employee from soliciting customers of his employer, the activity restricted must be confined to the class of customers with whom the employee had contact as part of his duties during the course of his employment. There can be no reason to restrict other unconnected activities except a desire to restrict competition, which the court will find an unacceptable restraint of trade.

The third is that, in a commercial transaction, the greater the value the covenantee receives for the covenant, the greater the extent of the covenant which is likely to be acceptable. This is particularly so where, tax considerations permitting, it is possible to allocate a specific and substantial part of the consideration for the transaction to the restrictive covenant.

The fourth is that, where employment contracts are concerned, the more senior the employee the greater the extent of the covenant which is likely to be regarded as reasonable.

The fifth is not to be too greedy. The draftsman should always resist his client's desire for covenants of large extent which turn out to be unenforceable.

The sixth is, where possible, draft with the doctrines of severance in mind, and include an express severance clause in the contract.

In the particular context of employment contracts, at the simplest, where dealing with a senior employee, three covenants, one covering trade secrets, one covering solicitation of customers and suppliers, and one imposing a general ban on competition, could all be included, on the basis that if one or more is declared unenforceable one or more of the others may survive.

In some cases the covenants tend to be drafted in the alternative or the draftsman includes two or more covenants which cover the same issue, except that they have a different extent, again on the basis that if the court finds one is unreasonable, it may choose to permit the enforcement of another with a lesser extent. It should be noted that there is a difference between applying the true 'blue pencil' test for severance by deleting a whole independent clause (*Rex Stewart Jeffries Parker Ginsberg Ltd v Parker* [1988] IRLR 483, CA) and asking the court either to take a few offending words out of a clause (usually not successful—*Attwood v Lamont* [1920] 3 KB 571) or, still worse, asking the court to rewrite the covenant to an extent that it finds acceptable (but see *Hinton and Higgs (UK) Ltd v Murphy and Valentine* [1989] IRLR 519, a Scottish case where this approach was partially successful).

14.5 Precedent 1

This precedent sets out a full, formal service contract. It is drafted for an executive director of a company, but it can, with appropriate adaptation, be used for any senior employee for whom a full contract is required. It should be remembered that, although this is a full precedent, no attempt has been made to exclude any terms which would be implied by the common law or statute, and that, of course, certain areas of employment legislation, to the extent that they apply to a senior salaried employee, such as the right not to be unfairly dismissed, are mandatory, so that neither the employer nor the employee can contract out of them.

The precedent starts with a full set of definitions, many of them being definitions found in the Companies Acts which are incorporated by reference. It should be noted that the definitions relating to groups of companies are based upon the simple concepts of holding and subsidiary companies as originally defined in the Companies Act 1985, and that the more complicated concepts relating to 'subsidiary undertakings', grafted onto that Act by the Companies Act 1989, have not been used, although it would be possible to use them if the draftsman felt that the particular circumstances of the case required it. The main use of the definitions is in relation to the non-competition clauses, and the clauses regulating rights as between employer and employee over confidential information and intellectual property rights; for this reason the definitions are rather elaborate and have to be drafted with particular care.

Clause 1 sets out the basic obligations of the employer to employ and of the employee to serve, in accordance with the terms of the rest of the agreement. Clause 1(2) provides for a contract of an indefinite duration which (subject to earlier termination for such matters as breach or insolvency, as specified later in the agreement) is terminable by either side by 12 months' notice.

In this precedent, as is usually the case, the same length of notice is to be given by employer and by employee. However, if one leaves aside the special issues which may in some cases arise when an employee gives no notice or short notice, and leaves, in breach of his contract, to work for a competitor (see *Evening Standard Co v Henderson*, above), the courts will not grant an injunction to prevent an employee resigning in breach of his contract and going to work for someone else. The most that the employer will be able to claim is damages, but these damages are unlikely in most cases to exceed the costs, if any, incurred by the employer in recruiting a substitute. It can even be argued that, since the employer would, presumably, have incurred such costs, in any event, although at a later time, if the employee had resigned with proper notice, he should not recover the whole of these costs, but only such increase in these costs, if any, which he can prove was caused because the employee left early.

Because of these considerations, most employers tend to regard notice periods as being more for the protection of the employee than for the benefit of the employer, so that, in practice, except in cases where the employee's presence is vital for a particular task, or there are aggravated circumstances surrounding his leaving to work for a competitor, the employee is usually allowed to leave at some mutually agreed date that has no particular reference to notice period. Some contracts of employment actually specify either that the employee may give a shorter period of notice than the employer, and/or that, in appropriate cases, the employer will waive his right to a full period of notice from the employee. This is only common sense, since the idea of trying to keep an unwilling employee at work during his notice period could well cause more damage to the employer than if he had let him go. The only practical way of tying up the employee for the period of his notice is by the 'garden leave' method discussed earlier (see *Provident Financial Group plc and Whitegates Estate Agency v Hayward*, and the suggested wording in cl 8(4) below). Because of this, some contracts of employment do include an express compulsory 'garden leave' clause, which provides that where the employee gives notice, the employer has the option to send him on 'garden leave' for the period of his notice.[16] However, if the employee breaches such a clause, the court will be unlikely to grant an injunction except to prevent the employee from working with a competitor. So far as breach of a 'garden leave' clause in other circumstances is concerned, it is hard to see that the employer has, in fact, suffered any damage at all, even additional recruitment costs, so that presumably the employee could ignore the clause with impunity and terminate his employment prematurely.

Some contracts of employment for senior staff are of a fixed duration, and such contracts have given rise to some case law surrounding the rights of the employee upon their termination. A contract is a fixed-term contract if it is stated to expire automatically upon a certain date or to last only for a specified period. The fact that the common law provides that the contract can be terminated prior to its expiry date (for instance for breach) does not prevent it being a fixed-term contract. Similarly, the contract does not cease to be a fixed-term contract even if the employer and/or the employee has an option to terminate it by notice earlier than the stated expiry date, or prior to the expiry of its specified period (*Dixon v British Broadcasting Corporation* [1978] ICR 357).

Under the employment protection legislation, the expiry of a fixed-term contract without its renewal counts as a dismissal for the purposes of redundancy payments legislation. However, although it also counts as a dismissal for the purposes of the legislation relating to the right not to be unfairly dismissed, such a dismissal is not automatically unfair. The 'dismissal' will be regarded as fair if the employer has a genuine reason for using a fixed-term contract and if the employee understood that his employment was not likely to be renewed when he entered into the arrangement (see *North Yorkshire County Council v Fay* [1985] IRLR 247).

Under s 197 of the Employment Rights Act 1996, where a fixed term contract has a term of one year or more, the parties can exclude the unfair dismissal legislation by agreement, and where it has a fixed term of two years or more they can exclude in addition the right to a statutory redundancy payment. This can either be by a clause in the contract itself, or by a later agreement entered into during the currency of the relevant contract of employment. However, in the latter case, the employee must receive good consideration for the waiver of his rights. It should be noted that, where the fixed-term contract has been renewed a number of times, in order for the waiver to be valid the last renewal of the fixed term must be for the requisite qualifying period (see *BBC v Kelly-Phillips* [1997] IRLR 571, EAT and *Housing Services Agency v Cragg* [1997] IRLR 380, EAT).[17]

Clause 1(3) of the precedent is merely a device to enable the draftsman to personalise what is otherwise a standard contract by including any special terms relating to a particular employee. Clause 2(1) specifies the duties the executive is to perform. Where the contract relates to an executive director, the wording can be very general, as is the case here, since it can be expected that a high level executive will change his role from time to time within the company, and will be responsible for different facets of its operations as his career progresses.

It is of course possible to be more specific, and to limit the sphere of duties by reference to a title (eg 'Finance Director') or a job description ('responsible for the operations and running of the company's manufacturing plant situated at [   ]'). Limitations by way of job title or description will, in many cases, entitle the employee to refuse to change his responsibilities, and to resign in response to the employer's breach of contract if the employer insists on the change. A common compromise is to use the flexible wording contained in the precedent, plus the initial job title or description.

Flexibility also applies to the location at which the employee's duties are to be performed. Clause 2(1) specifies no location at all, and provides that the executive would have to move around to different locations as his duties required, although some restrictions (eg only to locations within the UK) may be appropriate. If a change required him to relocate to another home then he would have to comply. Specification of an initial location, coupled with the flexibility clause, does not change the principle, but specification of a location with no flexibility would mean that the employee could refuse to move, if the change in location were substantial, and again resign, because of the employer's breach, if the employer insisted.

So far as the common law is concerned, the employer can change any term of the contract of employment if he gives a period of notice for the change equal to the period of notice by which he could terminate the contract. However, when the offer is made, the common law regards this as in effect termination of the current contract by due notice (which is all the employee is entitled to at common law) followed by an offer to re-engage on the new terms. Even if the employee refuses the variation, and resigns, the employee is entitled to no compensation since the employer could by due notice simply have terminated his contract and not offered him re-engagement on any terms whatsoever.

This analysis has no bearing on the employee's statutory rights to redundancy payments or to compensation for unfair dismissal (which may or may not be available depending upon the facts of the case), and, where the period of notice is short, the employer will be more concerned with his exposure in respect of these issues. However, lack of flexibility carries a heavy penalty at common law (in addition to any statutory rights to compensation) where the contract is for a fixed term, a large portion of which is unexpired, or has a long period of notice. In this case, if the employer's needs change, and he cannot reach agreement with the employee, he will not be able to terminate the relationship quickly without buying out the employee by paying him the balance of the remuneration he would have earned for the unexpired portion of the fixed term, or for the period of notice. Such payments are of course subject to the duty of the employee to mitigate his loss by finding another reasonable job as soon as possible, but, in these days of high unemployment, particularly where senior executives are concerned, this may not be feasible.

However, it should be noted that, even where clauses provide for total flexibility, there is at least an implied term at common law that the employer will exercise his rights reasonably. For instance, requiring a senior executive to take a significant demotion to a demeaning position without a good reason (such as incompetence) is not likely to be justifiable by reference to a flexibility clause, even if the other terms and conditions of employment remain the same.

The remainder of the clause deals expressly with the issues of loyalty discussed above. Clause 2(2) requires the employee to comply with all reasonable instructions from his employer. Clause 2(3) requires him to devote his whole time and attention during his working hours to his duties for his employer, and to refrain from competing with his employer during his employment. Clause 2(4) provides a standard exception to the ban on competing activity by permitting the employee to own a low level of investments in competing companies whose shares are publicly traded on a stock exchange.

The clauses as drafted would prevent the employee engaging in competing activities at all, but would not prevent him from doing other work either on his own account or for another employer if he could do so outside the working hours required to discharge his duties to his employer. This seems reasonable, but, in practice, where a high level employee is concerned, who is obliged to work all the hours necessary for the discharge of his duties (cl 2(3)), it is hardly likely that he will be able to undertake a second job on a regular basis.

Clause 3 deals with remuneration by way of a stated sum of money (paid in instalments) as a yearly salary (and cl 2(3) provides that there is to be no remuneration additional to the salary for overtime). Clause 3(2) deals with payment of a rateable proportion of the current instalment to the employee's personal representatives in the event of his death. Clause 3(3) deals with the question of salary reviews. The position taken in the clause is that a review will take place every year (unless the employee is under notice) and that there is no obligation to grant an increase. There is, however, correspondingly, no right on the part of the employer to decrease the employee's salary without consent.

One point which sometimes arises is whether the employee has a legal right to enforce any increase in salary awarded to him during the currency of the contract. Some commentators argue that the employee has given no consideration for the increase so that it cannot become a variation of the contract binding upon the employer. Others avoid the problem, by simply regarding the increase as a consensual variation, or attempt to construct consideration on the basis that the employee has, presumably, agreed not to give notice terminating his employment because he has been given the increase.

Clause 3(3) deals with the issue by building provisions relating to the variation into the original contract, so that the employee has given consideration for them at the time when he entered into the contract. As is normal, the employee is not permitted to receive a director's fees for any companies, within the employer's group of companies, of which he is from time to time a director. It is considered that his salary is sufficient compensation for the discharge of such duties, and cl 3(4) so provides.

Clause 4 deals with payment of expenses in a conventional way. Clause 4(3), which gives the employee the right to relocation expenses, is necessary if the agreement is to provide for flexibility of location as set out in cl 2(1).

Clause 5 deals with holiday entitlement, and cl 6 with sick pay and sick leave. The provisions of these clauses are standard examples of usual terms for senior executives, although details will obviously vary in each case. Clause 6(1)(*b*) and cl 6(2) pre-suppose, as is very often the case, that the employer takes out permanent disability insurance which provides the employee with a disability pension if he is rendered permanently incapable of work through accident or ill-health. Sometimes such pensions are provided through the employer's pension scheme. If they are not provided at all, then the employee may be able to obtain them through private insurance.

Whatever the situation, the draftsman has to consider the way in which the transition is made from sick pay (appropriate for temporary illness from which the employee will return to work) to permanent disability. Under cl 6 the employee transitions to a disability pension after six months, and this lasts until he can return to work, or until he retires, but it is important to realise that his employment is not terminated by reason of his disability. Such termination only occurs if for some reason he is not eligible for the disability pension (because the employer will not then wish to keep him permanently on the pay roll and pay his salary till retirement at the company's expense).

However, cl 6 is only illustrative. For instance, where the disability pension is paid out of the pension plan, the employer will usually have to terminate the employment before the employee can become eligible to receive the pension.

Clause 7 is a detailed confidentiality clause based on the definition of 'Information'. This is a very wide definition which covers both confidential information in the nature of trade secrets and other types of confidential information, so that both of the classes of confidential information discussed by the Court of Appeal in *Faccenda Chicken Ltd v Fowler*, above, are covered. This causes no problem during the currency of the employment, but gives rise to a question of the enforceability of the clause after termination of the employment as provided in cl 7(4).

As drafted, ignoring the words in square brackets, the post-termination obligation applies to all 'Information' as defined, unless it comes into the public domain. Many draftsmen would leave the clause at this, arguing that the express words would overrule the *dicta* in *Faccenda Chicken Ltd v Fowler*, above, relating to express clauses, since the case actually concerned an employment where there was no express clause. It can also be contended that the distinction between the two types of confidential information would not arise, since the employer would not attempt to enforce the clause after termination of the employment except where (at any rate in the employer's opinion) the 'trade secret' type of confidential information was concerned. Lastly, even if the court does consider the distinction and apply it, the offending provisions relating to confidential information other than trade secrets could be severed from the definition of information pursuant to the express severance clause contained in cl 11(2).

There is, however, a danger that a court might take the point that the post-termination clause as a whole went too far, that there was no possibility of severing some parts of the definition of 'Information', so that the part relating to trade secrets was separately enforceable, and that therefore the whole of the clause was void as in restraint of trade.

It must be admitted that this point is not usually taken by the draftsmen of these clauses. However, for the cautious draftsman, there are two possibilities. The first is to provide a separate post-termination confidentiality clause with a definition of 'Information' which covers the 'trade secret' type of information only. The second is to add the phrase in square brackets presently shown in cl 7(4), which cuts down the post-termination confidentiality obligation to the extent that the court is prepared to enforce it. Of the two approaches the first is to be preferred for clarity, but, whichever is used, the difficulty of defining whether a piece of confidential information is really worthy of protection as a trade secret still has to be faced. However, this is not a reason for not including such a provision since, even in its absence, the employer who wishes to rely on the general wording of the clause may well have to pass the test in *Faccenda Chicken Ltd v Fowler*, above, in any event.

The law in this area is unclear, and there are certainly problems with the division of confidential information into two classes on the principles set down in *Faccenda Chicken Ltd v Fowler*, above. For a further discussion of these problems and their possible connection with the legal principles relating to restraint of trade, reference should be made to Chapter 13.

The best course is probably not to ignore the problems in the case of senior employees, and to solve it in one of the two ways discussed above. However, so far as the majority of employees are concerned, the simpler course is to use a clause like that suggested in cl 1 of Precedent 3, which merely imposes a general obligation of confidentiality without particular reference to a distinction either between trade secrets and other confidential information, or between obligations during and after the termination of employment. The employer will then simply have to rely on the fact that even in the absence of an express clause imposing post-termination confidentiality obligations, the general law will impose such obligations to protect his 'trade secrets', following the principles in *Faccenda*.

Clause 8(1) deals with summary termination on the part of the employer. It is assumed that reciprocal rights are not necessary for the employee, since he has his common law rights to terminate the contract in the event of material breach, and, if the employer goes into liquidation, the employment will either be terminated by the liquidator or the contract will come to an end with the disappearance of the employer. In any event, since the employer (subject to the limited preferential rights granted to employees on insolvency) can no longer pay salary or compensation for termination of the contract, the whole issue is academic. Clause 9 deals with a solvent winding up and reorganisation of the employer, when the employee loses his rights to any compensation if he is offered a new contract on the same terms with the new resulting entity.

Clause 8(2) provides for automatic termination of the contract upon the death of the employee, or when he reaches retirement age. It is arguable that (following *Dixon v British Broadcasting Corporation*, above) the inclusion of a provision for automatic termination on reaching retirement age converts the contract into a fixed-term contract, since, at the time when the parties enter into it, they know it will, if not terminated earlier, terminate on the date the employee reaches retirement age. In strict theory this is probably the case, but it is of no practical consequence. Under s 64(1) of the Employment Protection (Consolidation) Act 1978 the protection of the legislation relating to the right not to be unfairly dismissed ceases upon reaching normal retirement age or (if there is no relevant normal retirement age) 65 for men and 60 for women. EEC law on equalisation of retirement ages for men and women for the purposes of pensions may, arguably, have some bearing on this provision, but there appears to have been no consideration of this issue in the UK yet. In any event (following *North Yorkshire County Council v Fay*, above), automatic termination at a specified age would, in general, be a fair dismissal for some other substantial reason, unless the age limit were set in such a way that it amounted to sex discrimination (eg 55 for women, 60 for men). Further, if desired, one could, (at least under the law as it currently stands as discussed earlier), insert a 'contracting out' clause pursuant to s 142(1) of the Act.

Clause 8(3) provides examples of post-termination non-compete clauses which rely upon the principles discussed above, and which should be appropriate in most cases. The draftsman must, however, decide the exact provisions of such clauses by precise and careful reference to the facts of each case using the principles set out above. In particular, cl 8(3)(*f*) may (although not with certainty) be appropriate for some senior executives, as discussed above, but should not be used in other cases. At least the drafting of cl 8(3), coupled with the severance provisions of cl 11(2), should enable the general non-compete clause to be severed in cases where the court refuses to enforce it, leaving the others intact.

It will be noticed that the restrictive covenants contained in this clause apply upon the termination of the employment 'for whatever reason'. In *D v M* [1996] IRLR 192, it was held that such a provision rendered the clause unreasonably restrictive and therefore void because any restrictive covenant 'which upon its face applies to the employer's benefit even where termination has been induced by his own breach is necessarily unreasonable'. This decision meant that, irrespective of whether termination was actually caused by the employer's own breach, any clause that was wide enough to cover this contingency was necessarily so unreasonable as to be void. This judgment was overturned in the Court of Appeal in *Rock Refrigeration Ltd v Jones* (1996) *The Times*, 17 October. The majority of the court said that the reasonableness of the words used (in this case it was termination 'howsoever occasioned') were irrelevant. If the contract was terminated by reason of the employer's repudiatory breach all of the employee's obligations under the contract, including the restrictive covenant, were discharged. It was therefore impossible to enforce a restrictive covenant after an employer's repudiatory breach, and a restrictive covenant could not be regarded as unreasonable merely because it attempted to achieve the impossible in one particular circumstance. Phillips LJ also suggested, relying on *Heyman v Darwin Ltd* [1942] AC 356 and *Photo Productions Ltd v Securicor* [1980] AC 827, that certain secondary contractual obligations could survive a repudiatory breach, if drafted widely enough, and a restrictive covenant operating after termination 'howsoever occasioned' might fall within this class, so an employer could enforce a restrictive covenant even after a wrongful dismissal. This is not so unfair as it might seem at first thought. The employee has his remedies for wrongful dismissal. which will put him in the same position as he would have been if the dismissal had been in accordance with the contractual terms. If damages do put him in this position, why should he not abide by the restrictive covenant which would have applied to him if the dismissal had been in accordance with the terms of the contract in the first place.

Based on the majority judgment in *Rock Refrigeration*, the restrictive covenants in the precedent will be enforceable with the use of the term 'for whatever reason' provided that the actual termination does not come about as a result of a breach by the employer. The suggestion of Phillips LJ that possibly restrictive covenants could be enforceable even where termination occurs as a result of the employer's breach, depends upon two propositions: first, that as a matter of legal principle a covenant can survive such a termination; secondly, that the covenant has been drafted widely enough (as in the *Securicor* case) to cover this eventuality. So far. there is no decision as to the first point, although

Securicor is persuasive. However, using the words 'for whatever reason' would seem to cover termination by reason of the employer's breach. Those draftsmen who would wish to preserve the possibility of contending, in any future proceedings, that a covenant should survive termination by the employer's breach, could rely on the current wording in the precedent or make it more explicit and perhaps include a reference to termination in these circumstances. In this case it would be wise to include the provision in a separate clause (eg 'The provisions of clause x (restrictive covenant) are hereby expressly provided to survive the termination of this contract and to be enforceable in the event that such termination arises by reason of a breach of this contract by the employer'). This should be coupled with a severance clause elsewhere in the agreement so that in case problems do arise in later litigation it can be severed and leave the restrictive covenant intact (see cl 11(2) of the precedent). Finally, cl 8(4) is a suggestion for a 'garden leave' clause.

Clause 10 deals with the employer's right to own intellectual property rights generated by the employee in the course of his employment. It proceeds on the basis of the analysis of the relevant issues set out above. It is assumed that, since the employee here is a director, the intellectual property and inventions that he generates will belong to the company, but cl 10(3) provides for any rights to compensation that he may have under the Patents Act 1977 as an employee inventor, as discussed above.

Clause 11 deals with a number of ancillary points. Clause 11(1) supersedes any previous contracts of service. Clause 11(2) provides a severance provision mainly for the purposes already discussed. Clause 11(3) provides standard notice provisions. Clause 11(4) makes the employer the employee's attorney for the purpose of executing various documents in order to vest or perfect the vesting of the ownership in the employer of intellectual property rights and inventions generated by the employee. Clause 11(5) provides for the survival of accrued rights and for the post-termination survival of relevant provisions (such as the non-compete clauses—cl 8(3)). Clause 11(6) additionally provides for the devolvement of such obligations (to the extent relevant) upon the employee's personal representatives in the event of the termination of the contract by his death. Clause 11(7) specifies applicable grievance and disciplinary procedures. Clauses 11(8) and (9) deal with standard interpretation clauses.

Finally, Sched 1 shows examples of special terms which might apply. In connection with pensions it should be noted that the old practice of requiring that staff employees become members of the company scheme as a condition of employment is no longer legal. All such membership is voluntary for any employee who is eligible.

14.6 Precedent 2

This precedent is a short form written statement of terms of employment which complies with ss 1–7 of the Employment Rights Act 1996 and with the EC Directive on Form of Proof of Employment Relationship (533/1991).

The contents of the precedent are self explanatory. It should be noted that the document itself is not a contract of employment, and does not purport to be an exhaustive record of all the terms of employment. However, it may form part of the contract of employment, or, in appropriate cases, it may be used as evidence of terms contained in such a contract.

The new legislation now applies to all employees unless their employment continues for less than one month (see ss 1 and 198). However, the sections do not apply to employment during any period when the employee is engaged to work wholly or mainly outside Great Britain unless the employee ordinarily works in Great Britain for the same employer or the contract of employment is governed by the law of England and Wales or Scotland (s 196). Currently the sections do not apply to seamen working on UK-registered ships under a crew agreement approved by the Secretary of State (s 199). Since the Act as a whole does not currently apply to offshore workers, although powers are contained in the Act for the Secretary of State to extend the Act such workers, ss 1–7 do not currently apply to offshore workers (see s 201). However, the current government have indicated their intention to change the law in this respect by exercising the power under s 201.

Although the employer is not in breach of his duty to give the statement until the expiry of a period of two months after the start of the employment (s 1(2)), the right nevertheless accrues once the employee has been in employment for one month (s 1(1) and s 198). The employer is required to give a statement to an employee even if his employment ends before the expiry of the relevant two-month period (see s 2(6)).

Under s 1(3), the statement must state the basic particulars of the employment—name of the employer and of the employee, the date when the employment began, and the date upon which the period of continuous employment began, taking into account any employment with a previous employer which counts towards the current period (eg with a subsidiary company of the employer) for purposes of continuity of employment.

Pursuant to s 1(4) it must also state the following terms of employment:

- rates of pay or method of calculating pay;
- frequency of payment;
- hours of work;
- holiday entitlement;
- terms relating to sickness or injury, and injury or sick pay;
- terms relating to pensions and pension schemes (including, under s 3(5), whether the employment is contracted out for the purposes of a retirement pension);
- length of notice required to be given by either side;
- the title of the job the employee is employed to perform, or, as an alternative, a brief description of the work the employee is employed to do;

- when the employment is not intended to be permanent the period for which it is expected to continue, or, if it is a fixed term, when it will end;
- the place of work, or, if the employee works at various places, an indication of that, and the address of the employer;
- any collective agreements which directly affect the terms and conditions of employment, including, where the employer is not a party, the persons by whom they were made; and
- if the employee is to work abroad for more than one month, the period for which he is to work outside the UK, the currency in which remuneration will be paid, details of any extra benefits or remuneration provided for working abroad; and any terms and conditions relating to his return to the UK.

Pursuant to s 3(1) the statement must also give details of disciplinary rules and grievance procedures (with the exception of those relating to health and safety at work matters: s 3(2)) which apply to the employee, including appeals procedures.

However, under s 3(3), details of disciplinary and grievance procedures need not be given to an employee if his employer has (together with any associated employers) less than twenty employees working for him on the date the relevant employee started employment. In this case, the employee need only be told to whom he should apply to deal with any grievance that he has.

It should also be noted that, under s 2(1), where there are no particulars relating to any of the above matters, the employer must note this fact in the statement.

Section 1(2) of the Act now provides that the statements about the matters listed above may all be given in instalments, provided that they have all been covered by the end of the requisite period of two months. However, under s 2(4), the following matters must be covered in one statement (called the Principal Statement):

- name of employer and employee;
- commencement and continuous period of employment;
- remuneration and working hours;
- holiday entitlement and holiday pay;
- job title or description; and
- place of work.

The statement or series of statements must set out full details of all the matters required to be covered except that (in relation to absence through injury or sickness, pension schemes and disciplinary and grievance procedures only) ss 2(2) and 3(1) permit the employer to incorporate in the statement, by reference, collective agreements or other documents (such as handbooks, policies or standing instructions) which contain the relevant details, provided that the agreements or documents referred to are ones which are 'made reasonably accessible to him'.

Section 6 provides that in ss 2–4 all references to a document or collective agreement being reasonably accessible to an employee shall be satisfied if the employee had reasonable opportunities of reading the document or collective agreement in the course of his employment or if it is made reasonably accessible to him in some other way. The commonest method is either to state to the employee that such documents can be seen at the personnel office, or else that they are on view on company notice boards. In addition, under s 2(3) the statement need not detail the terms relating to notice, but may instead refer the employee to the law or to any relevant collective agreement reasonably accessible to him.

Section 4 requires the employer to notify his employees in writing of any change in the particulars shown in their statement within one month of the occurrence of the change. If the change occurs because the employee is going to work abroad for more than one month, notice must be given before he leaves the country, if that is earlier than one month after the change. Again where the original information was communicated by referring the employee to a document or collective agreement which was reasonably accessible to him, the change can be dealt with by a similar reference.

Finally, if all of the terms remain the same, but the identity of the employer changes (ie because of a transfer of a business affected by the Transfer of Undertaking (Protection of Employment)Regulations 1981) then it is not necessary to issue a new statement, but merely to treat the change of name of the employer as a change to the existing statement and deal with it under s 4(6), (7) and (8). The revision must give details of the new employer, and restate the date on which the employee's period of continuous employment began.

14.7   Precedent 3

Precedent 2 is not a contract of employment, but it can contain statements of terms of employment other than those required by ss 1–7 of the 1996 Act, or it can be turned into a written contract of employment which satisfies those requirements, thus obviating the need for a written statement under s 1, but, at the same time, again incorporating additional terms.

Precedent 3 sets out a number of clauses which can be added to a statement of particulars or incorporated into a short form contract of employment. The matters dealt with in the specimen clauses are not exhaustive. Although most of them should be included in nearly all cases, there are situations where some would not be appropriate or others need to be added. However, in general, a combination of Precedent 2 and Precedent 3 would produce a reasonably comprehensive short form contract of employment for nearly all personnel below senior management levels. It should be noted that there are no express post-termination bans on competition or use or disclosure of confidential information, and these issues are left to the general law. At this level of personnel it is not generally appropriate to include such clauses, but relevant clauses from Precedent 1 could be used as necessary.

It is of course also possible to include some of the clauses from Precedent 3 into Precedent 1, if circumstances require it, to cover matters other than those already dealt with in Precedent 1.

14.8 Precedent 4

Finally, this precedent, for the sake of completeness, sets out a comprehensive clause governing confidential information, inventions and intellectual property rights, which can be incorporated in a consultancy contract.

Executive service contract

THIS AGREEMENT dated the [   ] day of [   ]
19[   ]
BETWEEN
(1) [   ] LIMITED whose registered office is at [   ]
(the 'Company') and
(2) [   ] of [   ] (the 'Executive').

In this Agreement the following expressions shall have the following meanings:

'Competing Activity' shall mean any business, trade or occupation the same as or similar to or in conflict or in competition with any activity carried on by the Group;

'Connected Person' shall in relation to the Executive be defined in accordance with s 346 of the Companies Act 1985;

'Director' shall be defined in accordance with s 741 of the Companies Act 1985 and shall include (where the context so permits a shadow director as defined in the said section);

'Employment' shall mean the employment of the Executive in accordance with the terms of this Agreement, and in particular, the terms of cll 1 and 2;

'Group' shall mean the Company, the Holding Company of the Company, and any company which is for the time being a Subsidiary of the Company or of the Company's Holding Company;

'Group Company' shall mean any company within the Group;

'Holding Company' shall be defined in accordance with s 736 of the Companies Act 1985;

'Information' shall mean all communications and all information whether written, visual or oral and all other material supplied to or obtained by the Executive from any Group Company during the continuance of the Employment and all information, reports, recommendations or advice given to any Group Company by the Executive in pursuance of his duties hereunder, and shall (without limitation of the foregoing) include any information from whatever source supplied to or obtained by the Executive concerning the trade secrets, customers, business associations and transactions, financial arrangements and technical or commercial affairs of the Group;

'Inventions' shall mean all patentable and non-patentable inventions, discoveries and improvements, processes and know-how, copyright works (including without limitation computer programs), new designs and the like discovered or created by the Executive in the course of or for the Employment or discovered or created by the Executive as a result whether directly or indirectly of anything done by the Executive in pursuance of his duties hereunder and/or (as the case may be) based whether directly or indirectly on any item of the Information;

'Securities' shall mean stocks, shares and debentures of all kinds;

'Subsidiary' shall be defined in accordance with s 736 of the Companies Act 1985.

IT IS AGREED as follows:

1   Employment

1.1 Subject to and in accordance with the following terms and conditions, the Company shall employ the Executive and the Executive shall serve the Company, such employment to be deemed to have commenced on [   ] and continuing thereafter unless and until this Agreement shall be terminated including without limitation by reason of termination in accordance with cll 1(2), 6(2), 8(1) or 8(2).

1.2 Subject to cll 6(1), 6(2), 8(1) and 8(2) this Agreement may be terminated by either party giving to the other not less than 12 months' written notice.

1.3 The Employment in addition to all other provisions hereof shall be subject to those special terms and conditions (if any) listed in Schedule 1 hereto.

2   Duties

2.1 The Executive shall perform such duties and exercise such powers in connection with the affairs of the Group generally as may from time to time be assigned to or vested in him by the Chief Executive Officer of the Company. The location at which the Executive shall perform his duties shall be also be specified to him from time to time in writing by the said Chief Executive Officer [provided that such location shall not be a place outside of [England] [the

UK] without the consent of the Executive]. The location at which the Executive shall perform his duties at the date of signature hereof is set out in Sched 1 hereto. The Executive shall be obliged to accept an appointment to serve from time to time as a Director of any Group Company.

2.2 In the discharge of such duties and in the exercise of such powers the Executive shall observe and comply with all reasonable lawful and proper resolutions, regulations and directions from time to time made or given by the said Chief Executive Officer (who shall, subject to cl 11(7), deal with all disciplinary matters relating to the Executive in accordance with the Company's Disciplinary Code attached hereto as Appendix [   ]); the Executive shall conform to such hours of work as may from time to time reasonably be required of him for the proper discharge of his duties under the Employment and not be entitled to receive any remuneration additional to that provided in cl 3 for work performed outside normal hours.

2.3 During the Employment the Executive shall (i) faithfully and diligently perform his duties hereunder, (ii) use his best endeavours to promote the interest and welfare of the Group, (iii) devote the whole of his time, attention and abilities during hours of work to the affairs of the Group, and (iv) not knowingly, without the Company's prior written consent, be directly or indirectly engaged or interested in any capacity (including without limitation through a Connected Person) in any Competing Activity.

2.4 Nothing in cl 2(3) shall prevent the Executive from being interested in any Securities, provided that:
  (*a*) where such Securities are listed or quoted on a Stock Exchange, and the company that issued the Securities carries on, or is the Holding Company of a company carrying on, any Competing Activity, the Executive may not hold more than [3 per cent] in nominal value or in number of a class of Securities so listed or quoted; and
  (*b*) the Executive or any Connected Person may not be interested in any unlisted or unquoted company which carries on any Competing Activity.

3   Remuneration

3.1 Subject to the provisions of cl 6 hereof the Executive shall be paid from the date hereof for his services hereunder during the continuance of the Employment a salary at a rate of £[   ] per annum payable in 12 equal monthly instalments in arrears on the last business day of each calendar month. Such salary shall be deemed to accrue rateably from day to day.

3.2 In the event of the death of the Executive during the Employment the

Company shall pay to his personal representatives a rateable proportion of the said salary for the period between the date of death and the first day of the calendar month in which such death occurred.

3.3 The said salary shall be reviewed annually by the Company (but with no obligation to grant an increase therein) during the continuance of this Agreement (provided that the first such review shall take place on [   ]) unless there is in effect a notice to terminate this Agreement pursuant to cl 1(2) or 6(2) hereof. Any revision to the said salary resulting from such a review shall be effective from the date of the anniversary of the signature of this Agreement in the year in which the relevant revision is made, and each such revision shall thereafter have effect as if it were specifically provided for as a term of this Agreement and the figure of £[   ] in cl 3(1) shall thereafter be deemed from time to time to have been amended accordingly. Unless the Executive otherwise consents in writing no review under this cl 3(3) shall result in a decrease in the said salary from the level at which it was immediately before such review.

3.4 The said salary shall be deemed to include any sums receivable as Director's fees or other Director's remuneration from a Group Company, and the Executive shall not be entitled to retain and shall account to the Company for any such sums actually received.

4 Expenses and car

4.1 The Company or a Group Company shall reimburse the Executive such travelling, subsistence, entertainment and other out of pocket expenses as shall from time to time be reasonably and properly incurred by him in the course of the Employment.

4.2 The Company shall in addition make available to the Executive a car during the Employment, of a make and model agreed with the aforesaid Chief Executive Officer, for both private and business purposes.

4.3 In the event that it is necessary for the Executive to move his residence in order to discharge his duties under the Employment from time to time, the Executive shall be entitled to relocation compensation in respect of expenses incurred as a result of such move in accordance with the Company's Relocation Policy attached hereto as Appendix [   ].

5   Holidays

The Executive shall be entitled in each calendar year to [twenty-five (25)] business days' holidays (in addition to statutory and bank holidays) to be taken at such reasonable time or times as may be approved by the Chief Executive Officer of the Company. Any days' holiday not taken at the end of a calendar year shall be lost and not carried forward to the next year unless the Chief Executive Officer otherwise agrees.

6   Sickness and accidents

6.1 When the Executive is absent from work due to ill health or injury the Company shall not, subject to cll 6(2) and 8(2), terminate this Agreement and the Executive shall be entitled to receive:

(*a*) for the first six months of such absence only his normal rate of remuneration (less any entitlement to statutory sickness or injury benefits);

(*b*) and thereafter the Executive shall (subject to cl 6(2) hereof) be paid benefits under the Company's Permanent Health Insurance Scheme in accordance with and subject to the terms and conditions thereof from time to time in force (the premium for which shall be paid by the Company), such benefits to cease upon the Executive returning to work or upon the Executive reaching [the age of] [normal retirement date (as defined in the Company's Pension Plan)] whichever first occurs.

6.2 In the case of any absence through ill health or injury which continues for longer than six months, where the Executive is for any reason disqualified from benefit under the said Permanent Health Insurance Scheme, the Company shall thereafter be entitled, after full consideration of the facts, to terminate this agreement by giving six months' written notice to the Executive.

6.3 During the Employment the Company will pay contributions to a private medical insurance scheme [of the Company's choice] [with a level of benefits comparable to those specified in Appendix] to enable the Executive, the Executive's spouse and eligible dependant children to be covered for benefits under such scheme in accordance with and subject to the terms and conditions thereof from time to time in force.

7   Confidentiality

7.1 The Information shall be treated by the Executive as confidential and shall not be disclosed by him to any third party without prior written consent of the Company nor used by him in any manner which may injure or cause loss either directly or indirectly to the Group, or may be likely so to do.

7.2 The Executive shall take all reasonable steps to minimise the risk of disclosure of the Information. All reasonable precautions shall be taken to prevent unauthorised persons having access to the Information and the Executive shall make arrangement for the proper and secure storage of the Information.

7.3 As between the Executive and the Company the Company shall have the sole right to publish any item of Information (whether or not originated by the Executive) *provided that* the Executive may publish any item of the Information originated by the Executive if permitted in writing to do so by the Company.

7.4 The obligations under this cl 7 shall survive the termination of this Agreement but shall cease to apply to any item of Information when and to the extent that [any general principle of law relating to or affecting the protection of confidential information prevents it so applying including without limitation by reason of the fact that] it has come into the public domain other than by reason of a breach of this clause by the Executive.

8   Termination

8.1 If the Executive shall:
- (*a*) commit any material breach of this Agreement;
- (*b*) be guilty of any gross misconduct or wilful neglect or any act of dishonesty in the discharge of his duties hereunder;
- (*c*) become bankrupt or make any arrangement or composition with his creditors;
- (*d*) be convicted of any criminal offence other than an offence which in the reasonable opinion of the aforesaid Chief Executive Officer does not affect his position as a Director of any company within the Group or cast doubt upon his future ability or fitness to perform his duties hereunder;

the Company shall be entitled by written notice to the Executive to terminate this Agreement forthwith.

8.2 This Agreement shall automatically terminate (and neither party shall have any claim against the other in respect of such termination) upon the Executive reaching [the age of] [normal retirement date (as defined in the Company's Pension Plan)] or upon the death of the Executive, whichever first occurs.

8.3 Upon termination of this Agreement for whatever reason but subject to the provisions of any substitute agreement entered into by the parties pursuant to cl 9:

(*a*) the Executive shall deliver to the Company all books, documents, papers, materials and any other property or assets relating to the business or affairs of the Group which may then be in the Executive's possession or under his control;

(*b*) the Executive shall forthwith and without any claim for compensation for loss of office resign any office of the Company or of any Group Company held by him including without limitation that of Director of the Company;

(*c*) the Executive shall not at any time thereafter represent himself as being in any way connected with the business of the Group;

(*d*) the Executive shall not for a period of [one year] thereafter without the prior written consent of the Company solicit or endeavour to entice away from employment with the Group any person who is an employee of any Group Company engaged in skilled or managerial work at the time of the termination of this Agreement;

(*e*) the Executive shall not within [the UK] for a period of [one year] thereafter without the previous written consent of the Company either on his own account or otherwise and whether directly or indirectly, solicit or entice the custom (in relation to goods or services dealt in or provided by any Group Company for which the Executive shall have carried out any of his duties hereunder) of any person who was a customer of such Group Company at any time in the period of [one year] immediately prior to the termination of this Agreement provided that this restriction shall not apply in relation to solicitations of the custom of any person, firm or company who is then, or who has within the period of [one year] immediately prior to the termination of this Agreement been a customer (other than by reason of any solicitation by, or other act of, the Executive) of any person, firm or company for or in association with which the Executive is working following such termination.

(*f*) the Executive shall not for a period of [one year] thereafter within [the UK] knowingly, without the Company's prior written consent, be directly or indirectly engaged or interested in any Competing Activity, in any capacity (including without limitation through a Connected Person) (except in the circumstances set out in cl 2(4) which shall be deemed to apply to this clause as if it, *mutatis mutandis*, had been incorporated herein);

8.4 If the executive should give notice to terminate this Agreement pursuant to Clause 1(2), the Company shall have the right to require the Executive not to attend for work or to carry out any duties for the Company during such period, provided that subject to this cl 8(4) all of the other provisions of this Agreement shall continue in full force and effect during such notice period (including without limitation those relating to the right of the Executive to receive remuneration hereunder).

9 Waiver of rights

If this Agreement is terminated because of the liquidation of the Company or any Group Company for the purpose of amalgamation or reconstruction and the Executive is offered employment with such amalgamated or reconstructed company on the terms of a substitute agreement not less favourable in all material respects than the terms of this Agreement (provided that the said amalgamated or reconstructed company is able to fulfil all the obligations of the said substitute agreement) the Executive shall have no claim against the Company or the Group in respect of such termination of this Agreement.

10 Inventions

10.1 All intellectual property rights throughout the world in the Information and the Inventions shall vest in and be the absolute property of the Company. Upon the request of the Company the Executive shall (at the expense of the Company) execute all documents and do all acts and things required to vest or perfect the vesting of all intellectual property rights in the Inventions and the Information legally and exclusively in the Company or any nominee or assignee of the Company.

10.2 All documents, forms, papers, designs or other records (in whatever form) concerning the Information and/or the Inventions (whether originally delivered to the Executive by any Group Company or originated by the Executive) are acknowledged by the Executive to be the sole property of that Group Company and the Executive undertakes to deliver up all or any of the same to the Company either on demand or pursuant to cl 8(3)(*a*) *provided that* the Company shall not make such demands as could reasonably be considered to hinder the Executive in the due performance of his duties under this Agreement while the same continues in force.

10.3 The operation of cll 7, 8(3), 10(1) and 10(2) shall be subject to such rights (if any) as the Executive may have in the Inventions under the Patents Act 1977.

11 Miscellaneous

11.1 This Agreement shall from the date of signature thereof operate in substitution of all terms and conditions of employment previously in force between the Company or any Group Company and the Executive (which shall be deemed to have been terminated by mutual consent as from the said date of signature) but without prejudice to the rights, liabilities and obligations (if any) of either party accrued prior to that date.

11.2 If any term or provision in this Agreement shall be held to be illegal or unenforceable, in whole or in part, under any enactment or rule of law, such term or provision or part shall to that extent be deemed not to form part of this Agreement but the validity and enforceability of the remainder of this Agreement shall not be affected. Without prejudice to the generality of the foregoing, each of the subcll (*a*) to (*f*) of cl 8(3) shall be construed as a separate undertaking and if one or more of the said subclauses is found to be unenforceable or in any way an unreasonable restraint of trade, that subclause shall be deemed not to form part of this Agreement, but the remaining subclauses shall continue to be valid and enforceable.

11.3 Any notice to be given hereunder to the Executive may be served by being handed to him personally or by being sent by recorded delivery first class post to him at his usual or last known address and any notice to be given to the Company may be served by being left at or sent by recorded delivery first class post to its registered office for the time being. Any notice served by post shall be deemed to have been served on the next day but one (excluding Sundays and statutory and bank holidays) following the date of posting and in providing such service it shall be sufficient proof that the envelope containing the notice was properly addressed and posted as a prepaid letter by recorded delivery first class mail.

11.4 The Executive hereby irrevocably appoints the Company to be his attorney in his name and on his behalf to execute and do any instrument or thing and generally to use his name for the purpose of giving to the Company (or its nominee or assignee) the full benefit of the provisions of cll 7, 8(3)(*b*) and 10, and in favour of any third party a certificate in writing (accompanied by a certified copy of this Agreement) signed by any Director or the Secretary of the Company that any instrument or act falls within the authority hereby conferred shall be conclusive evidence that such is the case.

11.5 The termination of this Agreement and/or the Employment howsoever arising shall (subject to the terms of any substitute agreement entered into by the parties pursuant to cl 9) be without prejudice to any right of action already accrued to either party in respect of any breach of this agreement by the other party and the definitions and cll 3(2), 7, 8(3), 9, 10 and 11 of this Agreement shall survive such termination.

11.6 The benefits and obligation of this Agreement shall devolve upon the Company's successors in business, and to the extent provided by cl 11(5) shall in the event of the operation of cl 8(2) in an appropriate case devolve upon the Executive's estate and his personal representatives.

11.7 Should the Executive have any grievance relating to the Employment, or wish to appeal against the outcome of any disciplinary proceedings relating to him, he shall initially raise the same in writing with the Chief Executive Officer aforesaid. Should he fail to receive satisfaction therefor the matter shall be referred to the board of directors of the Company, and, if a satisfactory resolution is still not forthcoming, the Executive shall have the right to raise the matter with an industrial tribunal or a court of competent jurisdiction for resolution as appropriate. All other disputes between the parties covering their rights, duties or obligations hereunder or the interpretation of any provision hereof shall be referred to a court of competent jurisdiction.

11.8 Any reference in this Agreement to an Act of Parliament shall be deemed to include any statutory modification or re-enactment thereof whenever made.

11.9 The headings of clauses and Appendices shall be disregarded in construing this Agreement.

11.10 The Appendices and Schedules to this Agreement shall constitute an integral part thereof.

11.11 Any reference in this Agreement to a clause, Appendix or Schedule shall be deemed to be to a clause, Appendix or Schedule of this Agreement.

SCHEDULE 1

1 The location at which the Executive shall perform his duties at the date of signature of this Agreement is [   ].

2 The Executive will be provided with petrol for private mileage travelled in the motor car referred to in cl 4(2).

3 The Executive will be eligible (from the start of the Company's [   ] financial year) to participate in a bonus scheme the details of which will be reviewed and set afresh for each financial year.

4 The Executive's employment is contracted out for the purposes of a retirement pension. From the date of signature hereof the Executive shall be eligible to join the Company's [   ] Pension Plan which provides death and retirement benefits for senior employees and their eligible dependants.

AS WITNESS this Agreement has been signed by or on behalf of the parties hereto the day and year first before written.

Signed by

COMPANY SECRETARY for and
on behalf of [   ] LIMITED

Signed by

Precedent 2

Written statement of terms of employment

Employer's Name [   ]
Address [   ]
Employee's Name [   ]
Address [   ]

STATEMENT OF TERMS OF EMPLOYMENT
THE EMPLOYMENT RIGHTS ACT 1996 [INCLUDING COLLECTIVE AGREEMENTS]

Copies of Company Policies, Company Handbooks, and other documents referred to in this Statement are available for your inspection in the Personnel Office during working hours.

Any alteration in the information contained in any of the documents referred to in this Statement, will be duly recorded in new issues of such documents within one month of the alteration taking effect. Any alteration in the information contained in this Statement will be notified to you in writing within one month of the alteration taking effect.

1   Date of commencement [and termination] of employment

Your employment with the Company commenced on [   ] 19 [   ] [and will terminate on [   ]] [is not intended to be permanent, but is expected to continue for [   ] [weeks] [months]].

[Your normal retirement date is your [   ] birthday. Unless otherwise agreed, and if you are still in employment on this date your employment will terminate automatically without notice on that date.]

2   Continuity of employment

Your employment with [   ], an associated company of the Company counts as part of your period of continuous employment with the Company. The date when that period of continuous employment began was [   ].

3   [Job title] [job description] and location

[The title of the job which you are employed to do is [   ]] [You are employed to carry out the following duties: [   ]] The location of your place of work is [   ]. [The Company reserves the right to change your place of work to any other place within [   ] miles of this location.]

4   Salary

Your salary is £[   ] per annum, payable by bank credit transfer in twelve equal instalments in arrears on the last working day of each calendar month.

5   Normal working hours

Your normal working week consists of 35 hours. Your normal working hours will be [9am–5pm] Monday to Friday [with one hour every day for lunch, to be taken between 12pm and 2pm].

6   Holidays

Your entitlement to annual holidays and to accrued holiday pay on termination of your employment is set out in the Company's Annual leave policy attached as Appendix A.

7   Sickness and injury

The conditions of your employment relating to absence due to sickness or injury, and to pay during periods of sickness and injury, are in accordance with the Company's Sickness and Accident Benefits Plan for Staff Employees.

634 Drafting Commercial Agreements

8   Pension

Your pension entitlement will be in accordance with the rules of the Company's Retirement, Death and Disability Benefits Plan, and your employment is contracted out employment for the purposes of a retirement pension.

9   Grievances procedures

If you have any grievance you can raise this first, either orally or in writing, with your Supervisor who will explain the steps to be taken if the matter cannot be resolved at this level and you wish to take it further.
A document setting out the grievance procedure is available for your inspection in the Personnel Office.

10   Disciplinary rules and procedures

The disciplinary rules applicable to your employment with the Company are set out in the handbook, 'Working with [   ]'.
If you are dissatisfied with any disciplinary decision you can raise this first, either orally or in writing, with your Supervisor who will explain the subsequent steps you may wish to take.
A document setting out the disciplinary procedure is available for your inspection in the Personnel Office.

[11   Notice

The notice required to terminate your employment is in accordance with the periods specified to you in writing by the Company or by the Employment Rights Act 1996 whichever is the greater.]

[12   Collective agreements

The following collective agreements directly affect the terms and conditions of your employment, and are available for inspection in the Personnel Office.]

[13   Working abroad

During your employment you will work at [the Company's Brussels Office at [   ]] for a period of [two months] from [   ] to

[   ]. The Company will pay for your travel expenses (including transport of a reasonable amount of personal effects) by air to Brussels. During this period your salary will continue to be paid in pound sterling, at the rate detailed in paragraph 4, but in addition the Company will pay you [weekly] in arrears an accommodation allowance of [   ] in Belgian Francs. On the completion of the period or earlier termination of your employment (for whatever reason) the Company will be responsible for returning you and your personal effects to the UK by air at its expense.]

14   The foregoing particulars in this Statement are correct as at [   ].

APPENDIX A
Annual leave policy

THIS STATEMENT DOES NOT CONSTITUTE A CONTRACT

I acknowledge receipt of my Statement of Terms of employment.
Date [   ] Signed [   ]
Please detach and return to Personnel Department.

Specimen clauses for employment contracts

1   Confidential information

I appreciate that in the course of my employment I may produce or obtain trade secrets and other confidential information relating to the Company's business (such as details of processes and materials, new products and plans, costings and customer lists) and I agree that I shall respect the confidences entrusted to me by not disclosing or using such trade secrets and other confidential information outside the Company without the Company's permission.

2   Inventions

I understand that if in the course of my duties I originate or help to originate, an invention falling within s 39(1) of the Patents Act 1977, or if in the course of my employment I originate or help to originate a design or copyright work (such as a drawing or computer program) the rights in that invention, design or work belong to the Company. I undertake to give to the Company as soon as possible full details of any such invention, design or work and I am prepared to give the Company any necessary assistance, for example by signing patent application forms or assignments, to ensure that such rights vest in the Company. I appreciate that I may have to give such assistance after leaving the Company's employment and agree that I shall do so at its expense.

3   Expenses

I understand that any travel and out-of-pocket expenses wholly and necessarily incurred by me on Company business, will be reimbursed to me by the

Company to the extent that they are allowable under the relevant Company Policy on Employee Expenses.

4   Security

I agree to comply with all security measures laid down by the Company, from time to time. I understand that a breach of security may, depending upon the circumstance, be treated as gross misconduct justifying immediate dismissal.

5   Conflict of interest

(*a*) I agree to abide by the Company's [Policy on Conflict of interest].

(*b*) In order to avoid any possible conflict of interest between my position with the Company and my relationships with third parties, I agree to seek the Company's permission before becoming involved with any company, firm or person which is or would be a competitor or supplier or customer of the Company.

(*c*) Similarly, if any member of my family or any other person in close personal relationship to me should become involved with any competitor, supplier or customer, in circumstances which could compromise my position with the Company, then I will draw this fact to my manager's attention as soon as possible.

6   Use of company facilities

I agree that I will not use, or cause to be used, the Company's property, facilities or resources for any purpose other than those of the Company.

7   Health and safety

I understand that I am responsible for taking reasonable care of the health and safety of myself and other persons who may be affected by my acts or omissions at work. I accept that I am also responsible for complying with all enactments, regulations and Company rules in this respect, including the Company's [Health and Safety at Work Manual].

8   Other paid work

I agree that I will not, during the continuance of my employment with the

Company and without the prior written consent of my manager, be engaged or have an interest, either directly or indirectly, in any trade, business or occupation which is or may be in competition with the Company and/or which would involve use of the Company's time, property, facilities or resources.

Precedent 4

Consultant's confidentiality clauses

1 (*a*) For the purpose of this Agreement the 'Information' shall mean:
all communications and all information whether written, visual or
oral and all other material (i) supplied to the Consultant by the Company, or any company controlled by, controlling, or in common control with the Company (such companies including the Company
being hereinafter collectively referred to as the 'Group') in pursuance of this Agreement, (ii) relating to any invention, improvement,
report, recommendation or advice given to the Company by the
Consultant in pursuance of his obligations hereunder, and (iii) concerning the business, associations, transactions or financial arrangements of the Group with any other persons or bodies, including other
technical or commercial co-operation agreements;

(*b*) the Information shall be treated by the Consultant as confidential
and shall not be disclosed by him to any third party without the
prior written consent of the Company, nor used by him for any purpose other than pursuant to and for the purpose of this Agreement,
and, in particular, the Consultant shall not use the information for
his own benefit;

(*c*) the Consultant shall take all reasonable steps to minimise the risk of
disclosure of the Information. All reasonable precautions shall be
taken to prevent unauthorised persons having access to the Information and proper and secure storage shall be arranged for any of
the Information in the form of documents, papers and the like;

(*d*) as between the Company and the Consultant the Company shall
have the sole right to publish any item of Information (whether or
not originated by the Consultant) *provided that* the Consultant may
publish any item of the Information originated by the Consultant if
permitted in writing to do so by the Company.

(*e*) Without prejudice to the generality of the foregoing subclauses in the event that whether before or after termination hereto the Consultant shall be retained by a competitor of the Company he undertakes not to disclose to such competitor any of the Information (whether or not originated by the Consultant)

2 (*a*) All intellectual property rights throughout the world in patentable and non-patentable inventions, discoveries and improvements, processes and know-how, copyright works (including without limitation computer programs), new designs and the like (discovered or created by the Consultant in the course of or for any work carried out by the Consultant in pursuance of his duties hereunder or discovered or created by the Consultant as a result whether directly or indirectly of such work and/or (as the case may be) based whether directly or indirectly on any item of the Information) shall vest in and be the absolute property of the Company. Upon the request of the Company the Consultant shall (at the expense of the Company) execute all documents and do all acts and things required to vest or perfect the vesting of such intellectual property rights legally and exclusively in the Company or any nominee or assignee of the Company.

(*b*) All documents, forms, papers, designs or other records (in whatever form) concerning the work carried out by the Consultant in pursuance of his duties hereunder and/or the Information (whether originally delivered to the Consultant by any company in the Group or originated by the Consultant) are acknowledged by the Consultant to be the sole property of that company and the Consultant undertakes to deliver up all or any of the same to the Company on demand *provided that* the Company shall not make such demands as could reasonably be considered to hinder the Consultant in the due performance of his duties under this Agreement.

Chapter 15

Teaming agreements

15.1 Introduction

This chapter is concerned with collaboration or teaming agreements, by means of which two separate and independent undertakings agree to work together to achieve a common objective. Such arrangements are to be distinguished from contractual joint ventures or partnerships in that they are entered into for a limited period of time and for a restricted and well-defined purpose.

The single precedent in this chapter is of a long form teaming agreement, under which two parties agree to work together on a tender for a major contract, on the basis that if the contract is awarded to them, its performance will be divided between them, one acting as main contractor and the other as a subcontractor.

Such arrangements normally require the parties to undertake to work exclusively with each other, for the purposes of tendering and of entering into the relevant main and subcontracts if the tender is successful. Because of this, competition law issues arise, both under UK and EC competition law.

So far as EC competition law is concerned, a collaboration or teaming agreement is simply a horizontal agreement between two or more undertakings which is potentially caught by art 85. The position, here, is relatively simple. If such an arrangement affects trade between member states then the Commission has jurisdiction to consider its effect on competition. However, such arrangements occur because undertakings (each of which can perform part of the tender, but none of which can perform all of the tender) have to combine if they are to take part in a bid at all. Thus, the existence of such combinations in most cases increases the number of tenders for the project, and promotes competition. The fact that the undertakings in a combination agree not to team up and bid with undertakings outside of their combination is a small price to pay. The only circumstances where this may not be the case is if a key undertaking, which alone in the market has the capability to perform part of the project, agrees to team exclusively in one combination. If this occurs, no other combinations will have the full capability to bid. However, absent this consideration, exemption under art 85(3) is likely to be forthcoming in the case of such combinations.

So far as UK competition law is concerned, the current regime is to be found in the Restrictive Trade Practices Act 1976. The Act is complicated, and since the complications surrounding teaming agreements under UK competition law currently relate to this Act, it is necessary first to analyse it in some detail. This is done in section 15.2 of this chapter. Although the Act is to be replaced by the new regime under the Competition Act 1998, the Bill is unlikely to become law before September 1998, will probably not come into force for another 12 months after that, following which there will be a transitional period. Thus consideration of the Act is still necessary at this stage. Some discussion of the Competition Act is contained in Chapter 6 (in relation to agency and distribution) and in Chapter 9 (in relation to mergers, acquisitions and joint ventures). A somewhat fuller analysis of the Bill and its effect on teaming agreements is set out in sections 15.4 and 15.5 of this chapter.

15.2   The Restrictive Trade Practices Act

The Restrictive Trade Practices Act has a formalistic approach. In other words, it catches agreements and arrangements (whether or not legally enforceable) not by reference to what they do or seek to do ('effects doctrine') but by reference to whether or not they contain certain specific restrictions and provisions, and are constructed in certain well-defined ways.

Particulars of agreements and arrangements which are caught by the Act must be furnished to the Office of Fair Trading ('OFT') before implementation, or within three months of signature, whichever is the earlier (see s 24 of the Act), or the restrictions contained in them, which make them registrable under the Act, are void (see s 35 of the Act). The OFT enters the agreements on a public register, and, unless they are considered not to contain restrictions which have a significant effect upon competition, they are referred to the Restrictive Practices Court.

An 'agreement' does not have to be in writing and it is not necessary that the parties to it should intend it to be legally binding. Any arrangement or understanding is an 'agreement' for the purposes of the Act if the parties to it have communicated with one another in some way and as a result of the communication each has intentionally aroused in the other an expectation that he will act or refrain from acting in a certain way. In other words, within the scope of 'agreement' is the type of understanding which, if not honoured, would expose the defaulter to criticism or cause him embarrassment (usually known as a 'gentlemen's agreement').

A registrable 'agreement' may take the form of a number of related agreements which, if examined individually, would not be registrable.

If an agreement is registrable, the whole of the terms of it, whether or not relating to the restrictions which make it registrable, have to be furnished to the OFT under s 24 of the Act. Insofar as the terms are recorded in writing, copies of all the documents are required; if any of the terms of the agreement are not in writing, a memorandum of those terms has to be furnished to the OFT.

The OFT will also refer to the Restrictive Practices Court any unregistered agreements or arrangements which it discovers as a result of its own investigations.

In doubtful cases it is usual to furnish particulars of the agreement to the OFT on a fail-safe basis. The OFT will then discuss with the parties concerned whether or not the agreement or arrangement actually is registrable in its view.

Before the Restrictive Practices Court, the parties may contend that the OFT was wrong in law to regard the agreement or arrangement as registrable. In addition there are various defences or exemptions from registration, which broadly relate to public interest or consumer benefit. If the Restrictive Practices Court considers that the agreement or arrangement is registrable, and that none of these defences apply, it will make an order forbidding the operation of the agreement or arrangement in question. If the agreement or arrangement is an unregistered one which has been discovered by the OFT it will also usually make a further order forbidding the parties from operation of any other registrable agreements or arrangements without first registering them. Breach of any of these orders is a contempt of court punishable by fines or imprisonment. There is, however, no penalty prescribed under the Act for operating an unregistered but registrable agreement, although third parties who have suffered damage as a result of its operation, may bring a civil action for recompense.

An agreement relating to goods is subject to registration if there are two or more parties to it engaged in business in the UK in the production, supply or processing of goods, more than one party to it accepts restrictions (that is, some limitation on his freedom to make his own decisions), and the restrictions concern certain specified matters. These relate to prices to be charged, quoted or paid, or recommended or suggested as the prices to be charged or quoted or paid for goods; conditions of sale; persons to whom or from whom goods may be sold or bought; and quantities or kinds of goods to be made, sold or bought.

Certain classes of agreements within the general definition above are not required to be registered. For example, agreements which are authorised by or under any statutes, agreements relating only to exports or to conditions of employment, certain patent and know-how agreements and licences, and most two-party contracts of sale and most sole agency agreements are exempt from registration.

An agreement relating to services is within the scope of the registration requirements if there are two or more parties to it engaged in business in the UK in the supply of services, two or more parties accept restrictions under it, and the restrictions relate to certain specified matters. These matters are charges, fees, prices, commission rates and so on to be paid for services; terms and conditions for the supply of services; the extent to or the manner in which the business is to be carried on; persons with whom business is to be transacted; areas or places in or from which business is to be carried on.

'Services' is widely defined as including any engagement (whether commercial or professional) undertaken and performed for gain or reward for any matter other than the production or supply of goods or the application to goods of any process of manufacture. The effect of this is to bring within the scope of the registration requirements every variety of service in which business is carried on, with certain exceptions which fall into two categories.

The exceptions from registration which relate to agreements and other relationships concerning goods also apply in general to those concerning services although there are some minor differences. Certain specific agreements and other relationships are also excluded—those relating to international shipping, aviation, road passenger transport, insurance and some financial matters, as well as those affecting the supply or acquisition of certain professional services and certain technical consultancy services in the field of engineering and technology.

'Information agreements' relating to goods (but not services) are also subject to registration. These are agreements between two or more persons engaged in business in the UK in the production, supply or processing of goods, with or without other parties, whereby provision is made for the furnishing by two or more parties of information about the prices charged or quoted, or to be charged or quoted, for goods which have been or are to be supplied, offered or processed or about the terms and conditions on which goods have been or are to be supplied or processed.

The Act contains special provisions relating to the activities of trade associations. Any agreement made by a trade association is deemed to be an agreement made between the persons who are members of the association, and, where any restriction is accepted under the agreement on the part of the association, that restriction is deemed to be accepted by each of the members of the association. Furthermore, any recommendation by a trade association to its members or to any class of its members as to action to be taken or not taken by them in a particular situation operates as if each member had agreed to take or not take that action. In either case, the result would be a registrable agreement if the other registration criteria mentioned above are satisfied.

Finally, although not registrable under the Act, agreements relating to exports which contain registrable restrictions have to be notified to the OFT.

A 'restriction' is nowhere defined in the Act beyond the statement that it includes 'any negative obligation whether express or implied and whether absolute or not'. A party to an agreement is considered to have accepted a 're-striction' if he has accepted any limitation on his freedom to make his own decisions. A restriction thus includes any term of an agreement which places any limitation on the way a party runs his business. A party has accepted a restriction if he feels that he has any obligations to refer to the terms of the agreement or to consult or notify a third party before he makes a decision about any aspect of his business whether it be in matters of research, technical or quality standards or specifications, procurement, production, distribution, selling or marketing.

Certain situations give rise to restrictions which may not always be easily recognisable as such—any obligation to buy a specified percentage of a party's requirements of a product from a certain source and any obligation to supply a specified percentage of a party's production are, in substance, 're-strictions'.

An agreement may not directly restrict a party but may instead confer a benefit on a party who refrains from taking particular action (for example the payment of a commission by the selected tenderer to another company which has not quoted on the invitation to tender) or impose a disadvantage on a party who does not refrain from taking particular action (for example the payment of a penalty for quoting at a price above an agreed level). This type of provision is also a restriction.

An undertaking to a competitor that a bid will not be submitted in response to an invitation to tender before a particular time or before some action is taken with the prospective customer or another person is a restriction.

Even prior to the coming into force of the new regime, there have been attempts by both past and current governments to simplify and streamline procedures under the Act, and to bring it in line with EC competition law. This has been effected by a series of statutory instruments: the Deregulation (Restrictive Trade Practices Act 1976) (Amendment) (Time Limits) Order (SI No 347), the Restrictive Trade Practices (Non-Notifiable Agreements) (Turnover Threshold) Order 1996 (SI No 348), the Restrictive Trade Practices (Non-Notifiable Agreements) (Turnover Threshold) (Amendment) Order 1997 (SI No 2944), the Restrictive Trade Practices (Non-Notifiable Agreements) (EC Block Exemptions) Order 1996 (SI No 349) and the Restrictive Trade Practices (Non-Notifiable Agreements) (Sale and Purchase, Share Subscription and Franchise Agreements) Order 1997 (SI No 2945). All of these statutory instruments are discussed in Chapter 6.10 and the last one is also discussed in Chapter 9.4.

15.3 The Restrictive Trade Practices Act and teaming agreements

From the above it will be clear that the two parties to a teaming agreement have entered into restrictions on their freedom to tender for the relevant project by their undertaking to team exclusively with the other party for the purposes of the project. Also, by their agreement to negotiate together the terms of the relevant main and subcontracts, on a pre-agreed basis, they have probably entered into restrictions relating to the prices terms and conditions on which they will perform the project if the tender is successful. This means that the teaming agreement is registrable under the Restrictive Trade Practices Act, and, because of the technical nature of the Act, the extent to which the agreement promotes or restricts competition is irrelevant. However, the Director General of Fair Trading can recommend to the Secretary of State that a registered agreement not be notified to the Restrictive Practices Court, if he is convinced that the agreement has no effect on competition (see s 21(2) of the Act). This is what often happens in relation to teaming agreements. However, such agreements still have to be registered which means that (unless a special dispensation for confidential commercial terms can be obtained) all of their terms will become public.

The parties to such agreements often assume that a request for confidentiality means that the whole of the agreement will be put on the confidential register (see s 23(3) of the Act). This is not the case. In nearly all circumstances, the parties have to point to specific commercial terms (usually but not always relating to pricing) which they consider would 'substantially' damage their legitimate business interests if made public. Such terms are then deleted from the copy of the agreement (see s 21(3)(*b*)) put on the register.

So far as the precedent is concerned, the inclusion of cll 3.2 (restrictions on both parties only to collaborate with the other), and 5.5, 6.1, 6.2 and 6.3 (requirements for both parties to conduct preparation of the tender and consequent negotiations with the customer together in consultation) are sufficient to make it registrable.

15.4   The new regime under Part I of the Competition Bill 1997

Part I of the Competition Bill 1997 changes the current regime radically. It repeals the Restrictive Trade Practices Act 1976, the Resale Prices Act 1976 and most of the Competition Act 1980. It replaces the current regime with two basic prohibitions. The 'Chapter I Prohibition' deals with anti-competitive agreements or concerted practices (referred to generally in this section as 'agreements') between undertakings or associations of undertakings. The 'Chapter II Prohibition' deals with abuse of a dominant position by an undertaking or undertakings. The Chapter I Prohibition is closely modelled on art 85, and the Chapter II Prohibition on art 86 of the Treaty of Rome. There is, however, a special Chapter II Prohibition covering abuse of a dominant position by national newspaper undertakings. The only substantial difference between the wording of the Prohibitions and that of the arts 85 and 86 is that the former confine the effect of the relevant activity to trade within the UK. The Prohibitions are obviously not concerned with the effect on trade with other member states of the EU (which is the province of the Treaty of Rome) or with the effect on international trade in general.

Breach of the Chapter I Prohibition or the Chapter II Prohibition will be punished by fines. In addition, where there is a breach of the Chapter I Prohibition, the offending provisions in the agreement concerned are void, as is the case with art 85. Third parties who are affected by such breaches are not given a specific right to seek compensation under the Bill, but it is considered that they will have an action against the offender concerned for breach of statutory duty. The Director General of the Office of Fair Trading will disclose information found in his investigations so that third parties will know they have been prejudiced. Also, where the Director General makes a finding of fact in the course of his investigations into a breach, the parties to the offending agreement (in the case of a breach of the Chapter I Prohibition) or the party guilty of the abusive conduct (in the case of a breach of the Chapter II Prohibition) will not be able to dispute that finding in any subsequent proceedings brought by an affected third party.

The Director General will continue to operate the new regime. He is provided under the Bill with significantly strengthened powers to investigate potential breaches of the two Prohibitions, and to make decisions, based on his investigations, that undertakings have in fact breached a Prohibition. In these circumstances he has powers to direct the undertakings to change or end the agreements or conduct in question and to impose civil penalties for such breaches in the form of fines. The directions and any fines imposed are enforceable by a court order on the application of the Director General. The Director General can act either on his own initiative or at the instance of affected third parties.

It should be noted that most utilities in the UK are regulated by their own Director Generals (eg for telecommunications, the Director General of the Office of Telecommunications). The Bill provides that the Director Generals of the regulated utility sectors will exercise over their respective utilities, *concurrently* with the Director General of Fair Trading, most of his powers under Part I of the Bill. The Bill provides that secondary legislation will spell out various procedures and regulations to avoid conflicts over the excersise of the concurrent jurisdiction.

The Bill provides for the setting up of a new Competition Commission to which appeals can be made against the decisions or directions made or fines imposed by the Director General. These appeals can be made either by undertakings to whom the decisions or directions apply or upon whom the fines have been imposed. Interested third parties can appeal against decisions or directions made by the Director General, but not in relation to fines imposed by him. Appeal lies from the Commission (with leave) to the Court of Appeal (for matters in England and Wales) to the Court of Sessions (for matter in Scotland) and to the Court of Appeal of Northern Ireland (for matters in Northern

Ireland). Appeal lies on a point of law and for a review of the level of fines. The Competition Commission will also replace and discharge the functions of the Monopolies and Mergers Commission. This issue is discussed in Chapter 9.

Certain types of agreement are exempt from the scope of both the Chapter I and Chapter II Prohibitions: mergers and acquisitions under the Fair Trading Act 1973, planning obligations under the Town and Country Planning Act 1990, compliance with legal requirements, agricultural agreements exempted from the operation of art 85, the coal and steel industries (regulated by the ECSC Treaty) and undertakings entrusted with the operation of services of general economic interest or having the character of revenue-producing monopolies in so far as the Prohibitions would obstruct the particular tasks assigned to that undertaking.

So far as the Chapter I Prohibition is concerned, the Director General is granted powers to exempt agreements on an individual basis, in the same way that the EC Commission can under art 85(3). Similarly the Secretary of State, acting on the recommendation of the Director General, is empowered by order to exempt certain categories of agreements from the Chapter I Prohibition. This type of exemption is identical to the block exemptions enacted by the Commission under Regulations pursuant to art 85(3) and EU Council Regulation 17/62, and the exemptions are also referred to under the Bill as block exemptions.

Agreements covered by the special competition provisions in the Financial Services Act 1986, the Companies Act 1989 and the Broadcasting Act 1990, and the rules of various professions are exempt from the Chapter I Prohibition. There is a provision in the Bill which would enable the exemption of agreements relating to land, but to date the precise width and definition of the exemption is still the subject of considerable discussion.[18] Finally there is a power to grant immunity to 'small agreements' (other than price-fixing agreements) from the penalties for breach of the Chapter I Prohibition. It will be necessary to define 'small agreements' in secondary legislation by reference to criteria such as market share and turnover. This would appear to enable the passing of legislation which has an effect equivalent to the Commission Announcement on Agreements of Minor Importance of 1997, although the precise wording of the Bill's provision means that, although parties to small agreements need not notify them, the Director General could still investigate them and require the parties to change the agreement or terminate it. There is a similar provision granting immunity for conduct of 'minor significance' in relation to penalties for breach of the Chapter II Prohibition.[19]

Any party to an agreement which might infringe the Chapter I Prohibition can apply to the Director General either for confidential guidance or a firm decision as to whether the agreement in question does breach the Chapter I Prohibition. The Director General is normally unable to reopen proceedings once guidance has been given or a decision made, unless the situation changes or he has not been given the full facts of the case. Similar provisions apply to parties who are concerned whether their conduct might constitute a breach of the Chapter II Prohibition against abuse of a dominant position.

One of the aims of the new regime is to align UK competition law as closely as possible with EC competition law. This can be seen by a number of harmonising provisions set out in various clauses of the Bill.

First of all there is the question of conflict between the Commission and the Director General in relation to art 85 and the Chapter I Prohibition. An agreement could breach either or both of these provisions depending upon whether it had an effect on trade in the UK or on trade between member states of the EU or both. Similarly agreements which might be subject to both provisions would require an application for exemption to both the Director General and the Commission. The Bill deals with this conflict in two ways.

First, if an agreement is exempt from the prohibition under art 85, or would be so exempt if it affected inter-state trade, it is also automatically exempt from the Chapter I Prohibition. This is called a 'Parallel Exemption'. The concept of Parallel Exemption thus covers agreements which are actually exempt under Commission or Council Regulations (ie block exemptions) or agreements which would have been so exempt if a Regulation would have applied except for the fact that the agreement did not affect inter-state trade. Exemption is also granted if an individual exemption has been granted by the Commission pursuant to art 85(3) either expressly or through the expiry of the relevant opposition period set out in an application made under one of the block exemptions containing a provision for short-form notification and exemption under a non-opposition procedure. It should be noted that the definition of 'Regulation' is tight and that parties would not be able to take advantage, under the concept of Parallel Exemption, of Commission Notices and Announcements.[20]

Secondly, where an application for exemption under art 85(3) has been made to the Commission, the agreement in question is treated as provisionally immune from penalties under the Bill for the period during which it is being examined by the Commission, provided that the Commission has not withdrawn the similar provisional immunity from penalties granted to agreements notified to it pursuant to Council Regulation 17/62.

This means that, although the Director General can investigate the agreement himself and presumably give directions in respect of it, he cannot impose penalties for the period when the agreement is under investigation by the Commission. If in due course the Commission gives an individual specific exemption under art 85(3) or otherwise finds that an EC Regulation applies to grant exemption or would have done if inter-state trade had been affected, then the agreement will receive automatic exemption under the first provision above, and the Director General will not be able to act in relation to it.

However, if a specific exemption is refused and no other Parallel Exemption applies, the provisional immunity to penalties granted by this provision will cease once the Commission dismisses the application. In this case, the party concerned will from then on be potentially liable to penalties under the Bill unless and until it submits an application to the Director General for exemption from the Chapter I Prohibition. Obviously, if at all possible, the second application should be submitted with no time lag. It might, however, be prudent to submit an application to the Director General for exemption from the Chapter I Prohibition in parallel with the application to the Commission on a fail-safe basis.[21]

The most significant provision, which applies to the whole of the new regime in general, and in particular to both the Chapter I and Chapter II Prohibition, requires that the Director General, and all courts and tribunals concerned with the new regime, operate the new regime on the basis of principles that are consistent with EC competition law.

The relevant clause (as currently drafted) states:

'(1) The purpose of this section is to ensure that so far as is possible (having regard to any relevant differences between the provisions concerned) questions arising under [Part I] in relation to competition within the United Kingdom are dealt with in a manner which is consistent with the treatment of corresponding questions arising in Community Law in relation to competition within the Community.

(2) At any time when the court determines a question arising under [Part I] it must act (so far as is compatible with the provisions of [Part I] and whether or not it would otherwise be required to do so) with a view to securing that there is no inconsistency between:
   (*a*) the principles applied and decision reached by the court in determining that question; and
   (*b*) the principles laid down by the [Treaty of Rome] and European Court and any relevant decision of that Court as applicable at that time in determining any corresponding question arising in Community Law.

(3) The court must in addition have regard to any relevant decision or statement of the Commission.

(4) Subsections (2) and (3) also apply to:
   (*a*) the Director, and
   (*b*) any person acting on behalf of the Director
   in connection with any matter arising under [Part I].

(5) In subsections (2) and (3) 'court' means any court or tribunal.

(6) In subsections (2)(*b*) and (3) "decision" includes a decision as to the interpretation of any provision of Community law.'

This provision is clearly the strongest possible indication that the principles of EC competition law should be applied within the new regime even if it does not go quite so far as to incorporate the whole body of EC competition law within the new regime. The provisions of subsection (3) would enable regard to be had to Commission Announcements and also to European Court case law and Commission decisions on the definition of relevant terms such as 'undertaking' or 'dominant position'. For instance, it would seem highly likely that the Commission Announcement on Exclusive Agency Agreements of 1962, together with the relevant European Court and Commission Decisions, would be applied to exclude most agency agreements from the ambit of the Chapter I Prohibition and that the Commission's guidelines on determining markets would be applied to decide the relevant market for questions surrounding breach of the Chapter II Prohibition.[22]

15.5   Transitional provisions under the new regime

The current timetable for the Bill means that it is likely to be enacted in September 1998. The issue which held up the Bill for some time was a suggestion that there should be an exclusion applying to most vertical agreements (see the discussion on the EC Commission Green Paper on Vertical Restraints in Chapter 6.9). This was promised by the DTI in 1997 when announcing the Bill, but so far it has proved difficult to reach agreement on a clear definition of the term so as to produce a suitable exclusion. The Bill now provides that the exclusion will be defined and introduced by way of secondary legislation. Once the Bill has been enacted Part I will only come into force on an appointed day, which will be 12 months after the enactment date.

Agreements made before the enactment date will be exempt from the Chapter I Prohibition for a transitional period of one year from the date that Part I comes into force. The Director General may extend this period in relation to particular agreements by up to twelve months if the parties apply to him for such an extension. However, it is important to note that agreements made before the enactment date will still be subject to the Restrictive Trade Practices Act, and the Resale Prices Act, both of which will only be actually repealed by Part I when it comes into force. Thus, in order to benefit from the transitional period an agreement must, if registrable, be registered under the relevant Act. Where an agreement does take advantage of the transitional period, the Restrictive Trade Practices Act or the Resale Prices Act will continue to govern it during that period.

Agreements made between the enactment date and the date Part I comes into force can also take advantage of the transitional period provided that (where registrable) they have been registered prior to the date Part I comes into force. The transitional legislation is now contained in Schedule 12 to the Bill, and is detailed and complex. The basic message however, is that in order to take advantage of the transitional period, agreements (where registrable) must be registered before Part I of the Bill comes into force. Otherwise such agreements run the risk of being used under the old regime and immediately caught by the new regime (with the potentiality for fines and prohibition) with no chance to amend the agreement of discontinue it during a period of grace provided by the transition period.

15.6   The new regime and teaming agreements

Given the above discussion it can be seen that the principles to be applied to teaming agreements under the new regime will be similar to those already applied to them under art 85 as discussed in section 15.1 above. The only point that needs emphasising is that currently care must be taken to register teaming agreements under the Restrictive Trade Practices Act in order to take advantage of the transitional provisions of the new regime.

15.7   Precedent 1

It is now possible to analyse the detail of the precedent itself. The recitals set out the intent of the parties to co-operate for the purposes of a particular pro-project, on the basis that one will be prime contractor and the other subcontractor. After the definitions, cl 2 sets out the basic obligations of the parties to collaborate for the tender. Clause 3 defines their relationship as one of prime and subcontractor, and states clearly that the collaboration is for this limited purpose only, and does not give rise to some broader joint venture or partnership. Clause 3.2, which restricts the parties to collaborate in respect of the project only with each other, has already been discussed as the clause which is mainly responsible for the requirement of registration under the Restrictive Trade Practices Act 1976.

Clauses 4 and 5 then deal with the allocation of work and the way in which the parties will prepare, submit and negotiate the tender. Clauses 5.6 and 5.7 should be noted particularly. If the parties cannot agree on the terms of the tender to be submitted, then either party may withdraw from the project without liability. However, this does not mean that the mutual obligations to consult together on the terms of the tender in cl 5.5 do not constitute a registrable restriction. It must be remembered that a restriction is any clog on the freedom of a party to make its own decisions, even if not in the last analysis legally binding, and the obligation to consult (even though the parties can withdraw if they are not satisfied with the results of the consultation), does constitute such a restriction.

The basic purpose of cl 6 is to bind the parties to enter into their respective contracts for the project upon the terms upon which they have tendered for it, subject to any mutually acceptable amendments negotiated with the customer between the time that he has notified the parties that they have been awarded the contract and the time when the formal contract documents are signed. In general, the subcontractor is required to accept any amendment to the main contract which has no effect on the subcontract, and is also required to accept any such amendment, which does affect the subcontract, and any amendment to the subcontract, unless, in either case, it is economically disadvantageous to him.

Clause 7.1 provides a cross-indemnity where one party permits the other to use its intellectual property rights for the purposes of the project, and that party is subsequently pursued by a third party who claims that its intellectual property rights have been infringed by such use. Clause 7.2 excludes any liability of one party to the other in respect of loss of profits or consequential loss. This provision is very important since it prevents arguments where one party blames the other for loss of the tender and then tries to sue for compensation for such loss. Clause 7.3 contains some further standard limitations on liability by way of monetary amounts. Clause 7.4 makes it clear that once the project is awarded to the parties their rights *inter se* are regulated only by the terms of the subcontract which, presumably, will contain suitable limitations of liability in respect of the performance by the subcontractor of his obligations thereunder. Clause 8 is a standard *force majeure* clause.

Clause 9 regulates the licensing of intellectual property rights between the parties for the purposes of performing the project. Clause 9.1 provides that each party retains ownership of its background, or pre-existing intellectual property rights, grants the other party a free licence to use such background for the purposes of tendering for the project, and, once the project is being performed, provides for the grant of further licences between the parties, and to the customer, for the purposes of the project. Clause 9.1 also imposes an obligation on the subcontractor not to incorporate in, or use for the performance of, its part of the project, intellectual property which it does not own or control. Clause 9.2 regulates the ownership and licensing of intellectual property generated during the course of a project (foreground). Each party owns the foreground it generates, unless it is an improvement on or development of the other party's background, and licences are granted to the parties, and the customer, similar to those granted in relation to the project in respect of background. Clause 9.3 provides for the continuation of the grant of relevant licences of intellectual property rights if a party withdraws from the project. Clause 9.4 ensures that equivalent provisions to Clauses 9.1, 9.2 and 9.3 are incorporated in the resulting subcontract.

Clause 10 provides rights in relation to the use and disclosure of confidential information between the parties for the purposes of the project, but presupposes that the parties will have already entered into a separate full confidentiality agreement (see Chapter 13, Precedent 1 or 2) for the purpose of protecting that information. Clause 11 regulates the use of the parties' staff seconded to the project.

Clause 12 prevents, in most cases, as is natural, the assignment by one party of its rights and obligations under the agreement without the consent of the other. However, such assignment is permitted to another group company or to a purchaser of the relevant party's business, if the phrases in square brackets are included. In this connection, such permission should not be given without studying whether the customer will permit it under the terms of the invitation to tender, or the main contract, as the case may be.

Clause 13 regulates publicity releases by the parties in relation to the project. It is usual in such collaborations for neither party to make such releases without, at the very least, consulting with the other.

Clause 14 deals with the difficult subject of withdrawal. Clause 14.1 permits withdrawal up until the submission of the tender. Clause 14.2 provides alternatives once this date has passed. If the first phrase in square brackets is used no withdrawal is possible. This is really the most practical arrangement, since the parties are now committed together to the customer in the terms of the tender, and one or both of them may even have had to put up a bid bond. The second alternative permits withdrawal for some fundamental reason, but this alternative, because of the uncertainty it generates, and the difficulty of defining a fundamental reason, is not to be recommended.

Clause 15 deals with duration and termination of the agreement. It contains the standard clause that no restriction which requires registration under the Restrictive Trade Practices Act is to take effect until particulars of the agreement have been furnished to the OFT in accordance with s 24 of the Act. This provision preserves the legal position, but it must be remembered that in this case either party would be free to co-operate with a third party for the purposes of tendering (despite cl 3.2) until the particulars are duly furnished.

It should be realised, however, that the Act catches 'gentlemen's agreements' as well as legally binding contracts. This clause is thus of limited value if the parties have some arrangement that they tacitly agree to operate pending registration. Since it is often difficult to prove that there is no such arrangement particularly in a teaming agreement, where the parties are working together from the time the agreement is signed, and perhaps before, it is best to regard such clauses as a fail-safe, and to furnish particulars of the agreement to the OFT upon signature whenever possible.

Subject to this, the agreement (unless earlier terminated for breach or by withdrawal of one of the parties) will terminate when the customer or the parties decide not to go ahead with the project, when the tender is lost to a third party, or when the tender is awarded to the parties (in which case the agreement is superseded, as between the parties, by the relevant subcontract).

Finally, cl 16 provides a notice clause, cl 17 a whole agreement clause, and cl 18 a governing law clause. Appendices provide for details of the allocation of the work on the project between the parties, and the form of subcontract if this can be agreed at this stage of the collaboration.

15.8   European Economic Interest Grouping

Finally, mention should be made of the European Economic Interest Grouping ('EEIG') which is a creature purely of European law. The EEIG appears to third parties in most respects as a legal entity which can contract and do business with them in its own right. However, so far as the members are concerned the EEIG appears more like a partnership. The purpose of the EEIG is not to act as a long-term full function joint venture (see Chapter 9) but rather to act as a vehicle for *ad hoc* co-operation between parties, situated in different member states of the EU, for a particular project or a particular activity. Thus where parties join together for a specific project, as envisaged in the teaming agreement used in this chapter, an EEIG would be one vehicle which they could use to tender for and take the project if successful. Details of the regime governing EEIGs is set out in Appendix 1 to this chapter.

Teaming agreement

THIS AGREEMENT is made the [   ] day of [   ]
19[   ] between [   ] whose registered office is at
[   ] (the 'Main Contractor') and [   ] whose registered office is at [   ] (the 'Sub-Contractor').

WHEREAS:

(A) [   ] (the 'Customer') [has issued] [is shortly expected to is-
sue] an Invitation to Tender (the 'ITT') in respect of a requirement for
[   ] (hereinafter referred to as the 'Project'); and
(B) the parties wish to work together with the Main Contractor as the intended
prime contractor and the Sub-Contractor as the intended subcontractor to the
Main Contractor for its Allocated Work (as hereinafter defined), to prepare
and submit a tender in response to the ITT, and, if such tender is accepted, to
enter into the resultant Contract and Sub-Contract (both as hereinafter defined)
for implementation of the Project, with the parties' respective responsibilities
being as described in this Agreement; and
(C) the parties wish to define their respective rights and obligations *inter se* in
respect of the preparation, submission and negotiation of the said tender and
the execution of the Contract and the Sub-Contract; and
(D) the parties also wish to express their intention to work together to submit
tenders for, and execute, subsequent phases of the Project subject to later specific agreement of the parties.

NOW THEREFORE IT IS HEREBY AGREED as follows:

1   Definitions

For the purposes of this Agreement the following expressions shall (unless the

context otherwise requires) have the respective meanings set out against them:
'Main Contractor', 'Sub-Contractor', 'Customer', 'ITT' and 'Project' shall
have the respective meanings hereinbefore ascribed to them;

'Party' means a party to this Agreement and 'Parties' shall be construed accordingly;

'Operational Requirements' means the Customer's statement of requirements
for the Project [Reference No [   ] dated [   ]] and
shall include any amendment to such statement issued by the Customer;

'Proposal' means the formal response to the Operational Requirements and
the ITT to be prepared by the Parties and to be incorporated by the Main Contractor into the Tender;

'Tender' means the tender to be submitted to the Customer by the Main Contractor in response to the ITT;

'Contract' means the contract (if any) to be entered into by the Customer with
the Main Contractor as a result of the Tender;

'Sub-Contract' means the subcontract to be entered into between the Main
Contractor and the Sub-Contractor as a result of the Contract, pursuant to the
provisions of this Agreement;

'Allocated Work' means, in relation to a Party, the work and obligations whose
initial scope is set out in outline in Appendix 1 to this Agreement and which
will be the responsibility of that Party to carry out as part of the Contract or, as
the case may be, the Sub-Contract;

'IPR' means patents, registered and unregistered design rights, semiconductor
topography rights and copyright of any kind and any other form of related
protection, statutory or otherwise, wherever in the world subsisting, and shall
include applications for any of the foregoing respectively; and

'Proprietary Information' means and includes designs, drawings, reports, specifications, procedures, instructions, software, and any other technical or commercial information and data.

2 Collaboration

2.1 The Parties hereby agree to collaborate with each other for the purposes of,
and upon the terms and conditions set out in, this Agreement and to observe
good faith towards one another in all matters affecting their dealings hereunder and interests herein.

2.2 This Agreement is entered into solely for the purposes of preparing and
submitting the Tender and entering into and performing the Contract and the
Sub-Contract. The responsibilities of the Parties with regard to the carrying
out of the Project shall be as set out in the Contract and the Sub-Contract.

2.3 It is the present intention of the Parties to collaborate with each other in making a tender for any subsequent phase of the Project unless the methods of procurement chosen by the Customer prevent such collaboration.

3   Relationship of the parties

3.1 The relationship of the Parties hereunder is one of potential main contractor and subcontractor in respect of the Project. No relationship of agency, joint venture or partnership shall exist or shall be deemed to exist between the Parties, and except as specifically provided herein no Party shall have the authority to bind the other Party without the latter's prior written approval.

3.2 While this Agreement is in force neither Party shall, whether in relation to its Allocated Work or otherwise, either itself or in association with any third party, make any offer to the Customer in response to the ITT or provide to the Customer or to any third party any information constituting or leading to any such offer or enter into any agreement with the Customer or any third party for the supply of goods and services for the Project (which offer and/or agreement competes with the Tender submitted or to be submitted in accordance with this Agreement) without first securing the written agreement of the other Party. [Notwithstanding the foregoing, nothing contained in this Agreement shall be deemed to prevent any Party from supplying goods or services in the normal course of its business other than in respect of the ITT or the Project.]

4   Allocation of work

The work which is to be the responsibility of the Main Contractor under the Contract and of the Sub-Contractor under the Sub-Contract shall generally be in accordance with the Allocated Work.

5   Preparation and submission of the tender

5.1 The Parties will work together in good faith to prepare the Tender so that it may be submitted to the Customer by the Main Contractor by the submission date stated in the ITT. Each Party shall appoint a Project Manager to co-ordinate its activities in connection with the Project and the Tender and all matters relating thereto including without limitation the management of the Contract and of the Sub-Contract as the case may be.

5.2 Each Party shall prepare those parts of the Proposal which correspond to that Party's Allocated Work and the Sub-Contractor shall assist the Main Contractor with the integration of its parts of the Proposal into the complete Tender documents under the guidance of the Project Manager appointed by the Main Contractor pursuant to cl 5.1 hereof. Each Party shall have sole responsibility and liability in respect of its part of the Proposal and for ensuring the accuracy and adequacy thereof and of all information and data therein.

5.3 The Tender will indicate that the Main Contractor will be the prime contractor and that the Sub-Contractor will be the subcontractor in accordance with the Allocated Work of both of the Parties as defined in Appendix 1 hereto or as subsequently agreed in writing between the Parties.

5.4 The Sub-Contractor will submit to the Main Contractor a priced offer, including a full statement of compliance or (as the case may be) non-compliance with the provisions of the ITT, in respect of its Allocated Work by such time as will enable the Main Contractor to integrate such offer into the Tender and to comply with any time limits required by the Customer in connection with the submission of the Tender or any part thereof, but the Sub-Contractor shall not be obliged to provide the Main Contractor with details of its rates of wages and salaries, overheads or profit. Such offer shall be valid for acceptance by the Main Contractor, and shall not be capable of being withdrawn, during the validity period of the Tender plus an extra period of [thirty (30)] days.

5.5 A final draft of the Proposal shall be reviewed by the Parties at the premises of the Main Contractor and agreed by the management of each of the Parties before incorporation into the Tender. Prior to submission of the Tender, the Sub-Contractor shall confirm to the Main Contractor its agreement to the content thereof and its commitment to fulfil those terms thereof which relate to or concern its Allocated Work.

5.6 The Tender will be substantially on the terms required by the ITT subject to any amendments agreed by the Parties.

5.7 Neither Party shall be liable to the other Party for or in respect of the consequences of any failure of the Tender or any part thereof to result in the Contract and/or the Sub-Contract (for any reason whatsoever) or for any withdrawal effected under the terms of cl 14 hereof.

5.8 Unless otherwise stated in this Agreement, each Party will bear its own costs, fees and expenses incurred in performing its obligations under this Agreement.

6   Negotiation and acceptance of the contract

6.1 Subject to the other provisions of this Agreement, negotiation with the Customer shall be conducted by the Main Contractor as the intended prime contractor, but the Main Contractor may request the participation therein from time to time of representatives from the Sub-Contractor. Such participation shall be forthcoming from the Sub-Contractor in a proper and timely fashion.

6.2 The Main Contractor will report progress in the negotiation of the Contract regularly to the Sub-Contractor and will consult with the Sub-Contractor on all relevant matters.

6.3 (*a*)   If the Main Contractor is awarded the Contract by the Customer, the Main Contractor will accept such award and will enter into the Contract on the terms and conditions set out in the Tender subject to such amendments (if any) thereto as are agreed between the Customer and the Main Contractor, but with the prior approval of the Sub-Contractor to the extent that it is affected thereby, such approval not to be unreasonably withheld or delayed. Without prejudice to the generality of the foregoing, it shall be considered reasonable for the Sub-Contractor to withhold its approval if the relevant amendment would have the effect of:
   (i)   significantly reducing the price payable to, or the rates chargeable by, the Sub-Contractor; or
   (ii)   constituting a fundamental change to the Tender or the Project; or
   (iii) constituting a significant increase or decrease in the Allocated Work of the Sub-Contractor; or
   (iv)   significantly increasing the risk appertaining to the Sub-Contractor's performance of its Sub-Contract and/or its ability so to perform.
(*b*)   If the Main Contractor wishes or is requested to make any amendments to the proposed Contract, as set out in the Tender, that would result in an amendment to the Sub-Contract, the Main Contractor shall advise the Sub-Contractor, with full details of the proposed amendment and the corresponding changes to the Sub-Contract, and shall give the Sub-Contractor every reasonable opportunity to be present at all relevant meetings with the Customer and to make representations to the Customer regarding the proposed amendments.

6.4 If and when the Main Contractor accepts and enters into the Contract, the Main Contractor and the Sub-Contractor will enter into and accept the Sub-Contract and the Sub-Contractor will be bound to the Main Contractor as prime contractor to fulfil as subcontractor the obligations assigned to it in the Sub-

Contract and will be entitled to the corresponding rights therein and benefits thereof.

6.5 The terms, conditions and prices of the Sub-Contract shall (subject to any changes thereto subsequently agreed by the Sub-Contractor pursuant to cl 6.3 hereof) be those terms, conditions and prices contained in the Sub-Contractor's offer under cl 5.4 hereof. The Sub-Contract shall contain provisions equivalent to those of cl 9 hereof as provided by cl 9.4 hereof. The Sub-Contract shall be [substantially in the form of the draft document contained in Appendix 2 to this Agreement, and shall be] set out in a formal contract intended to come into effect on acceptance of and entry into the Contract by the Main Contractor as provided in cl 6.4 hereof.

7 Liability

7.1 Each Party will indemnify and hold harmless the other Party from and against any and all claims, demands, proceedings and judgments made against such other Party (and any costs and expenses incurred by such other Party with the prior approval of the indemnifying Party in connection therewith) in respect of any infringement or alleged infringement by the other Party of any IPR of a third party arising directly or indirectly out of the use by such other Party in accordance with the terms of this Agreement of any information or data (including without limitation Proprietary Information) or IPR provided or licensed hereunder to such other Party by the indemnifying Party. The foregoing indemnity shall only apply if:

(*a*) the other Party informs the indemnifying Party promptly of any such claim, demand, proceeding or judgment which has come to the notice of the other Party and refrains from taking any action in respect of such claim, demand, proceeding or judgment without the prior written approval of the indemnifying Party; and

(*b*) the other Party places the entire direction and control of any such claim, demand, proceeding or judgment in the hands of the indemnifying Party and fully co-operates with the indemnifying Party in the defence or settlement thereof, and makes no admission to the claimant or otherwise which might prejudice the indemnifying Party's conduct thereof or of any negotiations for the settlement thereof; and

(*c*) the aforesaid information or IPR data is used only in the manner and for the purposes reasonably to be inferred from this Agreement.

Provided that the foregoing indemnity shall not apply to:

(i) any claim, allegation, demand, proceeding or judgment arising out of use of the aforesaid information or data or IPR in a manner or for a purpose not specified in or reasonably to be inferred from this Agreement; or

        (ii) infringement or alleged infringement attributable to any combination of the aforesaid information or data or any product derived therefrom with any other information, data or product.

The remedies contained in, and the other provisions of, this cl 7.1 constitute the entire liability of the indemnifying Party, and the other Party's exclusive remedies, for the infringement of IPR of a third party by information, data (whether or not Proprietary Information) and IPR provided or licensed hereunder to the other party to the indemnifying party, and in no event shall the indemnifying Party be liable for any special, indirect or consequential loss or damage or for loss of use, business, income, profits or contracts suffered by the other Party, as a result of any such claim, demand, proceeding or judgment.

7.2 Neither Party shall be liable to the other Party for any special, indirect or consequential loss or damage or for any loss of use, business, income, profits or contracts suffered by the other party regardless of whether or not the same results from any delay or failure by the first-mentioned Party in carrying out the first-mentioned Party's obligations under this Agreement.

7.3 Subject and without prejudice to cll 7.1 and 7.2, the total liability of each Party to the other hereof under this Agreement, whether arising in contract, tort or otherwise, shall be limited in respect of each event or series of connected events as follows:

    (*a*) for death of or injury to persons, no limit;

    (*b*) for loss of or physical damage to tangible property, [   ]; and

    (*c*) for all other matters, [   ].

7.4 The liability of the Parties to each other as prime contractor and as subcontractor in respect of the execution of the Project will be as set out in the Sub-Contract to the entire exclusion of this Agreement (including without limitation cll 7.1, 7.2 and 7.3 hereof).

8   Force Majeure

Neither Party shall be liable to the other Party in respect of any delay in performing or failure to perform any of its obligations hereunder if such delay or failure results from (i) acts or intervention of Government or Government agencies, (ii) fire, flood or explosion, (iii) Act of God, (iv) declared or undeclared war, or riots or civil commotion, (v) strikes or other industrial disputes, (vi) any act neglect or default of the other Party, or (vii) any cause outside its reasonable control.

9 Intellectual property rights

9.1(*a*) Each Party (the 'Owner') or its licensor owns and will continue to own all the Owner's Proprietary Information and other material which has been developed independently of the Project and this Agreement and all IPR therein (hereinafter together referred to as 'Background').

(*b*) Subject and without prejudice to cl 9.1(*c*) hereof and provided it is not prevented from doing so by any agreement or arrangement with a third party, each Owner will, free of charge but subject to the agreement of appropriate terms and conditions, grant to the other Party for the duration of this Agreement, in respect of such Background of Owner to which that other Party needs access in order to carry out its obligations under this Agreement, such rights to use and licences as are necessary for that other Party to carry out such obligations.

(*c*) Except with the express written consent of the Owner, Background belonging or available to an Owner may not be used by:

    (i) any party other than the other Party to this Agreement; or

    (ii) by the other Party to this Agreement other than in accordance with this Agreement.

The Sub-Contractor agrees that it will not without the prior written agreement of the Main Contractor utilise for the purposes of this Agreement and/or the Project Background in respect of which the Sub-Contractor has no right to grant to the Main Contractor the rights required so to be granted by this Agreement.

(*d*) The Parties agree with each other to grant [free of charge but subject to the agreement of appropriate terms and conditions] [on fair and reasonable terms to be agreed] [on normal commercial terms]:

    (i) to the Main Contractor and/or the Customer, rights to use and licences under such Background of the Sub-Contractor to which the Main Contractor and/or the Customer need access in order for the Main Contractor to perform, and/or the Customer and the Main Contractor to exercise their respective rights under, the Contract; and

    (ii) to the Sub-Contractor, rights to use and licences under such Background of the Main Contractor to which the Sub-Contractor needs access in order for the Sub-Contractor to perform, and/or exercise its rights under, the Sub-Contract;

but in each case only to the extent necessary to enable such performance and exercise.

9.2 (*a*) All Proprietary Information and other material developed in the preparation of the Tender or generally in respect of the Project under this Agreement, the Contract or the Sub-Contract, and all IPR therein (hereinafter together called 'Foreground') shall belong to the Party employing the inventor or originator of the same. If the inventors or originators are employed by both Parties, the Parties shall agree between themselves arrangements for the ownership and use of the relevant Foreground.

(b)   Clauses 9.1(*b*), 9.1(*c*) and 9.1(*d*) hereof shall apply to Foreground *mutatis mutandis* but subject to any variations thereto which are necessary to give effect to the terms of the Tender, the Contract and the Sub-Contract.

(c)   In the event that any Foreground is a specific development by a Party of the Background of the other Party then the developing party shall for a reasonable fee (which shall take into account any sum which has to be paid by the Customer or the Main Contractor to the developing Party under the Contract or the Sub-Contract in respect of such development or its use) assign such Foreground to that other Party and shall then (subject to the provisions of cl 9.2(*b*) hereof) have no further rights or interest in the same *provided that* this clause shall not prevent the developing Party from using fully and without restriction and for any purpose the know-how, techniques or processes it has used in carrying out such development and no such use shall constitute an infringement of the IPR of the other Party in such Foreground.

9.3 In the event that any Party terminates its involvement in the Project in accordance with the provisions of this Agreement or otherwise becomes unable to perform its obligations hereunder then:

(a)   the rights granted by that Party under cll 9.1 and 9.2 hereof shall continue in full force and effect to the extent necessary for the performance of the Project and the use and exploitation of the results thereof; and

(b)   that Party will enter into good faith negotiations to grant or procure the grant to the other Party, on fair and reasonable commercial terms, of rights to use any Background or Foreground of that Party which is necessary for the performance of the Project and the use and exploitation of the results thereof, including without limitation the submission of the Tender and the execution and performance of any contracts related thereto (including the Contract or the Sub-Contract as the case may be).

9.4 The Sub-Contract shall contain clauses identical to cll 9.1, 9.2 and 9.3 hereof, together with any additional provisions needed to implement the said clauses in accordance with their terms.

10 Disclosure of proprietary information and confidentiality

10.1 Subject and without prejudice to the provisions of cl 10.3 hereof, the Parties shall keep each other fully informed of all significant matters concerning the Tender, the Contract and the Sub-Contract, and each Party shall upon request make available to the other Party such of the first-mentioned Party's Proprietary Information as is reasonably necessary for the performance by that other Party of its obligations hereunder.

10.2 The points of contact with respect to the transmission and control of Proprietary Information disclosed hereunder are designated by each Party as follows:

      For the Main Contractor [   ]

      For the Sub-Contractor [   ]

Each Party may change its designation by notice to the other Party.

10.3 In addition to any requirements of the Contract and subject as provided in cl 9, the obligations of the Parties in respect of the confidentiality and restricted use of Proprietary Information disclosed under or in connection with this Agreement shall be as set out in the Confidentiality Agreement dated [   ] between the Parties which shall remain in full force and effect in accordance with its terms.

11 Staff

11.1 The staff to be allocated by each Party to the preparation of the Proposal and the Tender in accordance with the Allocated Work, will be suitably qualified, trained and experienced for their intended responsibilities.

11.2 Until six months after an employee of either Party ceases to work on the preparation of the Tender pursuant to this Agreement, the other Party will not solicit the employment of such employee.

12 Assignment

Neither Party will be entitled to assign all or any part of its rights and obligations hereunder without the prior written consent of the other Party [with the exception of an assignment to any other company (having its registered office within the UK) in the Group of Companies to which the assigning Party belongs, or to a purchaser of that part of the assigning Party's business which is engaged in the preparation of the Tender or will be engaged in the performance of the Contract or the Sub-Contract as the case may be]. The aforesaid consent shall not be unreasonably withheld or delayed and, in any event, shall be given unless the other Party, acting reasonably and in good faith, objects to the identity and/or involvement of the proposed assignee as being contrary to its commercial and/or business interests.

13   Publicity

Neither Party shall make use for publicity purposes of the name, or of any trade name or trademark, of the other Party, or of any information obtained under or in connection with this Agreement from the other Party, without the prior written consent of the other Party. Neither Party shall issue any publicity or other announcement in relation to this Agreement, the Project, the Contract or the Sub-Contract, without the prior written approval of the other Party of the form and content thereof, which approval shall not be unreasonably withheld or delayed.

14   Withdrawal

14.1 If a Party decides that [for what in its reasonable opinion are sound technical or commercial reasons] it wishes to withdraw from this Agreement before the submission of the Tender, it may so withdraw by notifying the other Party forthwith, in which case the Party concerned shall thereupon cease to participate in the preparation of the Tender and shall have no liability for the subsequent actions of the other Party.

14.2 After the Tender has been submitted to the Customer, a Party [may not withdraw from this Agreement.] [may only withdraw from this Agreement for reasons of a fundamental nature vital to the affairs of that Party, and the provisions of cl 14.1 shall apply to such withdrawal *mutatis mutandis.*]

14.3 Any withdrawing Party shall, without prejudice to its obligations under cl 9 hereof, co-operate with the other Party to the extent reasonably necessary to enable its role under this Agreement to be taken over by the other Party or by a third party.

15   Duration and termination

15.1 This Agreement and all rights and obligations hereunder will come into force on the date of this Agreement, except that any provision hereof which would but for this cl 15 be void for failure to furnish particulars of this Agreement to the Office of Fair Trading pursuant to s 24 of the Restrictive Trade Practices Act 1976 shall not take effect until the day following the day on which the said particulars have been so furnished as aforesaid. This Agreement and all such rights and obligations will remain in force (subject as provided in cl 15.2 hereof), until whichever of the following shall first occur:

(*a*) a decision by the Customer not to proceed with the Project, or a direction or requirement by the Customer to the Main Contractor or the Sub-Contractor to collaborate in respect of the Project with a third party or third parties or to proceed with the Project alone; or

(*b*) the Parties' decision not to submit the Tender; or

(*c*) the award of a contract in respect of the Project to a third party; or

(*d*) the failure of the Customer to award the Contract to the Parties within [30 days] following the expiry of the validity period of the Tender (as amended with the agreement of the Parties from time to time) unless the Parties agree in writing an extension of such period; or

(*e*) withdrawal of any Party under cl 14 hereof; or

(*f*) the acceptance and entry into the Contract by the Main Contractor, and the acceptance and entry into the Sub-Contract by the Sub-Contractor in accordance with cl 6.4 of this Agreement.

15.2 In the event of:

(*a*) a breach of this Agreement by a Party which is irremediable or, if remediable, is not remedied by that Party within thirty (30) days of service upon it by the other Party of notice specifying the breach; or

(*b*) a Party having a receiver or liquidator or administrator appointed or ceasing to trade or having an order made against it, or passing a resolution, for winding-up, or making any composition or arrangement with its creditors generally;

the other Party shall be entitled forthwith by notice to that Party to terminate this Agreement.

15.3 Termination or expiration of, and withdrawal from, this Agreement, for any reason, shall be without prejudice to all accrued rights liabilities and remedies.

16   Correspondence and notices

16.1 Subject as provided in cl 10.2 hereof correspondence relating to this Agreement shall be sent:

(*a*) For the Main Contractor to

[   ]

marked for the attention of

[   ];

(*b*) For the Sub-Contractor to
    [   ]
    marked for the attention of
    [   ].

16.2 All notices to be given hereunder shall be in writing and shall be sent by first class registered or recorded delivery mail, or by telex, facsimile or other electronic means in a form generating a record copy, to the address stated above, of the Party being served, or to such other address of which such Party may hereafter give notice to the other Party. Any notice sent by mail shall be deemed to have been duly served three working days after the date of posting. Any notice sent by telex, facsimile or other electronic means shall be deemed to have been duly served at the time of transmission.

17   Entire agreement

This Agreement supersedes all prior representations, arrangements and understandings between the Parties relating to the subject matter hereof and except as expressly provided herein is intended by the Parties to be the complete and exclusive statement of the terms and conditions of this Agreement. Any amendment to this Agreement must, to be effective, be in writing and signed by an authorised representative of each Party.

18   Governing law

The interpretation, construction and performance of this Agreement shall be governed exclusively by English law and the Parties expressly submit to the non-exclusive jurisdiction of the English courts.

AS WITNESS this Agreement has been signed for and on behalf of the Parties the day and year first before written.

SIGNED for and on behalf of
the Main Contractor
[   ]
Status [   ]

SIGNED for and on behalf of
the Sub-Contractor
[   ]
Status [   ]

APPENDIX 1
Allocated Work

The initial scope of the work and responsibilities to be undertaken by each of the parties in respect of the Project is as follows:
(*a*) MAIN CONTRACTOR
(*b*) SUB-CONTRACTOR
The precise scope of the Allocated Work will be as defined in the Proposal.

[APPENDIX 2
Agreed Form of Sub-contract
See attached (   ) pages.]

European Economic Interest Grouping ('EEIG')

1   Concept and origin

(a)   Concept

(i) Facilitate cross-frontier co-operation between businesses and organisations in the EU.

(ii) Overcome difficulties in previous possibilities for such co-operation arising from:
- the need to use company or other corporate structures or a contractual relationship; and
- the need to choose a national legal system determined by the economic or legal domicile of one of the partners, with other partners therefore being on unfamiliar and 'hostile' ground.

(iii) The EEIG is a separate entity whose creation and functioning are governed by rules which will, in the main, be common to all countries of the EU and which national laws cannot change in any way.

(iv) The EEIG allows partners of various national domiciles to combine part of their economic activities while at the same time preserving their legal and economic independence.

(b)   Origin

(i) EC Council Regulation No 2137/85.

(ii) Direct applicability throughout the EU.

(iii) Came into force on 3 August 1985, but EEIGs could not be established until 1 July 1989.

2 Nature

(a) Objects

(i) To facilitate or develop the economic activities of its members and to improve or increase the results of those activities.

(ii) By pooling activities, resources and/or services, members can develop their own economic activities and increase their profits.

(b) Restrictions

EEIGs cannot and must not:
- (i) be used to create a new activity which has no connection with the activities of its members; for this a corporate or other structure must be used;
- (ii) replace the economic activities of its members or become so important that such activities are taken over by the EEIG or become dependent on it;
- (iii) exercise, directly or indirectly, power of management or supervision over members' own activities or activities of another undertaking, particularly in fields of personnel, finance and investment;
- (iv) directly or indirectly, hold shares of any kind in a member, but it can hold shares in another undertaking if on behalf of the members and necessary for the achievement of the EEIG's objectives;
- (v) employ more than 500 persons;
- (vi) be used to make loans, or transfer property, to directors of companies, except to the extent permitted by the company laws of EU member states; and
- (vii) be a member of another EEIG.

(c) Ancillary nature and examples

(i) EEIG activities must be not more than ancillary to a common economic activity of each member, ie there must be a link between the activity of the EEIG and the activities of its members.

(ii) Examples of situations in which an EEIG could be used or useful:
- in response to an invitation to tender for a major public works contracts;
- for centralised joint R&D or other centralised joint activities such as promotion or marketing;
- as representation on or to, or at the creation of, standards bodies.

(*d*)   Profits

(i)   The EEIG exists to promote members' interests, not to make profits for itself.

(ii) This does not prohibit profits being made.

(iii) The EEIG is neutral as regards profits and taxation.

(iv) Profits and losses are taxable only in the hands of the members of the EEIG.

3   Implementation of EC Regulation

(*a*)   UK

(i)   European Economic Interest Grouping Regulations 1989 came into effect on 1 July 1989.

(ii) Regulations are necessary despite direct applicability of EC Council Regulation:

(*a*) to implement parts of the Regulation which leave certain provisions for national laws;

(*b*) for the purposes mentioned in s 2(2) of the European Communities Act 1972, ie enabling the implementation of the EC Regulation.

(*b*)   Other EU countries

(i)   Largely implemented.

(ii) The EEIG can only be registered in a country which has passed the necessary national legislation, but can then operate throughout the EU without restriction.

4   Setting up an EEIG

(*a*)   Membership

(i)   Available to persons, companies, firms and other legal entities in the member states of the Community governed by public or private law and who were engaged in an economic activity prior to the creation of the EEIG.

(ii) Must have at least two members belonging to different member states:

(*a*) companies, firms and other legal bodies must have their registered or statutory office and central administration in the EU; and

(*b*) natural persons must carry out any industrial, commercial, craft or agricultural activity, or provide professional or other services in the EU.

(iii) Must be limited to 20 members if registered in an EU member state whose implementing legislation so provides.

(iv) Must not include members of a class prohibited or restricted by such legislation on grounds of public interest.

(b)   Official address

(i) Must be situated in the EU.

(ii) Must be fixed either:

    (a) where the EEIG has its central administration; or

    (b) where one of the members has its central administration provided that the EEIG carries on an activity there.

(iii) The official address can be moved from one EU member state to another without affecting the legal capacity of the EEIG, subject to the publication of the transfer proposal agreed by all of the members of the EEIG and the absence of opposition from the competent authority if so provided for by the implementing national legislation.

(c)   Formalities

(i) Members draw up a contract including:

- its name, which must include 'EEIG' or 'European Economic Interest Grouping';
- its official address;
- its objects;
- its name, business name, legal form, permanent address or registered office and its number and place of registration, if any, of each member;
- any finite duration of the EEIG.

(ii) The contract is filed at the registry of the country in which the EEIG has its official address.

(iii) Other documents and particulars have to be filed at that registry, including:

- amendments to formation contract;
- notice of setting up or closing of any EEIG establishment;
- notice of the appointment of managers and the termination of such appointments;
- notice of assignment of a member's participation;
- winding-up decisions, liquidation etc;
- proposals to transfer official address; and
- any clause exempting new members from liability for debts incurred prior to admission.

These matters are published in the *Official Gazette*.

(iv) Filing of annual reports and accounts is not required.

5   Structure and operation

(*a*)   Freedom

Considerable freedom is allowed by the Regulation. The EEIG is organised and run according to the terms of its formation contract.

(*b*)   Members and managers

(i) Two compulsory organs:
- members acting collectively; and
- a manager or managers.

(ii) Formation contract may provide for other organs, eg supervisory body, board, committee etc; if it does, it must determine their powers.

(iii) Members acting collectively are the decision-making body; terms for decision-making are to be defined by the formation contract, but:
- each member must have one vote, but can have more, ie *pro rata* to financial contributions, so long as no one member has a majority;
- certain decisions must be unanimous: a transfer of the official address; an alteration of the objects, votes, contributions and other obligations, or any other aspect of the formation contract; and an extension of any fixed period of duration.

(iv) Manager or managers:
- appointment is either in the formation contract or by a decision of the members;
- powers are either set out in the formation contract or determined and defined by a unanimous decision of the members;
- even if they are published, limitations on manager's powers have no effect against third parties on whom the only binding limitation is a published limitation requiring the signature of one or more other managers; and
- acts of managers are binding upon the EEIG without limitation, even if beyond the objects defined in the formation contract.

(*c*)   Financing

(i) Considerable flexibility; no requirement for capital.

(ii) Formation contract can provide for contributions in cash or in kind or by way of services including technical knowledge contributions.

(iii) Members are free to decide in what proportions and by what methods each member contributes. If the proportions are not laid down in the formation contract, the members contribute in equal shares.

(*d*)   **Liability**

(i)   The EEIG can enter into commitments and will be liable to cover them with its own assets.

(ii)   If the EEIG defaults, members have unlimited joint and several liability for its debts and other liabilities of whatever nature, if:

- the debt is a debt of the EEIG; and
- the creditor has requested the EEIG to pay and it has not done so within an 'appropriate period'.

(iii)   Any clause in the formation contract excluding or restricting the liability of a member is ineffective against a third party.

(iv)   The contract between the EEIG and the third party could contain an enforceable waiver of joint and several personal liability of the members or a limitation to a specified amount.

(v)   It is unclear as to whether performance by the EEIG of a contract could be specifically enforced against a member.

(vi)   A member who has paid the debt of an EEIG can proceed against the other members for their shares.

(vii)   Withdrawing members remain liable for five years in respect of debts arising out of activities before the cessation of membership.

(viii)   New members can be exempted from liability for debts arising prior to admission to membership if the exemption is provided for in the formation contract or in a published instrument of admission.

(*e*)   **Insolvency**

EEIGs are subject to national laws governing insolvency and cessation of payment. In the UK, the provisions in the Insolvency Act 1986 concerning members' voluntary winding up apply to EEIGs as if they were companies registered under the Companies Act 1985.

(*f*)   **Other matters**

Matters concerning EEIGs which are not covered by the Regulations or by the formation contract or by subsequent decisions of the members, must be resolved by the application of the internal law of the EU member state in which the EEIG's official address is situated.

Chapter 16

Securities for debts

16.1 Introduction

A creditor's primary method of ensuring payment of his debts is the threat of legal proceedings which will result in a judgment debt that can be enforced in the last analysis by seizing and, if necessary, selling, any of the debtor's assets that the creditor can lay his hands on.

Some creditors will also attempt to threaten the debtor with proceedings for bankruptcy (if an individual) or for a winding-up petition (if a company), since failure to pay a debt after due demand is an act of bankruptcy and grounds for winding up. However, where such a course of action is used in a case in which the reason for non-payment is a genuine dispute over the amount of the debt, or a counter-claim of some sort, not only can the debtor resist the proceedings successfully, but the court will regard the proceedings themselves as an abuse entitling the debtor to an award of his costs in the action against the creditor (see *Re a Company (No 0012209 of 1991)* [1992] 2 All ER 797).

In any event, putting the debtor into bankruptcy or liquidation is a pyrrhic victory, since the creditor merely invites all of the other creditors to share in the spoils, and rarely achieves a payment of one hundred per cent of his debt.

Thus the primary aim of a creditor has to be to put himself in a position where he knows he will be able to obtain payment of his debt in full speedily, without dispute, and without resort to legal proceedings. His secondary objective is to ensure that, if proceedings are required, and the debtor cannot pay all of his creditors, he at least is paid in full.

Where the debtor is solvent, and the debt is truly due, sooner or later, either as a result of persistent applications from the credit control department or the debt collection agency, or, in the last resort, through legal proceedings, the debt will be collected. The real difficulty is how to collect in full from a debtor who cannot meet all of his obligations in full. Here the contest is not between debtor and creditor, but between creditor and creditor, and this is where the question of security for debts assumes its true importance.

The simplest way to solve these problems is to deal with honourable, solvent debtors who meet their obligations as they fall due, and there can be no substitute for proper credit vetting procedures which check out the status of customers before credit is given to them. After all, the best way to avoid bad debts is to deal on the basis of an advance payment, cash with order or an irrevocable letter of credit, where there is any doubt as to status. Naturally this ideal state of affairs is not usually commercially practical, and creditors must make use of all of the various means given to them either at law or under contract to ensure both payment and priority.

16.2   Guarantees

The first, and in some ways the best type of security, is the third party guarantee. If the debtor appears a bad risk, let him find a guarantor who is creditworthy. The obtaining of such a guarantee sidesteps all of the problems relating to the debtor, but, of course, those problems will then arise in relation to the guarantor. In the commercial world, the best guarantor is naturally a bank or other financial institution, and such guarantees can be obtained by commercial customers in return for a fee. Such guarantees are usually only forthcoming to cover customers whom the guarantor itself considers a good credit risk. Nevertheless, the financial institution acting as guarantor will often be the main lender financing the customer's business requirements, and will thus already have taken security over the whole of its customer's business in priority to all of the trade creditors, so that, in assessing creditworthiness for the purpose of giving a guarantee, it can take a more relaxed attitude than an unsecured trade creditor could.

The other circumstances where guarantees are usually obtained as a matter of commercial practice and prudence are by a holding company of its subsidiary's liabilities, and personal guarantees of the liabilities of a private limited company by its directors and/or shareholders.

The latter situation is particularly important since such directors or shareholders may well choose (whether or not fraudulently) to take assets from their company into their private ownership, with a consequent diminution of its creditworthiness. It should also not be forgotten that, even if the directors or shareholders are not themselves particularly creditworthy, if their company starts to come under some financial pressure, they are more likely to pay debts which they have guaranteed personally than those that they have not. Although there is obviously a fine line to be drawn here as to whether, in the event of subsequent insolvency, some kind of fraudulent preference has taken place, the creditor who has been paid in full is in a better position than one who has not. The liquidator or trustee in bankruptcy will have to institute proceedings to attempt to reclaim the payment, and during the ensuing dispute some acceptable compromise may be reached. One of the most important principles in any dispute between creditors in the situation of insolvency is that the creditor who has been paid or holds an asset is in a stronger position than one who does not. In this case possession may not be nine-tenths of the law, but it is certainly more than half.

16.3   Liens

The simplest instance of the worth to a creditor of possession of an asset as security can be found in the operation of the lien.

Apart from specialised usages (such as judicial or equitable liens) a lien is a creditor's right to retain possession of his debtor's chattels until the debtor pays his debt. It confers no power of sale. Liens can arise at common law, under statute, or by contract. Since they are founded on possession, the creditor must obtain possession by lawful means, and not for a purpose inconsistent with a lien (eg to sell). Assets subject to a lien cannot be seized by third parties claiming against their owner, nor can the owner's successors in title obtain possession, without paying the debt. The lien thus provides both the debtor, and, in the event of insolvency, the debtor's receiver or liquidator, with a powerful incentive to pay the debt in full, particularly where the chattel is worth significantly more than the debt in question.

Under general liens, the creditor can retain any property of his debtor coming into his possession regardless of its relationship to the debt. They arise at common law only in favour of bankers (against customers for unpaid loans), solicitors and stockbrokers (against clients for unpaid fees and charges, but only over instruments of title or other documents), and factors (against the principal for unpaid commission). Older cases suggest that in some parts of the country such liens arise, in other relationships, under local usage, but where such cases still hold good, burden of proof lies with persons asserting such liens.

Under particular liens, only property directly related to the debt can be retained. At common law today, the only important particular lien arises where a chattel is delivered to a workman to carry out work on it (which results in some improvement, not merely maintenance) for an agreed price. Once the work is completed, he can retain possession until he is paid. In practice the line between improvement and maintenance is hard to draw, but repair, particularly where new parts or materials have been installed in a machine in exchange for old, would normally fall on the side of improvement. For instance, it is arguable that where a garage services a motor vehicle, merely by adjustment and perhaps lubrication, the vehicle cannot be the subject of a lien for the cost of the service, while, if, in addition, new parts were exchanged for old, or a repair was carried out, a lien for the whole of the cost of all the work carried out would arise.

However, most tradesmen tend to assert a lien in practice, without regard for this fine line, and most of their customers are not sufficiently knowledgeable to contest it, whether they are really entitled to do so or not. The correct solution to this problem is to impose a contractual lien as part of the conditions for doing the work in question, in which case the distinction between maintenance and improvement will become academic.

The innkeeper's lien for unpaid accommodation charges (originally arising at common law but now regulated by statute) covers all the property of a guest brought into the hotel and is thus something between a general and a particular lien.

The unpaid seller's lien arises under the Sale of Goods Act. Although property has passed to the buyer, and even if he is in possession as the buyer's agent, the seller may retain possession of goods until he has paid their price, provided that he has not sold on credit, or, if he has sold on credit, either the period of credit granted has expired, or the buyer has become insolvent. The lien is lost on delivery to a carrier without reserving the right of disposal, or if the buyer lawfully obtains possession. The lien is of course also lost if the seller chooses to waive it, but the obtaining of judgment by the seller in an action for the price neither destroys the lien nor constitutes a waiver by the seller.

16.4   Pledge

A pledge is a type of bailment. Personal property capable of being delivered (usually therefore tangible) is deposited by a borrower (pledgor) with his lender (pledgee). The property will be returned upon repayment of the debt. Unlike a lien a pledge confers not only possession but also the right of sale (and power to confer title on a purchaser) if repayment is not made and the property reclaimed within an agreed period of time. Although the pledge arose at common law and was previously used widely, today the most familiar pledgee is the pawnbroker, whose activities are regulated by statute. The pledge is thus not today a common form of security in commercial transactions, but it should not be ignored in appropriate circumstances.

16.5   Mortgages

Under a mortgage of real or personal property the borrower (mortgagor) remains in possession of the property mortgaged. A legal mortgage transfers title in the property to the lender (mortgagee), together with a power of foreclosure and sale upon a default in repayment. On repayment (redemption) title is reconveyed to the mortgagor.

An equitable mortgage may be created by an express document agreeing, under certain circumstances, to transfer the legal title in the property to the lender, or by way of deposit of the instruments of title to the property in question with the lender. On default, under both types of equitable mortgage, the lender has the right, in equity, to compel the borrower to convey to him legal title in the property for the purposes of sale. Upon repayment the agreement is terminated or the instruments are returned as appropriate.

Today, in commercial transactions, the true legal mortgage (particularly in relation to personal property) has mostly been replaced by various forms of charges (which will be discussed below), but the equitable mortgage by deposit of instruments of title is still quite widely used, the most common being title deeds or certificates for real property and certificates for shares, debentures or loan stock, although other documents of title for goods, such as bills of lading, warehousekeeper's certificates or dock warrants, may be used.

However, care must be taken to distinguish between documents which are certificates (ie evidence) of title, and documents which give the possessor the right to take immediate possession of the goods concerned as security for the debt (eg a warehousekeeper's certificate made out to bearer), or whose deposit of itself transfers title to a *chose in action*, such as bearer bonds or bearer shares, or other negotiable instruments payable or endorsed to bearer. Deposit of the latter is regarded not as an equitable mortgage but as the giving of a pledge of the relevant goods or *chose in action*.

16.6   Charges

Under a charge the debtor gives his creditor the right to resort to identified property, real or personal, tangible or intangible, to satisfy the debt if not repaid. Neither possession nor title passes to the creditor, but, at common law, he had a right to call for the assignment of the property to him if the debt were not repaid when due. The more common remedy, mainly under statute nowadays, is to appoint a receiver who takes control of the property for the purpose of selling it, satisfying the debt, and handing the balance, if any, over to the debtor.

Charges can arise either as a result of agreement or by operation of law. In commercial circumstances the charges arising by operation of law which are most commonly met with are those imposed under the equitable doctrines relating to the tracing of property (and the proceeds thereof) which has been entrusted to a bailee or fiduciary and misapplied by him.

Express charges arising by agreement have now largely replaced the old true legal mortgage, particularly for real property, where the most common form of security is now the charge by way of legal mortgage provided by statute in relation to registered land. The equitable mortgage created by an express document has also largely been replaced by charges.

Express charges can be either fixed or floating. A fixed charge is created over specific assets. Apart from real property and capital assets businessmen find fixed charges impractical since assets (eg inventory) are constantly being replaced by others, so charges would have to be continually created and released. Instead a charge is created over all the assets of the business from time to time, or perhaps one or more classes of assets, such as book debts or inventory. This floating charge 'hovers' over the assets as they change in the course of trading until a default occurs. The charge then attaches to all the assets actually in the business at that time ('crystallises') and a receiver is then appointed of those assets.

It should be noted that such charges can cover deposits of cash held either in a bank or by some other person (eg a landlord as security for payment of rent). *Re Charge Card Services Ltd* [1987] Ch 150, a decision at first instance in the Chancery Division, held that a charge in favour of a bank of a deposit of cash held by that bank was invalid because it negated the obligation of the holding bank to return the cash to the depositor in accordance with the terms of the deposit. This principle was applied to all persons who held deposits of cash by way of security, whether banks or not. This decision, even though recently affirmed by the Court of Appeal in *Morris v Agrichemicals* [1996] 2 All ER 121 was overturned by the House of Lords in *Re Bank of Credit and Commerce International SA (No 8)* [1997] 3 WLR 909, HL. It is now possible for the holder of the deposit (whether or not a bank) to take a charge over the cash deposit.

16.7   Registration of mortgages and charges

The problem with all forms of mortgages and charges, whether they are security for commercial transactions or personal loans, is that the borrower remains in possession of the assets mortgaged or charged, and so continues to present an appearance of prosperity to other creditors who are not aware of the mortgage or charge. Further, in cases of fraud, the asset concerned may be disposed of for value to third parties who are ignorant of the existence of the mortgage or charge in question. The debtor then disappears with the proceeds of the disposal, leaving the original creditor and the innocent third party to a dispute over the asset concerned.

Desire for publicity to avoid fraud has resulted in the application of the concept of registration. There are various regimes for registration, some of which overlap to some extent.

First, all charges or mortgages created over real property by individuals or companies do not bind third parties unless registered in the appropriate land registry.

Secondly, all charges or mortgages created by a company over its undertaking or over any of its property, real or personal, tangible or intangible, are void against a liquidator, receiver and creditors unless registered in the Companies Registry, pursuant to ss 395–405 of the Companies Act 1985.

Thirdly, legal and equitable charges or mortgages by individuals of personal property which are created by an express document are regulated by the Bills of Sale Acts 1878 and 1882. In general terms a bill of sale is merely a document which creates a mortgage or charge over personal chattels. The Bills of Sale Act 1882 requires all bills of sale given as security for loans by individuals to be made in a prescribed form and registered in the Central Office of the Supreme Court. Otherwise they are void against all persons including the parties.

Since the Bills of Sale Acts apply only to individuals, the area of overlap which occurs between these three regimes relates to mortgages or charges over their real property created by companies. In order for these to be completely effective they must be registered both in the appropriate land registry and in the Companies Registry.

The status of equitable mortgages requires some consideration. So far as real property is concerned, they may be registered at the appropriate land registry, but, if they are not, on the usual equitable rules, they will not bind a transferee who takes for value in good faith without notice of their existence.

So far as registration by natural persons is concerned, an express document which creates a mortgage over personal property (whether legal or equitable) is a bill of sale, but an equitable mortgage by way of deposit of title certificates is not caught by the Bills of Sale Acts, because there is no bill of sale which the Acts can require to be registered.

So far as registration under the Companies Acts is concerned, s 395 of the Companies Act 1985 requires the registration of all securities 'created' by the company. Thus it makes no difference whether the charge or mortgage is equitable or legal nor how it is created. Although a legal mortgage or charge over real property can only be created by a deed, an equitable mortgage over real property can be created either by a deed or other express document or by deposit of certificates of title. In theory, any mortgage of personal property (legal or equitable) can be created orally (and perhaps later evidenced in writing) and an equitable mortgage of personal property can also be created by deposit of documents of title. However, since all of these securities are 'created', they must be registered. Unlike the Bills of Sale of Acts which bite only upon the actual document constituting the bill of sale, s 395 bears on the creation of the charge irrespective of the manner in which it is created.

Re Bank of Credit and Commerce International SA discussed but did not settle whether it is necessary to register charges over cash deposits. This turns upon whether a cash deposit is to be regarded as a book debt in terms of s 395. In some cases it may well fall within this definition, although arguably cash at bank does not. However, for the sake of prudence, it is better to register all such charges if at all possible.

Thus, only those charges arising over a company's property by operation of law need not be registered. This is particularly important in relation to retention of title clauses which are discussed below.

Statutory and common law liens are not registrable under any of the above regimes, since they arise by operation of law. Thus there can be no bill of sale under the terms of the Bills of Sale Acts, nor is there any security 'created' by the company in terms of s 395 of the Companies Act 1985. Additionally, pledges are specifically exempted from the Bills of Sale Acts and the companies registration requirements.

A contractual lien granted by a company does not require to be registered under s 395 of the Companies Act 1985. The issue was discussed, in a recent case, *Re Hamlet International plc and Re Jeffrey Rogers (Imports) Ltd* (1998) *The Times*, 13 March, ChD. In the case a warehousing company was granted a contractual general possessory lien, over goods stored from time to time in its warehouse by two customer companies, one of which subsequently went into administration. Coupled with the lien was a contractual right entitling the warehousing company to sell the goods of the two customers from time to time in its possession to satisfy sums owed to it by the customers in respect of warehousing fees. When the warehousing company attempted to sell such goods, the administrators intervened claiming that the contractual lien coupled with a right of sale amounted to a floating charge which was void for want of registration under s 395.

Hamilton J disagreed with this and held that the lien did not amount to a charge: therefore did not require registration and hence was enforceable. He based his reasoning on the New Zealand decision *Wattomo Wools (NZ) Ltd v Nelsons (NZ) Ltd* [1974] 1 NZLR 484 which dealt with a case concerning registration under the New Zealand legislation which was almost identical to s 395. Here the nature of a charge was defined as conferring a right to fetter or interfere with the grantor's title to the property affected. In his view a contractual lien could not be described as a charge for the purposes of s 395 because it had no effect on the ownership of the goods, which clearly remained with the company granting the lien. The rights granted to the warehouse company under the contractual lien only held good so long as the goods were in its possession. If possession was lost, the rights would disappear as well. This was not the case with rights granted under a charge since they would continue to subsist irrespective who had possession of the goods. So far as the right of sale was concerned, Hamilton J considered that its existence did not convert the lien into a charge, but that, even if he were wrong and the right to sell were of itself to be regarded as a charge, its lack of registration would not invalidate the right of the warehouse company to retain possession of the goods until its fees were paid. He also laid stress on the fact that the goods had not been delivered as a security or pledge, but for the purpose of distribution by the warehouse company on behalf of its customer companies to their customers.

Where a contractual lien is granted in a written document by an individual, since possession is not retained but transferred to the creditor, the lien should not be registrable in terms of the requirements of the Bills of Sale Acts either. Of course, an oral contractual lien granted by an individual cannot be so caught because no document which could possibly be a bill of sale exists in respect of the transaction in any event.

16.8 Retention of title clauses

The possibility of retention of title clauses in contracts for the sale of goods arises, under English law, from the sections of the Sale of Goods Act 1979 (ss 16, 17 and 19) which together permit the seller to delay the passing of title under the contract, even though delivery has taken place, until a specific condition (in this case, payment for the goods) has been fulfilled.

The clause is quite commonly used under systems of law in Europe (particularly in Germany) and it was as a result of a case involving a sale of goods with Dutch sellers that the clauses first came into prominence in the UK (*Aluminium Industrie Vassen BV v Romalpa Aluminium Ltd* [1976] 1 WLR 676).

These clauses are often used too enthusiastically and drafted far too widely for their effective operation under English law, as the line of cases since *Romalpa* has shown. One trap for the unwary, which must be avoided at all costs, is to fail to reserve the whole title in the goods, and only to reserve a beneficial or equitable interest, while passing the legal title to the buyer. This method creates an equitable charge which is void unless registered under the Companies Act 1985, s 395 (see *Re Bond Worth Ltd* [1980] Ch 228 and *Stroud Architectural Systems v John Laing Construction plc* [1994] 2 BCLC 276).

Such clauses also create a practical problem in that an unpaid seller, who has delivered goods under a retention of title clause, cannot sue for the price, since under s 49(1) of the Sale of Goods Act 1979 the seller can only sue for the price when title has passed to the buyer, unless (see s 49(2)) the price has to be paid on a 'day certain'. This problem can be avoided by inserting express provisions as to payment, providing for a 'day certain' on which payment is to be made. Retention of title clauses are most useful where one is dealing with goods which are easily identifiable as the property of the seller. Unique capital goods and equipment, very often with identifying serial numbers, is probably the type of goods for which these clauses are most useful.

Problems arise when the goods which are sold to the buyer are in fact more in the nature of commodity or consumer goods, and are purchased by him for the purpose of resale. In these circumstances, the express power of resale, as agent for the original seller, coupled with either s 25(1) of the Sale of Goods Act 1979 or s 2(1) of the Factors Act 1889, enables the buyer to transfer good title to his end customers. The seller then looks to his security by trying to obtain rights over the proceeds of sale in the hands of the buyer.

It seems clear from *Romalpa* and *E Pfeiffer Weinkellerei Weinkauf GmbH v Arbuthnot Factors Ltd* [1988] 1 WLR 150 that a right to the proceeds of sale does not arise under a retention of title clause just because title is retained, and that an express imposition of such a right amounts to the creation of a floating charge, which will be void if not registered (see *Tatung (UK) Ltd v Galex Telesure Ltd* [1988] BCLC 325 and *Compaq Computers Ltd v Abercorn Group Ltd* [1991] BCLC 484). However, it is possible to solve this problem by providing in the contract of sale merely that the buyer when selling the goods acts as the agent of the seller. Here, the right of the seller over the proceeds of sale arises under the operation of general legal principles (ie that an agent stands in a fiduciary relationship to his principal) which are triggered by the wording of the clause but are not created and imposed by an express provision in the clause itself (see *Romalpa* and *Welsh Development Agency v Export Finance Co Ltd* [1992] BCLC 148, CA). If the buyer wrongfully mixes the proceeds of sale with his own monies in a mixed bank account, the seller should then have a right to trace under the equitable principles set out in *Re Hallet's Estate* (1880) 13 ChD 696.

The problems created by s 395 of the Companies Act 1985 apply, of course, only to companies, and, since the reputed ownership provisions of the Bankruptcy Act 1914 were repealed by the Insolvency Act 1985, and not replaced in the Insolvency Act 1986, there is more scope for retention of title clauses which create security interests in the case of individuals. However, there are still considerable problems with the Bills of Sale Acts 1878 and 1882, which create an effect rather like s 395 of the Companies Act 1985—simple retention of title clauses do not have to be registered as bills of sale, but extended ones creating security interests probably do. General assignments of book debts (eg by the buyer of his subpurchasers' book debts relating to resale of the goods) are required by s 344 of the Insolvency Act 1986 to be registered under the Bills of Sale Act 1878. In practice, it is safest to assume that the same rules as to registration of security interests created by the retention of title clause apply to both companies and individuals.

A final problem encountered in such clauses is the question of easy identification of the seller's goods. If they are not unique and easily identified (for instance by serial numbers which can be linked to unpaid invoices) the seller may not be able to go to the buyer's premises, and point to the goods which are his property, which he is entitled to take away. If he cannot do this, the receiver, for instance, is not, as a rule, obliged to let him take an equivalent number or amount of goods of the same description from a mixed stock. This problem usually arises with commodities such as grain, or building materials, such as glass, brick, wood or nails, or components with no serial numbers or maker's marks on them.

This problem can best be solved by the seller imposing an obligation upon the buyer to keep the seller's goods separate and easily identifiable as the seller's property, until they have been paid for, and title has passed. If the buyer complies with this, each consignment owned by the seller will be stored separately until paid for. If this obligation is not fulfilled by the buyer (which is likely in practice often to be the case) and he mixes in the seller's goods with his own goods, then a wrongful intermixture will have taken place which results at common law in the seller and the buyer being tenants in common of the mixed store of goods. The seller can then take from the mixed store sufficient goods to satisfy his claim for the goods which belonged to him and were wrongfully so mixed (see *Indian Oil Corporation v Greenstone Shipping SA* [1987] 3 WLR 869). In appropriate circumstances such wrongful intermixture might also produce an equitable remedy under the principles in *Re Hallet's Estate*, above.

Many retention of title clauses have attempted to go further than the ones discussed above, but have nearly all come to grief upon the application of the principle that the clause created a security interest, which was then void for want of registration.

This is particularly obvious in the area of goods which are purchased, with the knowledge and, therefore, the express or implied permission of the seller, to be used in a manufacturing process which alters or destroys their substance. First of all, the original goods cease to exist as soon as the buyer starts working on them in the manufacturing process, so that the seller can no longer claim any title to them, and, then, any provision that he may have inserted in the clause to claim title to the end product, until he has been paid for the raw material, will be regarded as a security interest created by the clause, and therefore void if not registered. This was the case with resin sold to be used to make chipboard (see *Borden (UK) v Scottish Timber Products* [1981] Ch 25), leather to be made into handbags (see *Re Peachdart* [1984] Ch 131), yarn to be spun into fabric (see *Clough Mill Ltd v Martin* [1985] 1 WLR 111), cardboard to be made into cartons (see *Modelboard Ltd v Outer Box Ltd* [1993] BCLC 623) and fabric to be made into dresses (see *Ian Chisholm Textiles Ltd v Griffiths* [1994] 2 BCLC 291).

The only exception to the above rule seems to be in the area of large components or subassemblies which, while they have been assembled into part of a larger machine, have not been altered or worked upon so that they can be detached and restored to their separate existence in their original state. This was held to be the case with diesel engines in *Hendy Lennox (Industrial Engines) Ltd v Grahame Puttick Ltd* [1984] 1 WLR 485. This is an uncertain area of the law. Looking at *dicta* in *Re Peachdart* and *Clough Mill* it seems as if the criteria for the seller retaining ownership are not only that the subassembly must be easily separable, but that the seller must have carried out very little (preferably no) work to change or adapt the subassembly himself, as the very act of carrying out such work may create a proprietary interest in the subassembly for the buyer, and extinguish the title retained by the seller.

The remaining type of extended clause is one which is often called an 'all-monies' or 'all-accounts' clause, which provides that title in any one consignment of goods shall not pass until all sums owing by the buyer to the seller for that or any other consignments of goods shall have been paid. The clauses sometimes go as far as to impose a condition that all sums owing by the buyer to the seller under any contracts and in any capacity must be paid. Based on

Romalpa, Borden, Clough Mill and *John Snow and Co Ltd v DGB Woodcraft Co Ltd* [1985] BCLC 54, there seems no reason why such a clause is not a permissible condition for the passing of title under s 19(1) of the Sale of Goods Act 1979. However, this type of clause will require registration if it is to be enforceable and, in any event, creates many practical problems so that it is probably best avoided.

First, title may never pass in any of the goods until the business relationship is at an end, no more orders are placed, and all orders have been paid for.

Secondly, if at any time the buyer's account has a zero balance or goes into credit, title to all of the goods delivered up to that time will vest in him, to the extent that he has not already sold them, while from then on new goods delivered, will continue to be subject to the clause. The seller will then have to contend with a mixed stock of goods, some of which will belong to him and some of which will belong to the buyer, and with all the problems of separation and identification which this will entail.

Clauses imposing the duty to keep the seller's and the buyer's goods separate, may save the seller by creating a wrongful mixing of goods as described above. Nevertheless, in the circumstances of an all-accounts or all-monies clause, these concepts seem somewhat artificial, since both parties know that such separation will hardly be practical in the event of the zero balance or credit balance occurring—the buyer and the seller will probably not even know the exact date upon which such a balance occurs. For this reason there must be some doubt about the enforceability of such clauses. Indeed, in Scotland, 'all-accounts' clauses have been struck down as attempts to obtain security without possession and as thus falling outside the Sale of Goods Act 1979, by virtue of s 62(4) of the Act, which provides that the Act (and hence the rules on conditional passing of title) does not apply to 'a transaction in the form of a contract of sale which is intended to operate by way of mortgage, pledge, charge or other security'. The same approach was followed in *Compaq Computers Ltd v Abercorn Group Ltd* [1991] BCLC 484, where an all accounts clause was held to amount to the provision of a security for all debts from time to time outstanding between the buyer and the seller, notwithstanding that the clause attempted to characterise the relationship between the buyer and the seller as a bailment which imposed fiduciary duties upon the buyer by operation of law. The clause was thus held to be a floating charge, and, in the particular circumstances, void for want of registration under s 395.

16.9   Set-off

Finally, it is necessary to discuss the operation of the doctrine known as set-off.

Originally, under the English common law, there was no right of set-off as we understand it today. All that was permitted was that, where a running account existed between two parties, to which both debits and credits were posted as they became due, either party could call for the balance to be calculated and then pay or be paid the balance owing.

In the early 18th century Acts of Parliament were passed which provided that where there were mutual debts between two parties, and A claimed payment of his debt from B, B, as a defence against the action, could set off a debt owed by A to B. It was not necessary for the two debts to be part of one transaction or of related transactions, so long as the debts were mutual. This was taken to mean that the parties must be dealing with each other 'in the same right' (this was called 'the principle of mutuality'). For example two merchants who sold and bought goods between themselves, or who generally traded together, could set off the debts on both sides as mutual. Similarly a bank can be regarded as borrowing money from a customer when it takes a deposit, and the customer as borrowing from the bank when he takes a loan. Each debt arises under a separate and unrelated contract, but again all the mutual debts between the bank and the customer could be set off.

It should be noted that this statutory right of set-off was limited to debts— ie to claims for fixed and ascertained sums of money. It did not, by way of contrast, permit a debt to be set off against a claim for damages, for, say breach of contract, or for negligence, because a damages claim was for an unascertained sum (unliquidated) whose value would have to be proved to and accepted by the court.

However, equity extended the strict rules of the common law, and the precise wording of the statutes, and gradually developed a principle that in certain cases it was unfair, and justice would not be done, if a claim for damages could not be set off as a defence in an action to recover a debt.

At first equity proceeded on the principle that the debt and the claims for damages must arise out of the same contract. For instance, it permitted the setting off, against a claim for the purchase price for goods sold and delivered, a claim for damages for breach of the contract of sale because the goods were defective or not in accordance with the contract. This particular type of set-off is now expressly conferred by the Sale of Goods Act 1979 (s 53(1)(*b*)).

This principle was then extended to any situation where the two claims were so closely connected that it would work injustice if they were tried separately rather than in the same action. There are many decisions showing in particular cases whether a close enough connection exists or not. However, almost entirely equity kept to the principle of mutuality. One of the few exceptions here was that if A sued B, in his capacity as trustee for C, B could set off, as a defence against the claim, a claim that B had against C. In other words the court would go behind the legal title of the trustee A and consider the fact that C was the real beneficiary of A's claim against B so that it would have been unjust not to consider B's claim against C. Similarly an agent suing on behalf of his principal can be met by a set-off of a claim that the party he is suing has against that principal.

Following the fusion of the courts of law and equity in the mid-19th century, the principles of equity were held to prevail. However, the effect of the old statutes on mutual debts was also preserved, even though the original statutes were repealed.

From there, although many detailed decisions on particular points have been made, the law of set-off has been broadly based on the three following principles.

First, the parties must claim against each other in the same right and thus only debts which are mutual (ie arising out of unrelated transactions but between the parties in the same right) can be set off. (The principle of mutuality.)

Secondly, provided the parties are in the same right and the two claims arise out of the same contract, or are closely connected, a claim for damages can be set off against a debt, or another claim for damages.

Thirdly, the tendency has been to define more and more loosely the term 'closely connected' so that the operation of set-off has become more widespread, but the principle of mutuality has generally been preserved and interpreted in a restrictive way.

In practical terms, in an action for a debt, a defendant who is also a creditor of the plaintiff will set off the debt owed to him and counter claim if that amount exceeds the claim made against him. If the defendant has an unliquidated claim for damages the procedure may vary, although the principle is the same. As the amount which the defendant seeks to set off is unquantified, the court will want to be satisfied that the claim can be substantiated (on the balance of probabilities) as a matter of law (without actually determining the value of the claim). If the court considers that it is capable of substantiation, leave to defend will be given, usually unconditionally; if it is possible only (or less than probable but not wholly improbable) then the court can impose conditions (eg the defendant may be given leave to defend upon payment into court of part or all of the amount claimed by the plaintiff).

These rules are related purely to the situation where no insolvency is involved and all that it is sought to achieve is to prevent wasting the courts' time, and working injustice by bringing separately as two actions matters which should really be tried together. It should be noted that these rules do not require a previous agreement (express or implied by conduct) nor do they require a previous course of dealing where set-off has been accepted.

The following are some examples of where the claims are not 'in the same right'. For instance, if one takes the case of a banker and his customer, where the customer has opened an account as trustee for a third party, the bank would not be entitled to set off the credit on that account against debits on the customer's ordinary trading accounts. Similarly, where a liquidator of a company claims against a debtor of the company, it would not be possible for the debtor to set off another debt owed by the liquidator to the debtor (but otherwise unrelated to the company in liquidation) which has arisen, because the liquidator was carrying on a separate business on his own account and had purchased goods from that debtor. Another example would be where an executor sues on behalf of a deceased person's estate to recover a debt. The debtor could not set off, against the executor's claim, a debt which the executor owed in his personal capacity to that debtor.

Where one is dealing with a bankruptcy, or the liquidation of a company, there is a statutory duty to exercise set-off in appropriate cases, not merely as an option. It was said in one case that this was a positive absolute rule and that one could not prove in a bankruptcy or liquidation where there were mutual debts and credits until set-off in accordance with statute had been made, and then one could only prove for the balance of the account between the parties.

The current statutory provision relating to bankruptcy is s 323 of the Insolvency Act 1986, which talks about situations where there have been 'mutual credits, mutual debts or other mutual dealings' between the bankrupt and any creditor proving or claiming to prove a debt in the bankruptcy or liquidation. In this situation an account is taken of what is due from one party to the other, in respect of such mutual dealings, and the sum due from the one party is set off against any sum due to the other party. The balance of the account, and no more, is then allowed as a claim in the bankruptcy, or paid to the trustee in bankruptcy as appropriate.

The Insolvency Rules 1986 now contain the provisions applicable to companies in liquidation and are identical in substance. Both provisions can be traced back to s 31 of the Bankruptcy Act 1914, which means that all of the old cases on this section are still good law.

In these situations it is not necessary that the credits should be dependant one on the other nor that there should have been any specific agreement to this effect beforehand.

The material date at which one applies the rules of set-off, as distinct from the amount of the set-off, is the date of the receiving order in a bankruptcy, or the date at which the company is wound up, either by an order of the court, or through the passing of the relevant resolution in a voluntary liquidation.

The way the definition of 'mutual credits, mutual debts or other mutual dealings' has been applied in the cases shows that what is involved is that the claims on both sides should eventually result in a liability to pay money, but that at the time of the set-off it is not necessary for the exact amount of the debit to have been ascertained. Thus, a claim for damages (where the amount of the compensation has yet to be ascertained), can be set off against the fixed amount of a debt, and a future debt (ie not yet due) can be set off against a present debt. However, the principle of mutuality must be preserved.

The problem in a receivership situation is that the statutory rights of set-off on bankruptcy will only benefit an unsecured creditor once the debenture holder has been paid off as a preferred creditor in respect of his security. The question then arises as to what extent and in what way an unsecured creditor has the right to set off against the receiver any claims it has against the company so as to prevent the receiver collecting debts from that unsecured creditor.

The basic principle is that since, in the normal situation, the company or individual which created the charge or debenture under which the receiver was appointed can only charge whatever interest the company or individual itself has in the debts, if a right of set-off exists, as between the company or the individual and the unsecured creditor, before the floating charge crystallises and the receiver is appointed, then (since the receiver can have no better rights to the debt than the individual or company itself has) the receiver must exercise the charge over the debts subject to existing rights of set-off. The critical date is thus the date on which the floating charge crystallises.

In order to decide whether there is a right of set-off affecting the debts subject to the charge which the receiver is trying to collect, the receiver is not concerned to look at the laws of bankruptcy or winding-up. At this stage the company has not been put into liquidation nor, if one were dealing with a firm, or a sole trader, has a trustee in bankruptcy been appointed. Such appointment normally follows once the receiver has collected the secured creditor's debts.

In any case, even if a receiver and a liquidator are appointed concurrently, the receiver, acting for the secured creditor, will still have a superior right over the liquidator to pay the secured creditor first, and leave the residue of the company's assets to be dealt with by the liquidator for the benefit of the unsecured creditors. Thus, the sole question in all cases is whether the receiver has taken charge of assets which are already subject to the right of set-off under the general law or under a contract.

It is thus important to realise that the rights of set-off as described above can be extended by express or implied agreement, or even, in some cases by trade custom. For instance, where one or both of the parties is a member of a group of companies, the general law would not permit one company in a group to set off a debt owed to that company's creditor to another company in the same group, because the principle of mutuality would be violated. However, such a group right of set-off can be created expressly by contract. Similarly, the right of set-off can be extended to debts arising under different contracts between the parties even if, again, they are not acting under those contracts in the same right, and the principle of mutuality is violated.

Similarly, the right of set-off can be excluded or restricted by contract but such clauses are regarded as exclusion clauses which are regulated by s 3 of the Unfair Contract Terms Act 1977 (see *Stewart Gill v Horatio Myer Co* [1992] 2 All ER 257, CA and *Overland Shoes Ltd v Schenker International Deutschland GmbH* (1998) *The Times*, 26 February).

Finally, a note of caution should be raised in relation to payment by cheque and direct debit. Payment by cheque is treated as equivalent to cash payment. THus, unless the cheque itself is involved or there is a total failure of consideration, a party to a contract cannot resist payment of his cheque by setting up a counter-claim against the other party for a breach of contract.[23]

16.10 The precedents

The precedents are largely self-explanatory, and should be read in the context of the relevant commentary upon them. It should be noted that space forbids the inclusion in this chapter of the standard forms of charges and mortgages usual in commercial transactions, for instance floating charges securing debentures, or charges over real property by way of legal mortgage. Such documents are in standard forms which can easily be found in larger encyclopaedias of forms and precedents.

Precedents 1, 2 and 3 are of various forms of guarantees which can be adapted as appropriate for most commercial uses. It should be noted that Precedent 1 is not a true guarantee, but rather an undertaking to procure performance, and that cl 4 of Precedent 3 (if included) goes further than a normal guarantee by making the guarantor jointly and severally liable as principal with the debtor.

Precedent 4 is an arrangement which enables a trade seller to put his customer in possession of a stock of goods on consignment, thus, in effect, selling on credit, but retaining the title in the goods as security. Such an arrangement is really a variation on the retention of title clause. In such cases one of the most important clauses is cl 3, which imposes the obligation on the customer to insure the goods and store them so that they can be separately identified. Insurance is important. Although the seller may still have a sufficient insurable interest in the goods to retain cover under his own policy, this may not always be the case, and, if he has many such arrangements, the seller may not even find it cost-effective where his insurer is prepared to extend cover.

Precedent 5 is taken from an actual situation where a subcontractor had been given an order to fabricate a finished product that was required for the performance of the main contract. The subcontractor was likely to become insolvent, and its bank was about to appoint a receiver under the floating charge in its favour over the subcontractor's undertaking. This floating charge covered the inventory, work in progress and finished products not yet sold to the main contractor, and in which both title and possession remained with the subcontractor. In order to avoid seizure of these assets, and the consequent putting of the performance of the main contract in jeopardy, the main contractor entered into this agreement to purchase the assets and pay off the bank itself.

Such agreements, which should only be used as a last resort, are effective for a number of reasons. First, once they are concluded (and provided they do not constitute a transaction at an undervalue which can later be overturned) they are proof against a receiver or liquidator. However, as can be seen from the agreement, the requirements of separate storage and marking are absolutely essential, if, in practice, the purchaser is to be able to prove his title in the event of the subsequent appointment of a receiver or liquidator.

This sort of agreement, for which full value has been given, is not, in fact, particularly obnoxious to a receiver or a liquidator who is appointed soon after it has been executed, since he still has the relevant proceeds of sale.

As far as registration goes, this type of agreement does not create a charge or other security interest, and so does not require registration under s 395 of the Companies Act 1985. It should also not be registrable as a bill of sale when given by an individual because it is an outright sale for value, as a commercial transaction, and not an agreement for sale by way of security for a loan. However, since such transactions are comparatively rare, and the law relating to bills of sale is quite uncertain in these areas, it would be prudent, at the expense of a little trouble, to register such an agreement as a bill of sale, to avoid any doubt.

Precedents 6 and 7 are respectively short and long form retention of title clauses, while Precedent 8 is a payment clause which removes the problem, discussed in the commentary, of suing for the price before property in the goods has passed.

Finally, Precedents 9 and 10 are examples of contractual set-off clauses which extend the rights of set-off beyond the bounds normally granted by the general law. It is important to remember that such clauses should be proof against a receiver, but that they may not in all circumstances be proof, in their wider application, against the powers of a liquidator or trustee in bankruptcy who is required and entitled to apply the statutory provisions relating to set-off.

Precedent 1

Short form undertaking to procure performance by subsidiary

The company hereby unconditionally and irrevocably undertakes to procure the execution and delivery of each of the subsidiaries' agreements and of each instrument and agreement referred to therein by each of the company's subsidiaries party thereto and undertakes to procure the prompt performance or payment when due of each and every obligation and liability which any of them may have under any such agreement or instrument.

Precedent 2

Short form guarantee

In consideration of the vendor entering into this agreement guarantor hereby unconditionally and irrevocably guarantees to the vendor the due and punctual performance and observance by the purchaser of its obligations under this agreement and notwithstanding any other provision in this agreement this guarantee shall not be affected by the granting of time or other waiver or indulgence on the part of the vendor.

Precedent 3

Long form guarantee of trade debtor

Dear Sirs,

As [directors] [shareholders] of [   ] Limited of [   ] (the 'Company') we confirm to you that we wish you to supply goods to our company on credit, and that, in consideration of your agreeing so to supply such goods, we hereby jointly and severally undertake to and agree with you as follows:

1 We hereby unconditionally and irrevocably guarantee to you the due payment by the Company for all such goods as you may from time to time supply to it [but subject to the limitation that our liability under this guarantee shall not at any one time exceed the sum of £[   ]].

2 This agreement shall be and constitute a continuing guarantee to you for all debts whatsoever and whenever contracted by the Company with you in respect of goods to be supplied to it by you [but subject always to the above limitation].

3 You may without notice to us at any time and without in any way discharging us from our liability hereunder grant time or other waiver or indulgence to the company and accept payment from it in cash or negotiable instruments, in whole or partial satisfaction of any debts then due to you from the Company.

4 We agree and accept that you may treat us jointly and severally liable with the Company to you instead of merely the company's guarantor.

Dated this [   ] day of [   ]

                           (Signature and address of surety)

Yours faithfully,

(Signatures of directors/shareholders)

Precedent 4

Letter agreement for goods sold on consignment to a limited company

Dear Sirs

In order to provide you with a more efficient service and assist you to increase your trading with us we are prepared to sell the products listed in Appendix 1 to this letter (the 'Products') to you on a consignment stock basis on the following terms and conditions:

1 We will deliver to your premises at [   ] ('your premises') an initial stock on consignment of the types, sizes and quantities of the Products detailed in Appendix 2 to this letter. We will make further deliveries on consignment of such types and sizes at frequencies and of quantities as agreed between us from time to time. By agreement in writing this arrangement may also be extended to other sizes, types and quantities of Products.

2 The initial stock and all further deliveries under this arrangement ('the stock') will remain our property, and be held by you as bailee, but you are authorised to sell the stock to your customers, and each item of the Products will become your property and cease to be part of the stock either when you cut, process or perform any work on or with it, or deliver it to a customer, whichever happens first.

3 The risk in the stock will pass to you on delivery to your premises. In particular, all breakages will be for your account, unless notified to us within twenty-four hours of delivery, and we are satisfied that they occurred before delivery. You will arrange adequate insurance for the stock (and provide proof of insurance on request) and store it in such a way that it can be recognised as our property, if necessary by providing a separate area in your warehouse and appropriate notices.

4 You will permit us access to your premises on the last working day of each calendar month to count the stock. We will then issue you an invoice (payable at the end of the next calendar month) for the value (calculated on our trade price list as notified to you from time to time—current price list attached as Appendix 3 to this letter) of opening stock plus deliveries by us less closing stock for that month. VAT will also be charged on the invoice as appropriate.

5 Sales of items of the Products from the stock to you under this arrangement shall be upon our standard terms and conditions (copy attached as Appendix 4 to this letter) except where this letter is inconsistent with them, when this letter shall take precedence. When you sell items of the Products from the stock to your customers it is understood that you act on your own behalf and not as our agent, and that you are not authorised to make any statements, representations or warranties on our behalf.

6 You undertake, in return for the operation of this arrangement, that during the period of this arrangement you will not purchase or obtain the Products in the types and sizes covered by this arrangement from anyone other than us, and that therefore all quantities of such types and sizes of the Products on your premises are acknowledged to be covered by this arrangement and accordingly part of the stock.

7 This arrangement is personal to the parties and may not be assigned by either of us without the other's permission.

8 You will immediately disclose this arrangement to your bankers in writing (with a copy of your letter to them to be sent to us) and also, in due course, by including a note in your year-end accounts.

9 This arrangement can be ended by one month's notice in writing by either side, and will end automatically, without notice, if either side enters into liquidation, or has a receiver or manager appointed, or has any distress or execution levied on its assets, or compounds with its creditors, or takes or suffers any similar action in consequence of debt or insolvency. It may also be ended by either party immediately by notice given verbally or in writing if the other party fails to observe or perform, any of its obligations under this arrangement.

10 Upon the ending of this arrangement for any reason whatsoever, you will permit us to enter your premises and remove the stock then held by you. At that time we will perform a final count of the stock and issue you with an invoice (payable within 30 days) for VAT on and the value (calculated in accordance with para 4) of opening stock at the beginning of the calendar month in which this arrangement ends, plus deliveries during that month by us less closing stock as at the date of the final count.

If you are in agreement with the contents of this letter and wish to enter into this arrangement, please sign and return the enclosed copy of this letter, indicating the date on which you wish us to deliver the initial stock.

Yours faithfully,

ON COPY

We agree and accept the above arrangement for consignment stock. Please deliver the initial stock under the arrangement on [   ].

For and on behalf of [   ] Limited

Director

Agreement to purchase work in progress

1 Parties

1.1 [   ] Limited of [   ] ('Buyer').

1.2 [   ] Limited of [   ] ('Seller').

2 Definitions

2.1 The 'Stock Length Sections' are listed in Appendix 1.

2.2 The 'Stock Length Box Frame Sections' are listed in Appendix 2.

2.3 The 'Furniture' is listed in Appendix 3.

2.4 The 'Glazing Materials' are listed in Appendix 4.

2.5 The 'Fabricated Items' are listed in Appendix 5.

2.6 The 'Cut Lengths at Factory' are listed in Appendix 6.

2.7 The 'Cut Lengths at Painters' are listed in Appendix 7

2.8 The 'Materials' are collectively all of the items listed in cl 2.1–2.7 hereof inclusive.

2.9 The 'Effective Date is [   ].

2.10 The 'Items To Be Fabricated' are listed in Appendix 8.

2.11 The 'Additional Products' are listed in Appendix 9.

2.12 The 'Factory' means the Seller's factory at [   ].

3   Sale and purchase

3.1 Buyer agrees to purchase from Seller and Seller agrees to sell to Buyer the Materials for the price of £[   ] (Pounds [   ]) ('the Purchase Price').

3.2 Upon the Effective Date Buyer shall pay to Seller the Purchase Price by means of a telegraphic transfer from Buyer's bank to Seller's bank account details of which are set out below:
Bank:
Name of account:
Account number:

3.3 Immediately upon payment of the Purchase Price under cl 3.2 property in the Materials shall pass to Buyer, Buyer shall become the legal and beneficial owner of the Materials, and Seller shall cease to have any right, title or interest of any nature whatsoever in the Materials.

4   Marking

4.1 Buyer wishes to leave the Materials in the possession of Seller as bailee for Buyer in order for Seller to carry out the work on the Materials referred to in cl 5 below.

4.2 In order that the Materials be clearly seen to be held by Seller as bailee for Buyer marking and affixing of notices shall be carried out on the Effective Date immediately upon the passing of property under cl 3.3 by Buyer and SELLER as follows:
4.2.1 each of the unopened outer packages containing Stock Length Sections and Stock Length Box Frame Sections shall be marked with a label indicating that they are the property of Buyer;
4.2.2 any Stock Length Section and Stock Length Box Frame Section removed from its outer packaging shall be individually marked with a label indicating that they are the property of Buyer;
4.2.3 the Furniture and the Glazing Materials shall until delivered to Buyer in accordance with cl 5.3 (or until assembled into one of the Items To Be Fabricated under cl 5.1) at all times be stored in a separate area at the Factory set aside exclusively for their storage with a notice adjacent to that area indicating

that all items stored in that area are the property of Buyer;

4.2.4 all Fabricated Items shall be individually marked with a label indicating that they are the property of Buyer;

4.2.5 the Cut Lengths at Factory shall until assembled into an Item To Be Fabricated be stored while they are being worked on, on trestles pallets or other racks used exclusively for this purpose with a notice affixed to each rack trestle pallet or other rack indicating that the items stored thereon are the property of Buyer;

4.2.6 the Cut Lengths at Painters will when returned to the Factory and until assembled into Items To Be Fabricated be stored in the same way as if they were Cut Lengths at Factory;

4.2.7 in relation to the Cut Lengths at Painters Seller shall on the Effective Date send a letter (in the form set out in Schedule 1 hereto) signed by Seller which shall be delivered by hand by Seller to the painter at whose premises they are presently situated. Upon delivery Seller shall obtain from the said painter a signed copy of the said letter and deliver the same immediately to Buyer. Buyer shall then deliver a letter signed by them in the form set out in Schedule 2 hereto to the said painter.

5   Sub-contract work

5.1 On and from the Effective Date Seller shall work on and assemble the Materials into the Items To Be Fabricated as subcontractor for Seller.

5.2 Seller shall at no time have any property, lien or other interest of any nature whatsoever in the Items To Be Fabricated and Buyer shall continue to be the legal and beneficial owners of the Materials after they have been assembled into Items To Be Fabricated.

5.3 Seller shall complete the works under cl 5.1 and deliver all Fabricated Items, all Items To Be Fabricated and any Materials and Additional Products not then assembled into Items to Be Fabricated to [   ] not later than [   ].

5.4 As the Materials are worked upon so that packaged Stock Length Sections and packaged Stock Length Box Frame Sections are taken out of packages and, together with any of the same already unpackaged on the Effective Date, cut and painted, and are eventually assembled (together with Furniture and Glazing Materials) into Items To Be Fabricated, all of the same that are unpackaged and the cut and painted lengths produced from them shall be treated in all respects (and marking and the affixing of notices shall be effected in respect of them under cl 4.2) as if they were Stock Length Sections, Stock Length Box Frame Sections, Cut Lengths at Factory or Cut Lengths at Painters as the case may be.

5.5 All Items To Be Fabricated shall when assembled be treated as if they were Fabricated Items and marked under cl 4.2.4.

5.6 In order to produce all of the Items To Be Fabricated Seller shall procure as Buyer's agents the Additional Products and assemble them into the relevant Items To Be Fabricated. Buyer shall pay at the prices detailed in Schedule 3 hereto for each of the Additional Products on its delivery to the Factory and upon such delivery property shall pass to Buyer from the original seller. The Additional Products shall be treated and marked while at the Factory, and until they are incorporated into an Item To Be Fabricated as if they were Fabricated Items under cl 4.2.4.

5.7 Buyer's original Order for the supply of the Fabricated Items and the Items to be Fabricated (No [   ] dated [   ]) placed upon Seller is hereby cancelled, but without prejudice to the rights and liabilities of both parties arising prior to the Effective Date.

5.8 For the avoidance of doubt the Parties agree that:
5.8.1 Seller will not remove alter tamper with erase or obscure any label or notice affixed under cl 4; and
5.8.2 Seller is not and will not from the Effective Date until the delivery of the Items To Be Fabricated, the Materials and any Additional Products pursuant to cl 5.3 work on, or store, in the Factory any items which are of the same colour as any of the Materials or the Additional Products and any item which is coloured any of such colours shall be deemed to be one of the Materials, an Additional Product, and/or an Item To Be Fabricated even if it is not labelled marked or stored in accordance with cl 4.2 or not listed in Appendices 1–7 inclusive or 9.

[APPENDICES 1–9].

SCHEDULE 1
Seller's letter to painter

Dear Sir
This is to inform you that all of the items listed below which are currently at your premises for painting under Job Number [   ] have today been sold by us to [Buyer].
All future items sent to you for painting under Job Number [   ] will also be the property of [Buyer].
Please confirm by signing the copy of this letter that you will now hold all the aforesaid items to the order of and as bailee for [Buyer] and deliver them according to [Buyer's] instructions.

Yours faithfully

(Director of Seller)
ON COPY

I acknowledge receipt of this letter and agree to act in accordance with it.

Painting Sub-Contractor

SCHEDULE 2
Buyer's Letter to Painter

Dear Sir
We refer to the attached copy of the letter to you from [Seller].
The items listed in that letter, and any further items to be sent to you for paint-ing under Job Number [   ] are now our property. However, please redeliver them to [Seller] as our bailee at their factory at [   ].
Acting as our agents [Seller] will pay your invoices relating to work carried out under Job Number [   ].

Yours faithfully

(Director of Buyer)
ON COPY

I acknowledge receipt of this letter and agree to act in accordance with it.

IN WITNESS whereof the duly authorised representatives of the parties have signed this agreement on [   ].

For the Buyer [   ] (Mr [   ] director)

For the Seller [   ] (Mr [   ] director)

Precedent 6

Short form simple retention of title clause

Title to the goods shall remain with the Seller and shall not pass to the Buyer until payment in full for the same has been received by the Seller.

Precedent 7

Long form simple retention of title clause

Title to Equipment shall not pass to the Customer but shall be retained by the Seller until the Contract Price has been paid to the Seller in full by the Customer.

Until such time as title in the Equipment has passed to the Customer:

   (i) the Seller shall have absolute authority to retake, sell or otherwise deal with or dispose of all any or part of the Equipment in which title remains vested in the Seller;

  (ii) for the purpose specified in (i) above, the Seller or any of its agents or authorised representatives shall be entitled at any time and without notice to enter upon any premises in which the Equipment or any part thereof is installed, stored or kept, or is reasonably believed so to be;

 (iii) the Seller shall be entitled to seek a court injunction to prevent the Customer from selling, transferring or otherwise disposing of the Equipment;

 (iv) the Buyer shall store or otherwise denote the Equipment in respect of which property remains with the Seller in such a way that the same can be recognised as the property of the Seller.

Notwithstanding the foregoing, risk in the Equipment shall pass on delivery of the same to the Customer, and until such time as title in the Equipment has passed to the Customer, the Customer shall insure such Equipment to its replacement value [naming the Seller as the loss payee] [noting the Seller's interest on the relevant insurance policy] and the Customer shall forthwith, upon request, provide the Seller with a Certificate or other evidence of such Insurance.

Precedent 8

Payment clause for use with retention of title clauses

The Buyer shall pay for each consignment of the Products supplied to it here-under [by draft payable 60 days after the date of shipment from the UK Port of Exit], [30 days after the date of delivery to the buyer's premises] [at the end of the month following the month in which the relevant invoice is issued] or by such other method of payment as shall from time to time be agreed between the time of [shipment] [delivery] [issue] as aforesaid and the time that payment becomes due as aforesaid.

Payment shall fall due as aforesaid in respect of each consignment of the Products despite the fact that title therein has not passed to the Buyer and the Seller shall accordingly be entitled to sue for the price once the same is due notwithstanding the fact that the property in the said consignment has not so passed.

Where the Seller recovers possession of a consignment of the Products title in which has not yet passed to the Buyer such recovery of possession shall be without prejudice to the rights of the Seller to sue for the purchase price under this clause.

Precedent 9

Simple set-off clause

Whenever under the Contract any sum of money shall be recoverable from or payable by the Contractor, the same may be deducted from any sum then due or which at any time thereafter may become due to the Contractor under this or any other contract with the Customer. Exercise by the Customer of its rights under this clause shall be without prejudice to any other rights or remedies available to the Customer under the Contract, or otherwise howsoever, at law or in equity.

Precedent 10

Group set-off clause

Whenever any sum of money shall be recoverable from or payable by one party hereto or any holding or subsidiary company of that party (the 'paying group') to the other party hereto or any holding or subsidiary company of that party (the 'receiving group'), the same may be deducted by the paying group from any sum then due or which at any time thereafter may become due to the paying group from the receiving group under this Agreement or any agreement or contract between any member of the receiving group and any member of the paying group.'

Chapter 17

Dispute resolution and settlement agreements

17.1 Introduction

Commercial disputes can be settled by negotiation, resort to an expert or arbitrator, or by litigation. This chapter thus contains first precedents which can be used to record and implement a settlement which the parties have reached in respect of a dispute, and then provides precedents for clauses which prescribe and regulate the various formal methods of dispute resolution which are available to the parties as discussed above.

17.2 Settlement agreements

Settlement agreements in commercial situations are usually individually drafted documents which detail, often in some complexity, the particular settlement that the parties have come to. However, they also all have a common element in the central clause which releases the claims which are the subject matter of the dispute, and ensures that the parties cannot bring further proceedings or raise further issues relating to the subject matter of the dispute after the execution of the settlement agreement.

Precedents 1 and 2 are actual settlement agreements, from which some of the more personal details of the transactions have been removed for the sake of confidentiality, which illustrate the interworking between the commercial detail and formal aspect of such settlement agreements.

Both precedents are self-explanatory, but cl 5 of Precedent 2 which deals explicitly with the waiver of unknown claims should be noted.

17.3   Dispute resolution by negotiation

There is no particular need to insert a clause in commercial contracts to provide for a process of consultation or negotiation between the parties before they turn to more formal procedures for the resolution of disputes, but clauses providing for an escalation of disputes to higher levels of management are sometimes included as a way of avoiding an immediate breakdown in relations between the parties.

Another possibility is to provide for a more formal process of negotiation assisted by the mediation of a third party. This process has gained in popularity in the UK (having spread originally from North America) under the name of Alternative Dispute Resolution or 'ADR'. ADR involves the use of an impartial, specially trained third party who acts as a mediator to facilitate a mutually acceptable settlement between the parties. The mediator is given no power (even under contract) to impose a solution on the parties, who are free at any time to abandon the procedure and resort to more formal means of dispute resolution.

The procedure used under ADR can vary considerably. The mediator can act as a go-between for the parties, who do not, at least initially, meet face to face. He can also conduct formal joint settlement discussions. Additionally, the parties can opt for an 'executive tribunal' or 'mini-trial' where a formal presentation by each party is made to a panel made up of senior executives from each party with the mediator as the neutral chairman. The executives, who have normally not been involved in the dispute, then try to negotiate a solution with the assistance of the mediator. Another alternative is for the mediator to arrange for a hearing in which the parties present their cases to an expert or adjudicator who then renders a formal but non-binding opinion or judgment.

The key to the success of ADR is the expertise of the mediator. In the UK, various organisations, such as the Centre for Dispute Resolution, have been set up (by persons with commercial and arbitration expertise, often lawyers) to train and provide mediators, and to provide the ancillary services required to run a successful ADR negotiation.

ADR has to contend with the various formal legal problems concerning the invalidity of agreements which attempt to set up any system of dispute resolution which ousts the jurisdiction of the courts. This is one of the reasons why ADR has to be a non-binding process. The other reason why ADR is non-binding is that its whole spirit is an attempt at achieving a meeting of minds between the parties with a solution that leaves both of them feeling satisfied, rather than one a winner and the other a loser. Such a process can only work if the parties are willing to co-operate to achieve the result.

Where ADR is appropriate it can result in a substantial saving of cost and time over the normal processes of arbitration or litigation, and often keep alive a commercial relationship between parties who have to continue to do business with each other in the future. Although ADR clauses are now being included in contracts more frequently, it is not always the best course for ADR initially to be commenced before resorting to arbitration or litigation. Sometimes the preliminary processes of arbitration and litigation (particularly pleadings, discovery and witness proofing) need to be gone through in order to sharpen up the issues sufficiently for the parties to understand what are the real points of dispute between them. Sometimes, also, parties who initially have insufficient mutual goodwill, or no desire to reach a settlement, have a measure of realism forced upon them as the formal proceedings progress and they realise the expenditure of money, time and effort that is involved. It is thus just as common for the advisers on both sides of formal proceedings to have one eye open for the right moment to suggest ADR. After all, commercial lawyers have always prided themselves upon the fact that the most valuable service they provide to their clients in commercial disputes is not the services of a litigator, but the service of dispute resolution, and ADR is just a more formal and efficient way of providing that service.

Precedent 3 provides an example of an escalation clause. Precedent 4 is an informal mediation clause. Precedent 5 is a suggested ADR clause for inclusion in an agreement before disputes have occurred to provide for their resolution in advance by ADR. The various ADR bodies also provide standard clauses which can be obtained on application. The drafting of an ADR agreement to cover particular disputes after they have arisen is a more detailed task, which must be tailored to the particular circumstances of the dispute, and is outside the scope of this book, although, again, the various ADR bodies are prepared to assist in this connection if required.

Finally, it should be remembered that all such clauses are probably not enforceable in English law, as being no more than agreements to negotiate in good faith. Nevertheless in commercial contracts such clauses do at least signify an intention of good faith on the part of the parties which may be useful, when disputes do arise, in persuading the parties to undertake the prescribed form of negotiation, even if they are not legally obliged to do so.

Lord Woolf's proposals on the reform of civil litigation have given increased prominence to ADR. He proposes that the court should be required to ask the parties during the preparations for trial whether they have seriously considered ADR as an alternative to litigation, and, if not, to explain why they have not done so.

Since September 1996, following the issue of a Practice Direction in June 1996, judges in the Commercial Court can now, on their own initiative, decide that a case is suitable for ADR and adjourn the court proceedings for several months while ADR takes place. The summons for directions questionnaire asks the parties whether they have considered ADR, whether they have discussed it with the other side, and whether they think ADR would help to resolve their dispute. Prior to the Practice Direction, these questions were often ignored, but now that the parties realise an ADR order may be made, they tend to give the answers to these questions more serious thought, and come prepared to discuss the issue of ADR at the hearing on the summons for directions in a meaningful way.

The Commercial Court considers the possibility of making such orders at the hearing of every summons for directions and at the first *inter partes* hearing. The practice is not to issue an order for immediate ADR, but, as discussed above, to allow the case sufficient time to mature so the parties have enough information to assess their positions properly. Very often the appropriate time for ADR is after discovery is closed or after the exchange of experts reports or witness statements. As a result of this Practice Direction, the use of ADR orders and the successful resolution of litigation through ADR has increased in disputes before the Commercial Court.

The current government has encouraged the use of ADR orders in commercial disputes, and is supportive of their use as a part of case management by the judiciary as suggested in Lord Woolf's proposals for reform. However, although in favour of the courts encouraging parties to use ADR, the government has ruled out permitting the courts to impose mandatory ADR as an alternative to litigation.

17.4   Settlement by an expert

Where the parties are concerned to resolve a problem of fact, such as compliance with a technical specification, whether a particular standard of quality has been reached, the value of an item, or the proper drawing up of a balance sheet, it is possible to use an expert, and to provide that his decision is final and binding. In nearly all circumstances, except perhaps outright fraud or manifest error on the face of the award, there will be no right of appeal to the courts, and the rules as to the ouster of the jurisdiction of the court discussed above in relation to ADR have no application.

Precedent 6 is a standard example of the type of clause used.

17.5   Arbitration

Arbitration is a process regulated by the Arbitration Act 1996, which replaced the Arbitration Acts 1950, 1975 and 1979 for all arbitral proceedings commencing after 31 January 1997 which have their seat in England and Wales or Northern Ireland. Arbitration is today as formal as litigation, although, originally, it began life, like ADR, as an attempt to provide commercial solutions for commercial disputes in a practical and cost-effective way. The Arbitration Act 1996 represents an attempt to streamline arbitration and to make it more effective and efficient. However, a large-scale arbitration is still likely to be as expensive, if not more so, than litigation, particularly if it is in connection with international issues, since the proceedings will have the same amount of formality and complexity as litigation and, in addition, the parties will have to pay for the cost of the venue and the arbitrators, where at least the costs of the court and the judge are borne by the state.

There are, however, a number of circumstances where arbitration is appropriate where litigation is not.

First, the parties may require the formality and, indeed, some of the adversarial qualities, of litigation, but not the publicity. Here arbitration can be conducted in complete confidentiality unlike proceedings in court.

Secondly, there are industrial sectors where the custom of arbitration has become so widespread and accepted by the parties that it actually is a cheaper and more practical alternative to litigation. One reason for this is that an arbitrator can be granted certain powers which can normally not be exercised by the courts, such as the adjustment of contractual terms and conditions or the re-opening of architects' certificates. A further common reason is that an arbitrator can be appointed who possesses particular commercial or technical expertise which judges do not normally possess. Instances of this sort of acceptability can be found in the commodity trades and in the building industry.

Thirdly, arbitration is very often accepted as a means of solving international disputes where the parties cannot agree on a mutually acceptable legal forum for their dispute, but trust some organisation like the International Chamber of Commerce or the London International Court of Arbitration to be an impartial adjudicator.

Under English law, where a valid arbitration agreement in writing exists, unless both parties agree (tacitly or expressly) to ignore it, the courts normally require that the agreement be honoured, so that one party cannot ignore the agreement and proceed through the courts instead. The normal remedy available is for the defendant in the relevant legal proceedings to apply to the court for the action to be stayed. The plaintiff must then either proceed under the arbitration agreement, or give up his claim, as the court will no longer listen to him once the stay has been granted.

Under s 9 of the 1996 Act, the court must grant a stay of proceedings unless it is satisfied that the arbitration agreement is null and void, inoperative or incapable of being performed. Under the old legislation this provision only applied to international arbitrations. On an application for stay of proceedings in relation to a domestic arbitration the court had more discretion as to whether or not to grant a stay. Equivalent provisions were inserted in ss 85 and 86 of the 1996 Act, but they have not been brought into force and are likely to be repealed. Thus s 9 now applies to both international and domestic arbitrations. It must be emphasised that a stay of proceedings is not something the court will grant of its own volition, but only upon the request of the defendant in the proceedings. As a procedural point, the defendant will lose this right if he takes part in the proceedings to any extent other than merely entering an appearance, and then asking for the stay. Even the filing of a defence will be taken to be an assent to the legal proceedings, which is sufficient to waive the right to ask for a stay.

So far as further intervention by the courts is concerned, the 1996 Act has considerably reduced the extent to which the court can interfere in the award made by an arbitrator. So far as procedural matters and the conduct of the case are concerned the role of the court is to act in support of the arbitral proceedings to assist the arbitrator in the enforcement of the orders and awards that he makes. The court is not empowered to take over the proceedings and manage them itself. Challenges to an award may be made on the grounds that the arbitration tribunal did not have substantive jurisdiction (s 67) or on the grounds of 'serious irregularity' (s 68(1)) which is a term exhaustively and quite restrictively defined by s 68(2). The parties may not by agreement exclude the right to appeal to the court under these sections. The parties may also appeal to the court on a point of law, either as a preliminary point (s 45) or in relation to an award (s 69). However, this right is restricted. First, if the parties have agreed that the arbitration award should be given without reasons, then they are deemed to have entered into an agreement to exclude the court's jurisdiction under the sections (ss 45(1) and 69(1)). In any event no appeal can be brought unless all the parties to the proceedings agree, or with the leave of the court (ss 45(2) and 69(2)). Leave will only be given by the court under s 45 if it is satisfied that determination of the question is likely to produce substantial savings in costs and that the application was made without delay (s 45(2)). Under s 69 the court must be satisfied that:

(*a*) determination of the question substantially affects the rights of one of the parties;

(*b*) the question is one the arbitrator was asked to determine;

(*c*) that on the basis of the findings of fact in the award:

    (i) the decision was obviously wrong; or

    (ii) the question is one of general public importance and the decision of the arbitrator is at least open to serious doubt; and

(*d*) despite the fact that the parties agreed to go to arbitration it is just and proper in all the circumstances for the court to determine the question (s 69(3)).

The 1979 Act again provided for rather more intervention by the court in the case of domestic and certain special category arbitrations. These provisions (which broadly only allowed parties to contract out of their right to appeal to the court on questions of law if an exclusion agreement had been entered into after the commencement of the arbitration agreement) were reproduced for domestic agreements only in s 87 of the 1996 Act. Again this section has not been brought into force and is likely to be repealed. Thus the parties can exclude the court's jurisdiction on points of law in all cases in advance of the commencement of proceedings.

Finally, it should be remembered that although arbitration agreements are not treated as exclusion clauses for the purposes of the Unfair Contract Terms

Act 1977, arbitration agreements with consumers are subject to special treatment under the Consumer Arbitration Agreements Act 1988. This issue is discussed in Chapter 1.[24]

Precedents 7, 8 and 9 show standard arbitration clauses of varying complexity, which can conveniently be included in contracts, and which are based upon standard clauses provided by various organisations offering the services of arbitration.

In connection with Precedent 7, para (B), the sentence in square brackets should be noted. The rules of the London International Court of Arbitration provide for two arbitrators and an umpire unless the parties agree upon a single arbitrator. The sentence should therefore be inserted in appropriate cases. The choice between a single and multiple arbitrators, and upon whether to choose an umpire or a chairman in the case of multiple arbitrators, depends upon many issues, particularly whether the parties can agree upon one mutually acceptable arbitrator. However, if they can, the expense of the proceedings is obviously much reduced.

Precedents 7, para (B) and 8 refer to an arbitration pursuant to the Arbitration Act 1996. It is important to realise that Part I of the Act applies to all arbitrations having their seat in England and Wales or Northern Ireland, and that a great many provisions of the Act are mandatory. The other provisions (which mostly relate to procedural issues) provide for various matters relating to the conduct of the arbitration, which can be displaced by agreement between the parties, but which will apply in the absence of such agreement. The use of the short form clause in Precedent 7, para (B) would mean that there was no such agreement. However, the reference to the rules of the London International Court of Arbitration in Precedent 8 would displace the non-mandatory provisions of the Act to the extent that the Rules dealt with the same issues inconsistently with them.

In general the 1996 Act is written in good plain English and provides a comprehensive code for dealing with all issues surrounding an arbitration. Section 1 sets out the principles upon which the Act is based as follows:

(*a*) the object of arbitration is to obtain the fair resolution of disputes by an impartial tribunal without unnecessary delay or expense;

(*b*) the parties should be free to agree how their disputes are resolved, subject only to such safeguards as are necessary in the public interest;

(*c*) in matters governed by this Part the Court should not intervene except as provided by this Part.

Section 33 sets out the general duty of the tribunal:

(*a*) to act fairly and impartially as between the parties, giving each party a reasonable opportunity of putting his case and dealing with that of his opponent; and

(*b*) to adopt procedures suitable to the circumstances of the case, avoiding unnecessary delay or expense, so as to provide a fair means for the resolution of the matters falling to be determined.

Finally s 40 imposes upon the parties a duty to do all things necessary for the proper and expeditious conduct of the arbitral proceedings.

In the absence of agreement to the contrary the tribunal will determine its own substantive jurisdiction (s 30) and decide all procedural and evidential matters (s 34). Nevertheless there are many matters where the parties may well want to make special agreement, and in this case a more detailed arbitration agreement is required.

One very important issue which is subject to agreement is the basis upon which the arbitration tribunal proceeds to its finding. The tribunal is required to decide the dispute in accordance with the law chosen by the parties as applicable to the substance of the dispute (s 46(1)(a)) or, if the parties so agree, in accordance with such other considerations as are agreed by them or determined by the tribunal (s 46(1)(b)). In the absence of any choice of law or other agreement the tribunal will apply the law determined by the conflict of law rules which it considers applicable (s 46(3)). Section 46(1)(b) in effect confers upon the tribunal, subject to the agreement of the parties, the possibility of making a decision not on the basis of any system of law, but upon the basis of any other criteria, for instance in accordance with the tribunal's discretion as to what it considers fair and reasonable in all the circumstances of the particular case. Clearly if this basis is chosen appeal to the court on a point of law will become irrelevant. This opens up the possibility of 'amiable composition' tribunals in an way that before the passing of the Act would not have been possible because of the common law rules of public policy against ouster of the jurisdiction of the courts.

The other area where the parties are likely to want to make special arrangements is for the appointment of arbitrators, and in particular to decide how they shall be appointed, what their qualifications should be, how many of them there should be and whether (in the case of multiple arbitrators) a chairman or umpire should also be appointed. Although ss 15–27 set out detailed rules in this area, the parties are free to agree different rules if they wish. It should be noted that under s 23 a party has the right (which cannot be waived by agreement) to request the court to remove an arbitrator if there are justifiable doubts as to his impartiality, he does not possess the required qualifications, he is physically or mentally incapable of acting or he has refused or failed to properly conduct the proceedings or to use all reasonable despatch in conducting proceedings or making an award.

17.6   Scheme for Construction Contracts

The Scheme for Construction Contracts (England and Wales) Regulations 1998 (SI No 649) provides for a scheme of adjudication in respect of certain construction contracts under Housing Grants, Construction and Regeneration Act 1996. The Regulations came into force on 1 May 1998. Any party to a contract can refer a matter in dispute to an adjudicator specified in the contract or nominated by a nomination body (eg the RIBA) specified in the contract. Where the contract makes no specification the party concerned can apply to a nominating body for an appointment in any event.

The adjudicator, while required to take note of agreements reached between all the parties to the dispute on procedural and substantive matters, can go ahead in the absence of such agreement and decide the dispute in an inquisitorial manner, setting his own rules of procedure. If other parties refuse to comply with the procedure and requirements he sets, or object to his appointment, he can proceed to adjudicate in their absence and on the basis of what evidence he has available. He is empowered to decide questions of both law and fact. He is required to act impartially, in accordance with any relevant terms of the contract, to reach his decision in accordance with the applicable law in relation to the contract, and to avoid unnecessary expense. In addition to deciding the dispute he has powers to open up architects' certificates, direct parties to the contract to make payments and award interest thereon (subject to the terms of the contract).

His orders are capable of enforcement by the court as if they were an arbitrator's award pursuant to s 42 of the Arbitration Act 1996. However, his orders are in a sense interim orders, since, unless the parties otherwise agree, the parties are only required to abide by the orders until final determination of the relevant dispute by legal proceedings or arbitration (if the contract provides for arbitration or the parties agree to arbitrate). Nevertheless, speed and economy of the adjudication process may well find favour with contracting parties, as an alternative to expensive litigation or arbitration, at least in cases where the sums at stake are not very large.

17.7   Resolution through the courts

The process of litigation is obviously outside the scope of this book, but, as far as contractual provisions are concerned, no more than a simple choice of law and jurisdiction clause (such as cl 6 of Precedent 1) is required. It should be noted, however, that such a clause should be included even if a more specific dispute resolution clause (such as an arbitration clause) is included as well. There may well be circumstances where, in any event, the parties will need to resort to the courts, for instance to determine the validity and construction of the specific arbitration clause itself.

Precedent 1

Settlement agreement

THIS AGREEMENT is made the [   ] day of [   ]
BETWEEN [   ] of [   ] (hereinafter 'ABC') of the
first part AND [   ] of [   ] (hereinafter 'DEF') of the
other part.

WHEREAS:

(a) There are certain issues in dispute between the parties as to the following matters (hereinafter 'the Matters') that is to say:

(*i*) claims by ABC for damages for alleged breaches by DEF of the
non-exclusive distribution and franchise agreement between ABC
and DEF dated [   ] (the 'Distribution Agreement')
under which DEF granted to ABC rights to distribute adapt and
maintain certain products of DEF (the 'Franchise Products') as
therein specified;

(*ii*) claims *inter alia* by ABC for compensation relating to certain inventories purchased by ABC from DEF; and

(*iii*) claims by each party that the other party has or may misuse certain
trade secrets and proprietary information of the other (such trade
secrets and proprietary information of each party being detailed in
Appendix I hereto and hereinafter respectively referred to as the
'Disclosed Information' of the party in question) which each party
has disclosed to the other pursuant to the Distribution Agreement.

(iv) The parties have agreed as to settlement and disposal of the said
matters and issues as hereinafter provided on the terms of this Agreement.

NOW IT IS AGREED as follows:

1.1 In consideration of the implementation of the provisions hereinafter referred to ABC and DEF mutually and individually hereby waive, release and

relinquish all their respective rights or interest claimed in the Matters, whether such rights or interests arise by way of claim or counterclaim, and undertake each with the other that they will not in any of the matters whatsoever henceforth bring, lodge or pursue such claims or any part thereof, and that they will bring no further claims under any agreements or in respect of any obligations arising directly or indirectly out of or referred to in the said Matters.

1.2 ABC warrants to DEF that it has not assigned, charged, hypothecated or in any other way dealt with or disposed or purported to deal with its rights or interests in the Matters, whether by way of claim or counterclaim, and that its rights or interests remain vested in itself solely as beneficial owner, and will indemnify DEF in respect of any breach of such warranty.

1.3 DEF warrants to ABC that it has not assigned, charged, hypothecated or in any other way dealt with or disposed or purported to deal with its rights or interests in the Matters, whether by way of claim or counter claim, and that its rights or interests remain vested in itself solely as beneficial owner, and will indemnify ABC in respect of any breach of such warranty.

2.1 DEF will purchase from ABC for the sum of [   ] the spare part items listed in Appendix II hereto. The said spare part items shall be made available for collection by, or, on behalf of DEF from the premises of ABC at [   ] within 21 days of the date hereof whereupon the said price of [   ] shall be paid by DEF to ABC or as it shall direct not later than ten days thereafter.

2.2 DEF will purchase from ABC for the sum of [   ] the spare part items listed in Appendix III hereto. The said spare part items shall be made available for collection by, or, on behalf of DEF from the premises of ABC at [   ] within 21 days of the date hereof whereupon the said price of [   ] shall be paid by DEF to ABC or as it shall direct not later than 10 days thereafter.

3 DEF and ABC shall as soon as reasonably practicable after the date hereof co-operate in mutually satisfactory arrangements for the free transfer and assignment by ABC to DEF of the responsibility for service and maintenance towards those customers of ABC who use the Franchise Products.

4 ABC and DEF acknowledge and agree that the Distribution Agreement shall cease and determine with effect from the date hereof and all obligations of any party thereto past or present whether arising thereunder or in connection therewith shall be deemed to be fully discharged from the date hereof and neither party shall bring any proceedings or make any claim in respect thereof.

5 With regard to the Disclosed Information of each party, and without prejudice to the generality of the provisions of cl 1 hereof, the parties agree with each other as follows:

5.1 Each party (the 'receiving party') shall be free to use and disclose Disclosed Information received from the other party (the 'disclosing party') in all respects as if the same had been originated by the receiving party and all intellectual property rights (if any) in such Disclosed Information were owned by the receiving party.

5.2 The disclosing party grants to the receiving party immunity from suit from, and hereby undertakes that it will take no action against the receiving party in any court of law or other forum alleging or based on, any claim of infringement of copyright or other intellectual property right resulting from any use or disclosure whatsoever made by the receiving party of the disclosing party's Disclosed Information. The grant and undertaking pursuant to this paragraph is given to the receiving party both (*a*) for itself and (*b*) in the capacity of agent for any person (a 'user') whom the receiving party has either directly or indirectly (through another user) permitted to use and/or disclose the disclosing party's Disclosed Information, whether as sub-licensee or otherwise, to the intent that all such users shall benefit from and may enforce such grant and undertaking as if they were the receiving party and signatories to this Agreement.

5.3 The parties further agree that in respect of Disclosed Information disclosed by the disclosing party to the receiving party the disclosing party hereby grants the receiving party a free-of-charge, fully paid-up, irrevocable, worldwide, non-exclusive licence to do any act in relation to such Disclosed Information which would be an infringement of any copyright or other intellectual property right of the disclosing party, including without limitation copying, modifying and sub-licensing or otherwise using such Disclosed Information, including any code, design or other feature or information comprised therein or extracted therefrom.

6 This Agreement shall be governed by and construed in accordance with English law and each party agrees to submit to the non-exclusive jurisdiction of the English courts as regards any claim or matter arising under this Agreement.

IN WITNESS WHEREOF, the above Agreement has been signed by the duly authorised representatives of the parties the day and year first above written.

SIGNED for and on behalf of
ABC

SIGNED for and on behalf of
DEF

Precedent 2

Release agreement

This Release Agreement is executed between [   ] of
[   ] (hereinafter 'ABC') and [   ] of [   ]
(hereinafter 'DEF'), as of the last date indicated below upon which it has been
executed by both parties.

This Agreement is made with reference to the following facts:

A. ABC and DEF entered into an agreement dated [   ] (the 'General Agreement') for the sale and/or licence of computer equipment, software
and/or maintenance services.

B. Pursuant to the General Agreement, DEF placed certain orders on ABC
(hereinafter 'the DEF Orders').

C. ABC and DEF desire to fully and finally resolve by this Release Agreement
all claims, damages, payments or other matters arising out of or in connection
with the DEF Orders.

THEREFORE, the parties agree, in consideration of the mutual releases and
other undertakings and agreements herein contained, and for other good and
valuable consideration, the receipt of which by each party from the other is
hereby acknowledged, as follows:

1 This Release Agreement is made for purposes of compromise only, and neither the agreement nor anything done or said in connection herewith shall be
an admission or evidence of any liability, fact or matter concerning the disputes settled by this Release Agreement.

2 Concurrently with the execution of this Release Agreement, ABC shall deliver to DEF (i) a cheque in the amount of [   ], and (ii) a refund

of DEF's payment made upon shipment of the DEF Orders in the form of a credit note in the amount of [   ] which may be used by DEF only against any future invoice from ABC for goods or services rendered to DEF pursuant to any current or future agreement between the parties.

3 DEF, for and on behalf of itself and its predecessors, successors, assigns, principals, agents and representatives, does hereby relieve, release and forever discharge ABC and its predecessors, successors, assigns, principals, agents and representatives under the General Agreement ('Released Parties') from any and all claims, rights, debts, liabilities, demands, obligations, conditions, promises, acts, agreements, costs, expenses, accountings, damages, and actions, of whatever kind or nature, whether in law or in equity, whether known or unknown, which they have had, may now have or may hereafter have against the Released Parties for or by reason of any occurrence, matter or thing through and including the date hereof which arises out of or in connection with any of the DEF Orders, including, without limitation, any claims for damages for defective products or delays in deliveries, and any claim of misrepresentation which in any way relates, in whole or in part, to any of the DEF Orders.

4 ABC, for and on behalf of itself and its predecessors, successors, assigns, principals, agents and representatives, does hereby relieve, release and forever discharge DEF and its predecessors, successors, assigns, principals, agents and representatives under the General Agreement ('Released Parties') from any and all claims, rights, debts, liabilities, demands, obligations, conditions, promises, acts, agreements, costs, expenses, accountings, damages, and actions, of whatever kind or nature, whether in law or in equity, whether known or unknown, which they have had, may now have or may hereafter have against DEF for or by reason of any occurrence, matter or thing through and including the date hereof which arises out of or in connection with any of the DE2F Orders.

5 Without prejudice to the generality of the foregoing, it is expressly agreed and accepted by each of the parties to this Agreement that this Agreement is and is intended to be a general release of all claims between the parties hereto in respect of the subject matter of this Agreement including those claims which a party did not know or suspect to exist in its favour at the time of executing this Agreement, even if such claims, if they had been known to it, could have affected the terms of the settlement reached between the parties as contained in this Agreement. To the extent that legislation or any principles of law might provide otherwise than the first sentence of this clause, such legislation and principles are (to the extent permitted by law) hereby expressly waived and excluded by each of the parties to this Agreement, who admit to full knowledge and understanding of the consequences and effect of such waiver and exclusion.

6 DEF, on the one hand, and ABC, on the other hand, each acknowledge and agree that neither they nor their respective legal advisers shall provide a copy of this Agreement or disclose, disseminate and/or publicise, or cause or permit to be disclosed, disseminated and/or publicised, any of the terms and conditions of this Agreement, to any individual and/or entity not a party to this Agreement, except as follows:

(*a*) in response to an order of a court of competent jurisdiction, or in response to an appropriate subpoena or discovery request issued in the course of litigation;

(*b*) in response to an inquiry or order issued by a governmental or supra-governmental agency of competent jurisdiction;

(*c*) to the extent necessary to report income to appropriate taxing authorities and/or to contest the imposition of any tax by appropriate taxing authorities;

(*d*) to such parties' respective accountants and legal advisers;

(*e*) in connection with any litigation between the parties hereto relating to this Agreement; and/or

(*f*) to the extent required in order to comply with applicable securities or other laws and/or regulations.

In the event disclosure is necessary pursuant to the provisions provided above, the disclosing party shall apprise the third party to whom such disclosure is made of the confidential nature of the information and said disclosing party shall use its reasonable and good faith efforts to secure the confidentiality of the information provided to any third party.

7 In the event that any provision of this Agreement should be held void, voidable or unenforceable, the remaining portions shall remain in full force and effect.

8 This Agreement contains the entire agreement of the parties to settle the disputes referred to herein, and expresses the entire agreement between the parties in relation to the subject matter of this Agreement.

9 This Agreement shall be effective when each party has executed it.

10 This Agreement may be executed in several counterparts, each of which shall be deemed an original and all of which taken together shall constitute a single instrument.

11 Each party acknowledges and confirms that the preparation of this Agreement has been a joint effort of all parties and counsel for all parties and that it shall be construed fairly in accordance with its terms and shall not be construed for or against any individual party.

12 This Agreement shall inure to the benefit of, and shall be binding upon, the successors and assigns of the parties hereto, and each of them.

13 This Agreement shall be construed and enforced in accordance with the laws of England.

14 DEF, on the one hand, and ABC, on the other hand, each represents that it has full power to enter into this Release Agreement, and that it has not previously assigned, encumbered or in any manner transferred all or any portion of the claims, rights or property interest covered, mentioned or released by this Release Agreement.

Dated:

      ABC
      By:
      Title:

Dated:

      DEF
      By:
      Title:

Precedent 3

Dispute escalation clause

The Customer and the Contractor shall use their best efforts to negotiate in good faith and settle amicably any dispute that may arise out of or relate to this Agreement or a breach thereof. If any such dispute cannot be settled amicably through ordinary negotiations by appropriate representatives of the Customer and the Contractor, the dispute shall be referred to the Chief Executive Officers of the Customer and the Contractor who shall meet in order to attempt to resolve the dispute. If any such meeting fails to result in a settlement, the matter at the election of either party may be submitted for resolution [by arbitration pursuant to cl [   ] hereof] [to a court of competent jurisdiction].

Precedent 4

Mediation clause

Before resorting to [arbitration pursuant to cl [   ]] [legal proceedings] the parties shall attempt to settle by negotiations between them in good faith all disputes or differences which arise between them out of or in connection with this Agreement. The parties further agree that (provided both parties consider that such negotiations would be assisted thereby), they will appoint a mediator by mutual agreement, or (failing mutual agreement) will apply to the [President of the London Chamber of Commerce] to appoint a mediator, to assist them in such negotiations. Both parties agree to co-operate fully with such mediator, provide such assistance as is necessary to enable the mediator to discharge his duties, and to bear equally between them the fees and expenses of the mediator.

Alternative dispute resolution clause

Before resorting to [arbitration pursuant to cl [   ]] [legal proceedings] the parties shall attempt to settle in good faith all disputes or differences which arise between them out of or in connection with this Agreement, by negotiations between them in good faith, and, in the event of failure of such negotiations, by the use of the procedure known as Alternative Dispute Resolution ('ADR').

Where failure of negotiations in respect of such dispute or difference occurs the parties shall together refer such dispute or difference to [name of ADR body] for resolution in accordance with such of the ADR Procedures offered by [name of ADR body] as [name of ADR body] considers appropriate in all of the circumstances.

The parties agree to be bound by the relevant rules of [name of ADR body] relating to the conduct of the relevant ADR Proceedings, as if the same were incorporated in this Agreement. Each party shall bear its own costs incurred in the relevant ADR Proceedings, and one half of the fees and expenses of [name of ADR body], unless a different agreement is reached as part of any settlement arrived at as a result of the relevant ADR Proceedings.

Precedent 6

Expert clause

If any dispute arises under this Agreement between the parties with respect to [any matter within the expertise of a technical expert] [the compliance of the products supplied under this Agreement with the technical specifications set out in Appendix [   ]] then such dispute shall at the instance of either party be referred to a person agreed between the parties, and, in default of agreement within 21 days of notice from either party to the other calling upon the other so to agree, to a person chosen on the application of either party by the President for the time being of the [British Computer Society]. Such person shall be appointed to act as an expert and not as an arbitrator and the decision of such person shall be final and binding. The costs of such expert shall be borne equally by the parties unless such expert shall decide one party has acted unreasonably in which case he shall have discretion as to costs.

Precedent 7

Short form arbitration clauses

(A) Any dispute or claim arising out of this Agreement shall be referred to and resolved by the International Chamber of Commerce ('ICC') in Paris in accordance with the ICC Conciliation and Arbitration Rules. [The ICC shall decide which system of law shall be applied in relation to the dispute.]

(B) Any dispute or claim arising out of or in relation to this Agreement shall be submitted to the arbitration in London of the London International Court of Arbitration ('LICA') under and in accordance with the Arbitration Act 1996 and the rules of the LICA at the date of such submission, which rules are deemed to be incorporated by reference within this Clause. [The tribunal shall consist of a sole arbitrator.] The parties hereto acknowledge that service of any notices in the course of such arbitration at their addresses as given in this Agreement shall be sufficient and valid.

Precedent 8

Standard form arbitration clause

Any question or difference which may arise concerning the construction meaning or effect of this Agreement or concerning the rights and liabilities of the
parties hereunder or any other matter arising out of or in connection with this
Agreement shall be referred to a single arbitrator in London to be agreed between the parties. Failing such agreement within thirty days of the request by
one party to the other that a matter be referred to arbitration in accordance with
this clause such reference shall be to an arbitrator appointed by [the President
for the time being of the London Chamber of Commerce]. The decision of
such arbitrator shall be final and binding upon the parties. Any reference under
this clause shall be deemed to be a reference to arbitration within the meaning
of the Arbitration Act 1996.

Precedent 9

Long form arbitration clause under UNCITRAL rules

All disputes or differences which arise out of or in connection with this Agreement or its construction, operation, termination or liquidation shall be settled by arbitration. The award of the arbitrators shall be final and binding upon the Parties.

The venue of such arbitration shall be decided by the Parties to the dispute in each case.

If the Parties fail to reach agreement on the venue of such arbitration within five days then the arbitration shall take place at the Vienna Chamber of Commerce.

The arbitration shall be in accordance with the UNCITRAL Arbitration Rules in effect on the date of the referral to arbitration, except that in the event of any conflict between those Rules and the arbitration provisions of this Agreement, the provisions of this Agreement shall govern.

The Vienna Chamber of Commerce shall be the appointing authority save as provided below.

The number of arbitrators shall be three.

Each Party to the arbitration proceedings shall appoint one arbitrator. If within fifteen (15) days after receipt of the Claimant's notification of the appointment of an arbitrator the Respondent has not, by telegram or telex, notified the Claimant of the name of the arbitrator he appoints, the second arbitrator shall be appointed in accordance with the following procedures:

If the Respondent is the Purchaser, the second arbitrator shall be appointed by the [   ] Chamber of Commerce and Industry.

If the respondent is the Seller the second arbitrator shall be appointed by the [President of the Law Society of England and Wales].

If within fifteen (15) days after receipt of the request from the Claimant, the [Chamber of Commerce and Industry] [or the President of the Law Society of England and Wales] as the case may be has not, by telegram or telex, notified the Claimant of the name of the second arbitrator, the second arbitrator shall be appointed by the Vienna Chamber of Commerce.

The arbitrators thus appointed shall choose the third arbitrator who will act as the presiding arbitrator of the tribunal. If within thirty (30) days after the appointment of the second arbitrator, the two arbitrators have not agreed upon the choice of the presiding arbitrator, then at the request of either party to the arbitration proceedings the presiding arbitrator shall be appointed by the Vienna Chamber of Commerce and shall be of a nationality other than that of the Purchaser or the Seller. The arbitration, including the making of the award, shall take place in Vienna, Austria and (except in those cases where this Agreement expressly refers to the applicability of [English] law) the arbitrators shall resolve any such dispute or difference referred to them (excluding conflict of laws) in accordance with the substantive laws of Austria. All submissions and awards in relation to arbitration hereunder shall be made in [English] and all arbitration proceedings shall be conducted in [English].

APPENDIX

LATEST DEVELOPMENTS

This Appendix comprises footnotes from the previous chapters
and is current up to July 1998

1   A further recent example of a case based on this line of reasoning is *Rafsanjani Pistachio Producers Co-operative v Kauffmans Ltd* (1997) *New Law Digest Commercial Communication* 187, 19 December, where the QBD refused to enforce a contract with a clause stating that the price for the goods to be purchased was 'to be agreed before each delivery'.

2   This case was followed by a further Court of Appeal decision, *Hogg v Roper* (1998) *The Times*, 22 April, in which trustees escaped liability for negligent advice to their beneficiary in drawing up a will by relying on a general exclusion clause in the will excluding trustees from liability for negligence.

3   This decision has, however, to be looked at with caution in the light of a later decision, *Garston v Scottish Widows Fund and Life Assurance Society* (1998) *The Times*, 14 July, CA, where a tenant served a contractual notice to trigger a break clause and a statutory notice to request a new tenancy for the same premises. Both notices erroneously treated the grant of the lease as the date of commencement as opposed to the true date of commencement of the term. The court held that the statutory notice was invalid but, applying the principles in Mannai, the contractual notice was effective to determine the lease.

4   *White v Jones* was followed, on similar facts, in *Esterhuizen v Allied Dunbar Assurance plc* (1998) *The Times*, 10 June, but in this case liability was extended from a professionally qualified solicitor to a lay company which had assumed responsibility for drawing up a will.

5   The current emphasis on the importance of assumption of responsibility can be seen in the House of Lords decision in *Williams v Natural Health Foods Ltd* (1998) *The Times*, 1 May, where the director of a company was held not to be personally liable for a negligent misstatement made by the company because the plaintiff was unable to show any evidence of dealings between him and the director which could have given the plaintiff reason to believe that the director was assuming personal responsibility for his company's statements.

6   There has been some consideration of the Schedule in a recent unreported case, *Hunter v Zenith Windows* discussed in *Commercial Lawyer* (1998) issue 24, p 82, which suggests that an agent who spends his time supervising sales agents who

canvass a territory assigned to him, but who does not directly deal with customers himself, is still an agent (and not a secondary agent) for the purposes of the Regulations.

[7] In the recent case of *Duffen v FRA BO SpA* (1998) *The Times*, 15 June, the Court of Appeal held that an agent who was not entitled to rely on a clause in his contract specifying an amount of £100,000 as a termination payment (since it was held to be a penalty and thus unenforceable) could still pursue a claim for compensation under the Regulations (in addition to his common law rights).

[8] This has been shown to be the case in a recent decision in the Queen's Bench Division, *Moore v Piretta PTA Ltd* (1998) *The Times*, 11 May, where the learned judge applied the German method of calculation to an agency contract specifying payment of an indemnity on termination. It was held that the indemnity provided for in the Regulations applied to the whole currency of the agency, including any period before the Regulations took effect.

[9] A further example of how the Directive can override provisions in the law of a member state, that would prevent the operation of the relevant local enabling legislation, can be seen in *Bellone v Yokohama SpA* [1998] 9 Euro CL 8. Here the European Court of First Instance ruled that the Directive rendered invalid local legislation which made the validity of an agency contract conditional upon the commercial agent being entered in the appropriate register.

[10] See *Javico International v Yves Saint Laurent Parfums SA* [1998] 9 Euro CL 23, ECJ.

[11] It appears from a DTI press release in June 1998 that the government was largely successful in this attempt and that amendments to the Directive are now in the pipe-line, in order to make clear how the Directive applies to subcontracting and public/private sector transfers. There appears to be no prospect of an amendment to the Directive to reverse *Suzen*, although the outsourcing industry would like to see this. Further amendments to the Directive are discussed later in this Chapter.

[12] As a result of the government initiatives discussed above, it appears that the Directive will be amended to permit such agreed and negotiated variations where the business is insolvent and this is necessary to save jobs after the transfer.

[13] The suggested developments to the Directive do not appear to cover this point.

[14] Clause 14.7 will need consequential amendments in due course to refer to the relevant provisions of the new data protection legislation.

[15] Warranty 3.4(g) contains suggested wording to cover the new Competition Bill once it becomes law. The references to the old UK competition law regime in warranties 3.4(a), (d) and (e) should be retained for the time being given the nature of the transitional provisions under the Competition Bill discussed in Chapter 15.

[16] Given the recent Court of Appeal decisions in *Hutcheys v Coin Seed Ltd* [1998] IRLR 190 and *William Hill Organisation v Tucker* (1998) *The Times*, 8 April, it is desirable to insert an express clause. The right to send an employee on 'garden leave' in the absence of an express clause will not be implied into the contract in most cases, particularly where high level executives or employees who do skilled work (where the skills need regular exercise) are concerned. Clearly employers

remunerated partly on commission or piecework rates (where the remuneration is lost or diminished if no work is carried out) cannot be sent on 'garden leave' in the absence of an express clause.

[17]   It should be noted that the current government has raised in its White Paper of May 1998 (Fairness at Work) the possibility of abolishing the right of exclusion under s 197. If this happens all fixed term contracts will, upon expiry, offer the potential of an unfair dismissal claim, and considerations such as those set out in *North York-shire County Council v Fay* would always apply.

[18]   The Bill provides that the details will be specified in secondary legislation.

[19]   The Director General is empowered, and encouraged, under the Bill to issue OFT Guidelines on the operation of the Bill. Draft Guidelines on many topics are currently being issued for consultation and finalisation. Draft Guidelines OFT 225 on 'de minimis' agreements caught by the Chapter I Prohibition suggest that agreements (whatever the size of the undertakings concerned) which have 'no appreciable effect' should be exempt, and that, in any event, there should be a 'safe harbour' provision exempting agreements where the undertakings concerned have no more than a combined market share of 10 per cent, unless the industry concerned is split into a network of similar agreements where, although each set would be exempt if considered alone, the cumulative effect of such sets does in fact restrict competition. Other considerations to be taken into account in deciding whether any agreement should be regarded as 'de minimis' are how easy it is for competitors to enter the market in question, and the need to encourage co-operation between small and medium-sized enterprises. OFT 225 also contains advice on conduct that would be considered 'de minimis' in terms of the Chapter II Prohibition. Where the undertaking covered has a market share below 20–25 per cent it will not generally be regarded as in a dominant position. Its conduct will, in any event, be regarded of minor significance where its turnover does not exceed a specified amount (not yet fixed but £50m has been suggested), although the Director General may still investigate the conduct. It should be noted that this part of the OFT 225 Guidelines is unique to the Bill. EC competition law has no comparable arrangement.

[20]   However draft Guidelines OFT 226 currently state that the EC Commission comfort-letter, preceded by a notice in the Official Journal that the EC Commission intends to take no action, will be considered by the Director General as a Parallel Exemption unless particular UK concerns are involved or there is an appreciable effect on trade in the UK (even though no such effect on trade between member states) or the letter is one of 'discomfort'. In any event the Director General has stated that the EC Commission will be consulted before action is taken in such cases.

[21]   Draft Guidelines OFT 220 (para 6.5) suggest that such parallel applications should be made by annexing copies of the application to the EC Commission (known as Form A/B) to the proposed UK application form (to be known as Form N) and adding the specific additional information (if any) required by Form N on the UK market. Draft Guidelines OFT 227 suggest however, that dual notification will not

often be necessary, encourages prior consultation with the OFT in border-line cases, and points out that the OFT can, in any event, give a retroactive exemption. However, where the OFT gives no exemption in any particular case, any uncovered period between dismissal of the EC application and submission of the UK application, does open a potential for a fine under the UK regime. Dual applications may well be necessary in more cases than first anticipated after the reassurance of the OFT in draft Guidelines OFT 227. Certainly, prior consultation with the OFT is essential.

[22]   Some evidence of this can already be seen in draft Guidelines OFT 221 on market definition which follow very closely the 1997 EC Commission Notice on Definition of Relevant Markets.

[23]   This rule has recently been extended to payment by direct debit (see *Esso Petroleum v Milton* (1997) *The Times*, 13 February).

[24]   It should also be noted that ss 89–91 of the 1996 Act provide that a term in a contract with a consumer which amounts to an arbitration agreement, constitutes an unfair term for the purposes of the Unfair Terms in Consumer Contracts Regulations 1994 (SI No 3159) if it relates to 'a claim for a pecuniary remedy' which does not exceed an amount specified by order (currently £3,000). Section 90 extends the ambit of the Regulations, solely in relation to the topic of arbitration agreements, so that they apply (unlike other instances of the application of the Regulations) not only where the consumer is a natural person, but also where the consumer is a legal person.

Index

HK$1,473-
CONTIG